vcrZEITEN
TIMES gone by

State Archaeology in Rhineland-Palatinate

Generaldirektion Kulturelles Erbe Rheinland-Pfalz
Direktion Landesarchäologie (ed.)

vorZEITEN

TIMES gone by

State Archaeology in Rhineland-Palatinate

SCHNELL + STEINER

Imprint:
vorZEITEN. State Archaeology in Rhineland-Palatinate.

Published by the Directorate of State Archaeology
Axel von Berg and Michael Schwab

in cooperation with
Generaldirektion Kulturelles Erbe Rheinland-Pfalz, Direktion Landesarchäologie,
Generaldirektion Kulturelles Erbe Rheinland-Pfalz, Direktion Landesmuseum Mainz,
Generaldirektion Kulturelles Erbe Rheinland-Pfalz, Direktion Landesmuseum Trier,
Generaldirektion Kulturelles Erbe Rheinland-Pfalz, Direktion Landesmuseum Koblenz,
Historisches Museum der Pfalz zu Speyer,
Naturhistorisches Museum Mainz / Landessammlung für Naturkunde Rheinland-Pfalz,
Liebenstein-Gesellschaft e. V., Koblenz,
Museum bei der Kaiserpfalz, Ingelheim am Rhein.

Editors:
Axel von Berg and Michael Schwab

Catalogue concept:
Axel von Berg, Generaldirektion Kulturelles Erbe Rheinland-Pfalz, Direktion Landesarchäologie,
Peter Henrich, Generaldirektion Kulturelles Erbe Rheinland-Pfalz, Direktion Landesarchäologie, Außenstelle Koblenz,
Ulrich Himmelmann, Generaldirektion Kulturelles Erbe Rheinland-Pfalz, Direktion Landesarchäologie, Außenstelle Speyer,
Hans Nortmann, Generaldirektion Kulturelles Erbe Rheinland-Pfalz, Direktion Landesarchäologie, Außenstelle Trier,
Michael Schwab, Generaldirektion Kulturelles Erbe Rheinland-Pfalz, Direktion Landesarchäologie,
Marion Witteyer, Generaldirektion Kulturelles Erbe Rheinland-Pfalz, Direktion Landesarchäologie, Außenstelle Mainz.

English translation coordinated by: Franziska Dörr

Bibliographical information of the German National Library:
The German National Library registers this publication in the
German National Bibliography; detailed bibliographical data
can be accessed in the internet via http://dnb.dnb.de

1st edition 2020

Cover design: Anna Braungart, Tübingen
Typesetting: typegerecht berlin
Print: Gutenberg Beuys Feindruckerei GmbH, Langenhagen
ISBN 978-3-7954-3203-4

Further information about the publishing programme can be found on:
www.schnell-und-steiner.de

CONTENTS

THE BRONZE AGE

IRON AGE

ROMAN TIMES

EARLY MIDDLE AGES

THE MIDDLE AGES

THE MODERN ERA

Preface

There is hardly any area in Western Central Europe as rich in historical finds and monuments as the regions of Rhineland-Palatinate. On the occasion of seventy years of existence of our federal state and of state archaeology department, the year 2017 will be the »Year of Archaeology«.

Situated in the middle of Central Europe and acting as a mediator between north and south, west and east, Rhineland-Palatinate was in a key position for the early cultures. The history of Rhineland-Palatinate is a story of cultural diversity and encounters, in which the streams of persons, goods, and ideas have been characteristic through millennia until today.

This jubilee is not only celebrated with a State Exhibition in a central place at the Landesmuseum in Mainz. Various actions by involved citizens, associations, and initiatives shall in addition create awareness for our rich archaeological heritage and make it experienceable for all in different places within the framework of a discovery tour.

Communicating archaeological research is not reduced to only the presentation in museums – where the Landesmuseum in Rhineland-Palatinate with its important archaeological collections has pride of place –: It is also reflected in the display and valorisation of archaeological monuments and excavation sites off-road. The World Heritage Sites in the state are also vital in communicating our cultural heritage.

The Archaeological State Exhibition will particularly focus on regions and spaces and their differences and common features. An important portion of the presentation is dedicated to the topic of cultural encounters and flows, since past cultures in Rhineland-Palatinate never existed on their own and isolated, but were part of greater contexts in Europe. This topic can be understood differently as migration, occupation, and acculturation in individual epochs.

The companion volume for the exhibition comprehensively presents the diverse work of the State Archaeology, selected finds, and the latest research outcomes. The result is a standard work for Rhineland-Palatinate which is also of great importance for supra-regional research.

I would like to warmly thank all those involved for the work they have done, and I am pleased that the results of 70 years of archaeological research in Rhineland-Palatinate can now be made permanently available to the general public and international scholarship.

Prof. Dr. Konrad Wolf
Minister for Science, Further Education and Culture

Preface

Rhineland-Palatinate is this year celebrating its 70th birthday and 70 years of the State Archaeology Department with an extraordinary State Exhibition in Mainz entitled »vorZEITEN – Archaeological Treasures in the Rhine and Moselle Area«.

Because of the general public interest, the protection, maintenance, study, and communication of national archaeological heritage are legally the responsibility of state institutions. In Rhineland-Palatinate, this task is attributed to the General Department of Cultural Heritage (GDKE), along with the Department for State Archaeology (Direktion Landesarchäologie). The legal provisions are regulated by the Monument Protection Act of Rhineland-Palatinate.

Under the direction of the State Archaeologist, the Department for State Archaeology, with its four branch offices in Speyer, Mainz, Koblenz, and Trier, is in charge of studying, safeguarding and preserving the stock of our archaeological cultural heritage. The extraordinarily large number of archaeological discoveries of the past few decades and the variety of the documented finds and findings are evidence of no less than 400 million years of geology and about 800,000 years of human history. The history of Rhineland-Palatinate is thus one of cultural exchange and diversity characterizing the country to this day.

An important task is the study of the archaeological heritage and the scholarly processing of this research, so that the results of this work can be communicated and made accessible to the public in an appropriate manner. The long-term protection of archaeological monuments and legacies in the soil is today one of the most important duties of the State Archaeology Department with the aim of preserving reservations with intact archaeological finds and findings for future generations, given that the archaeological archive in the soil is finite and non-renewable and therefore needs to be protected.

Accompanying the State Exhibition, we now have a comprehensive survey of archaeology in Rhineland-Palatinate. Not only are the latest research results communicated to the reader in chronological order, the finds of the State Exhibition, which represent the wealth of Rhineland-Palatinate archaeology, are also explained in individual contributions from the beginning to the present time.

We offer particular thanks to the authors of the companion volume for their work, but also to all the staff at the various branch offices, who, with utmost commitment, carried out the excavations, recovered the finds, and processed the results.

Thomas Metz
Director General
General Department of Cultural Heritage

Dr. Dr. Axel von Berg
State Archaeologist Rhineland-Palatinate
General Department of Cultural Heritage

INTRODUCTION

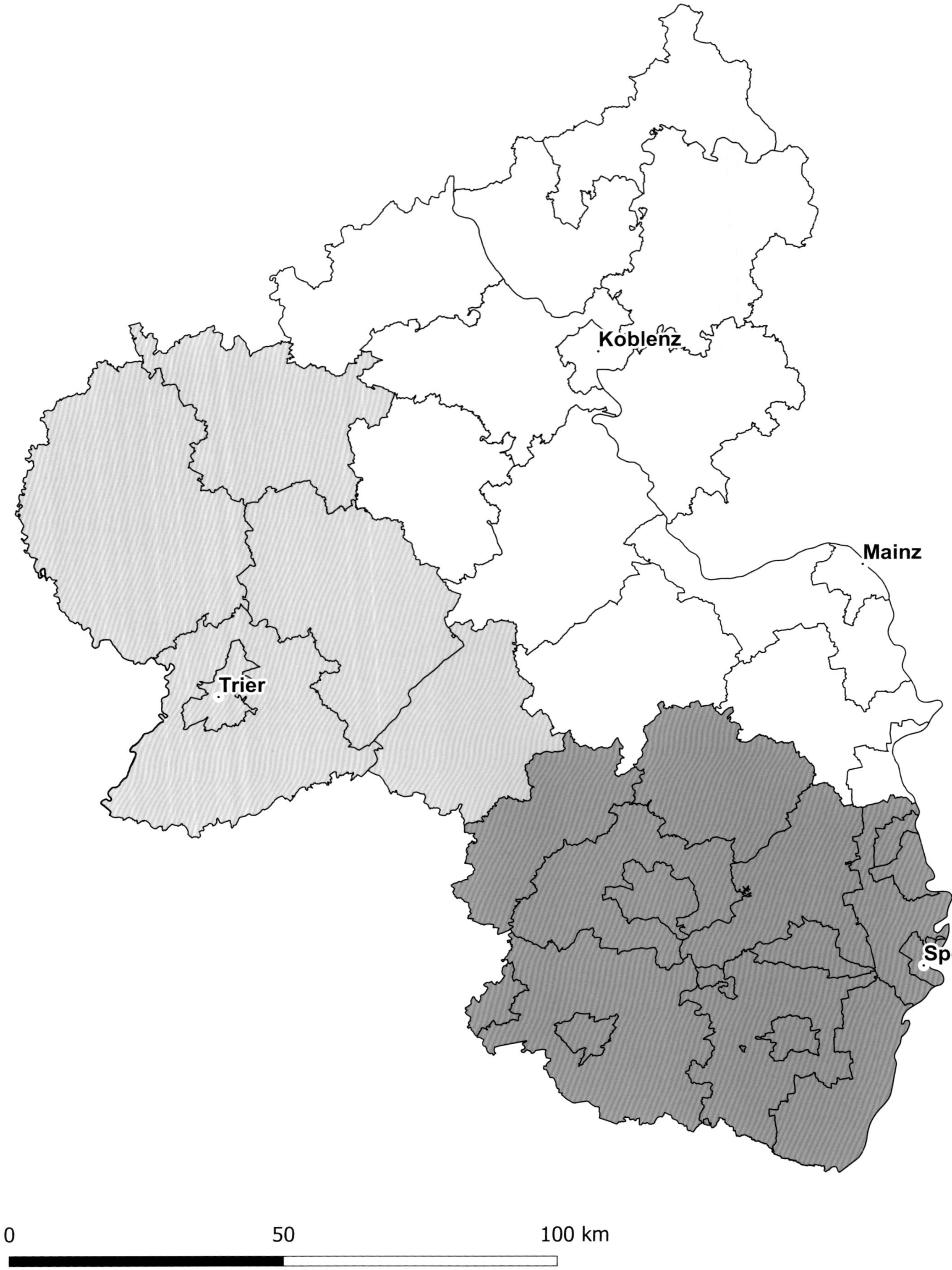
Koblenz
Mainz
Trier
Speyer
0
50
100 km

Rhineland-Palatinate changing through the ages – Landscape and early days

AXEL VON BERG

Archaeological monuments and findspots are part of our common historical inheritance and the history of us all. Given the general public interest, state institutions are responsible for the protection, maintenance, study, and communication of the local cultural property heritage within a legal framework. In Rhineland-Palatinate, the competent agency is the Generaldirektion Kulturelles Erbe (general department of cultural heritage), Direktion Landesarchäologie (department for state archaeology). The legal provisions are governed by the Denkmalschutzgesetz (monument protection act of Rhineland-Palatinate.

The most important task of the Department for Archaeology is to secure the stock of archaeological cultural monuments and preserve it for future generations. Another central task is the study of the archaeological heritage and its scholarly processing. Furthermore, the results of this work must be communicated and made accessible to the public in an appropriate manner. This applies to finds as well as to other objects visible or hidden in the soil and includes geological-paleontological monuments as well as all relics of human life and civilisation from its beginnings up to the era of the two World Wars. The long-term protection of archaeological monuments has priority in this context. In particular, the permanent conservation of archaeological legacies in the soil is one of the most important duties of the Department for State Archaeology today. Its aim is to preserve and provide reservations hosting intact archaeological finds and findings for future generations, given that the archaeological soil archive is finite and non-renewable, and therefore needs particular protection.

The four branch offices of the Department for State Archaeology in Koblenz, Trier, Mainz, and Speyer are coordinated by the State Archaeologist and dedicated to the study, safeguarding, and communication of archaeological monuments and sources in the German federal state of Rhineland-Palatinate.

Time and again archaeological finds and findings are cut into especially during earthworks, and they are then documented and, where possible, recovered by the Department for Archaeology before their final destruction. In such cases, excavations are only an emergency solution in order to preserve the findings for posterity, at least through documentation in word and picture, and to retain whatever finds that may be retrieved as archive material, evaluate them systematically, and communicate them to the public.

A characteristic feature of Rhineland-Palatinate is the extremely rich quantity of finds with the typical regional specialities of the various landscape sectors, such as the mining of raw

Map of Rhineland-Palatinate with the branch offices of the State Archaeology in Koblenz, Trier, Mainz, Speyer. (GDKE/Landesarchäologie/Koblenz/A.Schmidt)

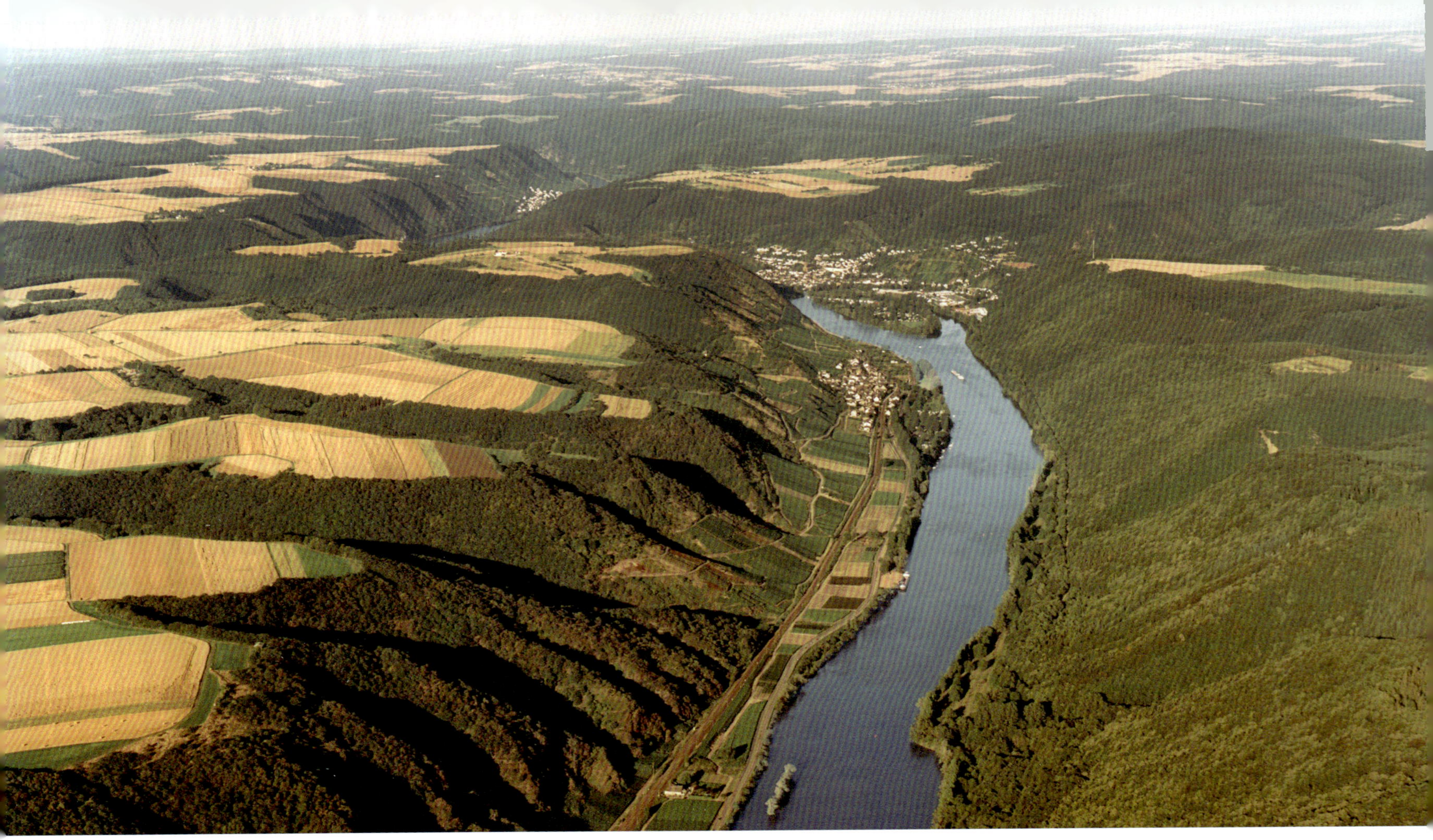

Fig. 1
Aerial photo with the Moselle valley cut deeply into the Devonian underground near Treis-Karden in the Cochem-Zell district. (Photo: A. Schmickler)

materials, the specific conservation conditions in the vast forest areas, the intensively used agricultural and viticultural areas, and the world heritage sites. Rhineland-Palatinate has been cultivated for ages.

The old cultivated landscape has its own characteristics that vary according to the region. Rhineland-Palatinate is situated geographically within the mid-range mountain zone and is structured by five major rivers – the Rhine, Moselle, Lahn, Saar, and Nahe. While the Rhine is still the most important north-south axis on the eastern flank, the Moselle opens up the west to France. The mid-range mountain areas of Eifel, Hunsrück, Westerwald, Taunus, and Palatinate Forest (Pfälzerwald) form core zones. The north of the state is structured by Tertiary and Quaternary volcanic structures, whilst wide plains dominate the south and Rhine-Hesse. Fertile soils, a mild climate, and rich deposits of raw materials offer favourable living conditions to this day and are the basis for a stable economy. It is no coincidence that Rhineland-Palatinate, with finds about one million years old, belongs to the earliest settled cultivated landscapes in central middle Europe. In the northern parts of the state alone, nearly 97,000 findspots are known, and their number is steadily growing with the use of the most modern prospecting methods, such as geophysics, aerial photography for archaeology, and the evaluation of LIDAR laser scans. There is a large number of unique archaeological monuments that are famous well beyond the borders of the state.

The typical character of a region and its settlement and use by man until today depend on its respective formation. The decisive element for the formation of a given landscape is its geological and climatological development since early days. The younger formation history is mainly determined by three factors: besides tectonics and volcanism, it is river development in particular that shapes the landscape and lastingly determines the life and economy of man in the area until today. The character of the landscape is defined by the

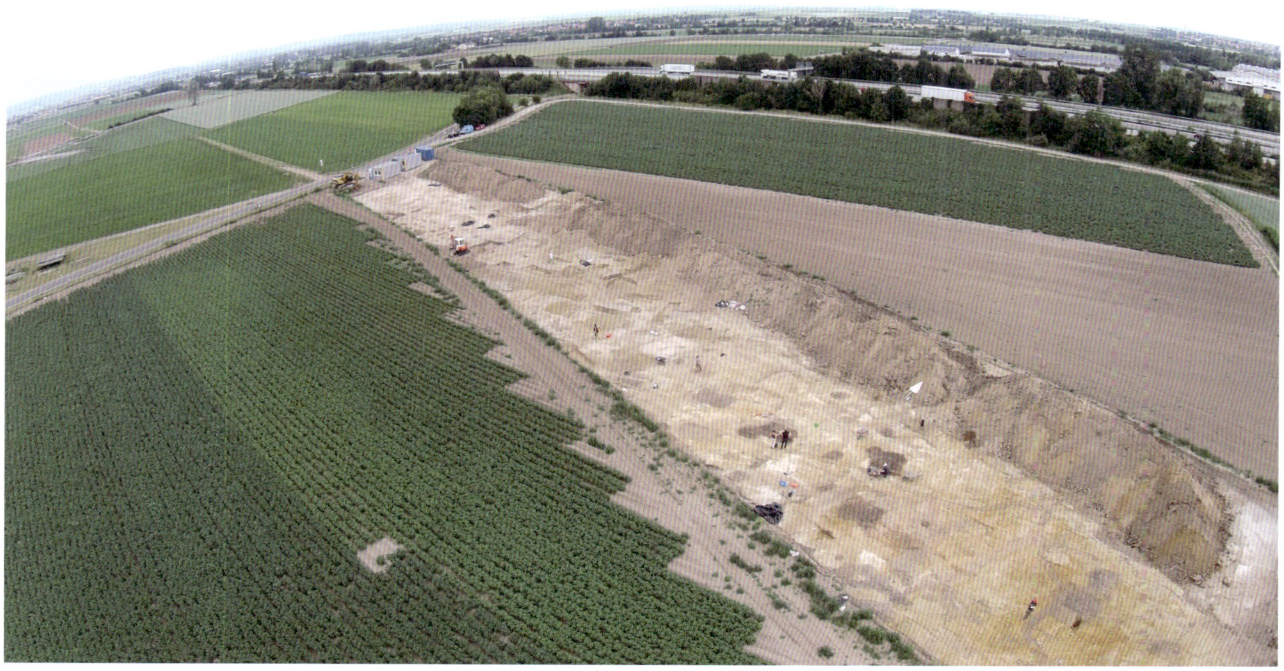

Fig. 2
Heßheim, Rhein-Pfalz distr. Excavation works for a bypass in the area of a medieval abandoned settlement (GDKE/Landesarchäologie/Speyer)

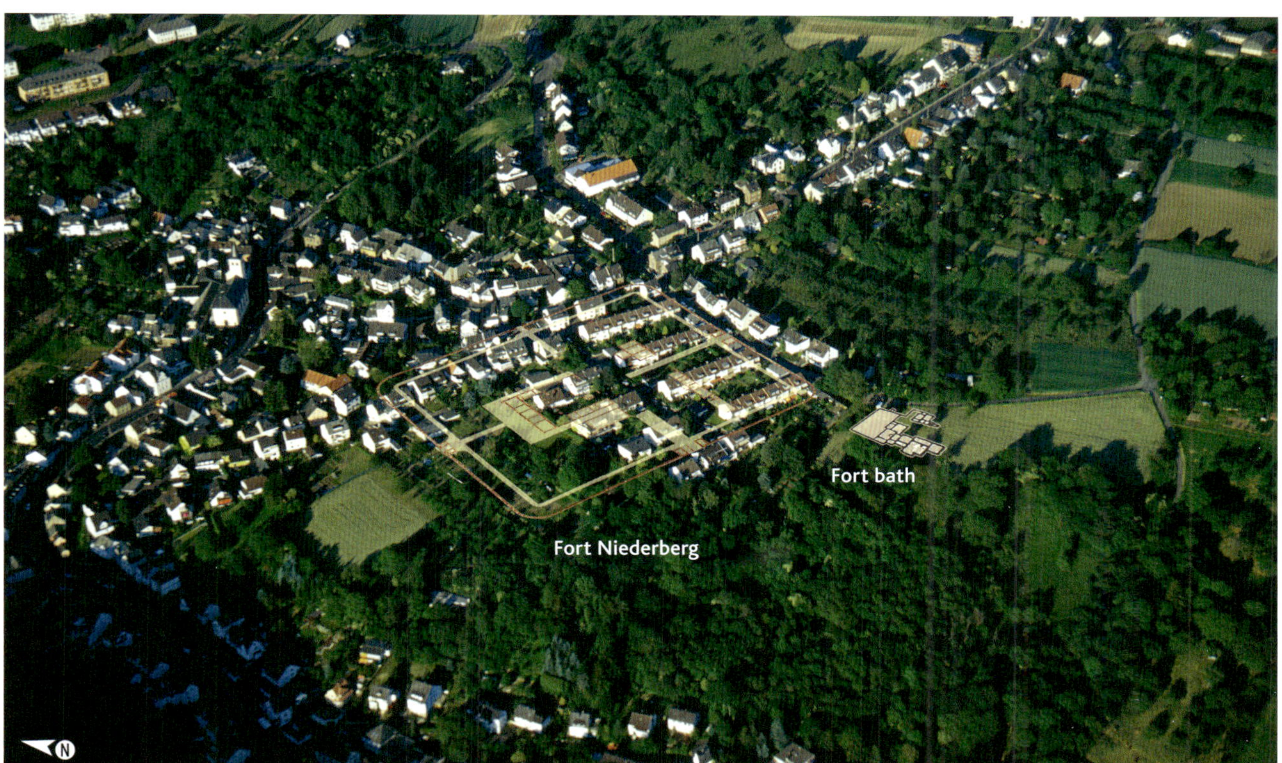

Fig. 3
Niederberg, city of Koblenz. Aerial photo with the fort marked in an area largely overbuilt with residential buildings at today's outskirts (GDKE/Landesarchäologie/Koblenz/C. A. Jost)

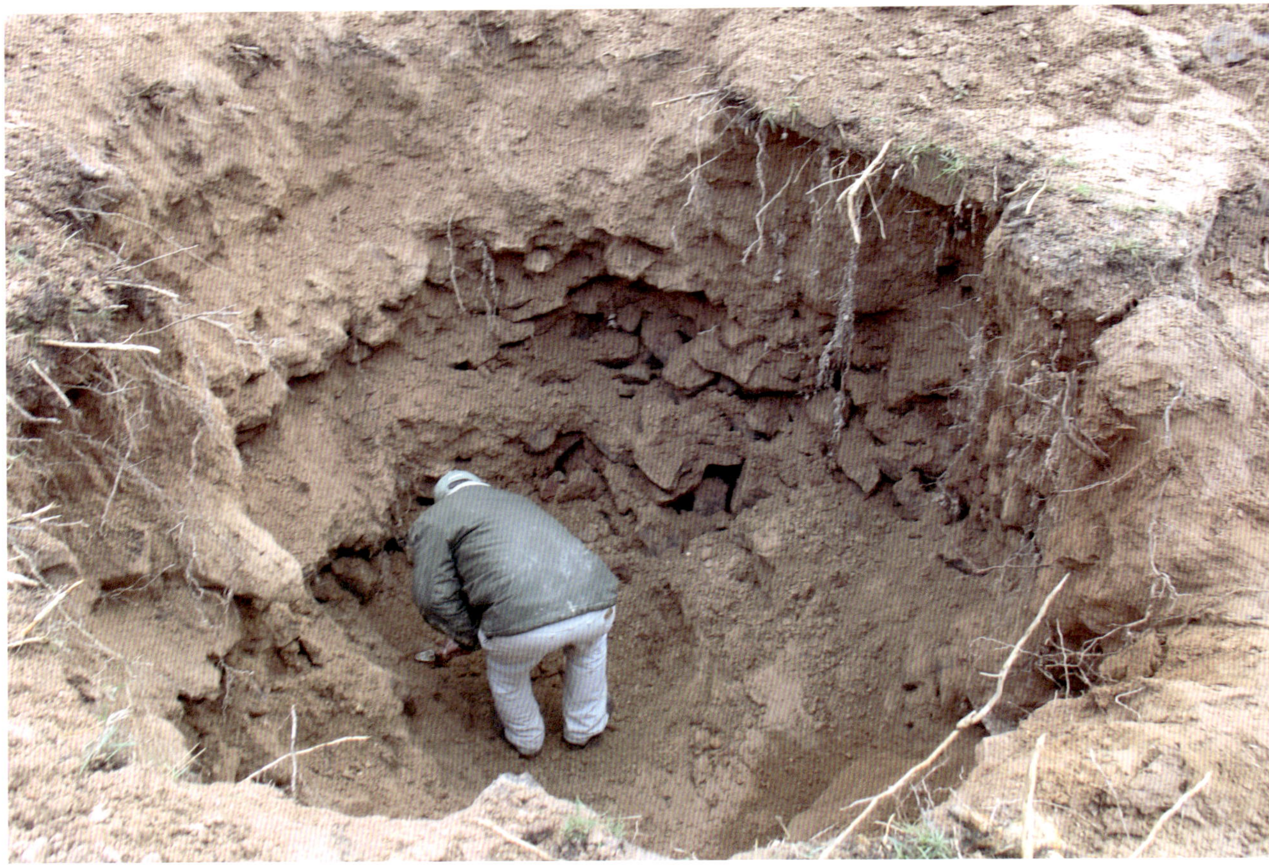

Fig. 4
Eisenberg, Donnersberg distr. Illegal excavation in a burial mound. The illicit shaft aimed at the central tomb of the mound. (GDKE/Landesarchäologie/Speyer)

mountain ranges and especially by the deep-cut river and stream valleys. The valleys of the Rhine, Moselle, Lahn, and Saar, which especially in the northern parts of the state are cut up to 150 m deep into the Devonian slate, were formed mostly after the end of the Tertiary and are a product of the eventful geology of the Ice Age. (Fig. 1)

The bedrock consists of old sediment formations, mostly Devonian clay slate and greywacke in the northern parts of the state, and mottled sandstone and limestones in the southern parts. The decisive development of the terrain structure and surface occurred only during the younger Tertiary and Quaternary epochs of earth history. The geology of Rhineland-Palatinate is mainly characterized by the north-south rift valley at the eastern side of the state, which is recognizable by the course of the river Rhine. This is where two intra-European plates push against each other.

The development of human civilization in Rhineland-Palatinate goes back nearly one million years. Thanks to its favourable position in a large river system, the land offered excellent living and settlement conditions to prehistoric man. The river valleys and their respective higher riversides were already settled from early times because of their convenient topography and accessibility. Especially at the crossings and fords and the streams flowing into the rivers, settlements developed continuously along the traffic routes. The big rivers were also important for cultural exchange as early trade routes: through the mid-range mountains via the Moselle to the west, the north-south connection along the Rhine, and via the Lahn to the east.

The history of a settlement landscape from the first appearance of man to the start of written records is studied through the legacies of the respective early cultures, which the soil has preserved like an archive until today. As a historical science, archaeological research tries to reconstruct daily human life in early times by means of the passed-down finds and findings, also in cooperation with other disciplines, espe-

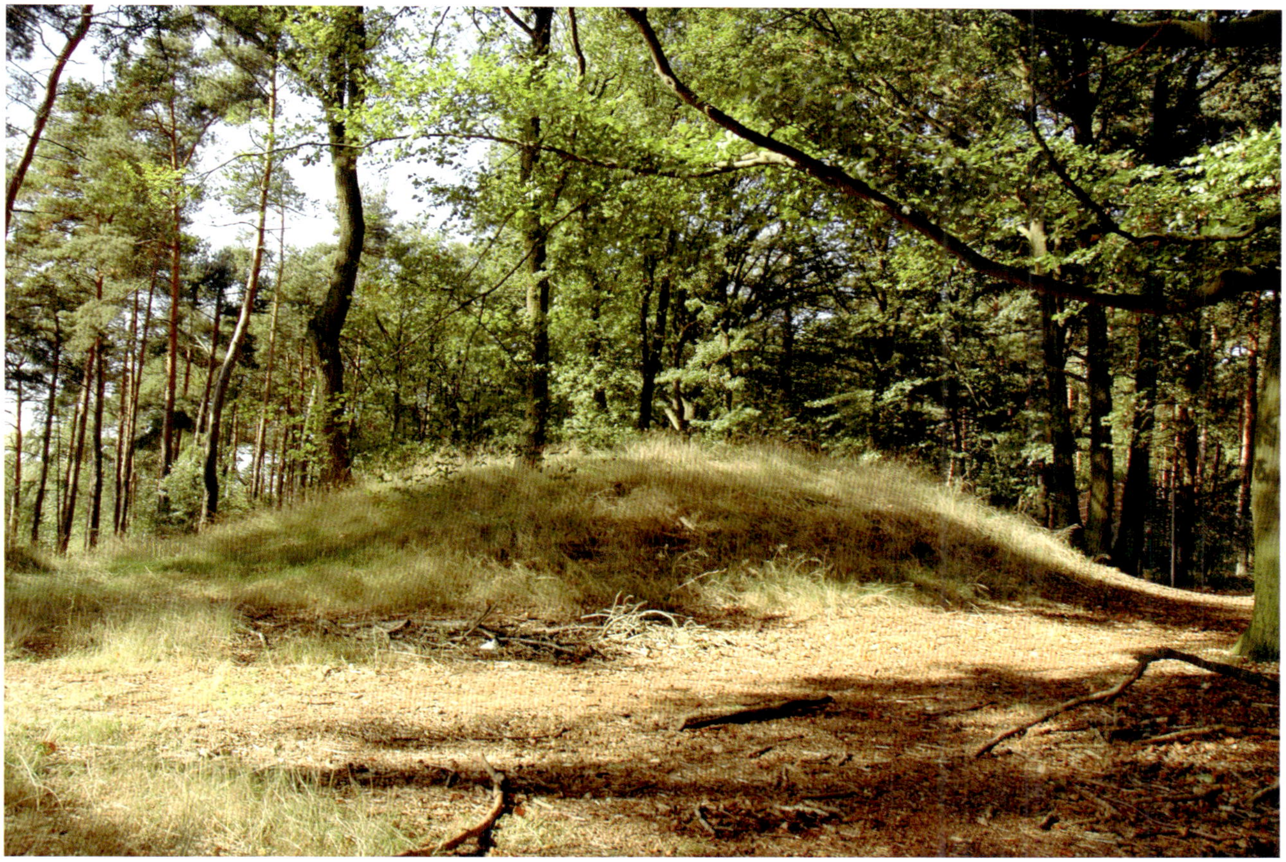

Fig. 5
Kobern-Gondorf, Mayen-Koblenz distr. Iron Age burial mound preserved intact in coppice forest. (GDKE/Landesarchäologie/Koblenz/M. Neumann)

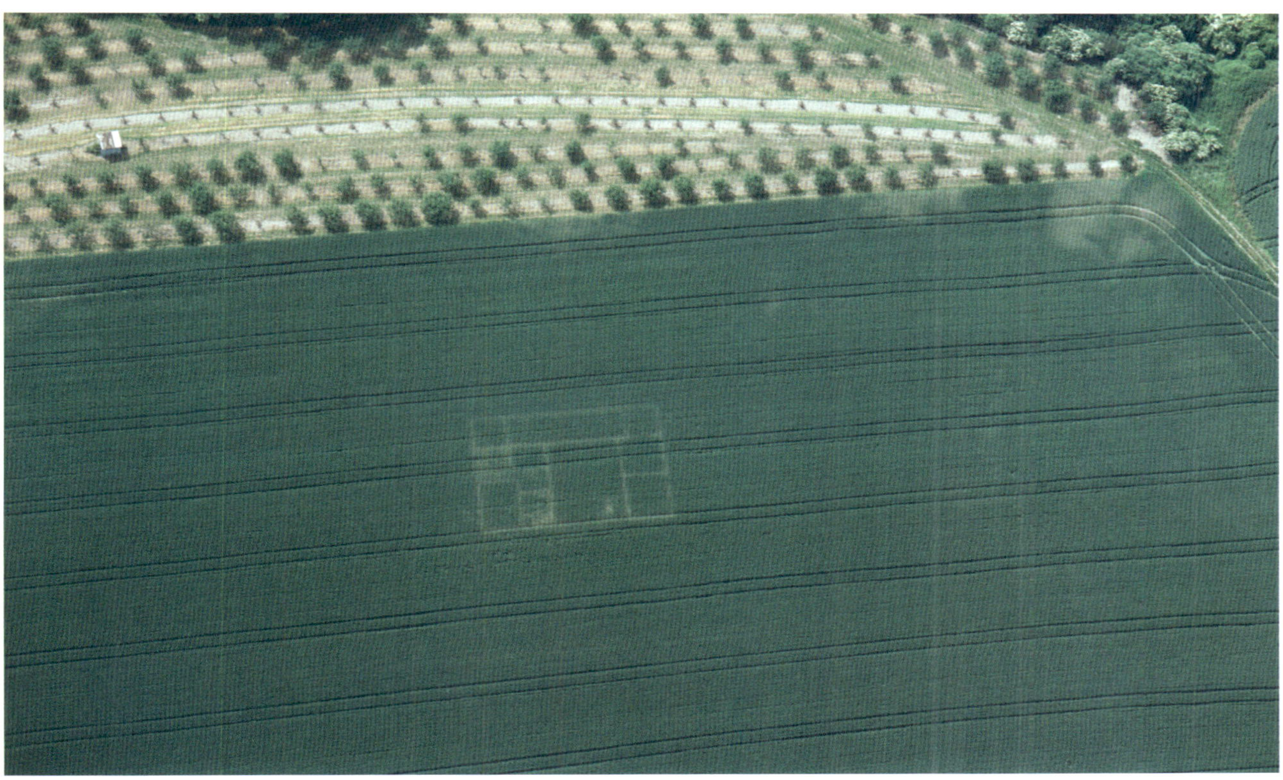

Fig. 6
Kobern-Gondorf, Mayen-Koblenz distr. Aerial photo with clearly recognizable ground plan of a Roman building in the growing grain. (Photo: R. Gensheimer)

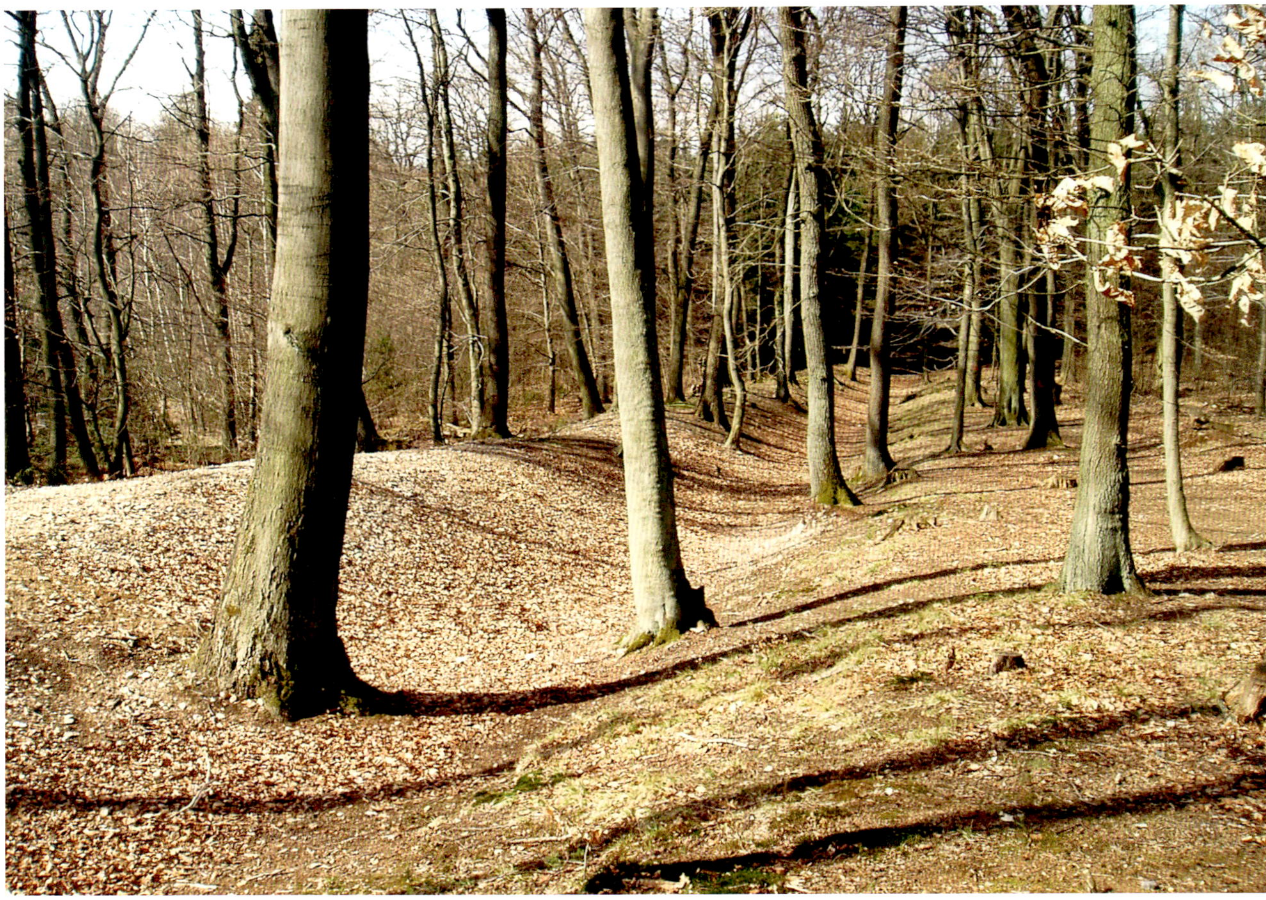

Fig. 7
Becheln, Rhein-Lahn distr. Ditch and rampart of the Upper German-Raetian Limes in high forest. (GDKE/Landesarchäologie/Koblenz/C.A. Jost)

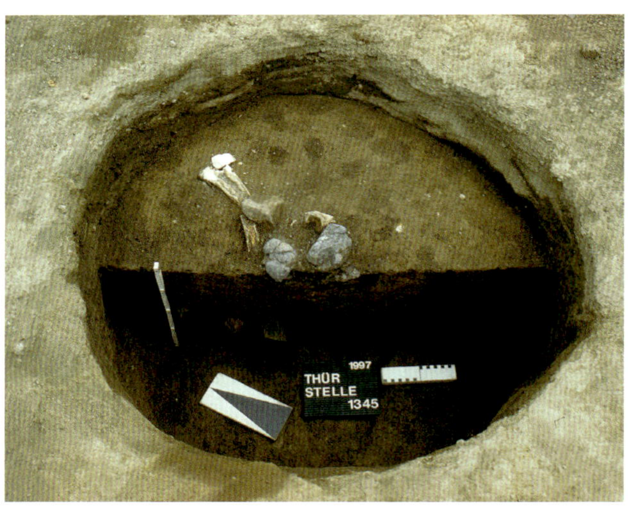

Fig. 8
Thür, Mayen-Koblenz distr. Iron-Age settlement pit with partially removed filling and find material during the excavation. (GDKE/Landesarchäologie/Koblenz/F. Gebert)

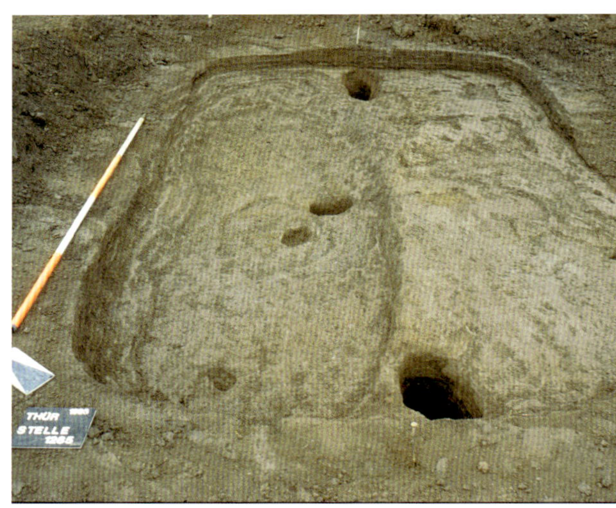

Fig. 9
Thür, Mayen-Koblenz distr. Iron-Age pit house after exposure. We can see the recess of the hut and the support posts of the roof on the narrow sides. (GDKE/Landesarchäologie Koblenz/F. Gebert)

cially natural sciences. No matter how rich the stock of monuments may be, the daily destruction of the relics is quite shocking: the stock of archaeological monuments is continuously being reduced through relentless interventions in so-far undisturbed soil as a result of the enormous land use of our modern world. (Fig. 2-3) The slow but steady destruction through intensive cultivation in agriculture and forestry, but also

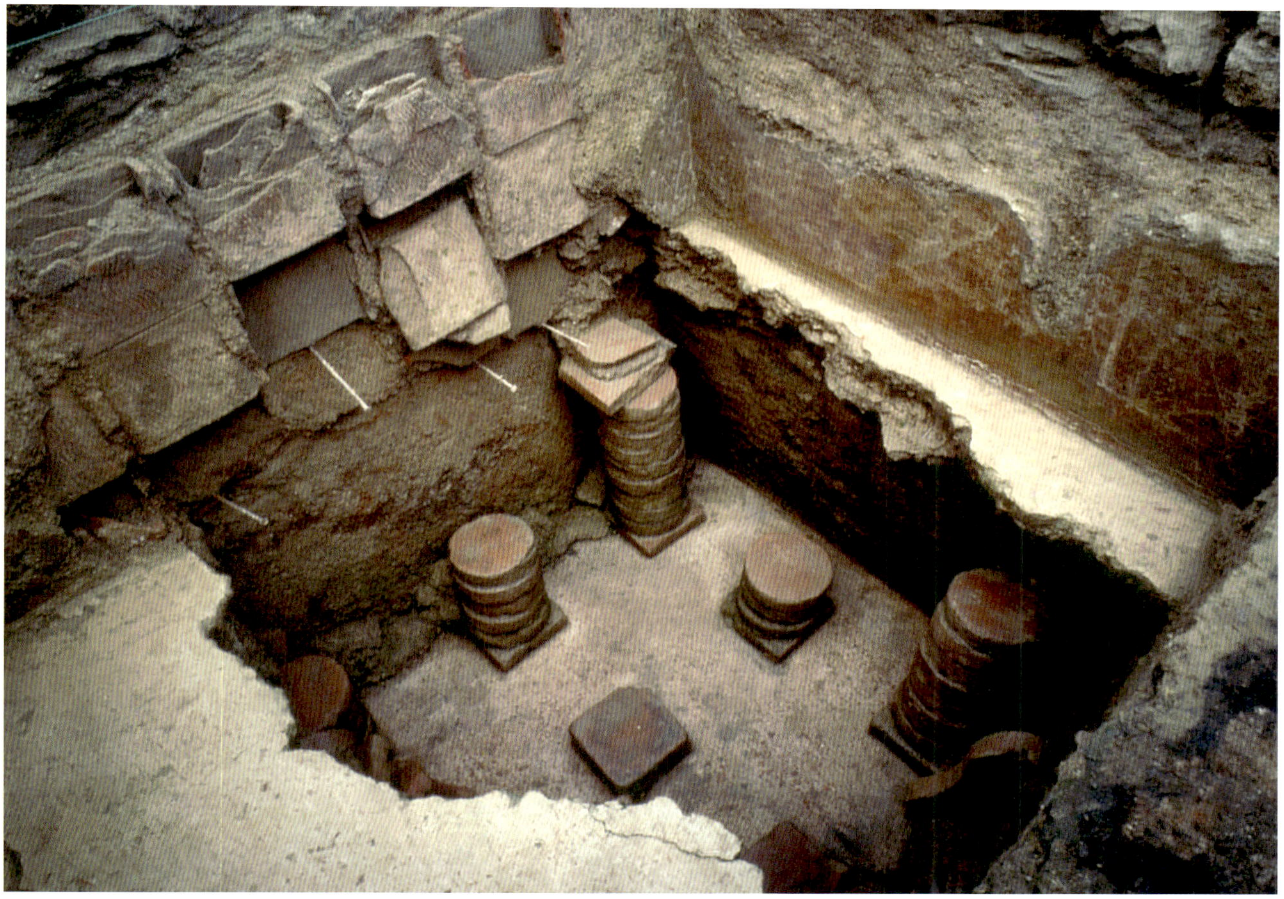

Fig. 10
Bad Neuenahr-Ahrweiler, Ahrweiler distr. View of an excavated room of the »Roman villa« with hypocaust, screen floor, and polychrome paintings on the rising wall. (GDKE/Landesarchäologie/Koblenz/H. Fehr)

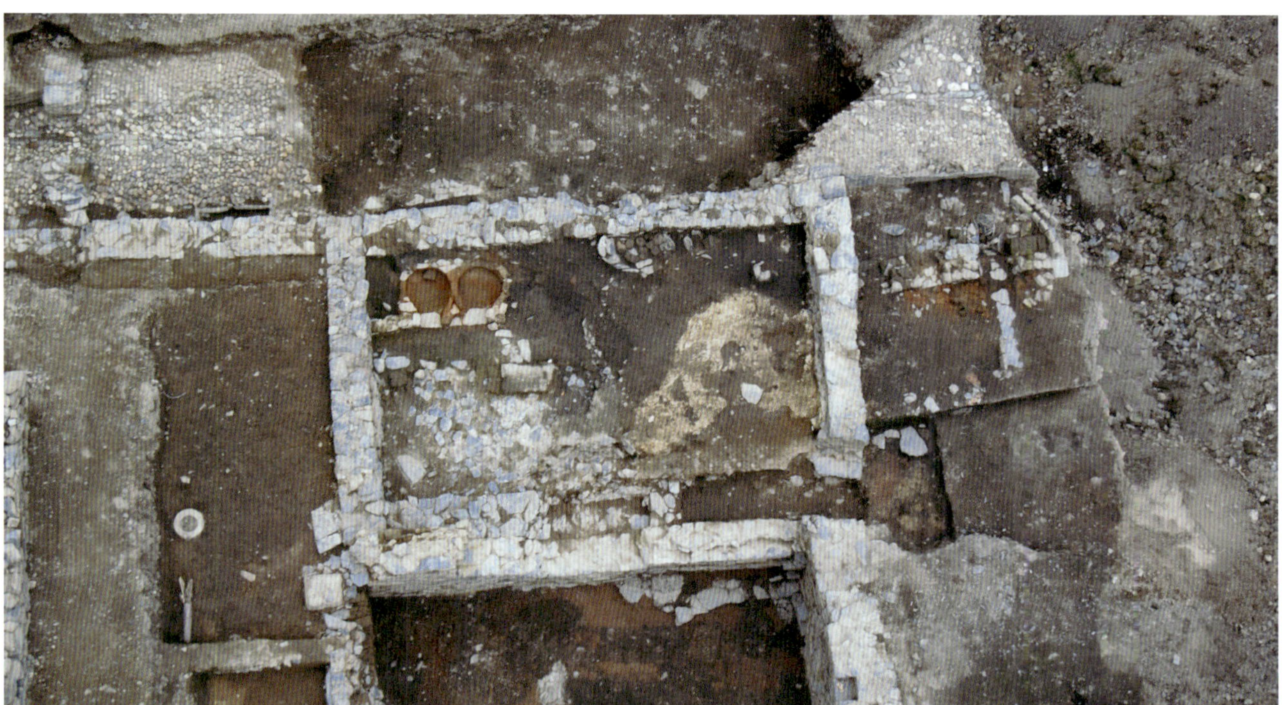

Fig. 11
Andernach, Mayen-Koblenz distr. Overview image of a medieval building complex. The foundations with the room divisions have been preserved. The central room has two hearths; parts of the screed floor are also preserved. (GDKE/Landesarchäologie/Koblenz/F. Brüninghaus)

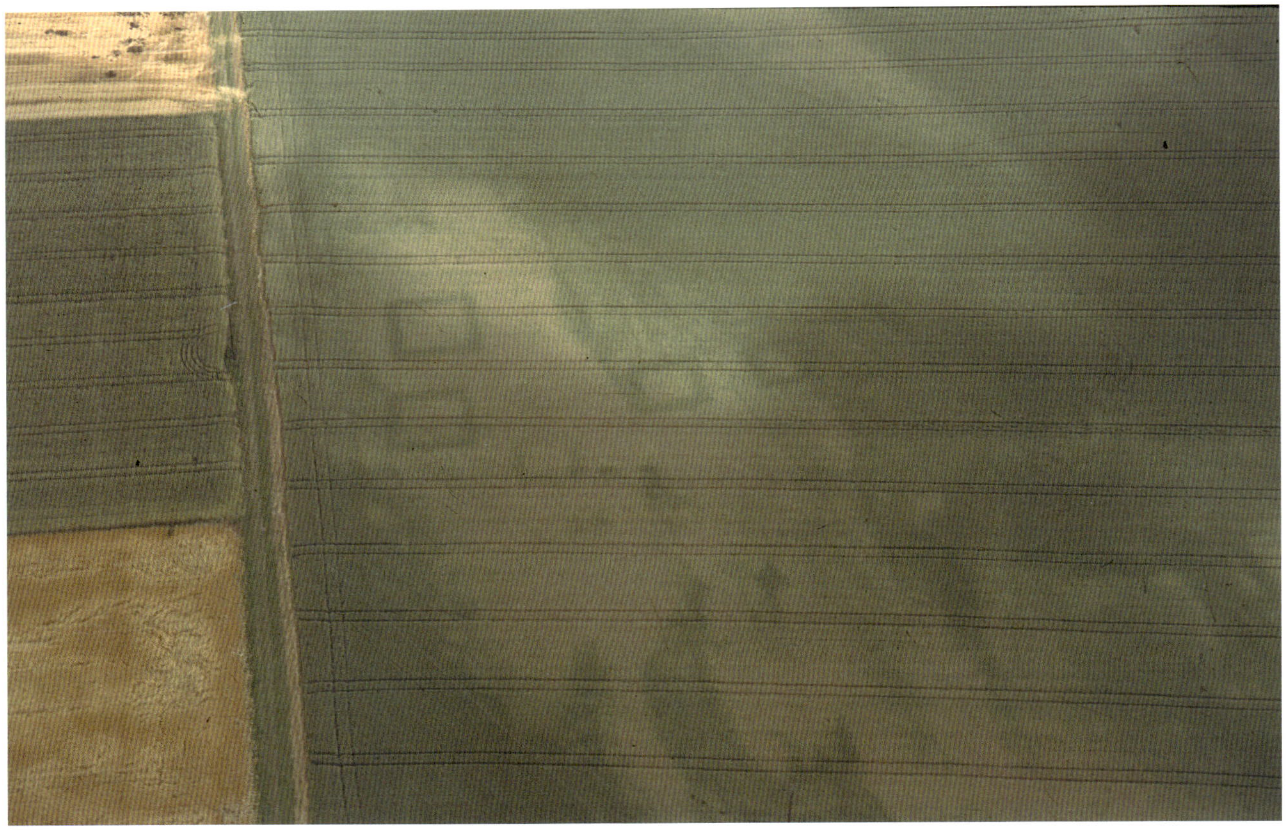

Fig. 12
Nickenich, Mayen-Koblenz distr. Aerial photo with several square enclosures of early Roman burial gardens in growing grain. (Foto: R. Gensheimer)

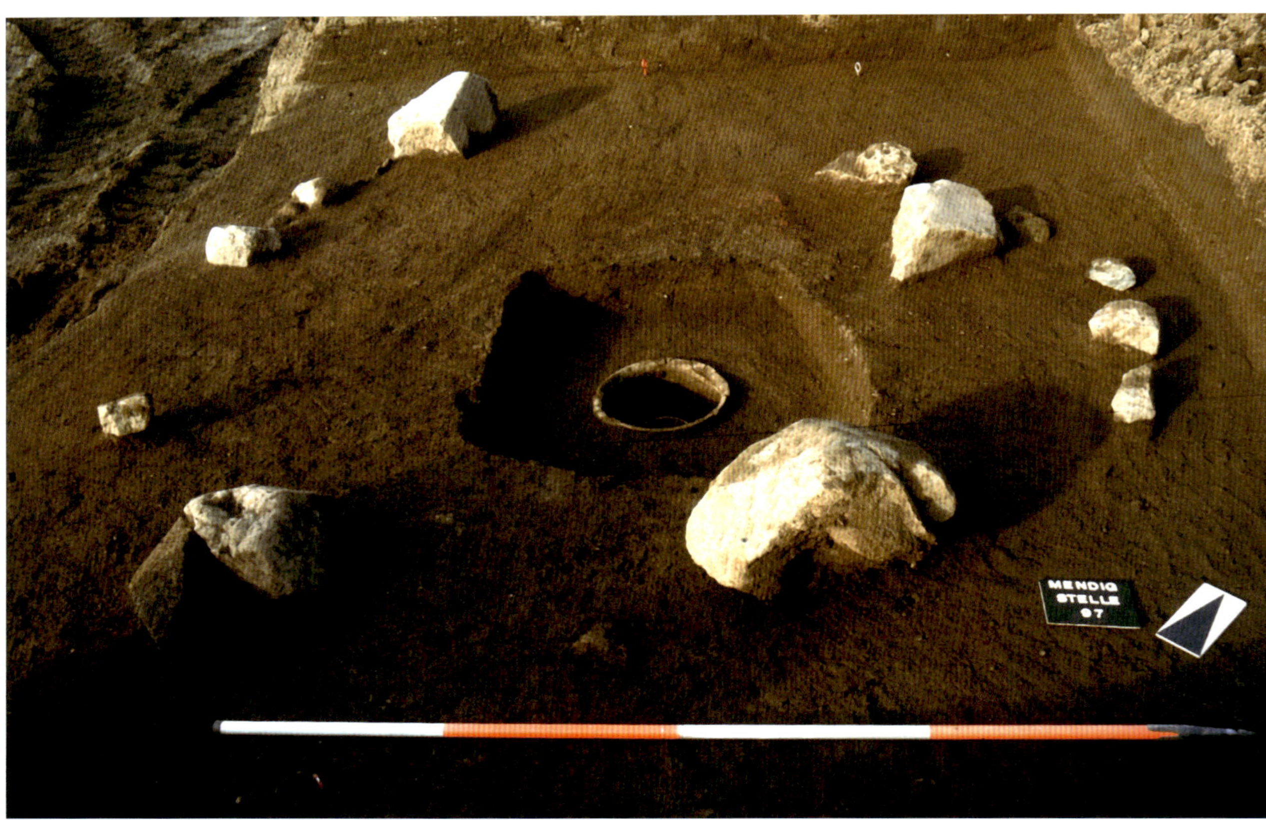

Fig. 13
Mendig, Mayen-Koblenz district. Urn grave in early excavation context. The concentrically arranged stones around the burial mark the former mound over the urn grave. (GDKE/Landesarchäologie/Koblenz/F. Gebert)

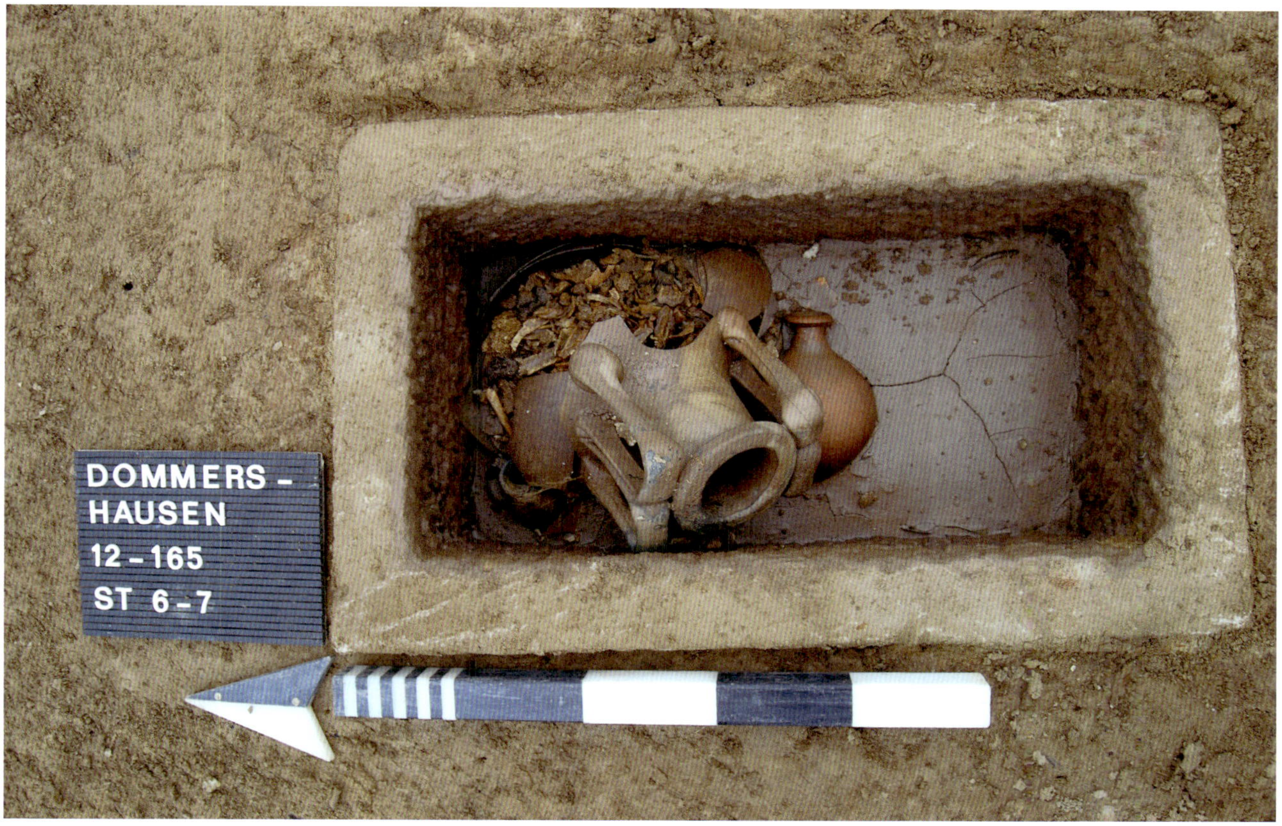

Fig. 14
Dommershausen, Rhein-Hunsrück distr. Sandstone ash box with the burial equipment of a Roman cremation after removal of the lid. (GDKE/ Landesarchäologie/ Koblenz/M. Gensty)

the destruction through illegal excavations by detectorists, continuously deplete the still intact inventory of monuments year by year. (Fig. 4)

The degree of preservation and transmission of archaeological objects and monuments in the field depends on several factors. The relics visible on the surface are relatively easy to recognize. They include the burial mounds often found in the state as the last visible witnesses of prehistoric burial sites (Fig. 5), as well as ramparts from prehistoric and early times, but also remains of Roman buildings (Fig. 6), which are still recognizable in forest areas and waste land zones as rubble strips or bumps. (Fig. 7) This group of monuments also comprises the early churches, castles and fortifications, and medieval-modern abandoned settlements and farmsteads. Trails, sunken roads, defensive dykes, and systems of farmland and terraces, but also the remains of earlier mining, all belong to the category of visible archaeological monuments.

It is much more difficult to recognize findspots hidden in the soil, which are far more frequent than the visible evidence. Since all houses and settlement structures in prehistoric times were made of wood, no observable traces of the settlements have survived. What can be found, however, are some discolourings in the soil indicating former wooden structures, such as the support posts of house constructions, pits filled in with man-made debris, and ditches of former enclosures. (Fig. 8-9) Remains of this type become visible in ploughed fields mostly as dark stripes, in which broken pottery and other find material is exposed by the plough. Stone buildings only existed during the Roman imperial period and for important constructions of Merovingian and Carolingian times, as well as during the following younger epochs. The massive stone building technique logically facilitates finding the remains hidden in the soil, since stone walls can be recognized more easily than simple discolourings in the soil in situ. (Fig. 10-11)

Besides settlement finds, grave finds are the second group of archaeological monuments not visible on the surface. These early witnesses of mortuary practices

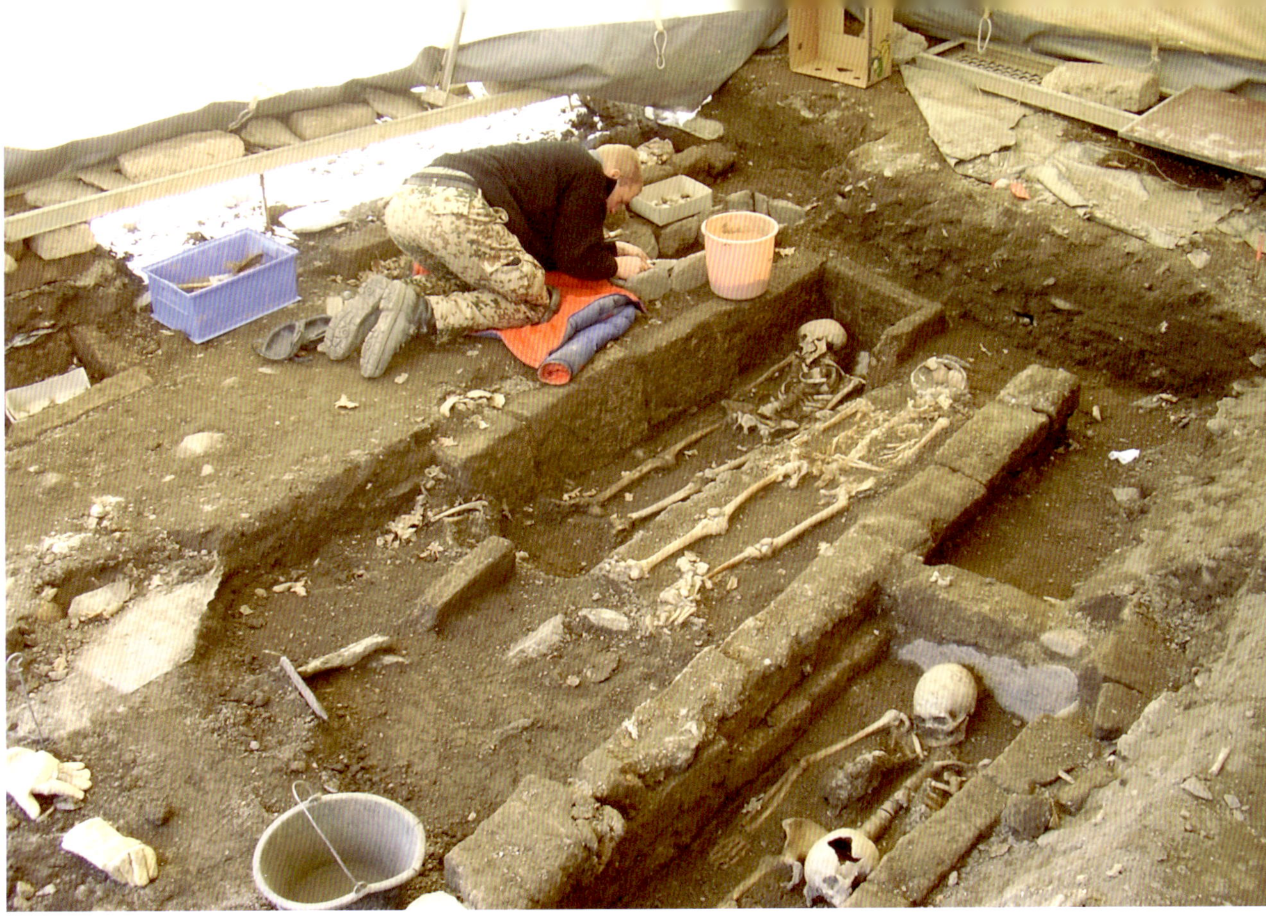

Fig. 15
Andernach, Mayen-Koblenz distr. Medieval inhumation graves near the Marienkirche during exposure. (GDKE/Landesarchäologie/Koblenz/F. Brüninghaus)

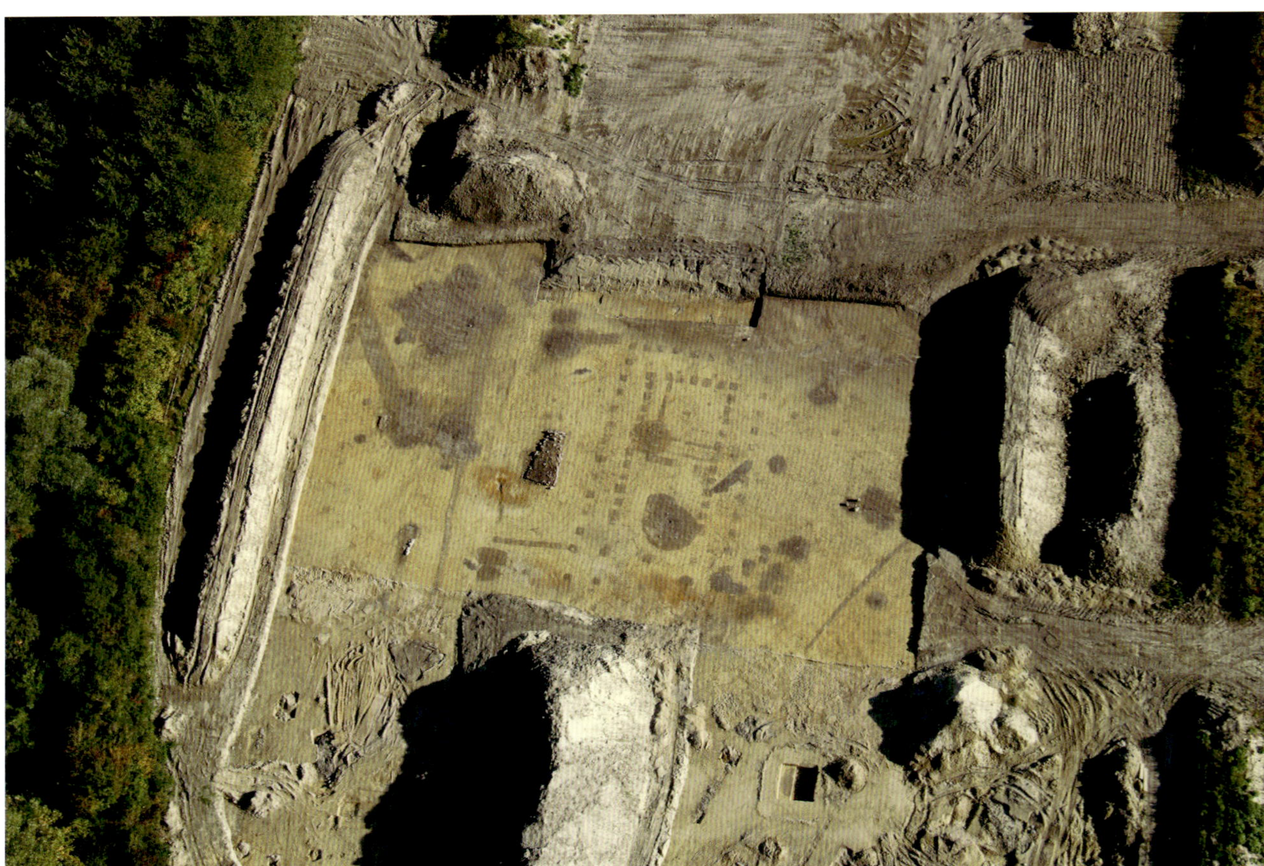

Fig. 16
Neuhofen, Rhein-Pfalz distr. Roman vicus. Exposure works in complex antique building structures. (GDKE/Landesarchäologie/Speyer)

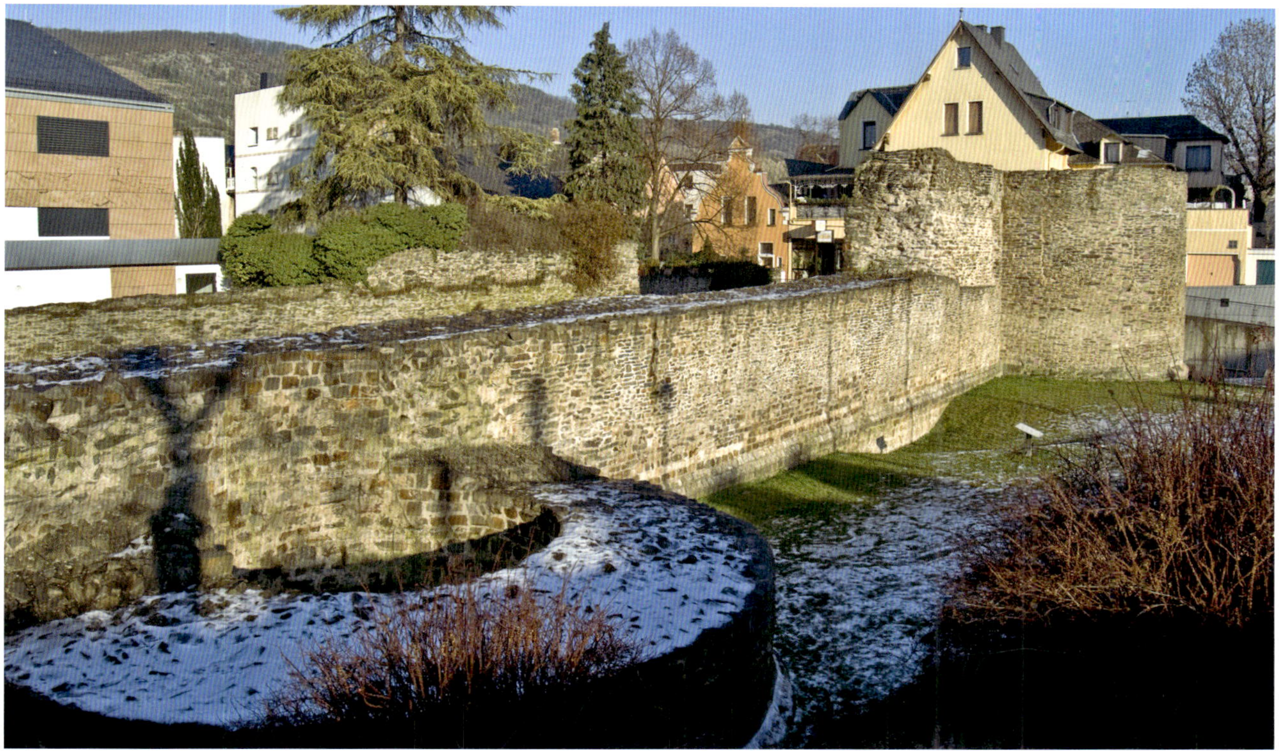

Fig. 17
Boppard, Rhein-Hunsrück distr. Part of the surviving late Roman fort wall with tower foundations. (GDKE/Landesarchäologie/Koblenz/H. Fehr)

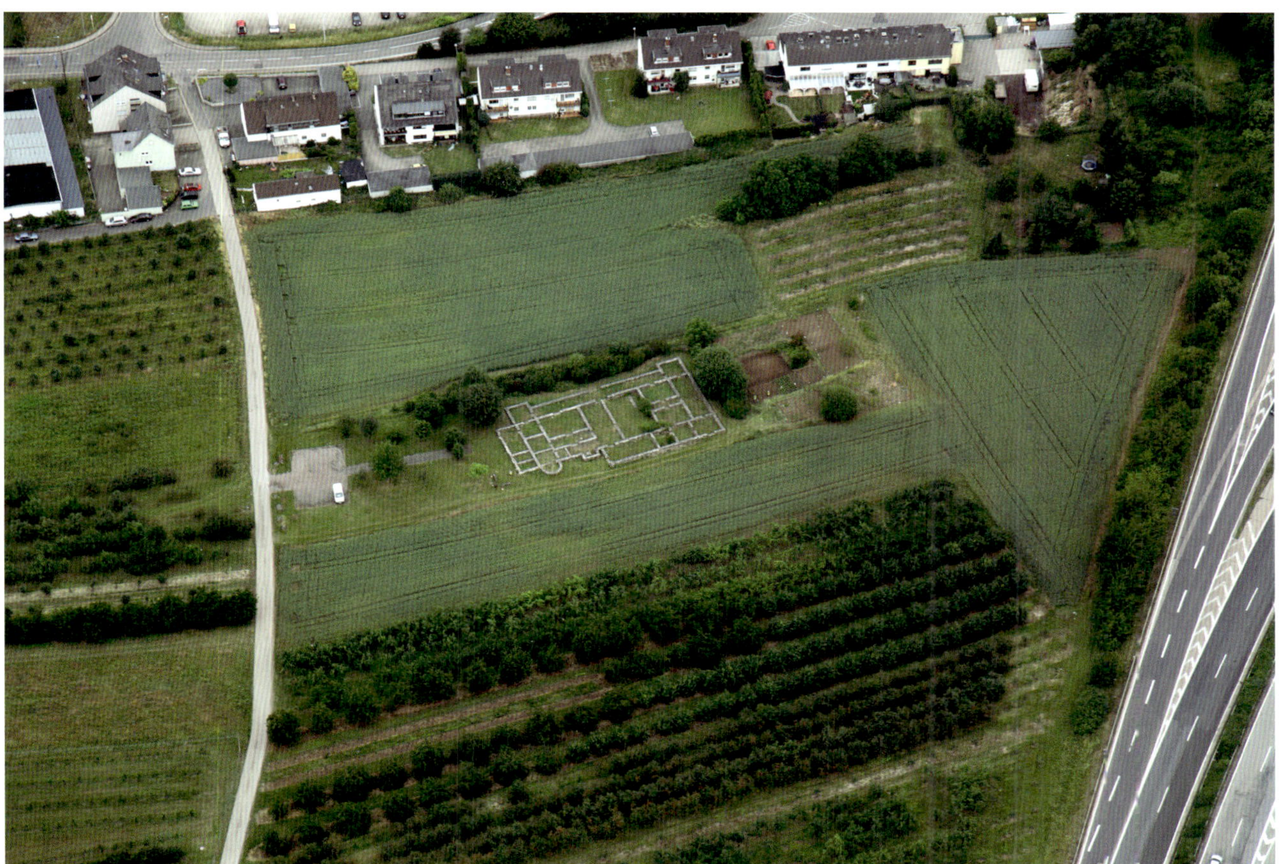

Fig. 18
Mülheim-Kärlich, Mayen-Koblenz distr. Aerial photo of a Roman villa visualised through walling-up according to the excavation findings. (Foto: R. Gensheimer)

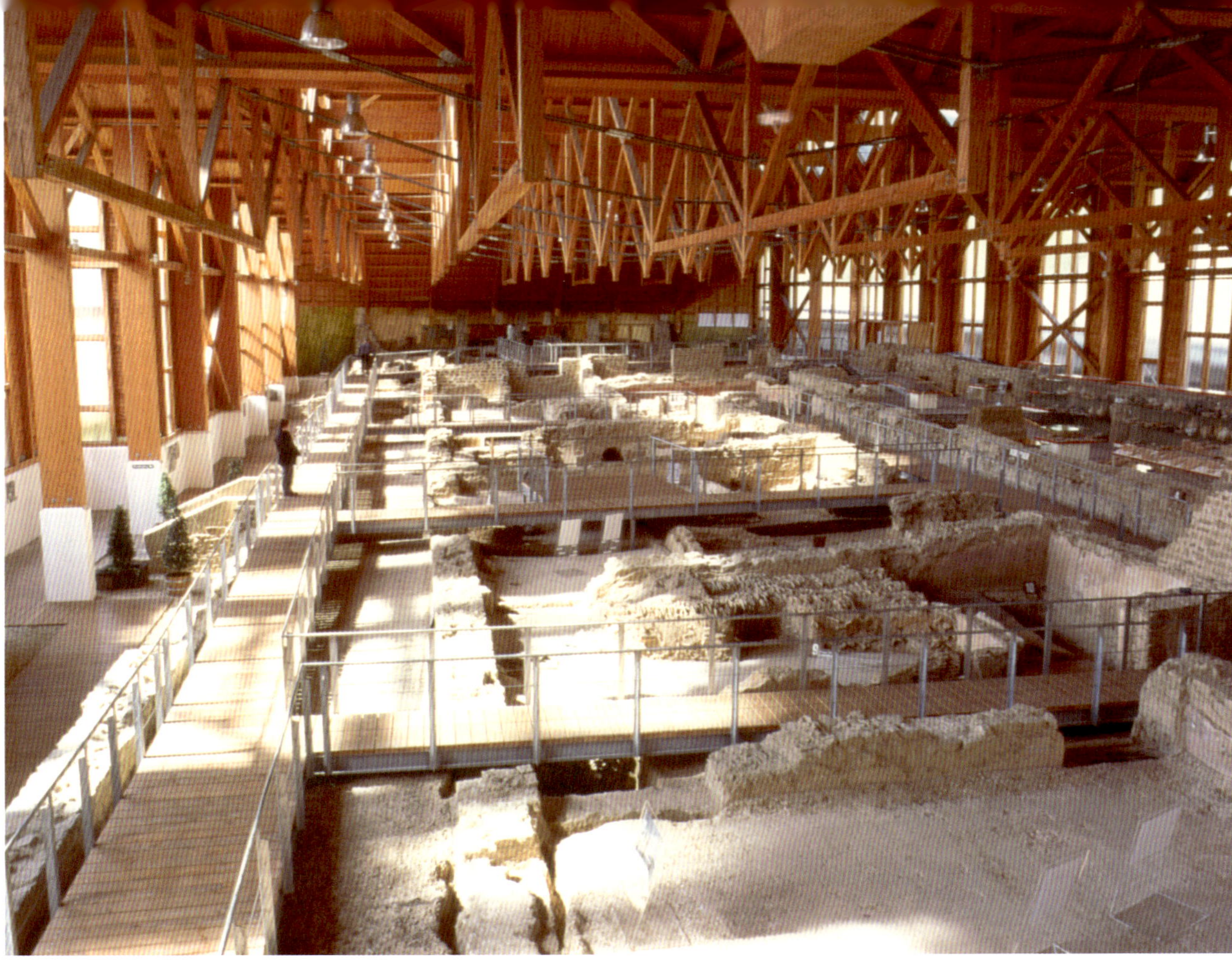

Fig. 19
Bad Neuenahr-Ahrweiler, Ahrweiler distr. Protective building over the »Roman villa« for a museum presentation of the original archaeological finding. (GDKE/Landesarchäologie/Koblenz/H. Fehr)

are particularly endangered because of their small size. Most of the time, they are only recognized through finds picked up from ploughed fields or through observation of earthworks during building measures. (Fig. 12-14) When evaluating the grave finds, archaeological research cooperates closely with anthropology: the examination of the age, gender or pathological changes of human remains permits drawing demographic conclusions regarding early settlement communities. (Fig. 15)

Another group of finds are the so-called »hoards« placed in the ground at different times to hide them or sunk in rivers and lakes as offerings. What is no longer visible are the traces of settlements from Roman and medieval times hidden under the old localities of today. The settlement layers preserved there usually facilitate the identification of a continuous sequence and formulation of differentiated statements about the historical development of a given locality. Archaeological research does not end with the start of written tradition – where a demarcation line may be drawn in Roman times already – but extends into modern times and the time of the World Wars and comprises everything that must be studied by archaeological methods.

The cultivated landscape is subject to constant transformation, since the requirements imposed by man on the landscape and nature change constantly, and the younger and most recent modifications of a landscape are particularly important in understanding the settlements of earlier epochs. These changes also provide the direct pre-conditions for assessing archaeological finds and findings in the field. Human interventions in the landscape have been occurring since early modern times, and in particular since the start of the industrial age in the 19th century. These include changes of the landscape through building measures, mining of mineral resources, expansion of villages, towns, and cities, development and industrial areas (Fig. 16), interventions in the vegetation, transformation of forest areas into agricultural land, and the adaptation of the landscape to the settlement requirements of modern man, but also river and stream regulations,

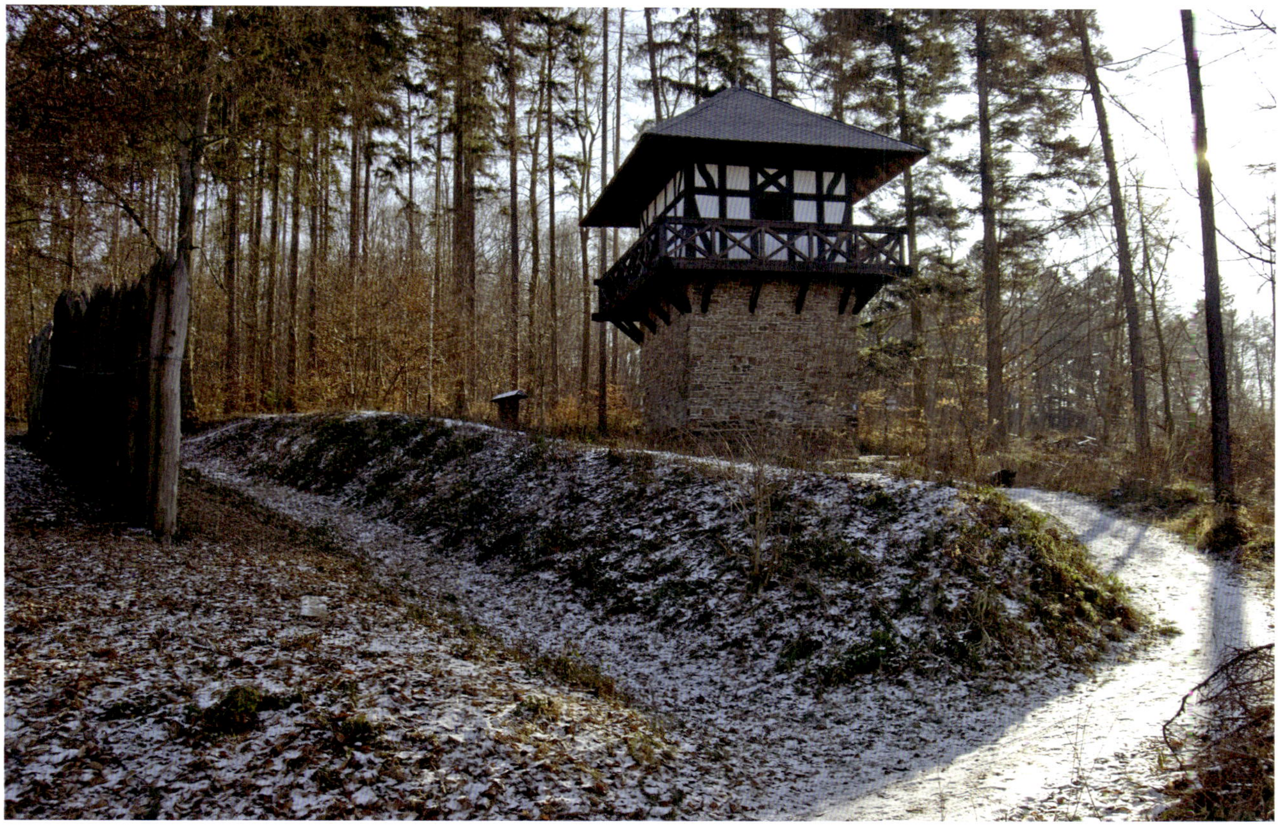

Fig. 20
Bendorf, Mayen-Koblenz distr. Older reconstruction of a Limes tower with palisade in the world heritage site »Upper German-Raetian Limes«. (GDKE/Landesarchäologie/Koblenz/C. A. Jost)

terrain modelling, drainage of wetlands, and land consolidation.

The communication of archaeological research is not reduced to presentation in museums only, for which nonetheless the state museums in Rhineland-Palatinate with their important archaeological collections are extremely important, but also includes the visualisation and valorisation of archaeological monuments in the field. (Fig. 17-19) In particular, the world heritage sites in the state play a key role in communicating its cultural heritage. (Fig. 20)

Rhineland-Palatinate is a young state and its borders only play a minor role as far as geological epochs and the cultures of pre- and early history are concerned. The State Archaeological Exhibition will therefore look mainly at regions and spaces with their differences and common features. Since the past cultures in Rhineland-Palatinate never existed alone and isolated, but as parts of larger cultural contexts, the presentation is above all dedicated to the topic of cultural encounter and cultural flow, which can be substantiated differently in individual epochs as migration, occupation, and acculturation. This topic, on the one hand, defines Rhineland-Palatinate in its position between cultural spaces, while on the other the subject is broad enough so as to not restrict the presentation of the varied archaeological work of the last decades. The position of the state in the heart of Europe, which is mainly characterized by the river Rhine as the north-south connection and the course of the Moselle from west to east, plays a key role here. The rivers Rhine and Moselle have been both bridges and borders of cultures in inter-European traffic routes since prehistoric times.

Bibliography

A. von Berg, H.-H. Wegner, Jäger, Bauern, Keltenfürsten. 50 Jahre Archäologie an Mittelrhein und Mosel. Archäologie an Mittelrhein und Mosel 13 (Koblenz 2001).

J. Kunow, H.-H. Wegner (Hg.), Urgeschichte im Rheinland. Jahrbuch des Rheinischen Vereins für Denkmalpflege und Landschaftsschutz 2005 (Köln 2006).

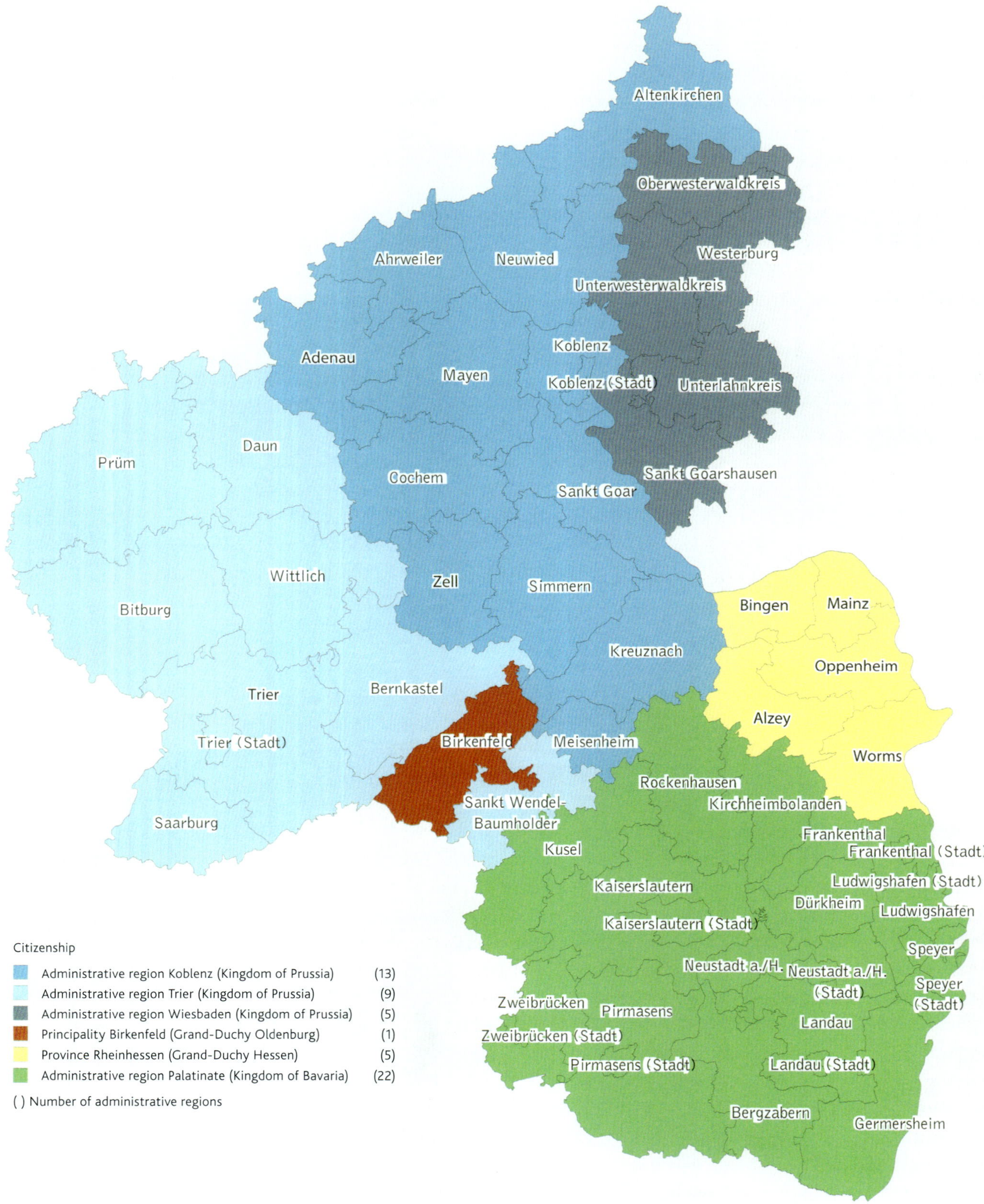
Altenkirchen
Oberwesterwaldkreis
Westerburg
Ahrweiler
Neuwied
Unterwesterwaldkreis
Koblenz
Adenau
Mayen
Koblenz (Stadt)
Unterlahnkreis
Prüm
Daun
Cochem
Sankt Goarshausen
Sankt Goar
Wittlich
Zell
Simmern
Bitburg
Bingen
Mainz
Kreuznach
Oppenheim
Trier
Bernkastel
Alzey
Trier (Stadt)
Birkenfeld
Meisenheim
Worms
Rockenhausen
Kirchheimbolanden
Sankt Wendel-Baumholder
Saarburg
Frankenthal
Frankenthal (Stadt)
Kusel
Ludwigshafen (Stadt)
Kaiserslautern
Dürkheim
Ludwigshafen
Kaiserslautern (Stadt)
Speyer
Neustadt a./H.
Neustadt a./H. (Stadt)
Speyer (Stadt)
Zweibrücken
Pirmasens
Landau
Zweibrücken (Stadt)
Pirmasens (Stadt)
Landau (Stadt)
Bergzabern
Germersheim
Citizenship
Administrative region Koblenz (Kingdom of Prussia) (13)
Administrative region Trier (Kingdom of Prussia) (9)
Administrative region Wiesbaden (Kingdom of Prussia) (5)
Principality Birkenfeld (Grand-Duchy Oldenburg) (1)
Province Rheinhessen (Grand-Duchy Hessen) (5)
Administrative region Palatinate (Kingdom of Bavaria) (22)
( ) Number of administrative regions

State Archaeology in Rhineland-Palatinate and more

MICHAEL SCHWAB

»The state of Rhineland-Palatinate comprises the greater districts of Koblenz, Montabaur, Rhine-Hesse, and Trier and the Palatinate.«

The spatial extent of the newly formed federal state of Rhineland-Palatinate is determined in its state constitution of 1947 through these few simple words. The greater districts of Koblenz and Trier were parts of the former Prussian Rhine Province; Montabaur formed part of the Prussian province of Hesse-Nassau; Rhine-Hesse was part of the former Great Duchy and later People's State of Hesse; while the Palatinate was Bavarian. (Fig. 1) Until 1947, all political and administrative decisions for these areas were made in Berlin, Düsseldorf, Darmstadt, Kassel or Munich. Each area therefore has its own history and tradition for dealing with archaeological cultural assets.

From the beginnings until World War II

Mainz

The »Collectanea antiquitatum in urbe atque agro Moguntino repertarum« by Johannes Huttichius, published in 1520, is the first work on archaeological finds in Mainz and surroundings. In 1645, Matthaeus Merian reports on Roman underfloor heating near Windesheim: the accuracy of the architecture shown is impressive to this day. In 1771, Father Joseph Fuchs publishes »Alte Geschichten von Mainz«: he conducts systematic excavations, and his work excels not only in the description of the objects, but also in criticism of the inadequate municipal care of archaeological cultural assets:

»The endless number of Roman monuments and antiquities in and around Mainz already made this town an open market place for Roman antiquities and rarities 400 years ago, from which many princes and important personalities decorated their cabinets«.

»Thousands of beautiful pieces were taken from Mainz to France England, Holland, the Netherlands, Lorraine, Upper and Lower Saxony, Hesse, Switzerland, Savoy, Sweden, and Russia.«

In Bingen and surroundings, Reverend Gärtler studies the city wall and the Roman villa in Bingen forest, 1764-1782. From 1798, Johann Friedrich Franz Lehne continues the work of

Fig. 1
Political affiliation of the territory of today's Rhineland-Palatinate around 1925. (LVerm-Geo RLP)

Fig. 2
Mainz, city of Mainz. Documentation of a canal from the time of Elector Johann Phillip von Schönborn. (GDKE/Landesarchäologie/Mainz/J. Dolata)

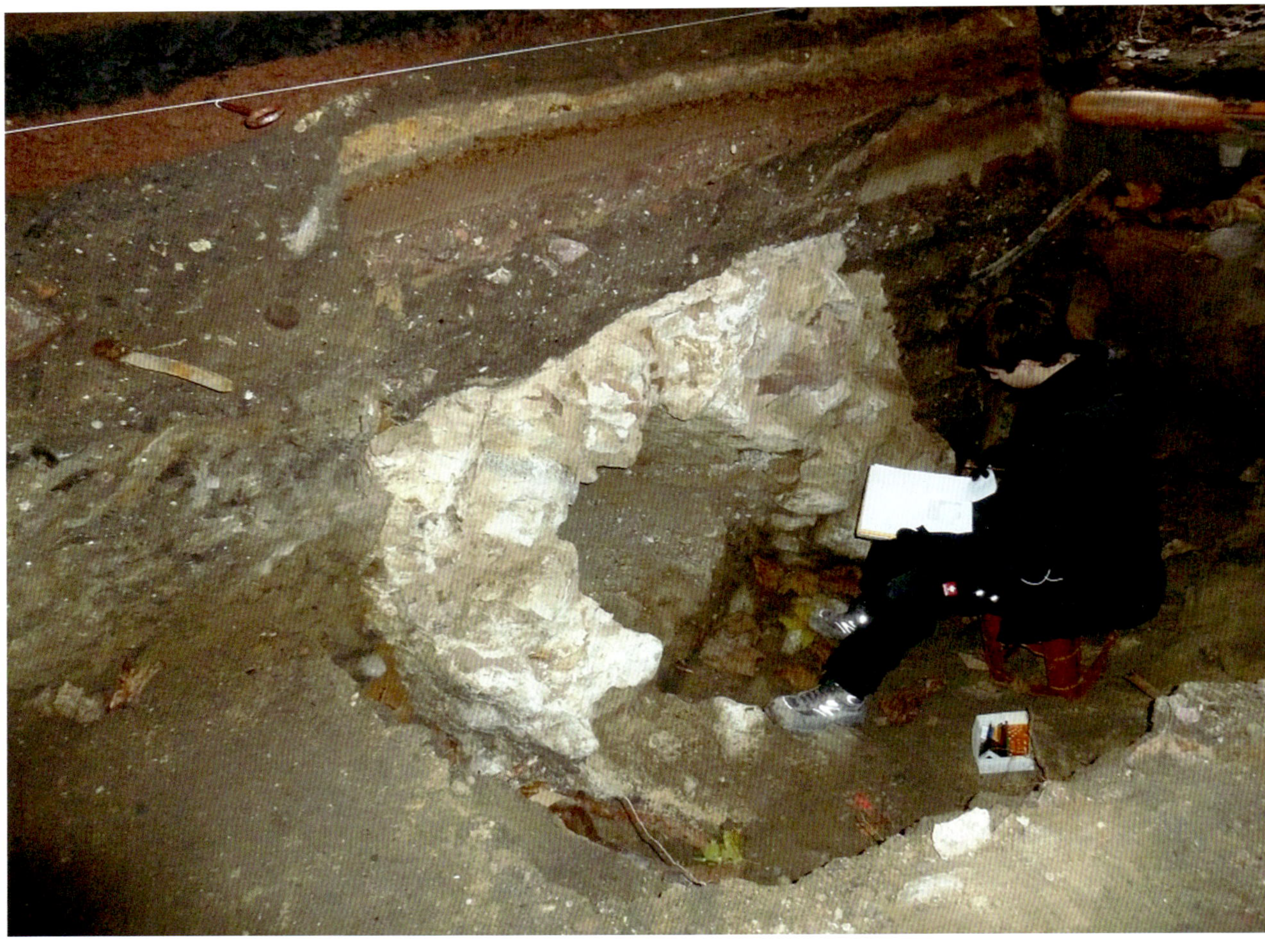

Fuchs. In 1802, the first archaeological finds are exhibited: they will become the basis of today's Landesmuseum in Mainz. Lehne also draws up the first overall archaeological map of Mainz. In 1844, the »Verein zur Erforschung der rheinischen Geschichte und Alterthümer in Mainz«, today's Mainzer Altertumsverein, is established, and the Römisch-Germanisches Zentralmuseum (RGZM) is opened eight years later. The »Antiquarisch-Historischer Verein für Nahe und Hunsrücken« is founded in Bad Kreuznach in 1856, followed in 1879 by the Altertumsverein in Worms. In Alzey, a museum is established in 1904 to present the finds from the local fort of late antiquity.

In 1884, the remains of the Roman stage theatre are discovered in Mainz. It is the first of many major Roman buildings found during subsequent years.

The »Gesetz, den Denkmalschutz betreffend« (monument protection act) is passed in 1902, followed in 1920 by the »Bekanntmachung über die Anzeigepflicht und die behördliche Genehmigung bei Ausgrabungen und Funden« (regulation on the obligation of disclosure and official authorization for excavations and finds). Together with the laws on the protection of archaeology, which follow later in all parts of the state, this regulation demands that (before the start of an excavation) there must always be a permit in hand. Even at that time, the importance of monument protection is thus recognized. In addition, regionally competent archaeological monument conservators are appointed to protect and study the archaeological finds and findings. Many finds can now be better processed from a scholarly viewpoint and meet with great interest from the public. Besides the »great« museums, many places of cultural mediation, which are of interest mainly to visitors from the region, are now also coming up.

In 1922, »at the urgent wish of the competent government office, the management of the RGZM reluctantly took over« the task of preservation of historical monuments as an additional duty. They were supported by historical societies and employees at the local museums.

Speyer

Beatus Rhenanus in 1531 already reports Roman finds in Speyer, and in 1542 King Ferdinand I visits the collection of the chairman of the Reichskammergericht, Wernher von Zimmern, who had placed it in the same spot where the Historisches Museum der Pfalz zu Speyer is located today.

In the 18th century, Duke Charles II of the Palatinate conducts systematic excavations, and the *antiquarium* in the Mannheim Palace becomes the home of many finds from the Palatinate. They will later be incorporated into today's Reiss-Engelhorn-Museen Mannheim. At that time, Georg Litzel gives detailed descriptions of Roman finds, inter alia of the fort in Altrip, where the Roman emperor Valentinian I stayed several times. The ceramics found there eventually gave rise to the term »Altrip-Horizont« (typical pottery of the period 370–425 AD), which is now well-established in archaeology.

As a result of the Congress of Vienna, in 1817 the Palatinate becomes part of the kingdom of Bavaria. An order for the protection of archaeological cultural monuments had already been issued in 1808, but clear efforts by the state for the protection and preservation of antiquities can only be seen when the Bavarians took over government. In 1826, an antiques hall is built in the cathedral garden of Speyer, and in 1869 the Historischer Verein (historical society) is set up, succeeding the »Geschichtlicher Verein der Rheinkreise«; it takes over the task of rescuing, collecting, and preserving archaeological finds in the Palatinate until 1956.

In 1908, the Kingdom of Bavaria passes the »Verordnung über Ausgrabungen und Funde von historisch merkwürdigen Gegenständen« (excavations act). This act will remain in force for the Palatinate – in spite of the formation of the federal state of Rhineland-Palatinate in 1947 – until the Monument Protection Act of 1978. The preservation of archaeological monuments is implemented by the Historisches Museum der Pfalz zu Speyer; archaeological scholars are employed by the museum.

Trier

Trier forms part of the French »Département Sarre« in 1801, when the »Société des recherches utiles du département de la Sarre à Trèves« is founded (today »Gesellschaft für nützliche Forschungen in Trier«); it is also in charge of archaeological matters. Since 1808, the society has conducted archaeological excavations and promoted the establishment of a collection of antiques. The transfer of the city to Prussian rule leads to the start of various excavation campaigns in 1816; for instance, at the amphitheatre and the imperial thermal baths. In 1875, the Prussian minister of culture combines the collection of the Gesellschaft with the Königliche Staatssammlung (Royal State Collection) set up in 1820. It forms the basis for the »Provinzialmuseum der preußischen Rheinprovinz«, today the Rheinisches Landesmuseum Trier, whose director is also in charge of the preservation of archaeological monuments in the Trier area. The building in Ostallee, where the museum can still be found today, is used for the first time in 1889, though the ever-increasing number of archaeological finds soon requires further building measures. Besides enlarging the exhibition and storage space, room is made for the staff. In 1914, the Prussian Excavation Act is passed for the regions of Koblenz and Trier; in 1920 the corresponding implementation rules follow. In 1937, the scope of activity of the museum in Trier is widened to the Birkenfeld district, which until then belonged to Oldenburg. The outbreak of World War II thwarts plans for a further enlargement of the museum.

Koblenz

Besides the museum in Trier, the »Provinzialmuseum der preußischen Rheinprovinz« is opened in Bonn in 1874. Until 1945 the museum caters for archaeology in the greater part of the then administrative district of Koblenz. In the former Hesse areas on the right bank of the Rhine, this task is assigned to today's Landesmuseum in Wiesbaden. The finds of that time can thus be visited in the museums in Bonn and Wiesbaden respectively.

In 1880, the »Altertumsverein Lahnstein« is set up. The origins of the »Verein für Geschichte und Kunst am Mittelrhein in Koblenz« go back to the »Verein für Kunst, Kunstgewerbe und Altertum für den Regierungsbezirk Koblenz«, founded in 1883. It effects the establishment of the »Schlossmuseum« with its departments of »Applied Arts«, »Arts« and »Antiques«.

The »Verein für Nassauische Altertumskunde und Geschichtsforschung« in Wiesbaden conducts the first archaeological studies, in particular for the regions on the right bank of the Rhine in northern Rhineland-Palatinate.

In 1880, a »Limeskommission« installed by the state for the study of the old Roman border is established in the Grand Duchy of Hesse; its research results are transferred in 1892 to the »Reichs-Limeskommission«. The »Deutsche Limeskommission«, set up in 2003 with the participation of the state of Rhineland-Palatinate, continues to build on this basic work. Since 2005, the 75 kilometres of the Limes situated on Rhineland-Palatinate territory are part of the UNESCO World Heritage site »Frontiers of the Roman Empire. Upper German-Raetian Limes«.

In 1911, the »Verein für Heimatpflege und Altertumskunde im Kreis Neuwied« is instituted; three years later, the Bodewig-Museum opens in Lahnstein, and in 1936 the »Altertumsverein Alt-Andernach«, founded in 1898, establishes the museum for the city. It is in particular the »Geschichts- und Altertumsverein für Mayen und Umgebung«, founded in 1904, that conducts archaeological excavations, the results of which are on display in a museum opened there in 1920/21.

State Archaeology in Rhineland-Palatinate after World War II

From 1945 on, the cities and localities are characterized by reconstruction. The creation of housing, the development of the economy and infrastructure, the acceleration of raw material extraction (e.g. pumice, gravel, and sand) and the growth in the »Miracle on the Rhine« have absolute priority in people's thoughts. As compared to the great opportunities and challenges of this time, the archaeological offices are utterly understaffed. The most important archaeological work can only be effectively carried out by focusing on priorities.

Fig. 3
The various official names of the institutions for the preservation of archaeological monuments in Rhineland-Palatinate, by the example of the Speyer branch office. (GDKE/ Landesarchäologie/ Speyer)

Because of their different historical development, the four areas of the state continue to conduct the preservation of archaeological monuments quite independently. (Fig. 3)

Mainz

By establishing a »French zone« on the left side of the Rhine and an »American zone« on the right, the end of World War II leads to the administrative separation of these areas. The organisational hour of birth of the Mainz State Archaeology Office coincides with the appointment of the director of the RGZM, »to take care of the archaeological heritage« in the administrative district of Mainz. For the time being, the organisational model of pre-war times is thus maintained.

During the reconstruction phase after World War II, the efforts made to record the archaeological traces of the city and its surroundings are concentrated on a few major excavation projects; for instance, the study of the Celtic-Roman burial ground in Badenheim and the forts of Alzey and Bad Kreuznach.

On the occasion of Prof. Dr. G. Behrens' retirement and the redefinition of the tasks of the RGZM, the ministry of culture of the state of Rhineland-Palatinate in April 1953 entrusts the Altertumsmuseum of the city of Mainz with the preservation of archaeological monuments in Rhine-Hesse.

From 1 April 1956, the department of archaeological heritage in Rheinhessen and the Kreuznach district finally has its own office (Landesdienst für Vor- und Frühgeschichte) within the premises of the Altertumsmuseum in the city of Mainz. The Landesdienst maintains a good level of cooperation between the preservation of archaeological monuments and the museum.

Until then, archaeological research and the presentation of the results to the public are inseparably linked: the museum and the Landesdienst in charge of the preservation of archaeological monuments work together in one institution. In 1963, however – with the exception of Trier – the museums and the preservation of archaeological monuments are being separated throughout the entire state.

In 1967, the state takes over the Altertumsmuseum in Mainz, which is renamed Mittelrheinisches Landesmuseum. The state now has overall responsi-

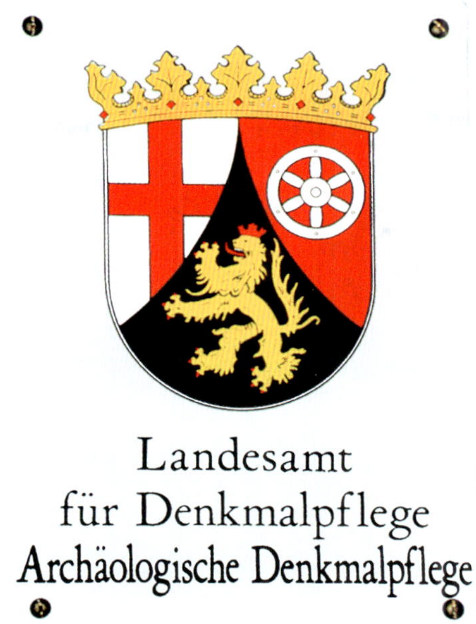
Landesamt
für Denkmalpflege
Archäologische Denkmalpflege

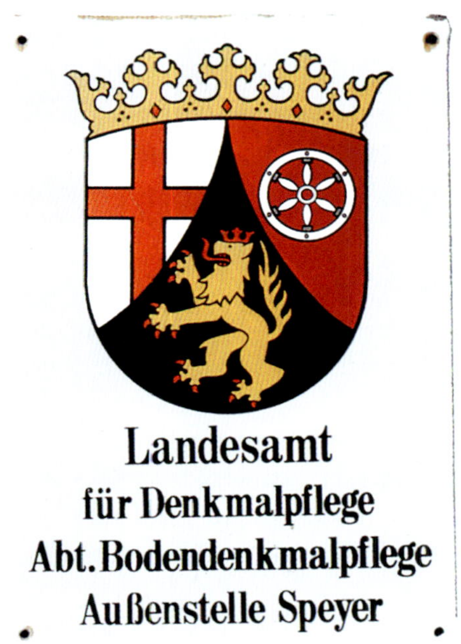
Landesamt
für Denkmalpflege
Abt. Bodendenkmalpflege
Außenstelle Speyer

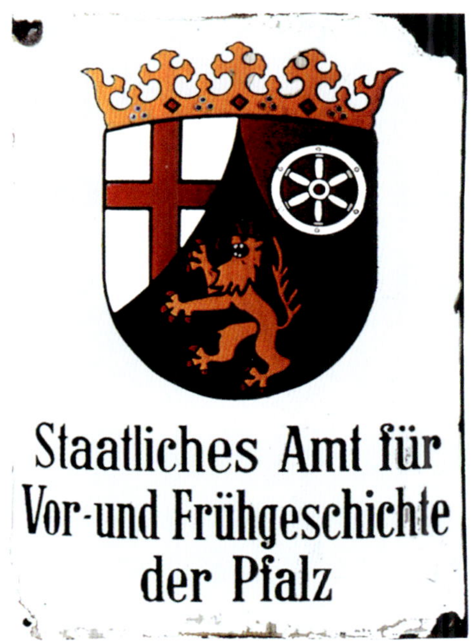
Staatliches Amt für
Vor-und Frühgeschichte
der Pfalz

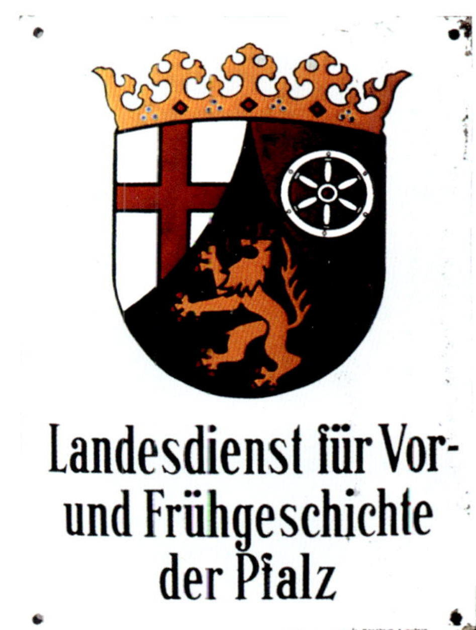
Landesdienst für Vor-
und Frühgeschichte
der Pfalz

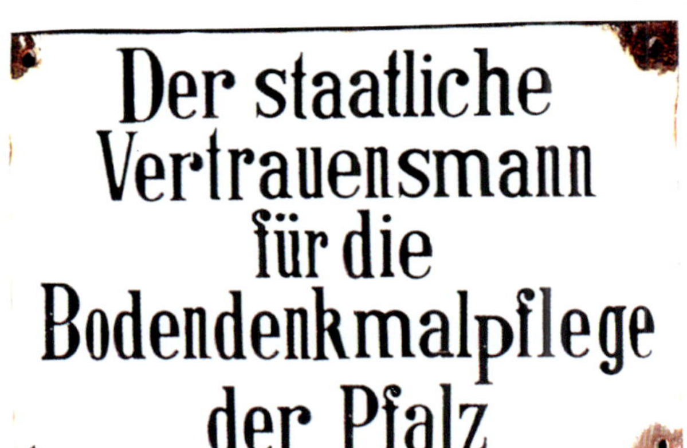
Der staatliche
Vertrauensmann
für die
Bodendenkmalpflege
der Pfalz

Fig. 4
Hechtsheim, city of Mainz. Unearthing of stone sarcophagi in 1978. (GDKE/Landesarchäologie/Mainz)

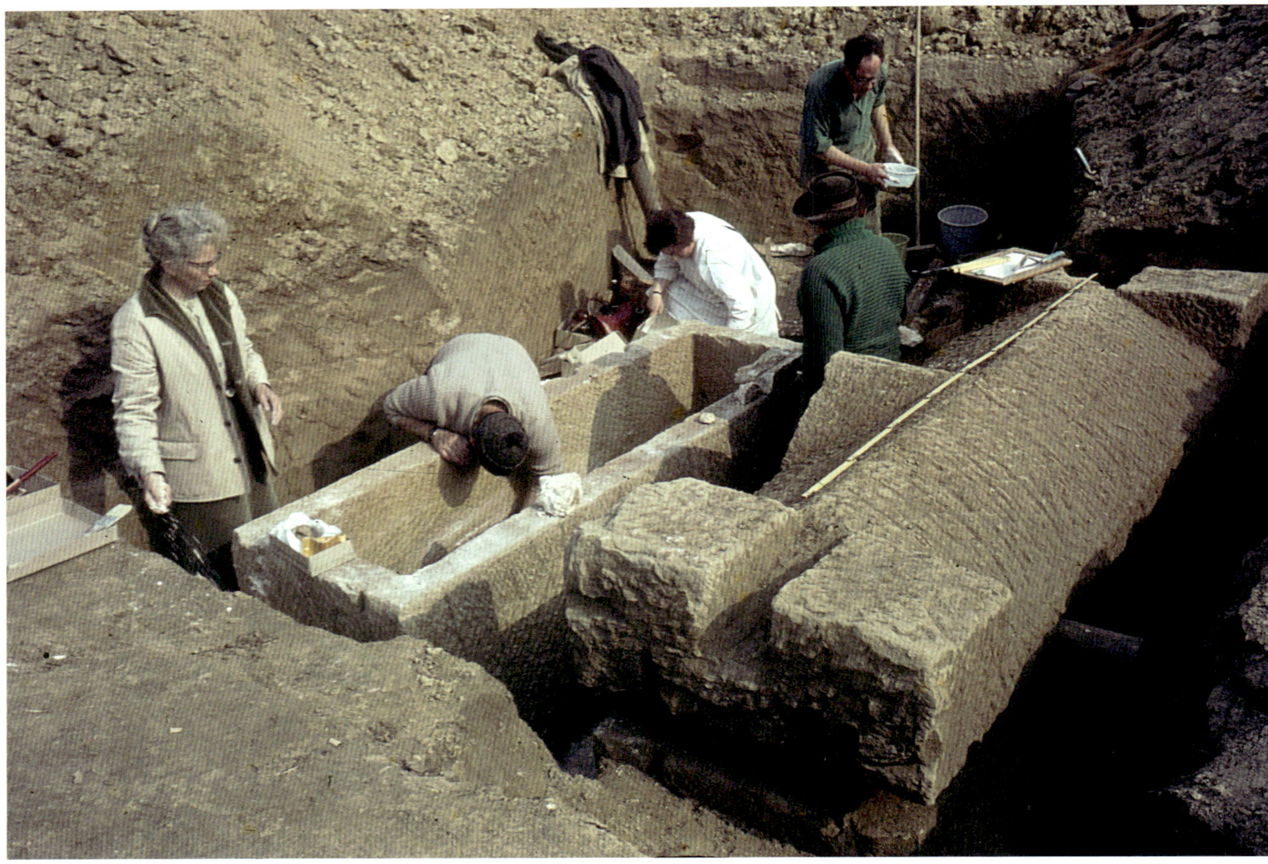

bility for the museum and the preservation of archaeological monuments, thus also for the study and presentation of the urban archaeological history of Mainz.

In 1970, the Landesdienst is renamed »Staatliches Amt für Vor- und Frühgeschichte«. The foundations are laid for archaeological documentation required to process the sources and for the function of the department as a »public agency«. The creation of inventories and the permanent storage of the archaeological finds are re-arranged, since this specific task of a museum now falls to the preservation of archaeological monuments after its separation from the museum.

Since the middle of the 1970s, more and more references and complaints can be found in the reports regarding the ever-widening gap between personnel and funding on the one hand, and the growing number of tasks in the field or the restorative and systematic evaluation of the excavation results on the other. The involvement of young people doing community service has offered some relief since 1977. (Fig. 4) Since the middle of that decade, discussion over a new state law for »the protection and care of cultural monuments in Rhineland-Palatinate« has been getting ever stronger. The objective is the creation of a uniform legal basis. The efforts of the four directors of the Staatliches Amt für Vor- und Frühgeschichte (offices for pre- and early history) in Rhineland-Palatinate – Dr. Eiden (Koblenz), Dr. Stümpel (Mainz), Dr. Kayser (Speyer), Dr. Schindler (Trier) – have above all and from the outset been directed at improving the legal conditions as well as content and organisational issues.

The law introduced in 1978 nevertheless falls short of the demands and expectations of the experts. It is true that greater possibilities are opened up through placing cultural assets under protection and by examining them scientifically prior to their unavoidable destruction in certain cases, and that the »Schatzregal« provisions introduced in 1986 regulate the destination of the finds, yet neither financial nor personnel improvement can be achieved. A particular problem is posed by the integration of the so-far independent Staatliches Amt für Vor- und Frühgeschichte into the

»Landesamt für Denkmalpflege«, which also comprises the preservation of architectural and art heritage the scientific methods and work procedures of the two disciplines are just too different. Only the Landesmuseum Trier can keep its special status and its own form of organisation.

In 1981, the famous Roman shipwrecks are discovered in Mainz. The processing is carried out in cooperation with the RGZM and it is the basis for today's Museum for Ancient Shipping in Mainz.

In 1982, during earthworks for a new office centre in Mainz-Weisenau, the Roman cemetery road is discovered. The excavations last until 1992, partly in cooperation with the German Research Foundation (DFG), and the results can be seen in situ. During building works, the city gate of late antiquity is found. This monument was also unearthed in situ in such a way that it can be seen by visitors. The same goes for the most important results of the excavations in the Isis and Magna Mater sanctuary in the inner city of Mainz (1999–2001).

As a consequence of further construction works (Fig. 2 and 5), other epochs (besides many Roman finds) can also be studied, such as the medieval »Alte Stromburg« in Stromberg (1984-1988), the medieval city quarters at Tritonplatz (1993) and Hopfengarten (2013), as well as a double body grave discovered and excavated in 2002 in Bad Kreuznach, which allows particular insights into the burial methods of the elites of the Urnfield Period.

Not only the processing of excavations already concluded, but also future building projects in the state capital are at the focus of the work there.

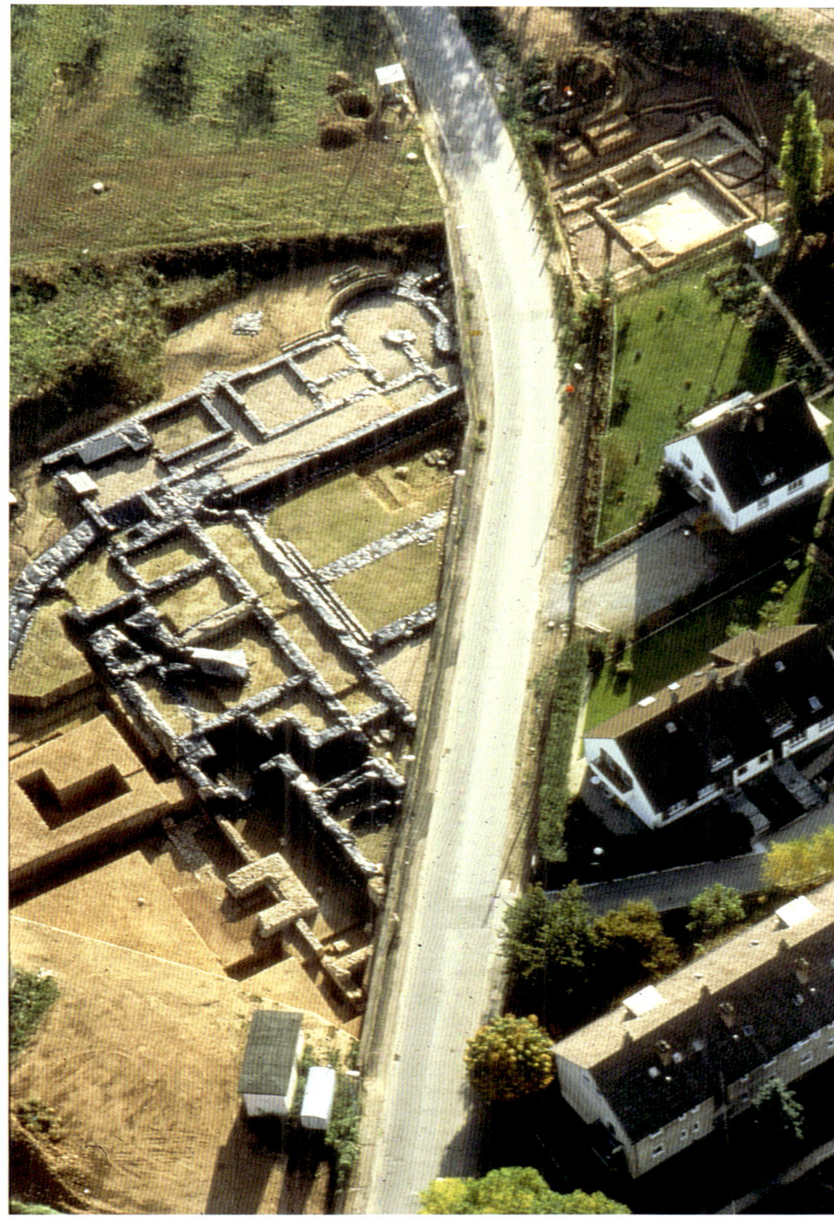

Speyer

The many major excavation projects are a peculiarity of the region. Contiguous settlement or production grounds over large areas could be unearthed and documented here. The late Celtic *oppidum* in Donnersberg (1974-1983), the Roman *terra sigillata* manufactory in Rheinzabern (1975-1996), and the early to high medieval settlement in Speyer »Vogelgesang« (1978-1982), where the study of the ceramic finds was only concluded in 1998, were at first funded by the German Research Foundation (DFG). Other collaborative partners followed later on.

The excavation on the Großer Berg near Kindsbach (1985-1990) opened up the only late antique height settlement completely known at the present time and was carried out in cooperation with the municipality of Kindsbach. In 1980/81, the Roman villas of Wachenheim and Ungstein underwent archeological investigation and today constitute attractions for cultural tourism in the region. During further regular excavations in the cemeteries belonging to the villas, particularly rich grave goods have been found time and again.

Annexes to the villas, where excavations are also

Fig. 5
Bad Kreuznach, Bad Kreuznach distr. Excavation of parts of a peristyle villa not yet destroyed by road works. (GDKE/ Landesarchäologie/ Mainz)

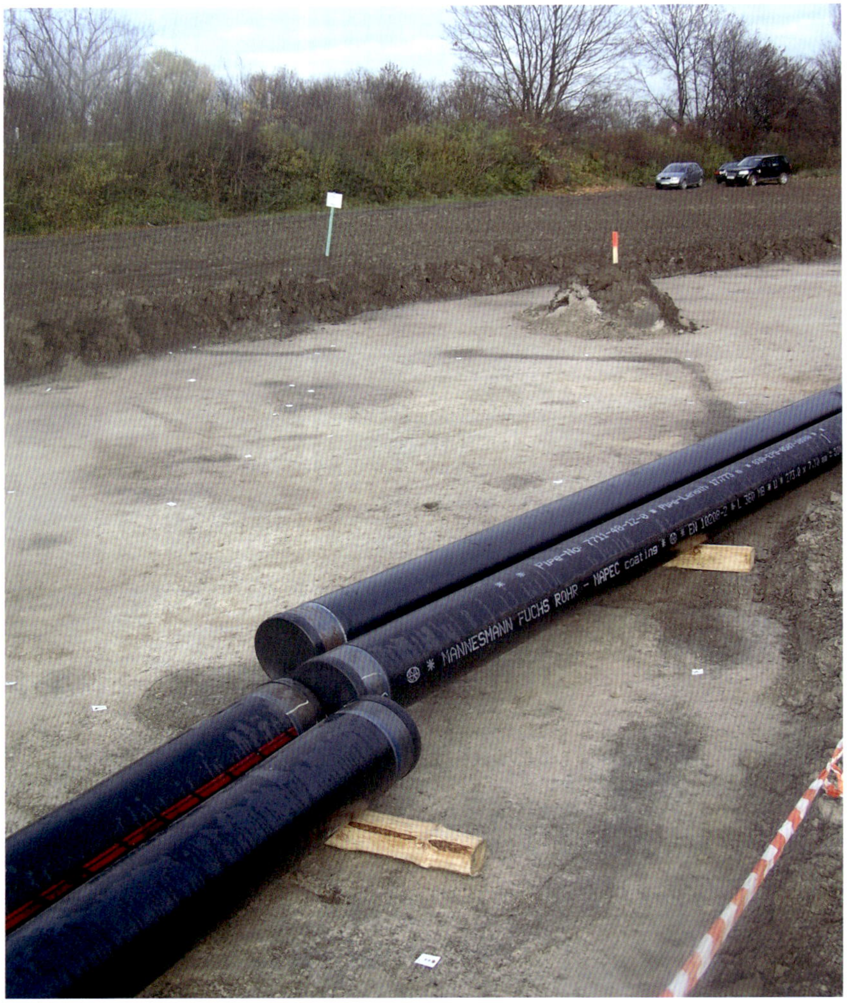

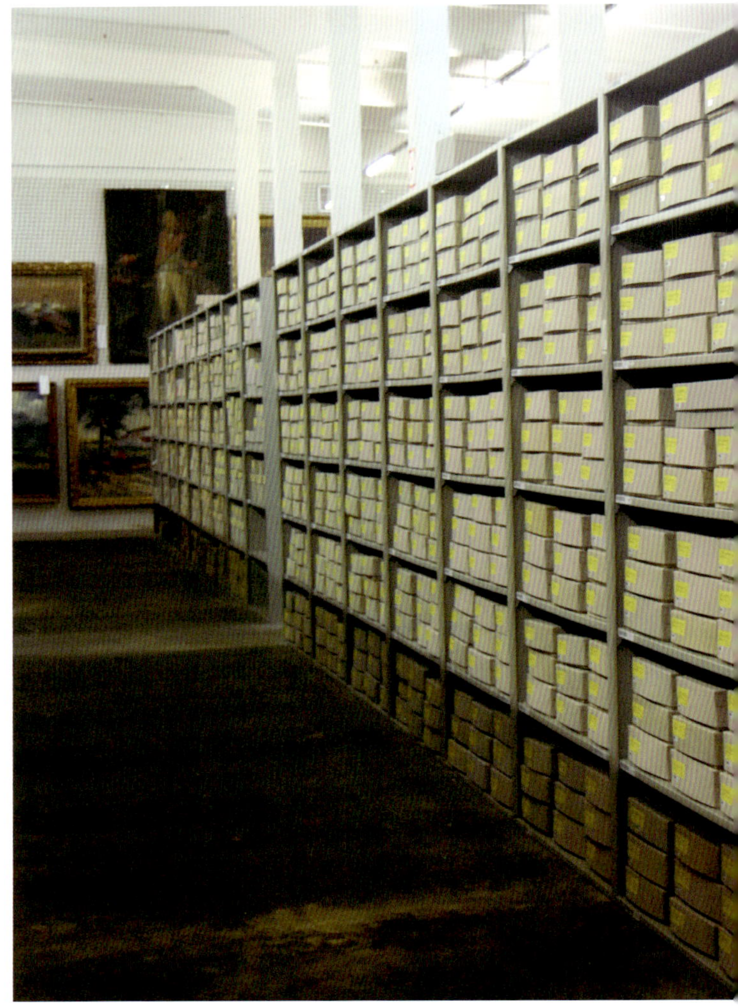

Fig. 6
After the top soil has been removed, ditches and pits show on the pipeline route. (GDKE/Landesarchäologie/Speyer)

Fig. 7
Speyer, city of Speyer. Parts of the new finds depot in the former cotton mill. (GDKE/Landesarchäologie/Speyer/B. Hünerfauth)

repeatedly conducted, show the importance of this region in Roman times; in fact, it is often referred to as »the biggest Roman winery north of the Alps«.

Even today, long-term excavation campaigns can only be conducted in cooperation with other institutions. This applies for instance to the excavations at the Linear Pottery ritual site of Herxheim (1995-2015) as well as that at Eisenberg, where a Roman industrial *vicus* with ironworking and a *burgus* from late antiquity have been undergoing excavation since 1992.

The new millennium brings new challenges. A section of the Ethylene- Pipeline South from Ludwigshafen to Münchsmünster (Bavaria) runs for 73 km (from Ludwigshafen to near Karlsruhe) on Rhineland-Palatinate territory. A total of 136 findspots are documented, with planning for the excavations (undertaken 2007-2009) having started back in 2004. (Fig. 6)

Long-term excavation campaigns conducted in cooperation with external partners have become routine in the meantime, as shown by the excavation of the grave field in the area of Speyer-Marienheim (2011–2014), used from the 1st to the 5th century AD and evidencing a particularly rich find of grave goods. The study of these excavations can only be undertaken with the financial means provided by collaborative partners.

Another problem of the State Archaeology concerns the proper storage of the finds. The depots will reach the limits of their capacity in the foreseeable future, and ever new building measures make the situation even more acute. In Speyer, however, a medium-term solution to this problem might be found with an »old acquaintance«, namely, sharing a storage facility with the Historisches Museum which was installed in a former cotton mill. Thanks to modern technology (bar code scanners, data bank management, etc.), finds required to be scientifically processed can now be retrieved and made available very quickly. (Fig. 7)

Trier

About 80 % of the museum building was destroyed during World War II, but since major parts of the collection had been evacuated in time, an exhibition could already be opened by 1948 in the Simeonsstift, which until then had accommodated the offices of the museum administration. The first exhibition in the building at Ostallee only took place in 1956. Besides the archaeological work in Trier, there was also work to be done in the surroundings.

The examinations of the Celtic-Roman grave field and the Roman vicus in Wederath-Morbach started in 1954, (Fig. 8) and the first campaign ended in 1985. In the years 2000-2011 and again 2014-2016, further excavations were required due to building projects. The excavations are supported by the DFG, by the universities in Kiel and Trier, and by the municipality of Morbach.

Contrary to developments in other parts of the state, the State Archaeology remained a part of the museum after 1963. The investigation of Roman urban development and of the »Kaiserthermen« (1960-1966) of late antiquity thus continued under one roof.

In 1970, the district of Birkenfeld was re-transferred from the Koblenz office to the care of the Trier State Museum. In 1971-1975, the fortified Celtic settlement of Bundenbach, the so-called »Altburg«, was examined with the DFG's financial support. Since 1972, the »Archäologische Trier-Kommission« has been in charge of the city's rich archaeological heritage. (Fig. 9) The new insights from all previous research and the excavations conducted at that time (St. Irminen 1970-1972 and St. Maximin 1978-1991) were processed by an inter-disciplinary professional body and made available for planning the future development of the city. During these years, studies were undertaken not only in Trier itself but also in other areas, as shown by the

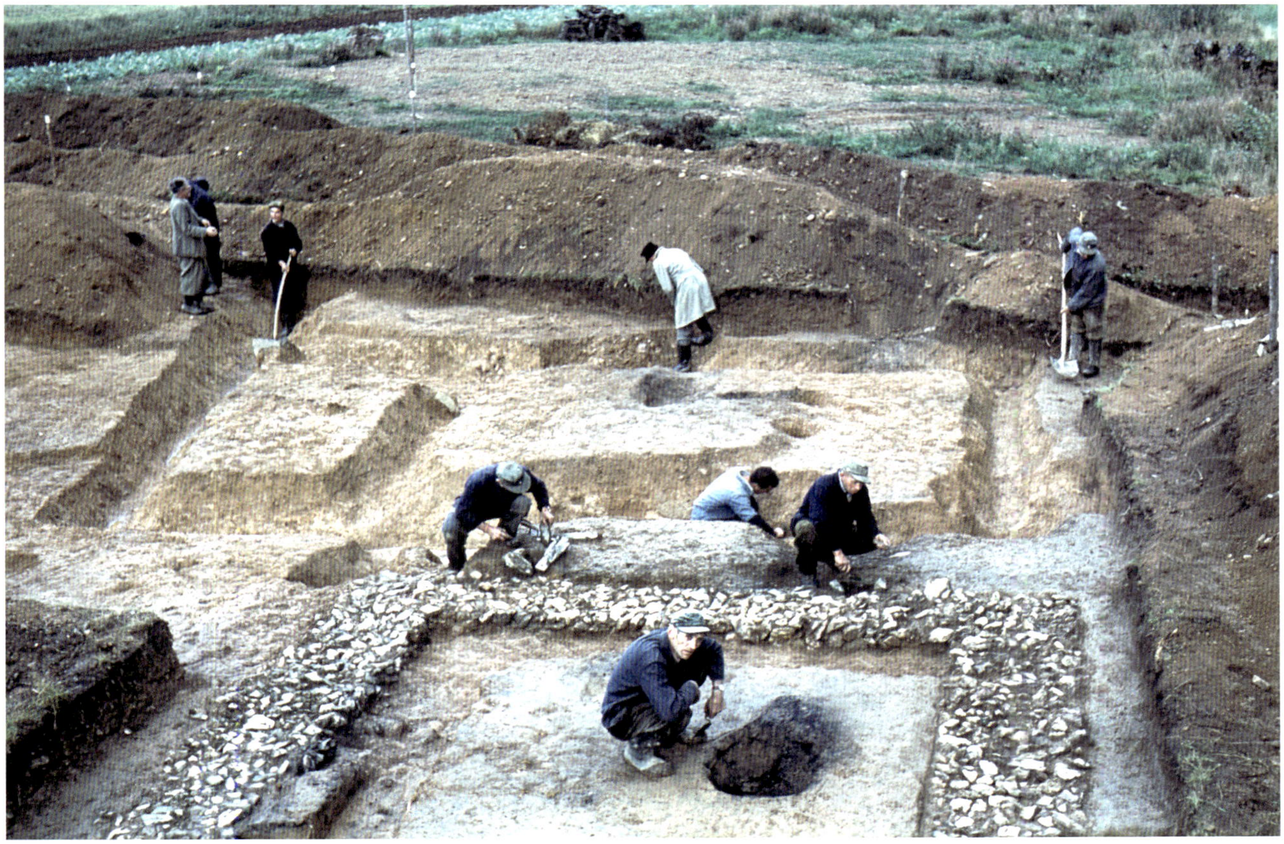

Fig. 8
Wederath, Bernkastel-Wittlich distr. Excavation work in 1958. (GDKE/Landesmuseum/Trier/H. Thömig)

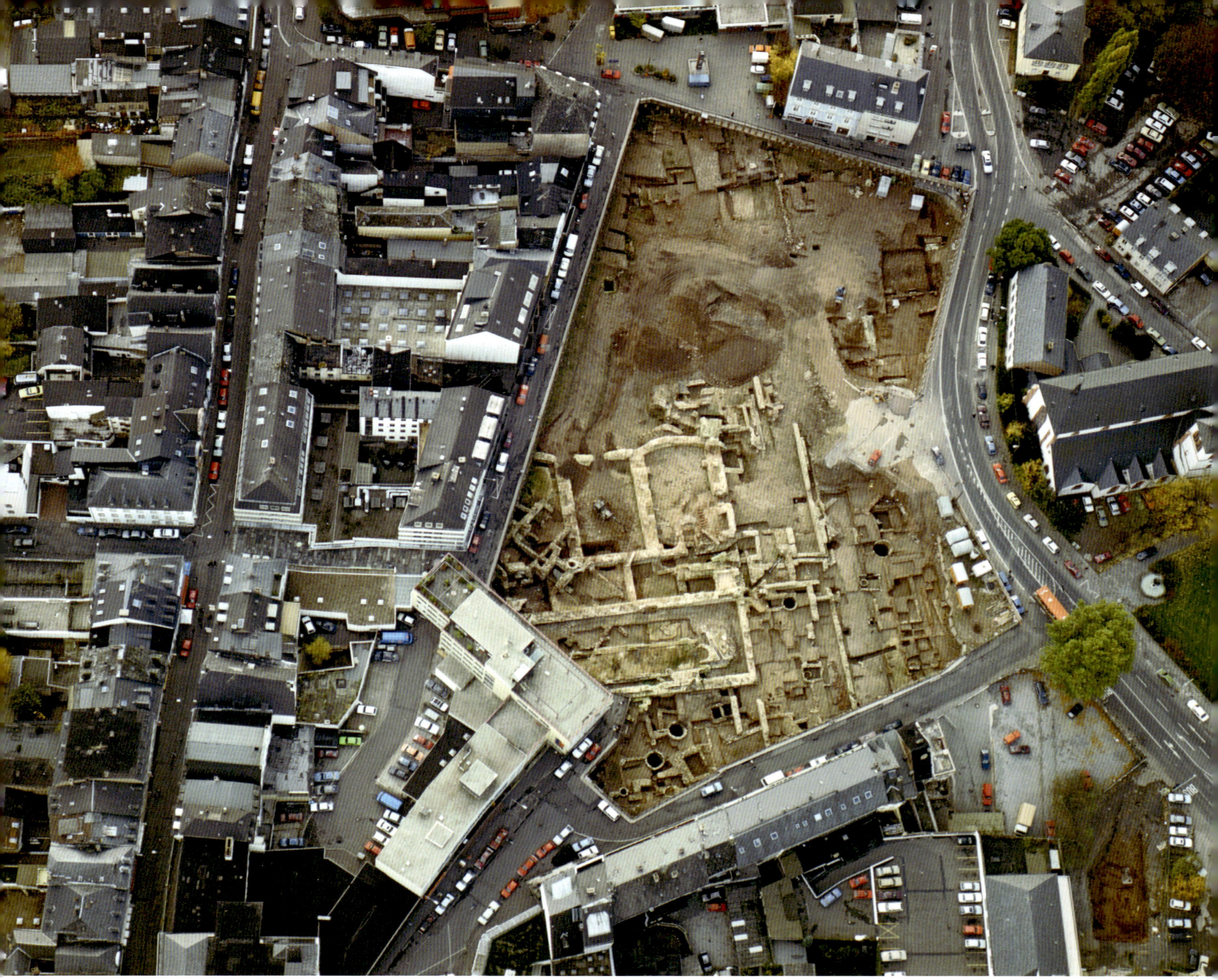

Fig. 9
Trier, city of Trier. Aerial photo of the Viehmarkt (cattle market) (GDKE/ Landesmuseum/ Trier/W. Bosl)

excavation on the early Celtic grave mound field of Bescheid/Beuren (1976-1979).

In 1986, the »Roman Monuments, Cathedral of St Peter and Church of Our Lady in Trier« became a UNESCO World Heritage site. It therefore comes as no surprise that the State Archaeology is involved time and again in building projects in the city. Trier's long history becomes more and more evident during excavations often carried out over many years: the Viehmarkt (cattle market) (1987-1991) and the Petrisberg (2002-2010) were examined archeologically; the Roman vicus and the sanctuary »Metzenberg« in Tawern were unearthed in 1986-1988 and 1994-1996 as a result of development projects in the area; in Piesport, the Roman wine press »Rusert« was examined archeologically in 1985-1986 and 1994-1995 as a pre-condition for agricultural measures, and excavations were conducted at the high medieval lowland castle »Alte Burg« in Dockendorf.

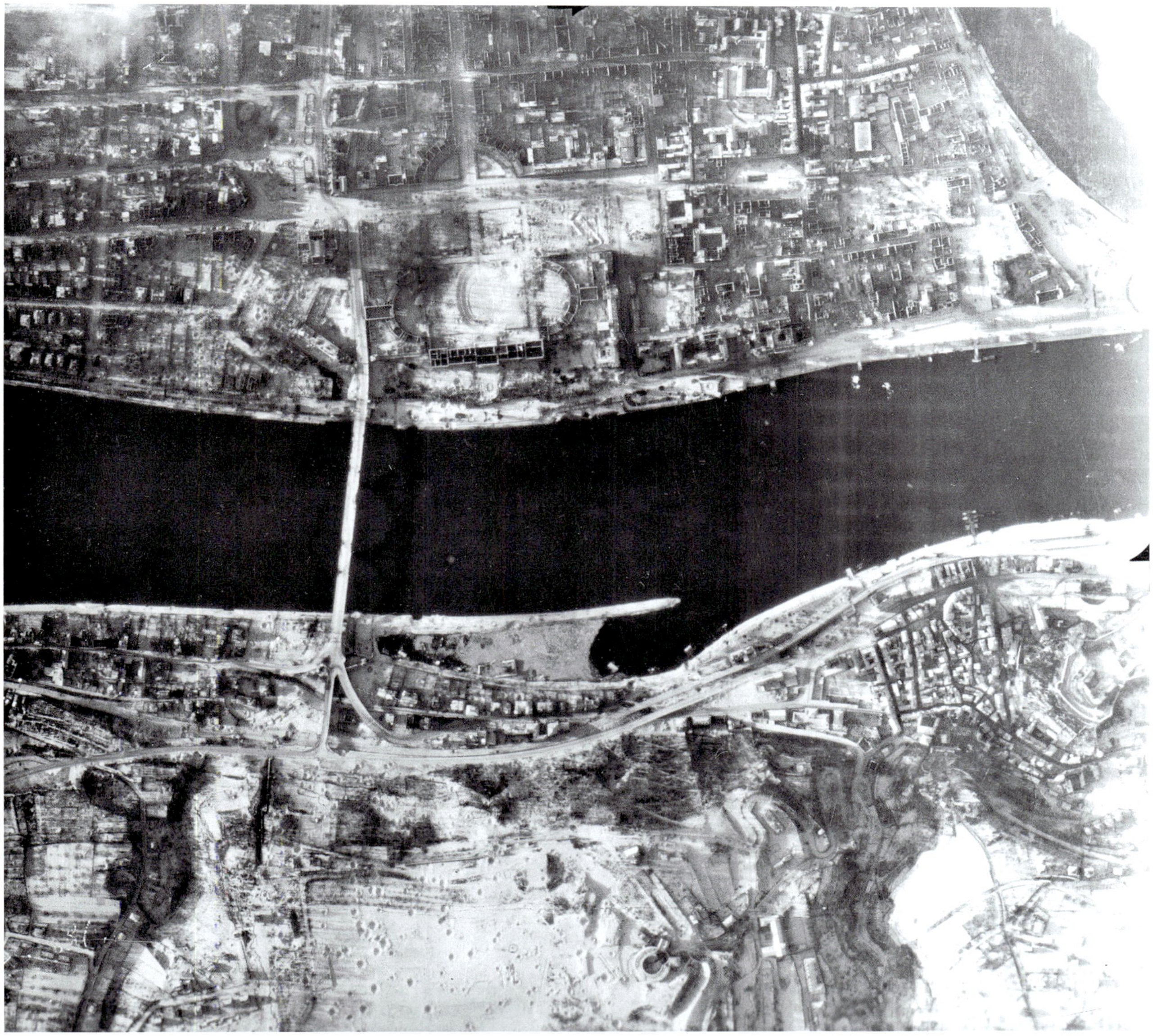

Fig. 10
Koblenz city. Aerial photo of the inner city destroyed during World War II. (GDKE/ Landesarchäologie/ Koblenz)

Koblenz

Nothing changed in the organization of the State Archaeology in the north of the state immediately after World War II. One scholar continued to work-at-home with the Rheinisches Provinzialmuseum in Bonn as »the territorial advisor of the Rheinisches Provinzialmuseum and state trustee for the district of Koblenz«. (Fig. 10) The work in those years was characterized by the traditionally intensive mining of raw materials, which even today is an important economic factor in the region. (Fig. 11)

Basalt is being mined near Mayen since the Neolithic. During antiquity, the region was renowned for the production of top quality pottery, whose raw materials were obtained directly from the region itself. The relevant findspots are now used for cultural tourism (Vulkanpark GmbH) and attract many visitors to the

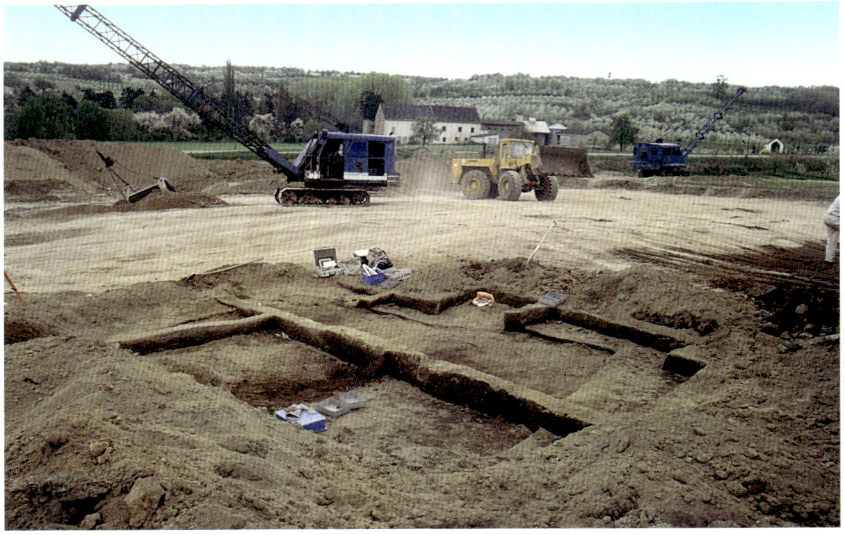

Fig. 11
Mülheim-Kärlich, Mayen-Koblenz distr. Excavation and documentation of the remains of a Neolithic house during pumice mining. (GDKE/Landesarchäologie/Koblenz)

Fig. 12
Rheinbrohl, Neuwied distr. Excavation of a watch tower at the Limes near Rheinbrohl. (GDKE/Landesarchäologie/Koblenz)

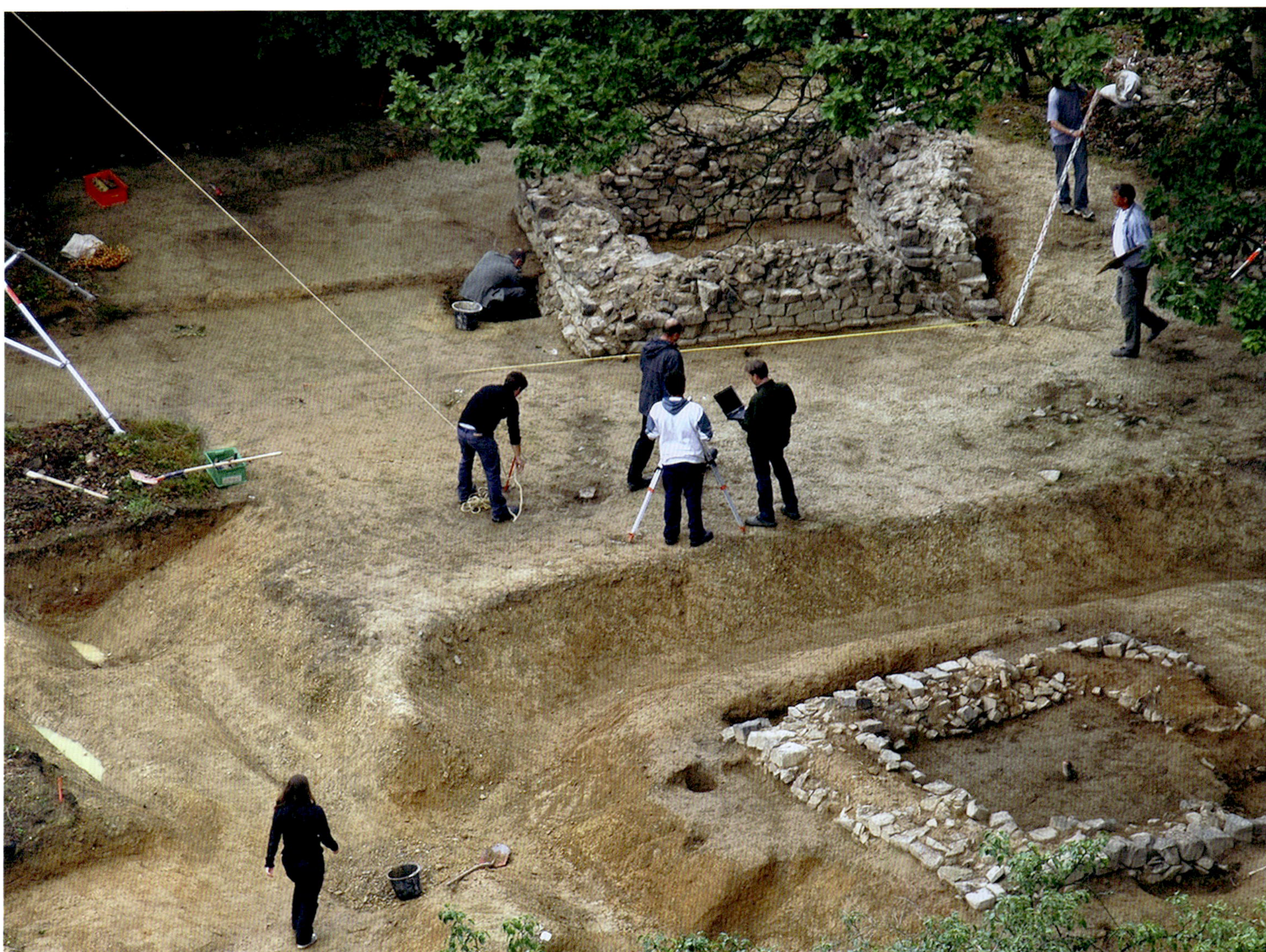

region every year. Pumice mining for the production of stones led to the discovery of the Frankish grave field of Saffig, the many finds west of Ochtendung, and also the ceremonial tombs of Lonnig, to name but a few. The emphasis of the research conducted in the areas of pumice mining was on the documentation of Iron Age settlements.

In preparation for the mining of lava deposits, the crater synclines of the eastern Eifel are investigated from an archaeological viewpoint, providing important insights into the life of early man in the Old Stone Age; the finds include the Neanderthal calvaria from the Wannenköpfe scoria complex near Ochtendung and the stone artefacts found along with it.

Even in areas where raw material mining does not play any role, finds turn up time and again to impressively reveal the development of this region into today's Rhineland-Palatinate. While the role of Kobern-Gondorf was already clear before the war due to its internationally renowned late antique and early medieval grave field, the Roman villa of Winningen and the early medieval grave field of Müden could be examined in the framework of street works.

The size of today's building projects is a mammoth logistic task for the State Archaeology. The evaluations of such major excavations often take years before they can be published and used for further projects. Months of excavations of the planned building areas precede the establishment of major new enterprises in Koblenz. During large-scale excavations in Polch (2014-2017), archaeologists found traces of human life dating from the Stone Age up to Roman times. The discovery of the late Palaeolithic settlements of Neuwied-Gönnersdorf and Andernach occurred during digging works for development areas; in this case, today's »Archäologisches Forschungszentrum und Museum für menschliche Verhaltensevolution Schloss Monrepos« in Neuwied was a long-term partner.

The often very early settlement of still extant localities and cities can be demonstrated time and again during examinations accompanying building works within the framework of renovations. In Andernach, Münstermaifeld, and Karden, the corresponding finds are the basis for new efforts by the municipalities regarding cultural tourism, with the aim of making these finds accessible to the public in their own museums or other exhibition venues.

In the north of the state, too, building activities will determine the policies and activities of the State Archaeology over the coming years. At the same time, the protection of the two UNESCO World Heritage sites located there will have top priority. (Fig. 12)

Earth History

The most junior member of the Department of State Archaeology is responsible for the oldest testimonies regarding our development.

The »Société des recherches utiles du département de la Sarre à Trèves«, established as far back as 1801 and still active today as »Gesellschaft für nützliche Forschung zu Trier«, is concerned with earth history. Subsequently, in 1834 the »Rheinische Naturforschende Gesellschaft zu Mainz« was established; it still exists today, and its collections formed the core of the Mainz Natural History Museum in 1910. Since 1988, the Landessammlung für Naturkunde Rheinland-Pfalz is also housed in the same building.

In 1840, the »Naturwissenschaftlicher Verein der bayerischen Pfalz POLLICHIA« was founded in Bad Dürkheim, followed in 1851 by the »Naturwissenschaftlicher Verein Coblenz«, in 1856 by the »Verein für Heimatkunde für Stadt und Kreis Bad Kreuznach« (which is expressly assigned natural history tasks as well), and in 1863 by the »Naturhistorischer Verein Zweibrücken«. The association POLLICHIA and the Verein für Heimatkunde Bad Kreuznach still exist today and led to the establishment of several museums, including the museum for the primeval world GEOSKOP in Thallichtenberg near Kusel.

The protection of archaeological evidence from a time when man was not yet present on this planet was already assured in the Prussian Excavation Act of 1914, since »excavations for items that are of concern for the primeval history of animal and plant life« had to be approved. However, this research field was included in the Monument Protection Act only in 1986. Not only the fossils, however, but also »evidence of earth history«, i.e. purely geological items, can be placed under protection.

Since 1989, the earth history staff have been active time and again in the entire state. Even before the department was set up, the so-called »Knochenhöhle«

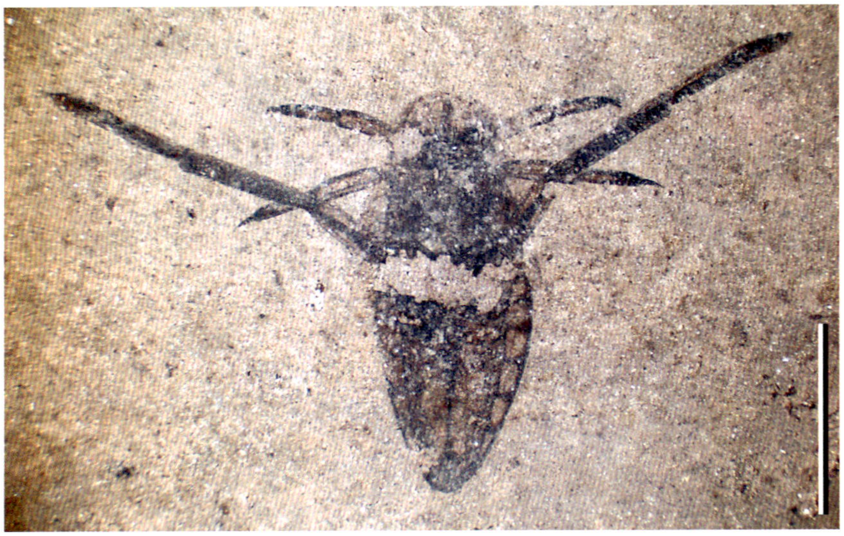

Fig. 13
Ruppach-Goldhausen, Westerwald district. Water bug (scale 5 mm) from the Tertiary Age. (GDKE/Landesarchäologie/Erdgeschichte/M. Poschmann)

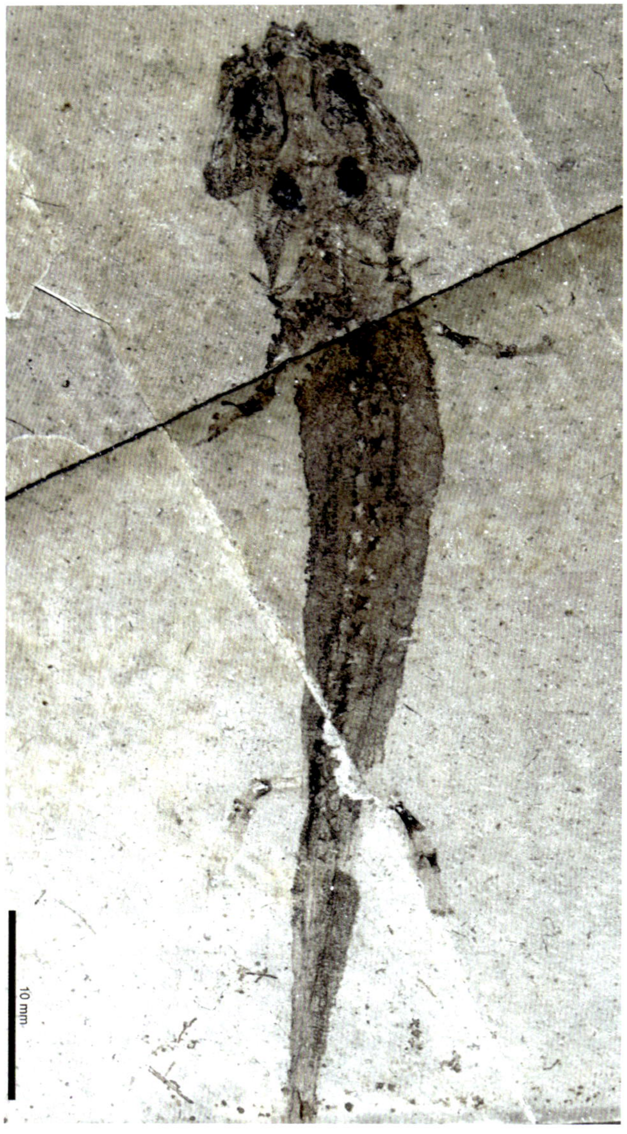

Fig. 14
Obermoschel, Donnersberg distr. Branchiosaurus *Apateon pedestris*, scale 10 mm. Rotliegend, found in 2013. (GDKE/Landesarchäologie/Erdgeschichte/K. Nungesser)

(bone cavern) was discovered in 1987 in a limestone quarry in Berndorf, with rich finds of snails and the bones of amphibians, small mammals, cats, horses, martens, bears, deer, and cattle from the Pleistocene. During the mining of loose and solid rock, one comes across finds (as in Willwerath, municipality of Weinsheim) that comprise a rich variety of early land plants, sea scorpions, fish remains, and ostracods from the Devonian Age. In Ruppach-Goldhausen (Westerwald), finely stratified sediments of a Pliocene crater lake were discovered for the first time in Germany, and in 2009 insects and plants from the Tertiary were documented during an emergency rescue. (Fig. 13) The long-term project Nahecaris studied life forms in the Hunsrück during the Devonian, when this region still formed the bottom of a sea. The centre of these studies was Bundenbach in the Hunsrück.

The department of earth history also supports the municipalities in implementing geo-touristic concepts. The Stöffelpark in Enspel, the new building of the »Devonium Waxweiler«, the conversion and new staging of the info centre for visitors at the Fell slate quarry, as well as the new staging of the info centre at the iron ore mine »Bindweide« (Steinebach/Sieg), all deserve to be mentioned in this context. The rescued »Strohner Lavaspaltenwand« (the »lava cracks wall« of Strohn) from a scoria volcano at the Wartgesberg was rebuilt in the Vulkanhaus Strohn. In addition, many geo-trails were developed and established.

Building projects time and again reveal new finds regarding earth history. Fish, large fresh-water sharks, amphibians, and large colonies of cyanobacteria from the Permian were found in 2005 in Unkenbach-Callbach. However, the undertaking of archaeological investigations does not automatically imply a building stop. Accompanying the construction of new roads in Pirmasens (2001-2004), arthropods, plants, mussels, brachiopods, sea lilies, and remains of fish and reptiles were rescued. On the basis of these finds, one can also demonstrate the change of the ecosystem in this region. Thanks to a very rare combination of coastal land plants and mud-dwelling marine animals, excavations in Kirchheimbolanden (2003-2006) were able to show that the region formed a sea coast during the Oligocene. In 2013 and 2014, during the construction of wind energy plants in Obermoschel in the Donnersberg district, mainly amphibians (Fig. 14) and trace fos-

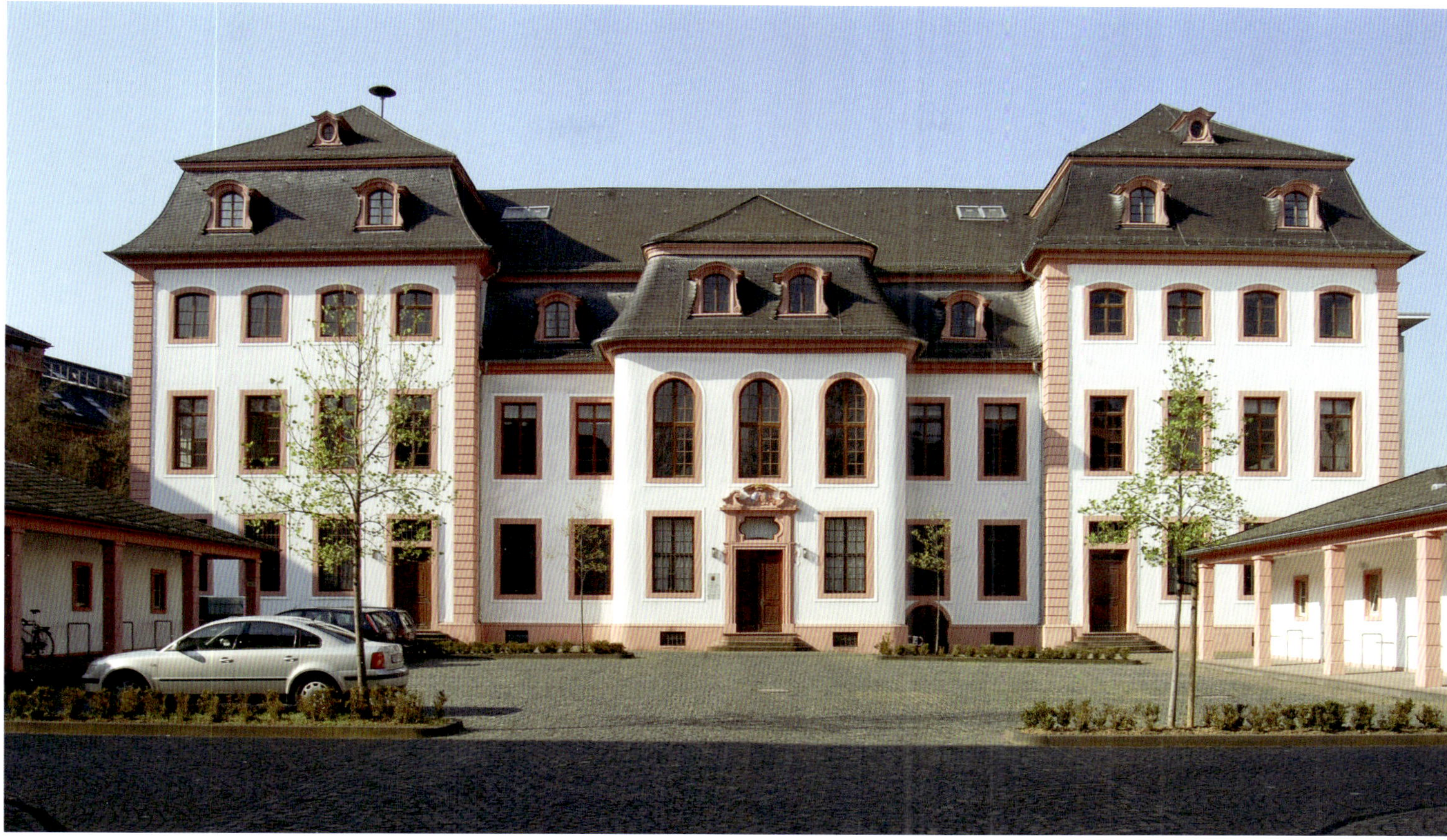

sils of the Permian were saved from destruction and a new species of brachiosaurus *(Leptorophus raischi)* was discovered in the process. Since 2016, the staff have been based in Mainz and Koblenz after an administrative change.

The General Department of Cultural Heritage of Rhineland-Palatinate (GDKE)

The GDKE was established on 1st January 2007. As a high state authority, it reports directly to the relevant ministry in Mainz. The seat of the new GDKE is Mainz (Fig. 15), while the central administration is housed in the Ehrenbreitstein Fortress in Koblenz.

The State Archaeology in Rhineland-Palatinate is today an independent department of the GDKE. The office of the state archaeologist has been at Ehrenbreitstein Fortress in Koblenz since 2013. (Fig. 16) With its branch offices in Koblenz, Mainz, Speyer, and Trier, and together with the staff of the earth history department, it serves, studies, and is generally in charge of the earth history and archaeological heritage of the entire state.

The financial resources of the State Archaeology are still scarce, but some of the funds can be saved by winning partners over for at least some of the projects. Major research institutions, such as the German Research Foundation (DFG), the Romano-Germanic Commission (RGK), the Römisch-Germanisches Zentralmuseum (RGZM), but also universities or local municipalities, can be won over as collaborative partners for excavations or the relevant evaluations. This is the case, for instance, for the excavations on the Martberg near Pommern, the evaluation of the finds from the fort at Neuwied-Niederbieber, and the hunting stations in Neuwied-Gönnersdorf. It was through these and many other excavations that the State Archaeology in Rhineland-Palatinate achieved an excellent scientific reputation, both national and international.

Fig. 15
Mainz, city of Mainz. The main building of the Generaldirektion Kulturelles Erbe Rheinland-Pfalz (GDKE/Landesdenkmalpflege/G.P. Karn)

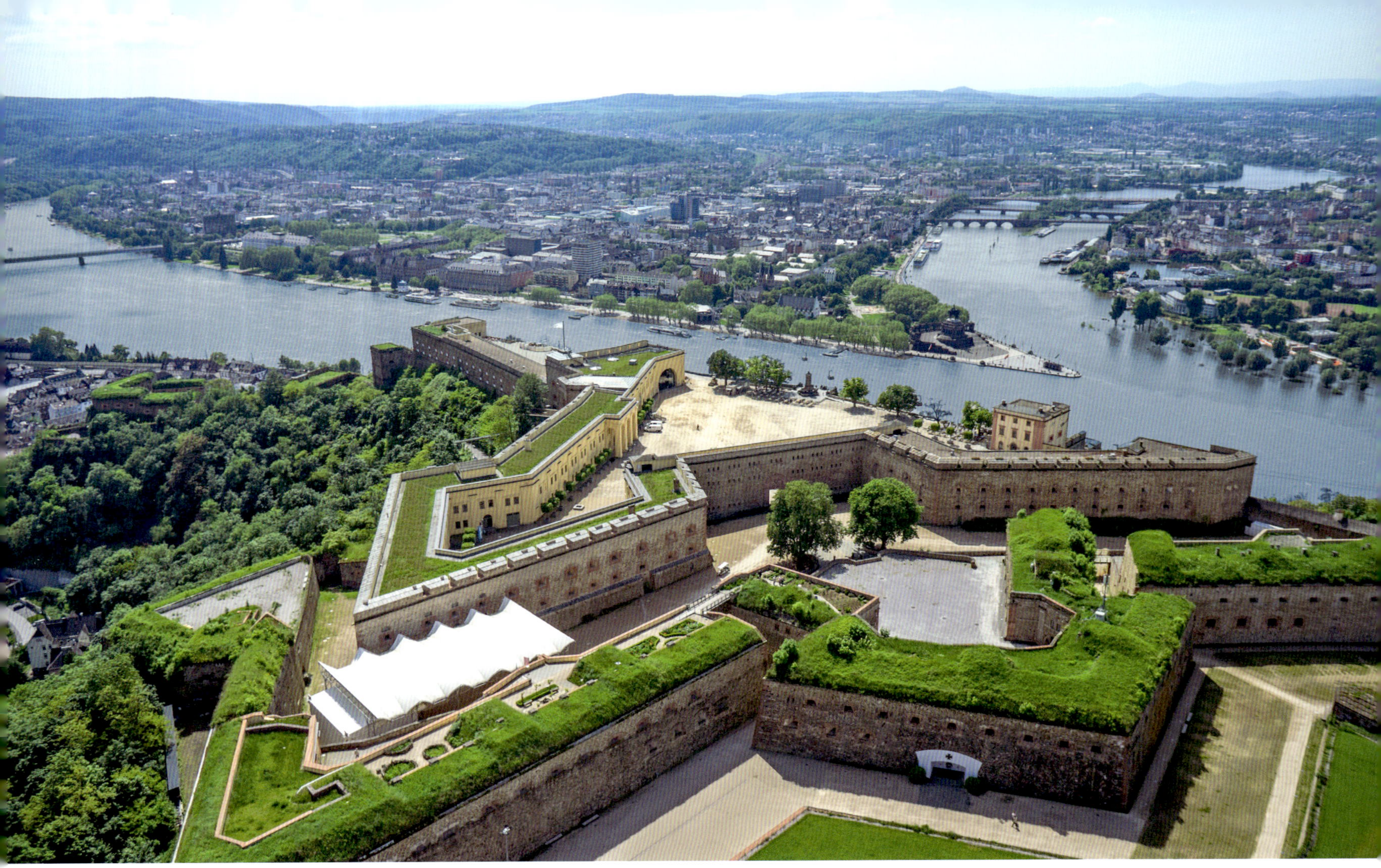

Fig. 16
Koblenz, city of Koblenz. Aerial photo of Ehrenbreitstein fortress. (Lufthelden)

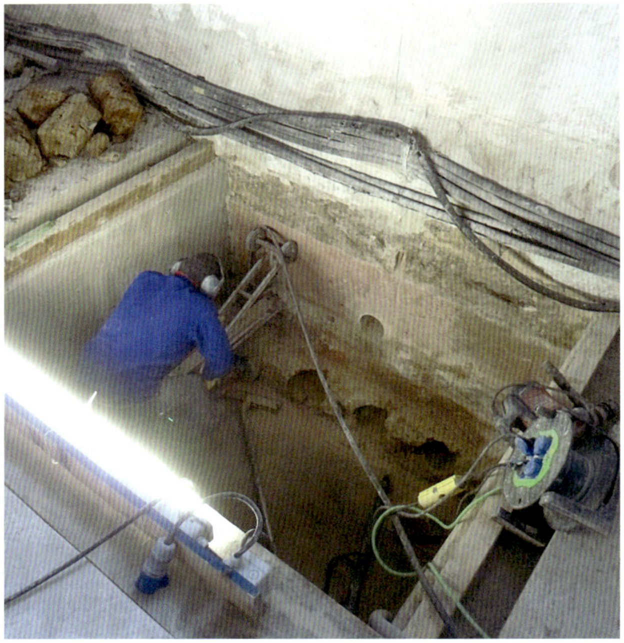

Fig. 17
Mainz, city of Mainz. Taking of drill cores for material and building research. (GDKE/Landesarchäologie/Mainz/J. Dolata)

During its seventy-year history, the State Archaeology has seen many changes, and each region had its own priorities. Today, archaeology is an interdisciplinary subject, where both the work with historical sources and the materials and insights from studies into other specialist areas are becoming more and more important. Zoology, botany, anthropology, DNA testing, CAD, photogrammetry, LIDAR scans, metallurgical examinations, and many other scientific research methods are now everyday tools for the archaeologist. At the same time, archaeology supplies study material for other fields of research. (Fig. 17)

Building measures, in particular, play a decisive role in the work of the State Archaeology. As a public agency, the State Archaeology has to enforce the protection of monuments before building works start. The objective is to prevent – through participation in the planning phase – the destruction of archaeological

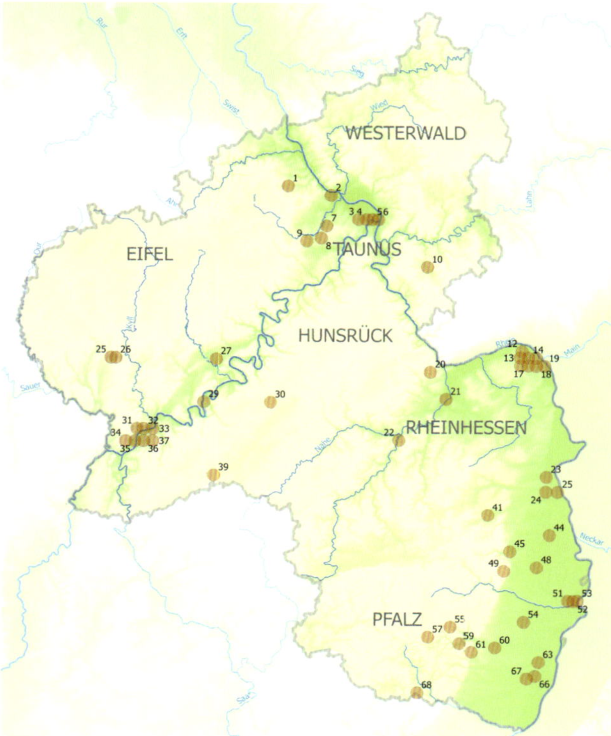

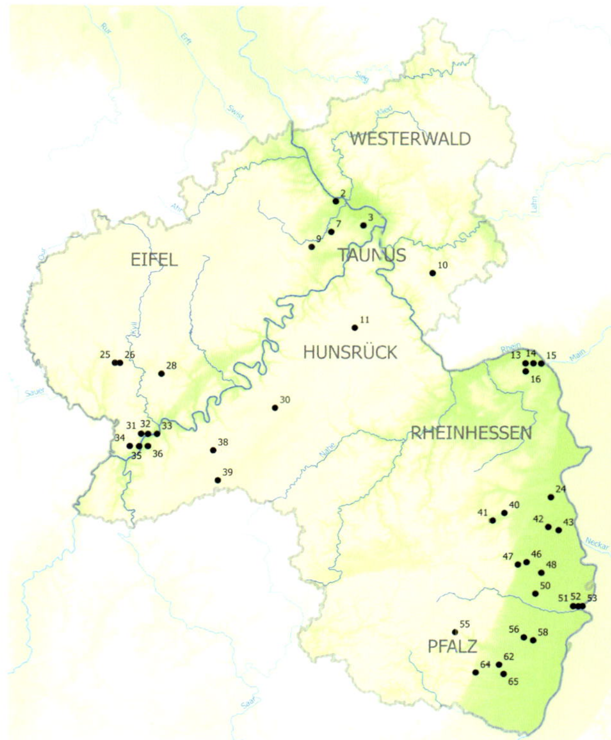

Fig. 18 (left)
Excavations by the Landesarchäologie Rheinland-Pfalz in 2016. (GDKE/ Landesarchäologie/ Schwab/Map basis: SRTM data (NASA) http://ows. terres-tris.de/osm/service)

Fig. 19 (right)
Excavations planned by the Landesarchäologie Rheinland-Pfalz for 2017. (GDKE/ Landesarchäolo-gie/Schwab/Map basis: SRTM data (NASA) http://ows. terrestris.de/osm/ service)

No.	Bounds
1	Niederzissen
2	Andernach
3	Koblenz
4	Koblenz
5	Koblenz
6	Koblenz
7	Ochtendung
8	Minkelfeld
9	Polch
10	Marienfels
11	Gödenroth
12	Mainz-Gonsenheim
13	Mainz
14	Mainz
15	Mainz
16	Mainz
17	Mainz
18	Mainz
19	Mainz
20	Waldalgesheim
21	Bretzenheim
22	Odernheim
23	Worms-Hernsheim
24	Worms
25	Worms
25	Bitburg
26	Bitburg
27	Wengerohr
28	Herforst
29	Neumagen-Dhron
30	Morbach
31	Trier
32	Trier
33	Trier
34	Trier
35	Trier
36	Trier
37	Trier
38	Prosterath
39	Hermeskeil
40	Quirnheim
41	Eisenberg
42	Heßheim
43	Frankenthal-Eppstein
44	Frankenthal
45	Niederzissen
46	Friedelsheim
47	Wachenheim
48	Assenheim
49	Deidesheim
50	Haßloch
51	Speyer
52	Speyer
53	Speyer
54	Freimersheim
55	Birkweiler
56	Hochstadt
57	Wilgartswiese
58	Zeiskam
59	Annweiler
60	Landau
61	Leinsweiler
62	Impflingen
63	Rülzheim
64	Klingenmünster
65	Rohrbach
66	Rheinzabern
67	Hatzenbühl
68	Nothweiler

finds. If this is not possible, the State Archaeology must have the developer include the expenses for archaeological excavations, documentations, and rescues in its calculation of the overall building costs and make the relevant funds available for these works. (Fig. 18–19)

It remains the task of archaeology to protect, document, research and communicate the traces of the past back to the beginnings of Earth's history and human life, in order to create a historical record of the unwritten times of our past.

Bibliography

A. von Berg, H.-H. Wegner, Jäger – Bauern – Keltenfürsten. 50 Jahre Archäologie an Mittelrhein und Mosel. Archäologie an Mittelrhein und Mosel 13 (Koblenz 2001).

J. Merten, Kurze Geschichte des Rheinischen Landesmuseums Trier, in: Rheinisches Landesmuseum Trier (Hrsg.), Fundstücke: Von der Urgeschichte bis zur Neuzeit. Schriftenreihe des Rheinischen Landesmuseums Trier 36 (Trier 2009) 218–225.

J. Merten, Das Rheinische Landesmuseum Trier 1920–1945: Ein Überblick, in: J. Kunow (Hg.), Archäologie und Bodendenkmalpflege in der Rheinprovinz 1920–1945. Tagung im Forum Vogelsang, Schleiden, 14.–15. Mai 2012. Materialien zur Bodendenkmalpflege im Rheinland 24 (Bonn 2013) 183–201

H. Bernhard, Zur Archäologischen Denkmalpflege in der Pfalz. Die Entwicklung des Amtes Speyer, in: H. Bernhard (Hg.), Archäologie in der Pfalz. Jahresbericht 2000 (Rahden/Westfalen 2001) 9–13.

EARTH HISTORY

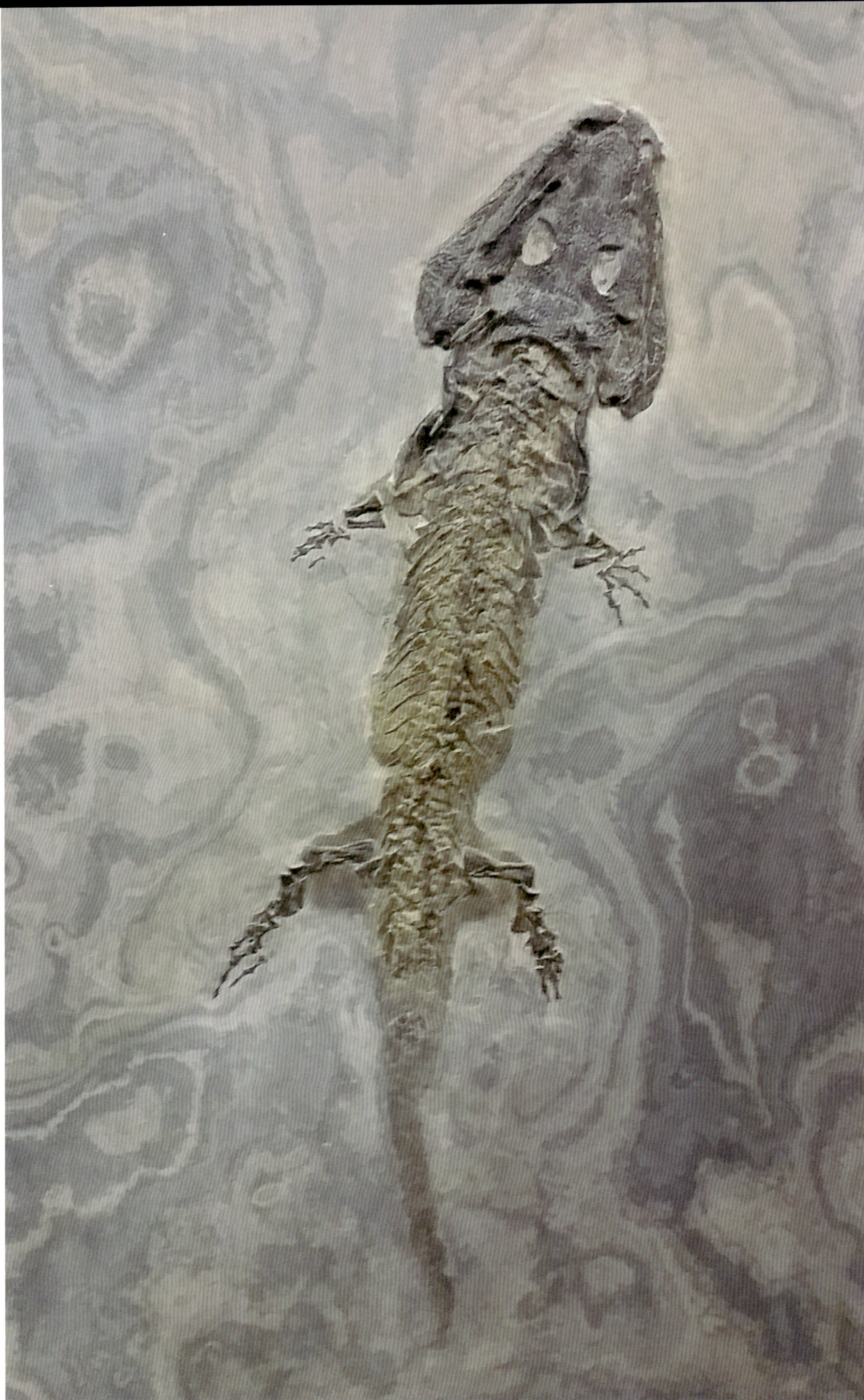

Earth History – a wide area

MARKUS POSCHMANN, HERBERT LUTZ

The history of the Earth comprises a period of approximately 4.5 billion years. It begins with the formation and development of our planet and also includes the present time with its man-made changes. Exploring earth's history is also future-oriented, since prognoses of future developments and their consequences can be deduced more reliably from the study of the past.

The Earth's historical record comprises geological aspects such as plate tectonics and volcanism, and involves the bio-scientific study of the evolution of organisms (palaeontology), there being no sharp distinction with archaeology. If we consider the dawn of mankind for example, this can only be explained by understanding plate tectonic processes, climate change, and the evolutionary adaptations associated with them. The cultural development of man also cannot be separated from climatic events. Examples are the »drying up« of the Sahara about 7000 years ago and the migrations caused by it; or the late antique/early medieval migrations of peoples whose causes are also linked to climatically challenging times.

In light of the enormous areas taken up as part of building measures, it is today more important than ever to preserve geological, predominantly paleontological testimonies for future generations and to document and study them as a matter of priority where they are in immediate danger.

Earth History in Rhineland-Palatinate

Because of the geological conditions typical for Rhineland-Palatinate, there are some natural priorities regarding the work of both State Archaeology/Earth History and the State Collection of Natural History attached to the Mainz Natural History Museum. The finds and findings trace the changes in the distribution of continents and oceans on our planet (palaeogeography), that continue till today, the changes in palaeoenvironments largely affected by this, as well as the evolution of plants and animals during the past 400 million years. (Fig. 1) The geological epochs (or periods) of Devonian, Permian, Triassic, Tertiary and Quaternary are particularly well documented in Rhineland-Palatinate. Sedimentary rock from the Age of Coal (Carboniferous) and the younger Mesozoic are less common however, and deposits from the Jurassic and Cretaceous, the age of the dinosaurs, are hardly to be found. Nevertheless, Rhineland-Palatinate is extremely rich in testimonies of earth's history, and we are only able to

Odernheim, Bad Kreuznach distr. The amphibian *Cheliderpeton lellbachae*. Rotliegend. (Naturhistorisches Museum der Stadt Mainz/Landessammlung für Naturkunde Rheinland-Pfalz/T. Engel)

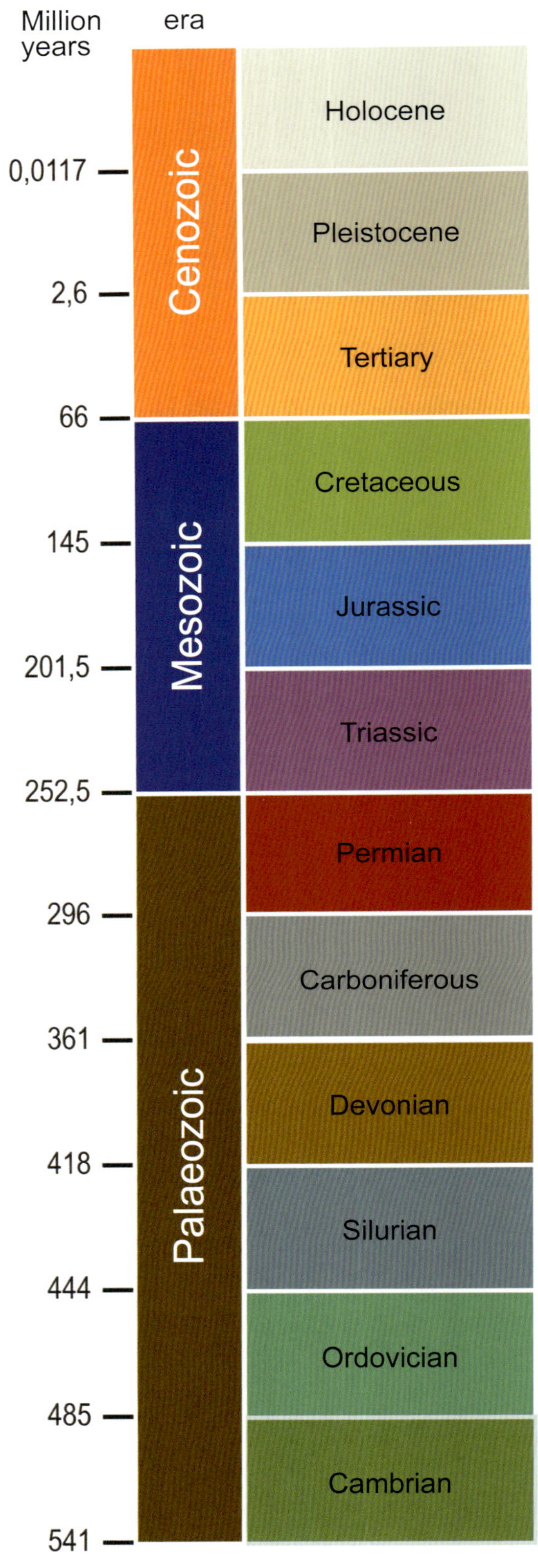

Fig. 1
Chronology of the geological periods without the Proterozoic. (by S. Treptow, Waldesch)

focus on some of them here. Besides impressive phenomena resulting from intensive volcanism and which are typical for the landscape - such as the cinder cones and volcanic maar lakes of the Eifel, or the basalt hills of the Westerwald - the particular focus of the work is on palaeontological finds and findings. Fossillagerstätten are of outstanding interest. These are rock strata that offer an extremely high amount of information due to the richness or quality of the preserved fossils.

The Lower Devonian: rich marine life and early colonization of the terrestrial realm

The approximately 418–392 million years old delta and sea deposits in the Lower Devonian of the Rhenish Slate Mountains, e.g. around Koblenz or Oberstadtfeld in the Eifel, are a classical topic of palaeontological research. Already at the middle of the 16th century Georgius Agricola wrote about finds of fossil lamp shells (brachiopods) near Koblenz. In the first half of the 19th century there were important studies on local fossil invertebrates such as brachiopods, mussels, trilobites, and sea lilies. They were fundamental and allowed a first structuring and chronology (biostratigraphy) of the Devonian rocks of the Slate Mountains. The flow of important discoveries and new insights has not ceased since then. Recently for example, a natural outcrop in the Holzbachtal near Seifen in the Westerwald provided fossils of a rare group of by now extinct echinoderms (Edrioasteroidea) related to starfish and sea urchins. The finds from the Holzbachtal are unique world-wide with regard to their preservation and variety. (Fig. 2) During the Lower Devonian, large rivers flowed from the Old-Red continent in the north into a shallow ocean basin south of the equator. The masses of sediment they carried and deposited were folded into the Rhenish Slate Mountains many million years later. In the river estuaries, living conditions were completely different from those in the shallow sea, characterized by frequent changes between fresh and salt water, falling dry and flooding. The organisms of the open sea areas, which were accustomed to constant conditions, could not survive here. Instead, we find inter alia fish and sea scorpions that lived in a mixture of fresh and salt water, land-dwelling arachnids, and early land plants. The latter developed a kind of shore

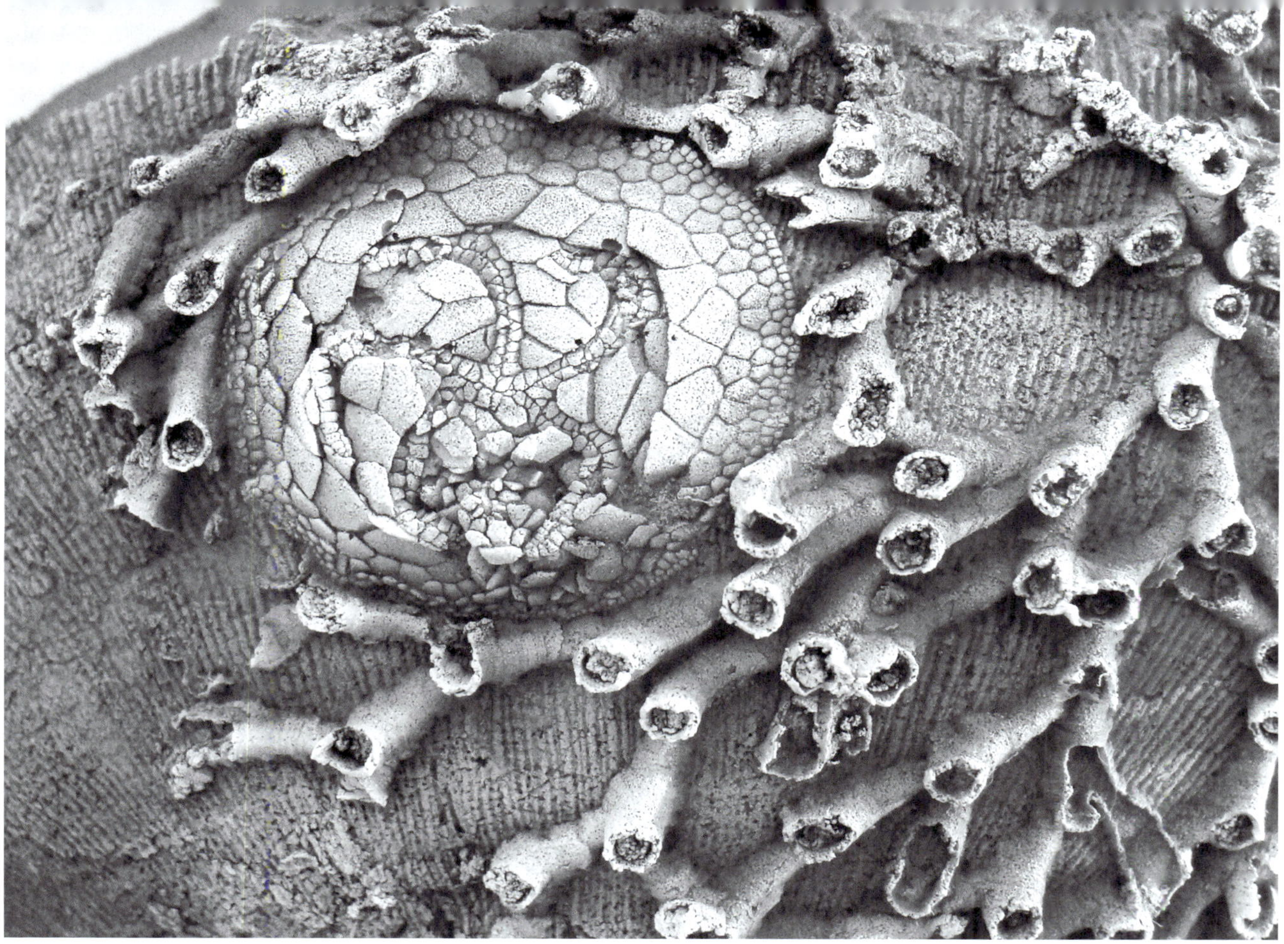

Fig. 2
Seifen-Holzbachtal, Westerwald distr. Edrioasteroid *Parakrama grebelae*, surrounded by corals. Lower Devonian. (P. Müller/ Freilingen

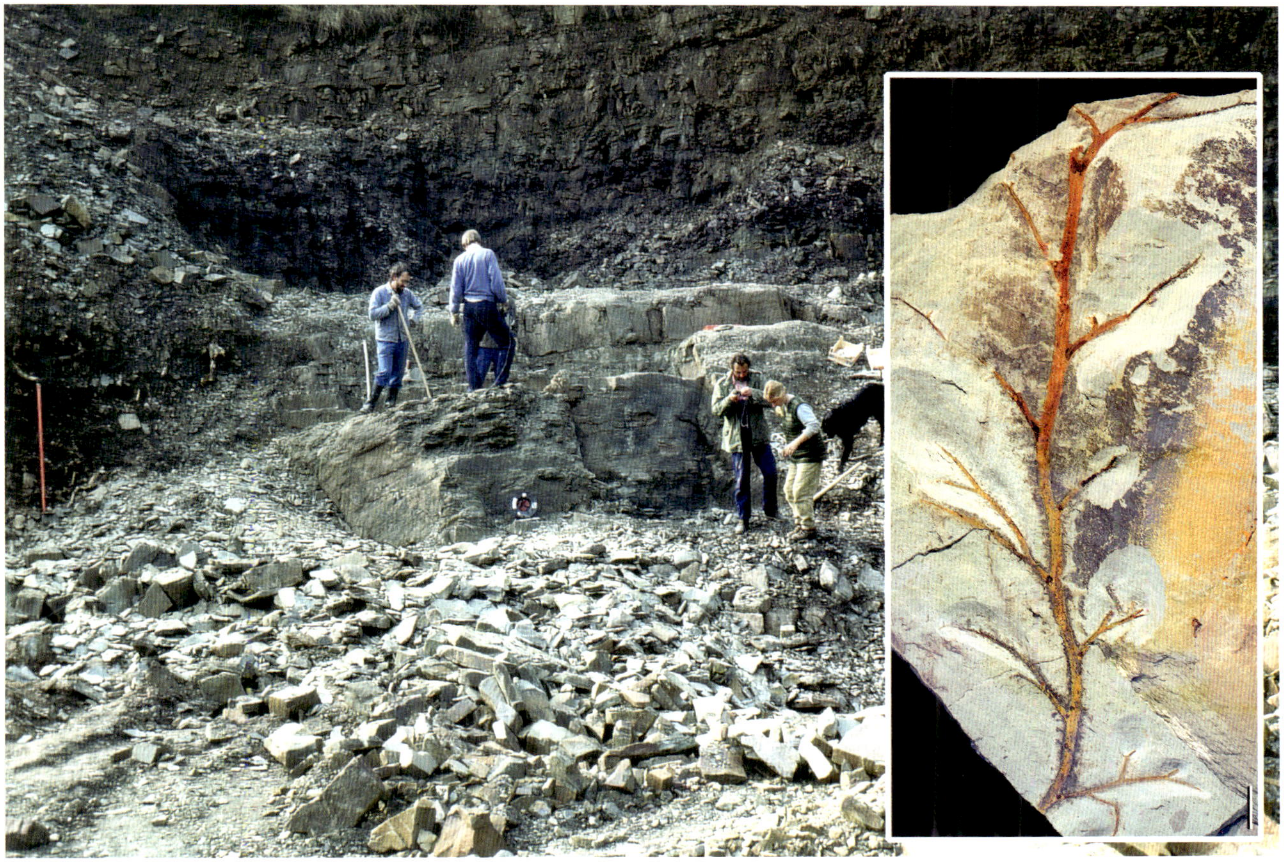

Fig. 3
Hermespand, Bitburg-Prüm distr. Rescue excavation by the Direktion Landesarchäologie / Erdgeschichte and the Naturhistorisches Museum Mainz / Landessammlung für Naturkunde in Lower Devonian rocks in a quarry. Early land plant »Psilophyton burnotense« (right/scale 10 mm). (Background: Naturhistorisches Museum Mainz/ Landessammlung für Naturkunde/ T. Engel. Photo insert: GDKE/ Landesarchäologie/ Erdgeschichte/ M. Poschmann)

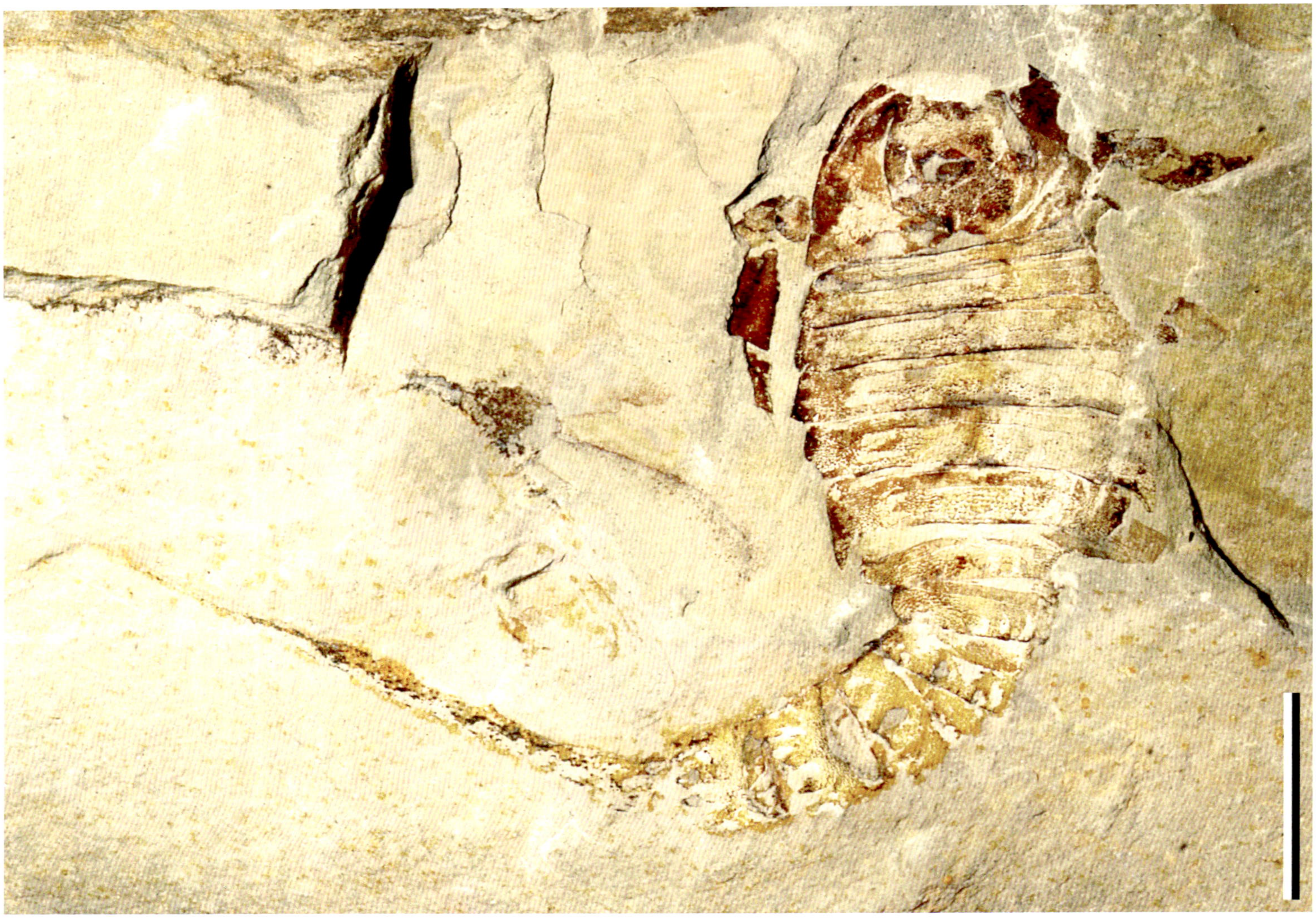

Fig. 4 Hermespand, Bitburg-Prüm distr. Sea scorpion *Adelophthalmus sievertsi* from the Lower Devonian (scale: 10 mm). (GDKE/Landesarchäologie/Erdgeschichte/M. Poschmann)

vegetation. The Rhenish Lower Devonian is one of the few sites world-wide that bears such rich witness of the early history of how the mainland was colonized. Numerous animal and plant fossils from these habitats came from rescue excavations, e.g. along the high-speed train line in the Westerwald or in quarries near Prüm in the Eifel. (Fig. 3) Many species of plants, sea scorpions (Fig. 4), and arachnids, some being the oldest evidence world-wide, are known exclusively from the Rhenish Slate Mountains.

The Middle Devonian: colourful reefs teeming with life

In the Eifel, approximately between Bad Münstereifel in the north and Prüm in the south, there is a series of geological structures known as the Eifel Synclines. The rocks found here are mostly of Middle Devonian age (392–383 million years ago) and were deposited in a tropical shallow sea. The water was clear, with high oxygen content and also well-lit because of its shallow depth of hardly 50 m. There was rich life under these conditions and in some places a large number of organisms formed extensive reefs. Sponge-like organisms, the so-called stromatopores, provided the greatest contribution to the development of these reef structures,

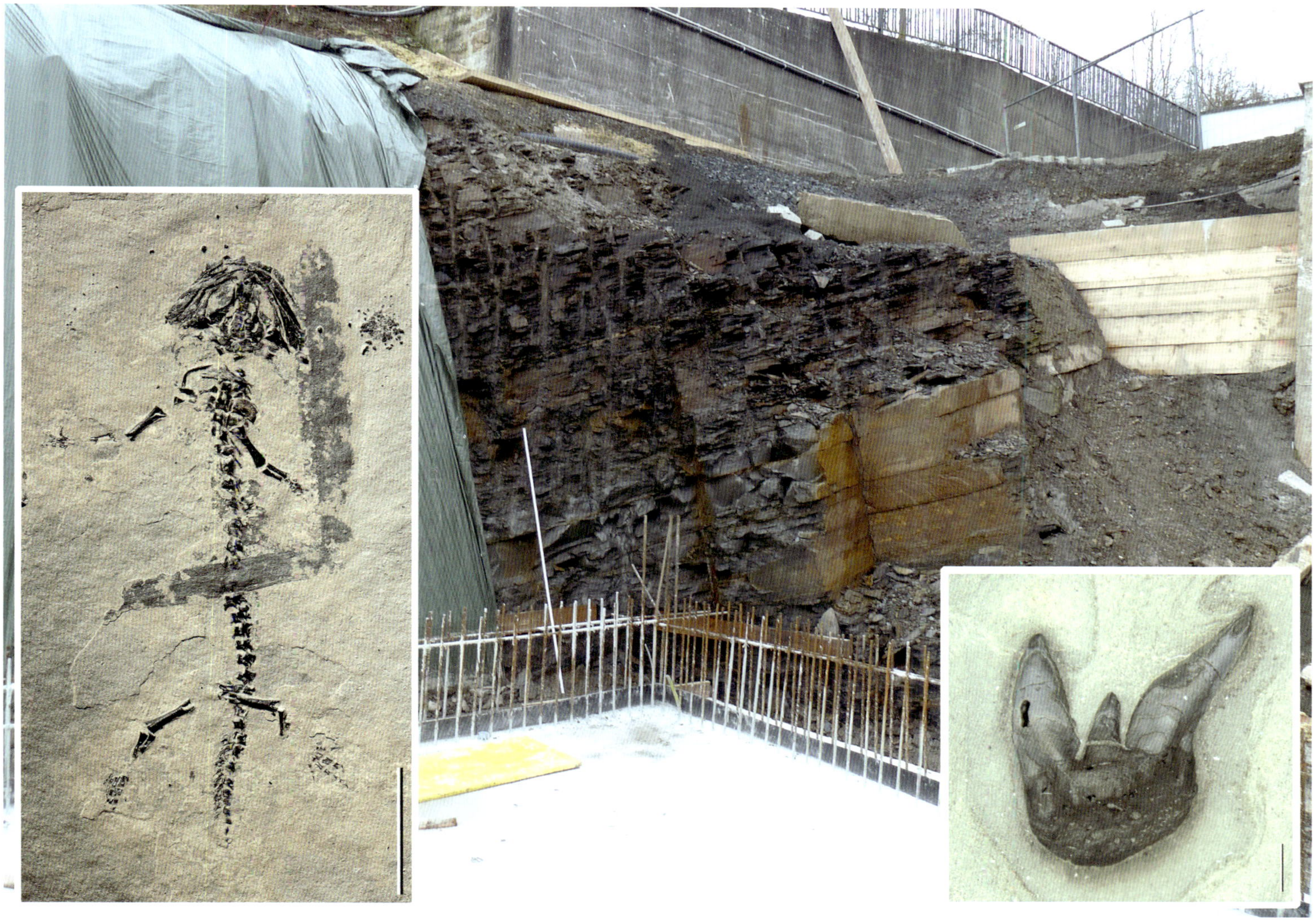

and to a smaller extent also corals; both belonged to groups that are now extinct. Brachiopods and sea lilies, the latter being relatives of star fish and sea urchins, lived here. In the vicinity of the reefs, for example in protected lagoons, algae, bryozoans, sea lilies, snails, and trilobites found ideal living conditions. Time and again, the fossil remains of these ocean dwellers are brought to the surface in the Eifel Synclines through road works, in building pits and quarries, but also through the ploughing of fields. Alexander von Humboldt is reported to have bought the woollen stockings of farmer women working in the fields so that he could store his abundant fossil finds when travelling the Eifel in the early 19th century. Today, many sites have been exhausted, and one hardly comes across such rich deposits of fossils. It is therefore one of the most important tasks of State Archaeology/Earth History to monitor ongoing building measures and to salvage fossils excavated there. In addition, well-known fossil sites, for example the famous »Trilobite fields« near Gees, must be protected by law against destruction through illegal excavations.

Rotliegend: sweet water lakes and marsh woods

The term »Rotliegend« is used in Germany to describe rocks from the geological period of the lower Permian (about 300–270 million years old). The name is de-

Fig. 5
Meisenheim am Glan, Bad Kreuznach distr. Sandstones deposited in rivers and dark-coloured lake sediments. Skeleton of the branchiosaur *Apateon pedestris* and plant remains (left, scale: 10 mm). Isolated tooth of the shark *Xenacanthus meisenheimensis* (right, scale: 2 mm). Rotliegend. (GDKE/ Landesarchäologie/ Erdgeschichte/ T. Schindler, M. Poschmann)

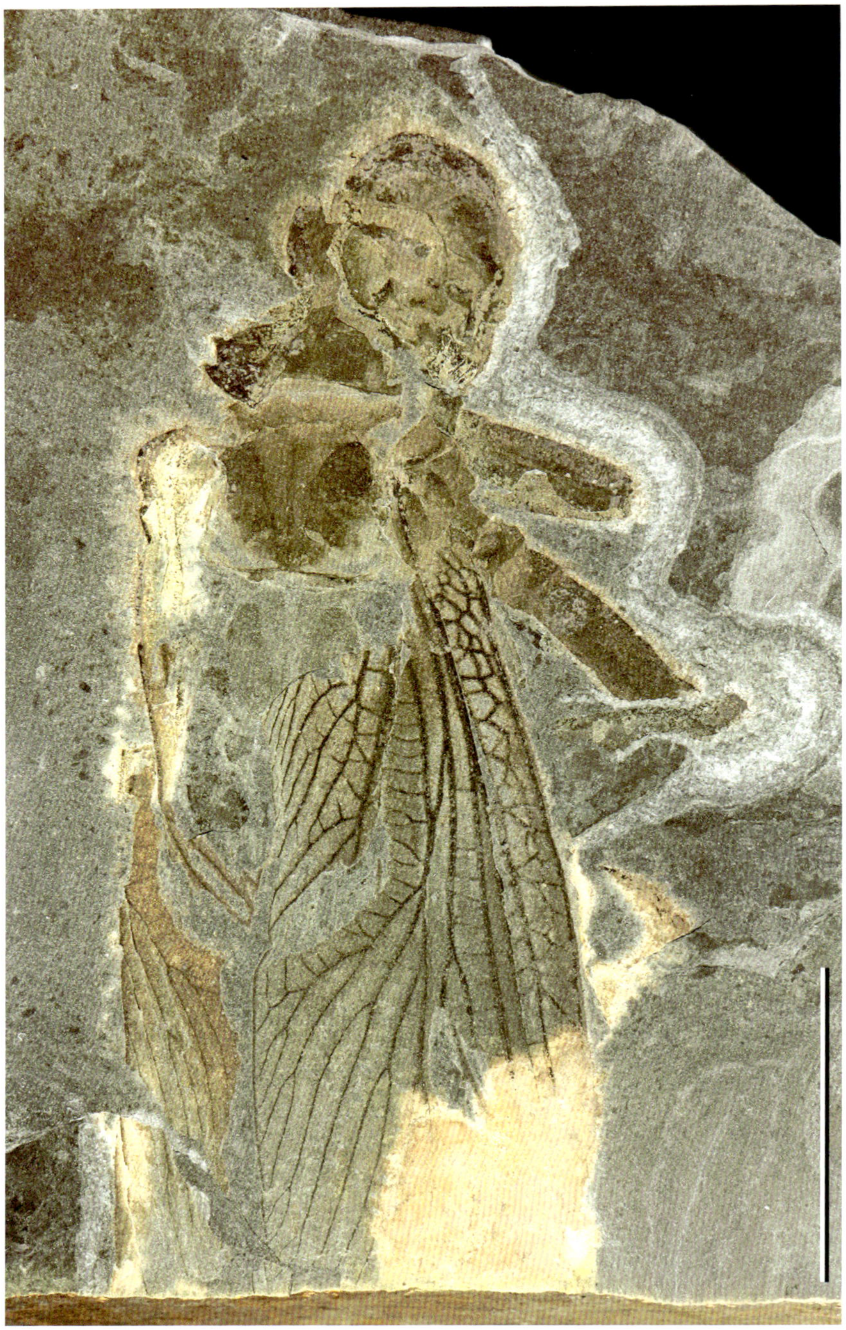

Fig. 6
Niedermoschel, Donnersberg distr. *Nosipteron niedermoschelensis*, a primeval relative of the grasshoppers (scale: 10 mm). Rotliegend. (GDKE/Landesarchäologie/Erdgeschichte/ M. Poschmann)

rived from the old mining term »rotes Todtliegendes«, which was used for rock strata below the so-called Kupferschiefer rich in ore. In contrast, these deposits were free of ore, i.e. 'dead', and often coloured red. In Rhineland-Palatinate we find such rocks in the Wittlicher Senke and in the Saar-Nahe basin. The latter extends south of the Hunsrück, approximately between Mainz and Kaiserslautern. Terrestrial deposits dominate here; i.e. besides rocks of volcanic origin there are sedimentary rocks that were deposited in rivers, in many small as well as large and deep freshwater lakes, and in swamps. Their fine-grained deposits crop out today in creek profiles, during road works and in building pits. (Fig. 5) They are extremely rich in fossils. The finds of plants in particular are internationally important. Comparably well-preserved and rich floras of this age cannot be found anywhere else in Europe. At the oxygen-free bottom of the deeper lakes, the conditions for preservation were so extraordinarily good that fish and amphibians have been preserved complete and sometimes even with remains of soft tissue such as skin shades and eyespots. In shallower waters, the currents were usually stronger, and due to decomposition gases the carcasses of vertebrates were more likely to float up to the surface where they then decayed. Here, invertebrate water dwellers, such as crustaceans and mussels, are better preserved. Where rivers or streams flowed into the lakes, remains of organisms were very quickly covered by mud and suspended particles and thus preserved. Besides the actual lake dwellers, various plants as well as land- and river-dwelling animals were transported there by the wind and water. As a result, the normally rare remains of land-dwelling insects (Fig. 6), amongst them also the oldest beetles in the world, are unusually frequent in particular lake deposits. In the Rotliegend of the Saar-Nahe basin, many spectacular finds were made during the last 150 years, where excavations by the Geological-Palaeontological Institute of the Mainz University played a major part. Amongst the particularly impressive fossils are temnospondyl amphibians of up to 2 m that resemble crocodiles, as well as complete freshwater sharks, which could even reach 3 m in length. On the occasion of salvage excavations, such as during road widening works near Unkenbach-Callbach (Fig. 7), amphibians, sharks (Fig. 8), and other fish can be recovered.

The Triassic: from desert-like river landscapes via a Muschelkalk sea to a varied coastal plain

Through the »travelling« of the continental plates (plate tectonics), the super-continent Pangaea had been formed during the Permian – an enormous con-

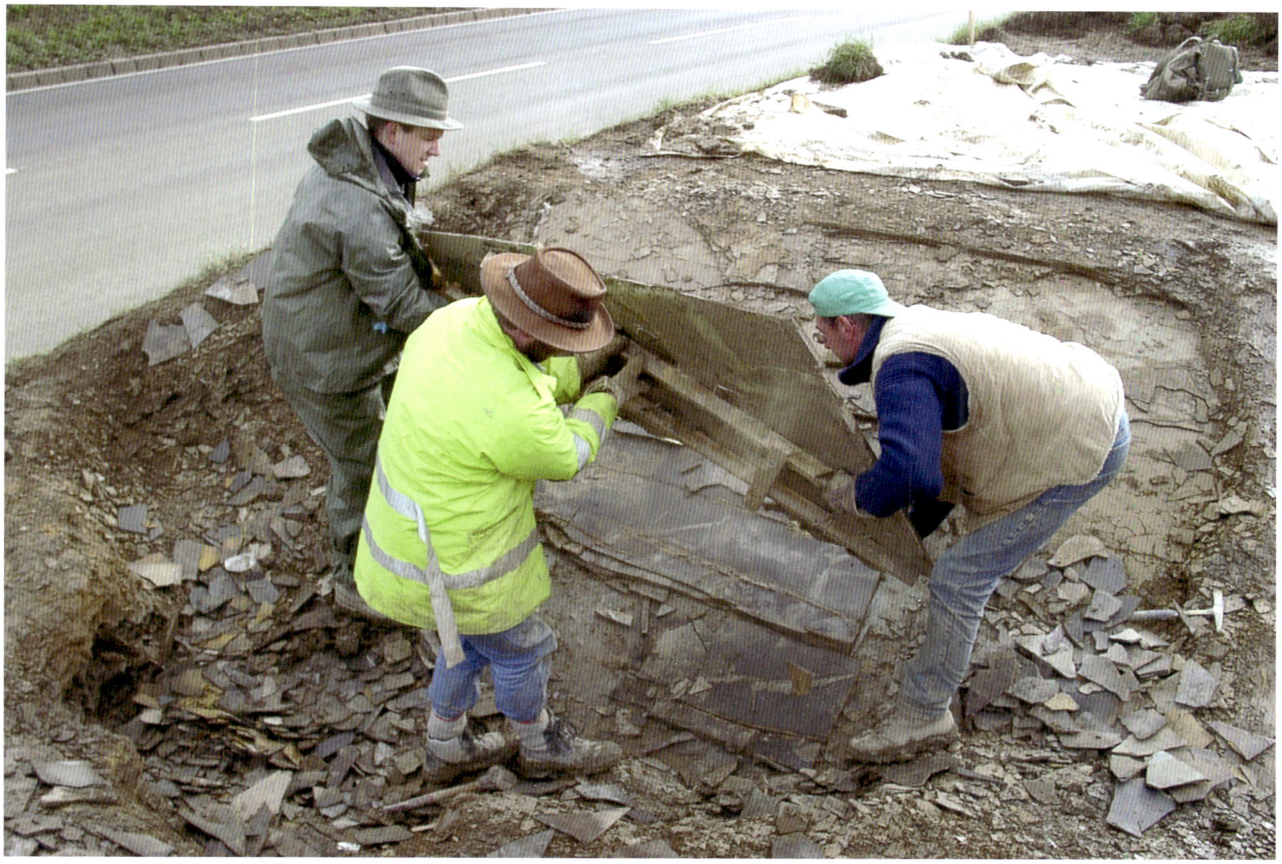

Fig. 7
Between Callbach, Kaiserslautern distr., and Unkenbach, Donnersberg distr. Rescue of a shark skeleton during road works. Rotliegend. (GDKE/Landesarchäologie/Erdgeschichte/K. Nungesser)

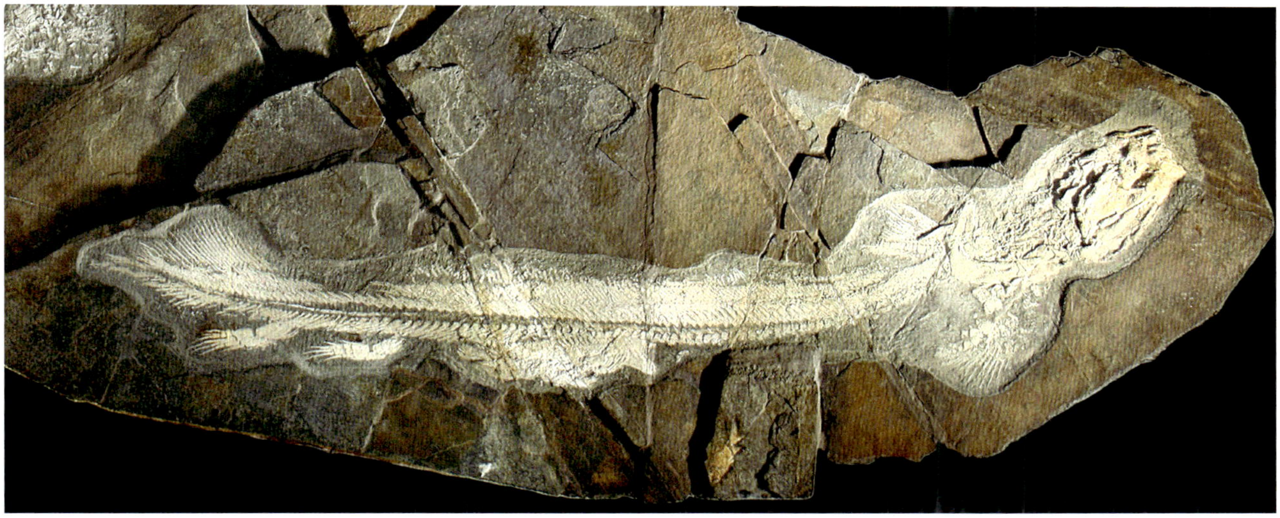

Fig. 8
Niederkirchen, Bad Kreuznach distr. Shark *Lebachacanthus colosseus* from Rotliegend lake sediments. The fossil-bearing rock was affected by hot magma, which changed the colour of the originally dark skeleton substance to white. »Fossil of the year 2011« of the Paläontologische Gesellschaft. (Naturhistorisches Museum Schleusingen/R. Werneburg)

tinuous land mass reaching from pole to pole. During the following Triassic period, this continent started to break up, leading to profound changes of the palaeogeography and environmental conditions. In Rhineland-Palatinate, the rocks of the Triassic period some 252–201 million years back can mainly be found in the Trierer Bucht and the Pfälzer Mulde. »Triassic« or »trinity« refers to the subdivision into Buntsandstein, Muschelkalk and Keuper. The Buntsandstein was formed in a desert-like environment, where rivers

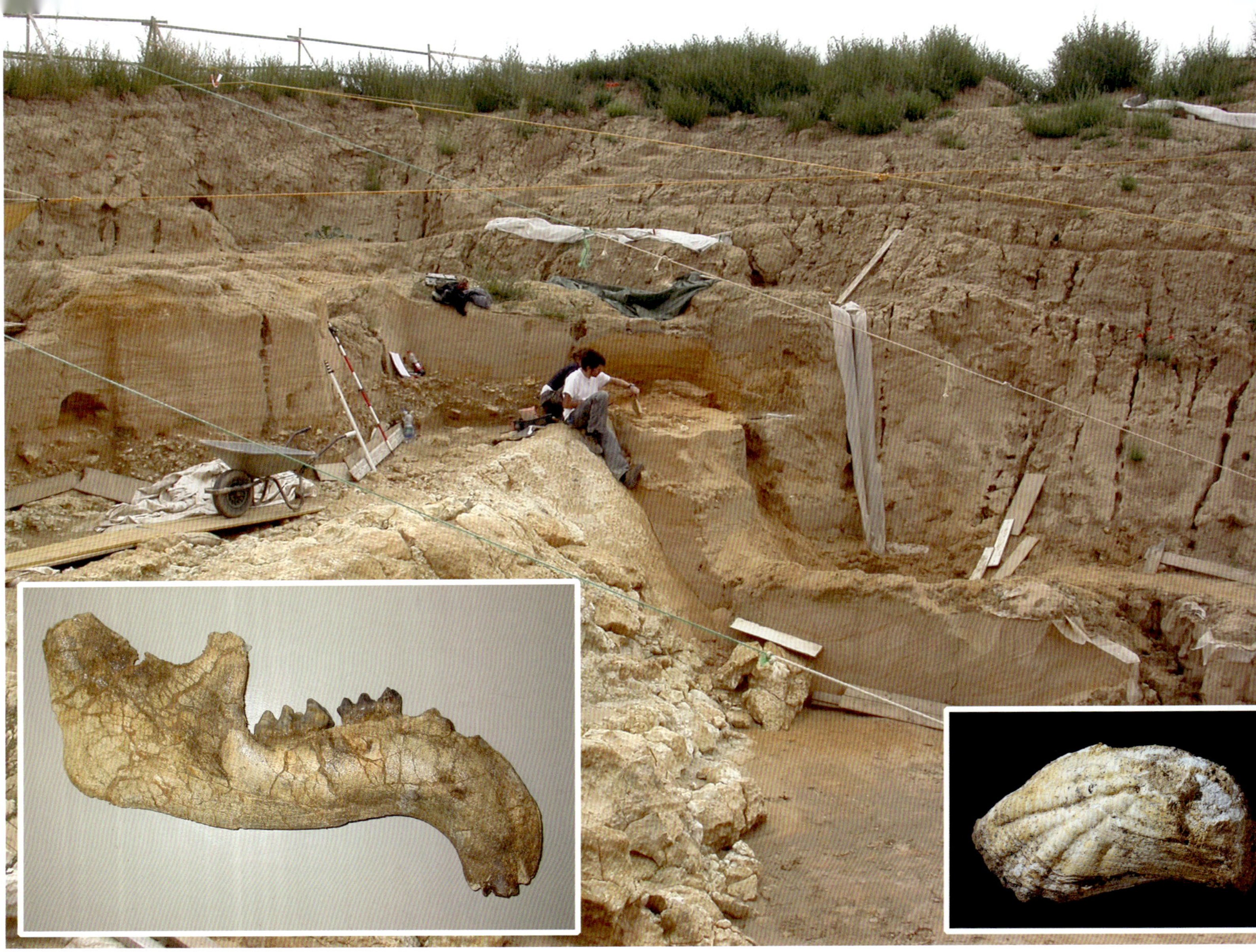

Fig. 9 Eppelsheim, Alzey-Worms distr. Scientific excavation in the Miocene deinotherian-sands. Lower jaw of a young tusk elephant *Deinotherium giganteum* (left, max. diagonal length: 64 cm). Pearl mussel *Plicatibaphia bavarica* (right, length of shell: 10 cm). (Naturhistorisches Museum Mainz/Landessammlung für Naturkunde/T. Engel)

nevertheless used to flow. Starting from the Middle Buntsandstein, the influence of incursions by the sea increased, eventually leading to the formation of the Muschelkalk. Later on, deposits reflecting a coastal plain with lagoons, lakes, and rivers dominated, and these are collectively called Keuper. During excavations accompanying road works, for example near Pirmasens, fossil arthropods, plants, and fish remains from the Buntsandstein, and mussels, brachiopods, sea lilies, and fish remains from the Muschelkalk sea were documented.

The Tertiary: sea coasts, rivers, and volcanic lakes

The Tertiary (66–2.6 million years ago) lies between a mass extinction at the end of the Cretaceous, which also wiped out the dinosaurs, and the start of the Ice Age. During the Tertiary, there were major fluctuations in sea levels and advances by the sea, which also left their traces in Rhineland-Palatinate. Many finds of fossil marine animals, from mussels via fish and shark teeth up to entire skeletons of sea cows, were discovered mainly in the Oligocene sediments of the Mainz Basin, which are about 30 million years old. The »Dinotheriensande« of Eppelsheim, which have been exploited in small sand mines for ages, became famous

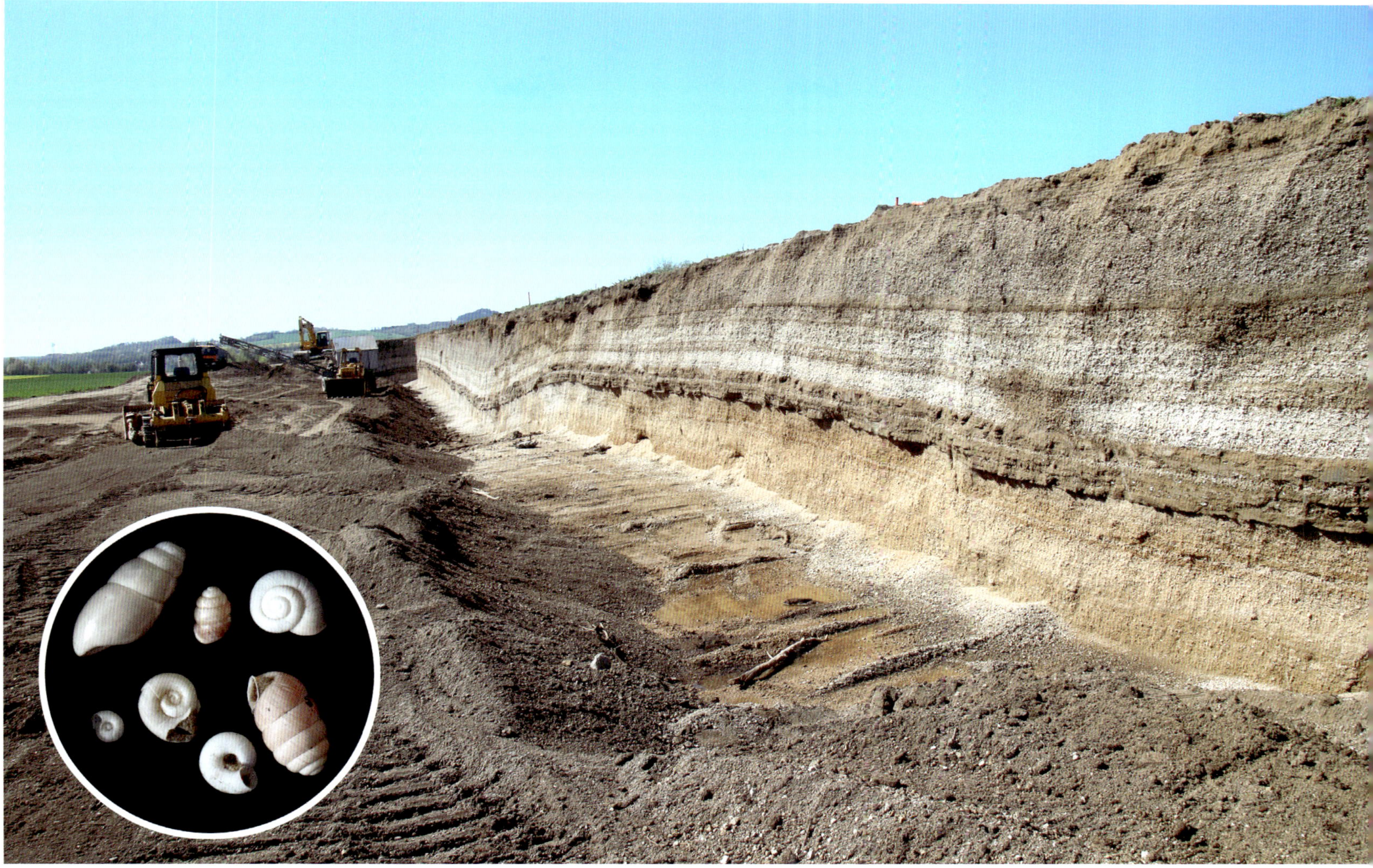

because of their diverse fauna. In these Miocene river deposits, evidence of about two dozen species of big mammals was found, amongst them sabre tooth cats, remains of apes, and the complete skull of the tusk elephant *Deinotherium giganteum*. Today, scientific excavations by the Mainz Natural History Museum/State Collection of Natural History are going on in the immediate vicinity of the original site. (Fig. 9) In volcanic maars and crater lakes like Eckfeld in the Eifel or Enspel in the Westerwald, deposits of quite diverse dating yielded important and particularly well-preserved finds of animals and plants. They grant us an insight into the evolution of the mammals, which took place at an accelerated speed during the Tertiary and led to the development of a particular diversity of species. The Eckfeld Maar, which has been systematically studied by the Mainz Natural History Museum/State Collection of Natural History since 1987, has long become world-famous. Marsupials, small primeval horses, four species of primates, and a still unique fossil louse were discovered here amongst others.

The Pleistocene: Pumice mining and crater troughs/Gravel extraction in the Upper Rhine valley

The Ice Age (2.6 million to 11,700 years ago) is characterised by a periodic alternation of cold and warm periods. During the cold periods, the area of Rhine-

Fig. 10
Miesenheim, Mayen-Koblenz distr. Late Ice Age Alleröd soil, about 13,000 years old, under the pumice tuff layers of the Lake Laach volcano. The environmental conditions immediately before the eruption of the Lake Laach volcano can be reconstructed from the various types of snails. (GDKE/Landesarchäologie/Erdgeschichte/M. Poschmann)

land-Palatinate was »wedged« between a glaciation area in the north, whose glaciers reached the Düsseldorf region, and the Alpine glaciers in the south, which reached far into the foreland. During warm periods, a re-forestation of the steppe and tundra areas is recognizable. Even hippopotami and water buffalo migrated to our area then. Today's appearance of the Rhenish Slate Mountains was mainly formed during the Upper Pleistocene by the Rhine and its tributaries cutting deep and narrow valleys into the Devonian bedrock. Sands and gravels of the Ice Age river terraces and especially of the Upper Rhine Graben provide rich finds of bones of big mammals from warm and cold periods, for example of elephants, rhinoceroses, deer, pigs, and bovids. During the cold periods, the wind blew fine erosion debris from the steppe landscapes sparsely protected by vegetation and deposited it again at protected spots. Such loess deposits can also be found in the crater troughs of the Eifel volcanoes and often hold rich finds of remains of small and large mammals, but also of invertebrates such as snails. (Fig. 10) Whilst marmots actually lived in the crater troughs, many bones of big mammals, such as horses, rhinoceroses, and bovids, were brought into the troughs by men as bag. Deposited strata of volcanic ash provide important datings and witness frequent eruptions and intensive volcanic activity in the western and eastern Eifel. The »eyes of the Eifel«, i.e. the maar lakes, are also due to this young volcanism. The finely stratified deposits at the bottom of these volcanic lakes represent a high-resolution archive and allow us, by using enclosed pollen grains and other fossils, to reconstruct the history of the climate and vegetation of the more recent past of the earth.

Bibliography

W. v. Koenigswald, W. Meyer (Hg.), Erdgeschichte im Rheinland (München 1994).

Landesamt für Geologie und Bergbau Rheinland-Pfalz (Hg.), Geologie von Rheinland-Pfalz (Stuttgart 2005).

The Hunsrück Slate and its fossils: Extraordinarily well-preserved variety 400 million years ago

HERBERT LUTZ, MARKUS POSCHMANN

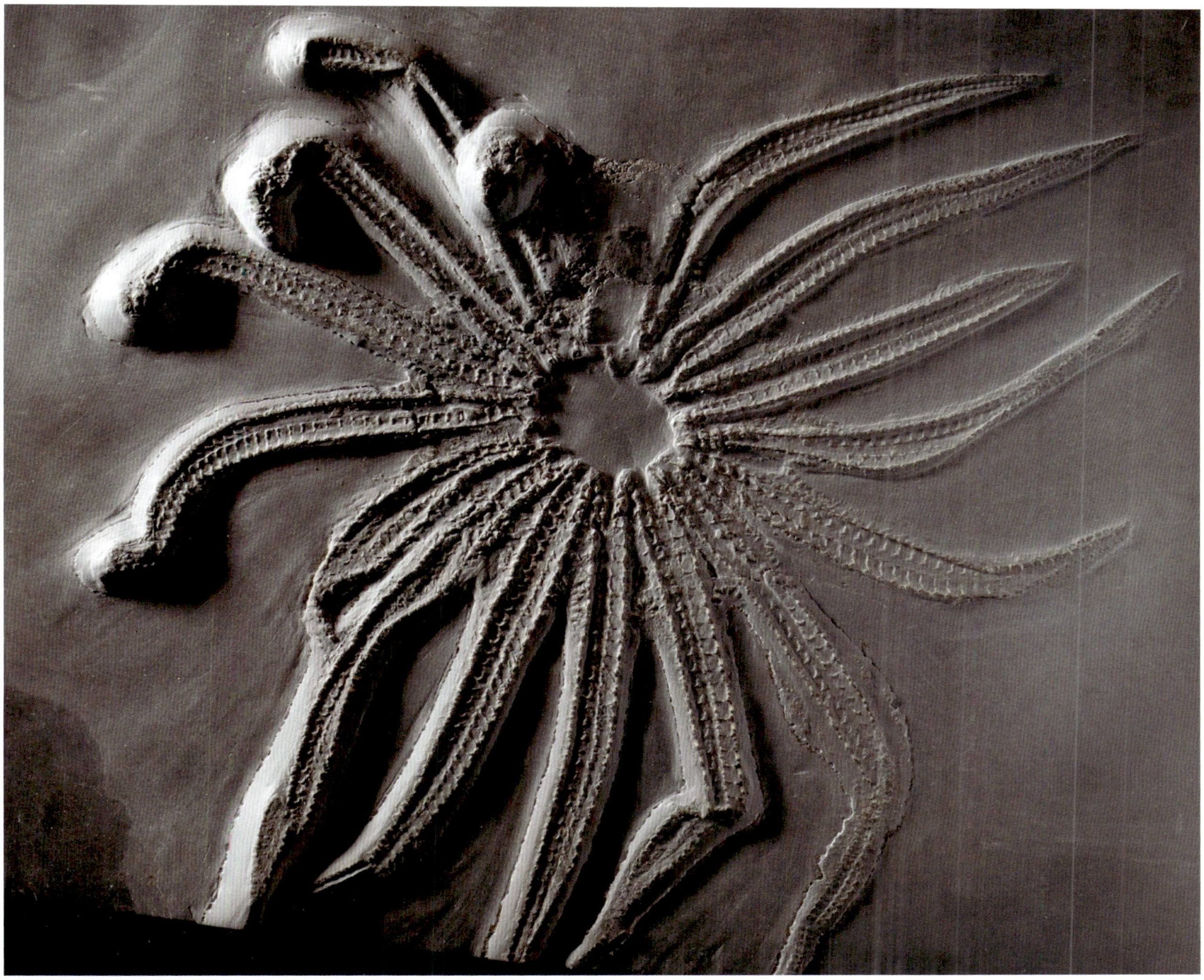

Fig. 1
Bundenbach, Birkenfeld distr. 16-armed starfish *Helian-thaster rhenanus*, colloquially also called »Sun star«. (Naturhistorisches Museum Mainz/ Landessammlung für Naturkunde/ B. Lischewsky)

During the Variscan mountain formation, the clays and silts that were deposited 400 million years ago at the bottom of the Hunsrück Slate Sea turned into »roofing slate«, which can be split into thin weatherproof slabs. These are used as shingles and roofing slate and are characteristic of numerous municipalities in the Hunsrück, the Eifel, and the Westerwald.

Many fossils were found in the slate, especially in the region around Bundenbach. At present, more than 270 species of marine animals are known. The

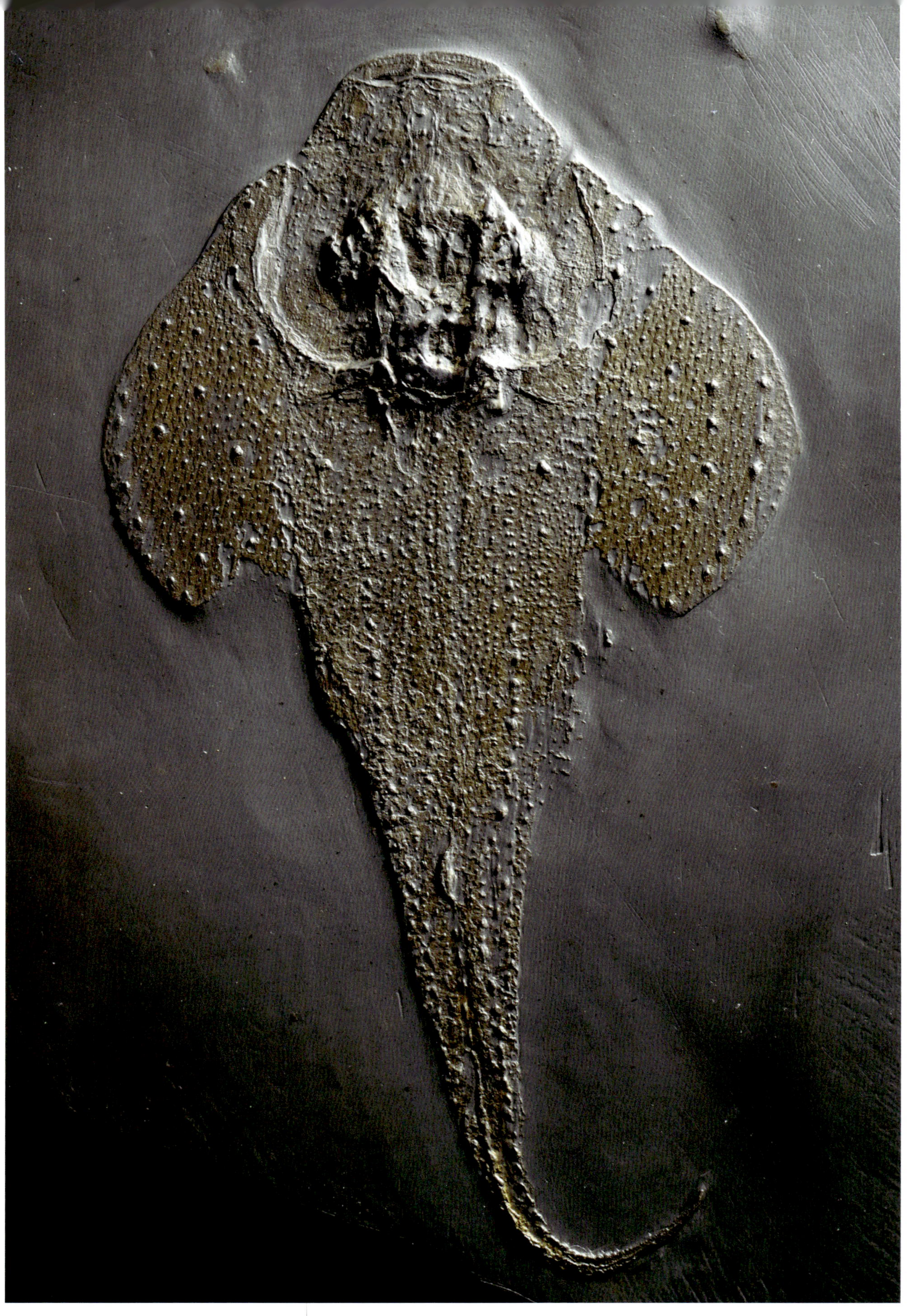

Fig. 2
Bundenbach, Birkenfeld distr. The ray-like shape of the »armoured fish« *Gemuendina stuertzi* seems to indicate that it was a bottom-dwelling animal. (Naturhistorisches Museum Mainz/Landessammlung für Naturkunde/B. Lischewsky)

painstaking and delicate work of recovering these from the slate began around 1850. Only then was their beauty revealed and their sale became a welcome extra income of the miners. As a result, many thousands of fossils found their way into private and public collections. In the meantime, the mining of roofing slate in the Hunsrück has practically ceased due to economic reasons. Since 1990, the study of the Hunsrück Slate has received fresh impetus both through the targeted collection activity of the State Collection of Natural History at the Mainz Natural History Museum and the »Project Nahecaris«, a research initiative of the then department of Earth History of the Directorate of State Archaeology. Today, this comprehensive special collection of the state enjoys top position world-wide. While in former times mainly the spectacular and filigree finds of sea lilies, brittle stars, starfish (Fig. 1), and of trilobites with legs or primeval fish (Fig. 2) were studied, today it is organisms that often appear inconspicuous and remained unnoticed previously that are collected and studied intensively. New species are being discovered time and again. Particularly outstanding specimens are so beautifully preserved due to having been rapidly covered by mud flows caused by storms or earthquakes. (Fig. 3) Finds optimally prepared with today's technologies and modern examination methods, such as micro-computer tomography, provide many details and allow important new insights. For example, the question at what depth of water the sediments of the Hunsrück Slate Sea were formed has still not been answered definitively. Whilst in previous times scholars had even presumed wadden sea-like conditions, one assumes today that we are dealing here with a habitat and depositional environment far away from the coast and in deeper waters.

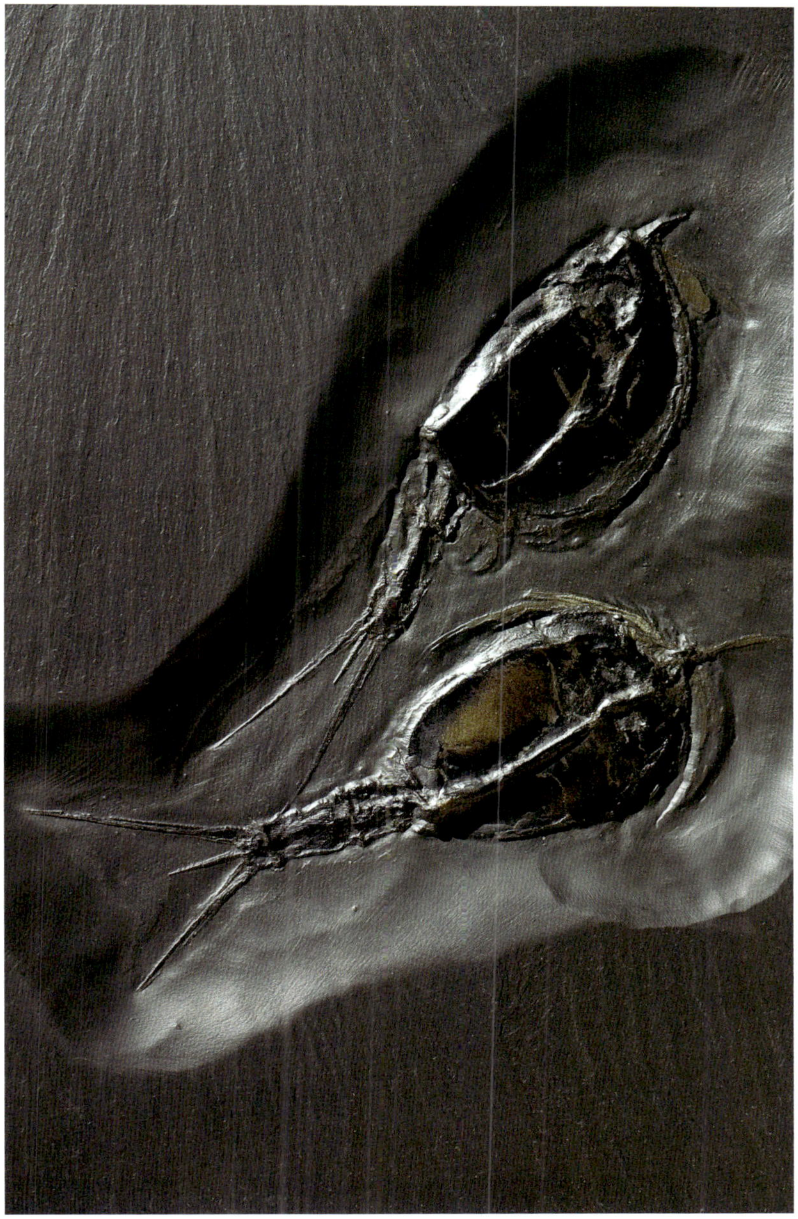

Fig. 3
Bundenbach, Birkenfeld distr. A »couple« of crabs *Nahecaris stuertzi* named after the river Nahe. (Steinmann Institut für Geologie, Mineralogie und Paläontologie/ G. Oleschinski)

Bibliography

C. Bartels/M. Wuttke/D. E. G. Briggs (Hg.), Projekt *Nahecaris* – Entschlüsselung devonischer Palaeo-Ökosysteme aus dem Hunsrückschiefer von Bundenbach. Metalla 9(2) (Bochum 2002).

G. Kühl/C. Bartels/D. E. G. Briggs/J. Rust, Fossilien im Hunsrückschiefer (Wiebelsheim 2012).

J. Rust/A. Bergmann/C. Bartels/B. Schoenemann/S. Sedlmeier/ G. Kühl, The Hunsrück biota. A unique window into the ecology of Lower Devonian arthropods. Arthropod Structure & Development 45 (London, Amsterdam 2016).

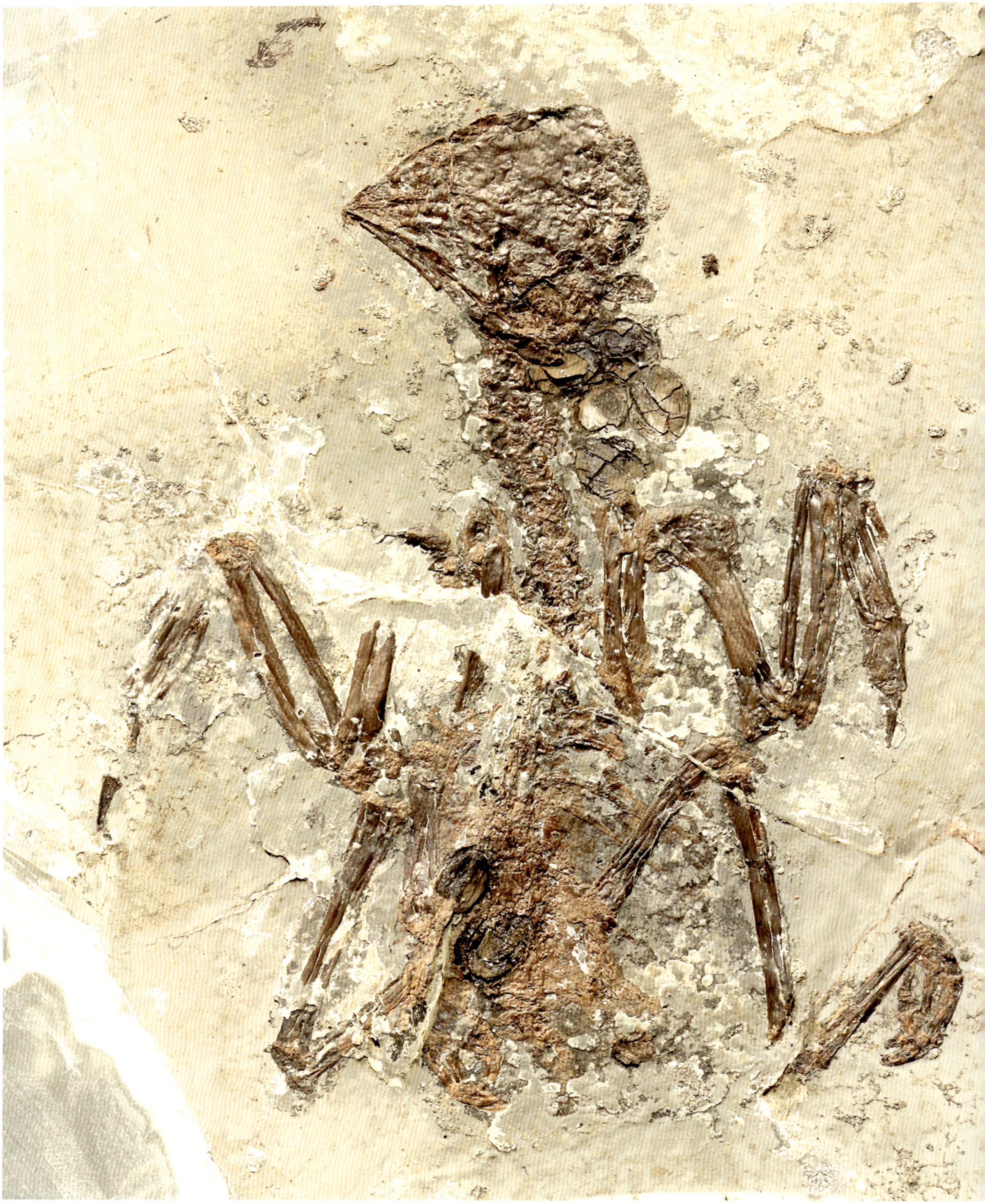

Fig. 1
Enspel, Westerwald distr. The mouse bird *Oligocolius psittacocephalon* died with food remains in its crop (scale: 10 mm). (GDKE/Landesarchäologie/Erdgeschichte/M. Poschmann)

Fossillagerstätte Enspel: Becoming and passing away in the scorching heat of volcanoes

MARKUS POSCHMANN, HERBERT LUTZ, AND PETRA SCHÄFERS

About 25 million years ago, enormous volcanic eruptions blew a funnel into the ground of today's Westerwald in the area of the municipalities of Enspel, Nistertal, and Stockum-Püschen. The crater eventually reached a diameter of more than one kilometre and was 200 m deep. At first, rocks slipped down the steep crater walls into the hole that had formed and partly filled it. Then a deep maar-like lake formed and acted as a trap for fossils. The carcasses of the lake-dwellers such as fish, frogs, and newts sank down to the bottom of the lake as did the remains of plants, insects, birds (Fig. 1), and mammals from the surrounding areas. Together, they were embedded there under quiet and oxygen-free conditions in the finely stratified sediment. The conditions for fossilization in these »oilshales« were so exceptionally good that some animals have been preserved literally with skin and hair on. Whilst crocodiles are only represented by their teeth, the »Enspel mouse«, a representative of the Eomyidae, an extinct family of rodents, shows a skin shade proving that it had gliding membranes like today's flying squirrels. (Fig. 2) Some insects display all their beautiful colours. (Fig. 3) Minute surface structures on their chitinous carapace still fulfil their function after 25 million years and reflect only certain spectral colours of sunlight. Even complex organic molecules such as chitin have been preserved almost unchanged in the sediments of Lake Enspel. An evaluation of the fossil plants, which show clear relationships to present flora in eastern Asia, revealed that the annual average tem-

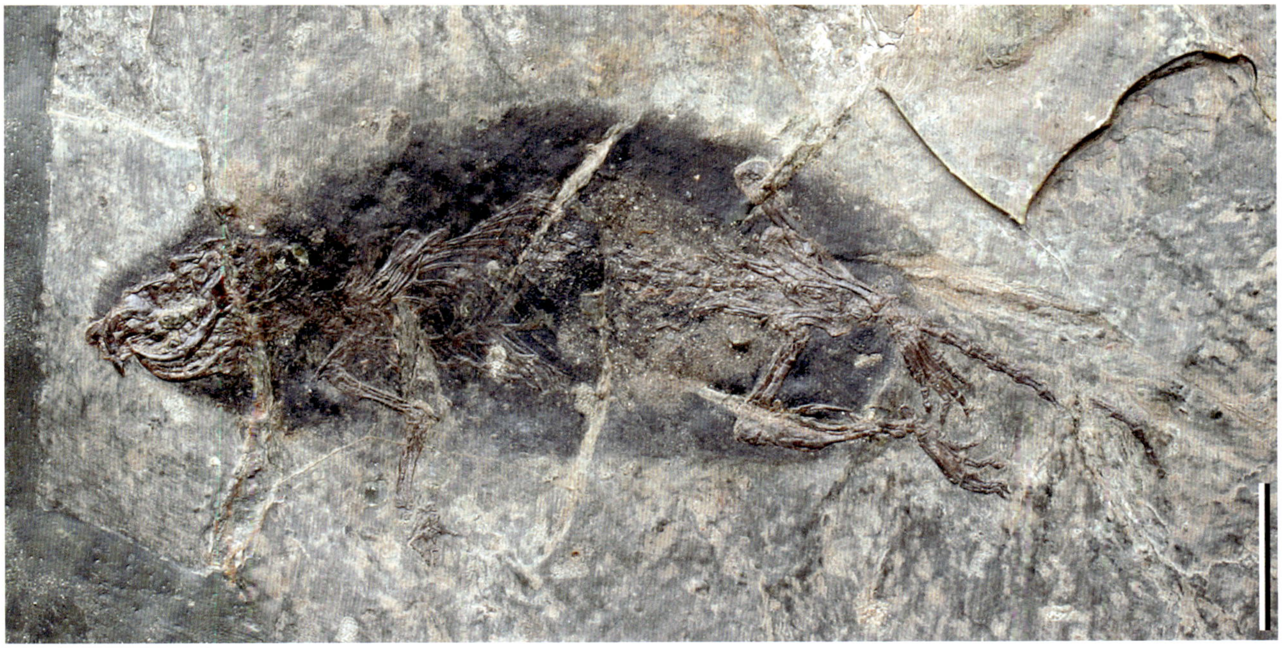

Fig. 2
Enspel, Westerwald distr. The »Enspel mouse« *Eomys quercyi* (family: Eomyidae) with an evident shadow produced by the skin and patagia between the hand and foot joint. This is the earliest geological evidence of a gliding rodent (scale: 20 mm). (GDKE/Landesarchäologie/Erdgeschichte/M. Poschmann)

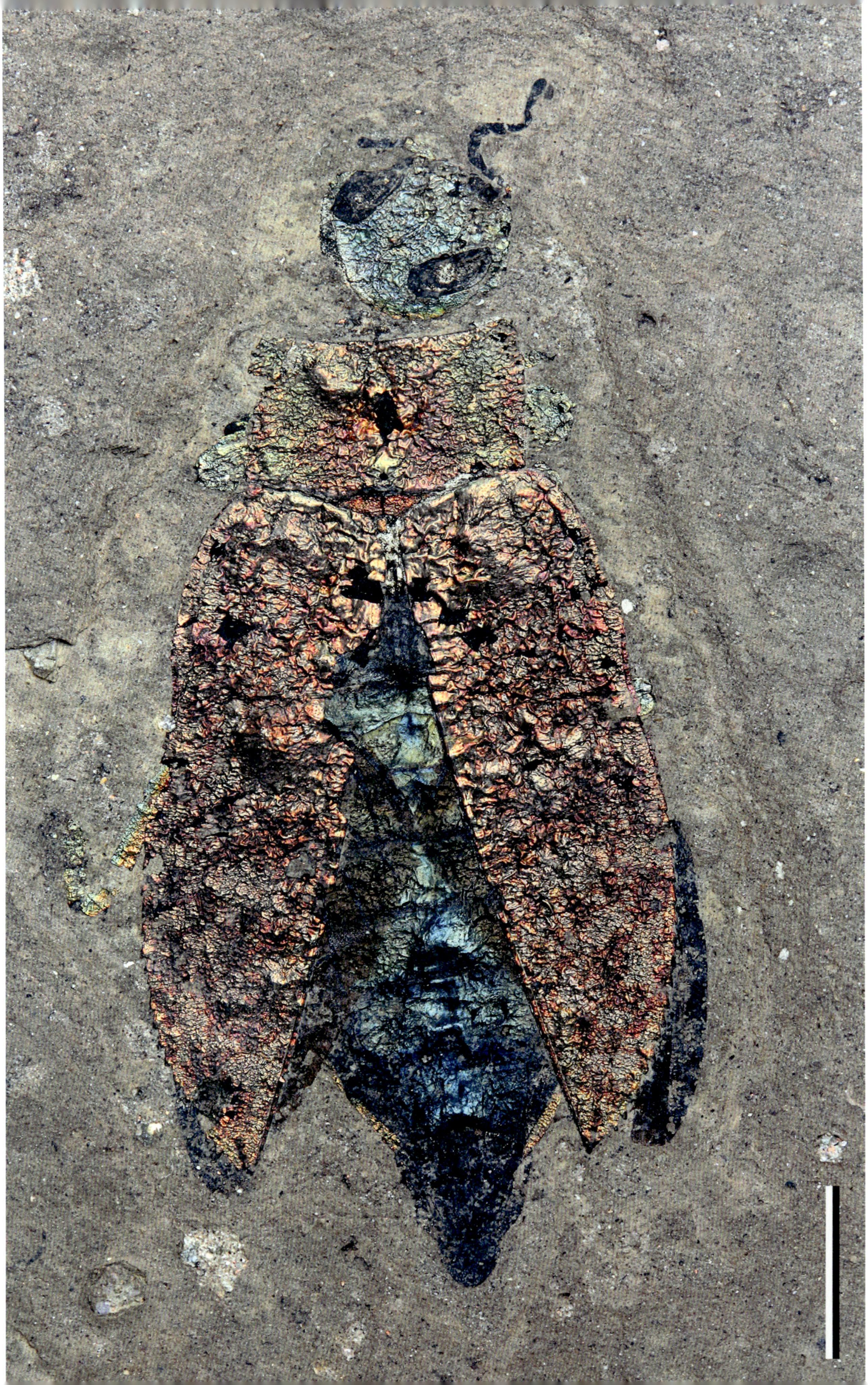

Fig. 3
Enspel, Westerwald distr. Fossil jewel beetle (family: Buprestidae), with clearly recognizable red, green, and blue structural colours (scale: 5 mm). (GDKE/Landesarchäologie/Erdgeschichte/M. Poschmann)

perature in the Westerwald at that time was approximately between 15 and 17 °C (today: 8 °C), with an average annual precipitation of 900 to 1355 mm/year (today: about 900 mm). The climate at that time can therefore be described as warm-moderate. The idyll of the Lake Enspel was time and again significantly disturbed by volcanic eruptions in the close vicinity. These events left clear traces in the form of layers of volcanic ash on the bottom of the lake. Afterwards, the fauna and flora recovered relatively quickly, as can be pieced together from the sequence of fossils in the consecutive layers of rock. After about 230,000 years, a catastrophe occurred, bringing the existence of Lake Enspel to an abrupt end, though at the same time contributing enormously to our knowledge about life in the Upper Oligocene of the Westerwald: once again, a volcano had erupted in the neighbourhood. Its basaltic lava flowed into the lake and filled the basin with a layer up to 100 m thick. This cap of hard basalt protected the soft lake deposits against destruction through weathering and erosion up until today. For more than 100 years this basalt has been quarried industrially, while gradually exposing the petrified bottom of the lake beneath. It is only because of the above that we can today peep through this unique window at a 25-million-year-old landscape shaped by volcanoes and its inhabitants.

Bibliography

M. Wuttke, D. Uhl, T. Schindler (Hg.), Fossillagerstätte Enspel – exceptional preservation in an Upper Oligocene maar. Palaeobiodiversity and Palaeoenvironments 90 (Berlin 2010).

M. Wuttke, T. Schindler, K. T. Smith (Hg.), The Fossil-Lagerstätte Enspel – reconstructing the palaeoenvironment with new data on fossils and geology. Palaeobiodiversity and Palaeoenvironments 95 (Berlin 2015).

The volcanism of the Eifel

AXEL VON BERG

The north of Rhineland-Palatinate is characterized by a large Quaternary volcanic area called the Eifel Volcanic Field. The geologically very young volcanism of the eastern and western Eifel began during the early Middle Pleistocene, some 600,000 years ago. The age of the existing Quaternary sediments is determined by means of different volcanic deposits of numerous eruptions, which can be precisely scientifically dated. Geologically, the Eifel Volcanic Field belongs to the continental »intraplate volcanism« and is situated on an old rising plate. Volcanism shifted from north to south in the course of its development. Here we have a connection with the rising of the Rhenish shield and the simultaneous sinking of the Lower Rhine Embayment. The landscape is characterized by at least 150 volcanoes, with mighty cinder cones usually structuring the terrain relief. (Fig. 2) They were formed by more than 1000 °C hot magma and volcanic ashes, which accumulated round the vents during the eruptions. The diameter of the base of these cinder cones is between 300 and 1000

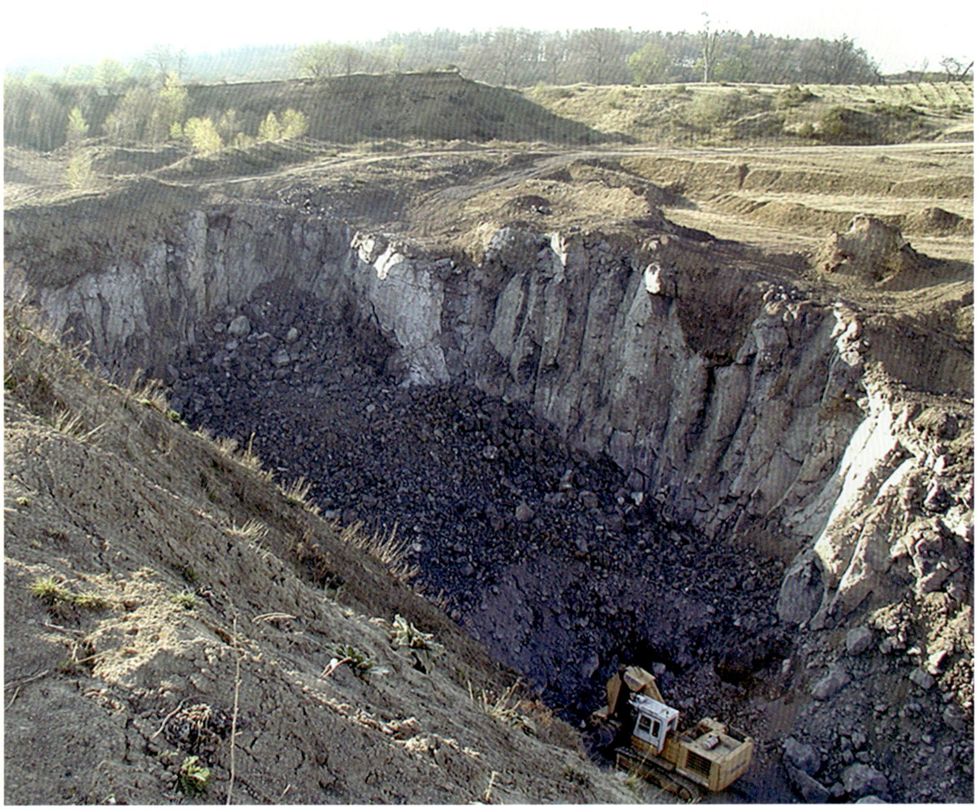

Fig. 1
Bassenheim, Mayen-Koblenz distr. View of the central vent of the slag volcano at the Schweinskopf with the lava solidified in columnar form. (GDKE/Koblenz/Landesarchäologie/M. Neumann)

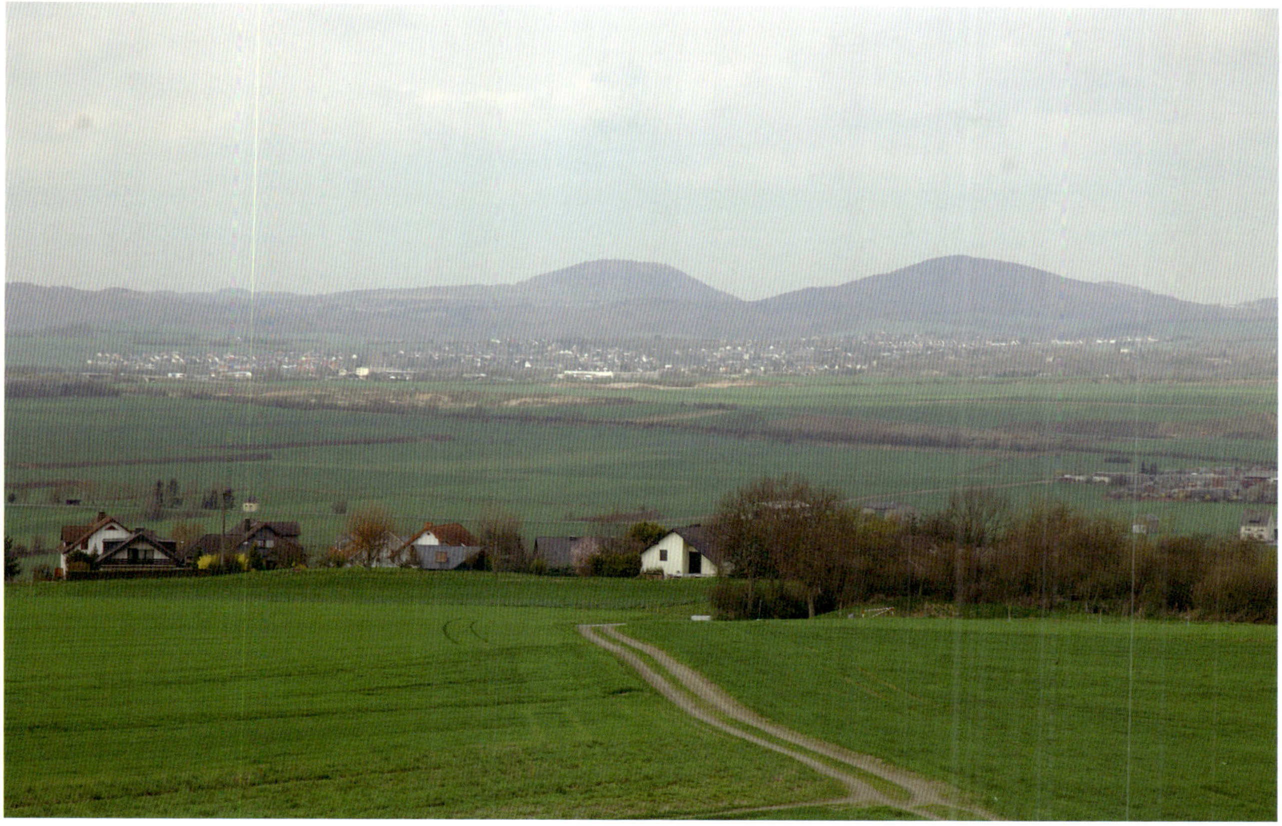

Fig. 2
Mayen/Ettringen, Mayen-Koblenz distr. View of the Hochsimmer and the Hochstein volcanoes. (GDKE/ Landesarchäologie/ Koblenz/ A. von Berg)

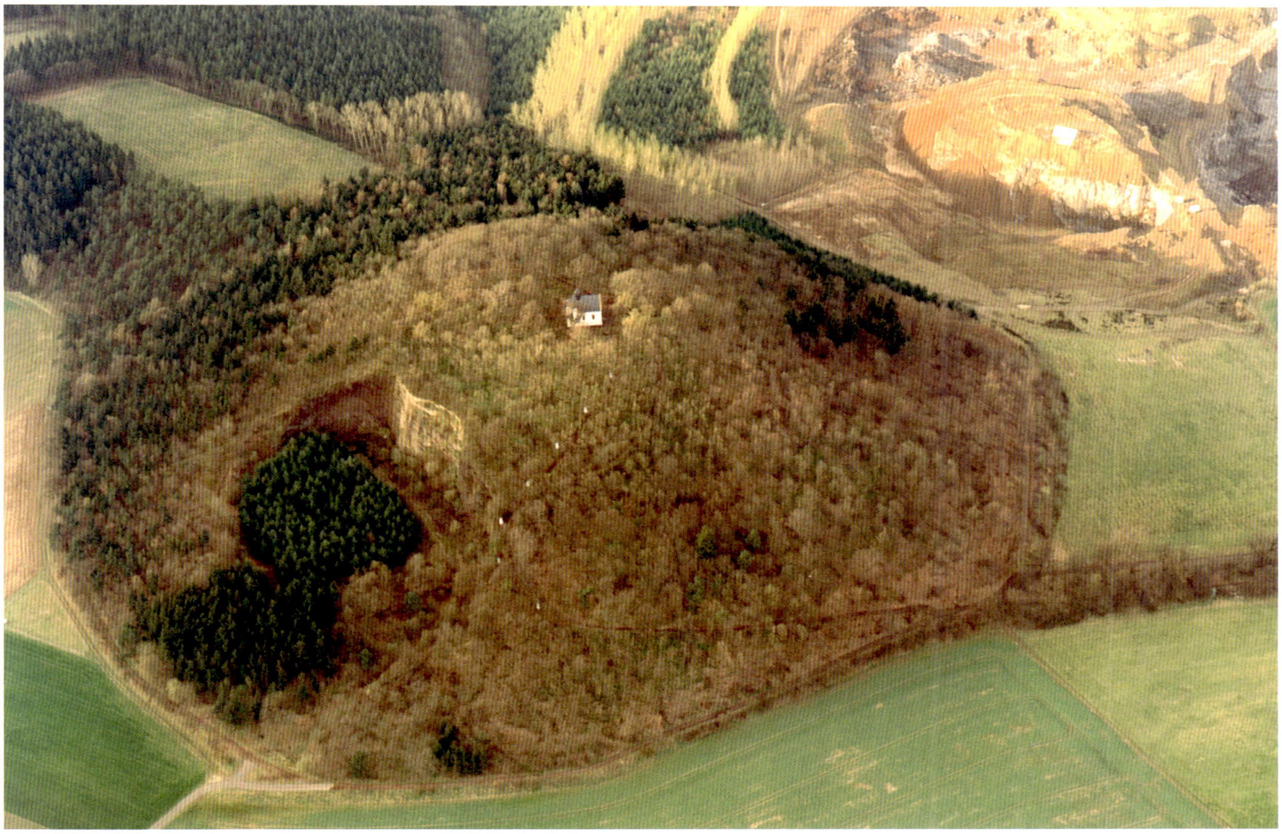

Fig. 3
Ochtendung/ Bassenheim, Mayen-Koblenz distr. Aerial photo of the Karmelenberg slag volcano; in the background: lava mining at the Schweinskopf. (GDKE/ Landesarchäologie/ Koblenz/ C. A. Jost)

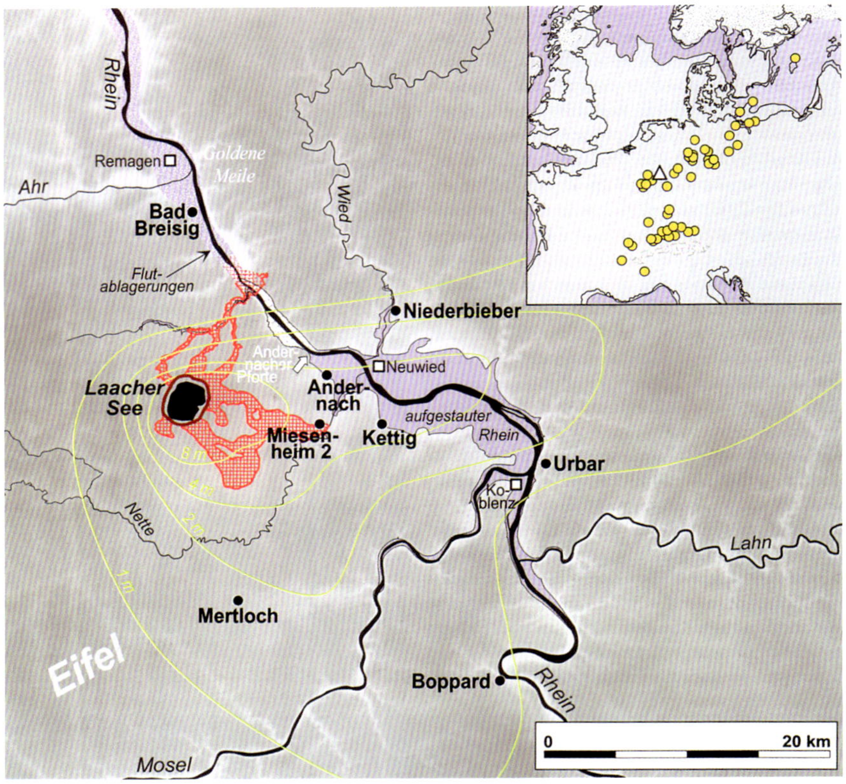

Fig. 4
Distribution of the ash layers of the Laach lake volcano and course of the ash flows near the crater. (after M. Baales, O. Jöris, H.-U. Schmincke)

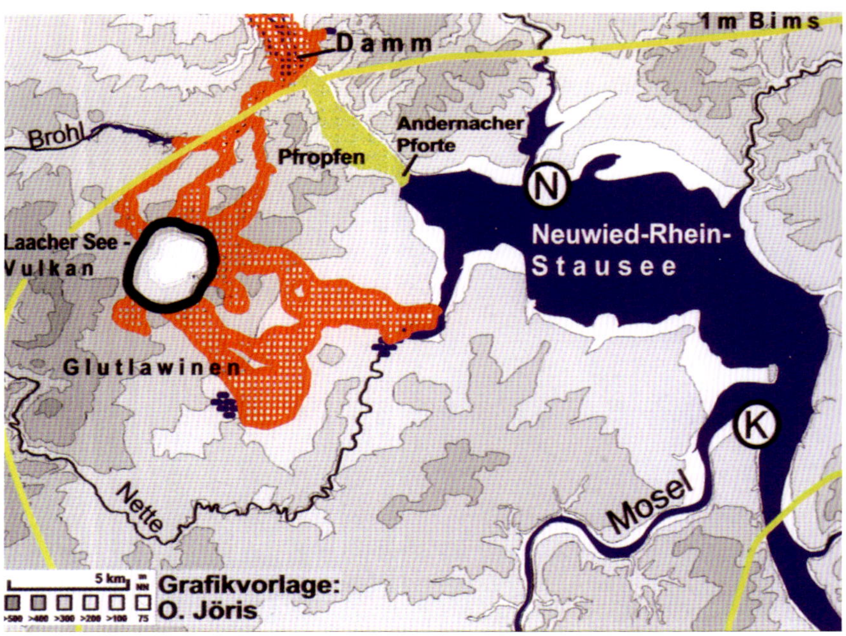

Fig. 5
Effects of the Laach lake volcano eruption in 10,966 BC with pumice layers, embers avalanches, the artificial lake in the Neuwied Basin, and the late Palaeolithic sites in the region. (O. Jöris, M. Baales, H.-U. Schmincke, C. Park and E. Harms)

m and they are between 50 and 200 m high. (Fig. 3) Lava often ascended through several volcanic chimneys close to each other, so some volcanoes form groups. From these cinder cones, lava streams started to flow towards the Rhine following the slope of the terrain. In addition to cinder cones, strong eruptions are recorded as further volcanic forms, and their enormous explosions produced pumice tuffs, which can be found as deposits all over Europe. In the case of these pumice volcanoes, the contact of magma and water led to »Plinian« eruptions, as described by Pliny the Younger when witnessing the eruption of Vesuvius in the year 79 AD. The material ejected, mostly pumice, still covers wide areas in Rhineland-Palatinate and is often several metres thick. Dust was introduced into the higher strata of the atmosphere and influenced the climate and environment for a considerable time. About 13,000 years ago, exactly in 10,966 BC, one of the biggest volcanic eruptions ever in Europe occurred at the spot of today's Lake Laach. (Fig. 4) Through the enormous explosion, large areas in Rhineland-Palatinate were buried under pumice tuff in a very short time. This layer is still 20 m thick in close vicinity of the vent. Clouds of glowing ash filled the valleys and led to trass deposits several metres thick. (Fig. 5) Usually, the structure of the pumice deposits is remarkably consistent, and the standard profiles show several eruption phases so far. (Fig. 6) The lower layers consist uniformly of white pumice tuff, the upper ones are sandy and grey. Several fine layers of ash, also referred to as »Britz«, structure the profile into different horizons. The wide distribution of pumice and ash makes this eruption an important marker horizon in Central Europe. The ashes of the Lake Laach volcano drifted through western and northern winds over several hundreds of kilometres to the south as far as Switzerland and even across the Alps as far as northern Italy, to the west as far as Belgium, and to the north east as far as the Swedish island of Gotland and to Poland. The increased sulphur content in the atmosphere and the »acid rain« connected with it led to a marked reduction in the growth of tree vegetation over a number of years, as indicated by the reduced thickness of tree rings of a fossil pine forest in western Switzerland. The eruption of the Lake Laach volcano probably also led to a short-term climate change in the northern hemisphere. During the middle eruption phase of the Lake Laach volcano, the eruption column consisting of hot ashes and gases and reaching heights of 20–40 km collapsed several times. As a consequence, hot, gas-rich avalanches of embers shot through the valleys round today's Lake Laach, filling them with trass deposits several metres thick. Pressure waves accompanying the eruption were responsible for the large-scale windthrow - uprooting trees in the area of the Neuwied basin. In 1980, a forest from the time of the Lake Laach volcano could be examined for the first time near Thür. In leeward positions such as near Kruft – where the mighty volcanic structure of the »Krufter Ofen« provided protection against pressure waves – birches and poplars were buried still upright, preserved either in the form of charred woods in airtight layers or as cavities in the volcanic ash. They represent more or less closed forests with many species of undergrowth. The remains of plants show typical floodplain vegetation, as in present day Sweden. When in the course of the eruption the avalanches of embers shot through the Brohl valley and across the Rhine, the course of the river was blocked by vast amounts of trass. The dam blocked the river up to Koblenz, forming a lake that had a surface of about 80 km², whilst downstream the riverbed fell mostly dry. While the volcano was still erupting over the course of only a few weeks, the dam burst, and enormous masses of water flowed down the Rhine valley.

During pumice mining in the area of Mertloch in

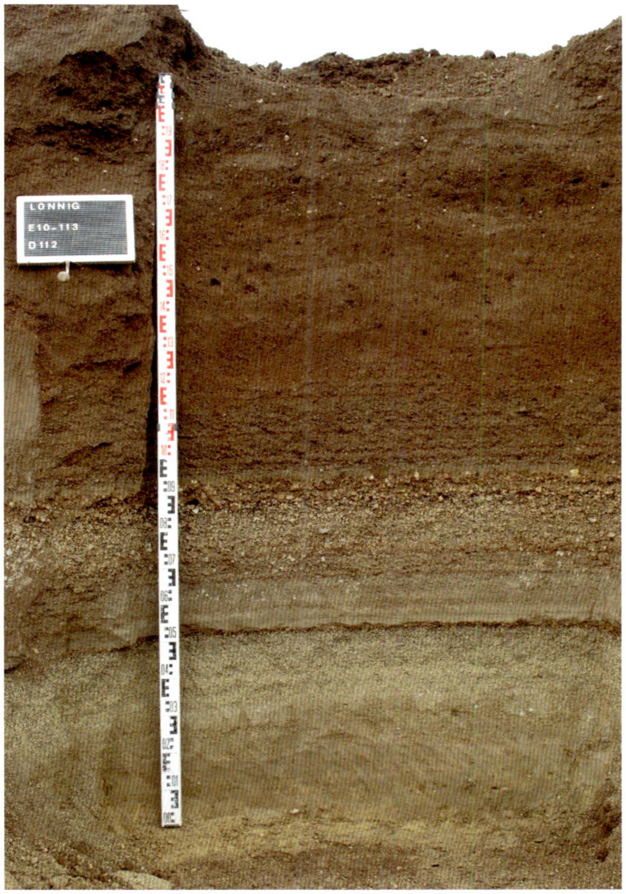

Fig. 6
Lonnig, Mayen-Koblenz distr. Cross-section of the pumice strata and ash layers of the Laach lake volcano. (GDKE/Landesarchäologie/Koblenz/A. von Berg)

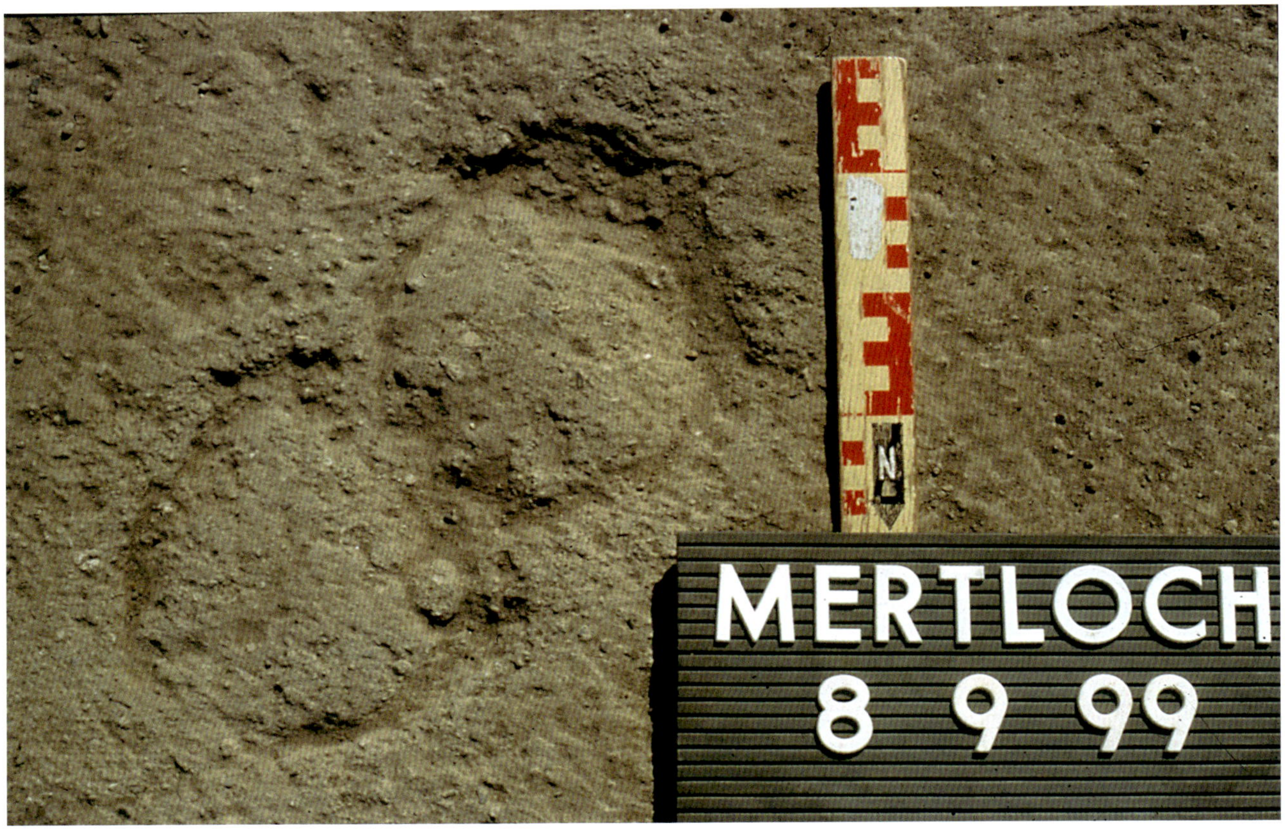

Fig. 7
Mertloch, Mayen-Koblenz distr. Animal track of a horse in the ash of the Laach lake volcano. (GDKE/Landesarchäologie/Koblenz/R. Eggers)

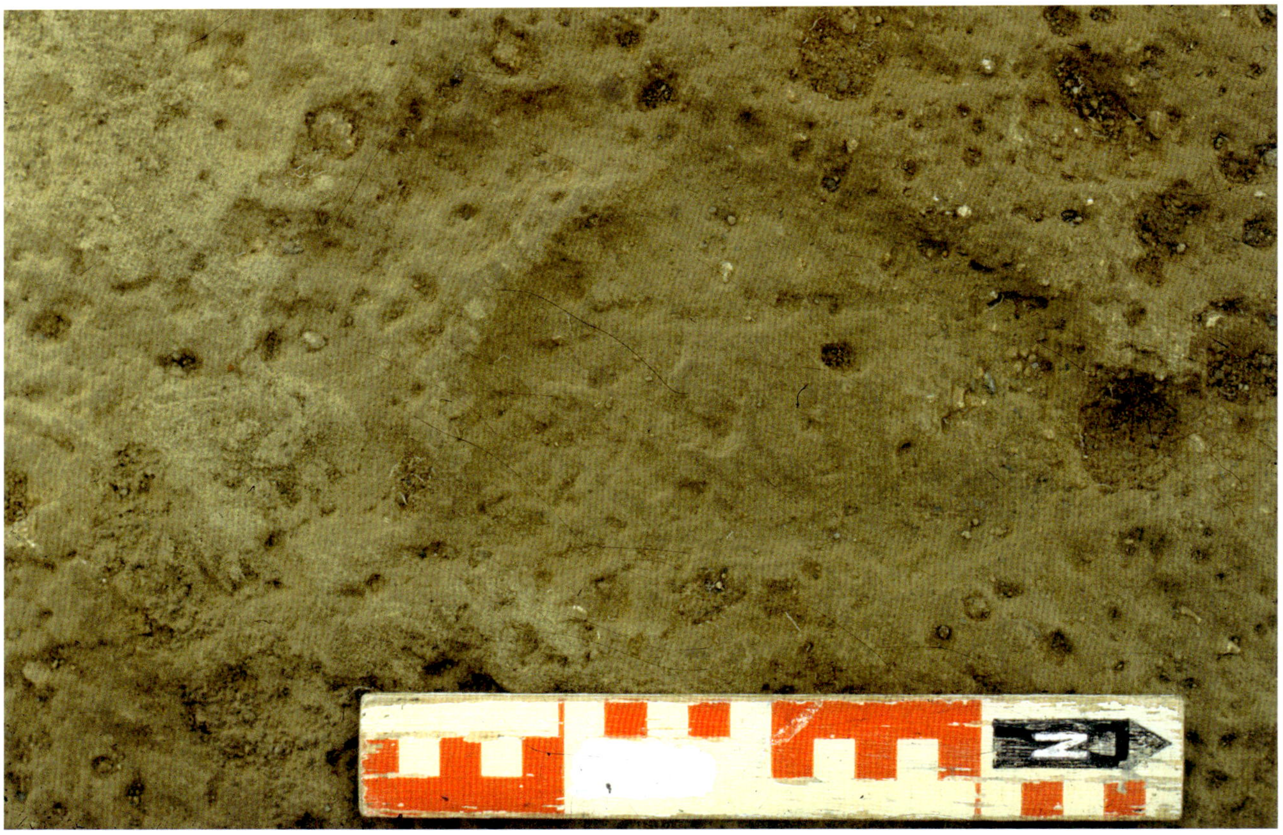

Fig. 8
Mertloch, Mayen-Koblenz distr. Animal track of a bear in the ash of the Laach lake volcano. (GDKE/Landesarchäologie/Koblenz/R. Eggers)

the Mayen-Koblenz district, some 15 km south-east of the eruption centre, numerous animal tracks could be documented on the surface of a layer of ash. Diverse tracks and trackways of Alleröd fauna from the end of the Ice Age were preserved over large areas as in a snapshot and were sealed again shortly afterwards with volcanic material. The tracks could be assigned to various animal species of the late Ice Age fauna 13,000 years ago, such as horse, brown bear, red deer, and capercaillie/wood grouse. (Fig. 7–9) Based on preserved footprints of young foals, the season of the volcanic eruption could be dated in agreement with other findings to the late spring/early summer of the year 10,966 BC. These were the first and so far only animal trackways that have been preserved from the time of Quaternary volcanic activity in the eastern Eifel.

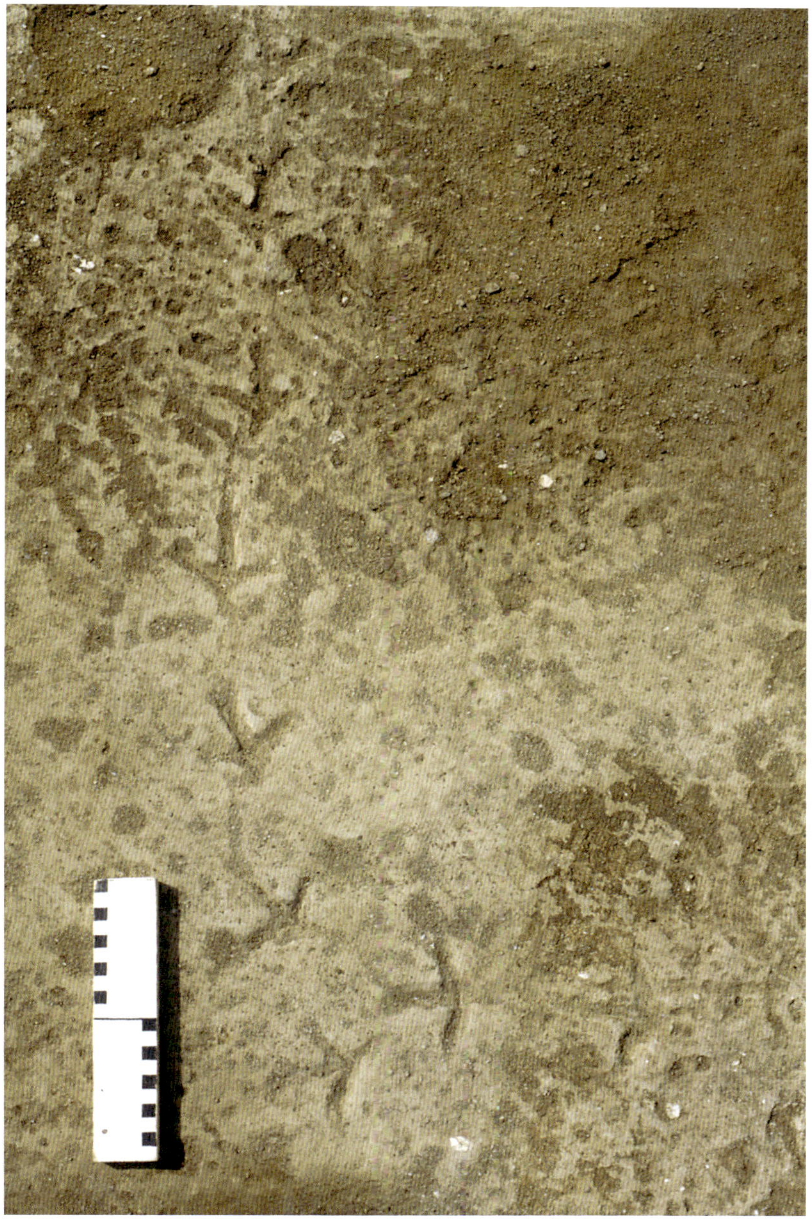

Fig. 9
Mertloch, Mayen-Koblenz distr. Tracks of a Black Grouse in the ash of the Laach lake volcano. (GDKE/Landesarchäologie/Koblenz/R. Eggers)

Bibliography

M. Baales, Archäologie des Eiszeitalters. Frühe Menschen an Mittelrhein und Mosel. Archäologie an Mittelrhein und Mosel Bd. 16 (Koblenz 2005).

M. Baales, O. Jöris, M. Street, F. Bittmann, B. Weninger, J. Wiethold, Impact of the Late Glacial Eruption of the Laacher See Volcano, Central Rhineland, Germany, Quaternary Research 58, 2002, 273 ff.

P. Bogaard, H. U. Schmincke, Die Entwicklungsgeschichte des Mittelrheinraumes und die Eruptionsgeschichte des Osteifel-Vulkanfeldes. In: W. Schirmer (Hrsg.), Rheingeschichte zwischen Mosel und Maas. deuqua-Führer 1, Hannover (1990) 166 ff.

G. Büchel, Die Maare im Vulkanfeld der Westeifel, ihr geophysikalischer Nachweis, ihr Alter und ihre Beziehung zur Tektonik der Erdkruste. Diss. Univ. Mainz (Mainz 1984).

W. Meyer, Geologie der Eifel (Stuttgart 1994).

H.-U. Schmincke, Vulkanismus. Wissenschaftliche Buchgesellschaft (Darmstadt 2000).

H.-U. Schmincke, The Quarternary Volcanic Fields of the east and West Eifel (Germany). In: J. Ritter, R.R. Christensen, R. Ulrich (Hrsg.), Mantle Plumes – A Multidisciplinary Approach (Berlin, Heidelberg (2007) 241 ff.

STONE AGE

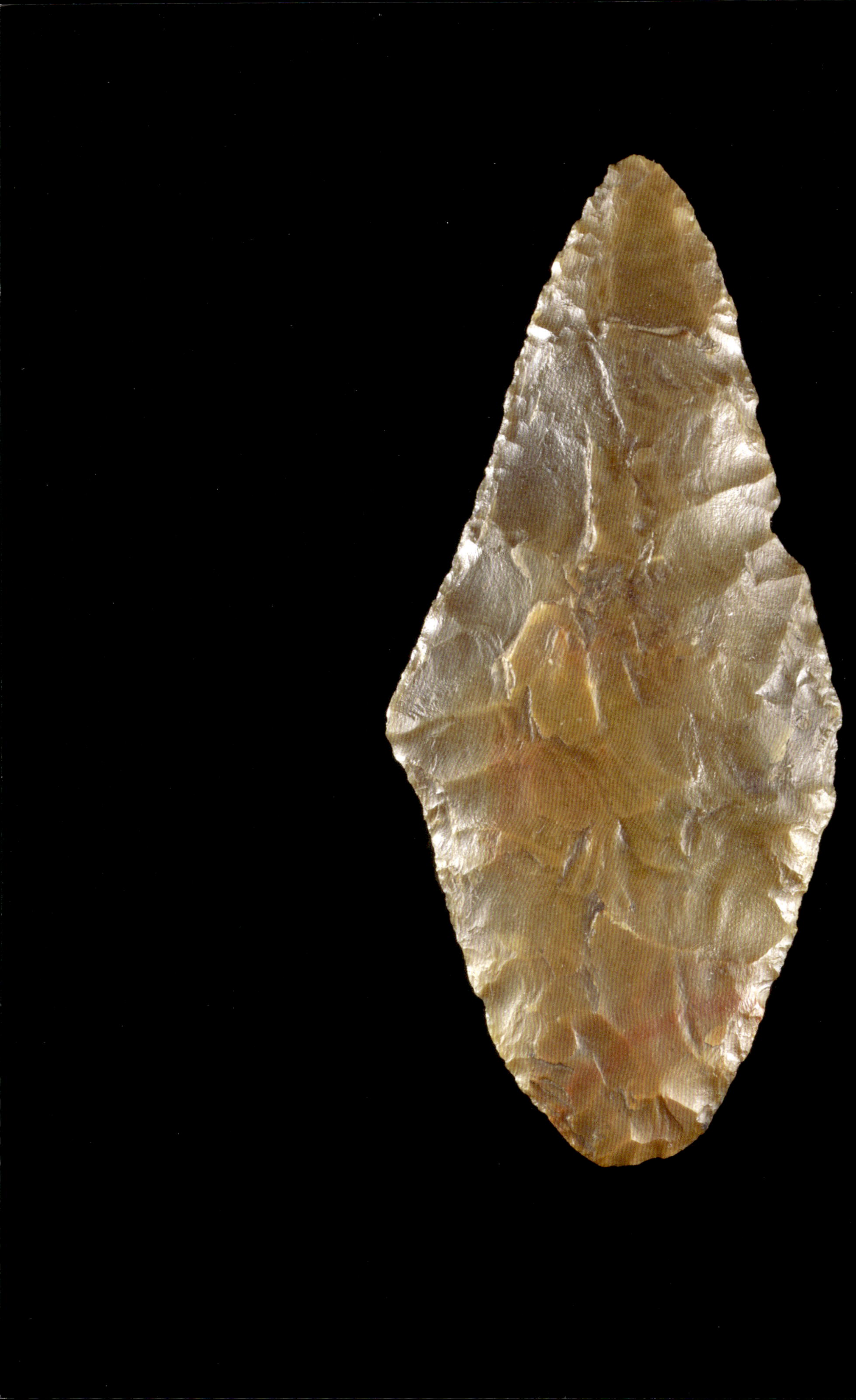

Early humans

AXEL VON BERG

The origins of mankind are to be found in the great savannahs of eastern Africa where the evolution of man began about 4 million years ago. Almost 2 million years ago, homo erectus evolved, an early human being who left Africa as early as 1.8 million years ago and whose descendants settled in Asia and Europe. The early history of man in Rhineland-Palatinate goes back, on the basis of current knowledge, nearly one million years and starts in the Pleistocene (Quaternary), also called the era of ice ages.

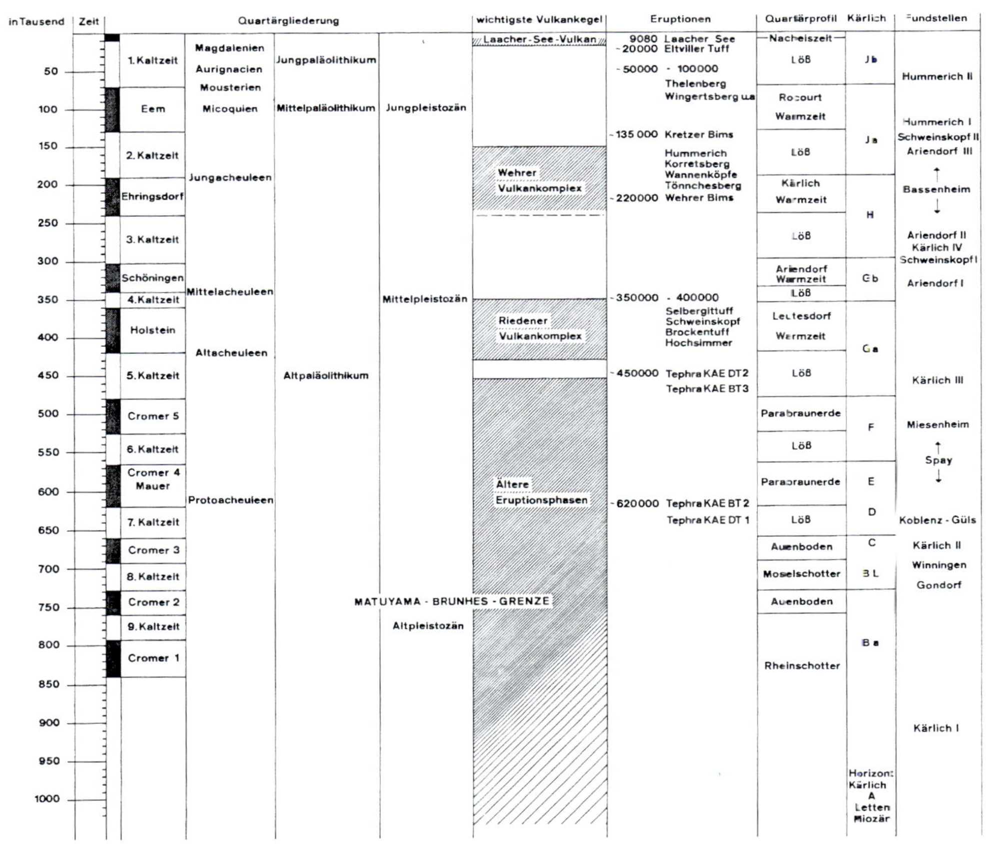

Fig. 1
Stratigraphy and time structure of the middle and young Pleistocene in Rhineland-Palatinate by means of the stratigraphy in the eastern Eifel and important find complexes of the early days in northern Rhineland-Palatinate. (GDKE/Landesarchäologie/Koblenz/ A. von Berg)

Kettig, Mayen-Koblenz distr. Lancet-shaped dagger blade made of western European flintstone. The blades were sharpened by retouching their edges and belong to the extraordinary finds of the Late Neolithic at the Middle Rhine (ca. 2000–1800 BC). (GDKE/Landesarchäologie/Koblenz/ W. Baumann, Höhr-Grenzhausen)

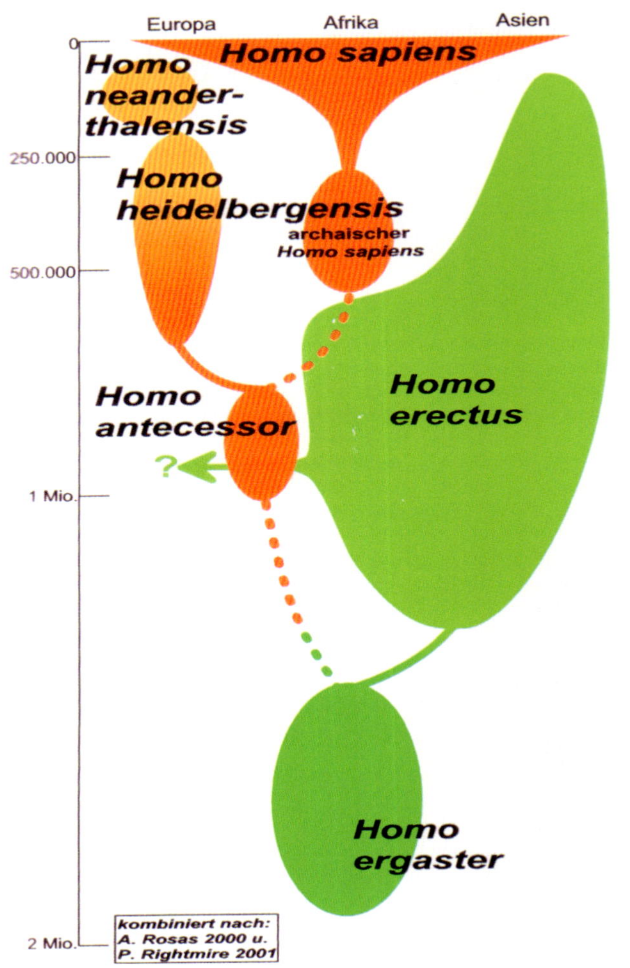

Fig. 2
Family tree of man with *homo heidelberghensis* and Neanderthal and the development towards modern man. (after O. Jöris, M. Baales; combined after A. Rosas and P. Rightmine)

The development of human culture during the unimaginably long periods of the Palaeolithic Age is hardly noticeable. Life was determined by its complete dependence on nature. Knowledge regarding the earliest settlement has increased considerably over the last few decades through detailed studies. With the development of new methods, dating, and correlation procedures involving geology, sedimentology, palaeontology and volcanology, the data regarding the recent and most recent past in earth's history, and thus also the earliest times of man, has been much refined and deepened. (Fig. 1)

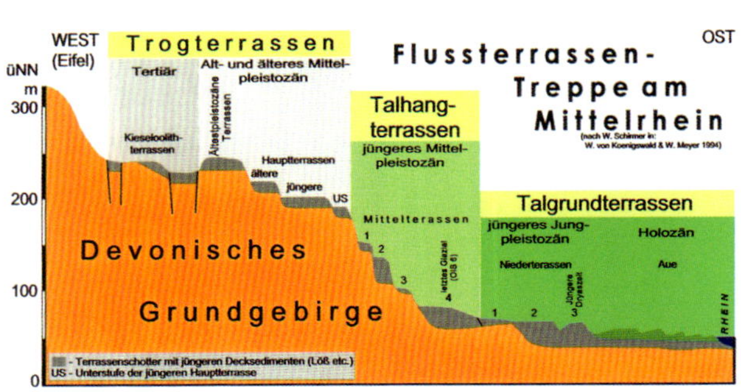

Fig. 3
Schematic cross-section through the river valley at the Middle Rhine with the different terrace formations. (after M. Baales, W. Schirmer, W. von Koenigswald and W. Meyer)

The first early humans reach Rhineland-Palatinate

The earliest archaeological evidence for the existence of early humans, *homo antecessor* and *homo heidelbergensis*, in Europe is about 1.2 million years old and associated with the so-called »Protoacheulean« of an early Palaeolithic cultural stage. Early man eventually reached the regions of Rhineland-Palatinate via the Near East and Southern Europe. (Fig. 2)

The Lower Palaeolithic

The oldest verified evidence for the presence of humans in northern Central Europe goes back to about one million years ago. Only from that time do we have some first indications of the spread of early man into the climatically moderate regions to the north of the high mountain ranges of Eurasia. The so-called »Jaramillo period«, when a particularly favourable and warm climate prevailed, plays an important role in this context. At that time, the European line of hominids, which later led to the evolution of the Neanderthals, separated from the African line. It seems that Europe north of the high mountain ranges was settled only during warm periods at first. During these moderate climate periods, deciduous forests with major grassy clearings covered large parts of Central Europe. Forest elephants, rhinoceroses, horses, deer, and cattle were indigenous to the region.

Archaeological evidence of this earliest settlement phase of our region is rare. Findspots are located mainly in northern Rhineland-Palatinate, such as Miesenheim, the clay pit of Kärlich, and also the main terraces of the Middle Rhine Valley and the Moselle.

Numerous findspots, mostly from the time of the Early and Middle Pleistocene, are in the areas of the river terraces of the Middle Rhine and the Moselle (Fig. 3), where, besides sites from the time of *homo*

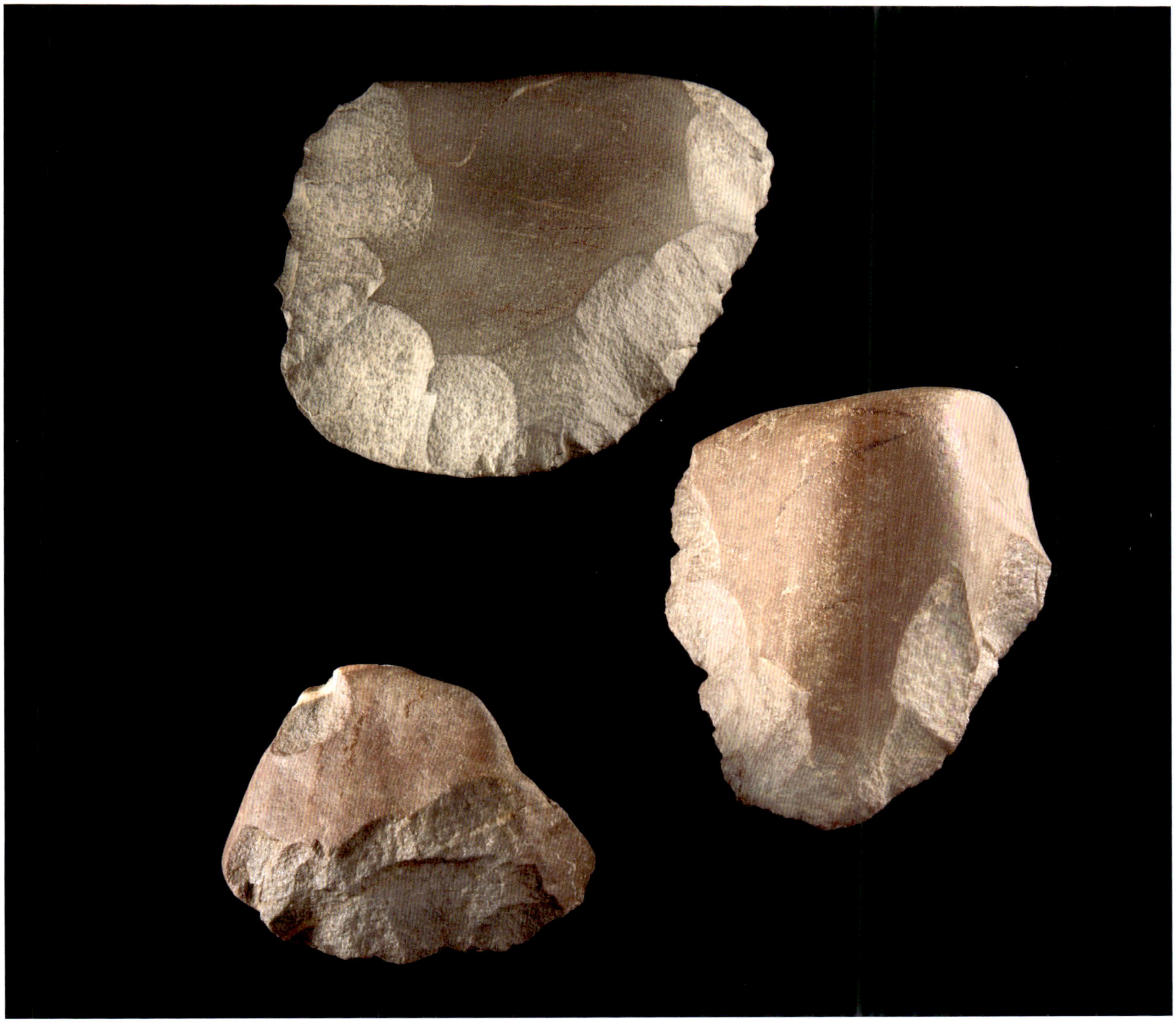

Fig. 4
Winningen, Mayen-Koblenz distr. and Karden, Cochem-Zell distr. Stone tools (hand axes: top and right, pebble tool: bottom left) of the early days from the main terraces of the Moselle. (GDKE/ Landesarchäologie/ Koblenz/W. Baumann, Höhr-Grenzhausen)

heidelbergensis with major series of artefacts, numerous individual finds were also made.

The oldest finds directly from or below the river gravel of the main terraces of the Rhine and Moselle are known from Kärlich, Winningen, Koblenz–Güls, and Spay. Their characteristic elements are the so-called »pebble tools«, mostly river gravel with sharply-hewn working edges, but also flakes of quartz and quartzite. These forms of tools were used for splitting and cutting and are typical for early Palaeolithic find groups.

The hand axe gradually became an all-purpose tool. (Fig. 4) Simply dressed hand axes were discovered at Winningen, Pommern, and Karden. Big game hunting was the most important livelihood at that time. These early forms of culture are represented by the early human *homo intercessor* and *heidelbergensis*. What we know so far is that these early finds originated from the river banks of the old Quaternary river systems of Rhine and Moselle. Dry river bank ledges, sand banks, and gravel zones of the rivers were ideal terrains for resting places. (Fig. 5)

A resting place of that time near Miesenheim in the Mayen-Koblenz district, with stone tools and hunting possibilities such as stag, deer, elephant, rhinoceros, cattle, and horse at the edge of a former water expanse, is among the oldest archaeologically explored places

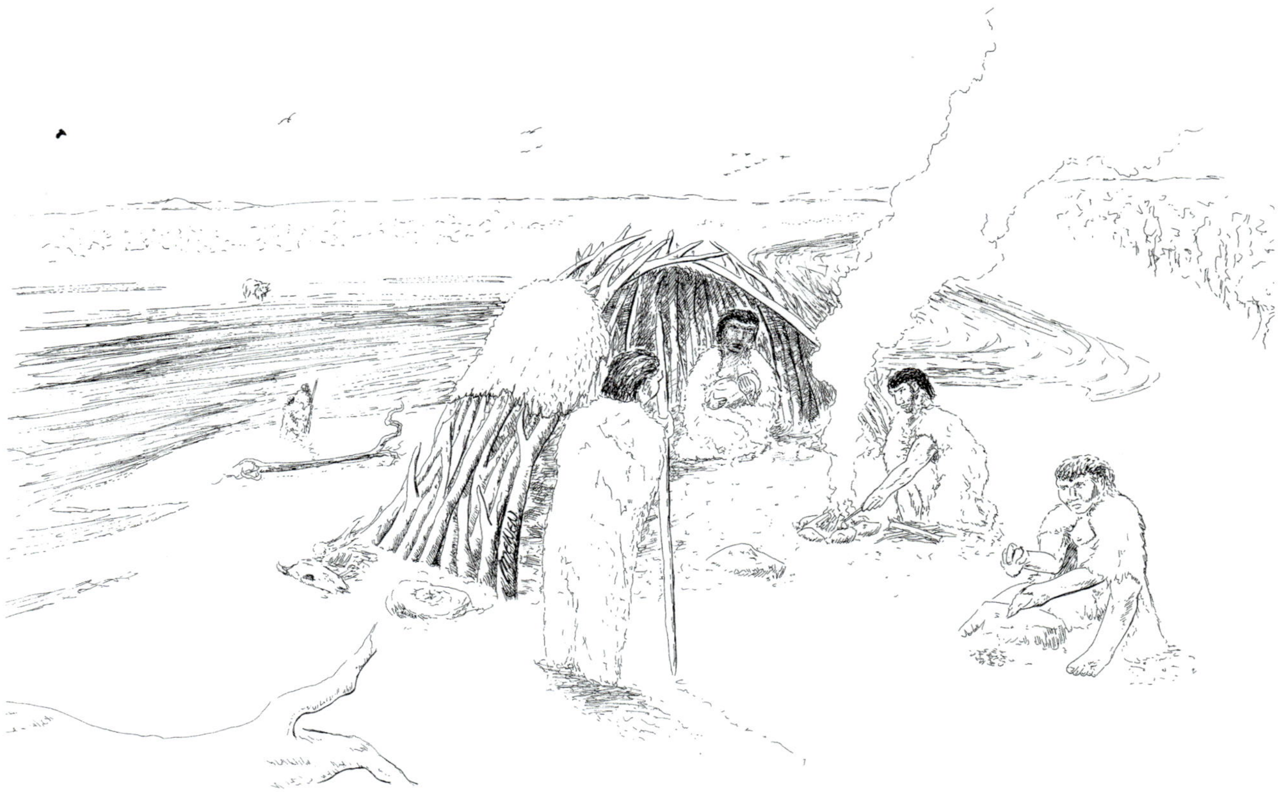

Fig. 5
Güls, city of Koblenz. Reconstructed camp site situation of the early days at the Moselle river bank. (GDKE/Landesarchäologie/Koblenz/M. Meinen)

of this kind in Germany. The unique find situation in Miesenheim I provides detailed insights into the life and environment of *homo heidelberghensis*. It is one of the few findspots of that time with surviving stone artefacts and animal bones, which were then covered by sediment more than 600,000 years ago. Today, the site lies on the eastern bank of the small river Nette in the eastern Eifel, some 3 km before it flows into the Rhine. At that time, the settlement was directly on the bank of the Rhine in a swampy terrain covered by alluvial forest. The stone artefacts found in Miesenheim were made in a simple manner from quartz, quartzite, and lydite. Two pieces show traces of fire. The expansion to the north beyond the borders of the original homeland of early man, i.e. the African savannah biotope, was only made possible through the systematic use of fire.

From around 450,000 years ago, there are indications that settlements in our state also occurred during cooler climatic phases. In the Kärlich clay pit, archaeologists examined parts of a findspot in the path of an old brook. Fragments of tusks and bones of the steppe elephant and a good number of stone artefacts of quartz and quartzite had been preserved, these being simply dressed cores and flakes. Early man lived in a steppe landscape, which developed in a dry climate with warm summers and very cold winters. In the same clay pit, a very well-preserved resting place on the banks of a former peat lake from the late period of *homo heidelbergensis could* be examined. The lake sediments with peat layers permit a reconstruction of the typical vegetation from the middle of a warm period – a time when the landscape was covered with deciduous forests, mainly hornbeam and oak. The many stone artefacts left behind were made from quartz and quartzite. There were cores and hammerstones showing that the artefacts were made in situ. The simple tools have a working edge knapped on one or both sides. The finds also included hand axes made from large quartzite scree. (Fig. 6) Numerous splitting wedges, so-called cleavers, consist of scree quartzite and feature a wide

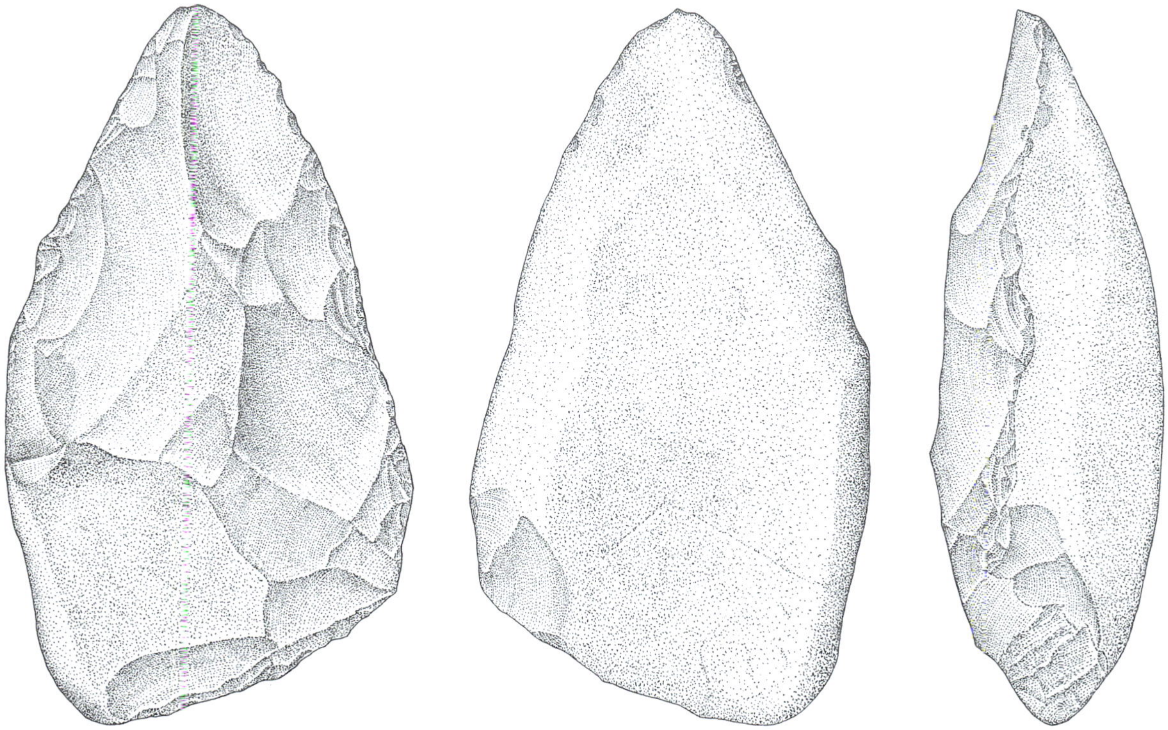

Fig. 6
Mühlheim-Kärlich, Mayen-Koblenz distr. Hand axe made of quartzite from the lake shore sediments of the hunting station from the late time of *homo heidelberghensis*. (after G. Bosinski)

cutting edge. In addition, there are flakes whose edges are splintered from use.

Large amounts of animal bones were found in the same area as the stone artefacts. These are mainly long bones and teeth of forest elephants, with a smaller quantity of bone remains of red deer, cattle, boar, and also of lion. The preserved animal bones, including the remains of at least eight elephants, are evidence of a moderately warm climate. Thanks to the advantageous conditions for good preservation, tools made of bone, wood, and antlers were also found. The lake was an attractive habitat for early man.

The position of the numerous pieces of wood on the site gives an indication of the oldest wooden construction of the region to date, probably the remains of a simple dwelling. The find situation fits well within a group of comparable sites with similar dating in Europe and the Near East and seems to indicate that the hunting of forest elephants played an important role at that time.

The Middle Palaeolithic

The following Middle Palaeolithic is the time of the Neanderthals in Rhineland-Palatinate. It began about 300,000 years ago, at the start of the third-last glacial period, and was characterized by a more careful and standardized technique of stone cutting. The human representative of the Middle Palaeolithic cultures is the Neanderthal, who for the following 250,000 years lived in the regions of the Rhine, the Moselle, and the Palatinate. During the developed phase of this period, about 150,000 years ago, decisive changes in the spectrum of forms occur: the rough and simple hand axes and pebble tools of the early age disappear and are replaced by specialized forms of tools such as points, scrapers, and purposely-made flakes. This is a time when the surface of lithic cores is prepared for the production of flakes, and the so-called Levallois technique becomes characteristic. Many pieces were also dressed and formed by retouching the edges with a hammerstone or ant-

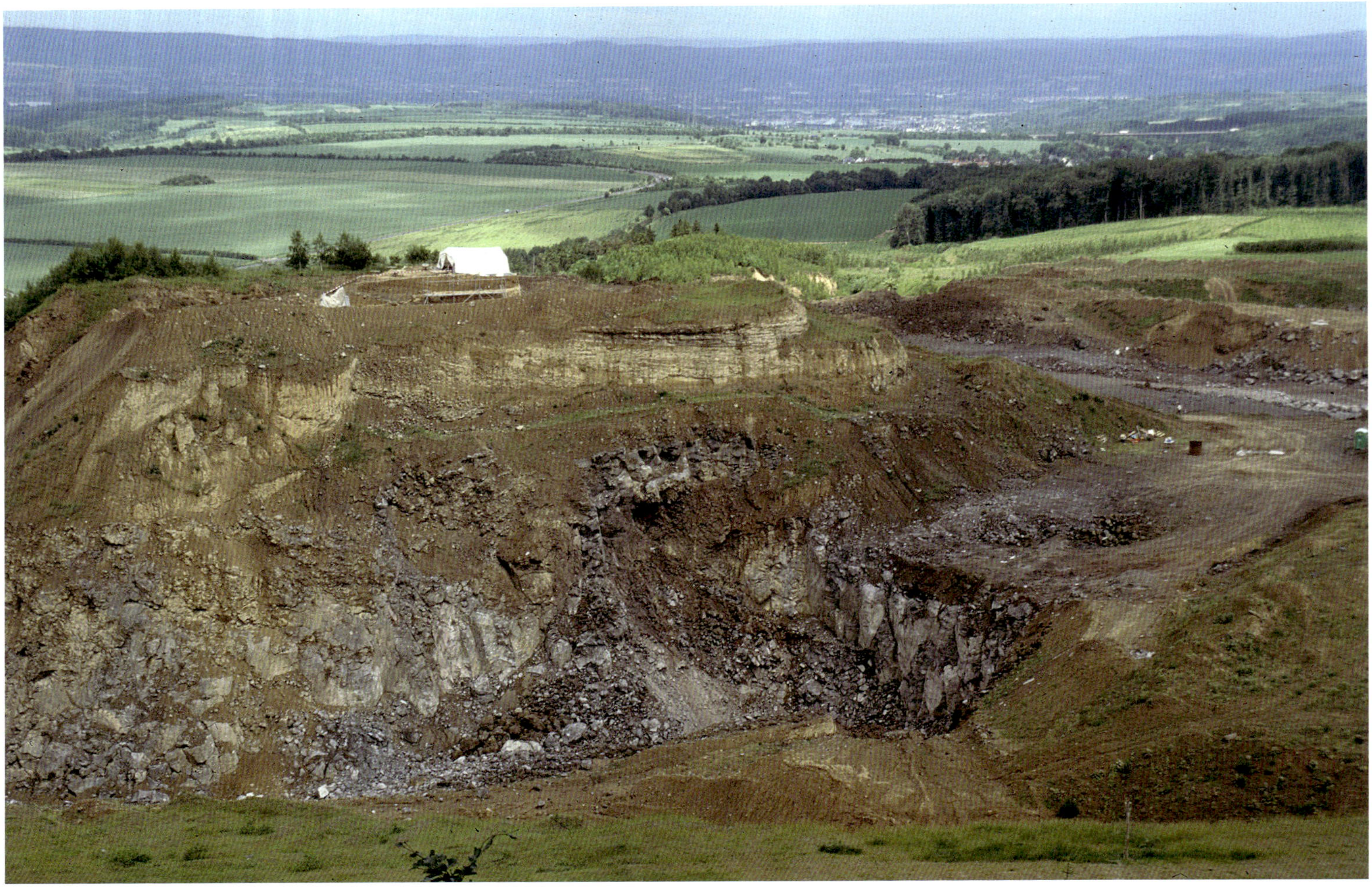

Fig. 7
Bassenheim, Mayen-Koblenz distr. Loess filling of the Schweinskopf scoria volcano during excavation works. The light filling with loess clearly contrasts with the dark lava of the volcano. (GDKE/Landesarchäologie/Koblenz/M. Neumann)

ler piece. A typical set of tools included scrapers with a retouched working edge and points that were used to equip wooden lances. Perfectly dressed flat hand axes continued in use. The Neanderthals developed progressive manufacturing techniques, which indicate a more differentiated and effective way of life at that time. The environment and the climate developed rather differently. The occasionally strong climate fluctuations of the Ice Age allow three cold periods and two warm periods to be identified for this time.

The physical build of the Neanderthal was very well adapted to the extreme conditions of a cold climate. The Neanderthal was of a much more robust physique and on average smaller than modern man. His strength and toughness made him a successful hunter of big game. Examinations of Neanderthal bones show that a major part of the nutritional requirements was obtained from animal proteins. The specialization of the Neanderthal in big game hunting is impressively demonstrated by his hunting spots: at least 52 wisents were killed on the banks of a river arm of the Wiesbach at the site of Wallertheim in Rhine-Hesse. Hunting big game was very dangerous, but it did provide high-quality and nutrient-rich food.

In Rhine-Hesse, the Palatinate, and at so-called flaking stations at the lower Nahe, stone workshops were examined which supplied a great number of artefacts. At such places, which were used time and again during the Middle Palaeolithic, large collections of stone artefacts were produced over time – mostly lithic cores and flakes as well as debris. Some core forms, especially the Levallois cores, which were prepared for only one targeted flake, are almost exclusively found at these flaking stations and are evidence of a targeted mass production of stone tools. These are mere work places: usable pieces were taken along and used at hunting stations. These work places are mostly found in spots where cleavable raw material was freely available on the surface.

The numerous cinder cones of the eastern Eifel with their deep crater funnels are of particular importance for scholarly research on the Palaeolithic. The crater fillings discovered and examined so far show similar sedimentation mechanisms, irrespective of their different datings. The loesses carried here by the wind during the cold periods slowly filled the original vent and offer the best clues for the dating of individual volcanic structures through the stratified soil horizons and the volcanic ejection layers of younger eruptions often found between them. Especially during the early filling stages, the hollows with temporary waterholes offered favourable dwellings for early inhabitants who according to the archaeological evidence visited the respective places repeatedly. Hunting stations in the hollows of the eastern Eifel volcanoes are known so far from the Schweinskopf near Bassenheim (180,000–65,000 BC) (Fig. 7), the Hummerich near Plaidt (130,000–70,000 BC), the Wannenköpfe near Ochtendung (170,000–70,000 BC), and the Tönchesberg near Kruft (115,000–70,000 BC). Since the sedimentations in such a hollow form (usually enclosed all around) occurred quite rapidly, the remains are normally well-preserved and allow conclusions to be drawn about the settling and hunting behaviour of the Neanderthals. Once the stratification of the sediments had ended, the fillings that developed there remained preserved in situ without any further shifting. The crater fillings of the eastern Eifel, which time and again are cut open in opencast mines, are extraordinary working places for both Quaternary geology and Palaeolithic studies and are unique research objects. After the volcanic eruption, the crater funnel, surrounded by steep crater walls, lay on top of the mountain. In time, due to the easy weathering of lava, the edges were eroded, and the crater funnel was levelled and sealed with pieces of lava and loess dust, which the wind had swept there in the dry climate of the cold periods. Thereafter, water collected on the bottom of the crater. The rest of the crater was then filled relatively fast. Lava slipped down from the crater walls and filled most of the lower areas of the hollow. However, it was above all loess that sedimented in the hollow forms. The structures of the loess, as well as the deposits of sediments of younger eruptions in the craters, can be particularly well stratified and dated. The hollow forms were sediment traps in which the deposits were extraordinarily well-preserved. Since the cinder cones of the eastern Eifel have different datings, the crater fillings usually reflect different periods. From the combination of the various fillings one can thus obtain a detailed outline of the last 600,000 years with changes in climate, environment, vegetation, and fauna. (cf. Fig. 1)

In the craters, numerous Palaeolithic resting and settlement places have been examined and documented. The hollows offered excellent conditions for settlements. Most of the finds are dated in the open steppe landscape of the penultimate cold period [oxygen isotope stadium (OIS 6)] and the last inter-glacial and early glacial (OIS 5). The high crater walls offered protection from the weather and the wide views from the edges of the crater were ideal for hunting. Since the sedimentation in the craters occurred relatively quickly, the respective finds are normally unusually well-preserved. The phase of favourable settlement conditions ended when the hollow was completely filled in.

The settlement places examined in the craters reflect the traces of occasional stays by man. Evidence of this is found in the form of both concentrations of hunting remains or stone artefacts and fireplaces or relics of former dwellings. In the hollow of the Schweinskopf near Bassenheim and also in the Wannenköpfe near Ochtendung, large stone circles of 2–3 m were documented, which can be conjectured as the former camp sites of simple dwellings. Remains of fireplaces around the camp sites were also observed. The hunting remains from around the camp sites give us an insight into behaviour patterns of the Palaeolithic. Besides organic remains, numerous stone implements are also preserved, affording unique insights into the use and processing of the raw stone material. Since the craters only hold volcanic rocks that are not suitable for toolmaking, all raw materials had to be transported into the craters. As a rule, local stone materials found in the respective terrace formations of the Rhine and Moselle were used for toolmaking. These are mainly varieties of quartz or quartzite of different quality. Non-local raw materials, such as flint, allow the reconstruction

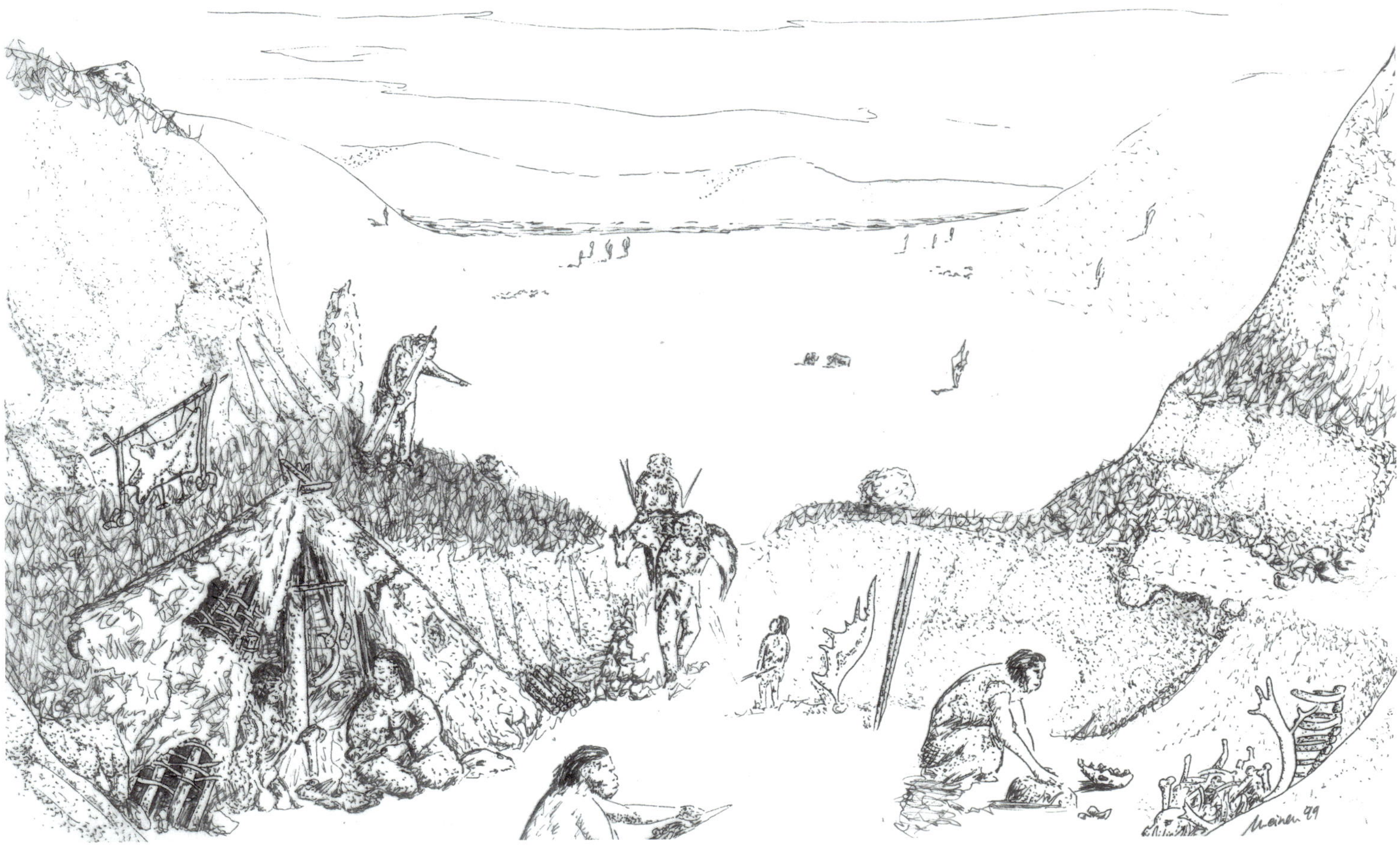

Fig. 8 Bassenheim, Mayen-Koblenz distr. Reconstructed camp site situation of the Schweinskopf scoria volcano. (GDKE/Landesarchäologie/Koblenz/M. Meinen)

of migration movements of these early humans. The migrations that presumably took place on a seasonal basis extended as far as the Meuse region, a radius of about 100 km, as repeatedly shown by a determination of the origins of the tools carried to the sites of this region. Most of the sites in the craters belong in the open steppe landscape of the cold periods. In this extreme biotope, the strategic position of the volcanic mountains for hunting purposes was an advantage. The high crater walls allowed seasonal herds of animals passing through each year to be spotted from far away. The settlement locations in the craters show mixed prey, with bones from different species, especially remains of rhinoceros (Coelodonta antiquitas), reindeer (Rangifer tarandus), horse (Equus sp.), red deer (Cervus elaphus), various types of cattle (Bos sp. or Bison sp.), and mammoth (Mammuthus primigenius). The type and condition of the hunting remains indicate that big game was mainly hunted beneath the volcanic cones in the open steppe landscapes (Fig. 8) The calvaria of an early Neanderthal was found in a crater of the Wannenköpfe near Ochtendung in the Mayen-Koblenz district.

Stratified Middle Palaeolithic finds are rarer in the higher areas of the middle-range mountains. In this context, the finds from the Buchenloch near Gerolstein or the multi-layer filling sediments of the Kartstein cave near Mechernich in the northern Eifel are important; they probably date from the early and middle sections of the last cold period. The most important finds come from the main cave of the Kartstein: a total of three Middle Palaeolithic layers containing remains of charcoal and fauna were documented under its collapsed eastern entrance. The late Middle Palaeolithic Kartstein III find complex, which together with part of the material from the Buchenloch leads on to the so-called »leaf-point industries« of the late Middle Palaeolithic, is the largest. Leaf-points are thin tools with pointed faces worked on both sides and used as knives or projectiles. The finds from the loess sequence at the Schwalbenberg near Remagen on the Rhine are also to be grouped with these leaf-point industries. These inventories from the end of the Neanderthal era show a new form of dealing with raw material, which finally seems to indicate a more intensive type of land use that will later characterize the behaviour of the anatomically modern man.

Bibliography

M. Baales, Archäologie des Eiszeitalters. Frühe Menschen an Mittelrhein und Mosel. Archäologie an Mittelrhein und Mosel Bd. 16 (Koblenz 2005).

A. von Berg, Älteres Paläolithikum aus dem Gebiet an Mosel und Mittelrhein. In: L. Fiedler (Hg.), Archäologie der ältesten Kultur in Deutschland. Ein Sammelwerk zum älteren Paläolithikum, der Zeit des Homo erectus und des frühen Neandertalers. Materialien zur Vor- und Frühgeschichte von Hessen 18, 1997, 227 ff.

A. von Berg, Ein Hominidenrest aus dem Wannenvulkan bei Ochtendung, Kreis Mayen-Koblenz. Archäologisches Korrespondenzblatt 27, 1997, 531 ff.

A. von Berg, S. Condemi, M. Frechen, Die Schädelkalotte des Neanderthalers von Ochtendung/Osteifel. Archäologie, Paläoanthropologie und Geologie, Eiszeitalter und Gegenwart 50, 2000, 56 ff.

A. von Berg, Frühe Menschen am Rhein. Altsteinzeit am Mittelrhein. Beiträge zur Rheinkunde 51, 1999, 1 ff.

A. von Berg, L. Fiedler, Altpaläolithische Funde von Winningen und Koblenz-Bisholder an der unteren Mosel. Archäologisches Korrespondenzblatt 13, 1983, 291 ff.

F. Bittmann, Vegetationsgeschichtliche Untersuchungen an mittel- und jungpleistozänen Ablagerungen des Neuwieder-Beckens (Mittelrhein). Jahrbuch des Römisch-Germanischen Zentralmuseums 38, 1991, 83 ff.

G. Bosinski, Urgeschichte am Rhein. Tübinger Monographien zur Urgeschichte (Tübingen 2008).

G. Bosinski, Die ersten Menschen in Eurasien. Jahrbuch des Römisch-Germanischen Zentralmuseums Mainz 39, 1995, 131 ff.

G. Bosinski, K. Kröger, J. Schäfer, E. Turner, Altsteinzeitliche Siedlungsplätze auf den Osteifel-Vulkanen. Jahrbuch des Römisch-Germanischen Zentralmuseums Mainz 33, 1985, 97 ff.

N. J. Conard, Tönchesberg and its Position in the Paleolithic Prehistory of Northern Europe. Monographien des Römisch-Germanischen Zentralmuseums Mainz 20 (Mainz 1992).

S. Gaudzinski, Wiesentjäger in Wallertheim. Zur Taphonomie einer mittelpaläolithischen Fundstelle in Rheinhessen. Jahrbuch des Römisch-Germanischen Zentralmuseums Mainz 39, 1995, 245 ff.

S. Gaudzinski, Kärlich-Seeufer. Untersuchungen zu einer altpaläolithischen Fundstelle im Neuwieder Becken (Rheinland, Deutschland). Jahrbuch des Römisch-Germanischen Zentralmuseums Mainz 43, 1998, 3 ff.

A. Justus, Der mittelpaläolithische Fundplatz »In den Wannen«. Jahrbuch des Römisch-Germanischen Zentralmuseums Mainz 47, 2002, 155 ff.

J. Kunow, H.-H. Wegner (Hg.), Urgeschichte im Rheinland. Jahrbuch des Rheinischen Vereins für Denkmalpflege und Landschaftsschutz 2005 (Köln 2006).

H. Löhr, Spuren des eiszeitlichen Menschen in der Eifel vor ihrem erdgeschichtlichen Hintergrund. In: H. Löhr, E. Lipinski, I. Koch, P. May (Hg.), Steinzeit im Gerolsteiner Raum (1990) 2 ff.

W. Meyer, Geologie der Eifel (Stuttgart 1994).

J. Schäfer, Der altsteinzeitliche Fundplatz auf dem Vulkan Schweinskopf-Karmelenberg. Diss. an der Univ. zu Köln (Köln 1990).

H.-U. Schmincke, Vulkanismus. Wissenschaftliche Buchgesellschaft (Darmstadt 2000).

M. Street, Plaidter Hummerich. An Early Weichselian Middle Palaeolithic Site in the Central Rhineland, Germany. Monographien des Römisch-Germanischen Zentralmuseums Mainz 45 (Mainz/Bonn 2002).

E. Turner, Miesenheim I. Excavations at a Lower Palaeolithic Site in the Central Rhineland of Germany. Monographien des Römisch-Germanischen Zentralmuseums Mainz 44 (Mainz/Bonn 2000).

The Ochtendung Neanderthal – The earliest human inhabitants of Rhineland-Palatinate

AXEL VON BERG

Fig. 1
Ochtendung, Mayen-Koblenz distr. Skull calotte of the early Neanderthal from the crater trough of the Wannenköpfe, outside. (GDKE/Landesarchäologie/Koblenz/W. Baumann, Höhr-Grenzhausen)

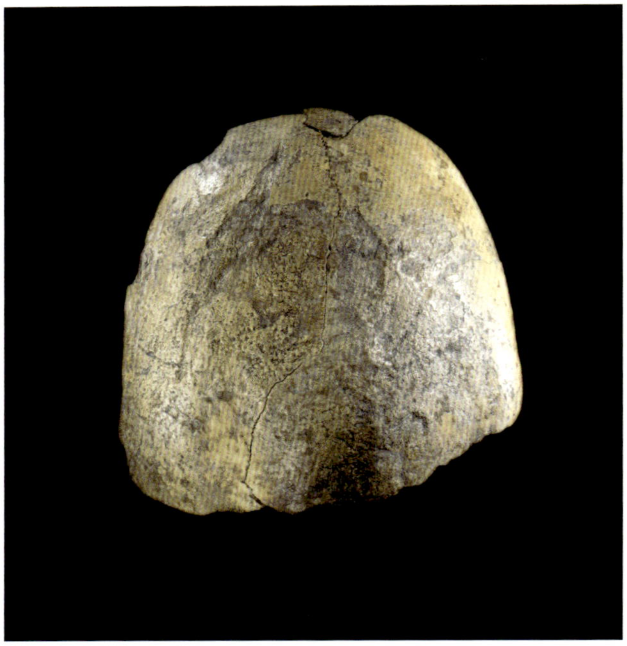

The Middle Pleistocene volcano group of the »Wannenköpfe« lies north of Ochtendung in the Mayen-Koblenz district. According to geological studies, the volcano group is to be dated at the beginning of the penultimate cold period some 200,000 years ago. Because of intensive lava extraction, many of these scoria cones have now disappeared except for a few remains. In spring 1997, a filling 30 m wide and 15 m deep in the northern pit section was cut into. The filling goes back mainly to the penultimate cold period. The fossilized human calvaria of an early Neanderthal (Fig. 1–2) comes from the middle layers of the hollow. Next to it were three stone artefacts, (Fig. 3) including a broad scraper made of silex, 6 cm wide and 4.5 cm long. (Fig. 3, top) This stone tool was made from grey-greenish Meuse flint and is typical for stone tools from the Middle Palaeolithic. The use of Meuse flint at the Wannenköpfe is evidence of the long-distance transport of raw materials as part of the migrations of hominids within a radius of 100 km between the Rhineland and the Meuse area. A small discoid core (5.0 cm × 4.0 cm) made of locally available grey-green fine grain Tertiary quartzite, with flakes systematically chipped off on one side (Fig. 3, centre), was also retrieved. The raw material came from the Pliocene crushed stones on top of the siliceous oolite terrace, of which large areas are exposed nearby. The finds inventory is completed by a flake of vein quartz (4.0 cm × 2.7 cm) with retouched edges on both sides. (Fig. 3, bottom) According to their morphology and typology, these artefacts belong in a typically Middle Palaeolithic finds context.

The most important find is the upper calvaria of a hominid preserved in three fitting fragments. (Fig. 1–2) At the edges, it shows clear traces of secondary reworking, which seem to indicate that the bone was used as an artefact. The preserved skull piece is 17.5 cm long

Fig. 2
Ochtendung, Mayen-Koblenz distr. Skull calotte of the early Neanderthal from the crater trough of the Wannenköpfe, inside. (GDKE/Landesarchäologie/Koblenz/W. Baumann, Höhr-Grenzhausen)

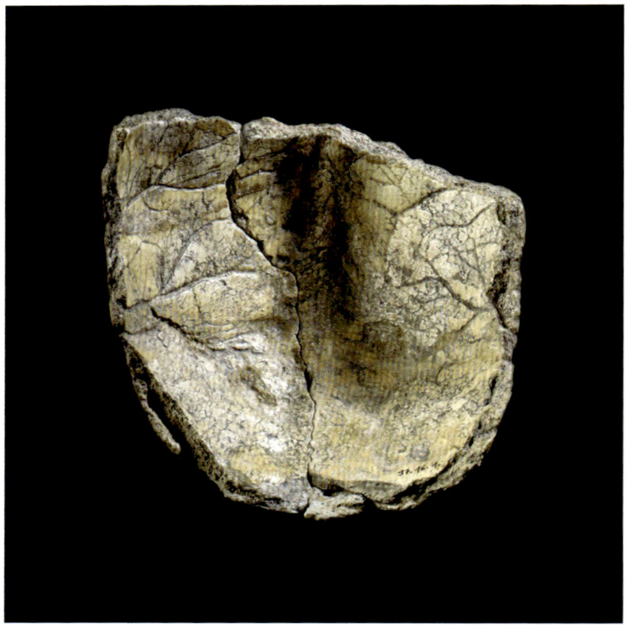

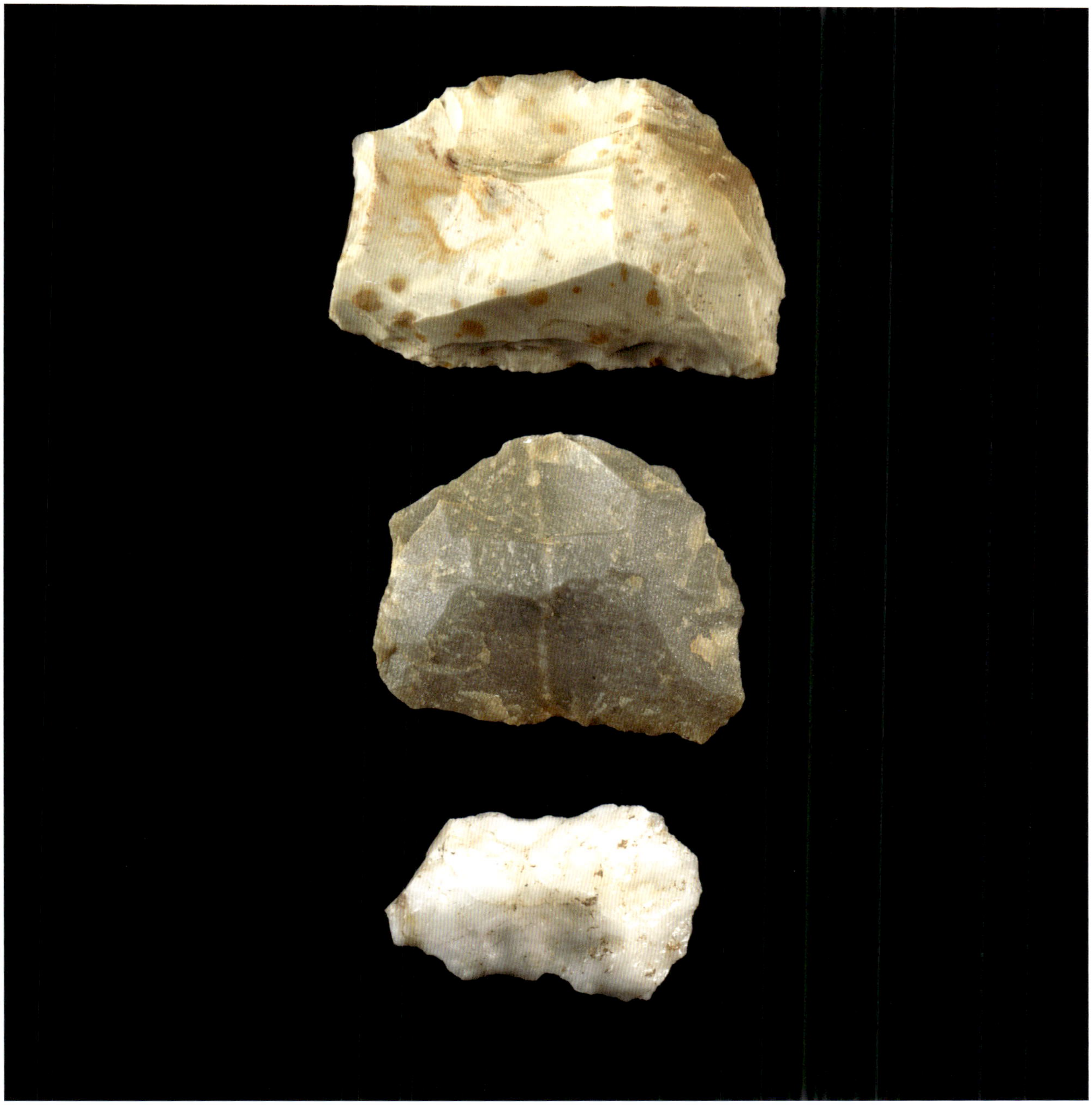

Fig. 3
Ochtendung, Mayen-Koblenz distr. Stone artefacts near the skull calotte from the crater trough of the Wannenköpfe. Top: Wide scraper made of Meuse flintstone; centre: discoid core of tertiary quartzite; bottom: flake of pebble quartz). (GDKE/Landesarchäologie/Koblenz/W. Baumann, Höhr-Grenzhausen)

and 14.5 cm wide and extraordinarily robust. What we have is the upper area of the skull with parts of the front skull cap (middle part of *Os frontale*) and of the lateral skull (*Os parietale*). The entire occiput (*Os occipitale*) and the facial skull *(Viscerocranium)* as well as the region over the eyes *(Torus occipitalis)* are missing. (Fig. 4) The cranial sutures are almost completely obliterated and the calvaria has an exceptional thickness of about 11.0 mm.

According to stratigraphy and scientific dating, the find can safely be assigned to the early phase of the penultimate cold period some 170,000 years ago. The find complex does not belong to a settlement horizon and is to be seen as an individually deposited find. On the basis of the geological findings, it appears that the oldest hominid remains from the Rhineland, so far, go back to the early glacial or the older section of the penultimate cold period (OIS 6).

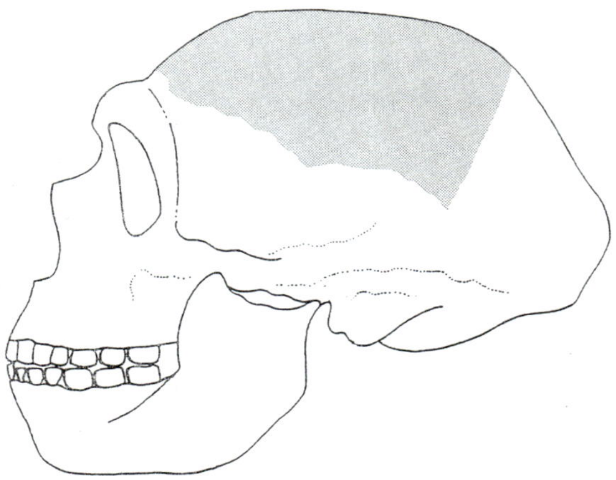

Fig. 4
Ochtendung, Mayen-Koblenz distr. Fitting of the skull calotte of the early Neanderthal into a reconstructed skull. (GDKE/Landesarchäologie/Koblenz)

Examinations of the calvaria gave indications that it was used as an artefact. This includes changes at the edges of the breaks and the outer skull area (Fig. 5), which can be observed in some parts. The bone edges show break spots and traces of blows, the edges are in part very much rounded and slurred. The surface and the rims of the calvaria show evident wear marks. According to the studies carried out so far, the finishings (especially in the front and parietal areas) were done on the already skeletonized bone. Traces of primary animal bites, particularly in the area of the skull cap, have become nearly unrecognizable by clearly visible secondary wear marks and the appearance of what can be understood as a form of polishing.

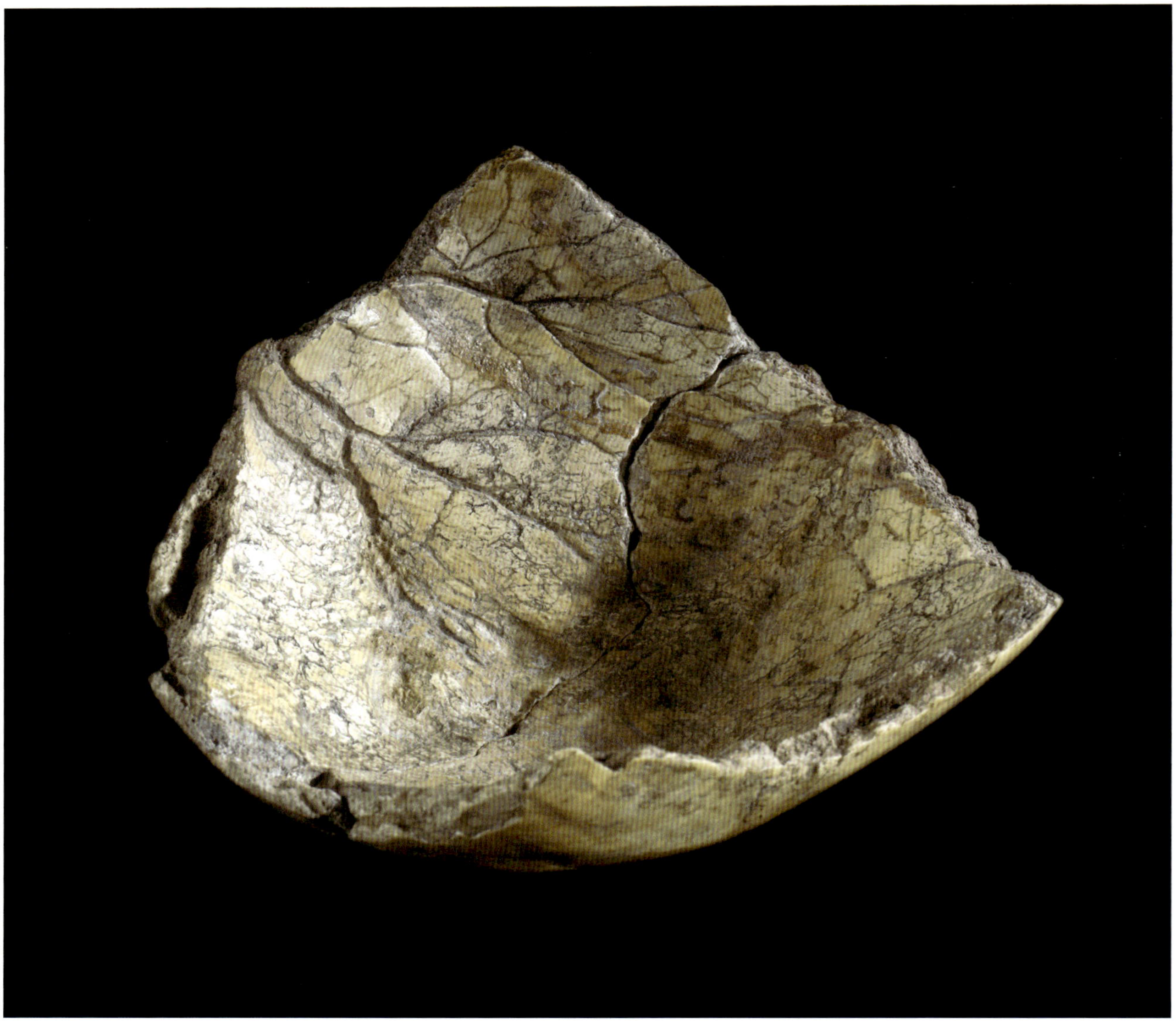

Fig. 5
Ochtendung, Mayen-Koblenz distr. Skull calotte of the early Neanderthal from the crater trough of the Wannenköpfe. Lateral view with secondarily altered bone edges. (GDKE/Landesarchäologie/Koblenz/W. Baumann, Höhr-Grenzhausen)

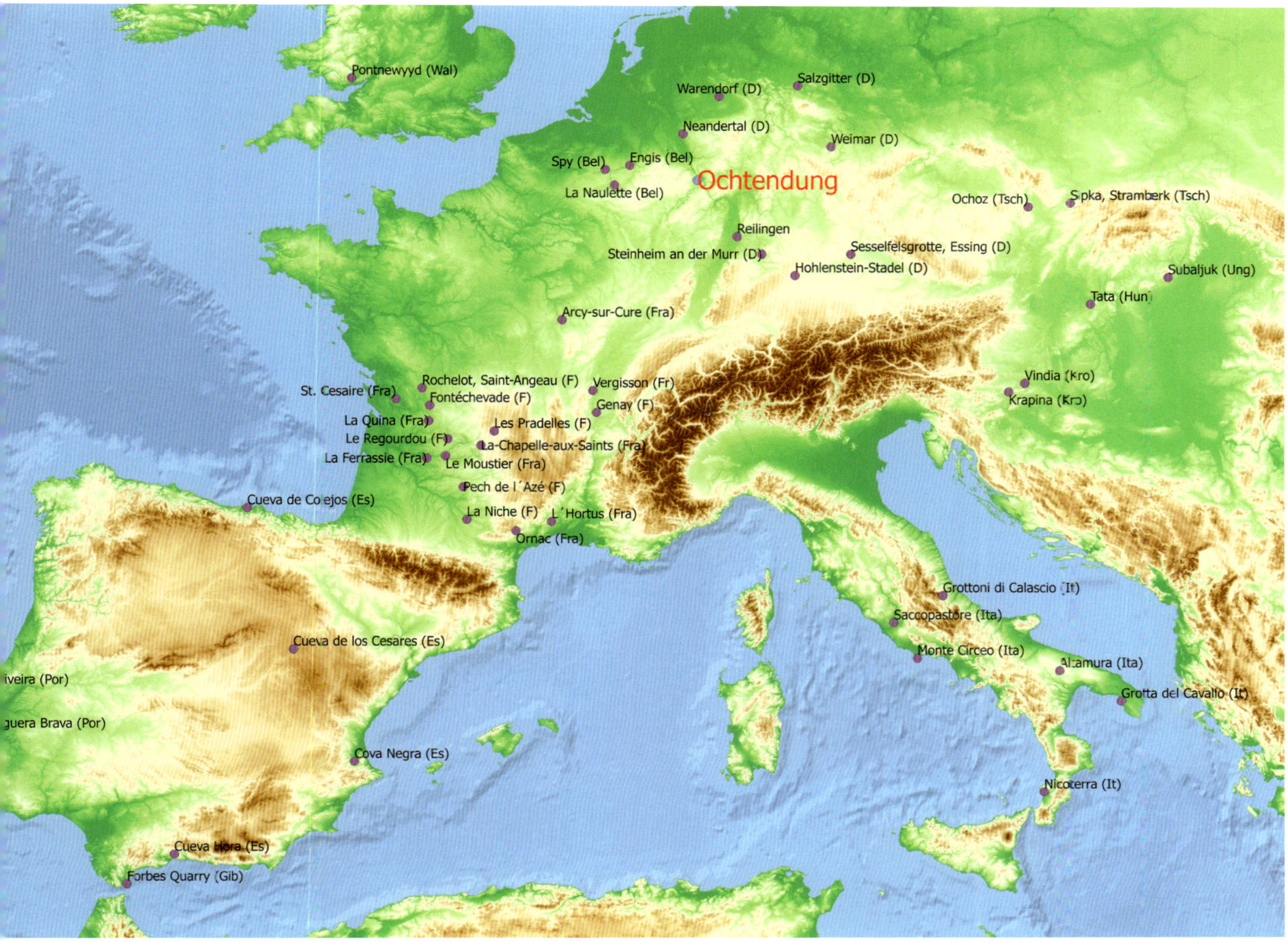

Fig. 6
Map of the most important Neanderthal finds in central Europe. (GDKE/ Landesarchäologie/ Koblenz/M. Schwab/ Map basis: SRTM-data (NASA) (ows.terrestis.de/osm/service)

The Ochtendung find goes back to an era from which only very few finds of human fossils are known so far. (Fig. 6) From a palaeo-anthropological viewpoint, the piece from the crater filling belongs to the early Neanderthals in Europe. The morphological characteristics of the skull thickness can be seen as evidence of the transition from the late *homo heidelbergensis* to the »classical« Neanderthal.

The entire complex can probably be interpreted as an isolated tool deposit outside the actual hunting camps. A burial can be excluded due to the find context.

Bibliography

A. von Berg, Die Schädelkalotte eines Neandertalers aus dem Wannenvulkan bei Ochtendung, Kr. Mayen-Koblenz. Ber. z. Archäologie an Mittelrhein und Mosel, Bd. 5, 1997, 11 ff.

A. von Berg, Ein Hominidenrest aus dem Wannenvulkan bei Ochtendung, Kr. Mayen-Koblenz. Arch. Korrbl. 27, 1997, 531 ff.

A. von Berg, S. Condemi, M. Frechen, Das Schädeldach eines Neandertalers aus der Kraterfüllung des Vulkans »Wannenköpfe«, Rheinland-Pfalz, Westdeutschland. Eiszeitalter und Gegenwart 50, 2000, 56 ff.

G. Bosinski, K. Kröger, J. Schäfer, E. Turner, Altsteinzeitliche Siedlungsplätze auf den Osteifel-Vulkanen. Jahrb. RGZM 33, 97 ff.

S. Condemi, Preliminary Study of the Calotte of the Ochtendung Cranium, Ber. z. Archäologie an Mittelrhein und Mosel, Bd. 5, 1997, 23 ff.

S. Flohr, A. von Berg, R. Protsch v. Zieten, Morphological Analysis of the Neanderthal Calotte from Ochtendung, Germany. Human Evolution 19 (1), 2004, 1–18.

M. Frechen, Eruptionsgeschichte und Deckschichtenfolge der Wannenköpfe-Vulkangruppe in der Osteifel. Eiszeitalter und Gegenwart 45, 1995, 109 f.

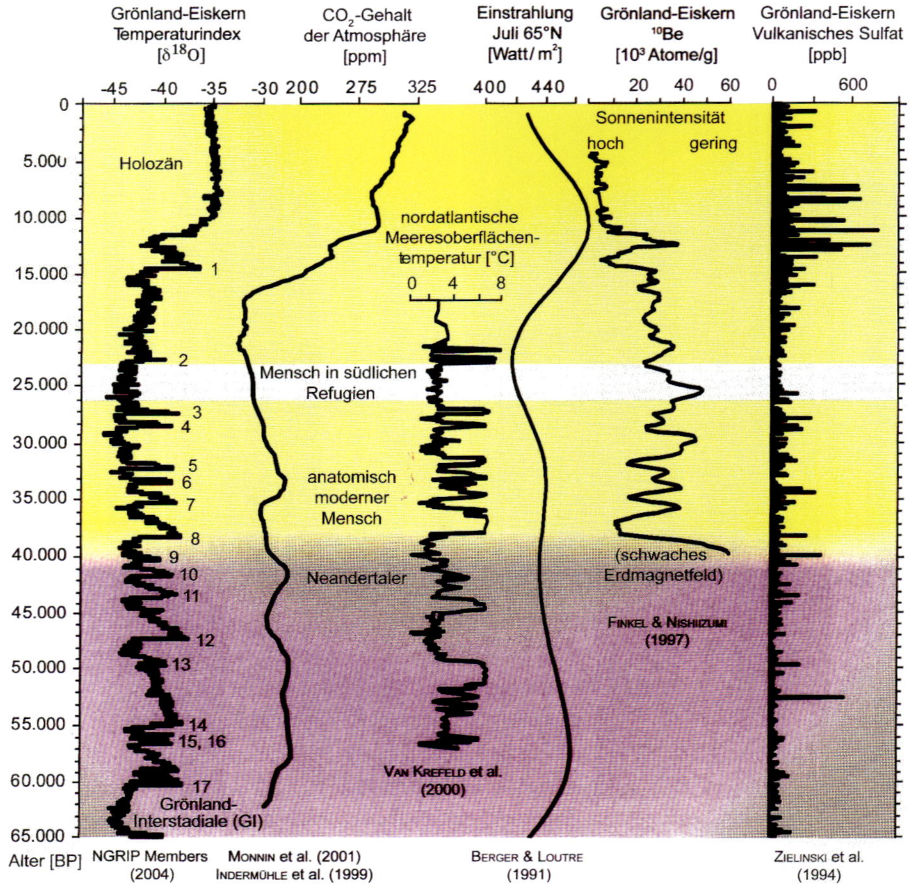

Fig. 1
Development of climate of the late middle Palaeolithic and the young Palaeolithic. (after F. Sirocko)

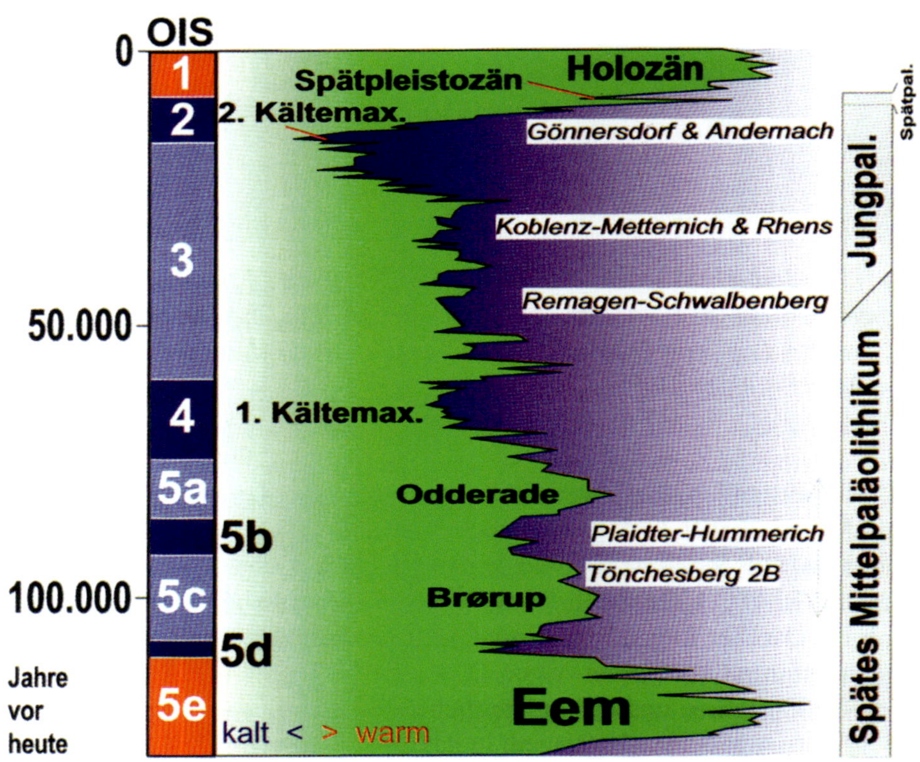

Fig. 2
Cold and warm phases in the middle and young Palaeolithic with important sites in northern Rhineland-Palatinate. (M. Baales and N. J. Sharkleton)

The era of the ice age hunters

AXEL VON BERG

The long phase of the Lower and Middle Palaeolithic was followed by the epoch of the Upper Palaeolithic; i.e., the younger Old Stone Age. The Upper Palaeolithic starts during the second section of the last cold period about 40,000 years ago, a time with a wet and mild climate. The development of the climate 60,000–25,000 years ago is characterized, also in Central Europe, by a quick change of cold phases and relatively short warm phases, (Fig. 1) which are referred to as GI (Greenland Interstadial), the cold phases as GS (Greenland Stadial). (Fig. 2) The often sudden changes between these two climate stages are usually associated with variations in the strength and scope of the Gulf Stream. Comparable developments in the intensity of the incident solar radiation and the CO_2 content of the atmosphere could also be observed. Lake sediments from the Eifel are now for the first time supplementing the few continental climate archives known so far. During that epoch of quickly changing environmental conditions, with vegetation changes from forested to non-forested areas, the anatomically modern man appeared for the first time in Europe. Finds from that early part of the Upper Palaeolithic are relatively rare so far, but finds from a resting place at the Schwalbenberg near Remagen in the Ahrweiler district grant us some insights into this time. The stone tools from the Schwalbenberg show the continuous typological transition from the Neanderthal to anatomically modern man. The hand axe and the purposely-made Levallois flake of the Middle Palaeolithic lose their importance: blades and blade implements now feature as standard tools. New and more effective technologies are employed by modern man, who slowly supersedes the Neanderthal. Typical stone tools of this time called »Aurignacian« are highly-perfected scraper forms, blades with retouched truncations, various burin shapes, and small retouched bladelets. Big projectile points made of bone, antlers, and ivory are also characteristic. Jewellery, such as pendants and pearls made of ivory or snail shells, complement the find inventory. Pictorial art is now also an important phenomenon: man depicts himself and his environment.

The Upper Palaeolithic brings about social changes and new developments, which are reflected especially in a completely changed culture. Most of today's scholars explain this marked revolution through the replacement of the Neanderthal by modern man. This process began about 43,000–42,000 years ago and was concluded around 30,000 BC. During the developed phase of the Aurignacian, all typical features of this new time are in place, including art, jewellery, music, and probably also religious ideas. In northern Rhineland-Palatinate, some typical stone implements and bone projectile points from the Buchenloch near Gerolstein can be assigned to the Aurignacian. Very similar finds come from the caves of the Lahn valley. A larger series of stone artefacts from the Aurignacian is known from the Trier area and the northern Eifel.

The middle Upper Palaeolithic – The cold arrives

In the early cultural history of Central Europe, the period of the Aurignacian ends at about 30,000 BC (GI 5), a time marker which in Central Europe corresponds to the last extensive tree coverage of the landscape. Between 30,500 and 26,000 BC it was cold in Central Europe, and after 25,000 BC a tundra landscape developed with poor vegetation and frequent loess accumulation. (cf. Fig. 2) Undoubtedly, this transformation of the landscape was accompanied by changes in the geographic range of the fauna – including game – and thus also of man. The »Gravettian«, as a new cultural stage in the Upper Palaeolithic, develops at that time with further innovations in tools technology as well as hunting and settlement behaviour.

The pollen profiles from the Eifel maars, crater lakes, show that during the last warm period (GI 3, 25,000 BC) there was yet another major increase in pine forests, which presumably spread over a grass steppe interspersed with birch trees. In this landscape, herds of horses and reindeer existed for the last time, with mammoth and polar fox dominating the subsequent tundra. This deterioration of the climate and transformation of the vegetation was accompanied by the world-wide advance of ice age inland glaciers, which at that time had already reached the Baltic Sea depression from Scandinavia. During this time, the frequency of loess storms increased continuously and around 24,000 BC reached a level which then remained rather constant till 18,000 BC. Compared with preceding times, the stone artefacts in the middle Upper Palaeolithic are characterized by a new method of producing regular blades and narrow bladelets, which shows only very slight differences between regions. Knives blunted at the back, so-called backed bladelets, appear as a new type of tool. The typical knife blades were insets as the points of weapons and other tools and the handles were made of wood and bone. The individual blades were fixed in a row one after the other with the back to the inside of a notch to serve as effective cutting tools and weapons. Projectile points with a bevelled basis on one or both sides were also a new development. They were used to tip thin wooden spears launched with a spear thrower. This tool was the most effective innovation in hunting technology in the developed Upper Palaeolithic: a staff with a barbed hook, in front of which the thin spear was placed. Through the lever arm of the sling, the spear acquired greater speed and penetrating power and became the most important weapon of subsequent times. The wide distribution of the spear sling may be an indication that this hunting technique was adapted to an open steppe-like landscape and to bigger game roaming the steppe in large herds.

The cold phases, with their extensive grasslands and at times enormous, but seasonally fluctuating availability of game, became longer and longer and forced man to lead a very mobile life. This mobility, however, allowed the establishment of far-reaching social networks, through which exchange relationships were cultivated over distances of many hundreds of kilometres. Evidence for this is provided on the one hand by items exchanged over long distances, such as decorative snails from the Mediterranean area, some examples of which were found in Mainz-Linsenberg or Sprendlingen in Rhine-Hesse. On the other hand, these contacts are manifest in a uniform style of plastically shaped »Venus« statuettes, whose best-known example is the famous »Venus of Willendorf«. Statuettes of this kind are found as far as Lake Baikal, but fragments were also found at the Linsenberg in Mainz. They were made from sandstone and are among the oldest works of art from the region. Stratigraphic data place the finds from the Linsenberg in Mainz at the beginning of a loess accumulation phase. Loess deposits and the Ca-increase caused thereby (at around 25,000 BC) are in fact the dominating signal in climate development, evidencing the start of dust storms and a reduction in the vegetation density with increasing cold and drought. Changes in the prey spectrum, i.e. increased hunting of big migrating mammals in herds, could have led to long migrations of humans and the spreading of uniform cultures. The settlement places, which are now inhabited for longer times, are often situated on a terrace above a river or stretch of water. The settlement was protected on the weather side by the mountain slope. A wide view of the surroundings allowed the targeted hunting of big game.

Settlement sites of that time were also examined near Koblenz-Mettemich and Brey on the Middle Rhine. Due to the extreme climatic conditions, regionally independent traditions developed after 25,000 BC in the regions better suited for settlements, which were usually separated from each other, as shown by their different forms and spectrums of implements.

There is only sparse evidence for a presence of man during the following high ice age, lasting throughout the millennia from 24,000 to 12,500 BC. It seems that from 24,000 BC on, large tracts of Central Europe were uninhabitable because of the extreme climatic conditions preceding the advancing glaciers. While most of Rhineland-Palatinate remained ice-free, small glaciers did develop in the higher areas of the medium-range mountains. Man retired to the south and held out the winter during the last glacial maximum in southern Europe, especially in the south of France, Spain, and Italy.

The glacial maximum of the last cold period

From about 22,000 to 14,000 BC, the last cold period reached its peak. Summer insolation on the northern hemisphere had reached its lowest point, and the big inland ice masses in Eurasia and North America had advanced far southwards. In northern Central Europe, the Fennoscandian ice shield, with a thickness of up to 2500 m at its centre, reached the area around Berlin; in the south, the Alpine glaciers stretched as a closed ice cover far into the area of the alpine foothills. Since immense amounts of water had turned to ice, the sea level was about 140 m below that of today. As a consequence, continental coastal areas, such as the southern North Sea, fell dry, so that the British Isles were joined to the continent and the North Sea coast was about 600 km more to the north than today, between Scotland and south Norway. The influence of rather stable continental high-pressure cells over the Eurasian continent led to a markedly dry-cold climate. During the winter half-year, precipitations reached Central Europe only rarely via south-western winds. The annual average temperature in our region was about –8 °C (the warmest summer month was 8 °C and the coldest winter month below –20 °C). Like in the arctic of today, one has to reckon for that time with permanently frozen soils (permafrost) for large areas of Central Europe. The vegetation period was restricted to only a few weeks, so there was a sparse, non-blanket plant cover. Most of the species of plants and animals were constrained at that time to refuges in south-west and south-east Europe.

While most scholars have so far shared the opinion that Central Europe remained unsuitable for settlement for some millennia after the last glacial maximum, a series of ^{14}C data from the open-air station at Wiesbaden-Igstadt in neighbouring Southern Hesse proves the presence of man at around 20,500 BC. During the following period, from 19,000 to 14,000 BC, we again see a lack of settlement sites in wide areas of Europe. During that time, intensive frost weathering and subsequent wind transport produced mighty loess deposits even in our region. (Fig. 3)

In the varve deposits of the Holzmaar near Manderscheid in the western Eifel, which go back to the end of the glacial maximum, various phases of differing loess accumulation intensity – due to strong loess storms – could be detected, starting at about 16,000 BC. In various profiles, the yellowish loess deposits of that time show one or more narrow stripes of volcanic ashes, which are referred to as »Eltville tuff« Because of their distribution, the Korretsberg near Kruft in the Mayen-Koblenz district in the Eastern Eifel was considered by some to be the eruption centre of the ash layer. The stratigraphic position of Eltville tuff in the sequence of sediments indicates that it was deposited very soon after a short warmth variation following the glacial maximum, which could correspond to GI 2. The climatic phase following the deposit of Eltville tuff is also characterized by a cold, though now markedly wetter, climate. Individual ^{14}C data from south German sites indicate settlement by man, albeit only sporadic, since that time.

The late Upper Palaeolithic – Resettlement of the territory begins

During the extreme cold phase from 18,000 to 15,000 BC, Central Europe was a permafrost landscape with hardly any vegetation, which offered very little food to many species of large mammals. Small animals were the only living creatures in the cold of the ice-age. Evidence of

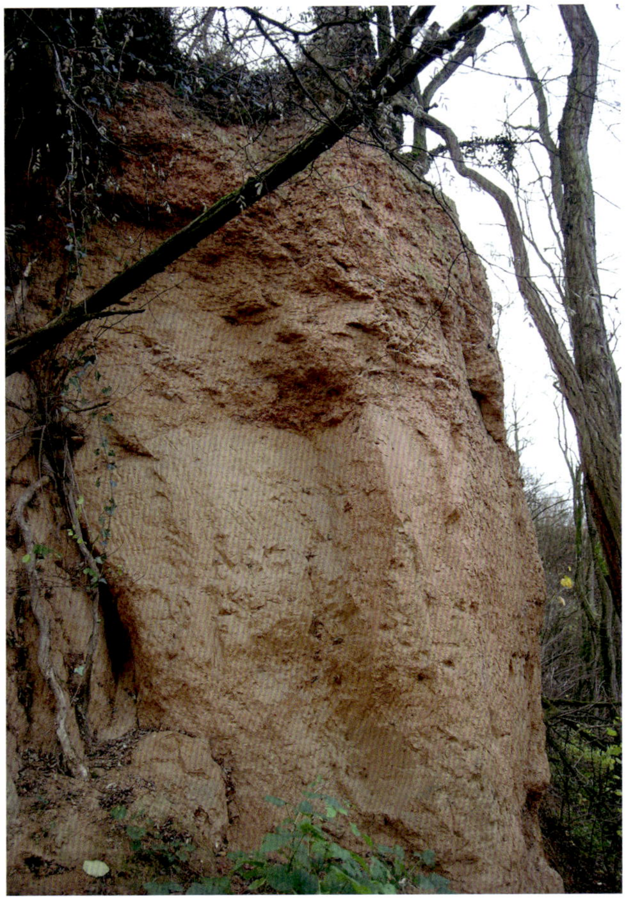

Fig. 3
Koblenz-Karthause, city of Koblenz. Cross-section of wind-blown loess deposits of the last cold period. (GDKE/ Landesarchäologie/ Koblenz/ A. von Berg)

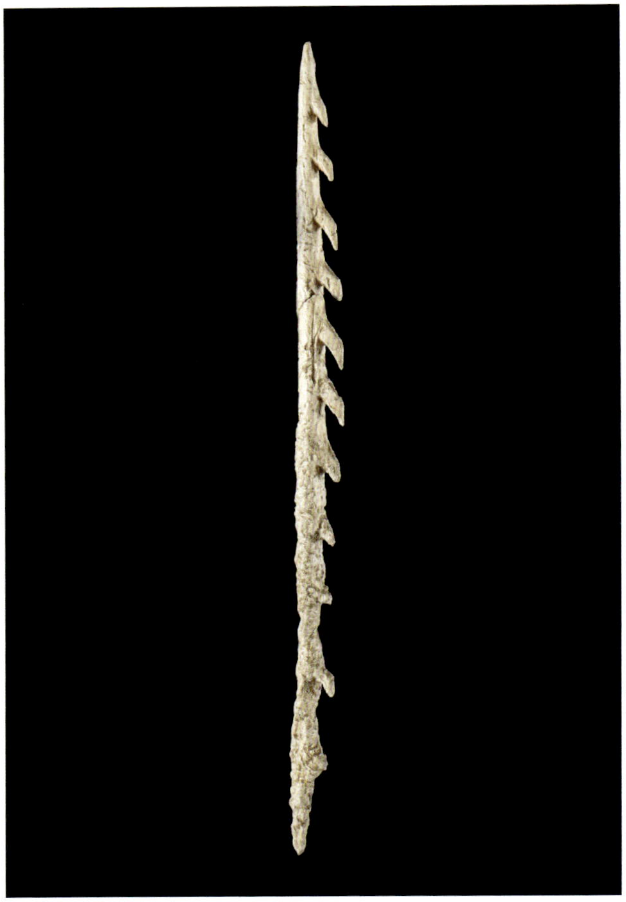

Fig. 4
Andernach, Mayen-Koblenz distr. Bone harpoon of the Magdalénien from the hunting station at the Martinsberg. (GDKE/Landesarchäologie/ Koblenz/W. Baumann, Höhr-Grenzhausen)

the presence of the mammoth in our region can again be found from around 15,000 BC. In the south, a first notable temperature rise starts around that time, and somewhat later the north is also slowly becoming warmer. Around 14,000–12,700 BC, the humans of the »Magdalenian« follow their game from its south-west European refuges up to Rhineland-Palatinate. At that time, large parts of Central Europe were open grass landscapes with low-growing species of trees and bushes where animal herds roamed. The most important sites of the Magdalenian are the hunting stations of Neuwied-Gönnersdorf and Andernach-Martinsberg in the Neuwied basin in northern Rhineland-Palatinate, with very complex settling and housing structures. The sites of Neuwied-Gönnersdorf and Andernach-Martinsberg allow us unique insights into the culture, way of life, and hunting habits of the late ice age communities. The camps were built on slopes half-way above the Rhine within view of each other. The hunting stations are from the time around 13,500 BC. Therefore, the late ice age expansion of man to the north already starts before the actual late glacial warming of the GI 1 interstadial. The pumice tuff of the Lake Laach volcano later preserved the sites and maintained them almost undisturbed until today. The extraordinary rich finds of both stations show that people frequented these convenient places time and again and probably also for longer periods.

The life of these late ice age hunting communities was governed by the open steppe landscape, rich in game, in addition to the changing seasons characterized by extreme variations in temperature. The average annual temperature at that time was far below –1 °C. For this period, one must assume a seasonally frozen ground, which would only start to thaw during the few weeks of summer. Among the bone remains, the researchers found indications that the groups of hunters stayed in the region both in summer and in winter. The origin of the raw materials for the production of stone implements shows that the late ice age hunters did not

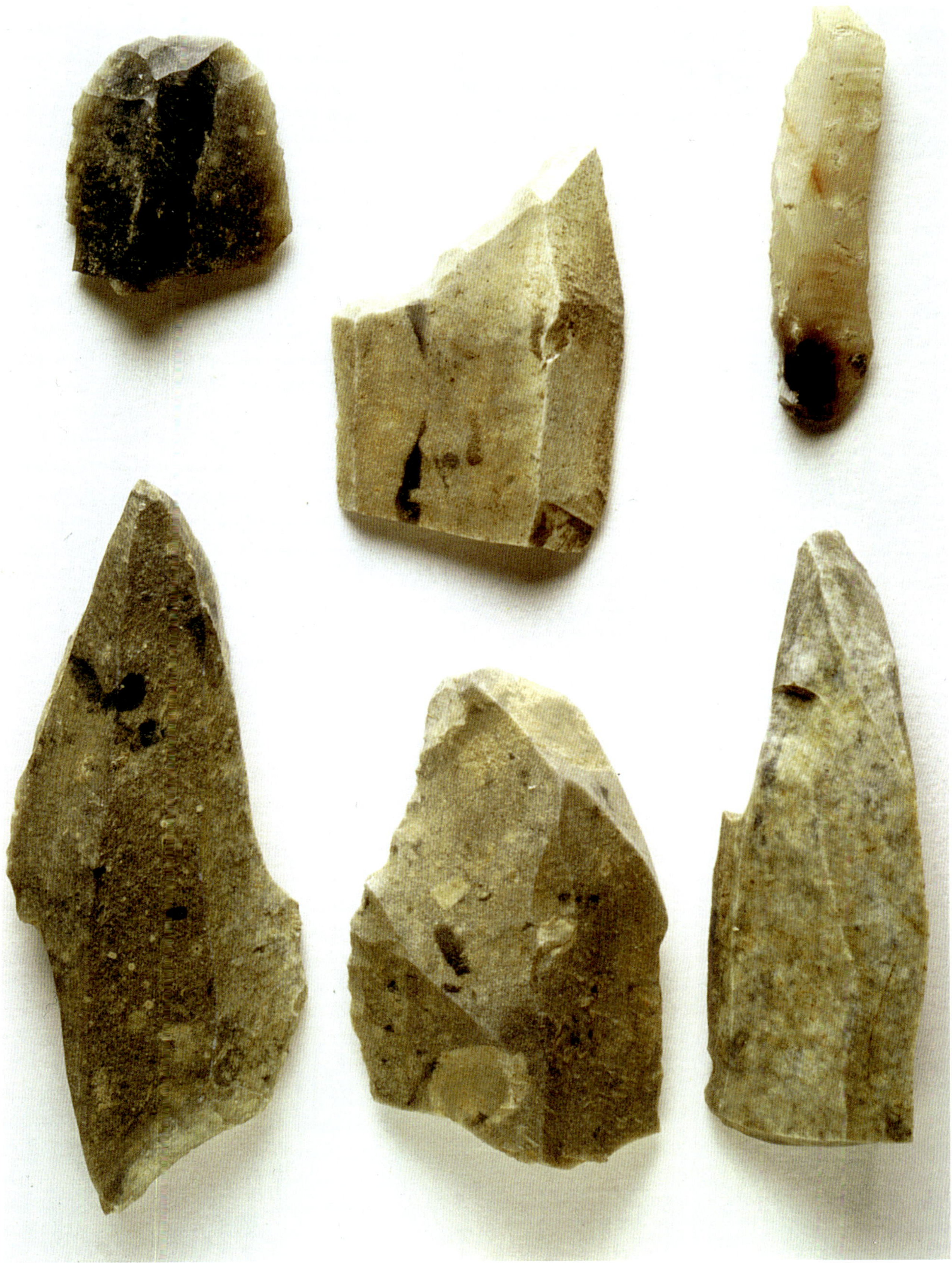

Fig. 5
Andernach, Mayen-Koblenz distr. Blade tools (burin, scraper, back knife) of the young Palaeolithic made of silex. (GDKE/Landesarchäologie/Koblenz/M. Neumann)

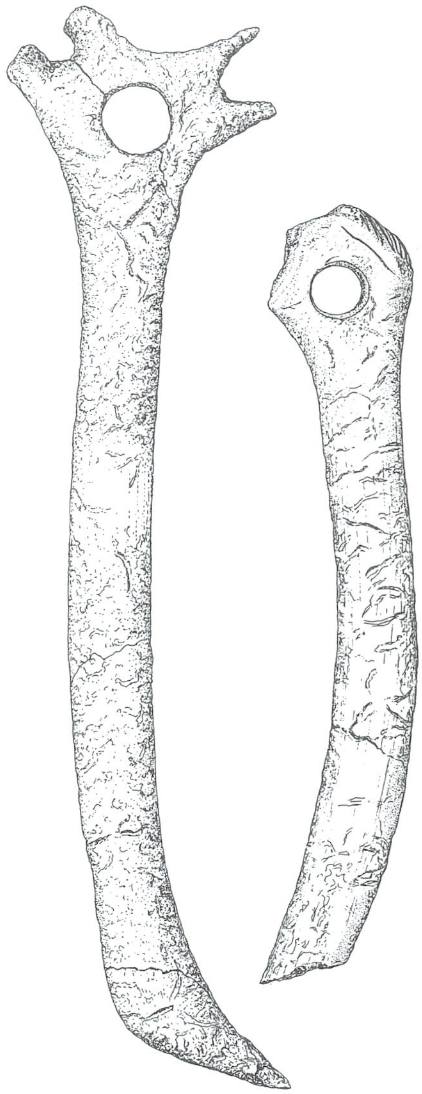

Fig. 6
Andernach, Mayen-Koblenz distr. Perforated batons. (after G. Bosinski)

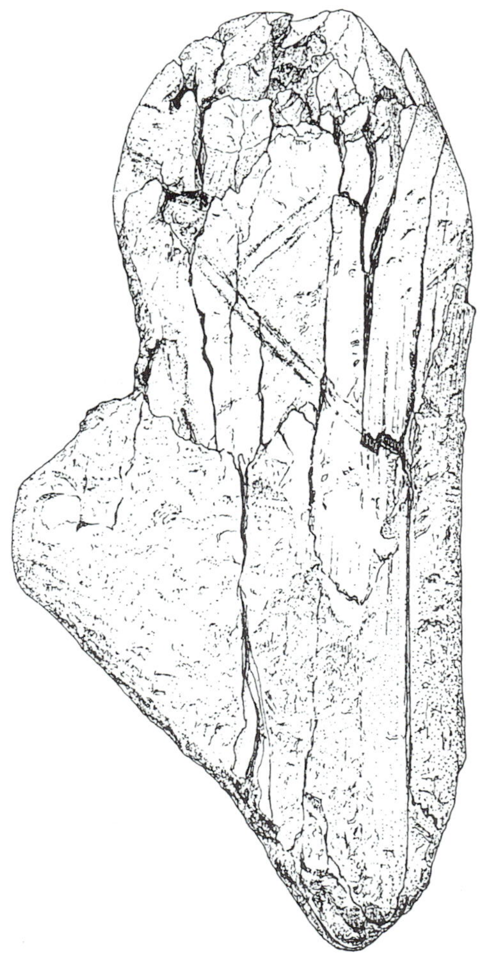

Fig. 7
Andernach, Mayen-Koblenz distr. Female figure of the young Palaeolithic made of mammoth ivory. (after G. Bosinski)

only dwell in the Middle Rhine area, but also roamed other regions, such as the Meuse region with its flint deposits. The most important hunting weapon in the Magdalenian was still the spear sling. The projectile points developed into thin harpoons with rows of barbs whose cone-like base was no longer permanently fixed to the shaft of the spear, so that the harpoon would come loose from the shaft after a hit. (Fig. 4) Horse and reindeer were the most important prey. Backed bladelets, burins, scrapers, drills, and splintered stone pieces were still the typical stone tools. (Fig. 5) So-called *bâtons percés* (perforated batons) as a new implement were probably used for straightening splints and shafts. (Fig. 6) New objects also include tallow lamp bowls and many appliances made of bone and ivory. The use of ground haematite as a colour powder has been proven as well, and all sorts of jewellery made from animal teeth strung into a chain as well as beads and pendants have been recorded.

Both sites became known primarily on account of figural engravings of men and animals on slate plates, as well as stylized ivory statuettes that are uniformly distributed as Venus figurines all over Europe at that time. (Fig. 7)

Bibliography

V. App, B. Auffermann, C. Hahn, C. Pasda, E. Stephan, Die altsteinzeitliche Fundstelle auf dem Schwalbenberg bei Remagen. Berichte zur Archäologie an Mittelrhein und Mosel 4 (Koblenz 1995) 11 f.

M. Baales, Archäologie des Eiszeitalters. Frühe Menschen an Mittelrhein und Mosel. Archäologie an Mittelrhein und Mosel 16 (Koblenz 2005).

G. Bosinski, Urgeschichte am Rhein. Tübinger Monographien zur Urgeschichte (Tübingen 2008).

G. Bosinski, Die große Zeit der Eiszeitjäger. Europa zwischen 40.000 und 10.000 v. Chr. (5. Mommsen-Vorlesung). Jahrbuch des Römisch-Germanischen Zentralmuseums Mainz 34, 1987, 3 ff.

G. Bosinski, Eiszeitjäger im Neuwieder Becken. Archäologie an Mittelrhein und Mosel 1 (Koblenz 1992).

G. Bosinski, Gönnersdorf und Andernach-Martinsberg. Späteiszeitliche Siedlungsplätze am Mittelrhein. Archäologie an Mittelrhein und Mosel 19 (Koblenz 2007).

H. Floss, Rohmaterialversorgung im Paläolithikum des Mittelrheingebietes. Monographien des Römisch-Germanischen Zentralmuseums 21 (Mainz 1994).

J. Hahn, Aurignacien. Das ältere Jungpaläolithikum in Mittel- und Osteuropa. Fundamenta A/9.

J. Kunow, H.- H. Wegner (Hg.), Urgeschichte im Rheinland. Jahrbuch des Rheinischen Vereins für Denkmalpflege und Landschaftsschutz 2005 (Köln 2006).

F. Sirocko (Hg.), Wetter, Klima, Menschheitsentwicklung. Von der Eiszeit bis in das 21. Jahrhundert (Stuttgart 2009) 129 ff.

W. Schirmer, Rheingeschichte zwischen Mosel und Maas. Deuqua Führer 1 (Hannover 1990).

M. Street, M. Baales, O. Jöris, Beiträge zur Chronologie archäologischer Fundstellen des letzten Glazials im nördlichen Rheinland. in: R. Becker-Haumann, M. Frechen (Hg.), Terrestrische Quartärgeologie (Boenigk-Festschrift) (Köln 1999) 426 f.

T. Terberger, Siedlungsspuren zwischen 20.000 und 16.000 B.P. am Mittelrhein? Vorbericht zu den Ausgrabungen an der jungpaläolithischen Freilandstation Wiesbaden-Igstadt, Hessen. Germania 76, 1998, 403 ff.

The hunting station of Neuwied-Gönnersdorf

AXEL VON BERG

The most significant Magdalenian site of the late Upper Palaeolithic is the hunting station of

Neuwied-Gönnersdorf at the eastern edge of the Neuwied basin in northern Rhineland-Palatinate, with its highly complex settlement structure. During the excavations of 1968–1974, round concentrations with stone material 7–9 m in diameter were uncovered; beneath them were small pits, which are to be interpreted as post holes of simple dwellings. They consisted of a basic structure of wood with vertical walls and a conical roof, which was supported by a strong central post. (Fig. 1) The entrance to the hut was usually in the south-east and the supporting structure was probably covered with animal skins. Up to ten or twelve people could be accommodated in any such hut, and there were fireplaces and cooking pits inside. The hunting station of Neuwied-Gönnersdorf gives unique insights into the culture, way of life, and hunting behaviour of late ice age communities 15,000 years ago. (Fig. 2) The camps were built halfway above the Rhine in so-called anticlinal positions within view of each other. The site of Neuwied-Gön-

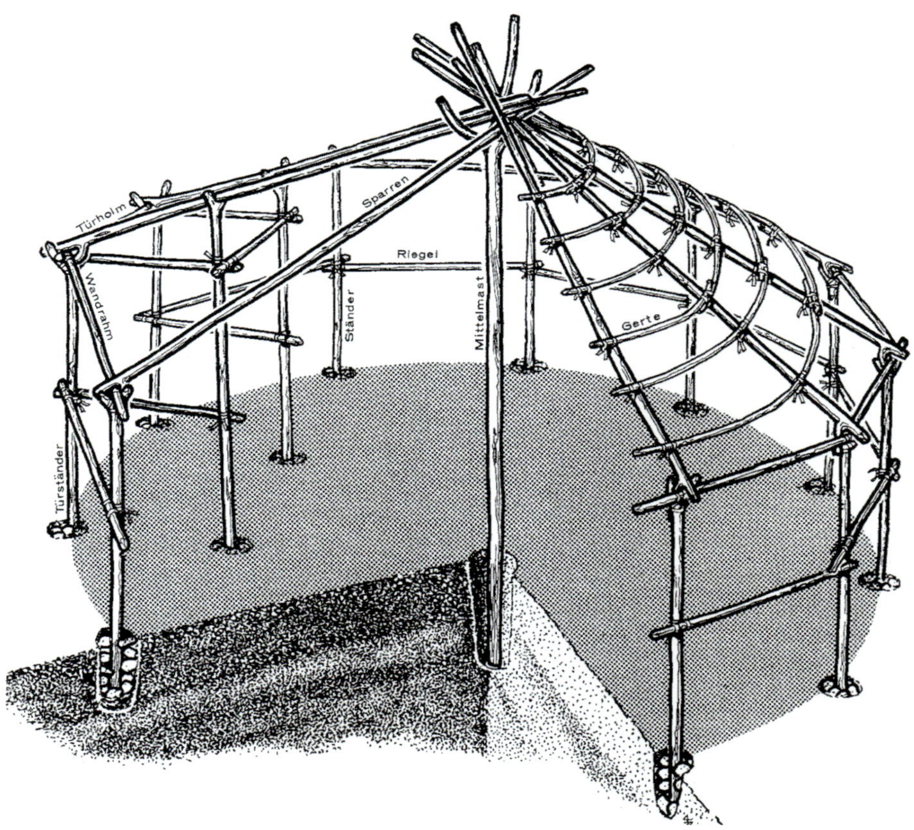

Fig. 1
Gönnersdorf, city of Neuwied. Reconstruction of a round hut of the hunting station according to the excavation findings. (after G. Bosinski)

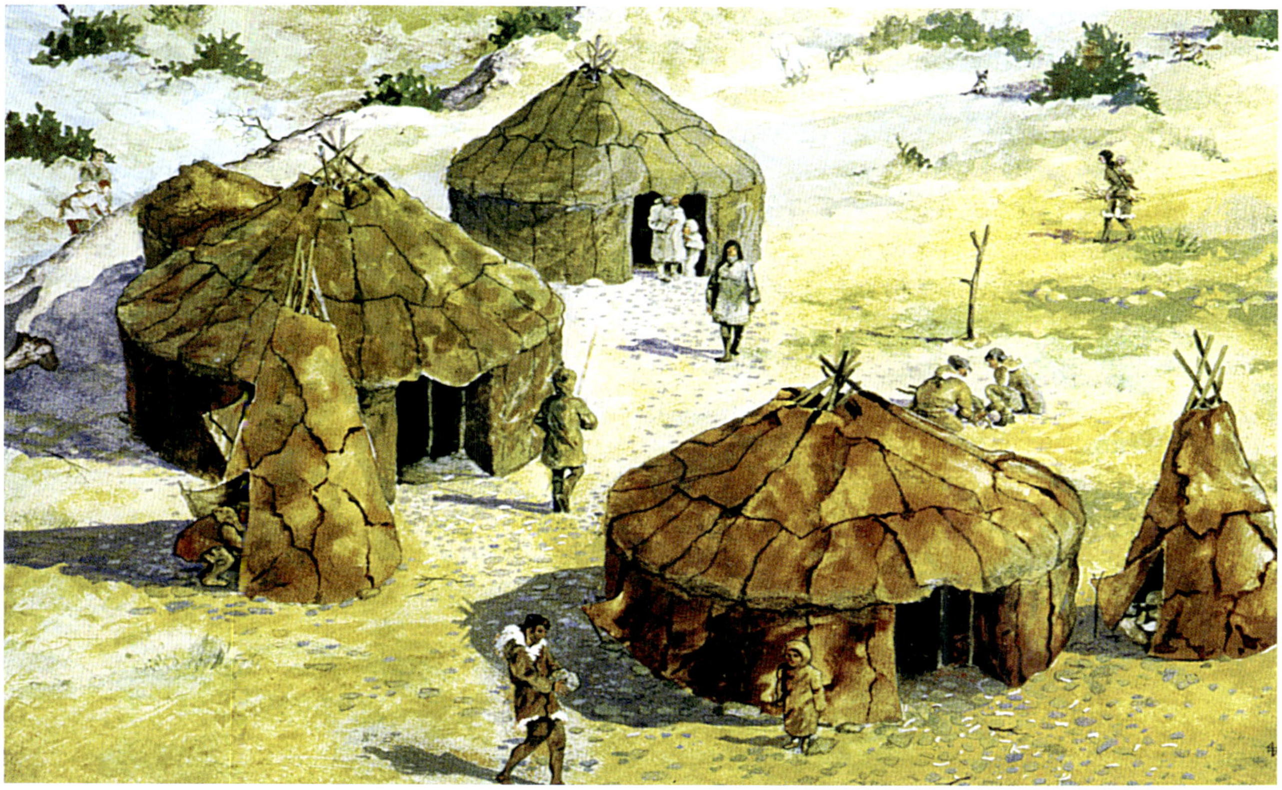

Fig. 2
Gönnersdorf, city of Neuwied. Reconstruction of the hunting station with different dwellings in the Ice Age tundra according to the excavation findings. (after G. Bosinski and D. Evers)

nersdorf can be dated to 3,500 BC approx. Therefore, the late ice age expansion of man to the north had already started before the actual late-glacial warming of the GI 1interstadial. Man followed the roaming animal herds to the north and gradually settled in the cold-period steppe. The pumice of the Lake Laach volcano later preserved the site until today, and the richness of finds shows that people frequented this convenient spot time and again and probably also for longer periods.

The life of these late ice age hunting communities was determined by the open landscape of the steppe, rich in game, as well as by the changing seasons characterized by extreme variations in temperature. The average annual temperature at that time was far below –1 °C. Seasonally, one must assume for this period a deep-frozen ground which would only start to thaw during the few weeks of summer. The slate plates of different sizes covering the floor of the individual dwellings, which were repeatedly found during excavations, could have served to stabilize the thawed ground during the summer months and as part of an insulation from the ground below in winter. The bone remains show that the groups of hunters stayed in Gönnersdorf both in winter and in summer. Typical stone tools are backed bladelets, burins, scrapers, drills, and splintered pieces used as chisels. (Fig. 3) Other objects include tallow lamp bowls made of slate, perforated rondelles, and many implements made of bone and ivory, such as sewing needles and points. All kinds of jewellery made from animal teeth threaded into chains as well as beads and pendants were recorded. A striking item are small decorative snails, which originated from the Mediterranean area and must have got as far as the Rhine through barter.

The hunting station of Neuwied-Gönnersdorf became known above all for the numerous figural engravings of men and animals on slate plates. Representations of strongly schematized female bodies in profile were often engraved in groups or pairs and interpreted as dance scenes. (Fig. 4–5) The best-known and truly unique slate engraving shows a group of dressed women in a row, probably a dance scene. One woman in the centre of the picture has a carrier on her back with a child in it. (Fig. 6) Unlike the representations of humans, the animals engraved on the slate plates

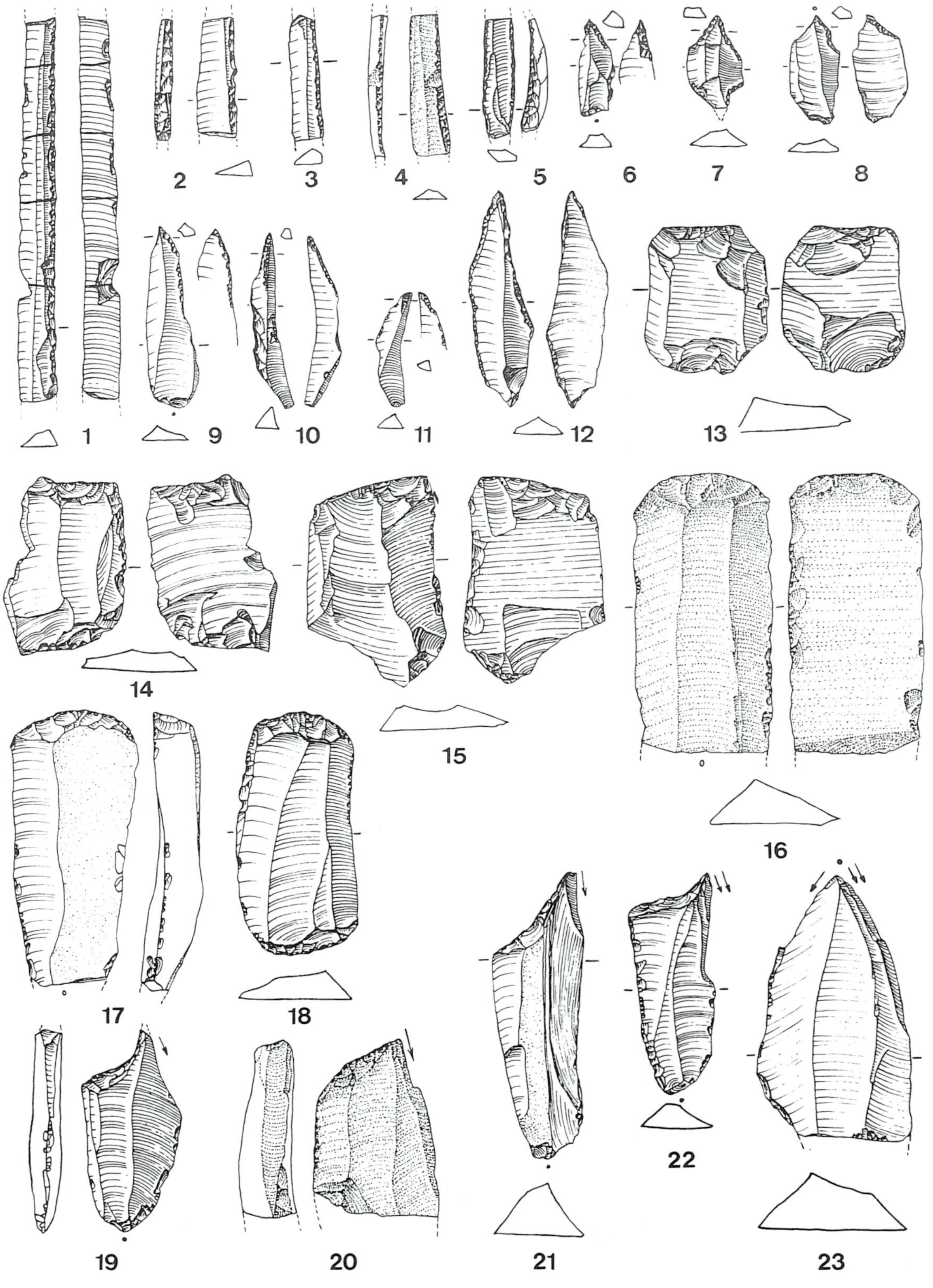

Fig. 3
Gönnersdorf, city of Neuwied. Typical stone tools from the hunting station. Back-blunted blades (1–5), drills/points (6–12), splintered pieces (13–15), scrapers (16–18), and burins (19–23). (after G. Bosinski)

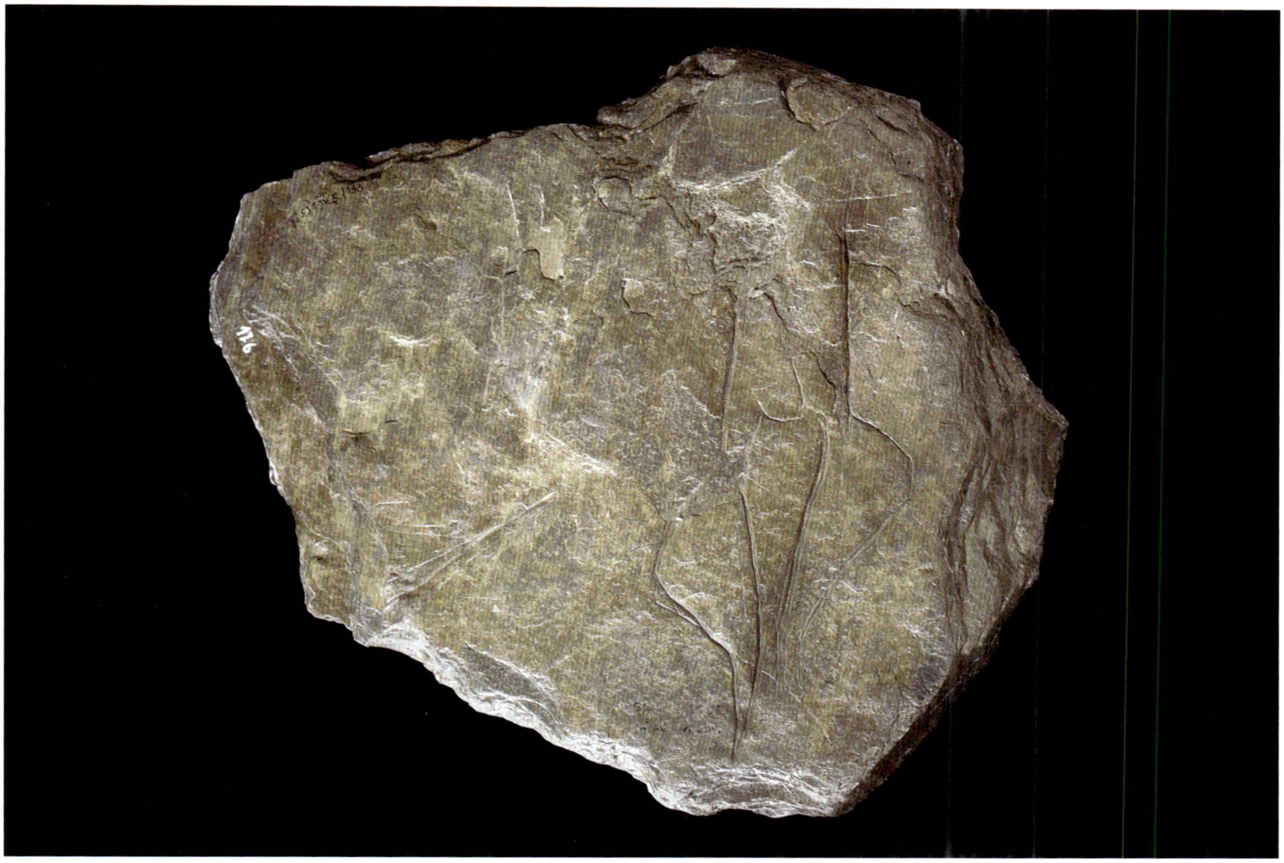

Fig. 4
Gönnersdorf, city of Neuwied. Engraved slate plate with schematic representation of two women facing each other (Plate 176). (GDKE/ Landesarchäologie/ Koblenz/ W. Baumann, Höhr-Grenzhausen)

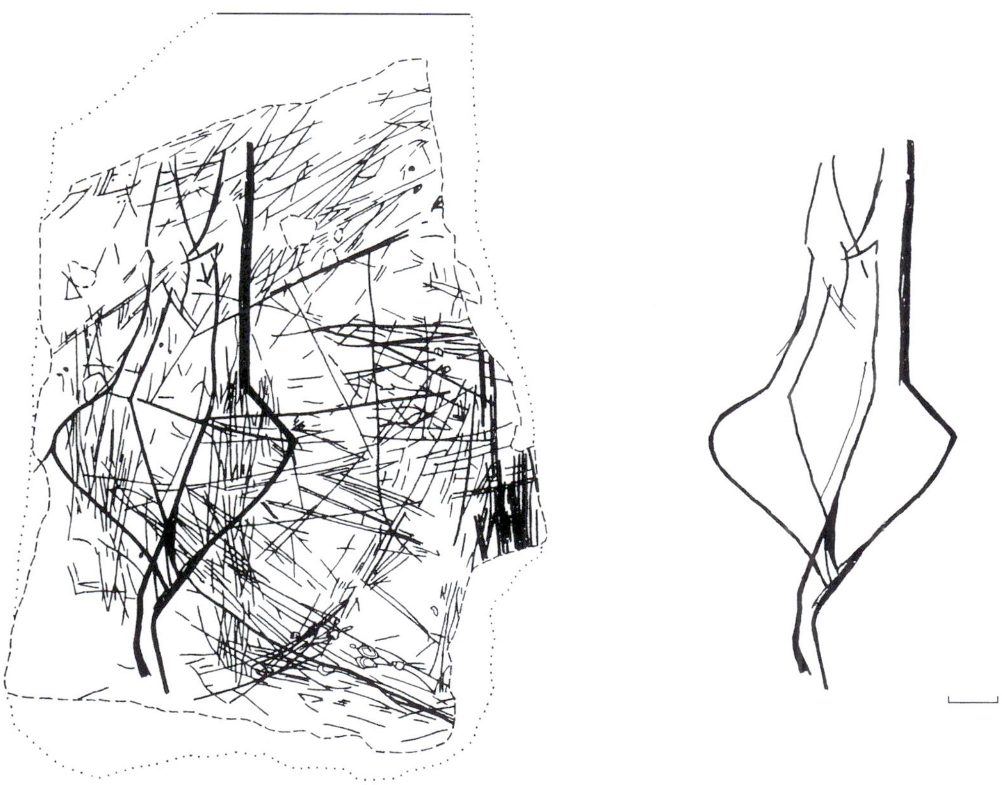

Fig. 5
Gönnersdorf, city of Neuwied. Rendering of the engravings on a slate plate with schematic representation of two women facing each other (Plate 78). (after G. Bosinski)

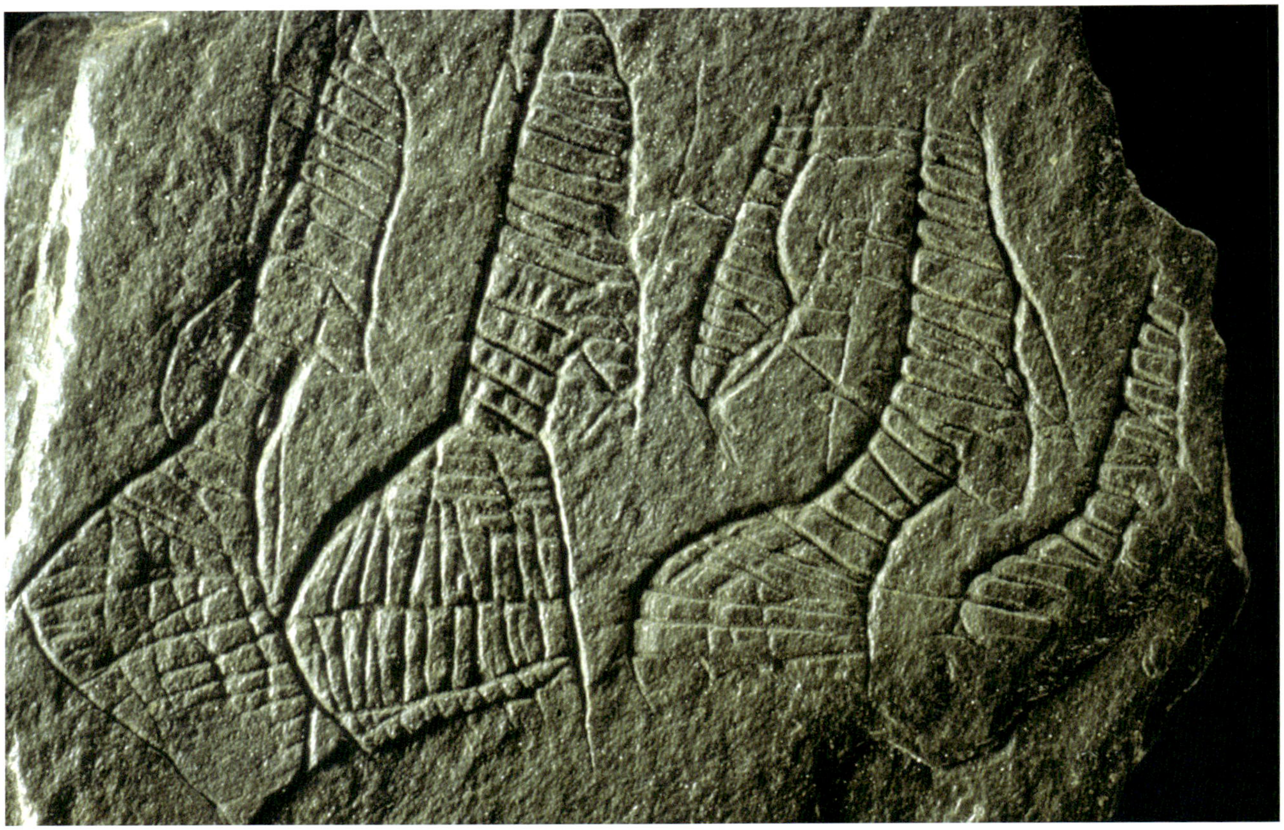

Fig. 6
Gönnersdorf, city of Neuwied. Engraved slate plate with dance scene of several women (Plate 87); the female in the centre right carrying a child on her back. (after G. Bosinski)

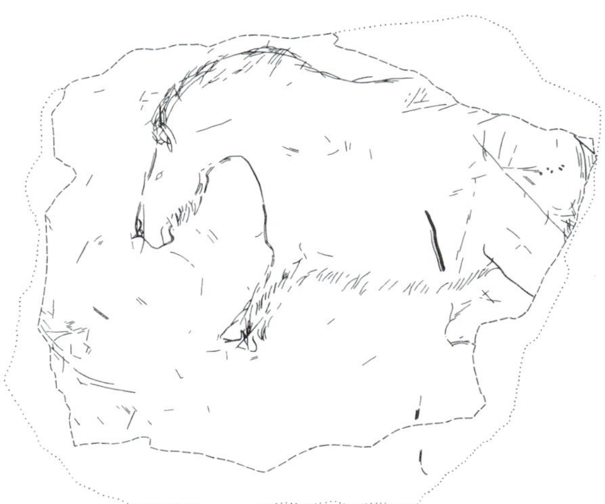

Fig. 7
Gönnersdorf, city of Neuwied. Rendering of an engraved representation of a horse on a slate plate (Plate 126). after G. Bosinski)

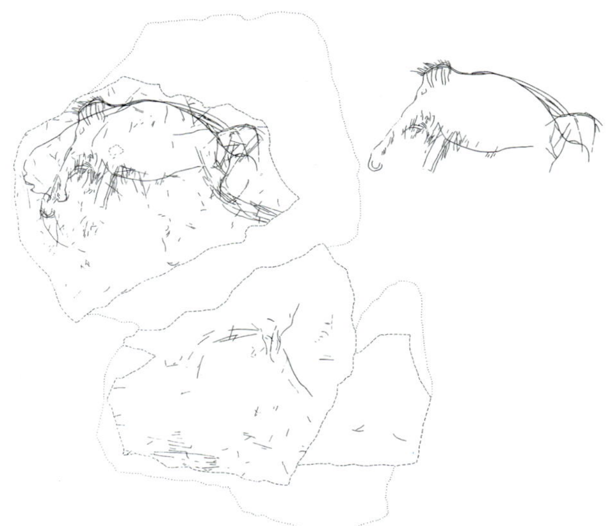

Fig. 8
Gönnersdorf, city of Neuwied. Rendering of an engraved representation of a mammoth on slate plate (Plate 112). (after G. Bosinski)

are shown in great detail and true to life. Many of the engravings show horses (Fig. 7), which were the main prey at that time, but also mammoth (Fig. 8), woolly rhinoceros and reindeer, wolf, and various species of birds. There is even an engraving of a young mammoth. (Fig. 9) Stylized statuettes of ivory were also found; in their typical form as so-called »rod-shaped Venus figurines« they were widespread all over Europe. (Fig. 10) The material retrieved in Neuwied-Gönnersdorf provides an important contribution to the interpretation of early image content in Europe for the structuring of ice age art.

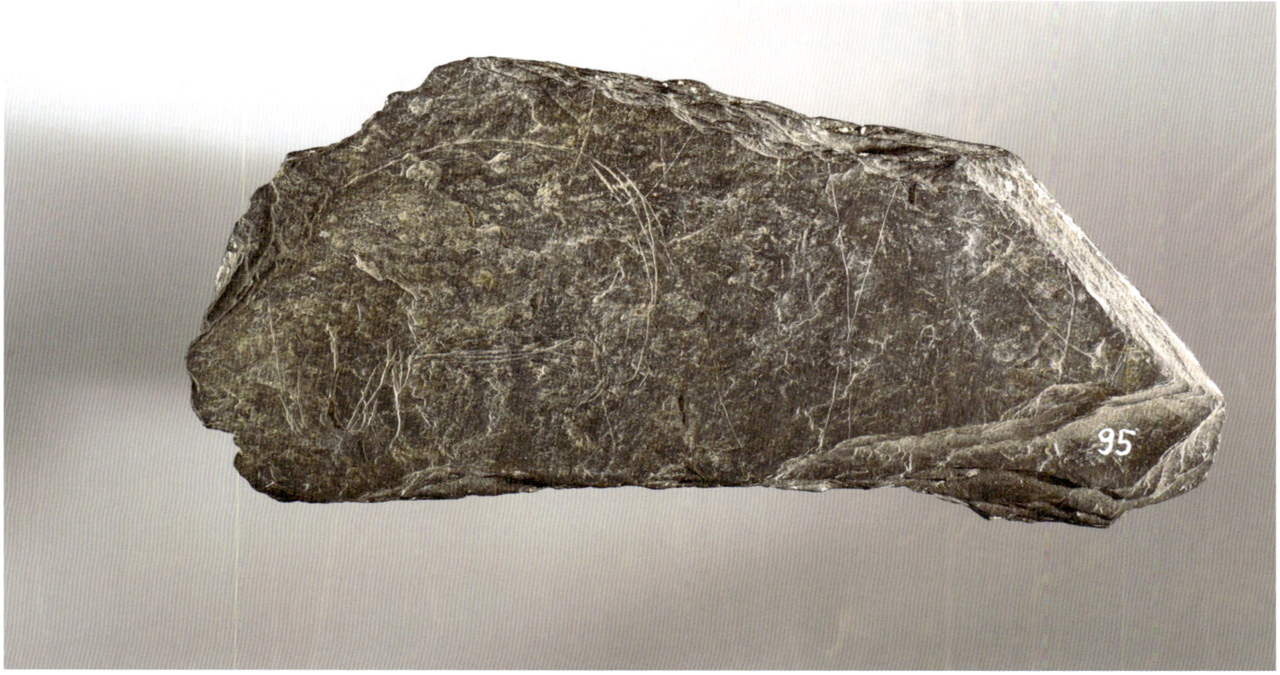

Fig. 9
Gönnersdorf, city of Neuwied. Engraved slate plate with representation of a young mammoth (Plate 95). (GDKE/Landesarchäologie/Koblenz/M. Neumann)

Bibliography

M. Baales, Archäologie des Eiszeitalters. Frühe Menschen an Mittelrhein und Mosel. Archäologie an Mittelrhein und Mosel 16 (Koblenz 2005).

G. Bosinski, Urgeschichte am Rhein. Tübinger Monographien zur Urgeschichte (Tübingen 2008).

G. Bosinski, G. Fischer, Die Menschendarstellungen von Gönnersdorf der Ausgrabung von 1968. Der Magdalénien-Fundplatz Gönnersdorf 1 (Wiesbaden 1974).

G. Bosinski, G. Fischer, Mammut- und Pferdedarstellungen von Gönnersdorf. Der Magdalénien-Fundplatz Gönnersdorf 5 (Wiesbaden 1980).

G. Bosinski, Die Ausgrabungen in Gönnersdorf 1968–1976 und die Siedlungsbefunde der Grabung 1968. Der Magdalénien-Fundplatz Gönnersdorf 3 (Wiesbaden 1979).

G. Bosinski, Die große Zeit der Eiszeitjäger. Europa zwischen 40.000 und 10.000 v. Chr. (5. Mommsen-Vorlesung) Jahrbuch des Römisch-Germanischen Zentralmuseums Mainz 34, 1987, 3 ff.

G. Bosinski, Eiszeitjäger im Neuwieder Becken. Archäologie an Mittelrhein und Mosel 1 (Koblenz 1992).

G. Bosinski, Gönnersdorf und Andernach-Martinsberg. Späteiszeitliche Siedlungsplätze am Mittelrhein. Archäologie an Mittelrhein und Mosel 19 (Koblenz 2007).

G. Bosinski, F. d'Errico, P. Schiller, Die gravierten Frauendarstellungen von Gönnersdorf. Der Magdalénien-Fundplatz Gönnersdorf 8 (Stuttgart 2001).

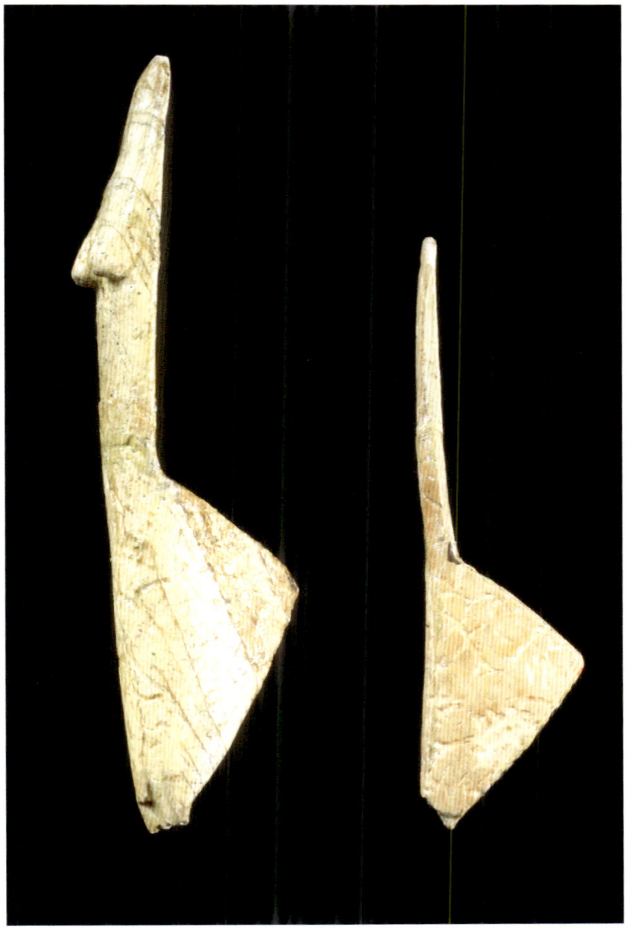

Fig. 10
Gönnersdorf, city of Neuwied. Two rod-shaped Venus statuettes, carved from mammoth ivory. (GDKE/Landesarchäologie/Koblenz/W. Baumann, Höhr-Grenzhausen)

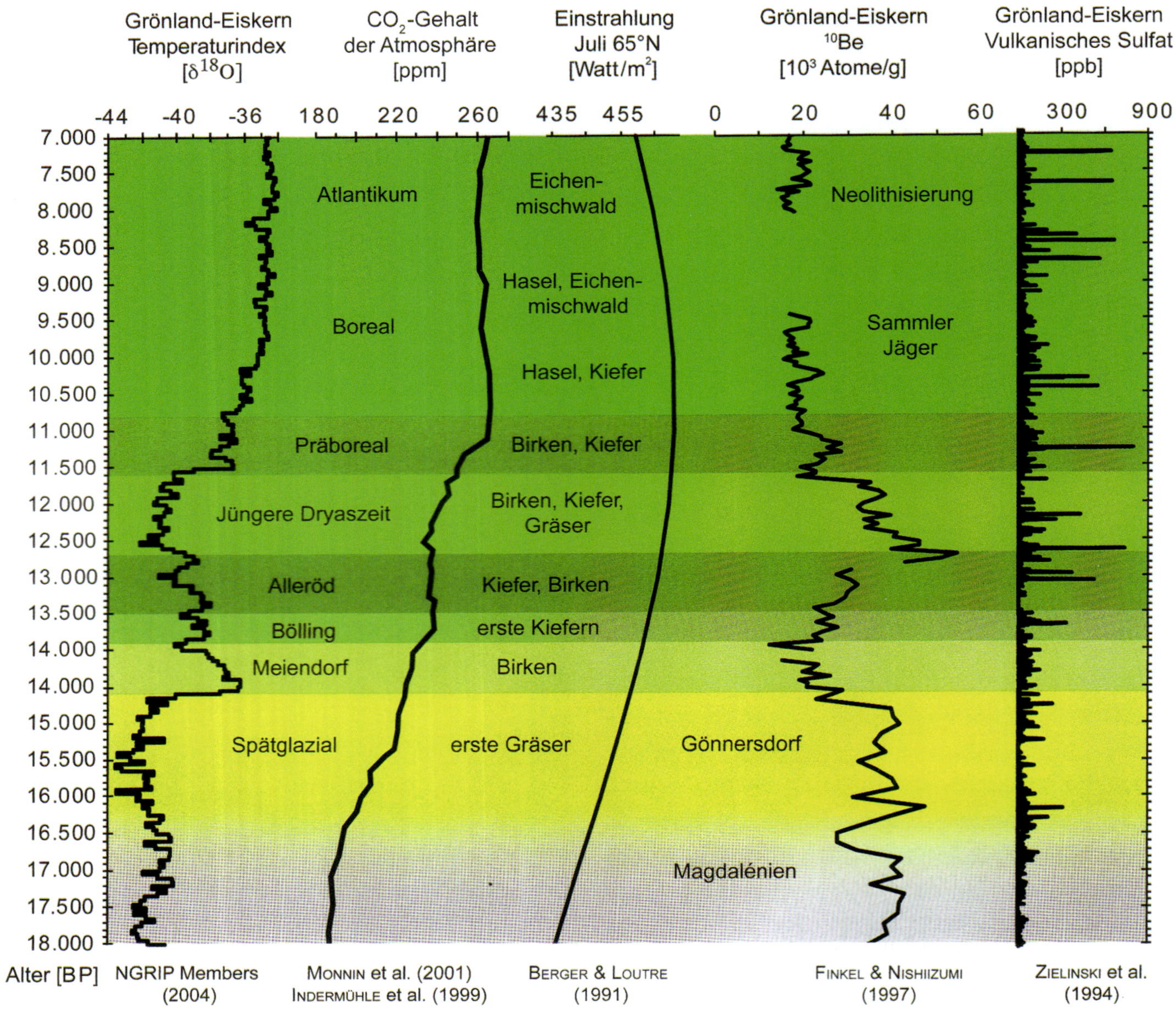

Grönland-Eiskern Temperaturindex [δ18O]
CO2-Gehalt der Atmosphäre [ppm]
Einstrahlung Juli 65°N [Watt/m2]
Grönland-Eiskern 10Be [10³ Atome/g]
Grönland-Eiskern Vulkanisches Sulfat [ppb]
-44 -40 -36
180 220 260
435 455
0 20 40 60
300 900
7.000
7.500
8.000
8.500
9.000
9.500
10.000
10.500
11.000
11.500
12.000
12.500
13.000
13.500
14.000
14.000
15.000
15.500
16.000
16.500
17.000
17.500
18.000
Atlantikum
Eichen-mischwald
Neolithisierung
Boreal
Hasel, Eichen-mischwald
Sammler Jäger
Hasel, Kiefer
Präboreal
Birken, Kiefer
Jüngere Dryaszeit
Birken, Kiefer, Gräser
Alleröd
Kiefer, Birken
Bölling
erste Kiefern
Meiendorf
Birken
Spätglazial
erste Gräser
Gönnersdorf
Magdalénien
Alter [BP]
NGRIP Members (2004)
Monnin et al. (2001)
Indermühle et al. (1999)
Berger & Loutre (1991)
Finkel & Nishiizumi (1997)
Zielinski et al. (1994)

The ice age comes to an end – Hunters conquer the forests

AXEL VON BERG

Around 12,700 BC, a marked increase in temperature over the northern hemisphere, with a warming of the North Atlantic within a short time, triggers the late glacial interstadial complex (GI 1). (Fig. 1) The clearly noticeable warming is accompanied by increasing solar intensity in the northern hemisphere. Within a few decades, the average annual temperatures rose considerably and reached values which by and large correspond to those of today. The climatic development of the following two millennia again shows a slight but continuous decrease of the average annual temperatures. Several cold snaps have been detected for the GI 1 interstadial complex; the climate changed within only a few decades and then the weather remained cold for a longer period. These cold snaps divided the warm phase into the Meiendorf (12,700–12,050 BC), the Bølling (12,050–11,580 BC), and the Allerød interstadial (11,580–10,700 BC). The warmer climate phase ends at around 10,700 BC. The cause of the fast warming at the start of the interstadial could be connected to a shifting of the Gulf Stream system further to the north, while the climate setbacks of that time, but also the climate change that occurred around 10,700 BC, were probably due to the short-term changes of the Oceanic stream patterns. In the northern hemisphere, enormous meltwater lakes formed ahead of the disintegrating inland ice. When these overflowed, huge amounts of fresh water flowed into the North Atlantic, at times pushing the Gulf Stream to more southern latitudes. The supply of Atlantic air masses was thus discontinued for large areas of the northern hemisphere, leading to a renewed reinforcement of the continental high-pressure areas that favoured dry and very cold winters.

In Rhineland-Palatinate, the tree pollen percentage increases considerably around 12,200 BC, indicating a dense tree cover. (see Fig. 1) The early warming phase at the start of the late glacial interstadial complex was still relatively dry, so it can be presumed that the vegetation cover still remained relatively scarce and wide areas were still covered by grass. Horse bones discovered time and again in sediments show that at that time large habitats untouched by man must still have existed. So far, there are only a few securely-dated find complexes from Rhineland-Palatinate that belong in the second half of the interstadial. The two most important finds come from the Rhineland. In both cases, these are human remains from burials. A grave find from Bonn-Oberkassel provided not only the nearly complete skeletons of an elderly man and a younger woman, but most importantly two carved art objects made of bone and the remains of a dog. Since that time, the dog, the oldest domestic animal, remains man's constant companion. A similar age is attributed to the formerly buried, red-discoloured

Fig. 1
Stratigraphic structure of the late young Palaeolithic and late Palaeolithic with development of climate and vegetation sequence. (after F. Sirocko)

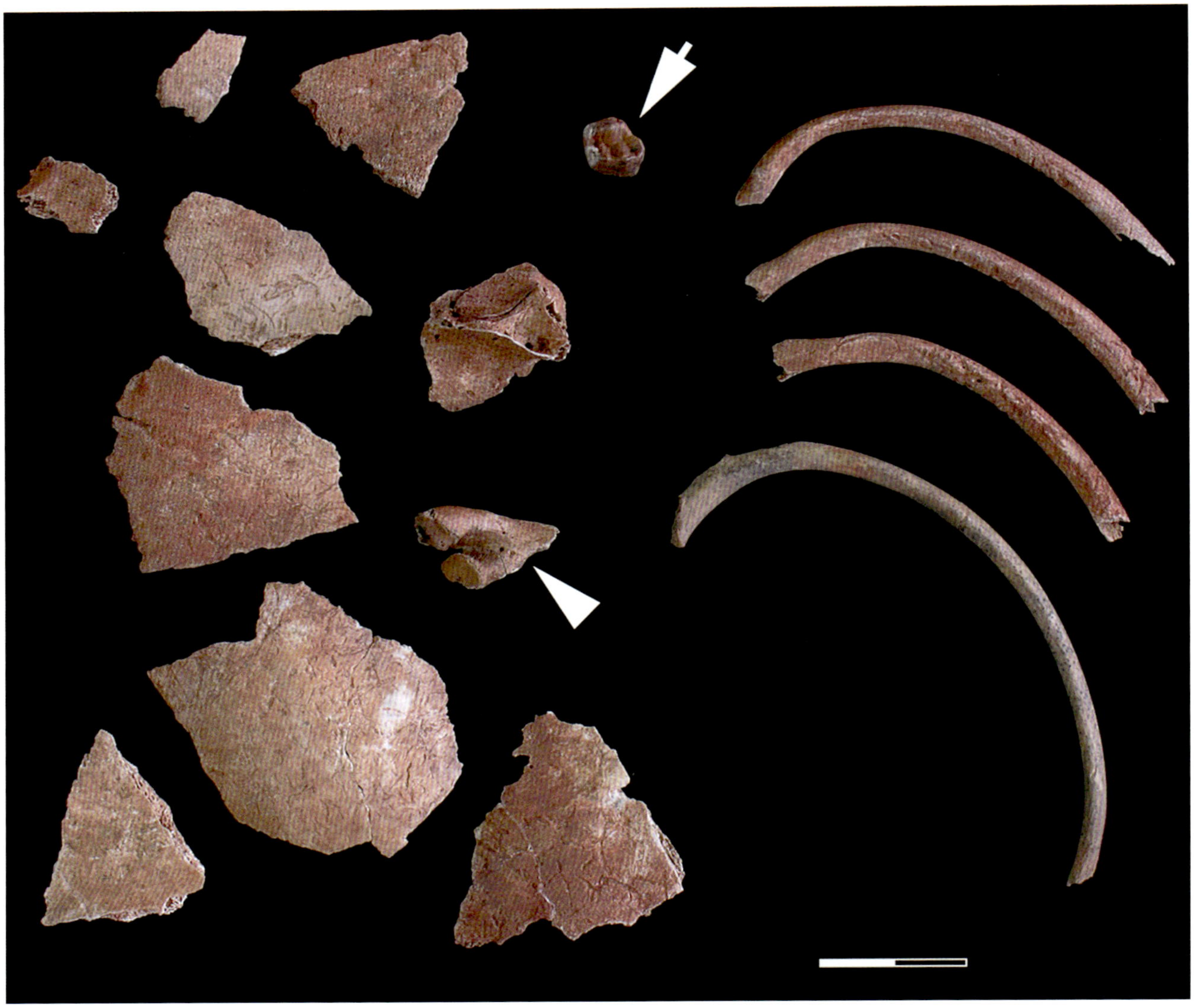

Fig. 2
Irlich, city of Neuwied. Late Palaeolithic burial remains of a child with bones coloured red. (GDKE/Landesarchäologie/Koblenz/M. Neumann)

human bones of several individuals and a child from a sand pit near Irlich, part of the borough of Neuwied. (Fig. 2) A perforated and decorated incisor of a stag and a projectile point made of bone were found as grave goods. The calibrated data of the individual parts of the skeletons placed them at around 12,500–11,200 BC.

After the following cold phase GI 1d, which lasted for about a century and during which the tree vegetation in our region receded almost completely and tundra-like steppes began to spread again, a warm phase lasting about 1200 years started at around 11,500 BC: it is termed the Allerød interstadial, after a Danish locality. This new stage led to yet another, very fast increase in the tree pollen curve, mostly from birch trees. The percentage of pine pollen in the evaluated diagrams increases only slowly after another climate setback. During the late Allerød, pine becomes the dominating tree species all over Central Europe. For this period, important finds are known particularly from northern Rhineland-Palatinate. The reason for this is the eruption of the Lake Laach volcano around 10,966 BC. As a consequence of this highly explosive eruption, the entire late ice age landscape on the Middle Rhine was covered with mighty volcanic pumice deposits several metres thick, and thus a large number of archaeological sites were covered up, preserved, and protected against later erosion.

Besides major settlement sites of the Allerød »Federmesser« (penknives, characteristic small quill-shaped backed flint points) groups at Andernach-Martinsberg, Kettig, Niederbieber, and Urbar, numerous other indications of the use of the landscape by late Palaeolithic man are known from this region. These include isolated fireplaces with finds as well as individual stone tools from the late ice age forests of Thür and Miesenheim in the Mayen-Koblenz district. It is assumed that in those days hunting with bows and arrows in the ever-thicker forests replaced the hunt practised using spear slings in the open steppes. The hunters were now armed with bow and arrow and could hunt effectively in the thicker vegetation. Among the retouched forms, backed points, so-called Federmesser (Fig. 3) prevail, which were fixed in the shaft with birch pitch. Backed blades, small scrapers, bladelets, and burins with truncation complement the tools of the trade of the late Palaeolithic man. The finds further include sandstone pieces with a ground groove, which were used to smoothen arrow shafts. Since fixed dwelling structures are missing, one must assume that the late ice age hunters lived in small, highly mobile communities that relocated their settlements after only a short residence time. (Fig. 4) Even large-scale settlement areas, like the ones on the Martinsberg in Andernach and in Niederbieber near Neuwied with many smaller settlement concentrations, seem to have seen only short-duration individual stays. Typical game were elk, deer, red stag, wild cattle, horse and beaver. Red fox, chamois, ibex and brown bear, boar and marten are also documented.

In the course of the eruption of the Lake Laach volcano in 10,966 BC, around 15 km³ of pumice and ash were produced in a short time. The pumice was deposited as fallout mainly over a large area of the Neuwied Basin and the Westerwald. Immediately after the Lake Laach event, hunters and gatherers of the younger Federmesser groups settled in the widening valley of the »golden mile« between Bad Breisig and Remagen (Ahrweiler district). So far, Bad Breisig is the only settlement site of the Middle Rhine Federmesser groups dated after the eruption of the Lake Laach volcano; according to typological comparisons, and because of its warm-temperate game with deer and red stag, it is still to be placed in the late Allerød interstadial.

Reindeer hunters of the Younger Dryas – The last return to glacial conditions in northern Europe

About 200 years after the Lake Laach eruption, Central Europe falls back for the last time into ice age climatic conditions for nearly 1200 years. The Gulf Stream stalled once again and threw Northern Europe into a

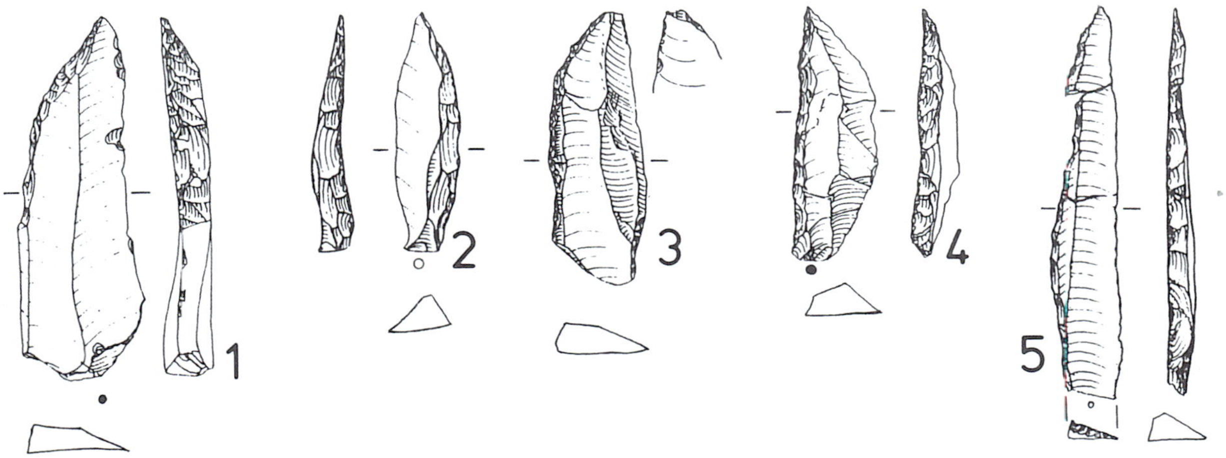

Fig. 3
Andernach, Mayen-Koblenz distr. and Niederbieber, city of Neuwied. Arrow points (1–5) with a retouched edge, so-called »penknives«. (GDKE/Landesarchäologie/Koblenz/M. Baales)

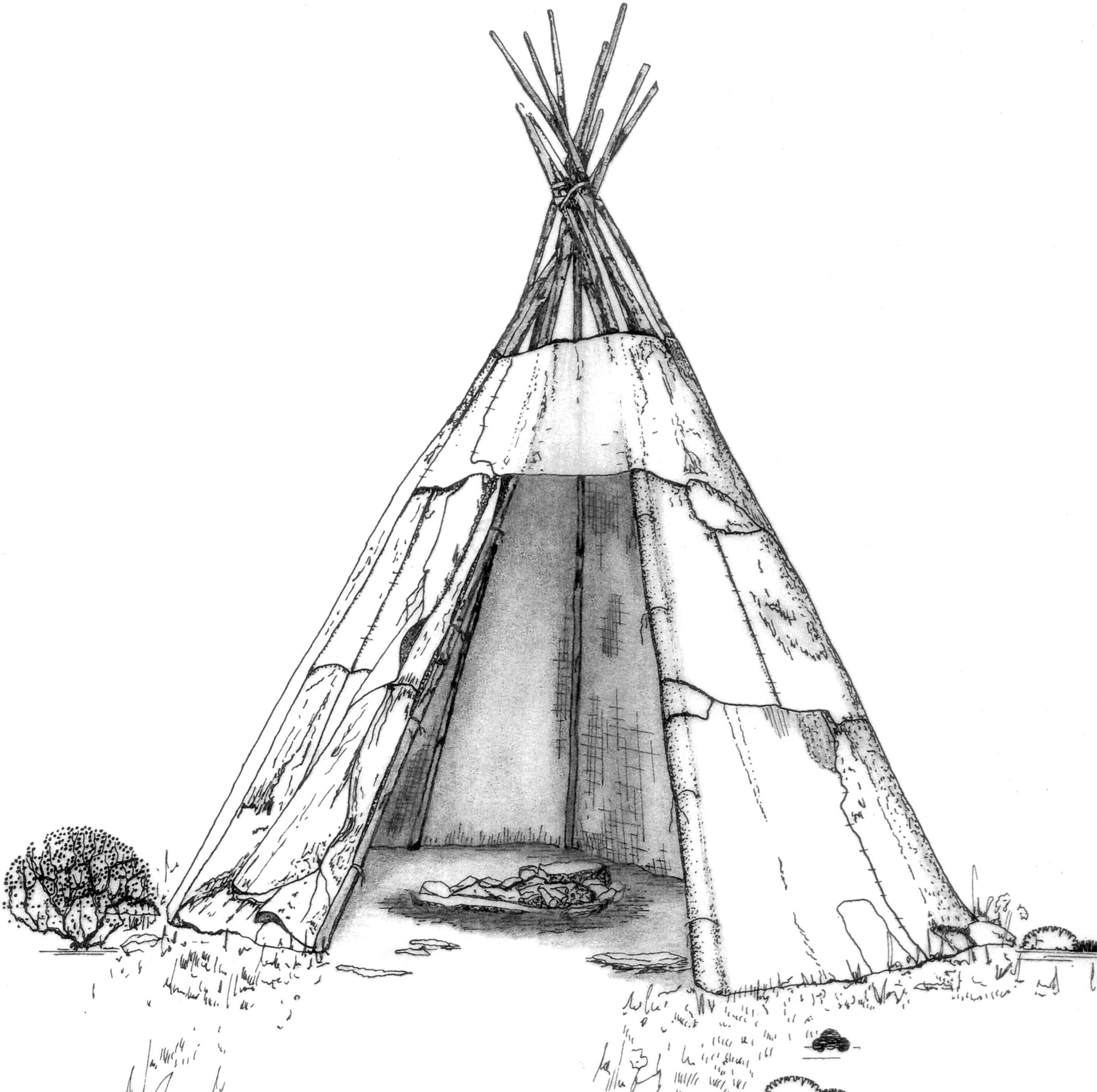

cold period called the Younger Dryas. The worldwide sea level at that time was still 60–70 m lower than today, and the average annual temperature was about 13 °C below that of our times. The vegetation was once again characterized by arctic conditions. The pollen analyses from core drillings in the Eifel maars show a clear reduction in tree pollen for the Younger Dryas. The beech and pine forests of the Allerød interstadial were significantly thinned out and pushed back, resulting in tundra-like open biotopes once again.

Because of these major climate changes, a different fauna developed in northern Central Europe as well. The forest fauna of the preceding Allerød gave way to animals of sub-arctic regions, and reindeer appeared for the last time in our region. While the »Federmesser groups« continued to exist in the warmer south, the »Ahrensburg Culture«, which was adapted to arctic conditions, advanced as far as northern Rhineland-Palatinate. Amongst the best-known tools are typical tanged points used as projectiles, as well as small microlith points with oblique end retouches called Zonhoven points, and also the usual repertoire of scrapers and burins.

The cold period of the Younger Dryas ended as abruptly as it had begun. In the ice cores of Greenland, the transition to the Holocene, our present warm stage, occurred at that time with a temperature jump of up to 8 °C in a short time. An important part of this development was certainly the shifting of the Gulf Stream towards the north. Between 10,200 and 9,500 BC, solar activity also increased considerably and has remained at a stable high over the entire Holocene, our present warm period.

The last hunters – The Middle Stone Age (Mesolithic) in Rhineland-Palatinate

The first part of the Holocene, starting in 9,640 BC, is referred to as Preboreal; the Middle Stone Age, the Mesolithic, begins. The last volcanic eruption of the Ulmen maar in the western Eifel at around 9,033 BC also falls in the early phase of the Holocene (Preboreal). From a climatologic viewpoint, this phase is characterized by general warming and a substantial withdrawal of the glaciers towards the north. The marked increase of tree pollens in the deposits of the Meerfeld maar in the Eifel is evidence of the warming that is now quickly taking place. As a consequence, the first large closed forest areas developed. While open post-ice age pine and birch woods were still characteristic during the Preboreal, the forests grew thicker during the following Boreal (8,000–7,100 BC); it is mixed oak forests of our time that now shape the landscape. A rich forest fauna with red stag, deer, aurochs, and boar is also backed by finds. The regions of the Middle Rhine and Moselle were now influenced more and more by the warm-stage climate we still have today.

The people of that time continued to adapt to the changing living conditions. Where settlement findings can be observed, they are mostly small find concentrations indicating a highly mobile way of life of small groups of hunters in the forests. Typical settlement sites with find inventories of that period are known especially from the mid-range mountain zones, from the peripheries of the Westerwald, and from the Eifel. The nomadic way of life continued, and the individual groups roamed a large territory and further refined the use of bows and arrows. The stone tools made of flint become smaller, and artistic points, triangles, and segments are used as arrow inserts. Because of their small size, these characteristic tools are also referred to as »microliths« and they remain typical until the first dawn of agriculture during the Neolithic.

Around 7,100 BC, the Boreal was succeeded by the Atlantic, the humid-wet climatic optimum of our warm stage. In many regions of Rhineland-Palatinate, the late Mesolithic slowly changes into the Neolithic with its characteristic economic forms: agriculture, livestock breeding, and a settled way of life. Whilst Mesolithic groups of hunters and early Neolithic people would still continue living side by side for some time, the early Neolithic »Bandkeramische Kultur« (Linear Pottery Culture) began to prevail on a large scale around 5,500/5,300 BC.

Fig. 4
Andernach-Martinsberg, Mayen-Koblenz distr. Schematic reconstruction of a tent dwelling of the late Palaeolithic according to the excavation findings. (GDKE/Landesarchäologie/Koblenz)

Bibliography

M. Baales, J. Vollbrecht, Kartstein. In: G. Bosinski, M. Street, & M. Baales, (Hg.), The Palaeolithic and Mesolithic of the Rhineland, Quaternary Field Trips in Central Europe 15, Band 2, INQUA-Congress Berlin, 1995, 941 ff.

M. Baales, Final Palaeolithic Archaeology of the Northern Rhineland and the Belgian Ardenne: State of Research. in: M. Dewez, P. Noiret, & E. Teheux, (Hg.), Actes du XIVème Congrès UISPP, Université de Liège 2001 / Acts of the XIVth UISPP Congress, University of Liège 2001, Sessions générales et posters / General Sessions ans Posters. BAR International Series 1240, 2004, 63 ff.

M. Baales, Archäologie des Eiszeitalters. Frühe Menschen an Mittelrhein und Mosel. Archäologie an Mittelrhein und Mosel 16 (Koblenz 2005).

M. Baales, O. Jöris, Zwischen Nord und Süd. Ein allerødzeitlicher Rückenspitzen-Fundplatz bei Bad Breisig, Kr. Ahrweiler (Mittelrhein, Rheinland-Pfalz). Die Kunde N. F. 52, 2002, 275 ff.

M. Baales, Der spätpaläolithische Fundplatz Kettig. Untersuchungen zur Siedlungsarchäologie der Federmesser-Gruppen am Mittelrhein. Monographien des Römisch-Germanischen Zentralmuseums 51 (Mainz, Bonn 2002).

M. Baales, O. Jöris, M. Street, F. Bittmann, B. Weninger, J. Wiethold, Impact of the Late Glacial Eruption of the Laacher See Volcano, Central Rhineland, Germany. Quaternary Research 58, 2002, 273 ff.

A. von Berg, Bestattungen des Spätpaläolithikums von Neuwied-Niederbieber im Neuwieder Becken. In: L. Giemsch, R. W. Schmitz (Hg.), Eiszeitjäger. Leben im Paradies. Europa vor 15.000 Jahren (Bonn 2014) 236 ff.

A. von Berg, Allerödzeitliche Feuerstellen unter dem Bims im Neuwieder Becken. Archäologisches Korrespondenzblatt 24, 1994, 355 ff.

A. von Berg, M. Baales, Tierfährten in der allerödzeitlichen Vulkanasche des Laacher See Vulkans bei Mertloch, Kr. Mayen-Koblenz. Archäologisches Korrespondenzblatt 27, 1997, 1 ff.

M. Bolus, Die Siedlungsbefunde des späteiszeitlichen Fundplatzes Niederbieber (Stadt Neuwied). Monographien des Römisch-Germanischen Zentralmuseums Mainz 22 (Mainz 1992).

G. Bosinski, Urgeschichte am Rhein. Tübinger Monographien zur Urgeschichte (Tübingen 2008).

G. Bosinski, Eiszeitjäger im Neuwieder Becken. Archäologie an Mittelrhein und Mosel 1 (Koblenz 1992).

G. Büchel, Die Maare im Vulkanfeld der Westeifel, ihr geophysikalischer Nachweis, ihr Alter und ihre Beziehung zur Tektonik der Erdkruste. Diss. Univ. Mainz (Mainz 1984).

G. R. Coope et al., Temperature gradients in northern Europe during the last glacial-Holocene transition (14-9 14C kyr B. P.) interpreted from coleopteran assemblages. Journal of Quaternary Science 13, 1989, 419 ff.

F. Gelhausen, J. Kegler, St. Wenzel, Latente Behausungsstrukturen im Spätpaläolithikum. Die Fundplätze Niederbieber I und IV, Andernach-Martinsberg 3, Berlin-Tegel IX. Die Kunde N. F. 56, 2005, 11 ff.

O. Jöris, B. Weninger, ^{14}C-Alterskalibration und die absolute Chronologie des Spätglazials. Archäologisches Korrespondenzblatt 30, 2000, 461 ff.

H. Löhr, Linksflügler und Rechtsflügler in Mittel- und Westeuropa. Der Fortbestand der Verbreitungsgebiete asymmetrischer Pfeilspitzformen als Kontinuitätsbeleg zwischen Meso- und Neolithikum. Trierer Zeitschrift 57, 1994, 9 ff.

J. F. W. Negendank, Pleistozäne und holozäne Maarsedimente der Eifel. Zeitschrift der Deutschen Gesellschaft für Geowissenschaften 140, 1989, 13 ff.

F. Sirocko (Hg.), Wetter, Klima, Menschheitsentwicklung. Von der Eiszeit bis in das 21. Jahrhundert (Stuttgart 2009).

M. Street, Ein Wald der Allerödzeit bei Miesenheim, Stadt Andernach (Neuwieder Becken). Archäologisches Korrespondenzblatt 16, 1986, 13 ff.

M. Street, Evidence for late Allerød ecology conserved by Laacher See tephra: Miesenheim 2, Miesenheim 4, Thür, Brohl Valley sites, Glees, Krufter Ofen, Wingertsberg. In: G. Bosinski, M. Street, & M. Baales (Hg.), The Palaeolithic and Mesolithic of the Rhineland. Quaternary Field Trips in Central Europe 15, Vol. 2 (W. Schirmer, (Hg.). 14. INQUA-Kongress Berlin 1995) 928 f.

M. Street, M. Baales, B. Weninger, Absolute Chronologie des späten Paläolithikums und Frühmesolithikums im nördlichen Rheinland. Archäologisches Korrespondenzblatt 24, 1994, 1 ff.

The Neolithic – Farmers and cattle breeders

AXEL VON BERG

The transition from the hunter cultures of earlier times to the agricultural cultures of the Neolithic represents a major revolution in the development of man in the 6th millennium BC. The finds from 5,600/5,300 BC at the latest prove that both culture and daily life had changed completely. One of the most important steps in this development is the transition from the forager cultures of earlier times to a settled way of life and a productive food economy and stock-keeping. It is the beginning of the domestication of wild animals and plants. At the start of the settlement period, spelt species such as einkorn and emmer were grown and intentionally cultivated. The cultivation of peas and lentils has also been proven. In order to gain land for agriculture and cattle breeding, people would choose fertile soils, and forest areas were time and again turned into arable land by slash-and-burn techniques.

The Neolithic had its roots in the Near East about 10,000 years ago. The causes of this development are a subject of controversy, but the climate change at the end of the last cold period unquestionably played an important role. According to latest studies, it was a short-term climate change 8,200 years ago, with droughts in the Near East and the Mediterranean area, which was decisive for the colonization of Europe and made Neolithic groups migrate to the north.

Due to the changed and more diverse vegetation, man developed the cultivation of grain from wild species. The surplus of carbohydrates led to an increase in the population, which eventually also led to the domestication of sheep and goats. Around 5,600 BC, the Neolithic economic and cultural concept finally reached the northern regions of Europe via the Balkans. Rhineland-Palatinate was also opened up from the Carpathian Basin during various waves of colonization. Immigration, accompanied by the spread of Neolithic ways of life, produced an adaptation of the foragers still caught in local Mesolithic traditions. Besides the fundamental economic changes, further developments of the material culture can also be observed. Stone tools were no longer only struck: the practice of grinding of stone tools is now an innovation. Ground and polished hatches and axes, which were sometimes perforated for mounting, are produced for the first time. These new forms of tools allowed the dressing and working of wood and beams for building large longhouses. Another novelty to be noticed is the manufacture of ceramic vessels which are often richly decorated. They were used both for storage and for daily use. The clay was formed freehand into vessels, smoothened, and kilned in an open hearth. Thus, the bases on which historical Europe would later build were already shaped in

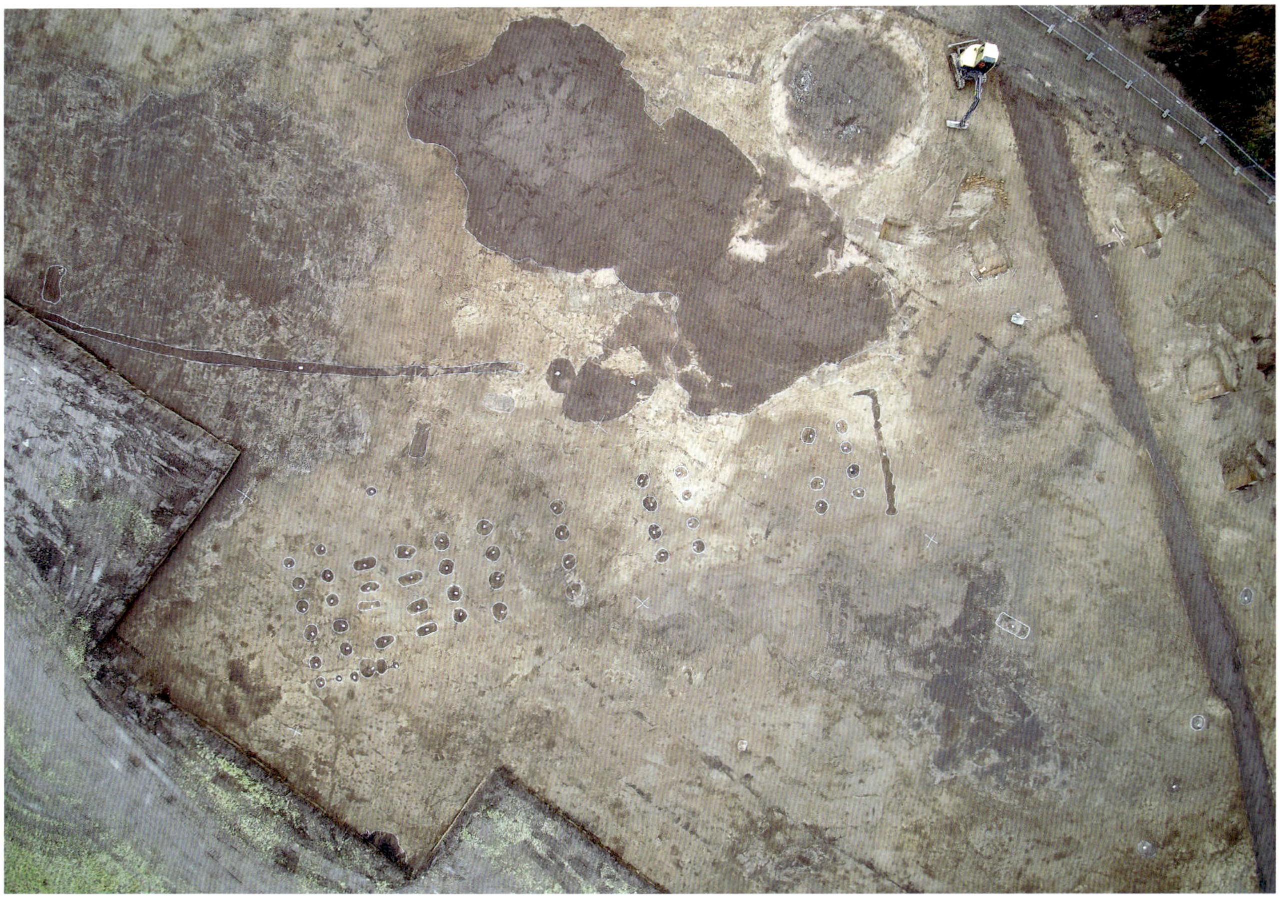

Fig. 1
Polch, Mayen-Koblenz distr. Aerial photo with Linear Pottery long house. The pole rows of the wall and roof construction are visible as discolourings in the soil. The large discoloured areas on the excavation area in the upper part of the picture are modern-time mining pits, above it a filled-in bomb crater of World War II. (GDKE/Landesarchäologie/Koblenz/M. Gensty)

the early Neolithic. The targeted cultivation of grain, the intentional breeding of productive livestock, and the keeping of domestic animals increased the natural provisions and at the same time led to new possibilities of gain.

The Early Neolithic – The »Linearbandkeramik« farmers

To name the individual stages of Neolithic culture, one uses either the names of sites or typical elements of form and decoration, mostly of pottery. The oldest cultural stage of the Neolithic is the »Linearbandkeramik« (LBK – Linear Pottery Culture). It comprises the period 5,600–4,900 BC. The culture is named after the typical incised linear decoration on ceramic vessels of similar shape repeatedly found in various sites. The forms were mainly round-bottomed jars, bowls, and bottles with different functions. As far as we know, the Linearbandkeramik originated in Hungary, in the sphere of influence of south-eastern European cultures, and between 5,000 and 4,500 BC also reached the mid-range mountains of the Rhine and the Moselle under the influence of a warm and sunny climate.

The most striking characteristic of the LBK are large wooden houses, about 8 m wide and up to 40 m long. (Fig. 1) The walls were braced with brushwood wattle and then extensively covered with clay. (Fig. 2) According to archaeological findings, about 45 massive oak trunks were used on average for the supporting scaffold. The houses were structured inside by crossbars, usually producing a four-aisled building as the basic form. Lengthwise, the houses were divided into three sections with farming, storage, and dwelling areas where extended families lived. The establishment of several settlement sites close to each other, which were often relocated after some time because the soil was

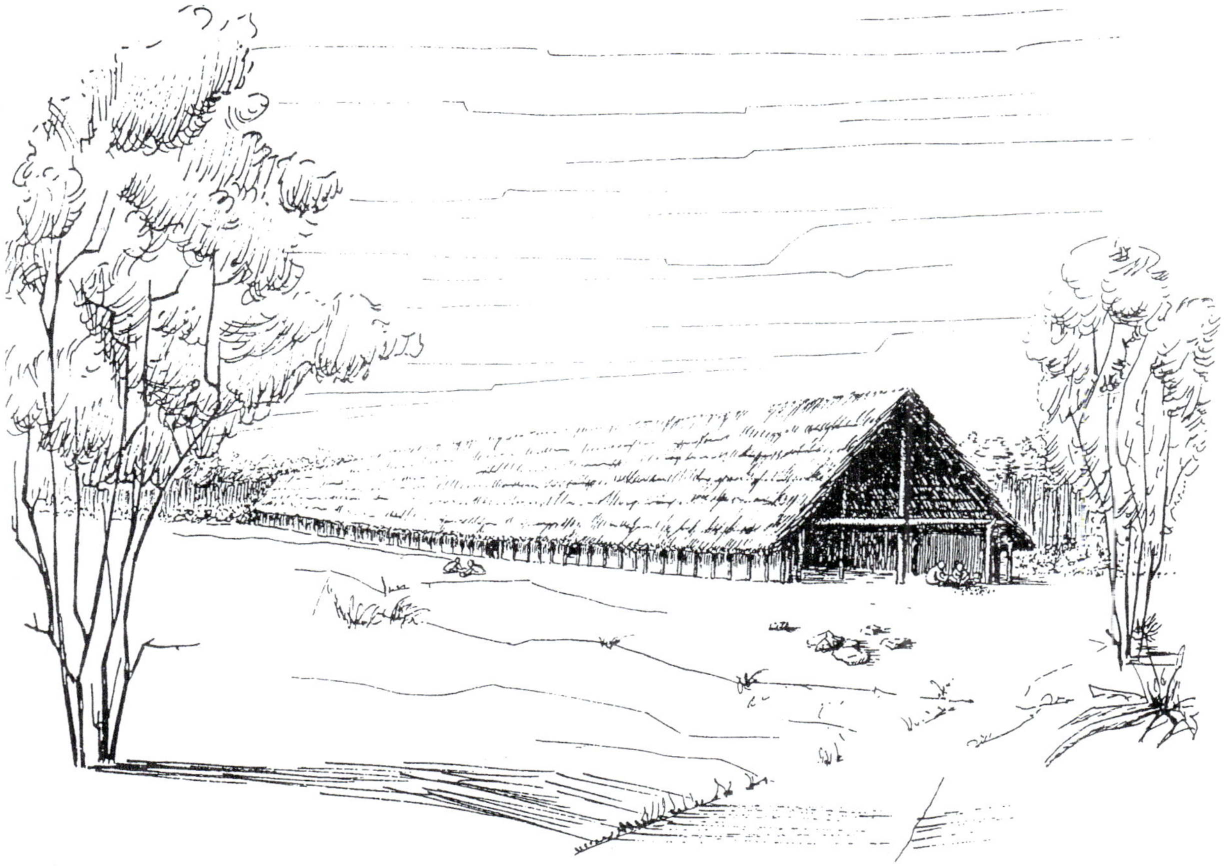

Fig. 2
Reconstruction of a Linear Pottery long house according to the excavation findings. (GDKE/Landesarchäologie/Koblenz)

no longer fertile enough, becomes typical for the settlement pattern of that time. Clearings to create settlement and agricultural areas in the originally closed forest created island-like zones in the landscape, which had a lasting influence on the local vegetation.

The grain cultivation of the LBK is based mostly on einkorn and emmer species. The grain was harvested using sickles with sharp flint segments inserted for efficient cutting. Besides the grain species rich in carbohydrates, pulses such as peas and lentils and oil plants such as linseed and poppy supplemented the food supply. The forest was also very important, not only as a supplier of wood but also for livestock farming. The preserved remains of bones from the Early Neolithic document mainly cattle, pig, sheep, and goat, introduced in their domesticated form by the first settlers. Specific forms of stone tools were developed at that time. These specifically include the adzes found in large numbers, i.e. stone tools made from rock that

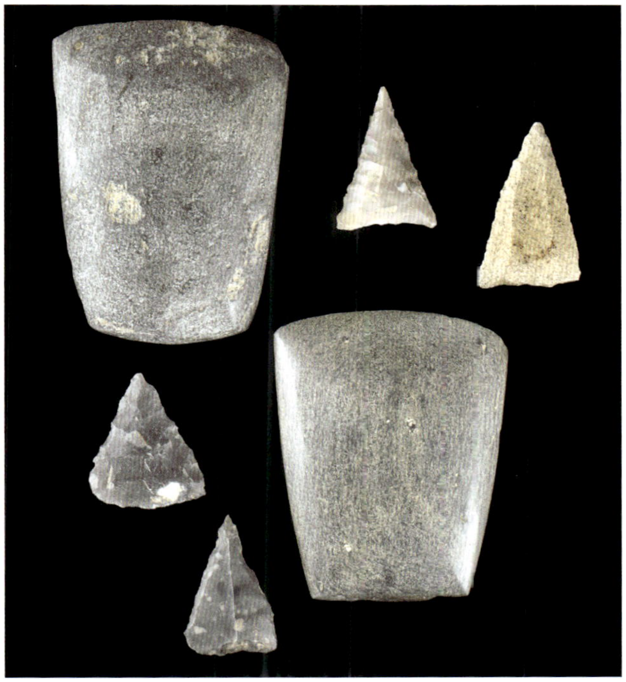

Fig. 3
Brieden, Binningen, Cochem- Zell distr. Trimbs, Mayen-Koblenz distr. and Koblenz-Metternich, city of Koblenz. Ground adzes made of rock and triangular arrow points made of flint from the early Neolithic. (GDKE/Landesarchäologie/Koblenz/W. Baumann, Höhr-Grenzhausen)

Fig. 4
Koblenz, city of Koblenz. Big splitting wedge made of rock with mounting hole of the Rössen culture. (GDKE/Landesarchäologie/Koblenz/M. Neumann)

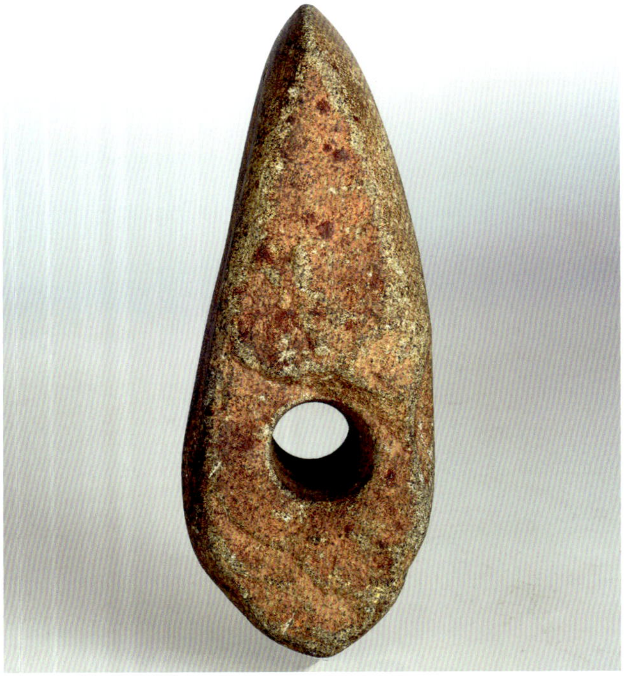

was ground and shafted transversely, with a flat lower and a convex upper side, which were mainly used for working with wood. Flint was employed for producing sharp blade tools. It has often been noticed that the raw material was rather uniform, indicating that a targeted exploitation of flint deposits was already taking place at that time. The grain mullers, which are now documented for the first time, were still small and flat and made from regional rock. The typical stone tool inventory included scrapers, chisels, and points made of flint and so-called »red iron ore«, which, when ground on a rough surface, produced a powder used as make-up because of its brick-red colour. (Fig. 3)

The society of the LBK remained constant over several centuries and shows quite little hierarchical differentiation. Burial grounds have been known since the middle LBK period. The burial settings are consistently furnished with stone tools and ceramic ware as grave gifts. Large settlements are also documented, showing that the relevant places were used continuously for up to 350 years and that trans-regional contacts were cultivated on the basis of individual family connections. In the late phase of the LBK, large earthworks with ditches and palisades were built. Among these, the earthwork of Herxheim in the Palatinate is exceptional.

Middle Neolithic – The »Rössen Culture«

With the transition to the Middle Neolithic, the documented archaeological finds and findings change. Whilst the LBK still persists in the northern parts of Rhineland-Palatinate, the Middle Neolithic already starts to develop in the southern parts of the state. In the north, a general decrease in population density is in evidence, accompanied by a reduction of the settlement areas used. The northern Upper Rhine area in the south of Rhineland-Palatinate, on the other hand, shows an enlargement of the settlement areas, which is explainable by the differing influences from north and south. The Middle Neolithic cultures, which dominate now, differ in many aspects from the older »Bandkeramik«. The change of style started in the south (in the Neckar and Upper Rhine area).

The Middle Neolithic is characterized by the large cultural region of the »Rössen Culture« (4,900–4,300 BC): while during the late phase the north is still under the influence of the regional »Bischheim Culture«, the south is mainly characterized by the south German »Großgartach Culture«. The form and ornaments of the vessels now clearly differ from the older epoch, with typical elements being conical beakers with a widely protruding rim. The pottery now generally shows deeper carvings and ornamentation. A new technical development of this time is the production of ground-flint axe blades. Flint axes are sharper and could be used longer than those made from rock of the preceding Bandkeramik period. In addition, big perforated wedges for splitting tree trunks complement the spectrum of tools. (Fig. 4) The type of economy practised and lifestyle remain largely unchanged and differ little from the older epoch. Changes in house construction begin to show with trapezoid longhouses, and the size of the houses grows considerably (up to 50 m in length). The striking size of the Middle Neolithic houses indicates several extended families living there. The buildings were covered with reeds, straw, or long wild grass, and erected in a post and wattle-and-daub technique. The individual frames were closed with wattle and daubed with clay. As with the developed Bandkeramik, it seems that several settlements of the same age were combined into bigger settlement groups, some of them fortified. The innovations in

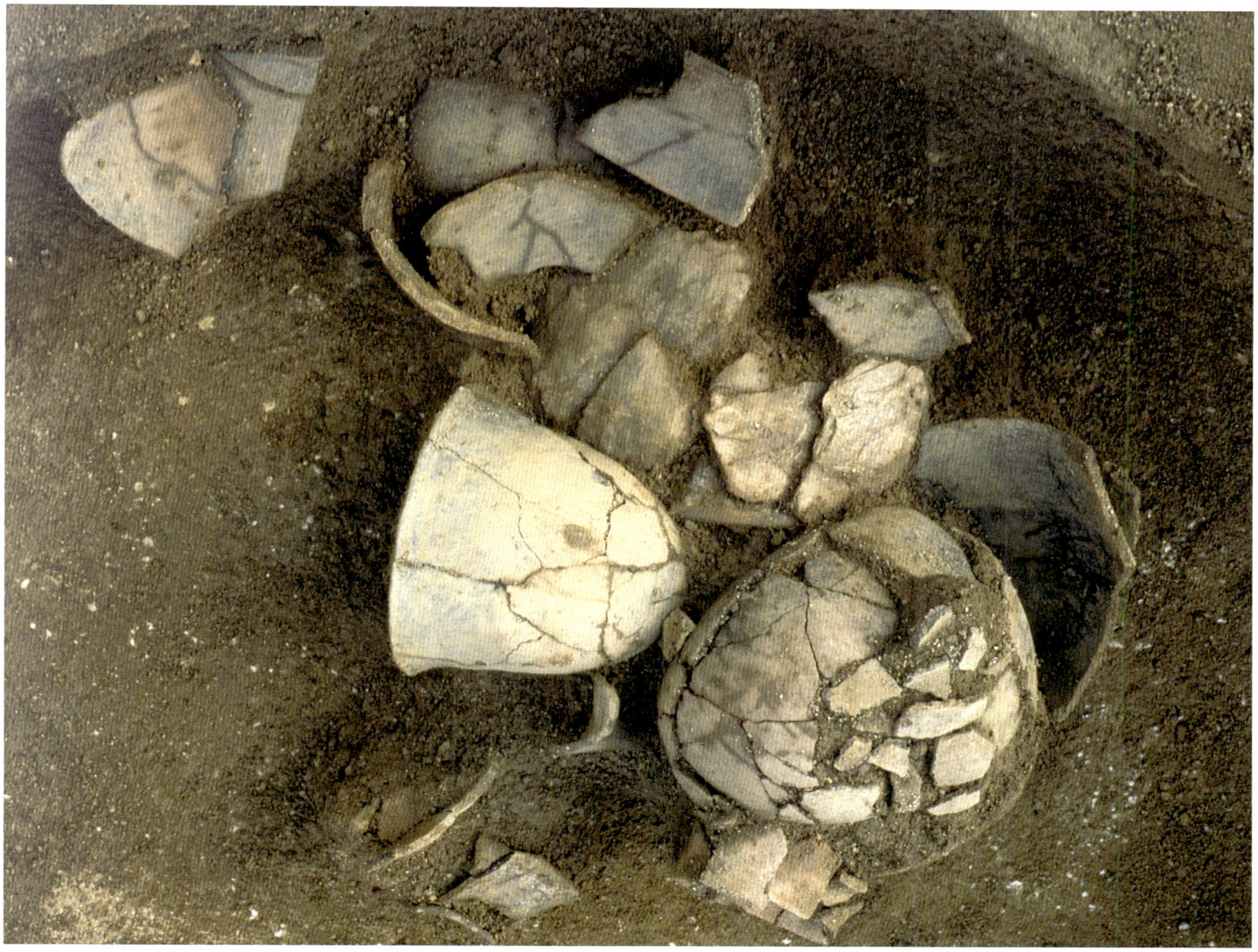

Fig. 5
Ochtendung, Mayen-Koblenz distr. Funnel-like beaker (tulip beaker) of the Michelsberg culture. (GDKE/Landesarchäologie/Koblenz/F. Gebert)

the economic system include an extended spectrum of cultivated plants, where, besides the old species of grain, the cultivation of barley is also documented.

Younger Neolithic – The »Michelsberg Culture«

The subsequent Younger Neolithic cultural group (Younger Neolithic, 4,300–3,500 BC) is called the »Michelsberg Culture« and developed from the older Middle Neolithic cultural groups. The »Michelsberg Culture« marks the beginning of the late phase of the Neolithic in Rhineland-Palatinate. Cultural changes affecting all areas of daily life can now be noted in Europe. Generally, there is an extension of the settlement areas into formerly uninhabited regions, including the uplands of the mid-range mountains. In agriculture, the ard plough is used from then on. This newly developed agricultural tool loosens the soil far better and allows a more efficient cultivation of grain. Lime trees dominate in the pollen diagrams, and in the spectrum of cultivated plants durum wheat appears beside einkorn and emmer, indicating western European influences.

The key pottery finds of this stage change considerably: most of them are left undecorated and their forms show greater variety, with new inventions such as the so-called tulip beakers making an appearance. (Fig. 5) Changes can also be noted in the forms of stone implements. New characteristic elements are the dagger-like pointed blade and large ground stone axes with oval cross sections. The first evidence of copper implements, originating in the Carpathian Basin and in Anatolia, also belongs in the Late Neolithic. Prestige

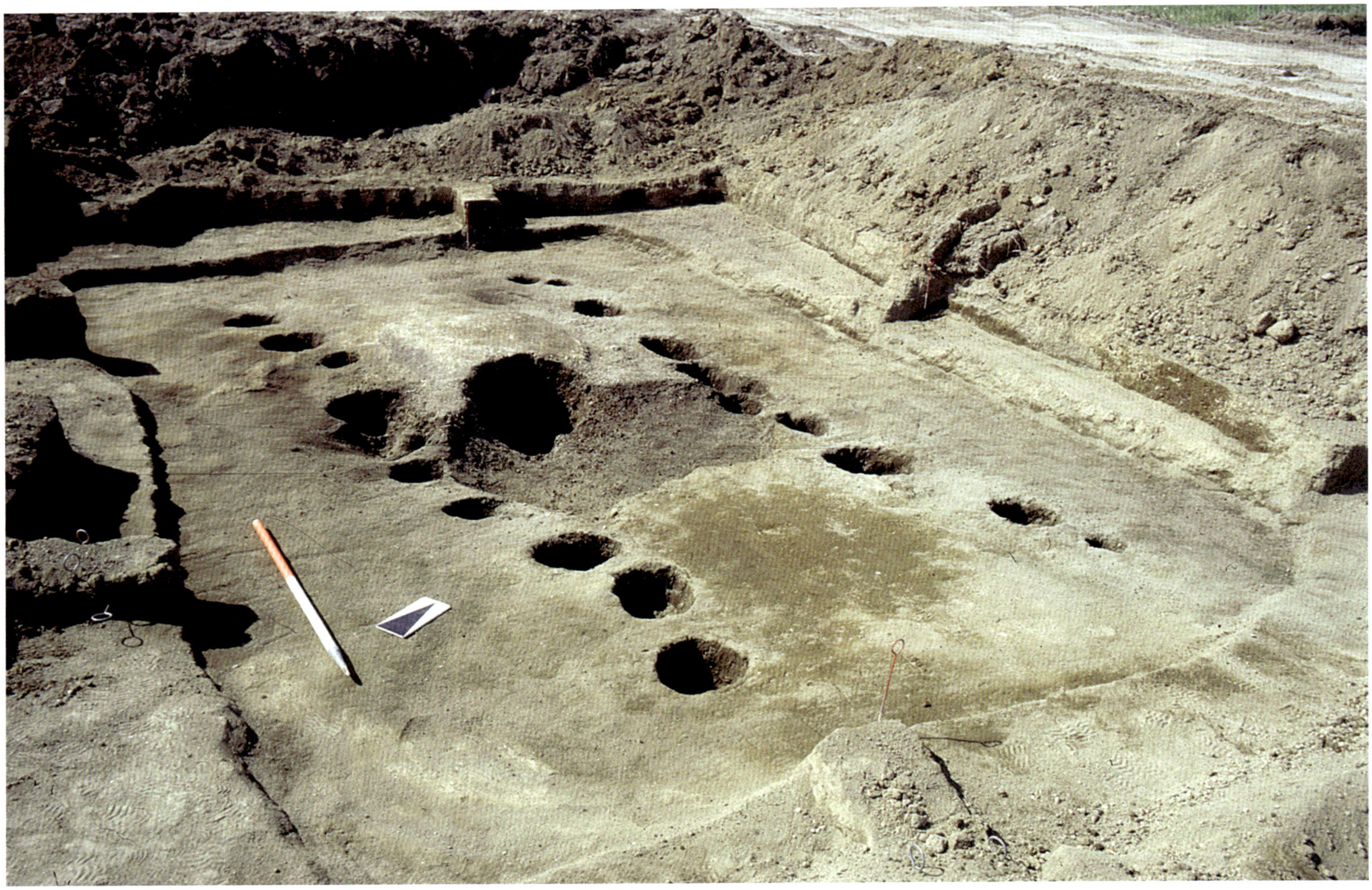

Fig. 6
Mülheim-Kärlich, Mayen-Koblenz distr. Footprint of a house of the Michelsberg culture with pole rows inside the sunken floor of the hut. (GDKE/Landes-archäologie/ Koblenz/ F. Gebert)

goods such as copper implements, amber or jadeite axe blades are long-distance trade products and are now more clearly traceable than in previous times.

A most remarkable feature is the general absence of burials. There are only a few indications from northern Rhineland-Palatinate for the construction of long mounds, which as a rule contained cremation burials.

The basic structure of the buildings is getting smaller, which might indicate a changed economic and social structure. (Fig. 6) Deposits of raw materials are now sought and exploited to specification, and the products derived from them traded over great distances. This leads to an increasing division of labour in society and might indicate a differentiation of the social structure with the emergence of a leading elite.

During this time, large fortification works are built, which have found their way into literature as so-called earthworks. These large installations, several hectares in size, enclosed with mighty ditches and palisades, served various purposes – among other things as a central square, cattle enclosure, cultic place, market-place, refuge fort. The earthworks mark the centres of individual settlement areas. They are communal works of considerable dimension, which could only be implemented and maintained by larger social groups consisting of several thousands of people. Huge sites of this kind are known mainly in northern Rhineland-Palatinate from Urmitz on the Rhine (Fig. 7) and from Mayen in the Vordereifel. (Fig. 8) The construction of such complex ditch systems is an indication of an emerging differentiated social structure. The development of trade routes took place at that time, when products and prestige goods were often traded over great distances.

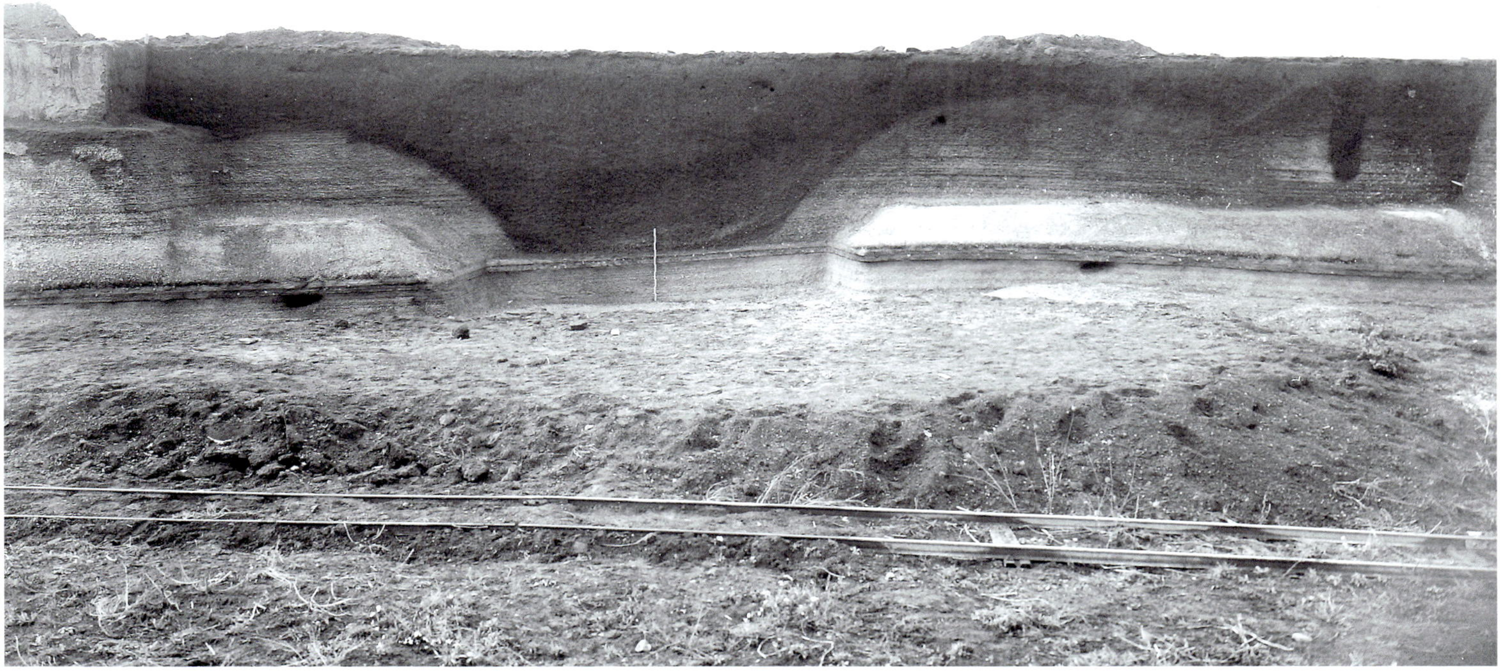

Fig. 7
Urmitz, Mayen-Koblenz distr. Cross-section of a pumice mine with the sole ditch and palisades of the Michelsberg period earthwork. (GDKE/Landes-archäologie/Landesmuseum Bonn)

Late Neolithic

It seems that the tradition of the Michelsberg Culture in Rhineland-Palatinate is interrupted at the end of the Younger Neolithic. Late Neolithic finds from the time around 3,500–2,800 BC are rarer than those from the older epochs of the Neolithic; the sites are reduced to only a few spots, which are also hard to trace archaeologically due to the highly undifferentiated material of the finds. It is not clear yet which factors produced this situation. Climate changes, caused by lower solar activity with a marked deterioration in the climate and the conflicts resulting therefrom, as well as economic shortages, led to migrations into other regions. The dramatic drop in the density of sites stretches from the Rhineland to the Upper Rhine Graben. It seems that Rhineland-Palatinate at that time was situated between the big cultural spheres of the Funnel Beaker Culture in the north, the Seine-Oise-Marne Culture in the west, and the Wartberg Culture in the east, the influences of which touched our region.

Alongside a few small-sized farmsteads with individual, mostly pit-houses, some burial sites (usually with collective graves) are also known. The economy is reduced mainly to animal husbandry in a possibly half-nomadic way of life. Because of the new climatic conditions, the landscape changes more and more to open grassland with thin oak forests.

Fig. 8
Mayen, Mayen-Koblenz distr. Outline plan of the Michelsberg earthwork with the typical ditch segments and passages of these multifunctional large buildings. (GDKE/Landesarchäologie/Koblenz/J. Eckert)

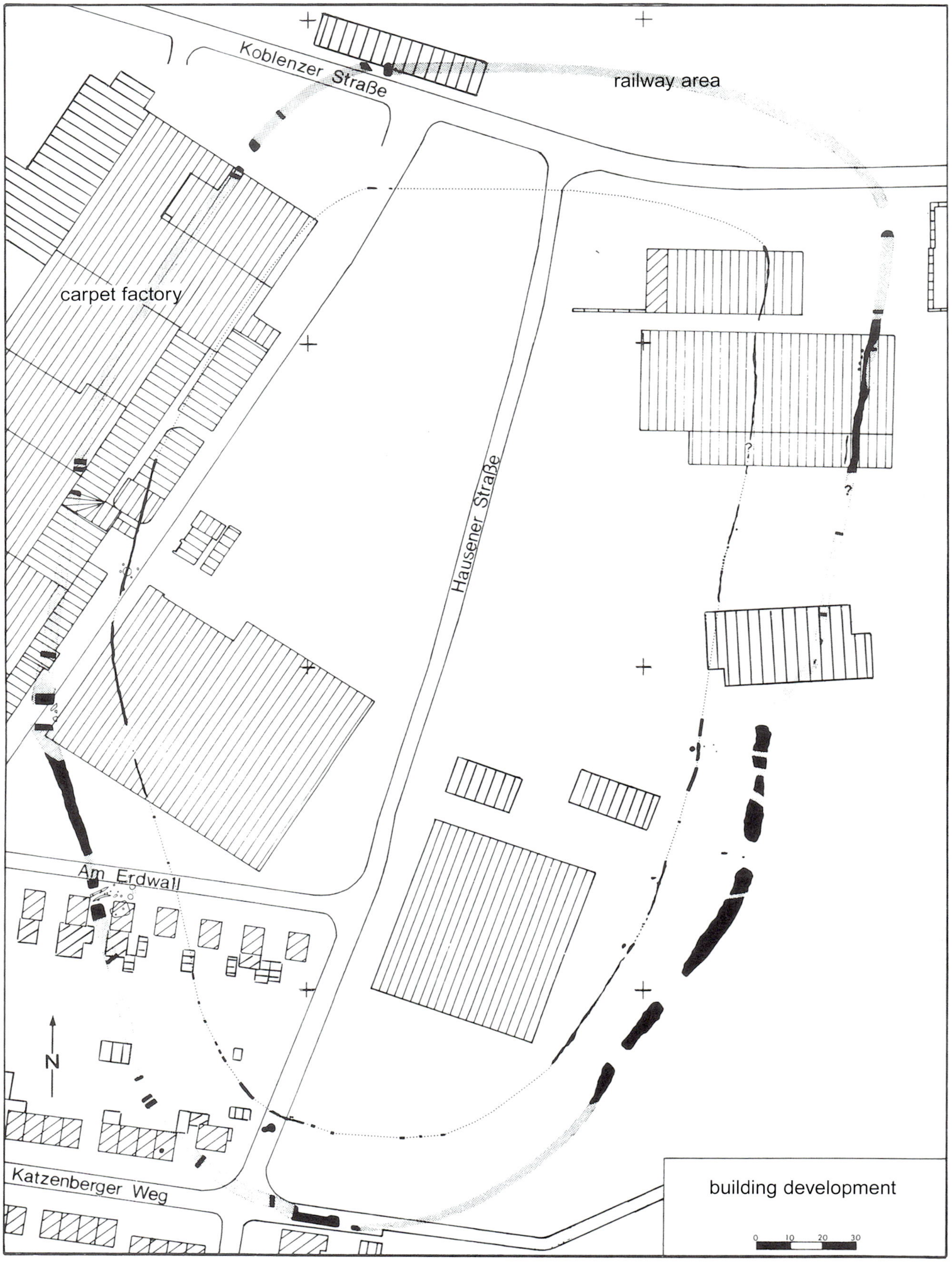

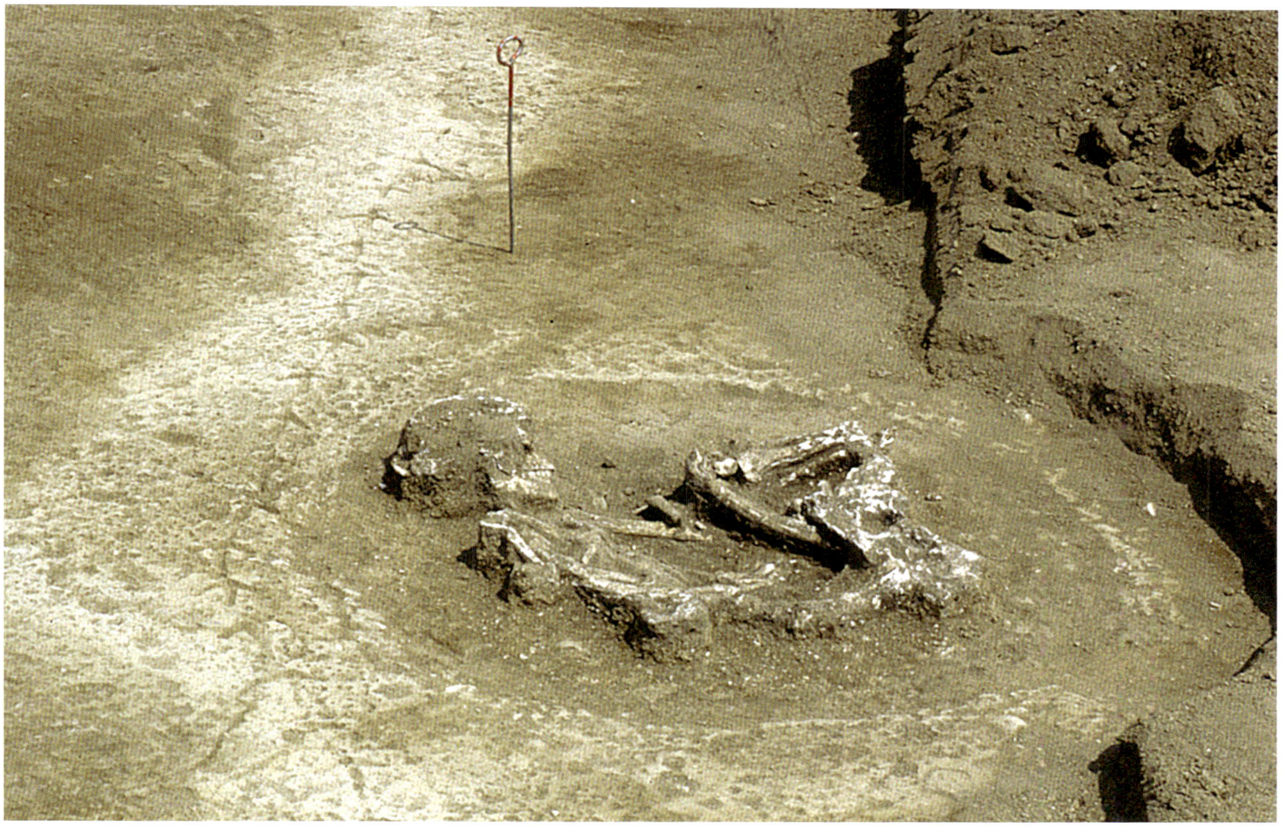

Fig. 9
Mertloch, Mayen-Koblenz. distr. Crouched burial of the end Neolithic. (GDKE/Landesarchäologie/Koblenz/F. Gebert)

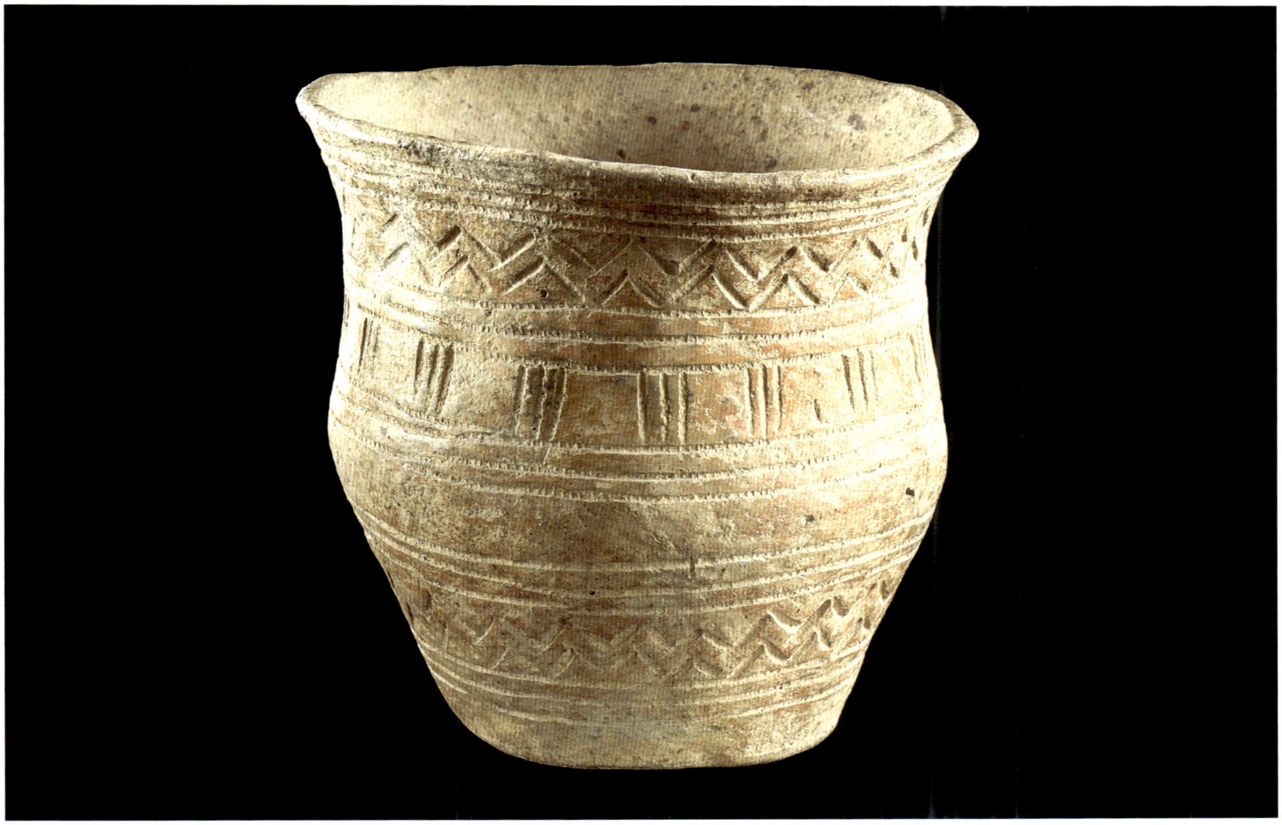

Fig. 10
Andernach, Mayen-Koblenz distr. Bell beaker decorated with lines and strokes and the characteristic S-shaped profile. (GDKE/Landesarchäologie/Koblenz/W. Baumann, Höhr-Grenzhausen)

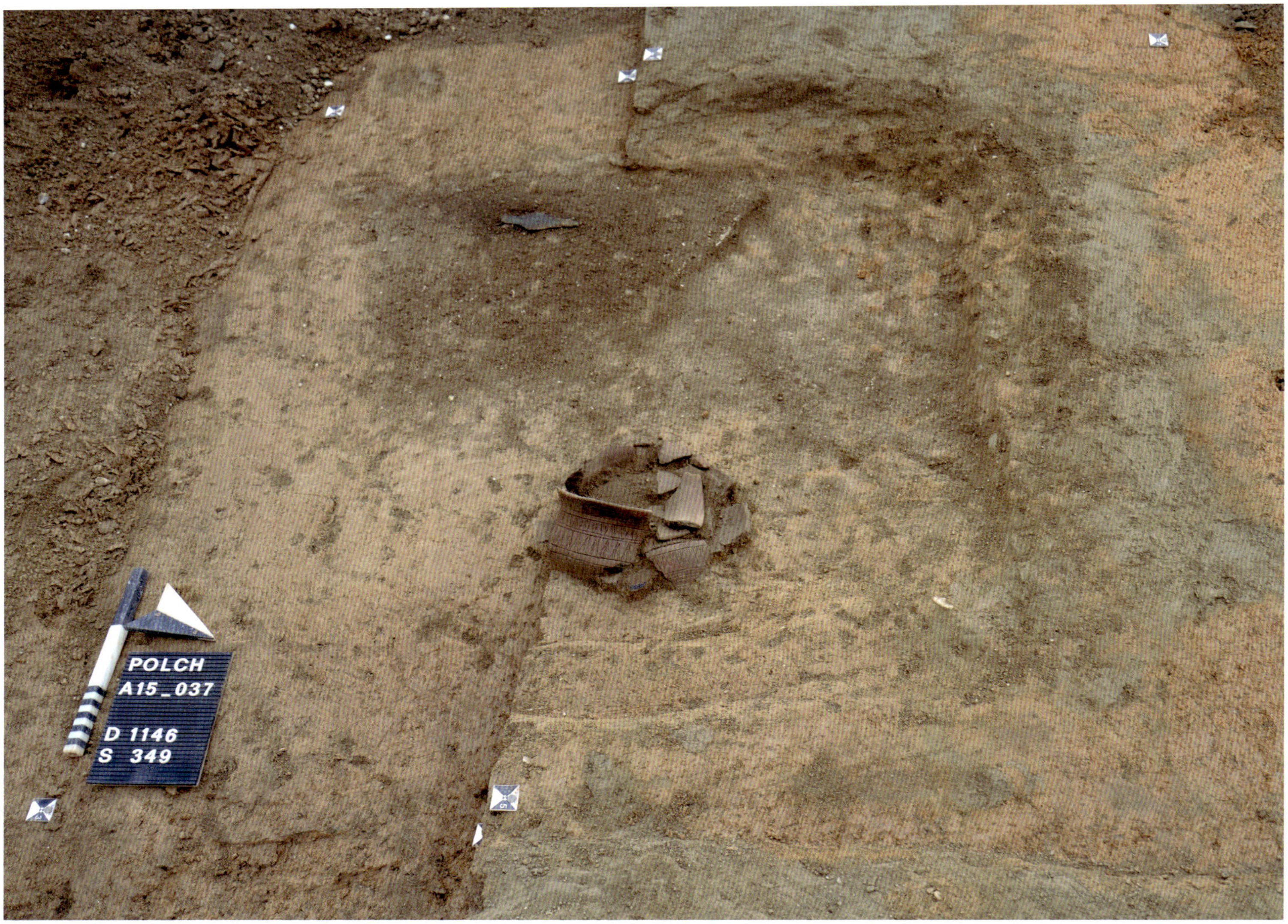

Fig. 11
Polch, Mayen-Koblenz distr. Burial of bell beaker culture in a square grave pit with richly decorated beaker and copper dagger. (GDKE/Landesarchäologie/Koblenz/M. Gensty)

End Neolithic – Corded ware and bell beakers

The youngest phase of the Neolithic (End Neolithic) is characterized by the so-called Beaker Cultures (2,800–2,100 BC). Rhineland-Palatinate is considered as a mixed area between the Corded Ware Culture from the northeast and the Bell Beaker Culture which originated in the west. Around 2,000/1,800 BC, the end phase of the Neolithic continuously develops into the Bronze Age. Except for a few settlement findings, the End Neolithic is mainly known from grave finds. While collective burials are normal for the Later and Late Neolithic, individual burial becomes typical for the End Neolithic. In addition, for the first time rich graves are vaulted by round burial mounds. Along with single cremation burials, the dead are buried in a crouched position and provided individually with grave goods. (Fig. 9) Bell beakers are characteristic for the pottery of this time, mainly appearing as grave goods. The beakers are typically decorated with circumferential cord impressions or stamped decorations. (Fig. 10) The use of the bow and arrow dominates at this time, and daggers made of flint or copper become a status symbol of the emerging warrior caste. (Fig. 11) Battle axes, ground from rock, are now prestige objects of a leading elite and show the further differentiation of society. The change in burial customs indicates that the individual had become more important than in previous times, when the group had priority. What is most striking is the large-scale inner-European distribution of »beaker cultures« with a lively cultural exchange. The older Corded Ware reaches from Poland to the Rhine, and the Bell Beaker Culture (starting around 2,400 BC) from the Iberian Peninsula to Hungary. The economic system continues to change: animal husbandry is more important than ever before, and settlements are established in an ever greater number of wet valleys and meadows. The elm and lime tree forests, which still dominated the Late Neolithic, developed into open oak woods with a very high hazel percentage during the End Neolithic. The change in vegetation into bright, open landscapes are not only due to climatic changes, but also to the transformation of the landscape by man. Large-scale slash-and-burn clearances to gain additional grazing areas required for cattle massively altered the landscape. Large rectangular enclosures, discovered time and again during excavations, indicate that sizable herds of livestock were kept. Remains of sheep, goats, and cattle dominate the spectrum of settlement debris. Horses acquire greater importance as riding animals at that time. According to the latest archaeological finds, the way of life of these people is based on small family groups. Few, simply constructed dwellings in small-scale settlement structures point towards a half-nomadic lifestyle. High quality shaped metal forms, which one comes across occasionally, testify to a developed knowledge of metal processing for certain regions or an integration in trans-regional trade routes. The social and ethnic structures are the basis for the later Bronze Age society. The local formation of groups, which can now be noted in the whole region, will remain characteristic for the subsequent prehistoric epochs.

Bibliography

A. von Berg, H.-H. Wegner, Jäger, Bauern, Keltenfürsten. 50 Jahre Archäologie an Mittelrhein und Mosel. Archäologie an Mittelrhein und Mosel 13 (Koblenz 2001).

H. Benecke, Der Mensch und seine Haustiere. Die Geschichte einer jahrtausendealten Beziehung (Stuttgart 1994).

U. Boelicke, Das neolithische Erdwerk Urmitz. Acta Praehist. 7–8, 1976–1977, 73ff.

M. Dorn-Ihmig, Untersuchungen zur Bandkeramik im Rheinland. Rhein. Ausgrabungen 15,1 Beitr. z. Urgeschichte im Rheinland I (1974) 51 ff.

J. Eckert, Das Michelsberger Erdwerk von Mayen. Ber. z. Archäologie an Mittelrhein und Mosel, Bd. 3, Beih. Trier Zeitschr. 14 (1992).

L. Fiedler, Formen und Techniken neolithischer Steingeräte aus dem Rheinland. Rhein. Ausgrabungen 19, Beitr. z. Urgeschichte des Rheinlandes 3 (1979) 53 ff.

A. Jürgens, Jungsteinzeit. In: H.-H. Wegner, (Hg.), Berichte z. Archäologie an Mittelrhein und Mosel 1, Beih. Trierer Zeitschr. 9 (1987) 31 ff.

W. Gebers, Endneolithikum und Frühbronzezeit im Mittelrheingebiet. Saarbrücker Beiträge zur Altertumskunde Bd. 27 u. 28 (Saarbrücken 1984).

A.J. Kahlis, J. Meuerers-Balke, Landnutzung im Neolithikum. In: J. Richter, E. Claßen, Geschichtlicher Atlas der Rheinlande. Beih. II/2.2 (Köln 1997) 25ff.

H. Löhr, Eine Übersichtskarte zum älteren Neolithikum im Moselgebiet. Archäologisches Korrespondenzblatt 16, 1986, 267 ff.

J. Lüning, Siedlung und Siedlungslandschaft in bandkeramischer und Rössener Zeit. Offa 39, 1982, 9 ff.

Th. Otten (Hg.), Revolution Jungsteinzeit. Archäologische Landesausstellung Nordrhein-Westfalen. Schriften zur Bodendenkmalpflege in Nordrhein-Westfalen 11, 1 (Darmstadt 2015).

J. Lüning, Die Michelsberger Kultur. Ihre Funde in zeitlicher und räumlicher Gliederung. Ber. RGK 48 (Frankfurt 1967) 1 ff.

F. Sirocko (Hg.), Wetter, Klima, Menschheitsentwicklung. Von der Eiszeit bis ins 21. Jahrhundert (Stuttgart 2009).

B. Weninger, E. Alram-Stern, E. Bauer, L. Clare, U. Danzeglocke, O. Jöris, C. Kubatzki, G. Rollefson, H. Todrova, Die Neolithisierung von Südosteuropa als Folge des abrupten Klimawandels um 8.200 CAL BP. In: D. Gronenborn (Hg.) Klimaveränderung und Kulturwandel in neolithischen Gesellschaften Europas, 6.700–2200 v. Chr. RGZM-Tagungen, Band 1 (Mainz 2005) 75 ff.

A. Zimmermann, J. Meureres-Balke, A. J. Kahlis, Das Neolithikum. In: J. Kunow, H.-H. Wegner (Hg.), Urgeschichte im Rheinland (Köln 2006) 159 ff.

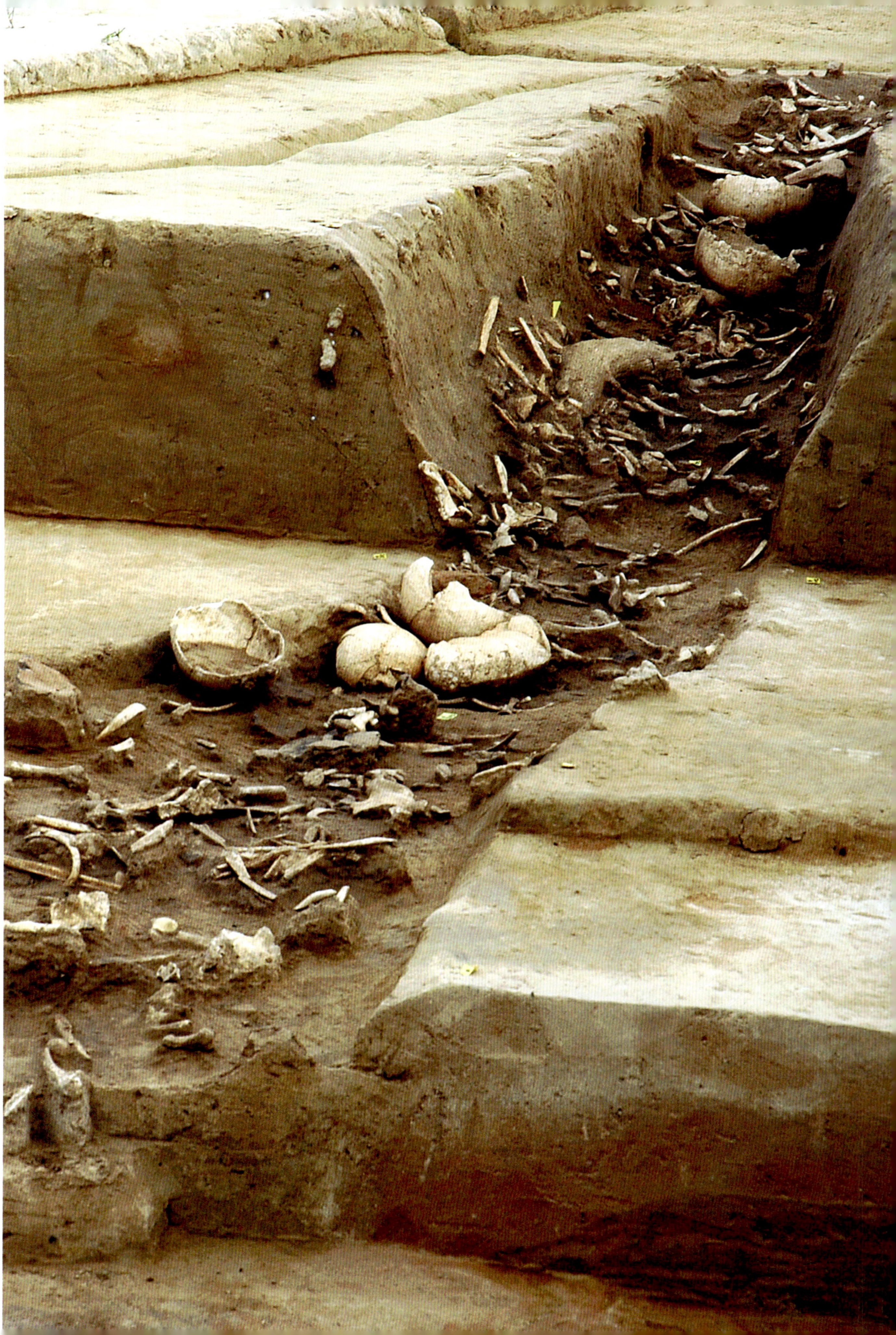

Fig. 1
Herxheim, Südliche Weinstraße distr. This large find concentration is an example of the composition of finds of human and animal bones as well as pottery fragments and stone tools. (GDKE/Landesarchäologie/Speyer/F. Haack)

Herxheim – a unique ritual place

ANDREA ZEEB-LANZ

During rescue excavations in the 1990s at the western edge of the village of Herxheim, Südliche Weinstraße district, the remains of a settlement of the Linearbandkeramik Culture (ca. 5,600–4,950 BC) were uncovered. While the traces of the settlement were rather unspectacular, the finds from the double ditch enclosing the Stone Age village were quite sensational: the remains of more than 500 individuals, who had apparently been ritually sacrificed, were found in major find concentrations in the ditches. (Fig. 1) After their violent death, the victims had been systematically cut up and de-fleshed. Then the actors of the bizarre ritual had meticulously smashed the cleaned bones into small fragments. The skulls received a special treatment: after removing the scalp and cleaning the skull of all soft tissue, the facial bones and the basis of the skull were chipped off by well-aimed blows with stone adzes, leaving intact only the skull cap, the so-called calotte.

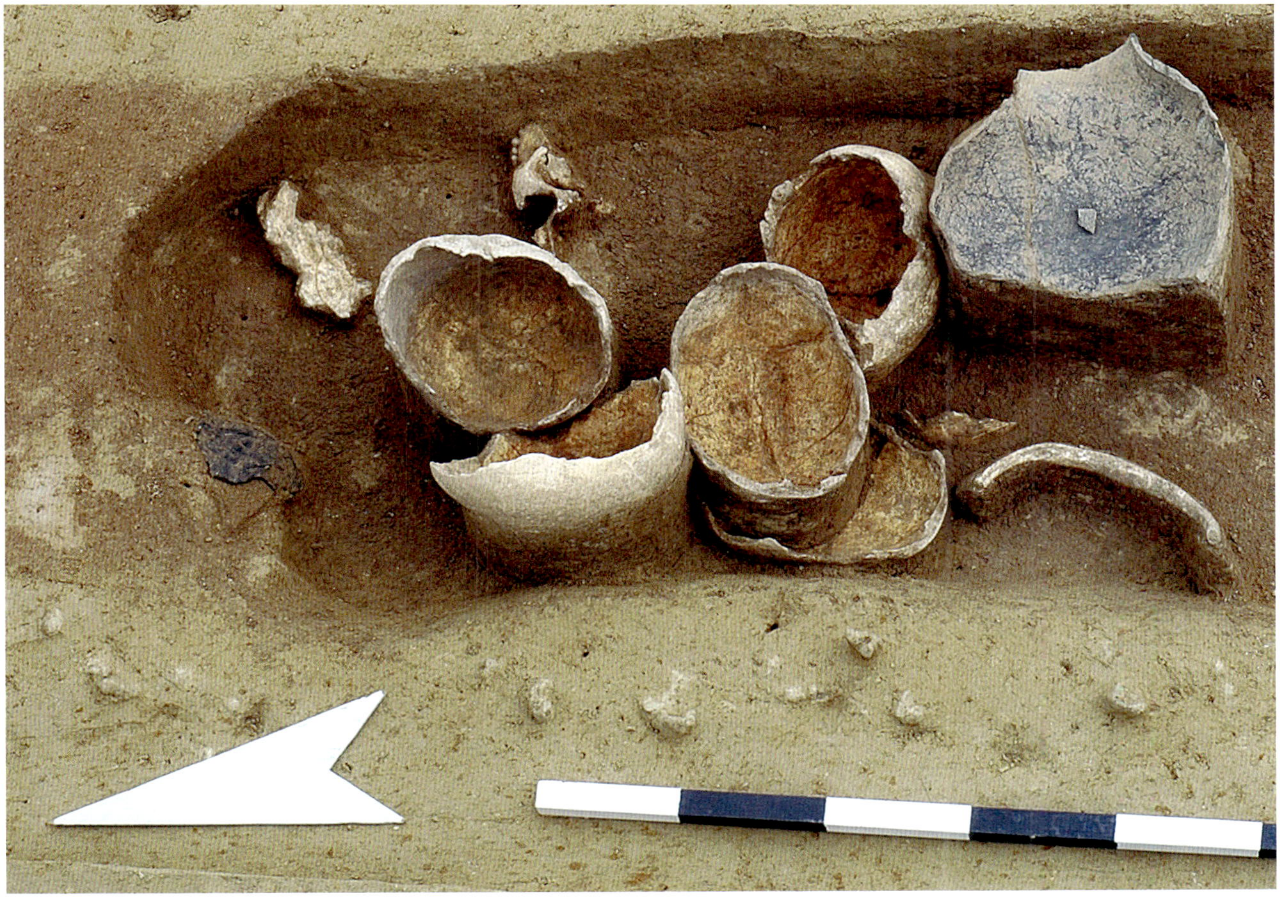

Fig. 2
Herxheim, Südliche Weinstraße distr. Concentration of human skull calottes in the inner ditch around the settlement; on the right side: a large fragment of a ceramic vessel. (GDKE/Landesarchäologie/Speyer/F. Haack)

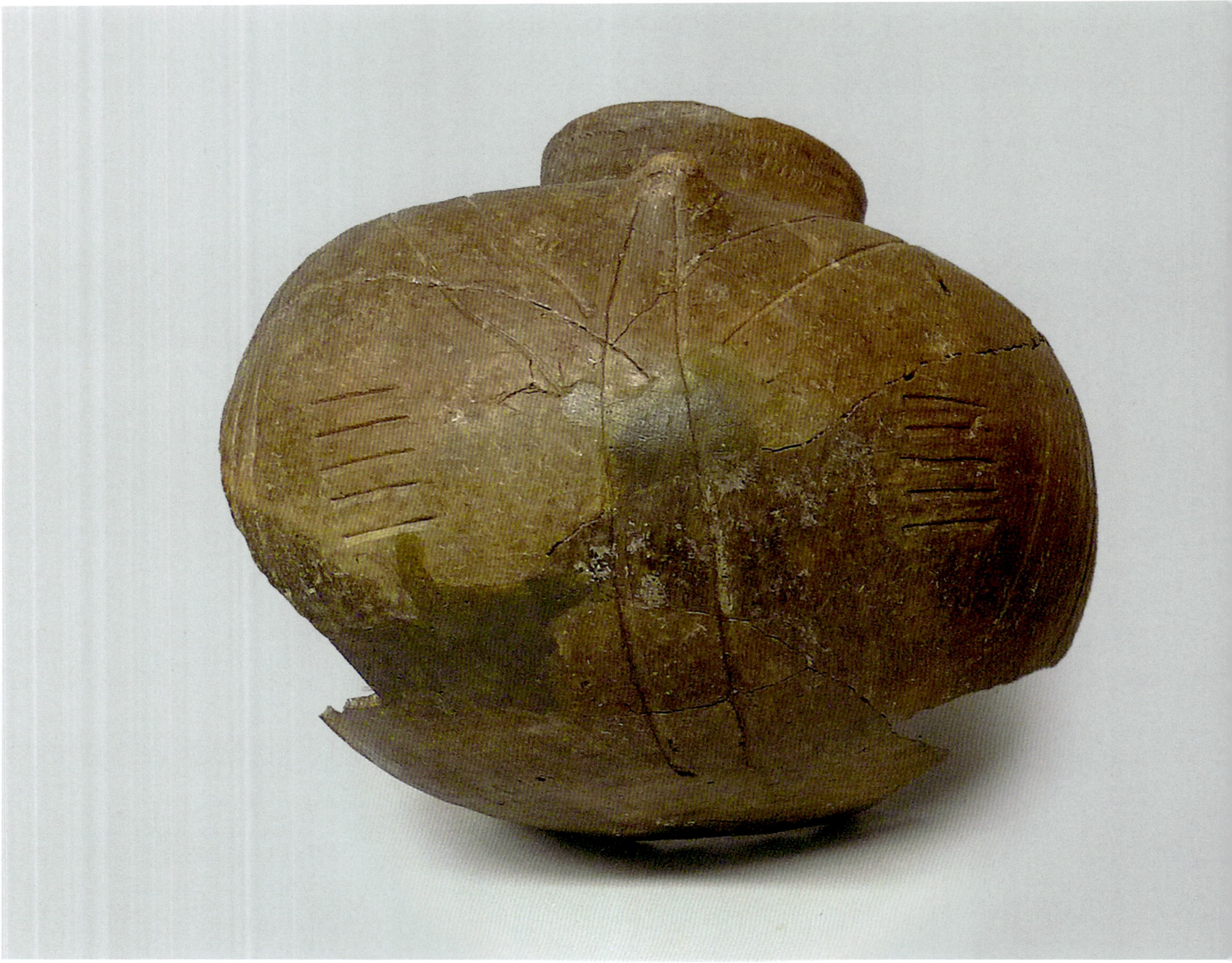

Some of these more than 400 calottes were found in nest-like arrangements. (Fig. 2) Except for these intentional settings, the bone fragments along with other finds had seemingly been thrown into the ditches randomly. The human finds have to be considered as ritual waste that also contained intentionally destroyed pottery, smashed stone adzes and flint tools as well as many shattered grinding stones.

Thus, the destruction of precious goods runs like a golden thread through the ritual events in Herxheim. Perhaps, ritual meals were held here – after the ceremonies, the entire ritual accessories would have been destroyed and disposed of in the ditches around the settlement together with the human bones. There are good arguments for the hypothesis that the flesh and marrow of the sacrificed individuals was consumed during the ritual; prehistoric cannibalism can, however, hardly be proven, so that the idea of a ritual sacrifice and processing of the individuals without their being eaten cannot be dismissed.

The decorated pottery is of the highest quality (Fig. 3) and originates from a variety of settlement regions of the Linearbandkeramik, some as far away as Bohemia. No other site of this culture shows such a large number of non-local vessels.

The identity of the dead is just as much of an enigma as the rituals. Strontium isotope analyses show that 90 % of the dead were not from Herxheim or the

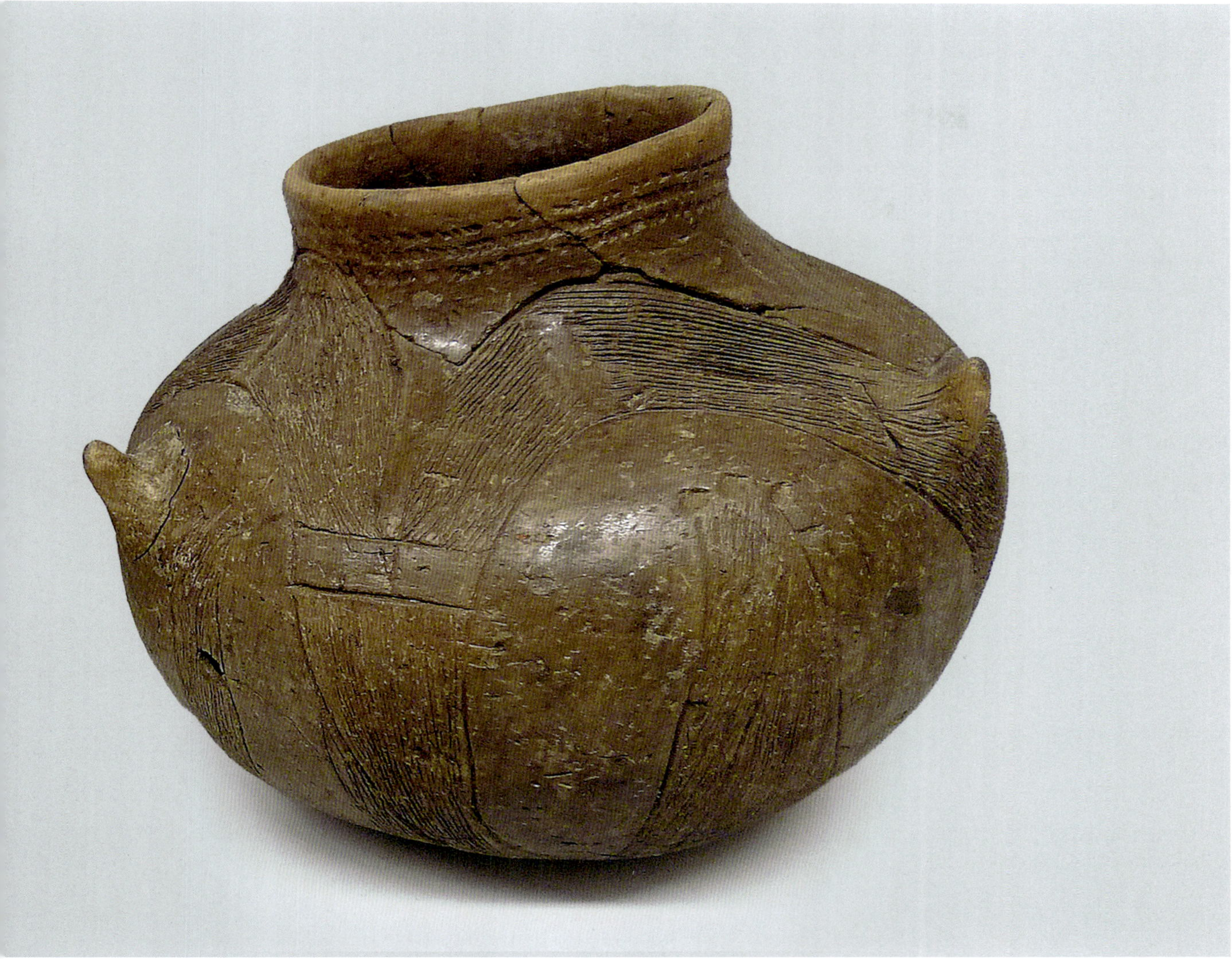

Fig. 3
Herxheim, Südliche Weinstraße distr. Two well-preserved examples of the magnificent pottery from the find concentrations. On the right side: a vessel with the hatching style of the Rhine-Main area; the vessel on the left side cannot be assigned to any regional Bandkeramik style. (GDKE/Landesarchäologie/Speyer/F. Haack)

near vicinity, but were born and raised in the higher realms of low mountain ranges. These must have been mountains with granite or gneiss bedrock, such as the Black Forest, Vosges, Harz or Taunus. Yet, to date no signs of Linearbandkeramik settlements were found in higher mountain areas anywhere in Central Europe. Analyses of mitochondrial DNA of the dead contradict the strontium isotope values, since the sampled individuals all possess the DNA typical for Linearbandkeramik people. This fundamental riddle in the scientific results has not been solved so far, and we do not yet know who the dead of Herxheim are.

Bibliography

A. **Zeeb-Lanz**, Gewaltszenarien oder Sinnkrise? Die Grubenanlage von Herxheim und das Ende der Bandkeramik. In: A. Zeeb-Lanz (Hg.), Krisen – Kulturwandel – Kontinuitäten. Zum Ende der Bandkeramik in Mitteleuropa. Beiträge der internationalen Tagung in Herxheim bei Landau (Pfalz) vom 14.–17.06.2007. Internationale Archäologie. Arbeitskreis, Tagung, Symposium, Kongress Bd. 10 (Rahden/Westf. 2009) 87–102.

A. **Zeeb-Lanz, F. Haack, S. Bauer**, Menschenopfer – Zerstörungsrituale mit Kannibalismus – Schädelkult: Die außergewöhnliche bandkeramische Anlage von Herxheim in der Südpfalz. Mitteilungen des Historischen Vereins der Pfalz 111, 2013, 5–53.

A. **Zeeb-Lanz (Hg.)**, Ritualised Destruction in the Early Neolithic – The Exceptional Site of Herxheim (Palatinate, Germany). Forschungen zur Pfälzischen Archäologie 8.1 (Speyer 2016).

THE BRONZE AGE

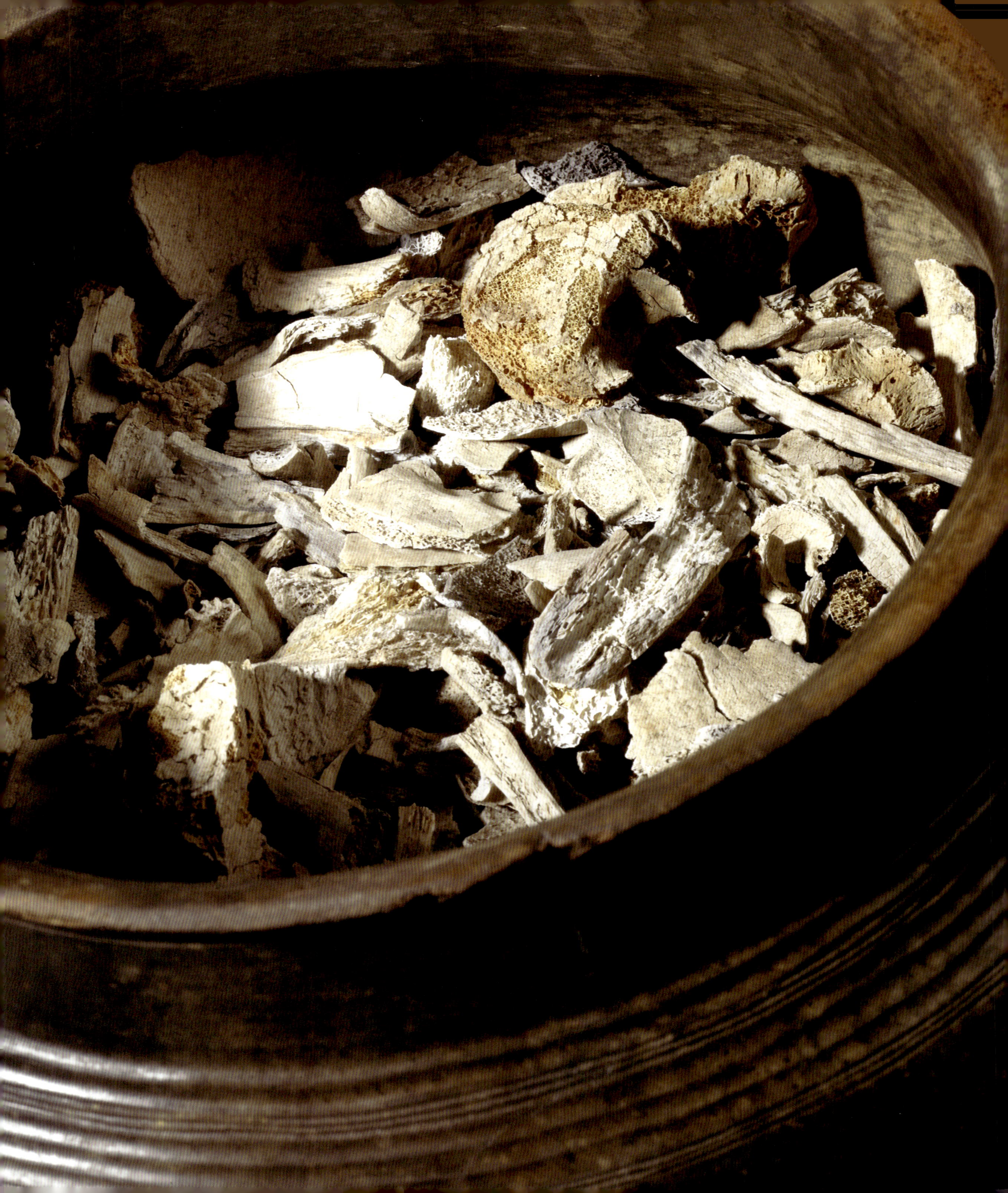

The Bronze Age and the Urnfield Period – Warriors, farmers, and bronze founders

AXEL VON BERG

The development from the Neolithic cultures with their regional features to the Bronze Age occurred gradually and continuously. Late Neolithic traditions remained in existence for a long period and characterized the cultural development of that epoch over several centuries. A clear north-south divide can be detected in Rhineland-Palatinate in this respect: while the southern parts of the state are influenced early on by the south-German/Alsatian Bronze Age groups, the north of Rhineland-Palatinate still persists in end-Neolithic Beaker Culture traditions.

The Bronze Age, as a cultural stage in itself, is divided into the Early Bronze Age and the Middle Bronze Age, also known as the Tumulus Bronze Age (with burials under grave mounds). The Bronze Age is a relatively short period of some 1200 years. The Early Bronze Age starts between 2000 BC and 1800 BC and leads on continuously to the Middle Bronze Age at around 1500 BC. This is then followed around 1200/1100 BC by the Late Bronze Age and the Urnfield Period, ending at around 800/750 BC.

The search for suitable raw materials and their targeted excavation and use already played an increasingly important role during the Neolithic period. Flint deposits were exploited in central mining areas and the silex produced was traded over wide areas. Knowledge about the respective deposit sites was vital for extracting the metal and for processing the ore at some later time. As early as the late Neolithic, copper was processed into weapons, implements, and jewellery, and traded over wide distances. The new material »bronze«, as an alloy of copper and tin, gained varying acceptance according to region, and the traditional raw material, i.e. stone, was still used in the production of tools throughout the entire Bronze Age. With bronze-processing as an indicator of the new age, new sources of raw materials had to be found and new inter-European trade relations were established. Goods such as salt and amber, and especially products from metalworking, became part of the long-distance trade, which in turn promoted cultural exchanges between the north and the south. Because of its geographical position between the main cultural spheres of the north and the south, Rhineland-Palatinate plays a key role in this respect. The decisive element was the course of the Rhine, which favoured cultural transfer between the north and the south along its banks and the surrounding hills and plateaus. As had been the case in the Neolithization process, the knowledge of metal processing spread from the Near East to northern Europe. Only pure copper was used at first; later, copper was alloyed with tin, lead, antimony, and arsenic, and eventually the char-

Ochtendung, Mayen-Koblenz distr. Ceramic urn with cremation burials of the late Urnfield period (9th century BC). The thin-walled vessel was very carefully formed by hand and to imitate metal vessels. (GDKE/Landesarchäologie/Koblenz/W. Baumann, Höhr-Grenzhausen)

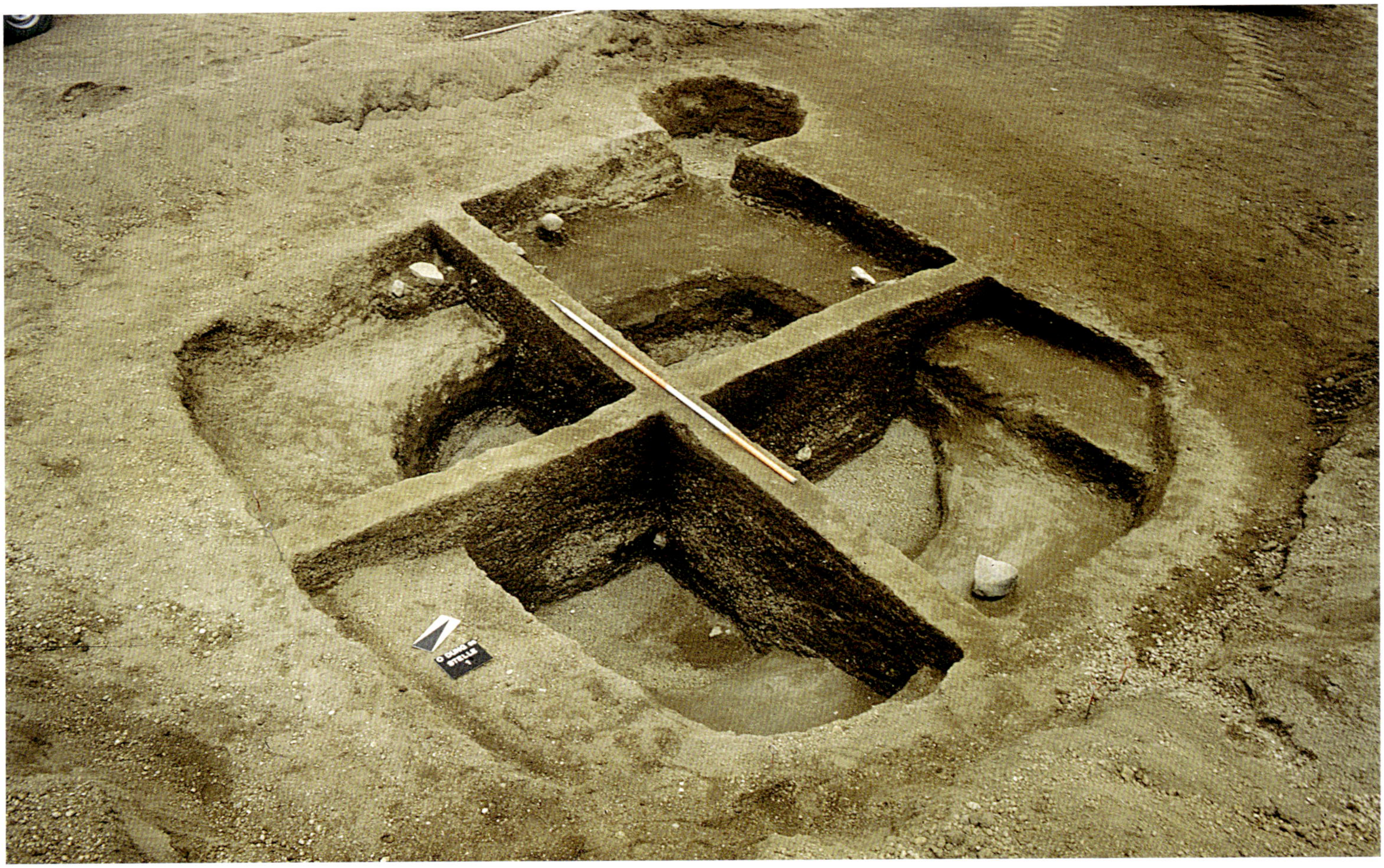

Fig. 1 Ochtendung, Mayen-Koblenz distr. Excavation finding of a pit house of the Early Bronze Age with the baulks not yet removed. (GDKE/ Landesarchäologie/ Koblenz/F. Gebert)

acteristic mixture of bronze with 70–90 % copper and 10–13 % tin (for casting alloys) was developed. Casting was done in moulds of one or more sections, in which tools, weapons, and jewellery were produced. Until the start of the Middle Bronze Age at around 1500 BC, more and more economic and technical innovations and an ever more specialized society developed in an environment characterized by animal husbandry.

Early Bronze Age

In Rhineland-Palatinate, the Early Bronze Age starts 2000 BC approx. and lasts until 500 BC approx., with the transitions being fluid and very different from region to region. While around 1800 BC the Palatinate is already a part of the South-German Early Bronze Age »Adlerberg Culture«, the north of Rhineland-Palatinate, as a peripheral area of the classic Early Bronze Age cultures, still belongs to the end-Neolithic beaker cultures with their marked regional features. Both the bell beaker and corded ware groups as well as the Nordic-influenced giant beaker groups continue as regionally splintered groupings and develop special forms during the Early Bronze Age which have eluded archaeologists so far. The Adlerberg group in the south, characterized by its tradition of crouched inhumation, only reached parts of the Rhineland and the Trier area and had little influence. Even though the development of the Early Bronze Age in the Rhineland is not clear, one can at least say that for the Saar-Moselle area some influences from the end-Neolithic »Single grave culture« and the »Bell beaker culture« continue until the end of the Early Bronze Age at around 1600 BC, and that only a few pieces imported from the south and the east have survived.

Whilst the south of Rhineland-Palatinate is defined by flat graves with standardized grave goods, being mostly crouched burials with bronze and ceramic goods according to the south-German pattern, it is far more difficult to determine the burial custom in northern Rhineland-Palatinate. Both cremation and inhumation graves have been found occasionally, with the equipment of beaker-like vessels and stone tools still following Neolithic models. The evident north-south divide is indeed characteristic of the entire Bronze Age.

The settlements are small and consist of a few pithouses. The hastily erected buildings seem to indicate itinerant farmers or semi-nomadic cattle breeders. The huts, which were often repaired and modified, could mean that the individual settlement spots were revisited at regular intervals and newly settled. The huts are small, with a square rectangular ground plan of usually 4 m × 3 m. (Fig. 1) The floors of the huts are generally sunken into the ground, and the wall and roof constructions are simple with few posts and poles. Bones of sheep, goats, and a few types of cattle are evidence that livestock breeding predominated, with the cultivation of grain having been somewhat secondary. As a rule, a settlement of that time consists of three to four staggered huts, mostly on ridges and heights. Long ditch works in the immediate vicinity of the settlements indicate fences and livestock pens for animal husbandry.

The Middle Bronze Age (Tumulus Bronze Age)

The Middle Bronze Age or Tumulus Bronze Age starts 1500 BC approx. and ends 1200 BC approx. with the dawn of the Late Bronze Age, which leads on to the Urnfield Period. The start of the Middle Bronze Age is specifically marked by changes in burial traditions, with a clear divide in this case as well.

The dead are now buried generally in a stretched-back position with a uniform north-south orientation. The generic term for this epoch is »Hügelgräberzeit«, since the burials during this time are all vaulted with burial mounds (tumuli). (Fig. 2) In addition, the mounds, some of them huge, come with grave chambers, houses for the dead, and ring ditches. The dead buried there are now provided with weapons or bronze jewellery depending on their gender. While the south is characterized by graves with combinations of rich goods and period costumes, the graves of the north have only a few individual pieces. The goods include cloak pins, bronze daggers, and bronze axes.

The settlements are dominated by small farm areas with one-storey half-timbered dwellings, pithouses, and settlement pits. The buildings are small, and the settlement areas show only a few structures, which may be indicative of a way of life determined by mobility. The late Neolithic trend of remaining mobile instead of permanently settling continues. The specialisation was still animal husbandry, as was the case during earlier epochs, with cattle, sheep, and goat dominating. While the south is characterized by rich pottery sets with combinations of channelled and parallel incised lines as decoration, the ceramic of the north is often limited to simple forms, mostly high beakers following end-Neolithic traditions. Silex artefacts still determine the spectrum of tools in the settlements, with old Neolithic pieces being often reworked and reused.

Urnfield Period

With the dawn of the Late Bronze Age around 1200 BC, the entire cultural structure changes within just a short time. The following centuries are dominated by the Urnfield Period as a cultural stage in its own right, with a rich cultural heritage. As already indicated by the name of the epoch, the inhumation of the older Bronze Age is discontinued in favour of cremation. On the basis of stylistic similarities of pottery and also of metallic dress components, the finds are assigned to a bigger, western-oriented »Rhenish/Swiss/eastern French« group of finds, which also highlights the corresponding wide communication framework of that time. Diverse links to neighbouring regions and a lively exchange of goods are dominant features of this pan-European cultural epoch. Characteristic of the period are cremations and the burial of the remains in urns placed in larger grave fields. According to the current state of research, the Urnfield Period evolved continuously from the Tumulus Period of the Middle Bronze Age in Rhineland-Palatinate just as in other regions. It emerged around 1100 BC as a cultural development in its own right, based on fundamental changes in the

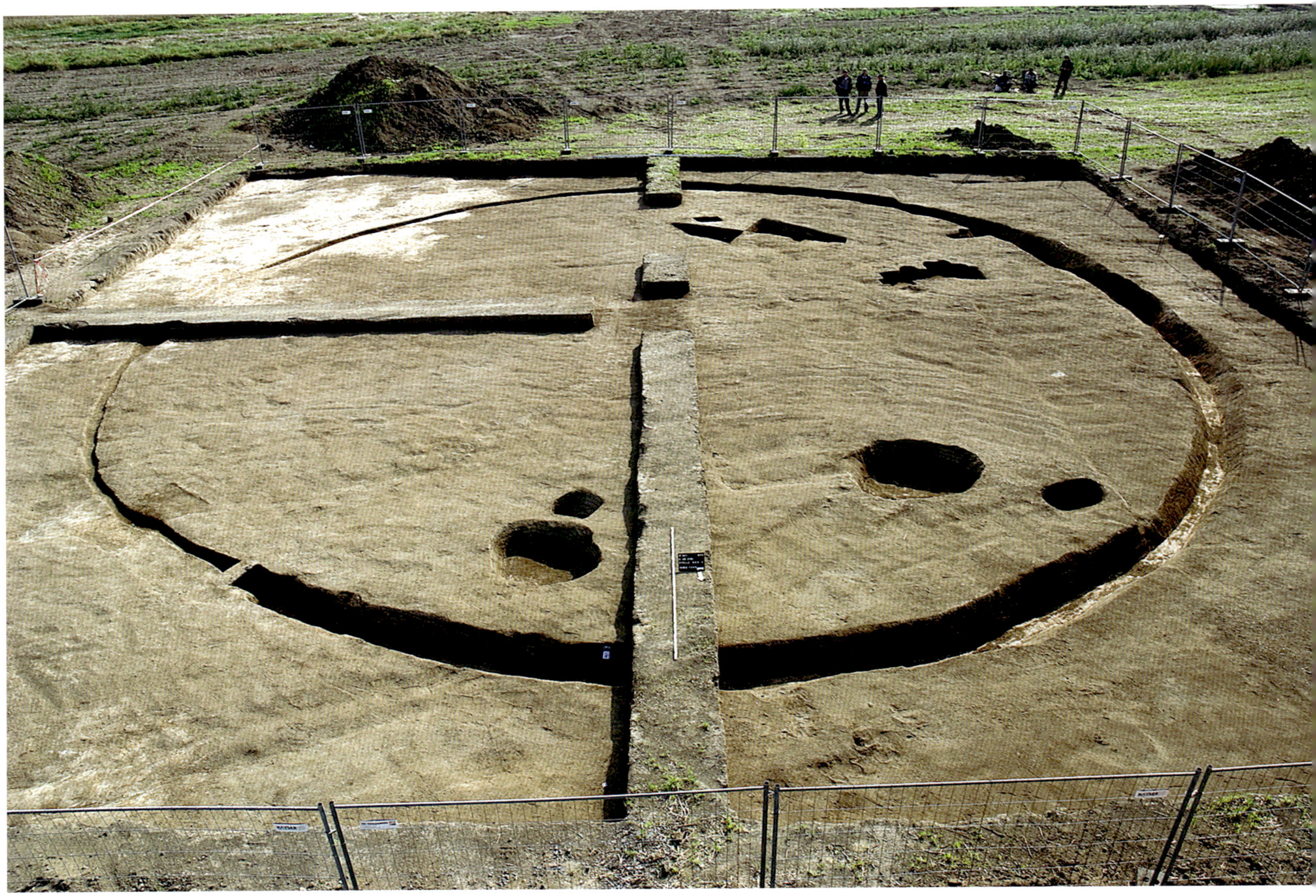

Fig. 2 Kobern-Gondorf, Mayen-Koblenz distr. Circular ditch and burial pits of a Bronze Age burial mound in excavation finding. (GDKE/Landesarchäologie/Koblenz/M. Neumann)

social system and on new spiritual and religious ideas. It ends at around 850/750 BC and leads steadily on to the Iron Age. The Urnfield Period shows a very uniform structure over several centuries, only to diversify again towards its end into regionally dissimilar groups. Different influences from neighbouring regions continue to be distinctive features. The north bears many characteristics from the Lower Rhine area and Westphalia; the Trier area absorbs western European influences; the eastern sites of the Main and the Hesse Lowlands have an impact on Rhine-Hesse; while the Palatinate is once again characterized by south-German influences.

The Urnfield Period belongs to those prehistoric epochs in Rhineland-Palatinate from which very many finds have been preserved, most coming from graves, but also from settlements and depositions. There was vibrant trade – even across the heights of the mid-range mountains – between the Middle Rhine Basin and Rhine-Hesse in the east, the Palatinate in the south, and the Trier area in the west, in spite of individual characteristics and relationships.

As important transport routes from the north to the south and the west, the river valleys of the Rhine and the Moselle were vital elements. With the beginning of the Early Iron Age in the 8th century BC and the slow development of early Celtic civilisations, the south gradually separates from the cultural development in the Middle Rhine Basin, Rhine-Hesse, and the Trier area,

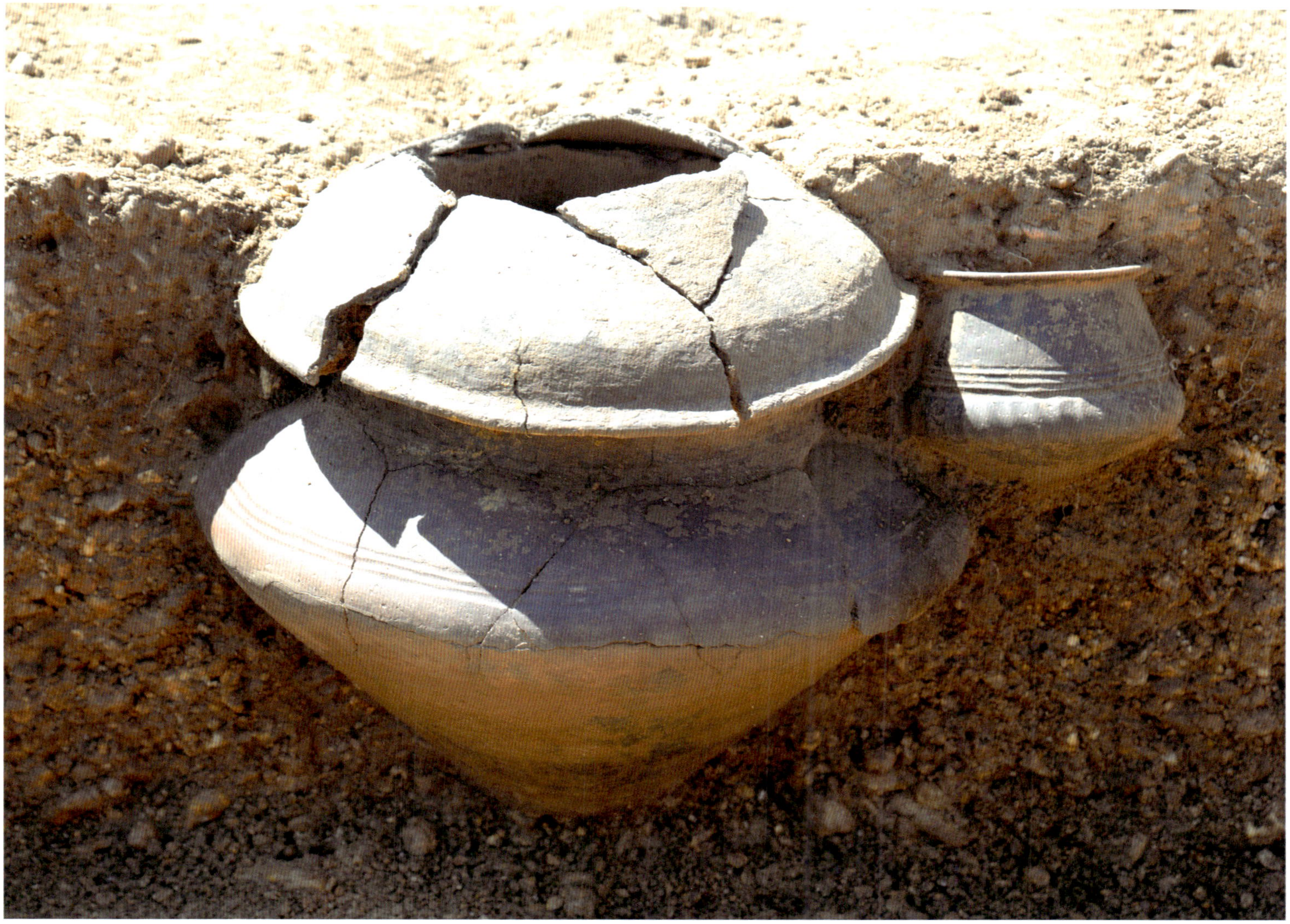

while the Palatinate opens up more and more to the influences from southern Germany and finds other orientations in the cultural structure of that time.

In mortuary practices, the single burial as a cremation grave becomes the norm. (Fig. 3) The graves of men and women can now no longer be distinguished directly by the grave goods and dress components because of significant changes in grave accoutrements. The combinations of grave goods during the Middle Bronze Age, with their clearly gender-specific objects, have disappeared almost completely.

Necropolises from that time were examined in large numbers in Rhineland-Palatinate, and the finds are rich. Characteristic forms of vessels found are conical bowls, bevelled bowls with folded walls, so-called »Schulterbecher«, and biconical cylinder-necked vessels. The shapes of these vessels are completely new and distinguish the »new era« by their form. Rich single burials in chambers with bronze weapons and gold jewellery stand out from the simple urn graves and announce the development of a noble class in Rhineland-Palatinate as well. Thanks to weaponry, the graves can be assigned to the Urnfield Period warrior graves known from the entire Urnfield Culture circle.

Both the pottery, with its typical variety of decoration, and the bronze items allow a further subdivision of the Urnfield Period into a late phase of its own. The appearance of pottery with combinations of chip-

Fig. 3
Polch, Mayen-Koblenz distr. Urn burial with shoulder beaker as grave good in excavation finding. (GDKE/Landesarchäologie/Koblenz/M. Gensty)

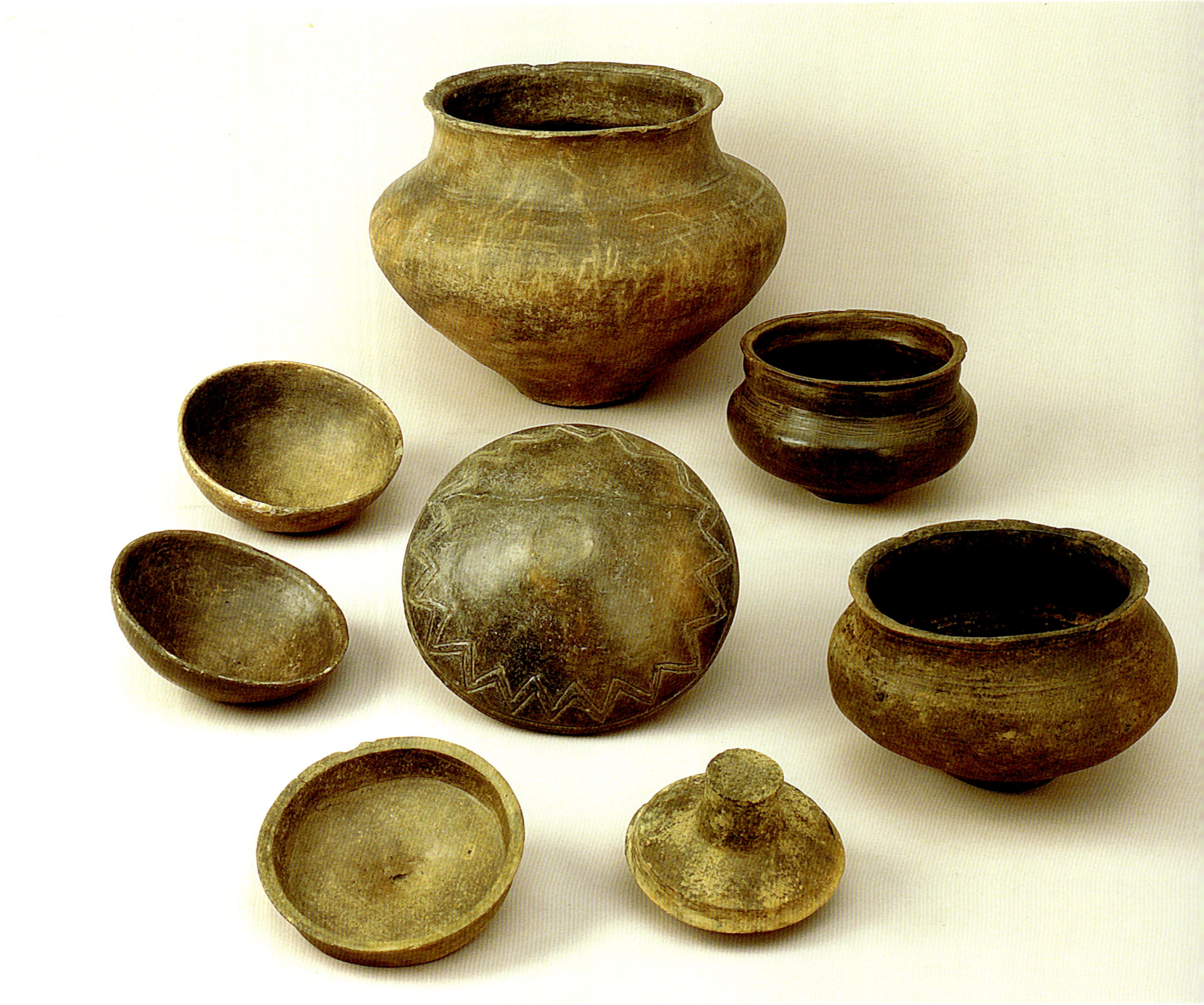

Fig. 4
Heddesdorf, city of Neuwied. Equipment of a late Urnfield culture cremation grave with a set of crockery. (GDKE/Landesarchäologie/Koblenz/ M. Neumann)

carved and parallel-incised lines as decoration leads on to the younger Urnfield complex. (Fig. 4) The transitions to the younger Urnfield Period are again fluent. In the north of Rhineland-Palatinate, the last Urnfield horizon leads to the early Iron Age »Laufelder Gruppe« that at first remains clearly within the Urnfield Period traditions. At that time, the south of Rhineland-Palatinate is increasingly influenced by the south-German early Hallstatt Period. In the late Urnfield Period, burial mounds in the old tradition, which are characteristic of the following Iron Age, are used in growing numbers once more. (Fig. 5)

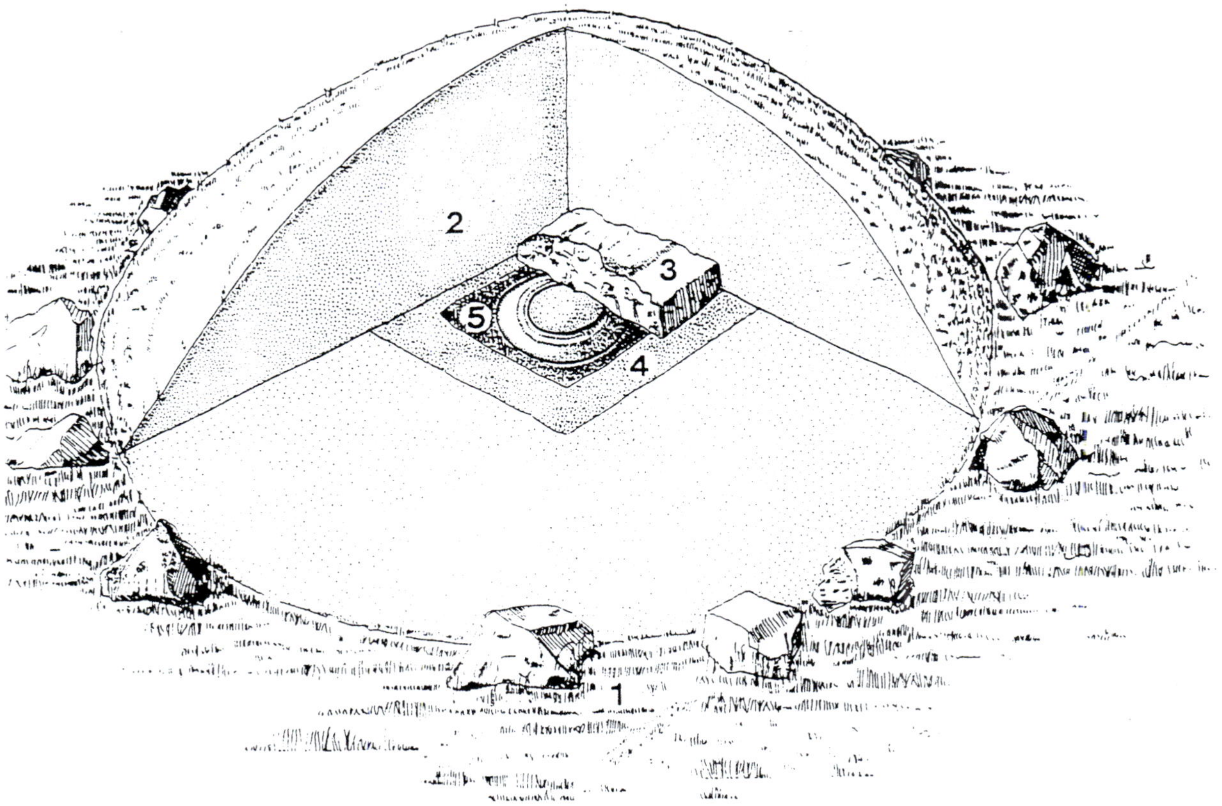

Fig. 5
Grave mound from the late Urnfield period with central cremation burial, reconstructed according to excavation findings.
1. stone circle
2. mound
3. stone cover
4. grave pit
5. urn burial
(GDKE/Landesarchäologie/Koblenz)

Economy

Agriculture and animal husbandry were the economic bases of the Urnfield Period settlements. The many animal bones retrieved from pit fillings are evidence of the breeding of cattle, sheep, goats, and pigs. Bone remains of horses, used for riding or as draught animals, are also known. Loom weights and numerous spindle whorls show that textiles were manufactured in the settlements, and various hoards with blanks, ingots, and semi-finished products as well as tools for bronze working indicate differentiated metal crafts. (Fig. 6)

Ring ditches

Ring ditches are a specific category of monuments in Rhineland-Palatinate. Especially in the Middle Rhine Basin, in Rhine-Hesse, and in the Trier area, numerous ring and double ring systems were found with individual pits or shafts in the centre and often filled with fire debris. Other ring ditches show postholes and layouts of former buildings in the middle. The proximity of these systems to concentrations of settlements or necropolises is striking. It is possible that these ring ditches represent cult sites and served ritual purposes.

The image-bearing finds from the Urnfield Period provide interesting insights into basic ideas of the heavens and early astronomy, which were quite obviously oriented to the sun as the central element. The ring ditch system also documents the importance of the sun for the people of that time, since the openings were usually oriented to the rising or setting sun at the time of the winter or summer solstice.

Depositions

Besides ring ditches, depositions represent a further important source from that time. The storage finds

Fig. 6
Ochtendung, Mayen-Koblenz distr. Bronze socketed axes of the late Urnfield period from a hoard find. (GDKE/ Landesarchäologie/ Koblenz/W. Baumann, Höhr-Grenzhausen)

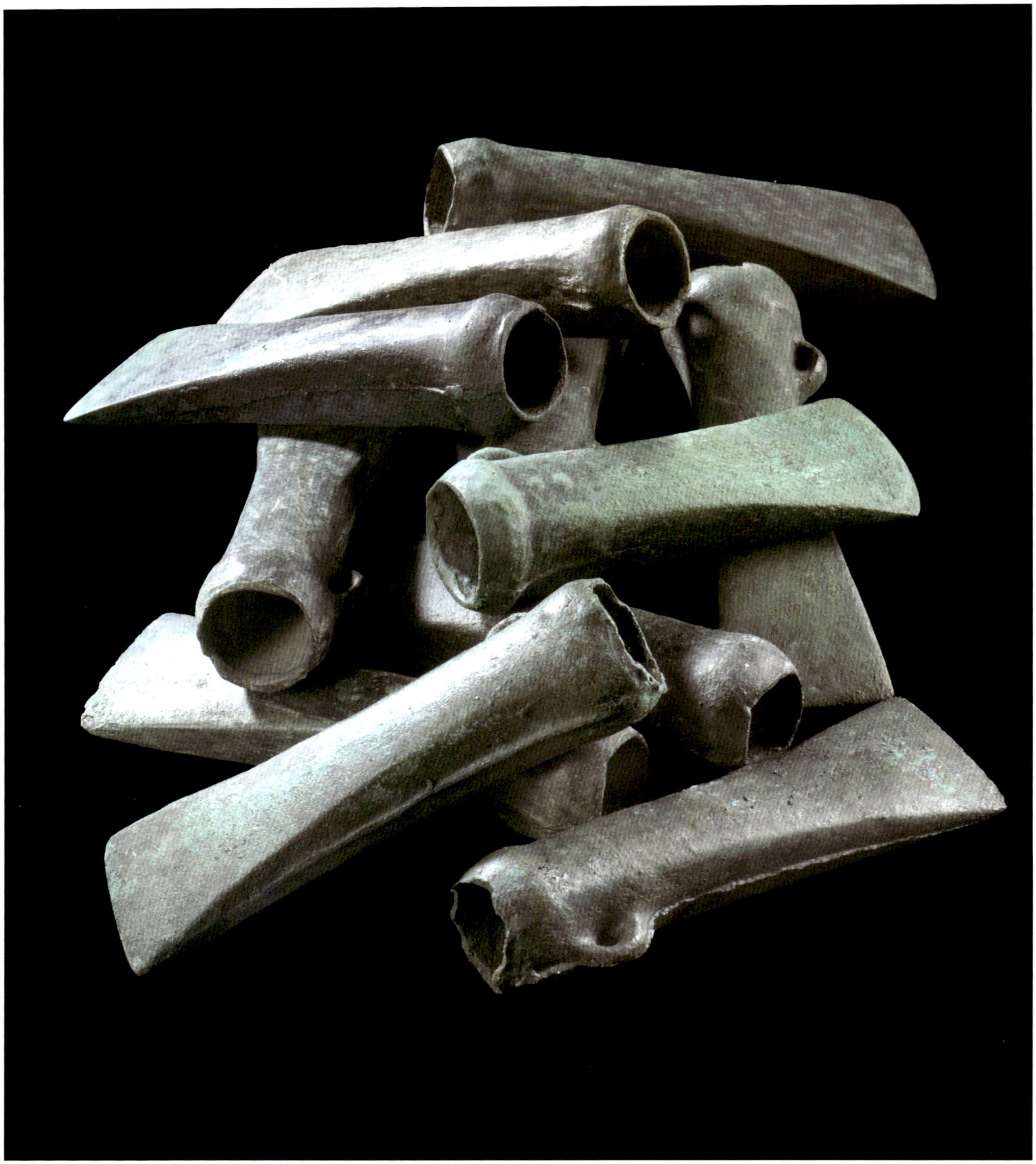

form the first group of depositions. The selection of finds and the conditions under which the depositions were made point towards the safeguarding of certain objects. Besides bronze appliances, metal ingots and semi-finished products were buried as well, indicating hoards made by artisans or merchants. (Fig. 7)

Another group are votive finds, deposited both in water and on land, mostly at selected spots. The con-

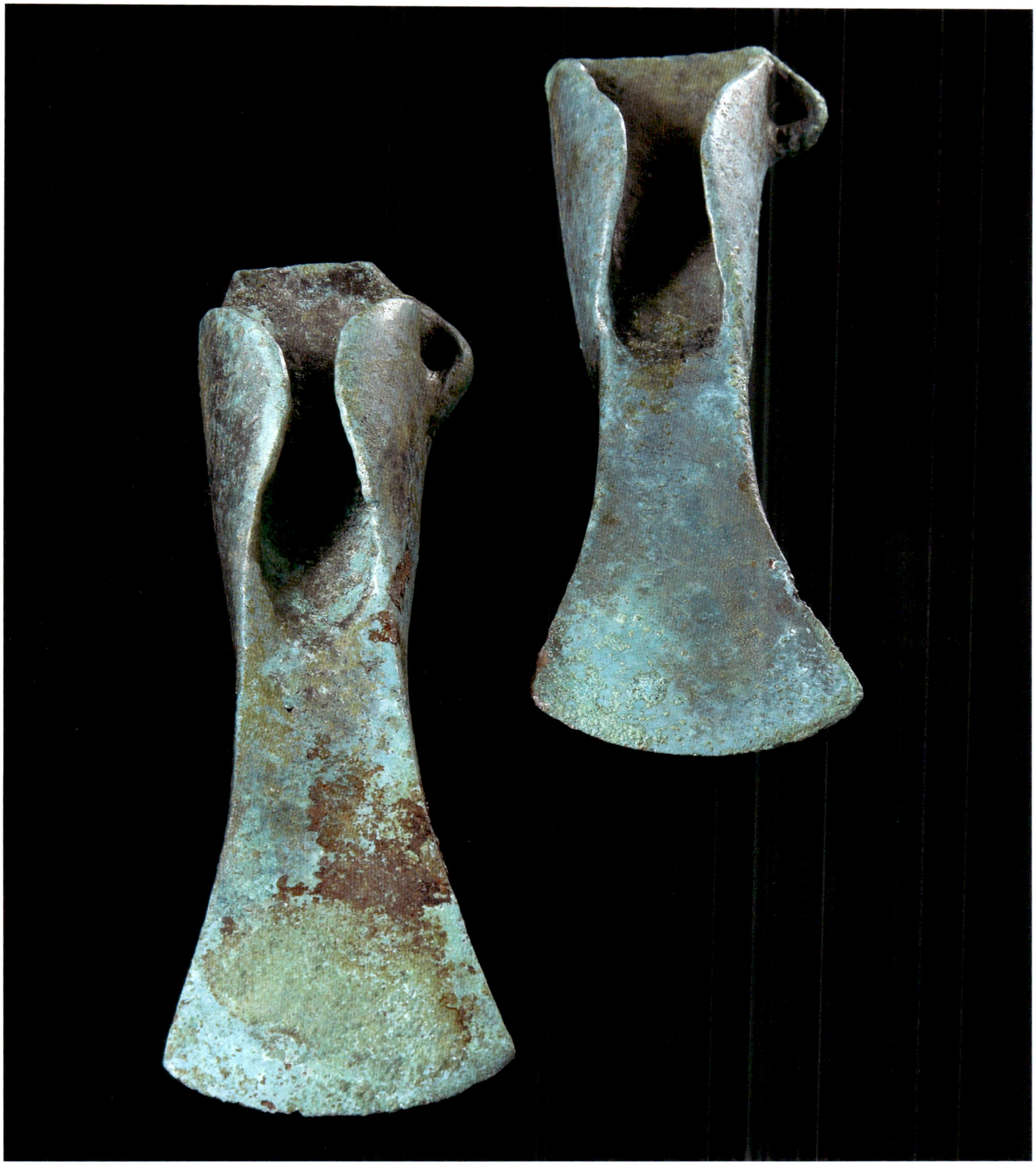

Fig. 7
Ochtendung, Mayen-Koblenz. distr. Bronze winged axes from a hoard find. (GDKE/Landesarchäologie/Koblenz/W. Baumann, Höhr-Grenzhausen)

secrate finds represent the majority of depositions and are generally found in wetlands and waterways. Many depositions were found at the mouths of rivers and near old fords along the major rivers. A ritual motive is generally considered to be the reason for these objects, as a form of equipping oneself for the afterlife, as offerings or votive gifts.

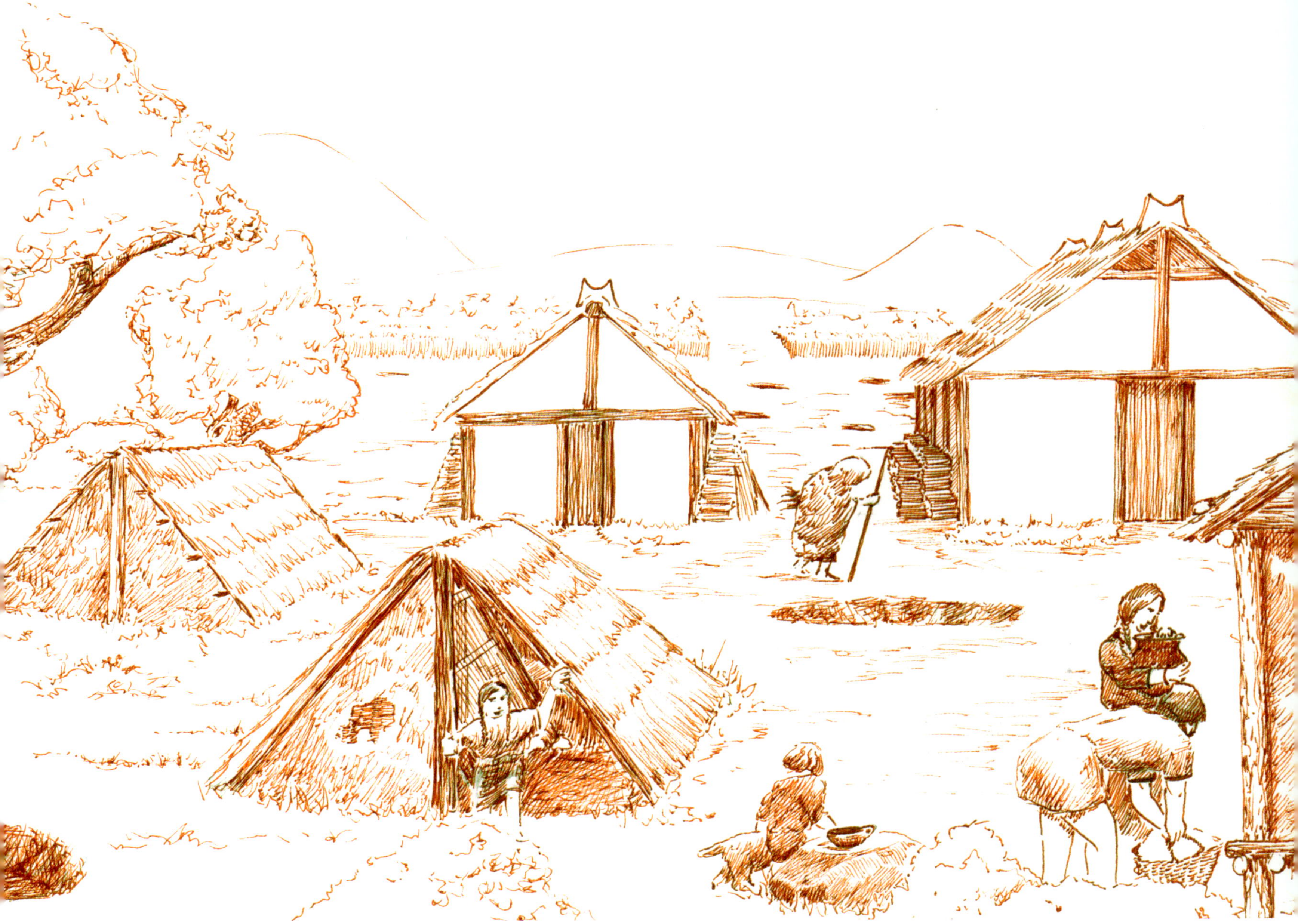

History and characteristics of settlements

While a pastoral economy with a partly nomadic way of life dominated during the previous late Neolithic and Bronze Ages, agriculture developed as the economic basis during the Urnfield Period, and as such it is an indication of stable climatic conditions. The sediment cores from the maars of the Eifel show grain pollen throughout the entire Urnfield Period and document the agricultural use of fertile soils also in higher areas of the mid-range mountains. At that time, large beech forests developed, with the common beech dominating the forest vegetation from around 1850 BC. Low sediment rates in the maar cores indicate that the Urnfield Period was generally a time with few floods or extreme weather conditions. The climatic conditions began to deteriorate only with the onset of a phase of poor solar activity at around 800 BC, just at the threshold of the subsequent Iron Age.

The ritual worship of the sun during the Bronze Age and the Urnfield Period is a persistent feature. This phenomenon is understandable against the background of developments in solar activity: from 2200 to 800 BC, the powerful solar activity shows only minor changes. The last strong ^{14}C-production peak was around 2800 BC at the start of the late Neolithic, with

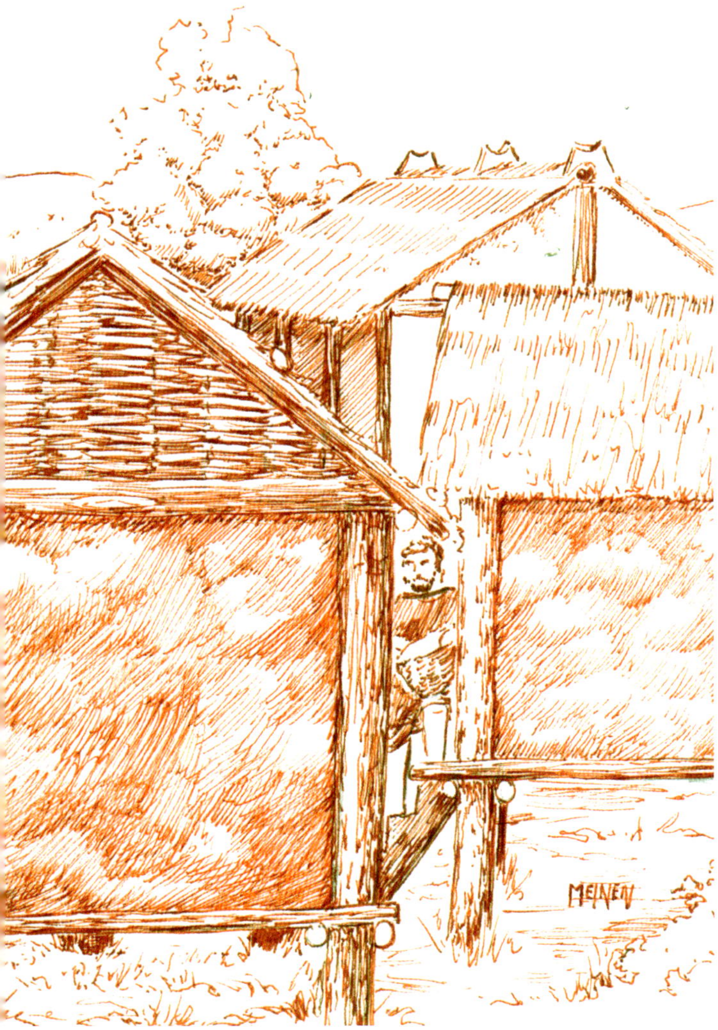

Fig. 8
Urnfield period farm with dwelling and farm buildings, reconstructed according to excavation findings. (GDKE/Landesarchäologie/Koblenz/M. Meinen)

the next coming as late as around 800 BC, at the transition to the Iron Age. So it seems that the people of the Urnfield Period were spared cold, rainy summers and lost harvests, which are characteristic of phases with low solar activity.

Settlements

The settlement structure is largely characterized by individual farmsteads. One can distinguish large rectangular buildings and smaller square layouts. Targeted large-scale excavations in Rhineland-Palatinate revealed several complete granges of the Urnfield Period, which as a rule extended over 500 m^2. The farmsteads usually consist of one larger rectangular building and a smaller number of farm buildings, barns and pit-houses. (Fig. 8) The almost uniform size of the settlements seems to indicate a form of society based on small family groups.

During the late Urnfield Period, hill-fort settlements begin to reappear as protected permanent settlements and seats of noblemen, who controlled the sources of raw materials and the trade routes and would now protect their sphere of influence through fortified locations. Hill-fort settlements are known especially along rivers and in mid-range mountains rich in ores and they developed almost exclusively in the late period. One of the causes of the changes at the end of the Urnfield Period was a distinct deterioration of the climate towards the sub-Atlantic, which had far reaching consequences for the subsequent Iron Age.

Bibliography

A. von Berg, Untersuchungen zur Urnenfelderkultur im Neuwieder Becken und angrenzenden Landschaften, Bd. 1 und Bd. 2. (Marburg 1987).

A. von Berg, Die Bronzezeit. In: J. Kunow, H. H. Wegner (Hg.), Urgeschichte im Rheinland (Köln 2006) 212 ff.

A. von Berg, F. Sirock, Der »Sonnenkult« der Bronzezeit 1500–800 BC. In: F. Sirocko (Hg.), Wetter, Klima, Menschheitsentwicklung. Von der Eiszeit bis in das 21. Jahrhundert (Stuttgart 2009) 129 ff.

A. von Berg, Bemerkungen zur Chronologie der Urnenfelderzeit im Neuwieder Becken. Ber. z. Arch. an Mittelrhein und Mosel 2 (Koblenz 1990) 63 ff.

M. Bemmann, Zur Bronzezeit im linksrheinischen Neuwieder Becken. Pellenz Museum I, 1981, 23 ff.

M. Eggert, Die Urnenfelderkultur in Rheinhessen. Gesch. Landeskde. Bd. XIII (1976).

H. E. Joachim, Die Hunsrück-Eifel-Kultur am Mittelrhein. Beih. Bonner Jahrb. 5 (Köln, Graz 1968).

D. Zylmann, Die Urnenfelderkultur in der Pfalz. Grab- und Depotfunde, Einzelfunde aus Metall. Veröff. d. pfälz. Gesell. z. Förd. d. Wiss. 72 (Speyer 1983).

The Late Bronze Age grave field of Schifferstadt

RÜDIGER SCHULZ

The site was discovered in 1995 in the framework of a targeted inspection to find a route for the high-speed connection Ludwigshafen-Metz-Paris. Owing to a salvage excavation performed using the most modern examination techniques, a section of the largest urn grave field of the Late Bronze Age in the Palatinate with 47 burials was recorded. (Fig. 1)

The graves are without exception large ceramic urns containing contained bone remains of the cremated dead and their grave goods for the afterlife.

Only en- bloc recoveries could be performed, since nearly three millennia of storage in the periodically wet and very elastic loam soil, together with the stress on the soil from agriculture, had very much affected the large urns.

While unearthing, one particular urn burial (find 54) already stood out due to its good state of preservation. The cover plate, preserved in fragments, and a vessel outside the urn were quite special finds. Three complete blue-green ring-shaped glass beads with a diameter of 9 mm and a further fragment caused particular interest. (Fig. 2) The date of around 1100 BC derived from the ceramic emphasizes its importance: these are the oldest glass objects, the oldest glass pearls, in Rhineland-Palatinate. This is the reason why this burial is so extraordinary, which circumstance is further underlined by other finds. Six more, even smaller glass beads and 17 small spiral rolls of bronze wire were found among the grave goods. They presumably formed a chain with a total length of about 22 cm. Yet another item confirms the outstanding status of this burial: a four-sided bronze staff, approx. 30 cm in length, with a spiral head and a flattened end of the Neuenstadt type. Its main area of circulation was, as far as we know, in the northern Upper Rhine area including Hesse, Rhine-Hesse and northern Württemberg. The object from Schifferstadt completes

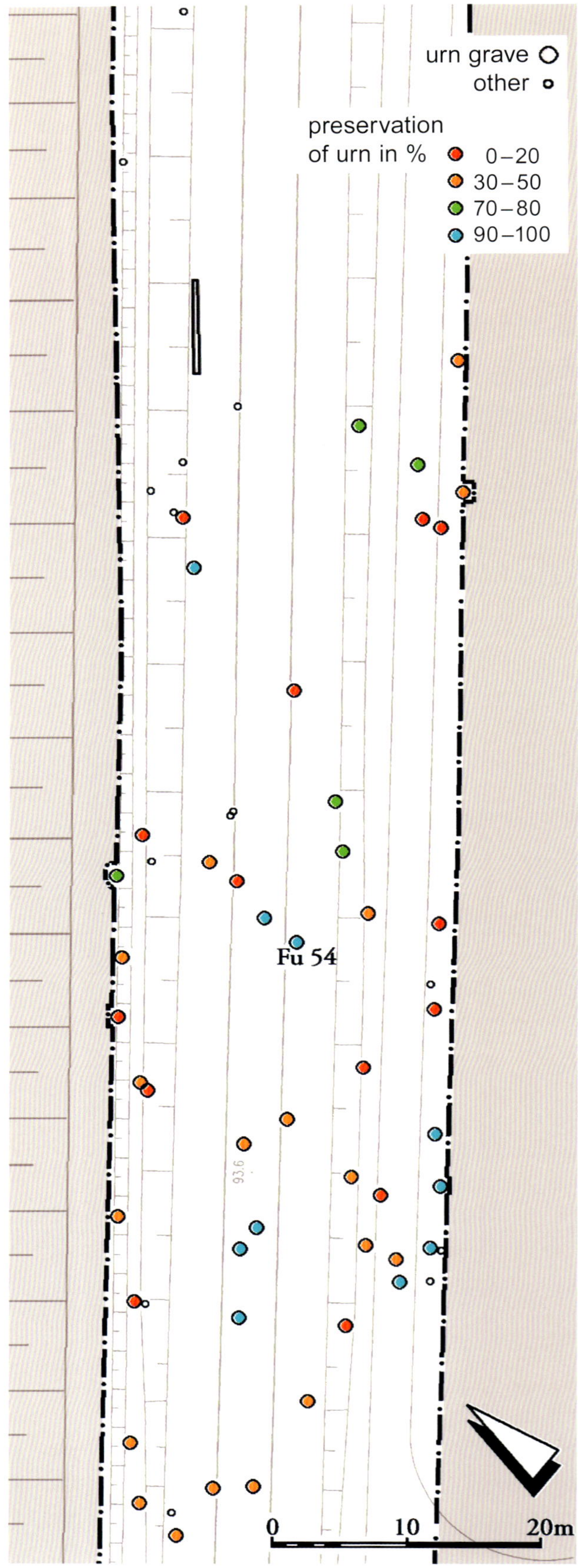

Fig. 1
Schifferstadt, Rhein-Pfalz district. Map of excavations in the grave field with grave 54 in the center. (GDKE/ Landesarchäologie/Speyer/ Winkelmann)

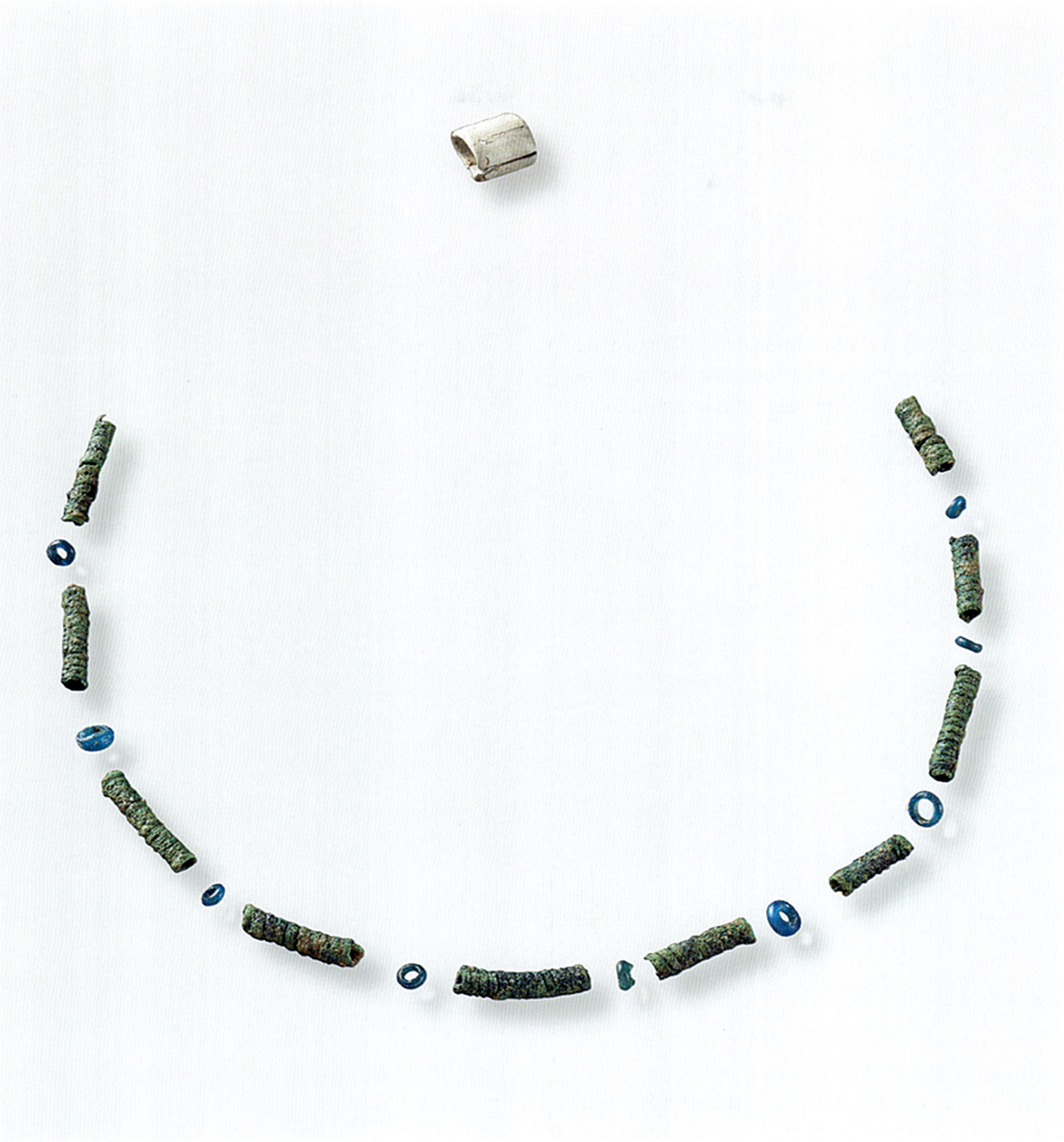

Fig. 2
Schifferstadt, Rhein-Pfalz district. Glass finds and small spiral rolls forming a chain, from burial 54. (GDKE/Landesarchäologie/Speyer/Winkelmann)

the distribution in the southwest. The discovery of a cockle is also unique in the Palatinate. It was worked as a pendant, and the manner by which it was processed and later worn indicates that it can be connected with the chain described above. The archaeologists also found a cloak pin, a perforated cockspur, and a bone bead as well as two non-local pebbles.

The ceramic grave goods (Fig. 3) – a larger bowl with a kinked edge turned inwards, the bottles, and the double-conical handled pots with wide, nearly horizontal

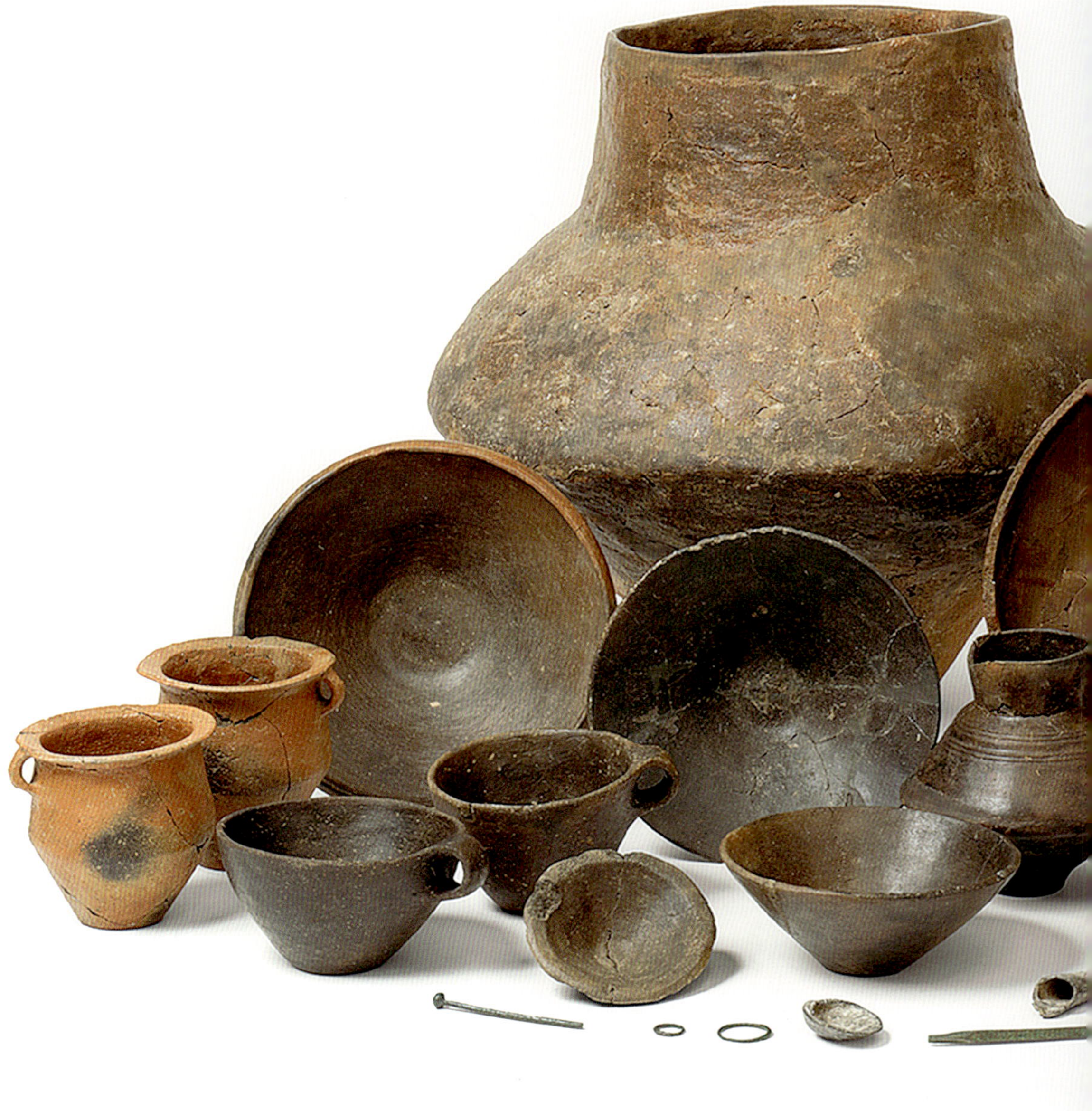

Fig. 3
Schifferstadt, Rhein-Pfalz district. Pottery and jewelry of burial 54. (GDKE/ Landesarchäologie/Speyer/ Winkelmann)

rims – stand out from the forms otherwise prevailing in the Palatinate through their form, decoration, and the working of their rims, and reflect rather the forms of the Lower Main-Swabian (right of the Rhine) and north-Württemberg Urnfield groups.

The other ceramic objects, including four small conical bowls fitting into each other – the smallest with a double-bevelled skewed edge – and the conical cup with handles complement the ceramic grave goods. A double set of crockery was evidently added to the urn for the burial. (Fig. 4)

The find complex is made up of elements from the neighbouring northern and eastern-southeastern form groups of the Urnfield Culture. The glass beads are imports, the glass mass probably coming from Persia. In the context of the other grave goods, the person buried here must have been someone of a high social and economic standing.

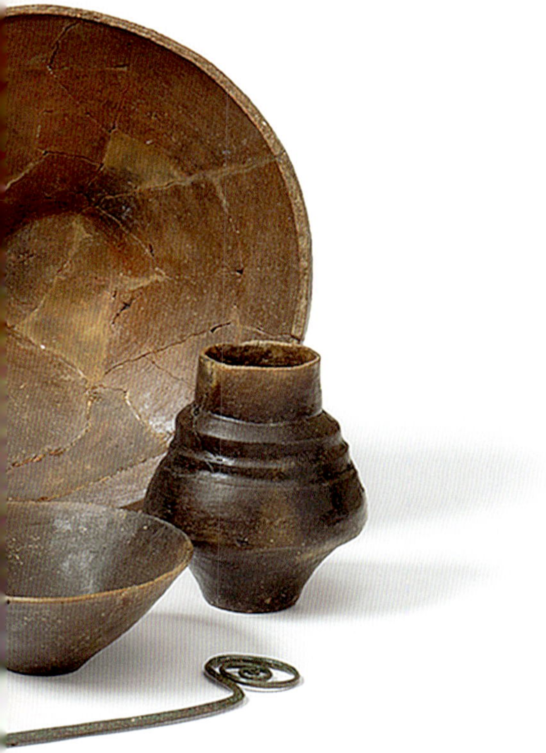

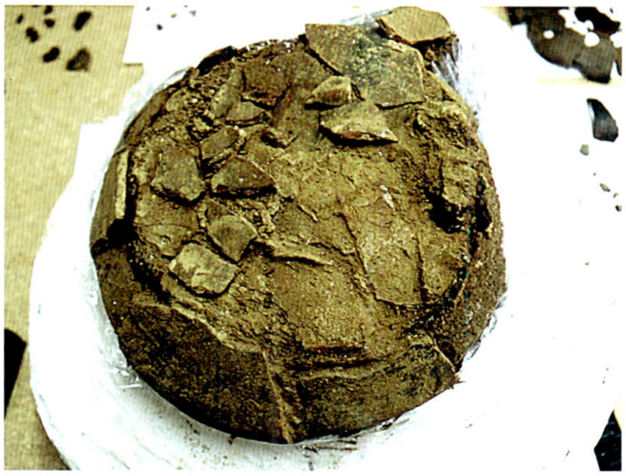

Fig. 4
Schifferstadt, Rhein-Pfalz district. Block excavation of an urn with cover bowl. Scientific drawing of the position of the various items in the urn. (GDKE/Landesarchäologie/Speyer/Winkelmann, Eschmann)

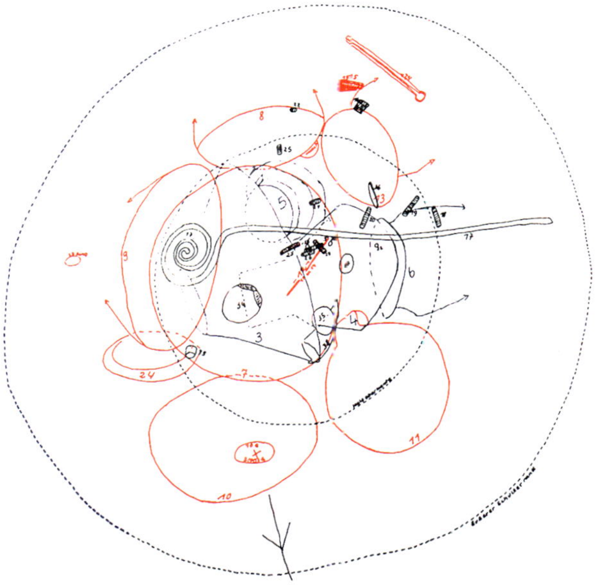

Bibliography

W. Kubach, Die Nadeln in Hessen und Rheinhessen, Prähistorische Bronzefunde XIII, 3 (München 1977) 487 f.

D. Zylmann, Die Urnenfelderkultur in der Pfalz, Grab- und Depotfunde, Einzelfunde aus Metall, Veröffentlichung der Pfälzischen Gesellschaft zur Förderung der Wissenschaften in Speyer (Speyer 1982) 72.

The Hohenberg – an extraordinary Late Bronze Age hilltop settlement in the southern Palatinate

MARC BENTZ

Where the river Queich breaks through the eastern edge of the Palatinate Forest, the first hillfort of the Urnfield Period in the Palatinate was discovered in 2014 above the Queich valley. (Fig. 1) The summit is 551.9 m high and can be spotted from far away. It is surrounded by the municipalities of Birkweiler, Albersweiler, Queichhambach, and Annweiler in the Südliche Weinstraße district. (Fig. 2) The strategically favourable position of the Hohenberg at the gateway to the Queich valley shows clear parallels with other hilltop settlements in Southern Germany. The initiative for its foundation was probably taken by powerful warrior noblemen, who in this manner gained the possibility of not only protecting and subduing the immediate surroundings of their settlement, but also of ensuring control of traffic and trade over the main road network.

This manorial aspect is emphasised in the first place by its high position and the enormous efforts required for building the entire system on the Hohenberg. Two defensive terraces, which also contributed to increasing the settlement area, encircle the entire upper mountain area. (Fig. 3) Up to three more section terraces to the west and the east were added near the summit.

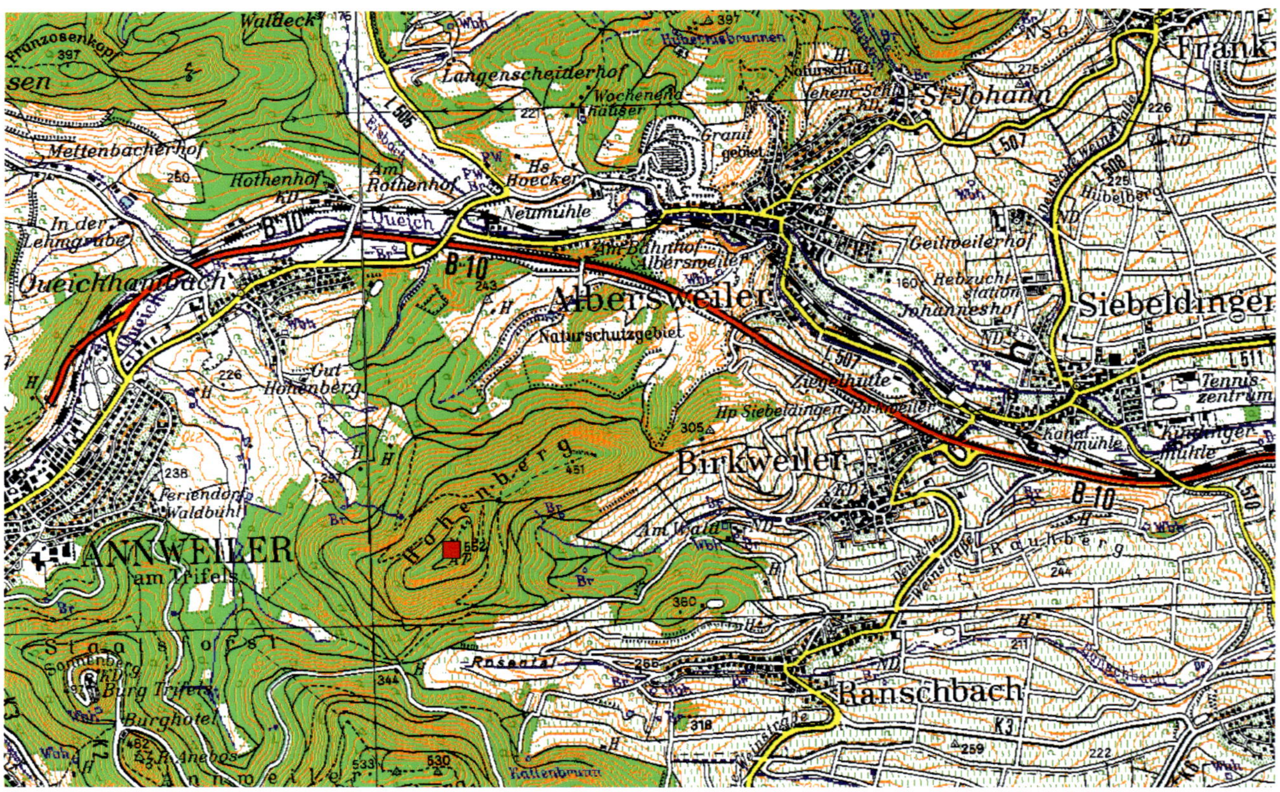

Fig. 1
Hohenberg, Südliche Weinstraße distr. Topographical map with findspot. (GDKE/Landesarchäologie/Speyer/M. Bentz)

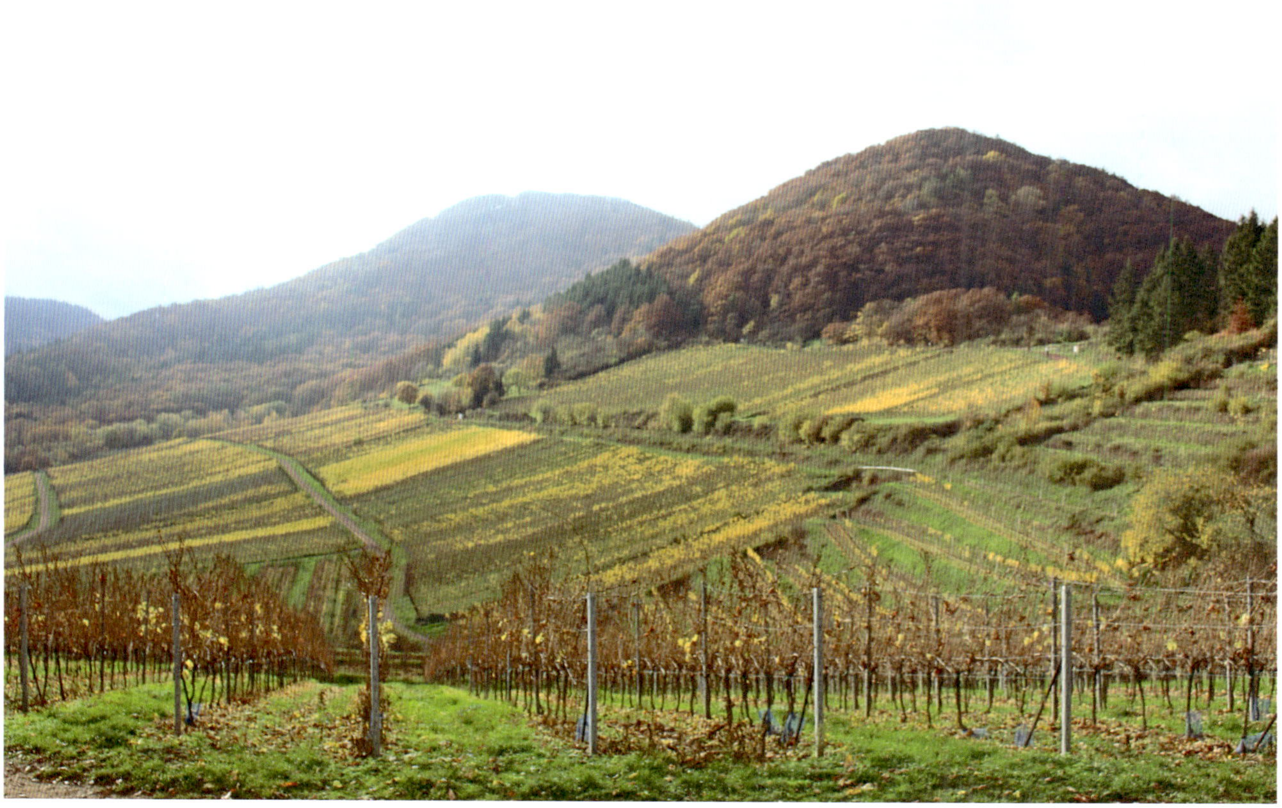

Fig. 2
Hohenberg, Südliche Weinstraße distr. View from the east. In the foreground: the »Kleine Hohenberg«. (GDKE/Landesarchäologie/Speyer/M. Bentz)

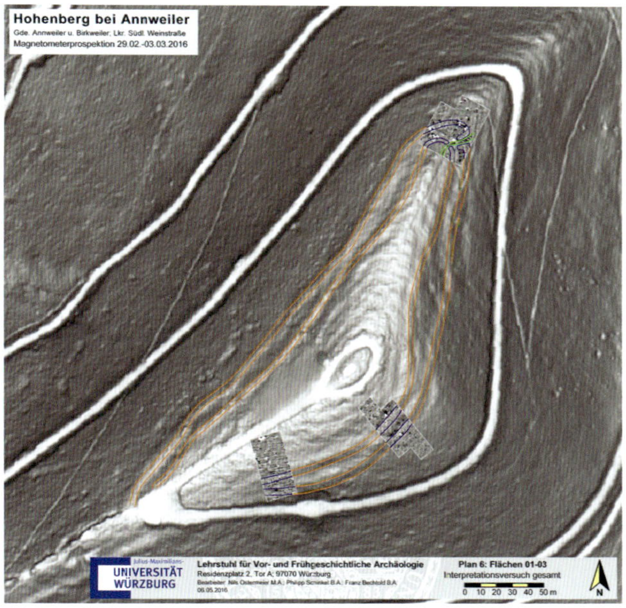

Fig. 3
Hohenberg, Südliche Weinstraße distr. LIDAR-scan with magnetometer survey areas. (Scan LVermGeo; Map LSVFA Julius-Maximilians-Universität Würzburg/N. Ostermeier)

Some construction elements of the two main terraces could only be explained after a first excavation campaign conducted in 2016 by the Speyer branch of the GDKE. (Fig. 4–6) Both terraces follow a largely analogous building principle, which also suggests that they were erected more or less at the same time. Two dry-stone walls, each running parallel to the mountain slope, form the end of the terrace down the slope. The walls stand directly on the natural Bunter sandstone rock. Immediately behind the walls, a 50–60 cm thick layer of smaller sandstone pieces was heaped up. (Fig. 7) It must have served to level the surface of the terrace, stabilize the dry walls, and also as a gravel layer. This provided an effective safeguard against water logging, say from rain. This 5 m wide surface of the gravel formed at the same time the historic floor level and walking surface on which the settlement was erected.

The construction of the dry walls can be dated in the late 11th respectively 10th century BC by means of the ceramic fragments from the settlement horizon resting here. (Fig. 8–9) Some of the rescued ceramic also shows extreme heat effects, which means that a major destructive fire may have sealed the end of the hilltop settlement at some time during the 9th century BC. A

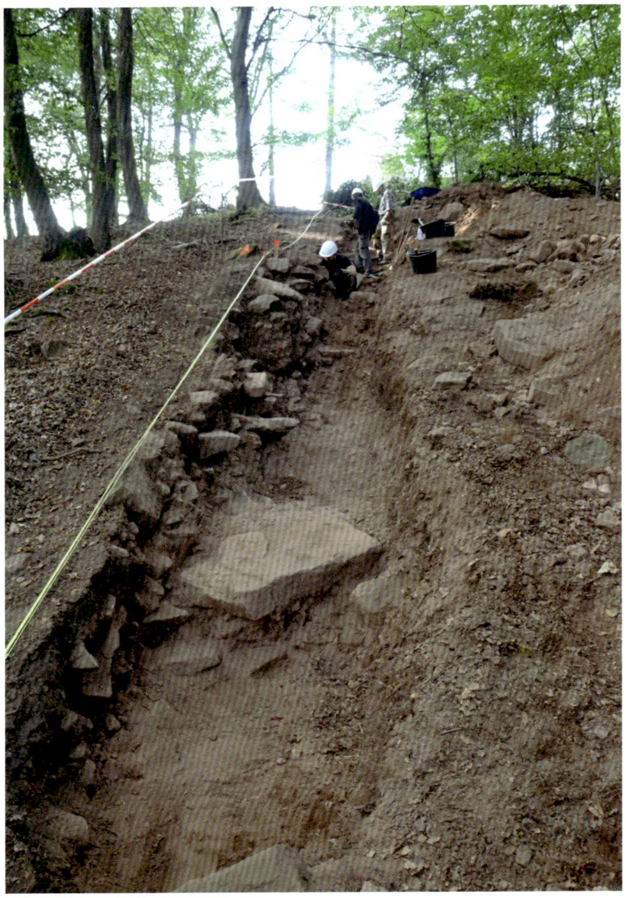

Fig. 4 Hohenberg, Südliche Weinstraße distr. Sondage trench through the settlement and defence terraces of the Late Bronze Age hilltop settlement. (GDKE/ Landesarchäologie/Speyer/ M. Bentz)

limited, irregular grey infill could also be observed in the gravel layer of the outer main terrace that could be interpreted as the aftermath of another, though somewhat earlier fire.

The mountain maintains its outstanding importance during the 9th century BC, as shown by several hoards with bronze objects deposited in the area of the two main terraces, including richly decorated arm rings, axes, chisels, sickles, knives, and plano-convex bronze ingots. (Fig. 10–12) With the nine multi-object deposits recovered here – mostly depositions of winged axes and socketed chisels in pairs – the number of securely confirmed Late Bronze Age finds in the Palatinate has nearly doubled. Nearly all bronze finds are of a high quality and show few if any traces of use. An interpretation of these deposit finds as votive gifts in the sense of an intentional sacrifice to the gods in order to protect the complex against enemies seems quite plausible, especially since the bronzes were deposited in pairs. At the same time, they reflect a certain conflict potential at the end of the Urnfield Period, which would also provide the context of some lost lance points as well as some shot off arrow points along the slopes. (Fig. 13–15)

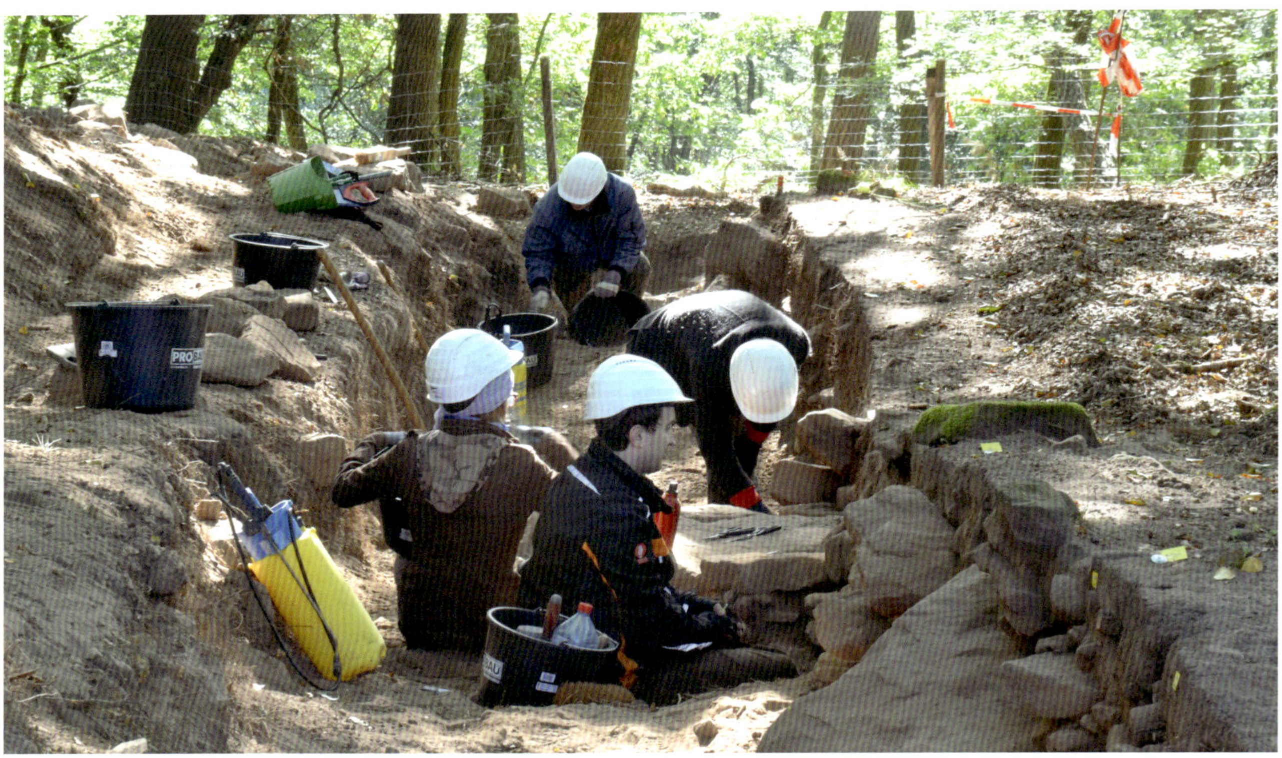

Fig. 5 Hohenberg, Südliche Weinstraße distr. The excavation team cleaning the profile. (GDKE/ Landesarchäologie/Speyer/ M. Bentz)

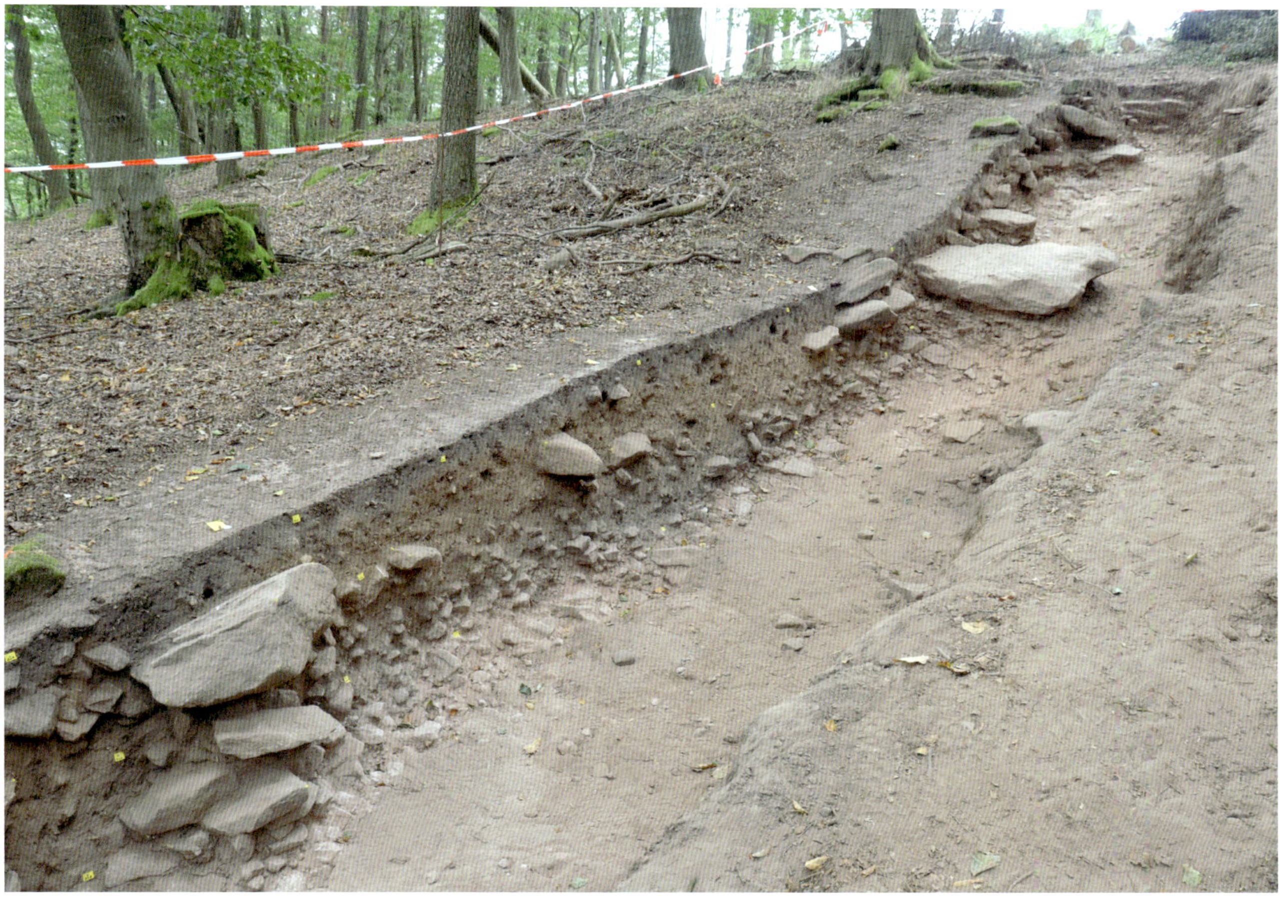

Fig. 6
Hohenberg, Südliche Weinstraße distr. Cleaned profile: on the left side of the picture is the dry wall of the 2nd main terrace; the respective terrace with a gravel layer (stone packing) and the red-brown settlement horizon follows to the right. On the right side: the slope area and the 1st main terrace. (GDKE/Landesarchäologie/Speyer/M. Bentz)

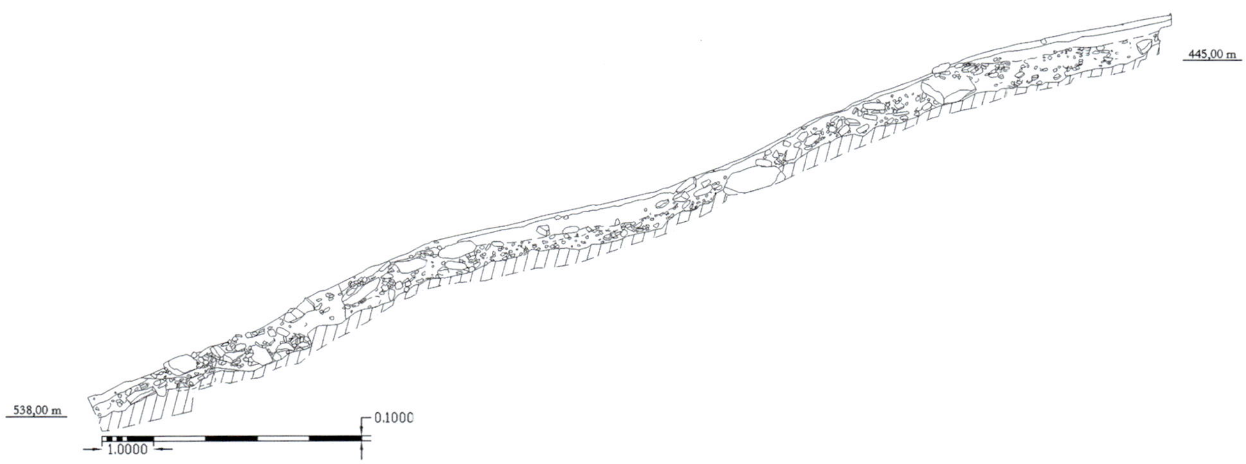

Fig. 7
Hohenberg, Südliche Weinstraße. distr. Complete profile of the settlement and the defence terraces. (GDKE/Landesarchäologie/Speyer/U. Mayer)

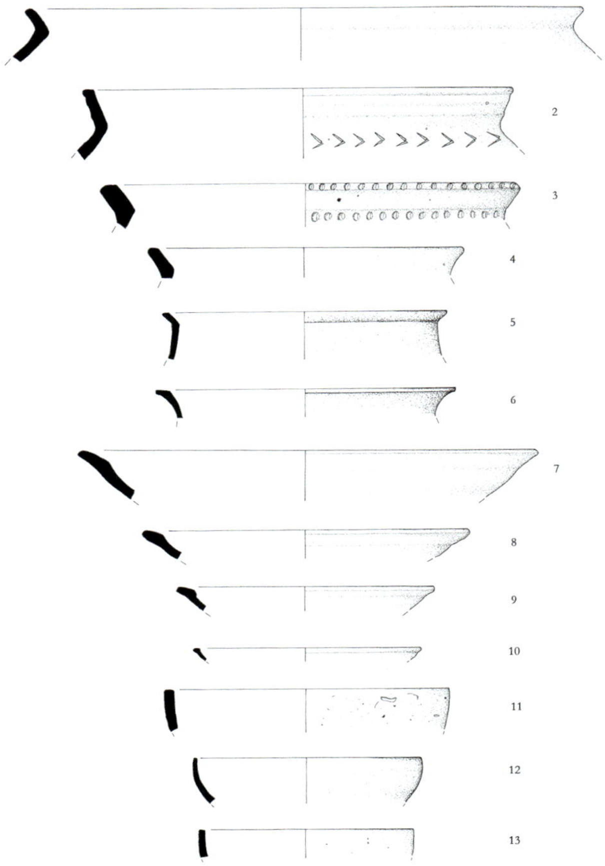

Fig. 8
Hohenberg, Südliche Weinstraße distr. Rim fragments from the area of the settlement terraces. (GDKE/Landesarchäologie/Speyer/M. Bentz)

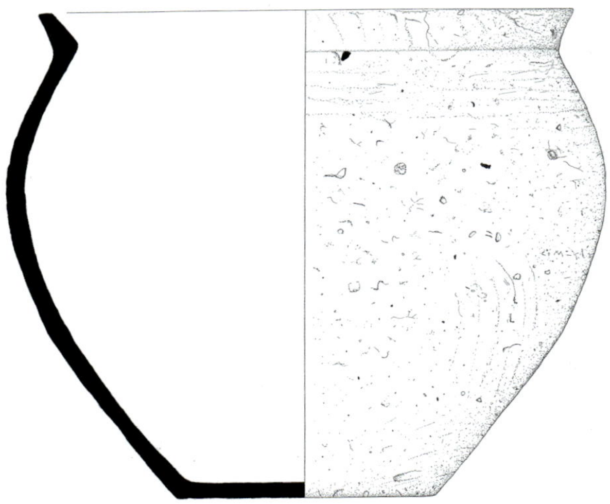

Fig. 9
Hohenberg, Südliche Weinstraße distr. Rough ceramic pot from the area of the 2nd main terrace. (GDKE/Landesarchäologie/Speyer/M. Bentz)

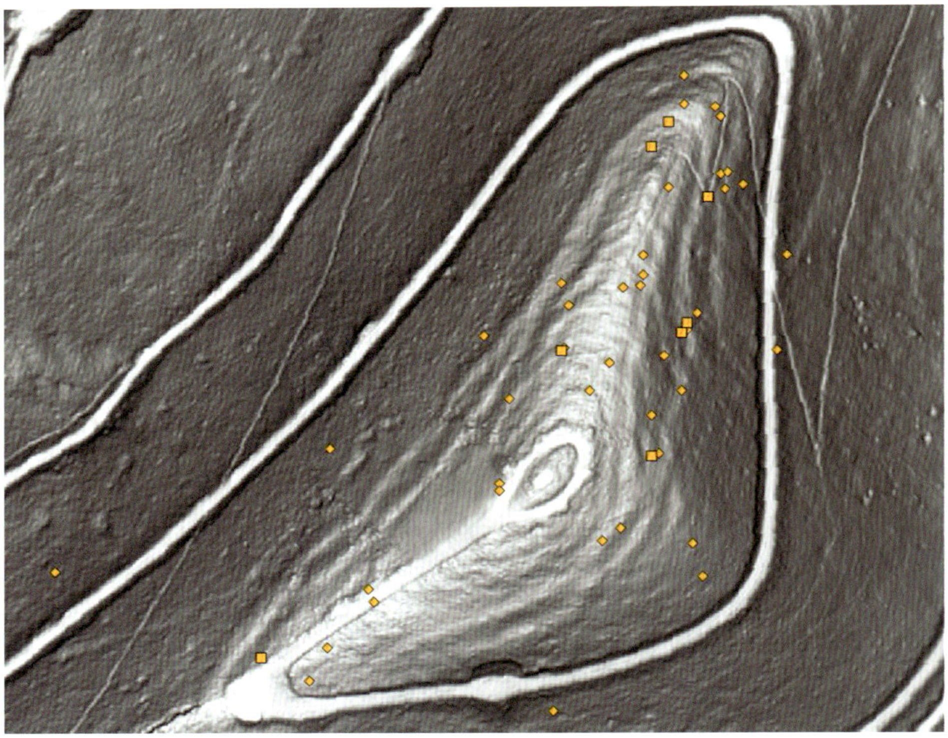

Fig. 10
Hohenberg, Südliche Weinstraße distr. LIDAR scan with distribution of the bronzes. Large rectangles: depots; small diamonds: individual bronzes. (Scan LVermGeo; Map GDKE/C. Schuppert)

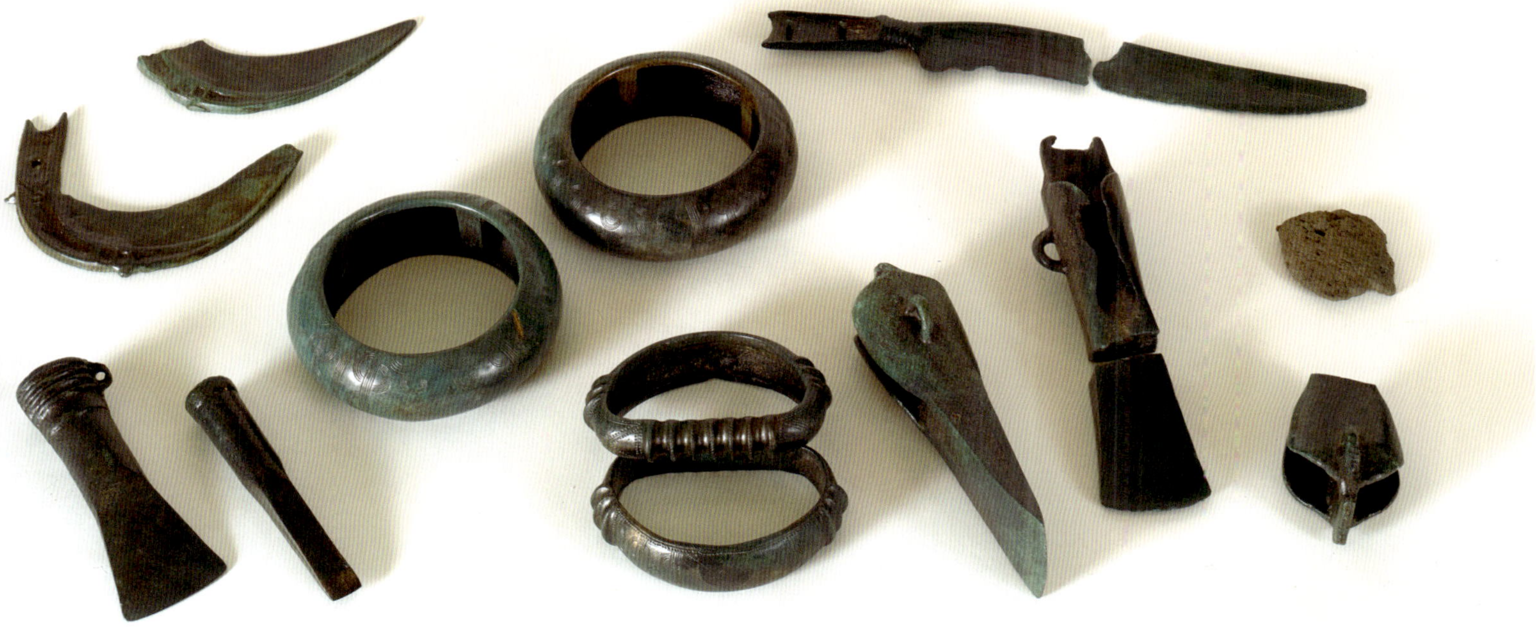

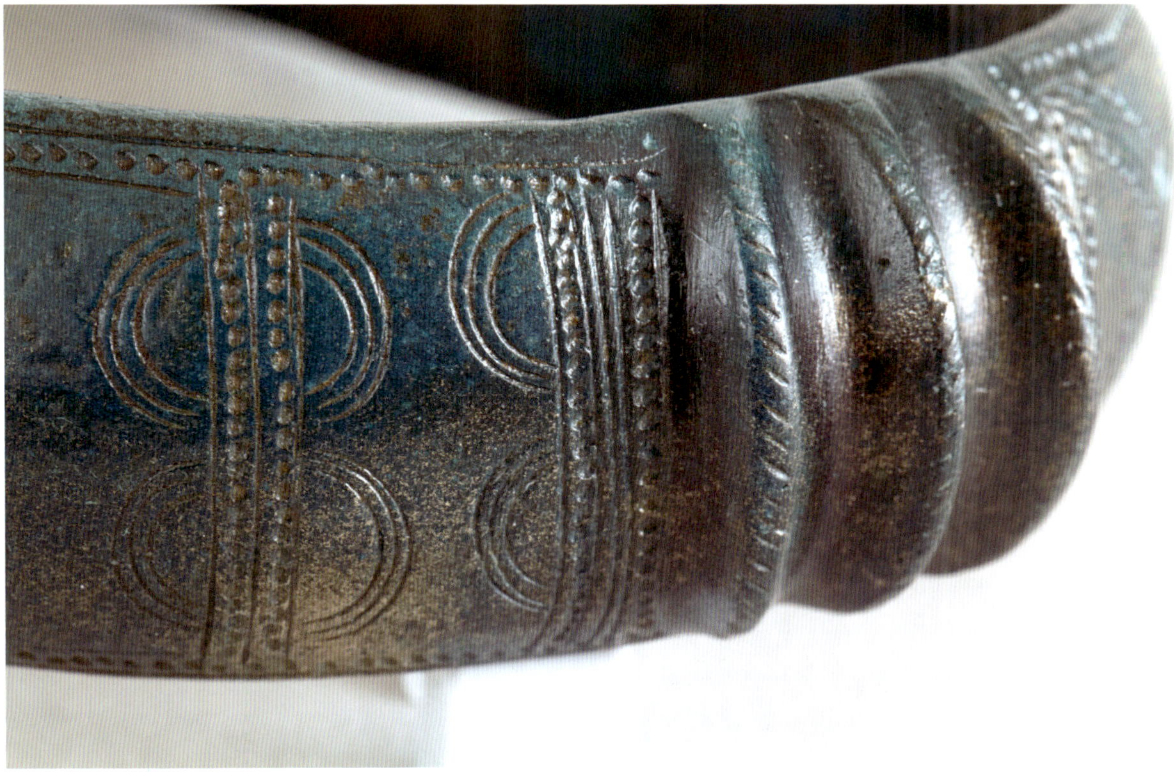

Fig. 11
Hohenberg, Südliche Weinstraße distr. Multiple finds depot (depot I) from the area of the 1st main terrace. (GDKE/S. Fitting)

Fig. 12
Hohenberg, Südliche Weinstraße distr. Close-up of the bangle from depot I. (GDKE/S. Fitting)

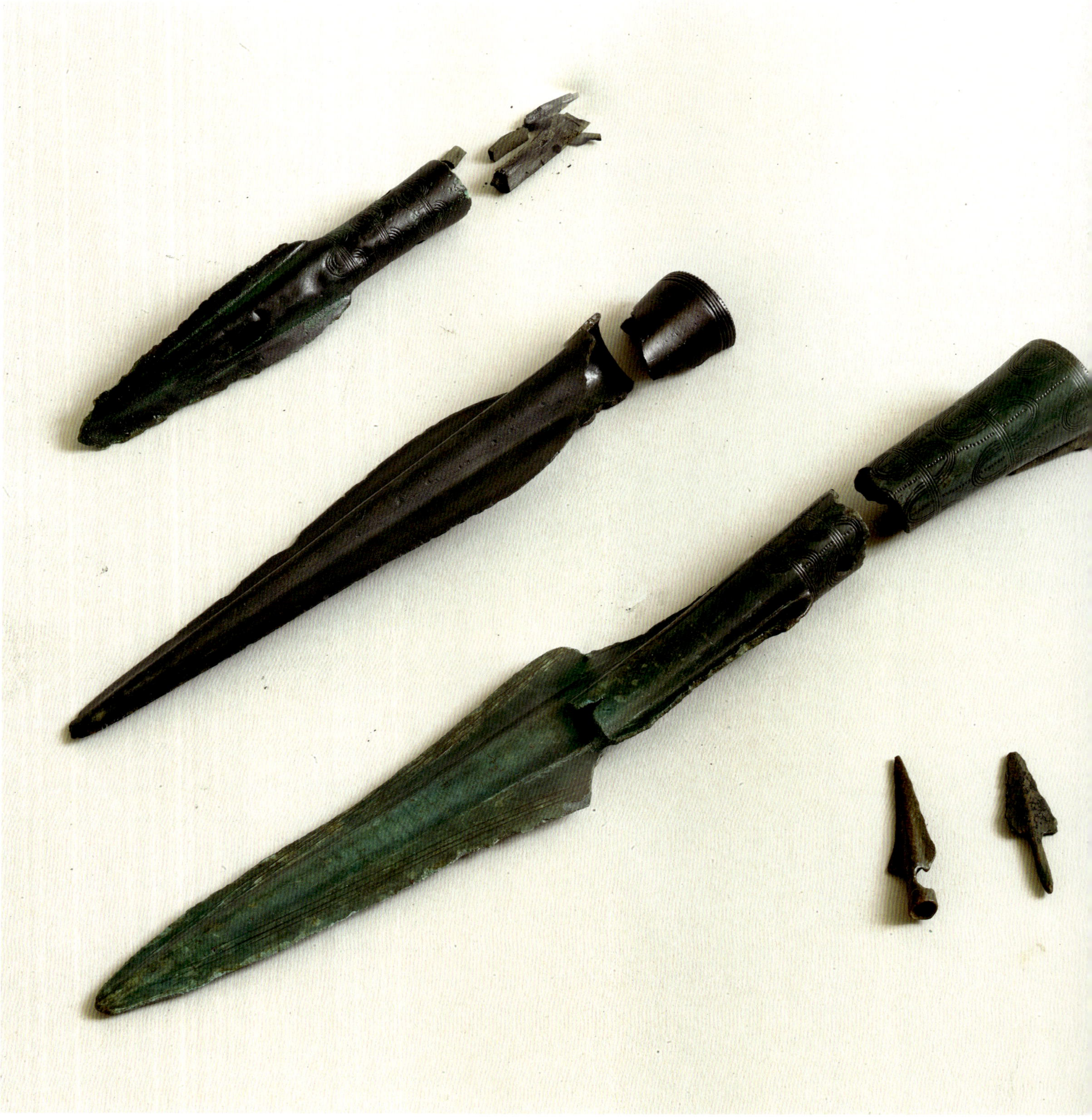

Fig. 13
Hohenberg, Südliche Weinstraße distr. Lances and arrow points (selection). (GDKE/S. Fitting)

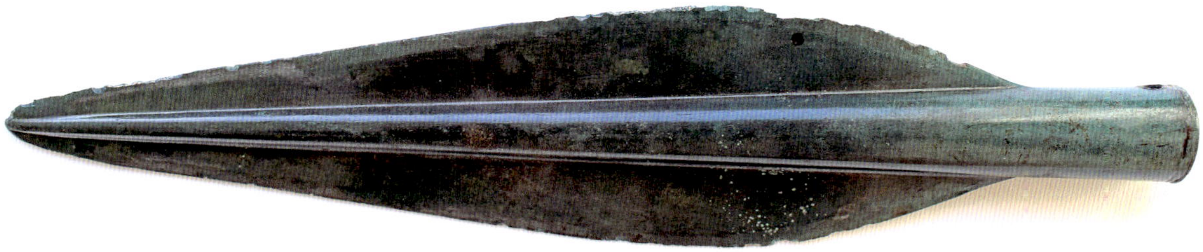

Fig. 14
Hohenberg, Südliche Weinstraße distr. Lance from the presumed gate area. (GDKE/ Landesarchäologie/Speyer/ M. Bentz)

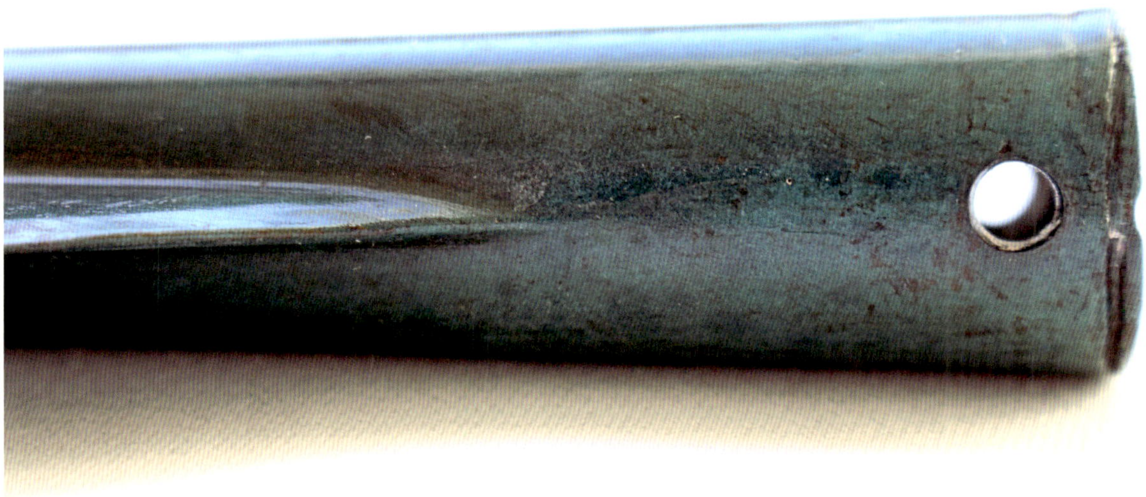

Fig. 15
Hohenberg, Südliche Weinstraße distr. Close-up of the lance (shaft hole). (GDKE/ Landesarchäologie/Speyer/ M. Bentz)

Bibliography

M. Bentz, J. Braselmann, Eliten, Kult, und Krieg am Ende der Bronzezeit. Archäologie in Deutschland 4, 2015, 60 f.

U. Grünwald, Die Spätbronzezeit in der Pfalz. Forschungen zur Pfälzischen Archäologie in der Pfalz 2 (Speyer 2017).

A late Urnfield Period bronze hoard from the Karmelenberg near Ochtendung

AXEL VON BERG

The most prominent elevation in the Middle Rhine and the Moselle area is the Quaternary volcanic structure of the Karmelenberg near Ochtendung in the Mayen-Koblenz district, where the Koblenz branch office of the Department for Archaeology of Rhineland-Palatinate discovered the hitherto biggest late Bronze Age metal hoard of northern Rhineland-Palatinate directly at the southern gently sloping foot of today's group of farms (the »Karmelenberger Höfe«). (Fig. 1) Not only the find itself, but also its circumstances and history are extraordinary, since the actual site was a victim of volcanic pumice quarrying already 40 years ago, and the surface of the area had been repeatedly disturbed and changed.

The history of the find of the bronze hoard starts in the year 1963: a digger operator was preparing the parcel of agricultural land for pumice excavation, removing the topsoil over the pumice tuff at the site and

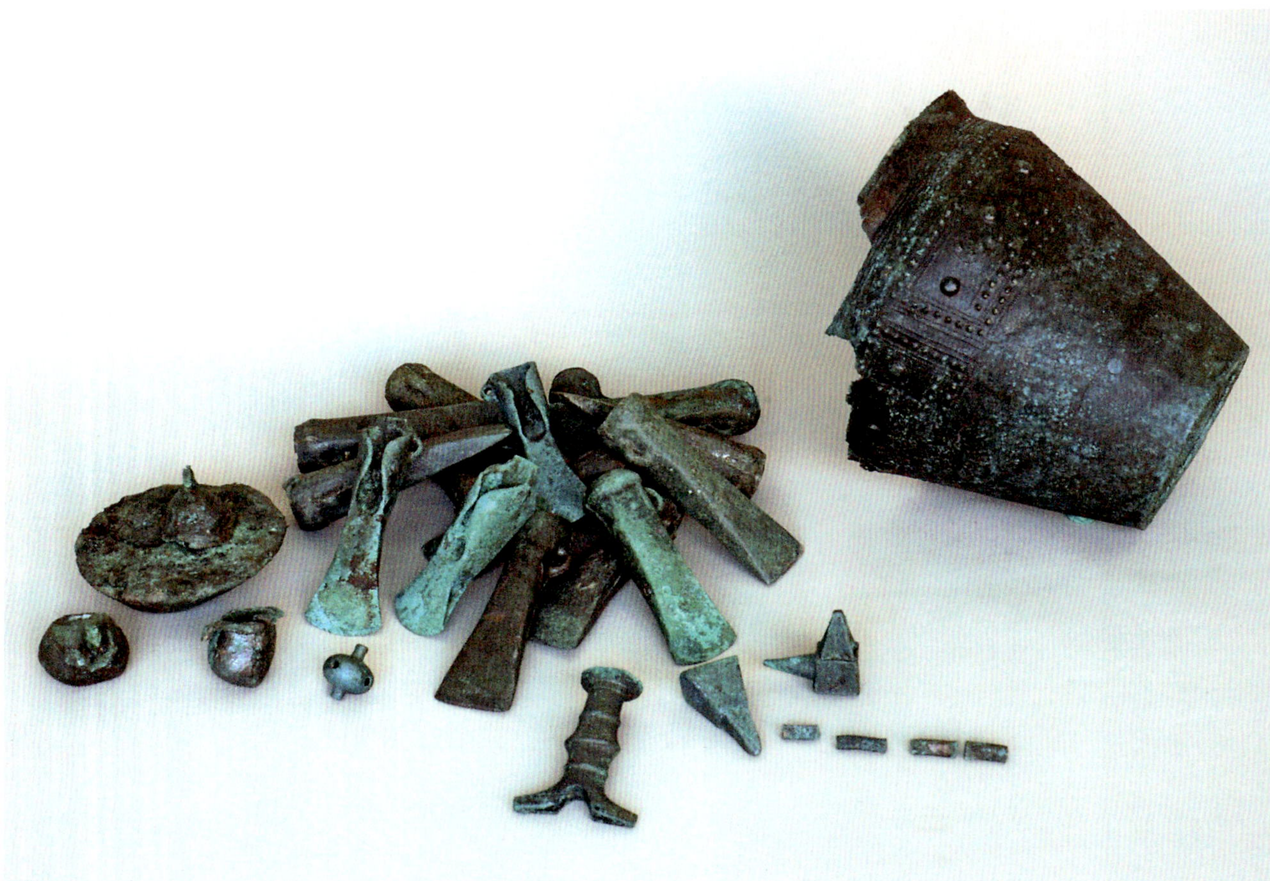

Fig. 1 Ochtendung, Mayen-Koblenz distr. Hoard find of the late Urnfield period from the Karmelenberg. (GDKE/Landesarchäologie/Koblenz/M. Neumann)

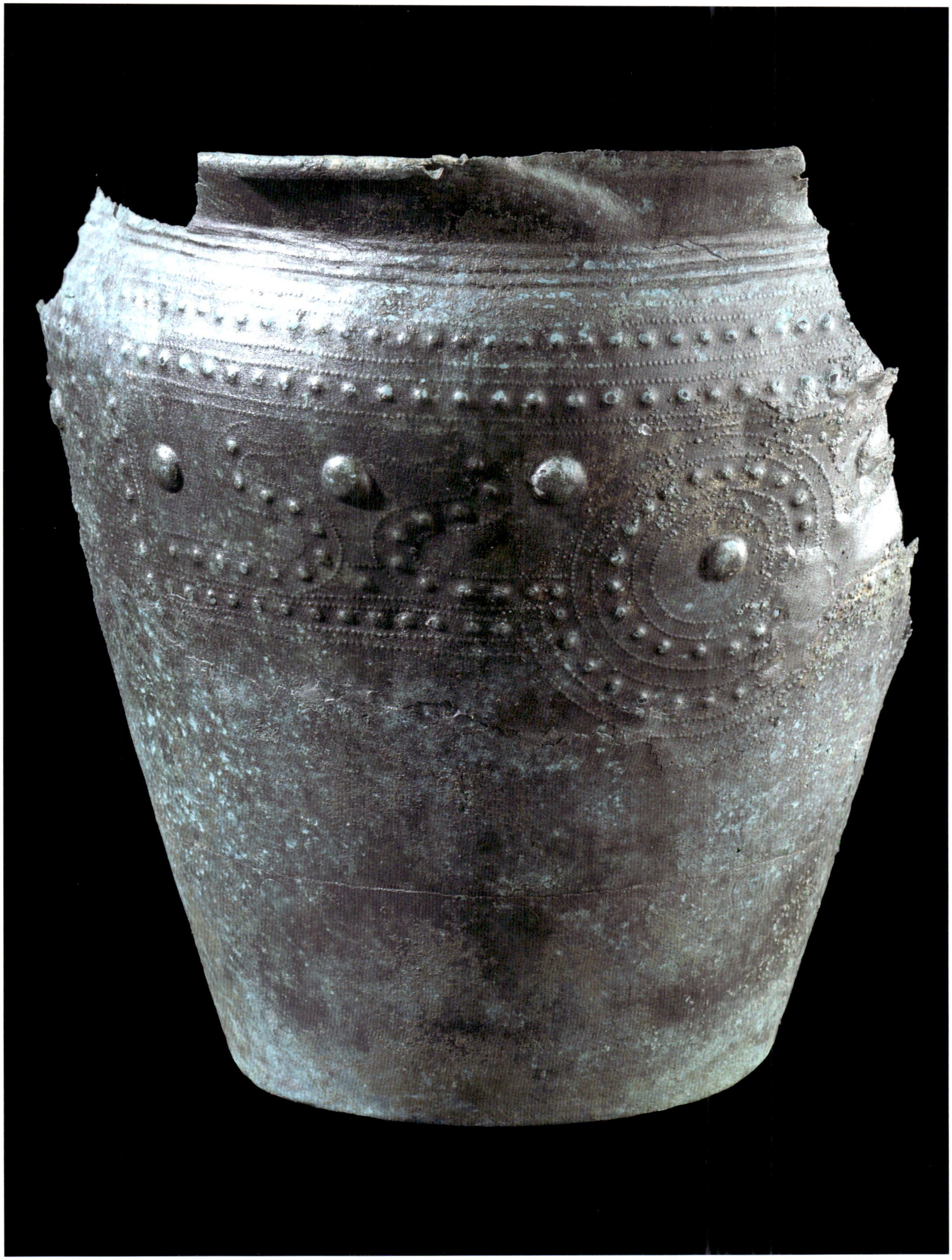

Fig. 2
Ochtendung, Mayen-Koblenz distr. Bronze situla. (GDKE/Landesarchäologie/Koblenz/Fotostudio Baumann, Höhr-Grenzhausen)

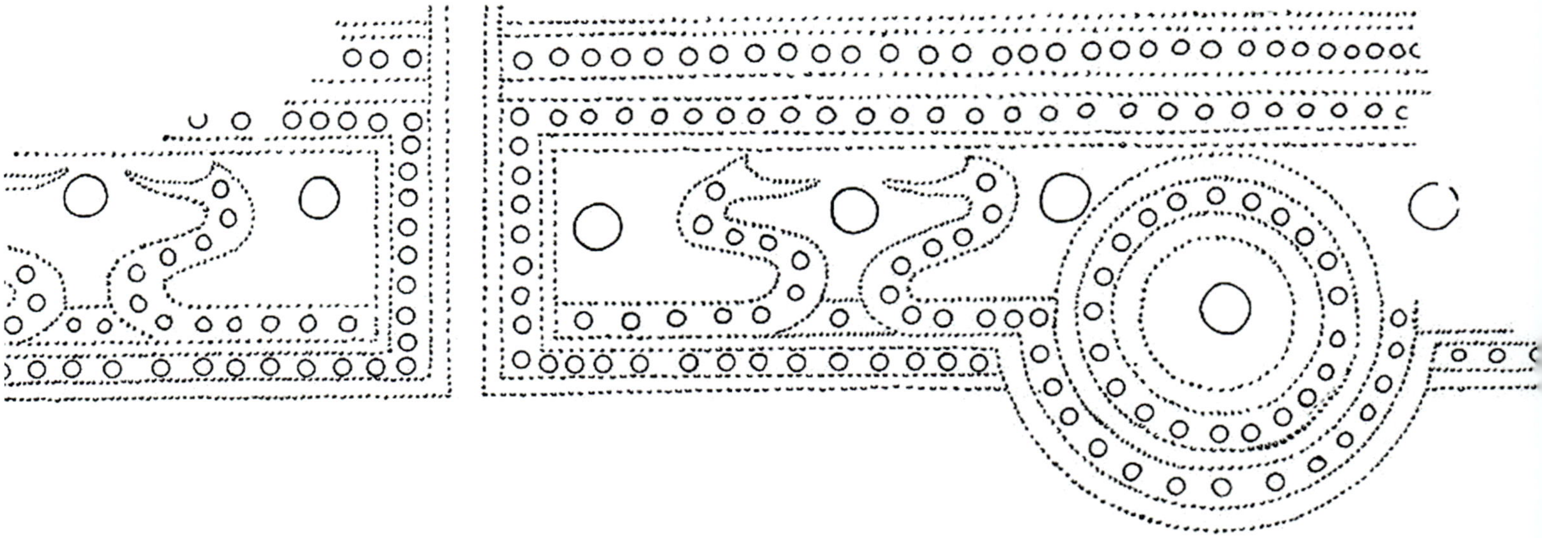

Fig. 3
Ochtendung, Mayen-Koblenz distr. Drawing of the sun barque motif on the bronze situla. (GDKE/Landesarchäologie/Koblenz/M. Meinen)

depositing it in parallel rows next to the field. The 2 m thick pumice layers were then excavated and loaded on trucks. After that, the stored topsoil was distributed over the area and the land re-used for agricultural purposes. When levelling the surface, the operator came across a bronze lance point with a green patina and took it home. He gave it to his two sons, who unwittingly polished it to a shine, stuck it on a broom handle and kept on throwing it into the wooden barn door until the point broke and ended up in the domestic waste. One year later (1964), a farmer found a bronze socketed axe when he was harvesting potatoes in the same field. The exact site was forgotten over the years, but 40 years later the Koblenz branch of the Department for Archaeology came to know of the two individual bronze objects: the site was generally indicated as »south-west of the Karmelenberg«. The indications of a possible hoard at this place grew stronger. During the mapping of surface-scattered shards of a large late Urnfield Period settlement at the southern foot of the Karmelenberg, which was also destroyed unrecorded 40 years ago by pumice mining, two more socketed axes were discovered on the surface within a limited area of 30 m × 30 m. It was thus possible to define the position of the former depot quite accurately. The mappings of the individual finds of the destroyed settlement revealed that the hoard had originally been buried at the periphery of the settlement.

The exact survey and examination of the site led to the discovery of the actual hoard, which was still in place 40 cm deep in the levelled topsoil of the old mine yield. In 1963, the vessel was pushed with the bulldozer into the excavation material next to the field, then levelled again on the excavated area after the pumice had been removed, subsequently ploughed over for 40 years, and in spite of that preserved until today.

The archaeologists discovered a thin-walled bronze vessel, its upper edge damaged by the plough, in which several bronze objects had been compactly deposited. (Fig. 2) The top layer consisted of bronze axes and below them were ingots, offcuts, two bronze anvils, a sword hilt and parts of a large cloak pin. The find included twelve socketed axes, ten of which were of the same form and origin, with some of them not completely finished. The casting seams had not yet been removed and the edges had not been sharpened. There were also three winged axes, the hilt of a full-grip bronze sword as a specialty – it is a hilt with three raised ridges for a »Dreiwulstschwert«, also a raw product – and the top of a pin with a globular head (»Bombenkopfnadel«).

Two small bronze anvils, used for toreutic metalwork, are also interesting. One anvil has grooves suitable for wire drawing. A round bronze ingot weighing more than 1 kg is particularly impressive. This is raw bronze material, which was kept for smelting after having been poured into a sand form. Then there were three smaller bronze cast objects: they are residual material from casting processes, i.e. valuable raw material to be used for further casting processes, as well as fragments of arm rings, which had been crushed for smelting. The conical bronze sheet bucket is made from two parts riveted together. The shoulder of the vessel is decorated with punched bumps and shows the bird barque motif, which was popular at that time in Central Europe. (Fig. 3) Metal analyses have shown that the bronze vessel was manufactured in the region.

All the finds belong to the 9th century BC at the end of the Urnfield Period. According to the composition of the hoard, this was the deposit of a bronze founder, a metal worker, who at that time knew how to produce the different tools and appliances on site. Comparative finds extend across western Europe and southern Germany as far as the Hungarian area.

The unusually rich hoard must be seen in connection with the early cult centre around the Goloring and the Karmelenberg as an early aristocratic residence. Together with larger village-like settlements in the vicinity, a centre populated by various groups of families and clans, who settled there over several centuries, is traceable here since the late Bronze Age.

Bibliography

A. von Berg, Hort im Acker. Archäologie in Deutschland 5, 2004, 58.

A. von Berg, Ein späturnenfelderzeitlicher Bronzehort vom Karmelenberg bei Ochtendung, Krs. Mayen-Koblenz. Archäologie in Rheinland-Pfalz 2005, 31 f.

IRON AGE

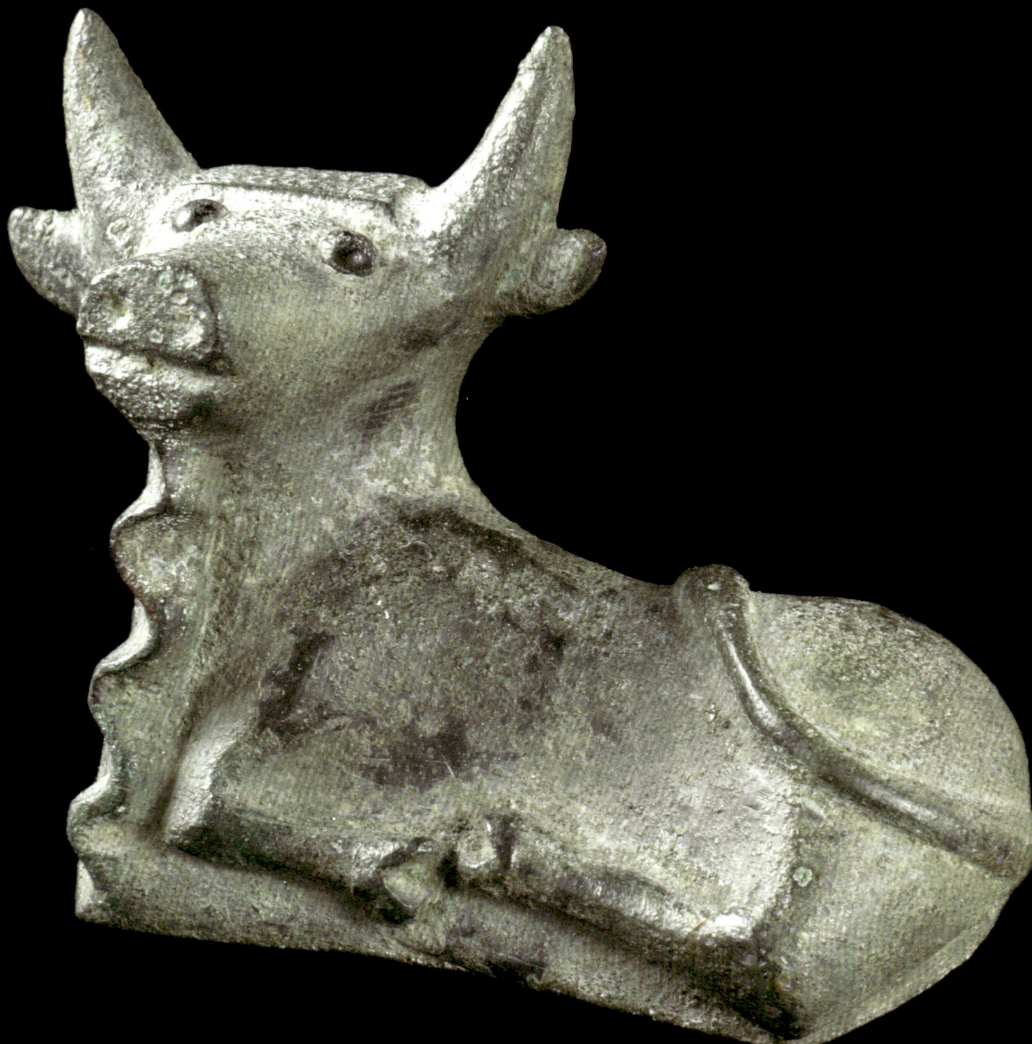

The Iron Age

HANS NORTMANN

Beginnings and foundations

Iron has been in use in Central Europe since the 8th century BC, becoming indispensable by the 5th century BC when the production chain was mastered to a high technical level. Regionally available iron ores were now strengthening the economic power of the upland areas.

The first two centuries appear at first as a hardly conspicuous continuation of late Bronze Age conditions. Grave finds, which become more and more numerous and revealing, still afford the easiest access to the epoch. From the 6th century BC until 250 BC at the latest, the custom of burying all the dead in mounds (Fig. 1) prevails. So far, we still do not know how exactly the communities, which can be traced through their cemeteries, follow the late Bronze Age settlement conditions. A clear continuity can, however, be noted from the 6th century BC onwards, which will continue unbroken into Roman times.

There is also a climate change between the Bronze and Iron Ages, accompanied by a reduction of forests seemingly caused by human activity. The settlement of large areas of the uplands, which apparently takes place only at this time, might, however, indicate only an extension of animal husbandry with the creation of new pastures. The wide-ranging occupation of the land, as witnessed by the occurrence of barrow cemeteries, leaves out only a few nutrient-poor regions and is hardly surpassed even during younger epochs.

The early Iron Age, using the example of Hunsrück and Eifel

The barrow cemeteries of the 6th–3rd century BC in the north of the state show a regular continuity. Despite many changes in customs at this time, a core of identity can be said to run through the constancy of those local communities.

Complete barrow cemeteries in the uplands had a diameter between 800 and 2000 m. For the respective settlement communities, wide catchment areas of up to 18 km^2 – though certainly smaller in valleys – with their main path network can be reconstructed. With an average life expectancy of only 22 years, one can determine some 4–9 youngsters and adults or 2–5 males living there on average. The total population of today's state during the early Iron Age and probably until the beginning of Roman times can thus be calculated as being only a few tens of thousands.

Thür, Mayen-Koblenz distr. Solid bronze bull figure from the Late Iron Age (1st century BC). The head with the horns is slightly raised, the fur is indicated by a rough bronze surface. (GDKE/Landesarchäologie/Koblenz/W. Baumann, Höhr-Grenzhausen)

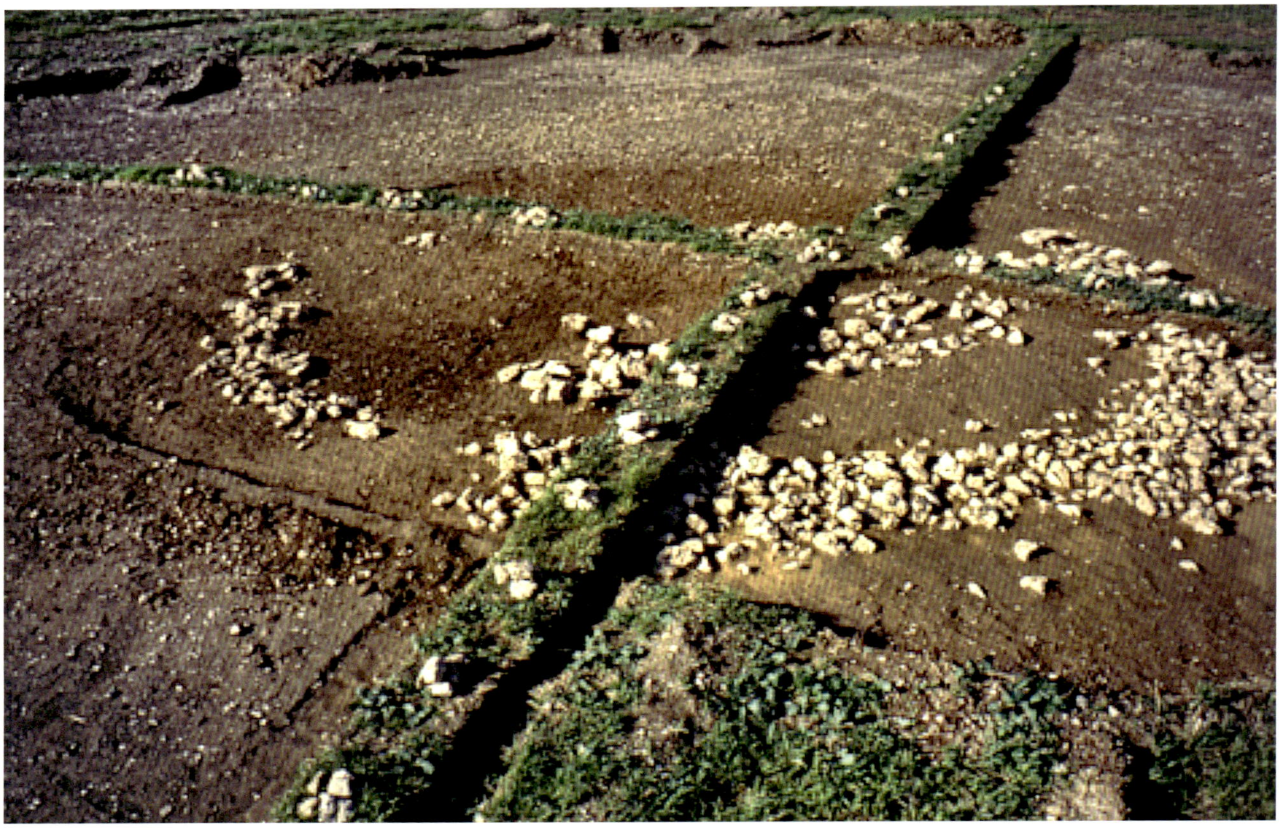

Ill 1
Pellingen, Trier-Saarburg distr. High-ranking warrior burial around 400 BC. Stone circle and stone packing of the grave mound are severely damaged by agricultural use (deep ploughing). (GDKE/Landesarchäologie/Trier)

The mounds erected over a single grave were subsequently often used for secondary burials, and casually distributed new barrows were placed next to them. After the urn graves following the tradition of the late Bronze Age, uncremated burial takes hold in the 6th century BC, until cremation prevails again in the 4th century BC. It will be practised until far into the Roman epoch even after the barrow tradition was abandoned at around 250 BC.

Most graves contain at least one set of equipment for food and drink. The pottery chosen for this purpose is very elaborate, with diverse, small-sized local styling seen especially during the 5th–4th centuries BC, some of it worked on the potter's wheel for the first time. The transition from traditional household manufacture to commercial production will however still take several centuries.

Women often reveal their identity through their garb decorations, which also show their status and prosperity. The form and composition of bronze neck and arm rings follows large-scale trends as well as regional preferences.

The prestige of a man is frequently expressed through his set of weapons, which also correspond to his social status indicating a prevailing self-conception as a warrior.

Luxury graves and contact with the Mediterranean world

During the 6th century BC at the latest, the charm of the advanced Greek-Etruscan civilizations also captivates the regions north of the Alps. It is especially the aristocratic elites living between Swabia and Burgundy who display an increased need for representation, which is reflected in luxury graves and a network of stately fortifications. To this end, not only luxury goods from Mediterranean workshops are regularly imported, but also local craftsmen are challenged to acquire new technical skills. However, these phenomena stop rather abruptly at the start of the 5th century BC.

During the 6th century BC, the Middle Rhine-Palatinate area had not yet visibly participated in the arti-

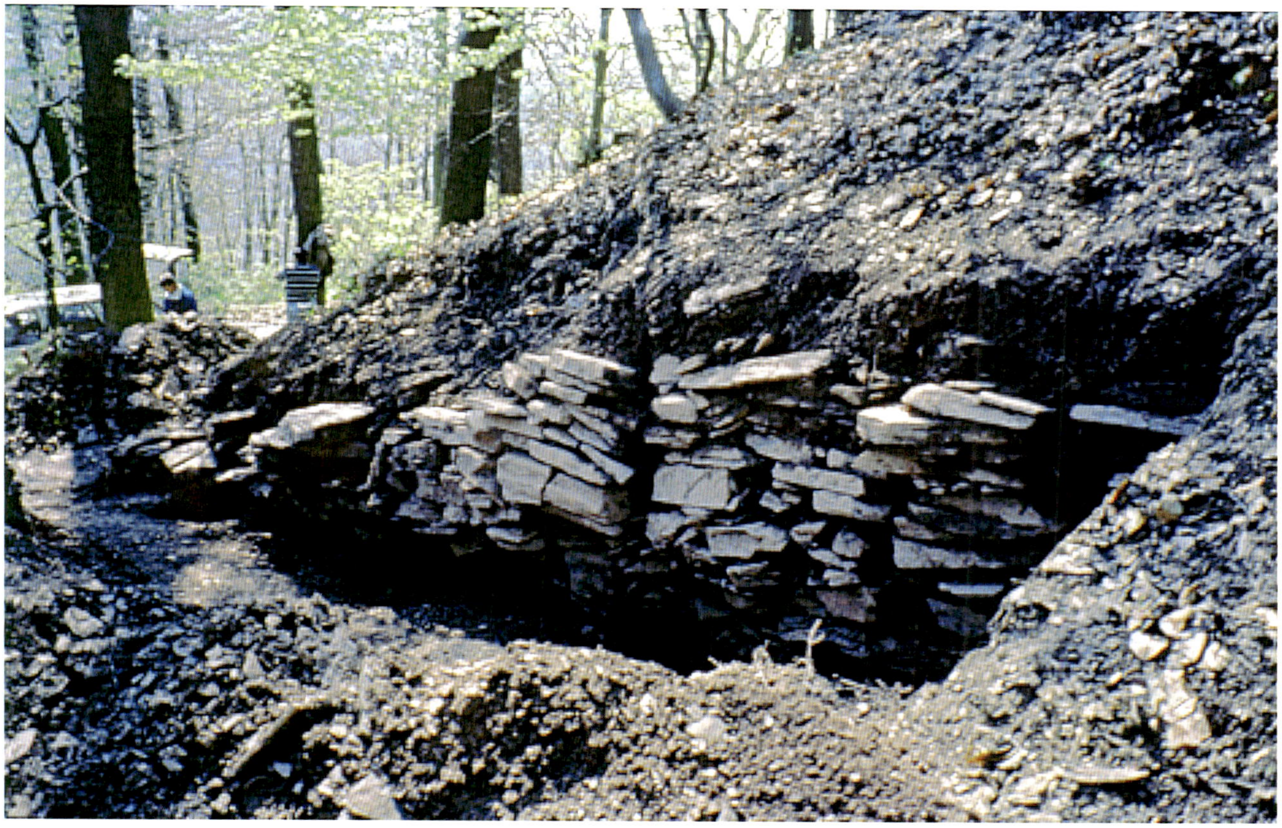

Fig. 2
Erden, Bernkastel-Wittlich distr. Celtic defensive wall (around 300 BC). The dry wall shows the typical vertical slots of past timber struts. (GDKE/Landesarchäologie/Trier)

sanal-cultural upturn of its southern neighbourhood. This changed at around 520 BC, and a comparable cycle lasting 180 years began in the former peripheral area. The main characteristics are once again a demonstrative emphasis on the native elites and frequent contact with southern Europe. The foundations for a typical Celtic culture are laid in this process.

The beginning of this development is marked by the construction of fortifications in the style last known from the Bronze Age. Two ›forts‹ in Befort, Luxembourg (near the German border), and Kirnsulzbach (Bad Kreuznach district), built at around 514 and 509 BC respectively, are representative of a large-scale wave of fortified seats. These bases used by the respective local ruler have an average catchment area of 10 – 15 km in diameter. The defence walls, stabilized with timber struts (Fig. 2), are the only stone constructions of the epoch and have both a military and a representational function. Although they were probably inspired by the stately fortifications of the Swabia and eastern France, the local forts were hardly occupied permanently, and around 450 BC they are already abandoned.

Simultaneously, other graves were built that differ from the majority in an unprecedented way, especially by a display of foreign luxury goods. The main characteristics are the addition of chariots (Fig. 3), metal vessels, mostly from upper and central Italy, and gold and other outstanding items of craftsmanship. Another noticeable feature is an exclusive position away from the normal cemetery. Undoubtedly, these ›luxury graves‹ distinguish persons from the leading class. Most of them are warriors, but luxury graves of women, boys, and girls indicate that it was ultimately the family connection that determined a person's status. All of these striking burials appear only for a short time, in particular at a local level, and cannot be explained solely with the representation of the social gradient. Luxury graves are a recurring phenomenon in various epochs and spaces, which also includes the older luxury graves of the north-western Alpine periphery mentioned above. The Middle Rhine region does in fact register the greatest density of luxury graves during the period 520 – 340 BC, but it thus also belongs to a zone of cultural dawn and upheaval stretching from Bohemia

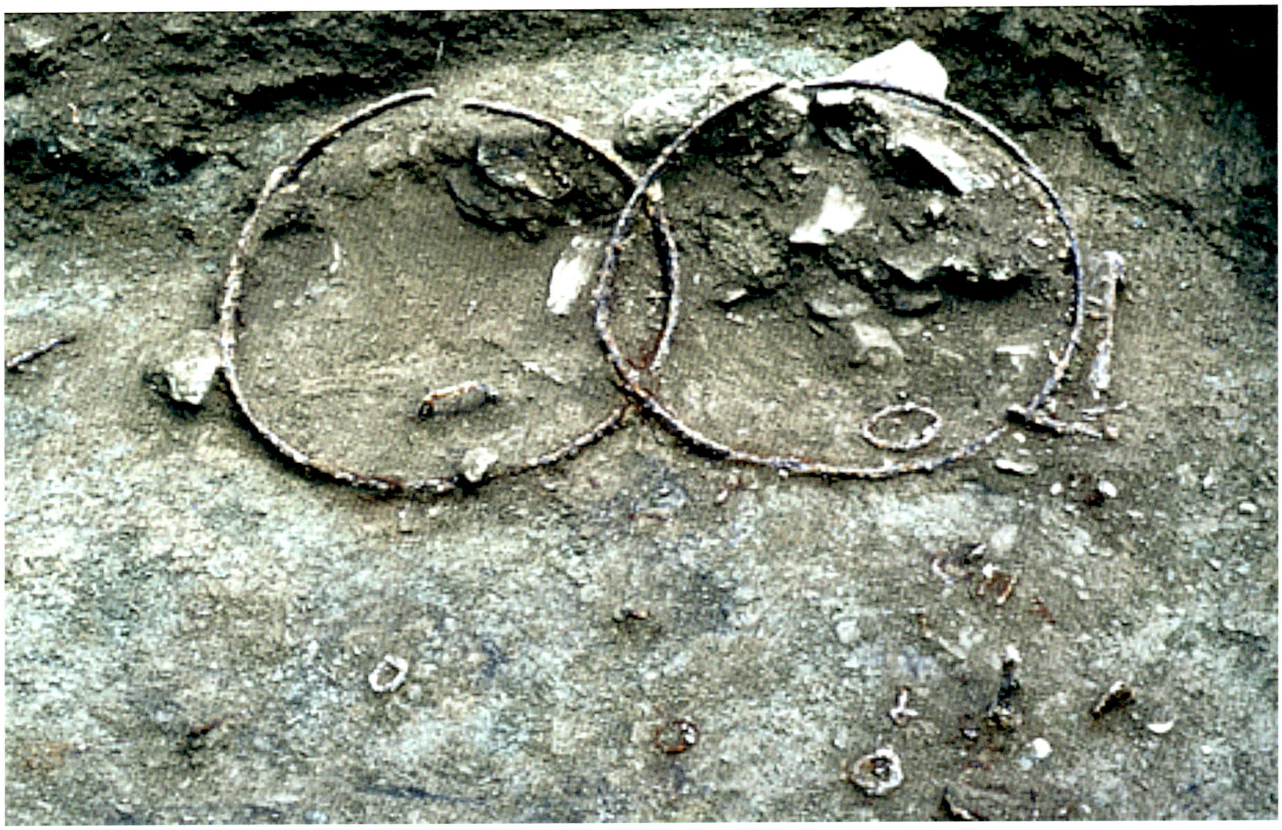

Fig. 3 Bescheid, Trier-Saarburg distr. Iron-hooped wheels of a Celtic battle chariot in a grave chamber. (GDKE/Landesarchäologie/Trier)

to the Champagne. The members of the local elites, who are distinguished in this manner, have a share in a supra-regional network of relationships scarcely recognisable in ordinary burials.

Luxury graves separated from the ›ordinary‹ cemetery are still situated demonstratively and recognizably at the natural access to a settlement area indicating the deceased quasi as a representative of his community. Evidently, each of these small groups of 4–9 persons was temporarily highlighting the status of their heads in such a conspicuous manner. The constancy of these local communities is not recognizably broken up by the emergence of luxury graves and given the small size of the groups a deeply graded social hierarchy is hardly to be expected. Superior ranks or bigger social units than these local communities are elusive so far.

The fascination with the Mediterranean cultures plays a key role in all this. It can be assumed that the trigger for coveting exotic luxury goods or foreign habits was in the Upper Rhine transit zone of the 6th century BC, but so far we know precious little about the mechanisms of the presumably indirect and probably also rather one-way trans-Alpine contacts. In the Middle Rhine-Palatinate area, at least 90 known bronze vessels represent Mediterranean table luxury. Festive drinking bouts provided the framework for demonstrating a distinguished Mediterranean lifestyle so as to enhance the status of the owner and host. The demand for such display objects brought about not only metal and ceramic imitations, but also an enormous artisanal and artistic boost. Here, too, luxury graves as a transculturally recurring phenomenon can be interpreted in the sense of a general behaviour pattern. According to this idea, it is indeed the direct experience of the Mediterranean world, which is considered superior, that challenges the self-esteem of the leading class. From this viewpoint, luxury graves serve to demonstrate the seeming self-assurance of insecure elites amongst themselves and vis-à-vis their community, and also indicate the assimilation of this encounter.

The foundation of a Celtic culture

Together with Etruscan bronzes, various components of Mediterranean imagery are also transported to Central Europe. Until then, this cultural space hardly ever had experience of pictures, probably because of religious taboos. The inflow of a southern European imagery of men, animals, mythical creatures, and plants had an enormous impact on the new surroundings from about 450 BC. The Mediterranean motifs were only vaguely understood and picked up and transformed by local artisans. This ›La Tène style‹ evolved through a break with tradition and can be regarded as a wholly new spiritual-religious orientation; for the first time, it establishes an independent Celtic form of expression, which will remain effective for centuries and is characteristic for the entire Celtic world.

In this new creation, a small repertoire of rather schematic images is combined with organic swelling motifs. The closeness of this not easily accessible ›art‹ to religious or magical ideas is instantly recognizable. But most of the contents hinted at continue to be enigmatic for us today. Much of the evidence is of a small format and applied in an artisanally masterful manner on objects of daily use. These are mainly representational pieces found in luxury graves, which bear witness to the self-esteem of the leading class buried there. The elite promotes and uses the new style as a means of expression and thereby interacts on a European level.

The Middle Rhine zone probably played a decisive role in the development of that Celtic style, which is accepted within a few decades between western Bohemia and the Champagne.

Between the early and the late Iron Age

Around 340 BC, the phenomenon of luxury graves is discontinued in Central Europe. It would seem that the crisis of self-esteem, which had been the basis for it, was overcome and no longer required a demonstrative compensation. Simultaneously, there is a general reversion to cremation burials with rather poor residues at first. Accordingly, during the further course of the Celtic epoch, there are hardly any artistically outstanding remains to be found in the Middle Rhine zone. Even the formerly conspicuous connections to the Mediterranean area regress completely for at least a century. Irrespective of this, there is rather a return to normality, to be noticed in particular at the local level: the traditional barrow cemeteries are documented for nearly another century without discontinuities. The transition to simple cremation cemeteries without mounds, starting around 250 BC, may represent a certain break from the archaeological point of view, but not historically. Besides the locations in valleys and basins, which were always favoured for settlement, the upland settlements and their local social continuity appear, at least in the Hunsrück, to be uninterrupted.

The level of craftsmanship previously reached is also maintained, in so far as may have been required, for instance, in the manufacturing of arms. Potters' wheels become the priority tool for the manufacture of finer ceramics. Glass pearls, rings, and inserts, which were at one time rare, appear more and more as mass articles.

The end phase of the luxury graves tradition is followed by a new start, which also signals constancy and consolidation through its continuation into the later period of the Iron Age: during the 4th century BC, a second wave of fort building can be recorded. Their position, size, and form of fortification do not differ in principle from the older forts of the 6th century BC, but these younger forts will be used long-term up to the 1st century BC and thus repeatedly renovated. With their dense internal constructions (Fig. 4), they were evidently also important settlements.

Tribe formation and urban beginnings of the late Iron Age

From the 2nd century BC, new developments determine the likely continuous settlement in small traditional communities within the manageable catchment area of regional fort domains. Like everywhere else in the Celtic world, few large fortified settlements emerge. The Roman conqueror Caesar will later use the term »oppidum« for them, which has connotations of a ›city‹. Internal areas of 30–240 ha (Fig. 5) and catchment areas of around 60 km in diameter give some idea of the so-far unprecedented dimension of the social or-

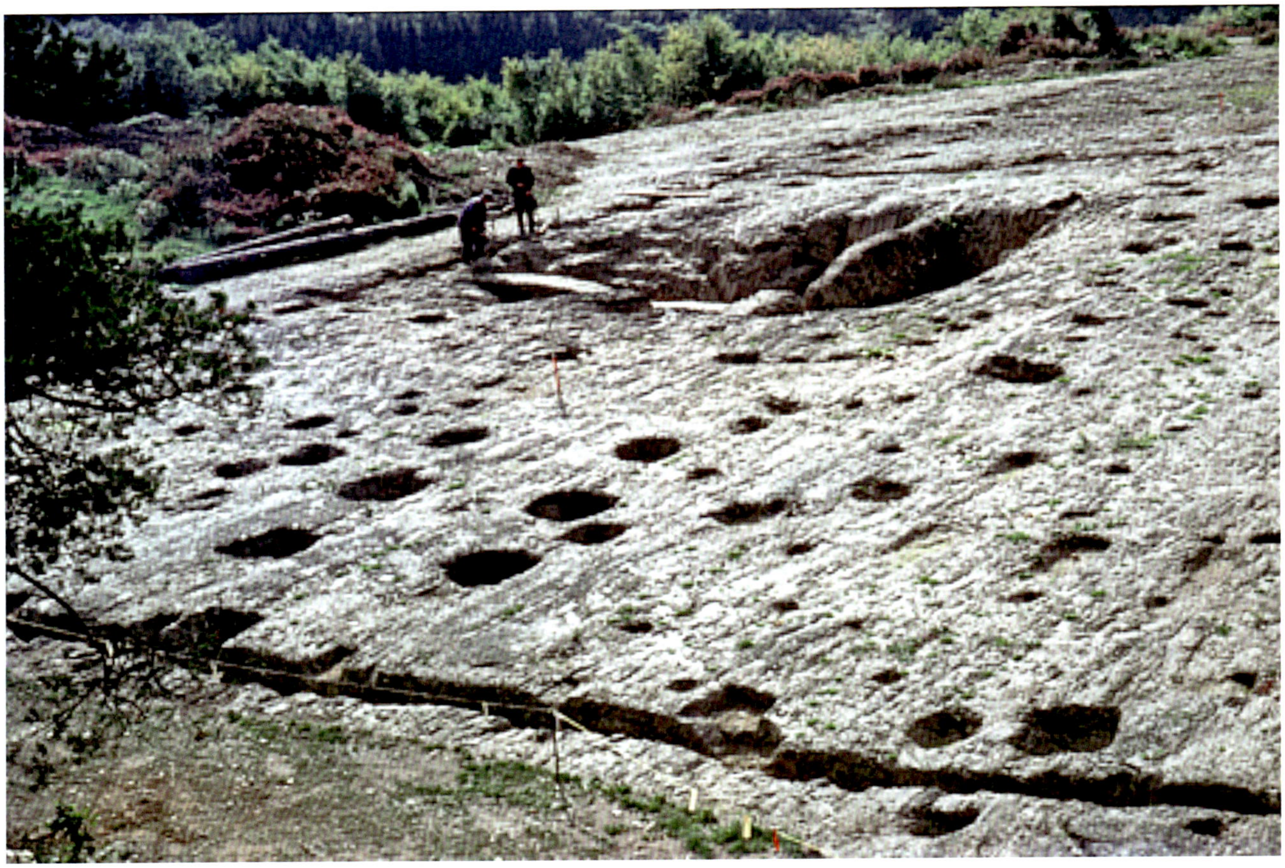

Fig. 4 Bundenbach, Birkenfeld distr. Perfectly preserved post settings cut into the rock of the former buildings of a Celtic castle (4th-1st century BC). (GDKE/Landesarchäologie/Trier)

der behind it. The internal constructions and the stone defence walls largely correspond to older forts.

Anticipating the political conditions described by Caesar during the occupation of Gaul, it is also possible to perceive the basis of the new centres: it is the Celtic or Gallic tribes organized as aristocratic tribal states. Of the four oppida known in the area of the state, three (plus the oppidum »Titelberg« in Luxembourg) are to be attributed to the tribe of the Treveri based between the Meuse and the Middle Rhine: Wallendorf »Kasselt«, Kastel, and Pommern »Martberg«. These four centres will initially retain their importance even after the conquest by the Romans.

The huge structure on the »Donnersberg« in the Palatinate is a different matter, since it was abandoned before the Roman conquest. It probably reflects the upheavals that contributed to the start of the Gallic War (58–50 BC), especially the advance of ›Germanic‹ tribes into the Upper Rhine, where they settled in Rhine-Hesse and the Palatinate as »Vangiones«, »Nemetes«, and »Triboci«. And indeed graves from the subsequent period with their roots on the other side of the Rhine in the northeast have been found in the Upper Rhine Plain.

The foundation of the oppida around 130 BC represents not only an architectural, but also a social feat. Therefore, the likely background may in fact be the consolidation of those tribal structures about which Caesar would first write a century later. The deep roots of these centres in the regional tribal identity also have a public-religious component, since all Treverian oppida will remain important sanctuaries until the end of the Roman period.

It remains doubtful for the time being whether the newly established centres had already played, from their foundation, the city-like economic role they would assume later; that is, as a location of specialized crafts, as a market place, and as a hub of long-distance trade, but certainly also as consumers who could only exist through an exchange with a rural hinterland, or

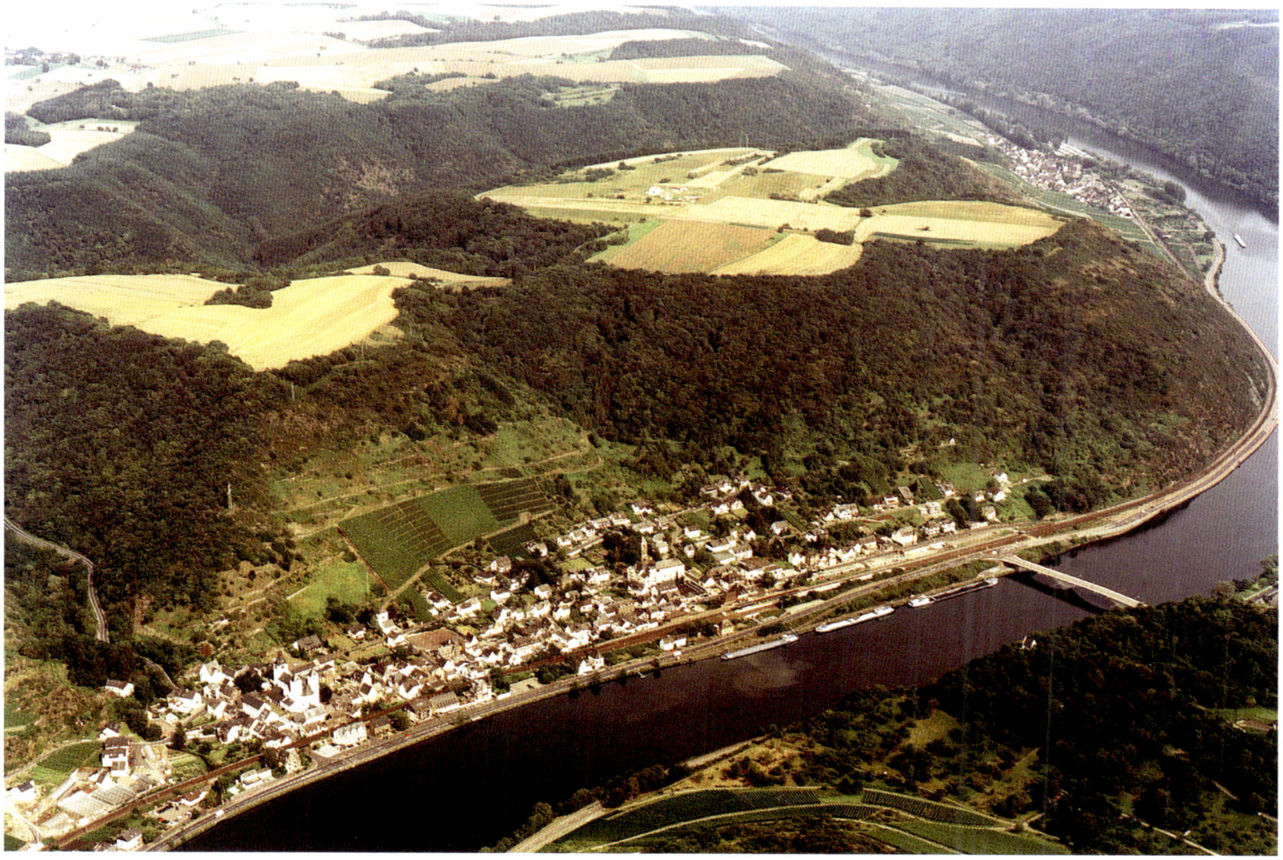

Fig. 5
Pommern, Martberg, Cochem-Zell distr. Aerial photo of the plateau above the Moselle with the 70-ha *oppidum* of the Treverians and the Gallo-Roman sanctuary. (GDKE/Landesarchäologie/Koblenz/A. Schmickler)

as main buyers of luxury goods, including wine (amphorae) and drinking vessels from the Mediterranean.

About one century before the foundation of oppida, the Celtic tribes had already begun their own coinage, following Greek-Hellenistic models at the outset. The monetary economy that developed around the oppida decisively changed the whole economy. It offers insights into a variety of minting authorities and the economic networks of various sub-regions. Coins are also nearly the only image carriers of the late Celtic world and thus provide some kind of access to the spiritual life of the time. One assumes that the coins were mostly minted in the oppida.

Around the middle of the 1st century BC, the forts are abandoned, presumably as a late consequence of increasing concentration of social and political life in the oppida.

The Roman submission of Gaul

The occupation of all Gaul up to the Rhine by the Romans (58–50 BC) under Caesar was in no way absolutely predictable. Discord and inner-tribal rivalries, particularly noticeable within the aristocracy of the Treveri, contributed to the defeat. These momentous events have left remarkably few archaeological traces, except for a probable Caesarian military camp in the Treverian area near Hermeskeil. The efficiency of the Roman military machine is however demonstrated a generation later by the two-legion camp Trier-»Petrisberg«, built in an incredibly short time; it probably was the main base of the Roman troops for the suppression of a first Treverian revolt in 30–29 BC.

The Celtic tribes – in our state the Treveri in the north and the Mediomatrici in the south – largely continued to exist as social units even after the defeat. Only their territory in the military zone along the Rhine was lost permanently and developed differently both politically and through massive immigration. In cemeteries of the old tribal areas, the political-military upheaval does not begin to show until at least one generation later with first approaches to the lifestyle of the conquerors, and only in the medium-term with a far-reaching romanization. In this process, the tribal aristocracy with greater open-mindedness adopts some elements of Mediterranean lifestyle, for e.g. wine, as status symbols.

Bibliography

R. Echt, Das Fürstinnengrab von Reinheim. Saarbrücker Beiträge zur Altertumskunde 69 (Bonn 1999).

H. Nortmann, Die ältere Eisenzeit (780–250 v. Chr.). In: Kreuz, Rad, Löwe. Rheinland-Pfalz. Ein Land und seine Geschichte 1 (Mainz 2012) 101–115.

H. Nortmann, Wie viel Gefolge hat der ›Fürst‹? Keltische Gesellschaft und Demographie in der Region Trier. In: M. Koch (Hg.), Archäologie in der Großregion. Archäologentage Otzenhausen 1 (Nonnweiler 2015) 91–108.

H. Nortmann, Frühlatènekunst in der Mittelrheinzone – Charakter, Umfeld, Entstehung. Archäologisches Korrespondenzblatt 46, 2016, 213–231.

H. Nortmann, Befestigungen der Eisenzeit im Hunsrück-Nahe-Raum. Forschungsstand, Fragen und Hypothesen. Trierer Zeitschrift 71/ 72, 2008/ 09, 15–25.

A. Zeeb-Lanz, Der Donnersberg. Eine bedeutende spätkeltische Stadtanlage. Archäologische Denkmäler in der Pfalz 2 (Speyer 2008).

H. Heinen, Trier und das Trevererland in römischer Zeit. 2000 Jahre Trier 1 (Trier 1985).

A. Haffner, Gräber – Spiegel des Lebens. Schriftenreihe des Rheinischen Landesmuseums Trier 2 (Mainz 1989).

R. Gleser, Studien zu sozialen Strukturen der historischen Kelten in Mitteleuropa aufgrund der Gräberanalyse. Die keltisch-römische Nekropole von Hoppstädten-Weiersbach im Kontext latènezeitlicher Fundgruppen und römischer Okkupation. Saarbrücker Beiträge zur Altertumskunde 81 (Bonn 2005).

H. Löhr, Das frührömische Militärlager auf dem Petrisberg bei Trier. Funde und Ausgrabungen im Bezirk Trier 35, 2003, 21–30.

H.-H. Wegner, Die jüngere Eisenzeit (250 v. bis um Christi Geburt). In: Kreuz, Rad, Löwe. Rheinland-Pfalz. Ein Land und seine Geschichte 1 (Mainz 2012) 117–128.

S. Hornung, Ein spätrepublikanisches Militärlager bei Hermeskeil (Lkr. Trier-Saarburg). Vorbericht über die Forschungen 2010–2011. Archäologisches Korrespondenzblatt 42, 2012, 205–224.

The luxury graves of Bescheid and Worms – witnesses of a cultural upheaval

HANS NORTMANN

By way of example, we will be looking here at three burials from the years around 400 BC in the Rhine Plain (Worms) and on the heights of the Hunsrück (Bescheid, Trier-Saarburg district). These graves were not isolated but belong to a large grave zone (Fig. 1), which was used continuously at least during the 6th–3rd century BC or even longer (Worms). The aim of the examinations performed during recent building work, which were concluded in Bescheid and only partially conducted in Worms, is to understand what went on in the history of the settlement communities buried here.

Weapons and a female jewellery set among the burial equipment on the one hand show the gender-specific self-perception of the populace. The graves of the two warriors and the woman are, however, also outstanding ›luxury graves‹ and thus characteristic of their time. Within the surroundings of a normal cemetery, members of the local leading family were thus honoured for a short time through particularly lavish equipment. The question arises of why the social status was demonstrated in such a conspicuous manner and only during these few decades.

The typical equipment of the luxury graves consisted of artisanally elaborate weapons, jewellery, and items for representational purposes, often made of gold or upgraded with gold. The manufacturing of the smooth golden arm rings, the perforated belt hook or the chariot alone requires more specialist knowledge and work than one could and would afford in previous years. The two-wheeled, light parade chariots of many luxury graves, like the one in Bescheid, underline above all the status of distinguished persons.

A representative bronze vessel, an exotic drinking tableware from upper and central Italy, is added to the equipment of nearly all luxury graves. Especially in the form of Etruscan wine flagons with their rim animals, tendrils, flowers, and palmettes (Fig.2), these vessels are unmistakable representatives of a foreign lifestyle allowing the owner to present himself before guests and peers as a man of the world. Even the local clay pot with handles, of little practical use, can only be understood as an imitation of a southern metal amphora. The laborious procurement and reproduction of these luxury objects alone signifies for Central Europe a new and simply overwhelming perception of the Mediterranean world. Moreover, this seems to provide a key to the ostentatious, although time-limited demonstration of one's self-perception in luxury graves.

The Mediterranean images and plant ornaments of the Etruscan showpieces clash with a non-pictorial and decisively plain art practice in the Middle Rhine zone. This encounter soon triggered its own forms of expression in a kind of chain reaction. With the gold decorative disc (Fig. 3) and the perforated belt hook, the warrior grave of Worms contains two not only aesthetically appealing answers to southern art: we can also say that the peculiar, still non-pictorial motifs are probably alluding in a symbolic manner to a world view of its own, even if its contents still remain quite enigmatic. This artistic creation probably marks a break with tradition and a new start that may reach into the religious sphere. The first Celtic style and the basis for an all-Celtic stylistic idiom develop in this way within a few decades. Ancient tradition in Italy refers to the alien intruders who cultivate this style there as »Celts«. By inference, we call the still anonymous relatives on the Rhine and Moselle: Celts.

Fig. 1
Bescheid, Trier Saarburg distr. and Hernsheim, city of Worms. Grave mounds with ceremonial graves (red) in connection with the completely or only partly known normal burials of the 6th–3rd century BC. (GDKE/Landesarchäologie/Trier)

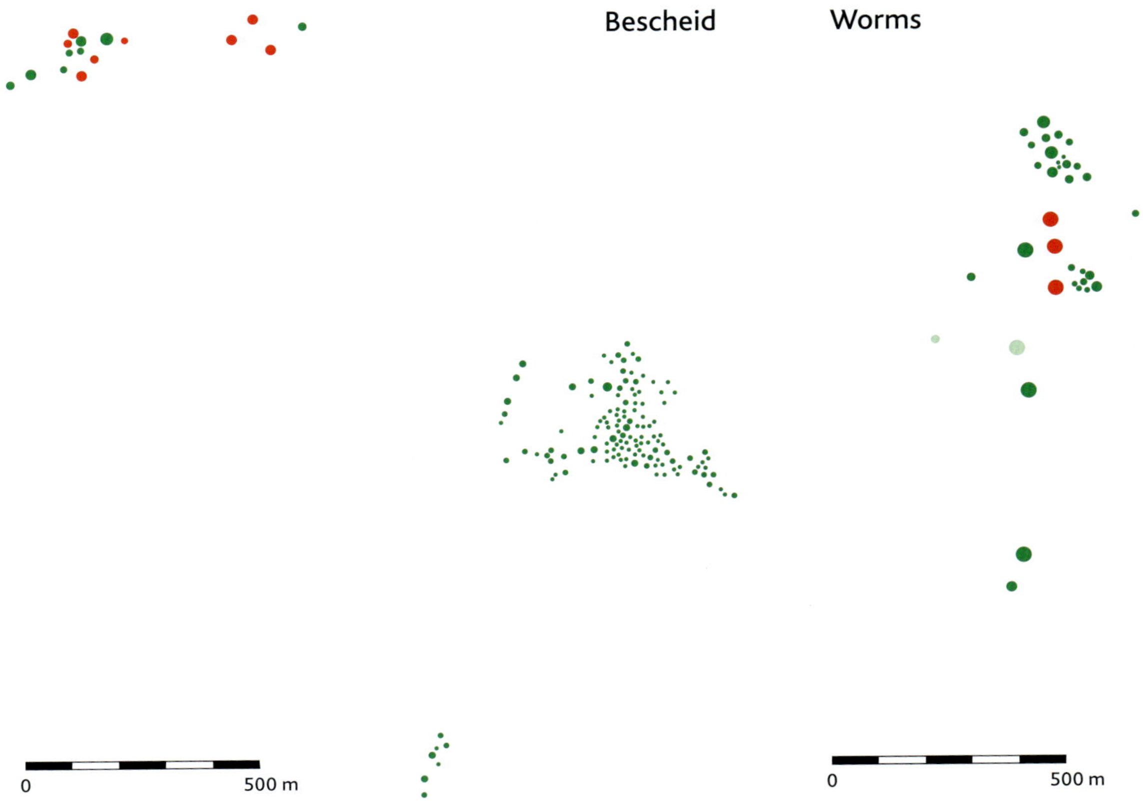

Fig. 2
Bescheid, Trier Saarburg distr. (right) and Herrnsheim, city of Worms (left). Decorated Etruscan bronze jugs and plant motifs from the neck and handle attachments. (GDKE/Landesarchäologie/Trier)

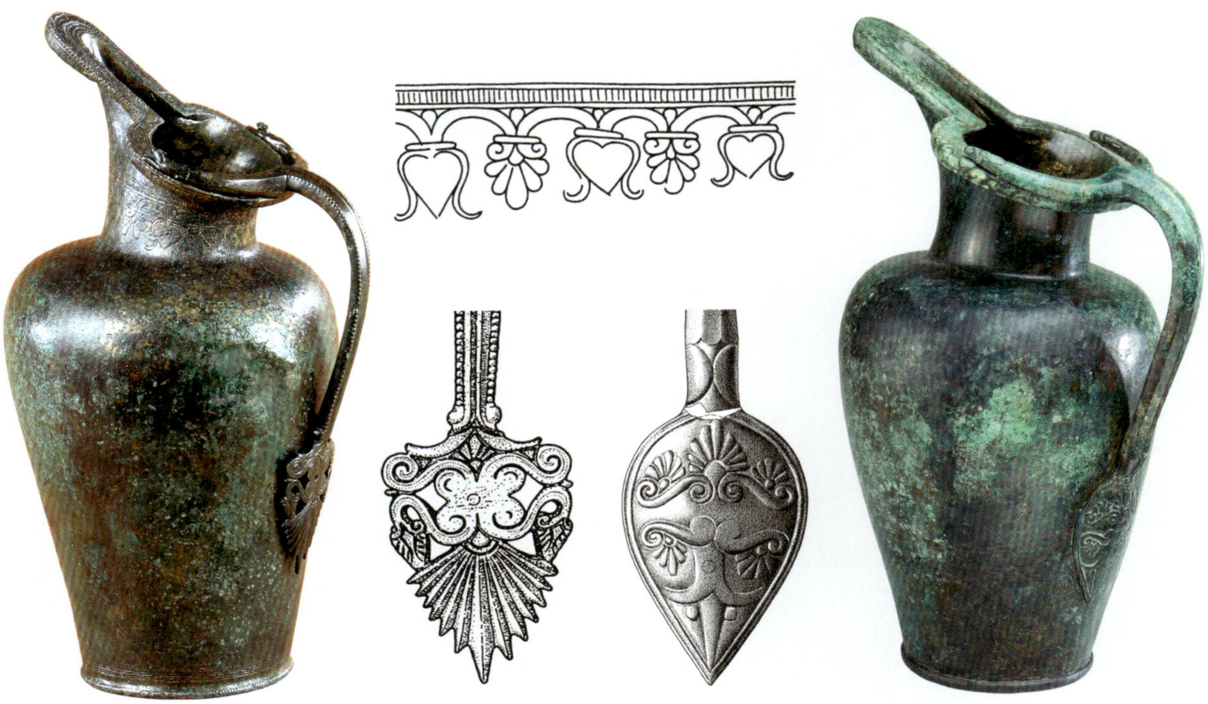

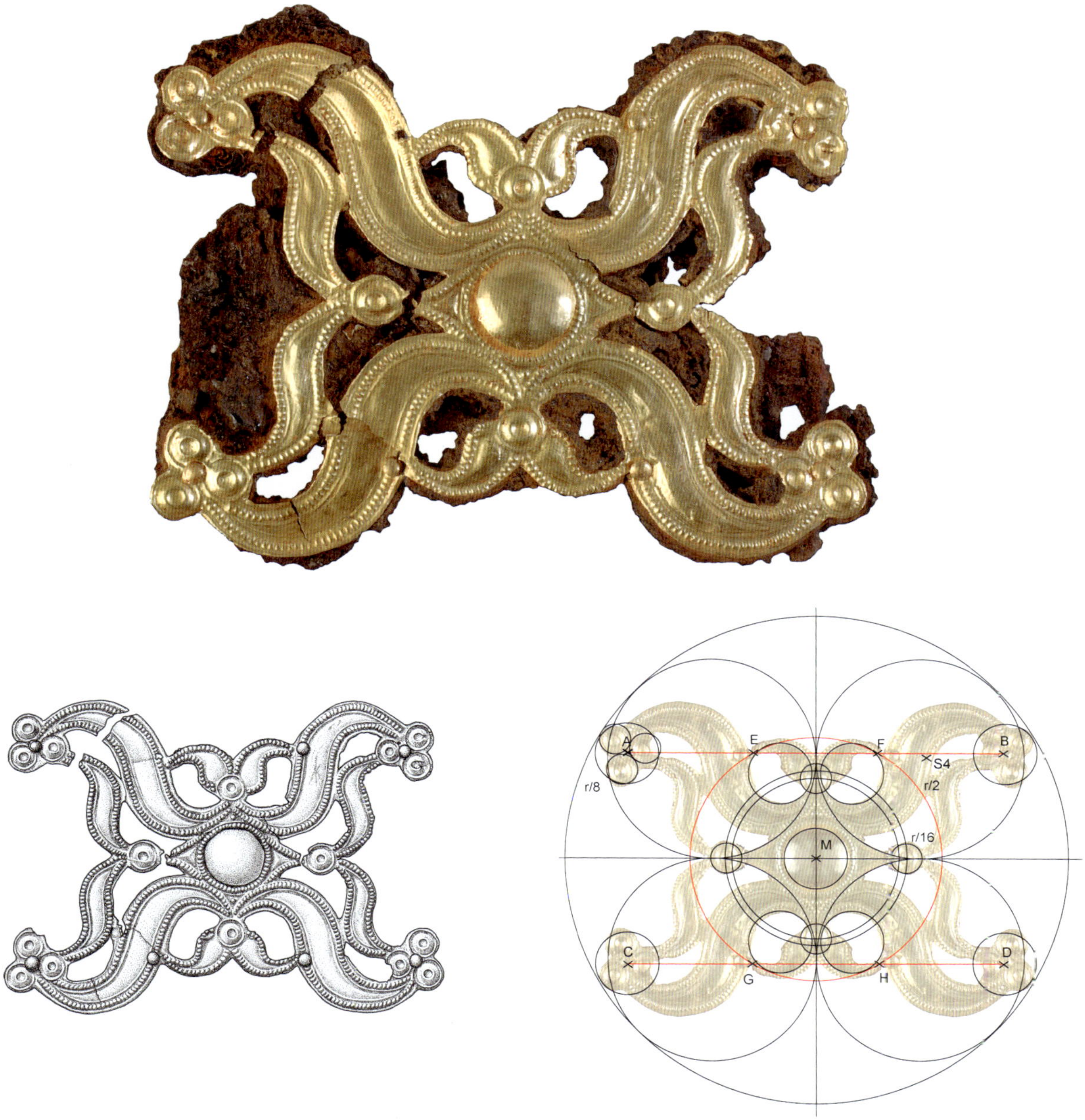

Fig. 3
Worms-Hernsheim, city of Worms. Decorative gold disc with typical Celtic transformations of Etruscan motifs; bottom right: the circle scheme on which it is based. (after Brücken 2014)

Bibliography:

R. **Cordie-Hackenberg**, Das eisenzeitliche Hügelgräberfeld von Bescheid, Kreis Trier-Saarburg. Trierer Zeitschrift Beiheft 17 (Trier 1993).

A. **Hafner**, M. **Lage**, Die frühkeltische Prunkgrabnekropole von Bescheid »Bei den Hübeln«, Kreis Trier-Saarburg. Trierer Zeitschrift 71/72, 2008/ 2009, 27–142.

D. **Zylmann**, Die frühen Kelten in Worms-Herrnsheim (Mainz 2006).

G. **Brücken**, Eine neu gefundene Goldscheibe vom Typ Weiskirchen aus dem Gräberfeld Worms-Herrnsheim. Archäologisches Korrespondenzblatt 44, 2014, 495–508.

ROMAN TIMES

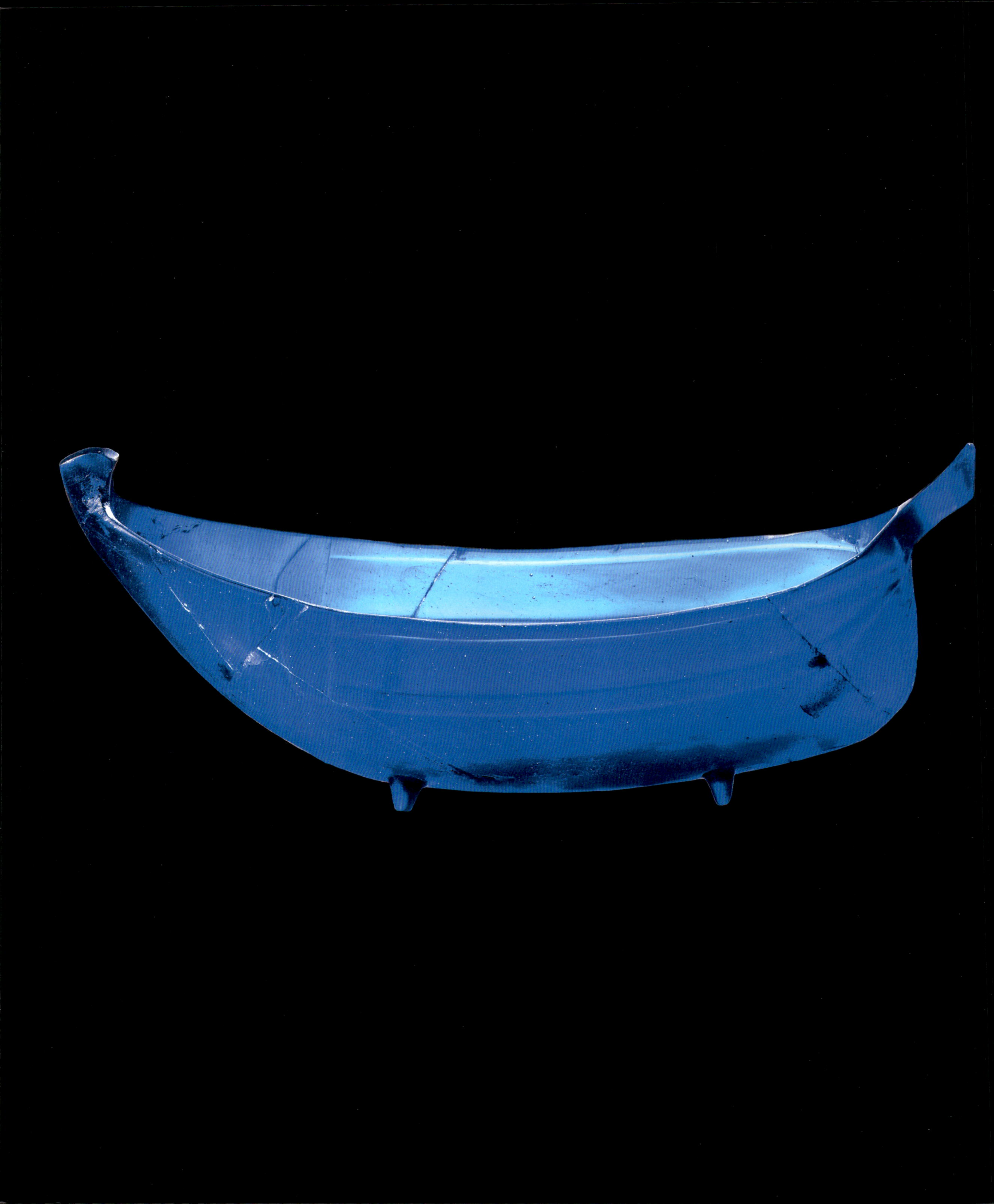

The early and middle periods of the Roman Empire

PETER HENRICH

Today's Rhineland-Palatinate once belonged to the Roman provinces of Gallia Belgica from 85 AD, Upper Germany/*Germania superior* and Lower Germany/*Germania inferior*. We know of the Celtic tribes of the Nemetri, Vangiones, Mediomatrici, Treverians, Caerosi, and Ubii from pre-Roman times.

The Upper Germanic-Rhaetian Limes

With the construction of the Upper Germanic-Rhaetian Limes at the end of the 1st century, the Roman military presence is massively strengthened in Rhineland-Palatinate. The areas on the right side of the Rhine, from Rheinbrohl on the Rhine to Eining on the Danube, are secured in several stages of construction with a total of 120 forts, around 900 watch towers, ramparts, trenches and palisades, and a wall in Rhaetia. The fort locations along the Rhine south of Remagen are abandoned. In Rhineland-Palatinate, the Roman border with the Germanic tribes now runs from Rheinbrohl to Holzhausen at the Hesse border, with an overall length of 75 km. We know of a total of nine cohort forts, ten small forts and 132 tower locations. Since 2005, the Limes has been a UNESCO World Heritage Site.

The Limes was constructed in stages. At first, wooden towers secured a path free of trees marking the border. A palisade was later erected as a clear borderline, which could only be passed at certain places. In the middle of the 2nd century, the wooden towers were replaced by stone towers, and finally a rampart-ditch system reinforced the palisade or existed simultaneously with the latter. (Fig. 1)

The best-known Limes fort in Rhineland-Palatinate is located in Neuwied-Niederbieber. It was destroyed in the years 260-270 AD during battles either between Germanic tribes and Romans or during inter-Roman conflicts. Parts of a standard were found in the battle debris and the well-known head of a dragon standard was retrieved in the *vicus*. The fact that after more than 170 years of Limes research new discoveries are still being made is demonstrated by the discovery of a new Limes fort located for the first time in 2016, during geophysical surveys south of Marienfels in the Rhein-Lahn district. After the incursions by Germanic tribes and the upheavals of the 3rd century, the Rhine along its entire length once again becomes the border of the Roman Empire.

St. Aldegund, Cochem-Zell district. Bowl made of deep blue transparent glass in the form of a ship with high bow and stern (4th century AD). Grooves and bulges on the outside are meant to indicate a wooden hull. (GDKE/Landesarchäologie/Koblenz/W. Baumann, Höhr-Grenzhausen)

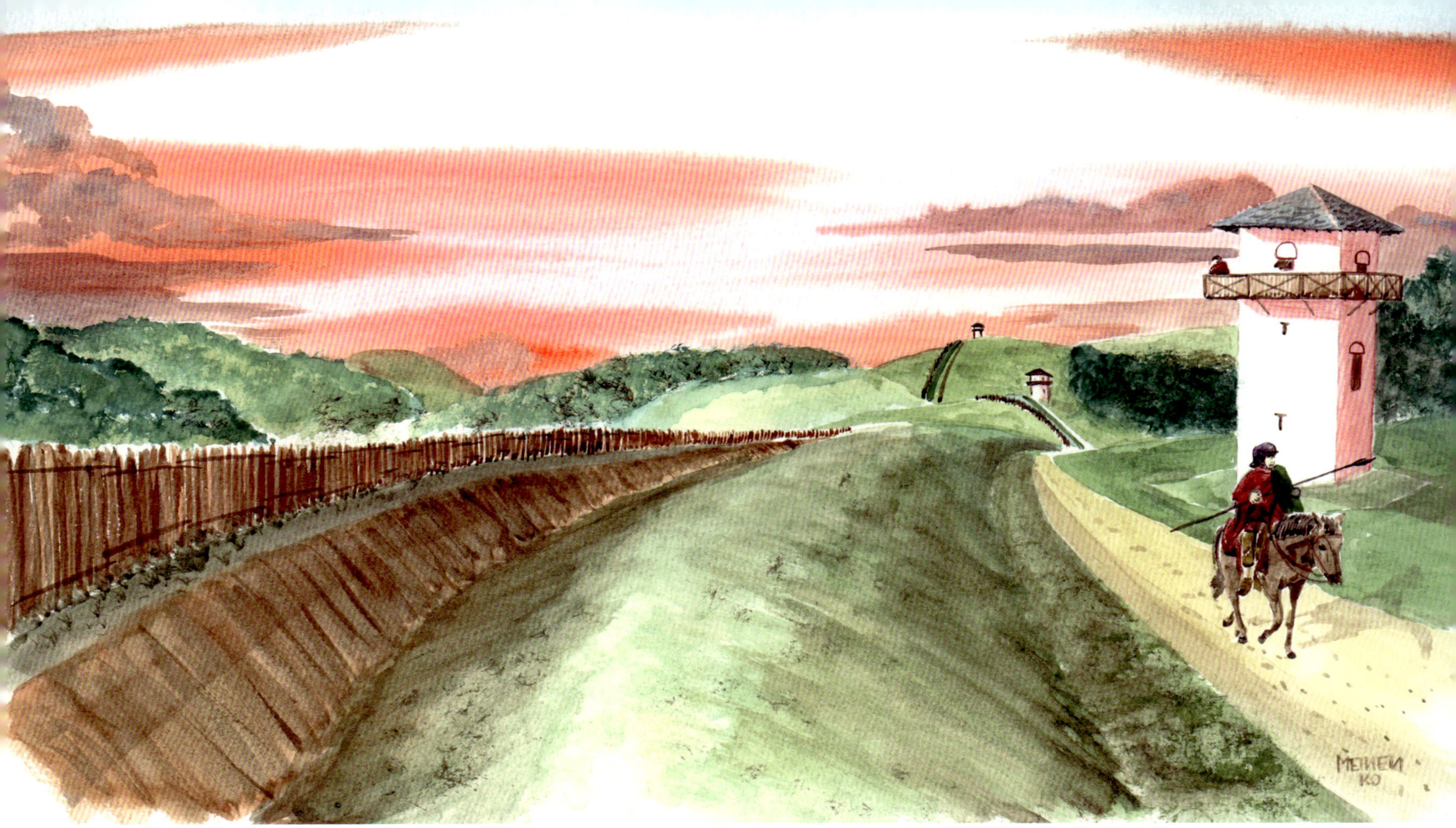

Fig. 1
Reconstruction of the Limes during the last extension phase 4. (GDKE/Landesarchäologie/Koblenz/M. Meinen)

Sanctuaries

Numerous Gallo-Roman sanctuaries (Fig. 2) are known in the area of today's Rhineland-Palatinate. They normally consist of several temples surrounded by an enclosing wall. Typical temple layouts are those of the Gallo-Roman gallery temple with a rectangular central room *(cella)* and a gallery, as well as small, square, rectangular or even polygonal temples, consisting of one room. A statue of the worshipped deity was placed in every temple. (Fig. 3–4) Besides the Roman goddesses and gods, local deities were also worshipped. Numerous terracotta figures, for instance, show that mother goddesses were worshipped, although one does not always know their names. In addition, a fusion of the names and attributes of Roman and Gallic deities is no exception for Gaul, but rather the rule. As regards temple areas, a distinction must be made between the sanctuaries which had already been frequented since pre-Roman times and those erected in the 1st century AD. An example of a sanctuary with Celtic roots is the Martberg near Pommern on the Moselle. Numerous small finds such as fibulae and coins, but also architectural findings, bear witness to both traditional rites and new Roman-Italic influences. In this context, one should also mention the Gallo-Roman sanctuary in the Celtic *oppidum* of Kastel-Staadt. At the start of the 2nd century, a theatre of the Gallo-Roman type is built there next to the central temple. (Fig. 5–6) In Gaul, these theatres, whose layout differs considerably from the classic Roman type, are found in or directly near sanctuaries, and were used for all kinds of assemblies including theatre performances, though they were mostly used in the context of rituals for pageants and other festivities. In Rhineland-Palatinate, theatres of this kind are documented through inscriptions in the *vici* of Bitburg/Beda and Wederath/Belginum.

The sanctuaries without archaeologically traceable Celtic origins are mostly smaller temple areas which date from the middle of the 1st century AD. Examples of this are Pelm »Judenkirchhof«, Bremm »Calmont« or the temple area of Tawern. Coins, fibulae, and ter-

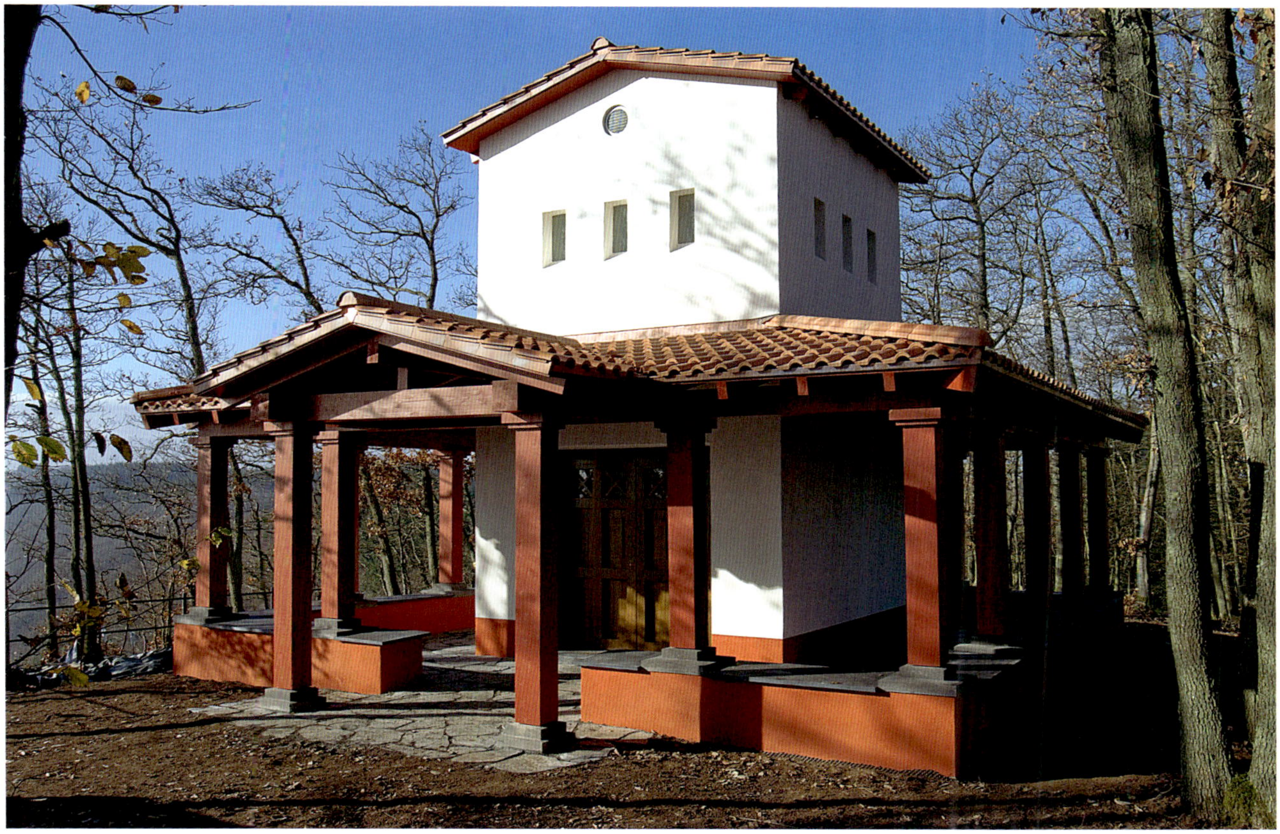

Fig. 2
Bremm–Calmont, Cochem-Zell district. Reconstruction of a Gallo-Roman temple. (GDKE/Landesarchäologie/Koblenz/C. A. Jost)

racotta statuettes were sacrificed in the sanctuaries in large numbers as votives to the gods. There are also regional votives which are typical for certain sanctuaries, such as the miniature vessels specially made for rituals (Fig. 7) and intentionally damaged coins from the Martberg, or coin-like lead votives from Nierstein-Schwabsberg. The end of the rituals and thus the end of the sanctuaries are to be dated in the 4th century. We do not yet definitively know whether the reasons for this are to be found in the growing Christianisation, the plundering by Germanic tribes, or in a general transformation of society.

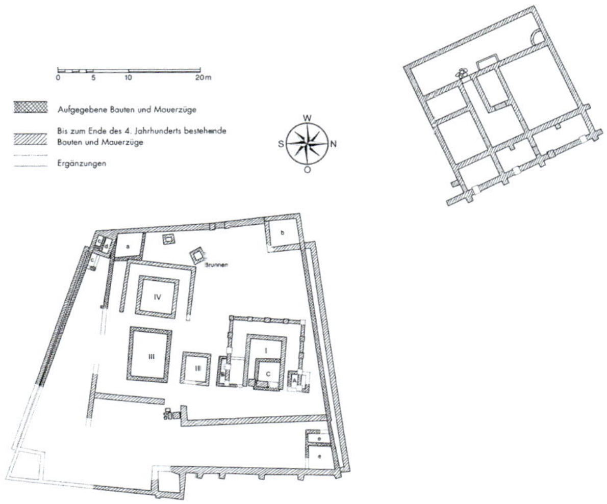

Fig. 3
Tawern, Trier-Saarburg district. Plan of the Gallo-Roman temple area. (GDKE/Landesmuseum Trier/S. Faust)

Villae rusticae

In terms of numbers, farms *(villae rusticae)* dominate the sites of Roman times documented archaeologically in Rhineland-Palatinate.

These *villa* sites, comparable to isolated farms of today, as a rule consist of a main house and several ancillary buildings, which are used as stables, barns or sheds. They were surrounded by a wall or a hedge. The graves were usually located outside the farm enclosure. The porticus villa with pavilions (*Eckrisaliten*) (Bollendorf/Stahl type) can be considered as the stereotypical

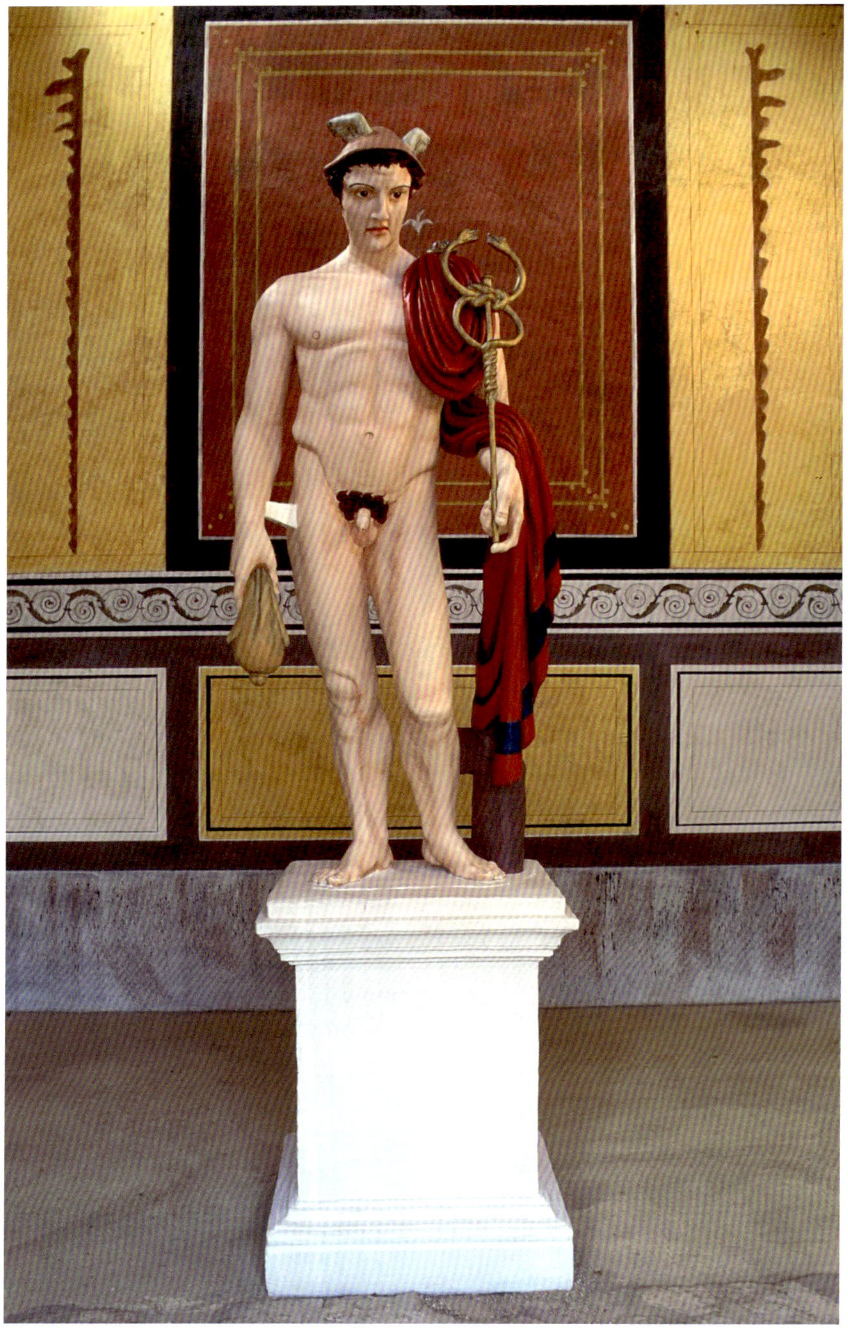

Fig. 4
Tawern, Trier-Saarburg district. Reconstructed statue of the god Mercury in the temple area. (GDKE/Landesmuseum Trier/ Th. Zühmer)

basic form for the main building, documented in large numbers in north Gaul and the neighbouring territories. This is a building with a central hall, surrounded by several rooms, baths and the two pavilions. The latter are connected by a colonnade *(porticus)* and form a front façade of at least 25–30 m in length. (Fig. 8) Examples of this building type are the villas of Bingen and Bodenbach (Phase 1). In the direct vicinity of the main house there are two or more ancillary buildings without a well-defined orientation to the main house. These villa sites are referred to as »dispersed« farm sites. Villas of the axial yard type are the second most important kind. They are characterized by numerous ancillary buildings arranged in two rows axial to the main house. The area covered by the ancillary buildings is normally larger than 5 ha and can be as much as 16 ha, as can be seen by the example of Gillenfeld. (Fig. 9) These villas have a basic structure with a working area comprising the ancillary buildings *(pars rustica)*, which is separated by a wall and entrance from the *pars urbana* where the main house stands and into which the owner could withdraw. The front of the main building is longer than 60 m. Here, too, one often finds pavilions, though in this case these consist of several rooms. Many of these main buildings evidently follow the basic concept of the Bollendorf/Stahl type, but the buildings are three to four times as big. The pavilions, which usually consisted of one room, are now formed by several rooms. Furthermore, these sites were often decorated with rich mosaics, marble plates, and stucco. Examples of axial yard villas are Gillenfeld »Römerberg« or Mendig »Lungenkärchen«. Because of their size, finish, and topographical position, these luxurious villa sites served as status symbols and bear witness to the great need of their owners for representativeness. Tunnelled water supplies for a constant provision of fresh water to individual large villas are also to be considered in this context.

The economic basis of the villas was agriculture, animal husbandry, and the sale of stone material in the form of mill stones or building material. Agricultural production was supplemented by the production of wine (which had significantly increased since emperor Probus) in numerous wine press houses in the Moselle or in the Palatinate (e.g. in Piesport and Bad Dürkheim-Ungstein).

The earliest stone villas in Rhineland-Palatinate are documented for the 1st century AD. We can assume, however, that the big axial yard sites in particular – like that of Borg in the neighbouring Saarland – had predecessor wooden buildings of the Latène period, which were later rebuilt and enlarged in stone. After only a few securely documented villa locations of the first half of the 1st century, the number of estates increases continuously towards the end of the century, reaching a maximum in the 2nd and early 3rd centuries. Only the incursions by Germanic tribes in the 3rd century affect the economic boom on the supra-regional level so much that numerous estates are abandoned.

Villages *(vici)*

Besides *coloniae* (civilian colonies, veterans' settlements) and *municipia* (civilian towns with administration), in Roman times there were also settlements in the country with clearly lower legal status, which are referred to as *vici*. The modern translation as »village« should not convey the wrong impression, since these *vici* – as central places several hectares large for commerce and trade, but also in connection with sanctuaries – formed the backbone of the Roman economy in the provinces together with the villas. Typical for

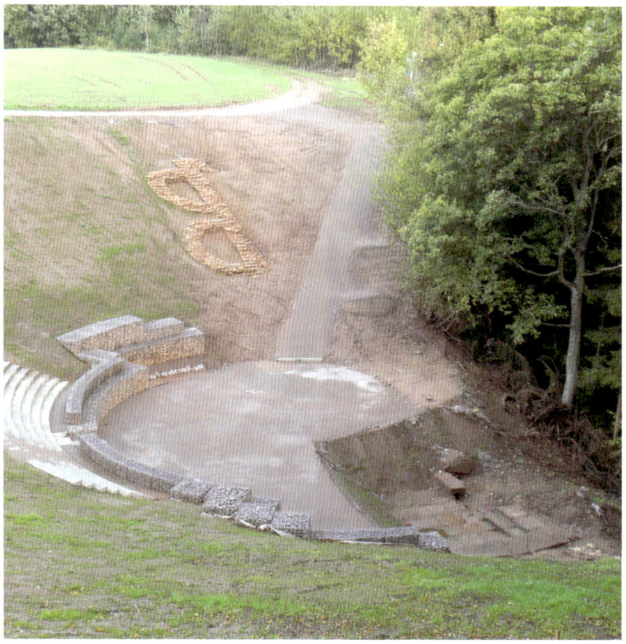

Fig. 5
Kastel-Staadt, Trier-Saarburg district. Gallo-Roman theatre. Survey photo after the excavations. (GDKE/Landesarchäologie/Trier/B. Kremer)

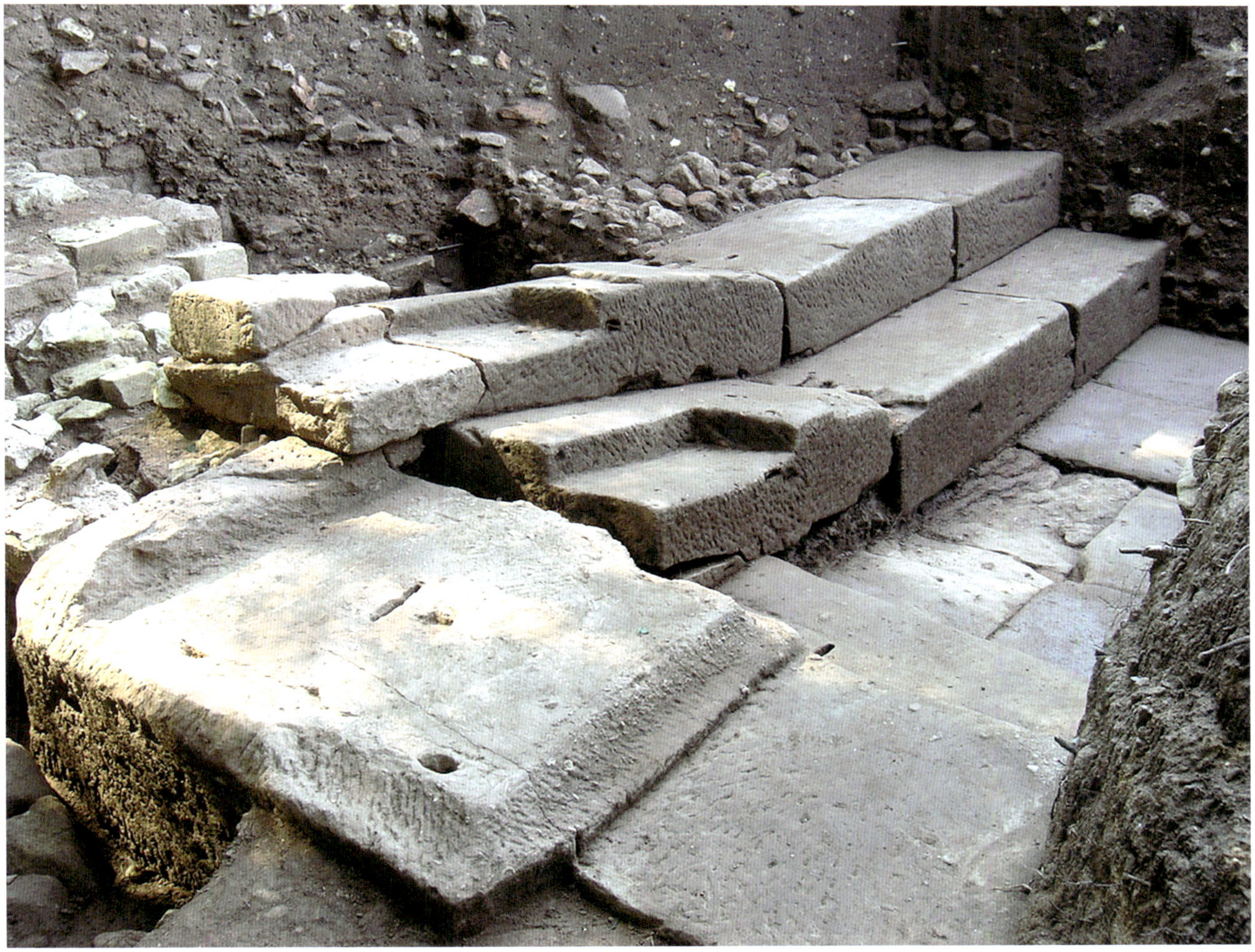

Fig. 6
Kastel-Staadt, Trier-Saarburg district. Detail of the seating steps and the stairs during the excavations. (GDKE/Landesarchäologie/Trier/B. Kremer)

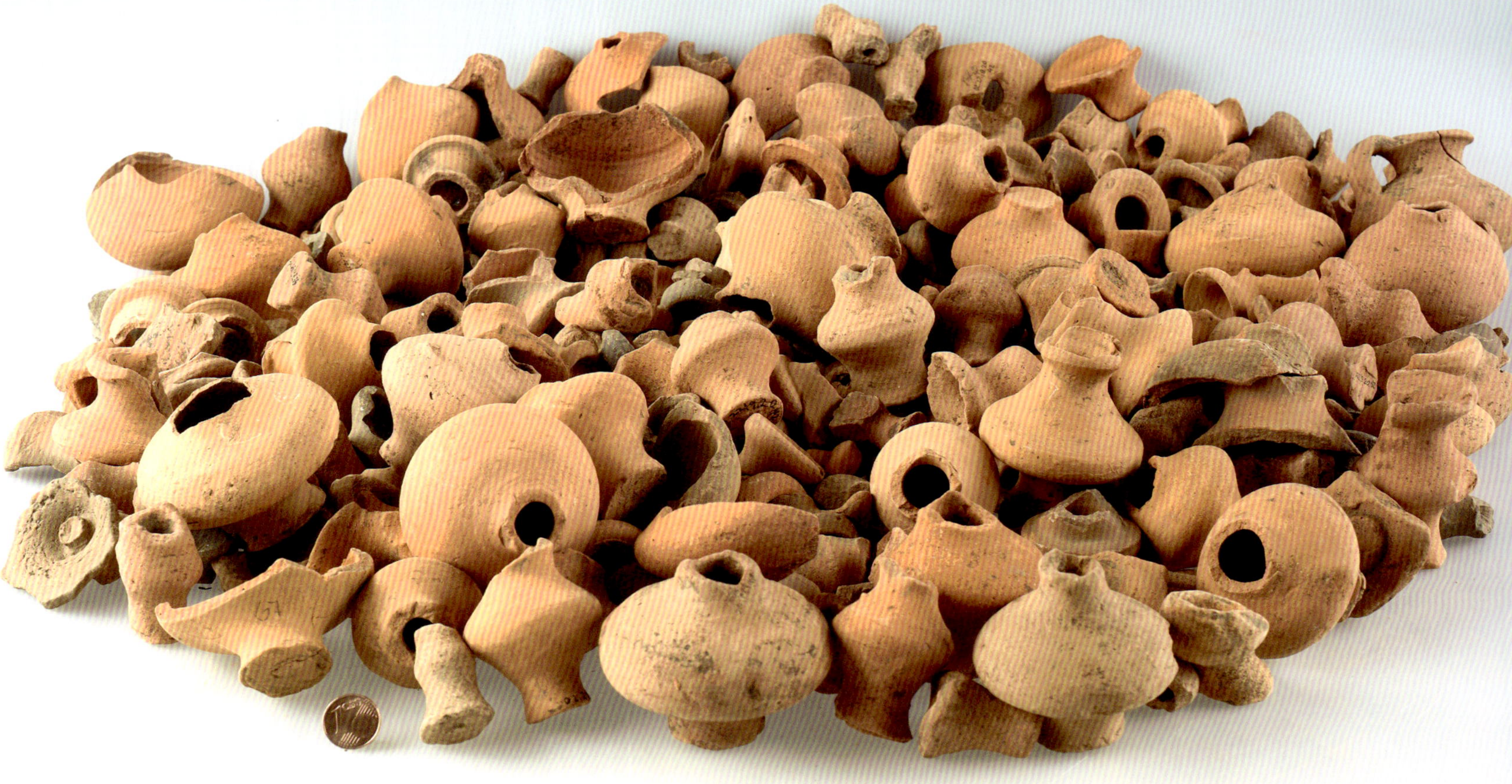

Fig. 7
Martberg, Cochem-Zell district. Miniature vessels from the sanctuary. (GDKE/Landesarchäologie/Koblenz/M. Neumann)

this form of settlement are long, rectangular houses, so-called strip houses, which were oriented towards the road with one narrow side. The houses were connected by a colonnade *(porticus)*. (Fig. 10) In the part of the house facing the road there was a shop, behind it living and utility rooms. The back of the plot was used as a garden. Latrines and technical installations, such as stoves etc., are also documented. Depending on its size and importance, a *vicus* included sanctuaries, theatres, and thermal baths as public buildings.

Unlike modern villages, no agriculture was practised in the *vici*. Commerce and services were the economic basis for the inhabitants *(vicani)*. For this reason, the *vici* developed in places with much public attendance, for instance on important long-distance routes (e.g. *Vicus Belginum*) or near important supra-regional sanctuaries (e.g. Kastel Staadt, Martberg). Some of the *vici* also became supra-regional or even international suppliers for certain products, because they were close to certain raw materials. Examples of this are Rhein-

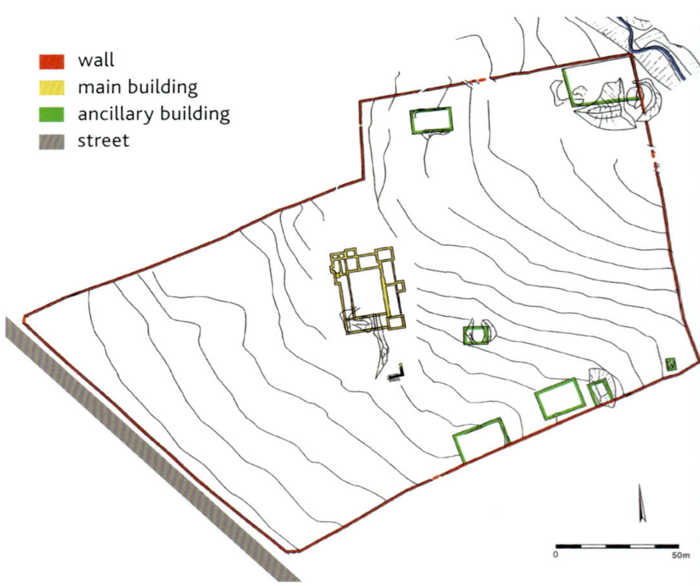

Fig. 8
Bingen, Mainz-Bingen district. Villa complex. The ancillary buildings are east of the main building with pavilions and porticus. (GDKE/Landesarchäologie/Mainz/Chr. Scherer/B. Spannring)

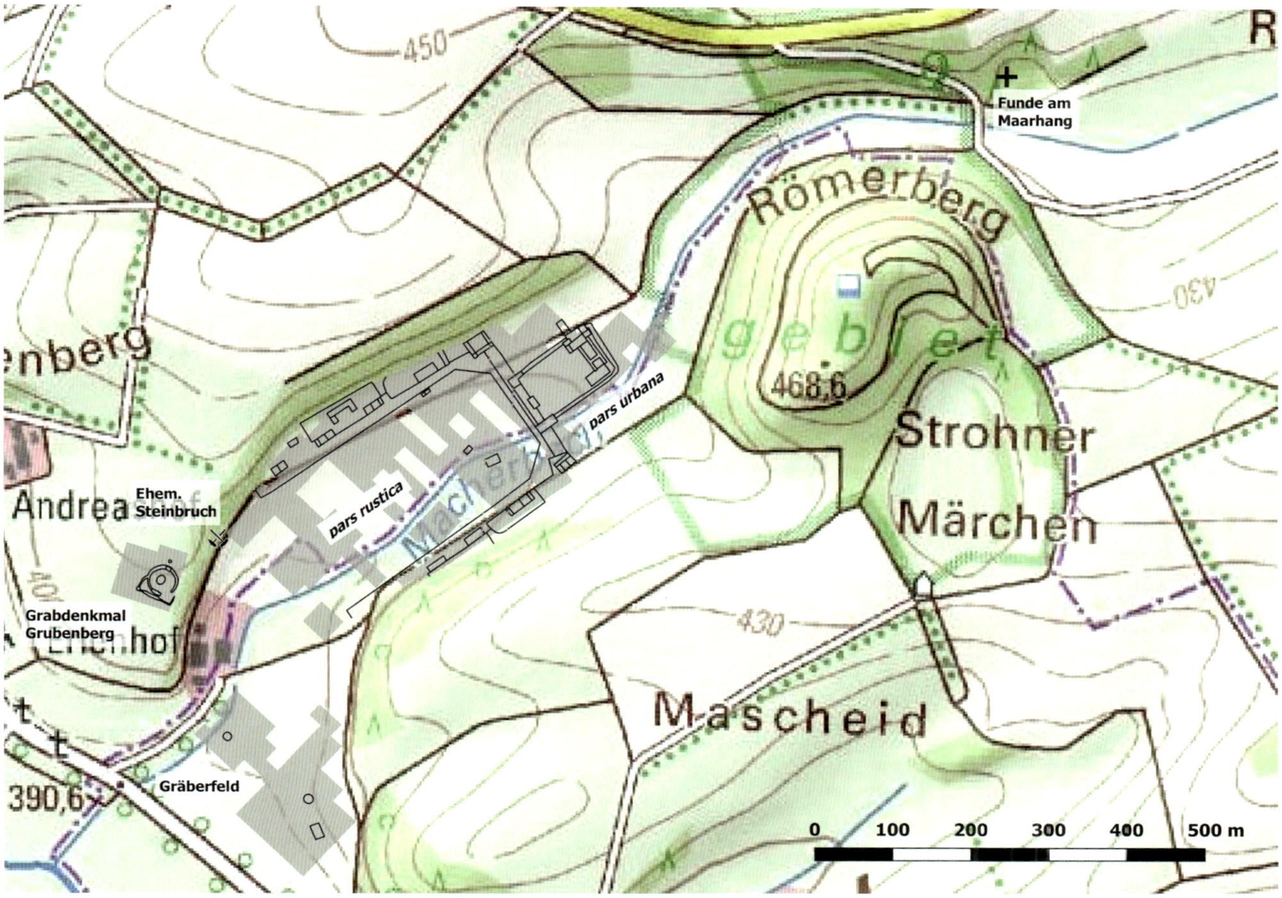

Fig. 9
Gillenfeld, Vulkaneifel district. Axial yard complex »Römerberg« with main building in the pars urbana and ancillary buildings in the pars rustica. (C. Mischka)

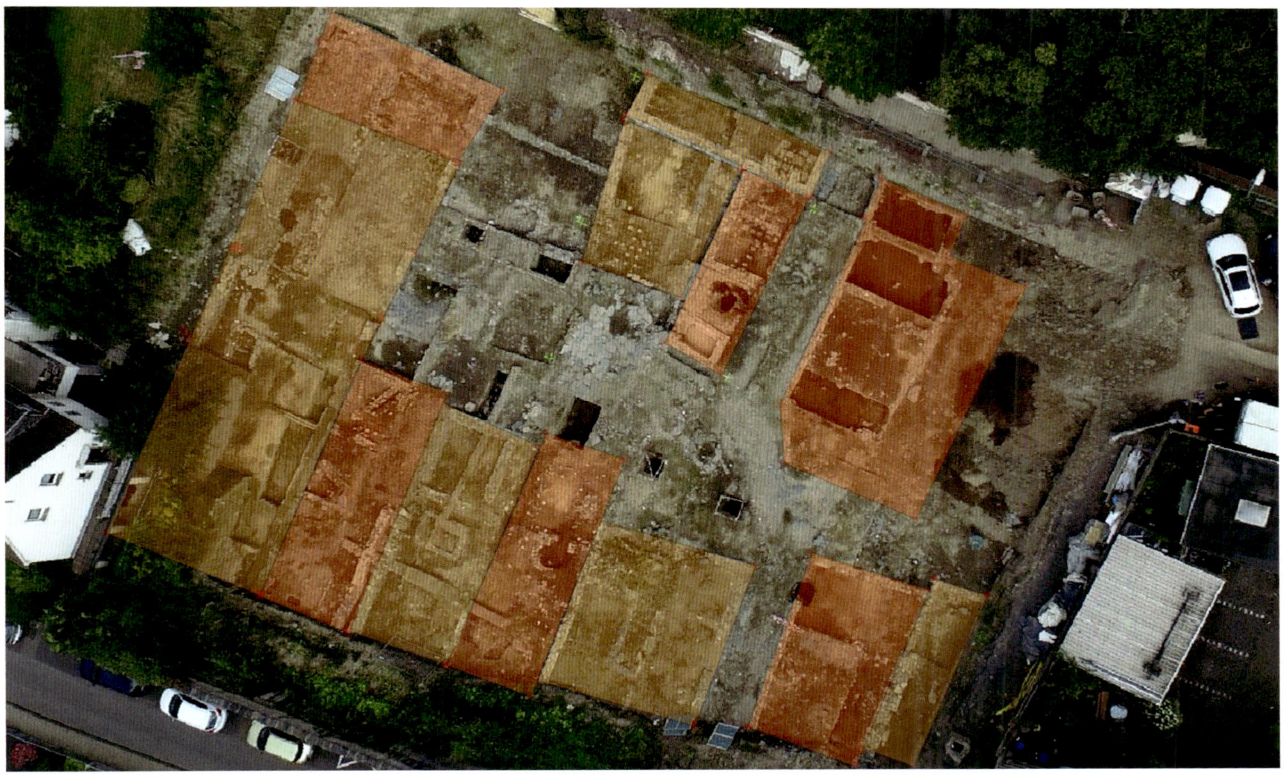

Fig. 10
Andernach, Mayen-Koblenz district. Vicus structure with strip houses. (H.-J. Du Roi)

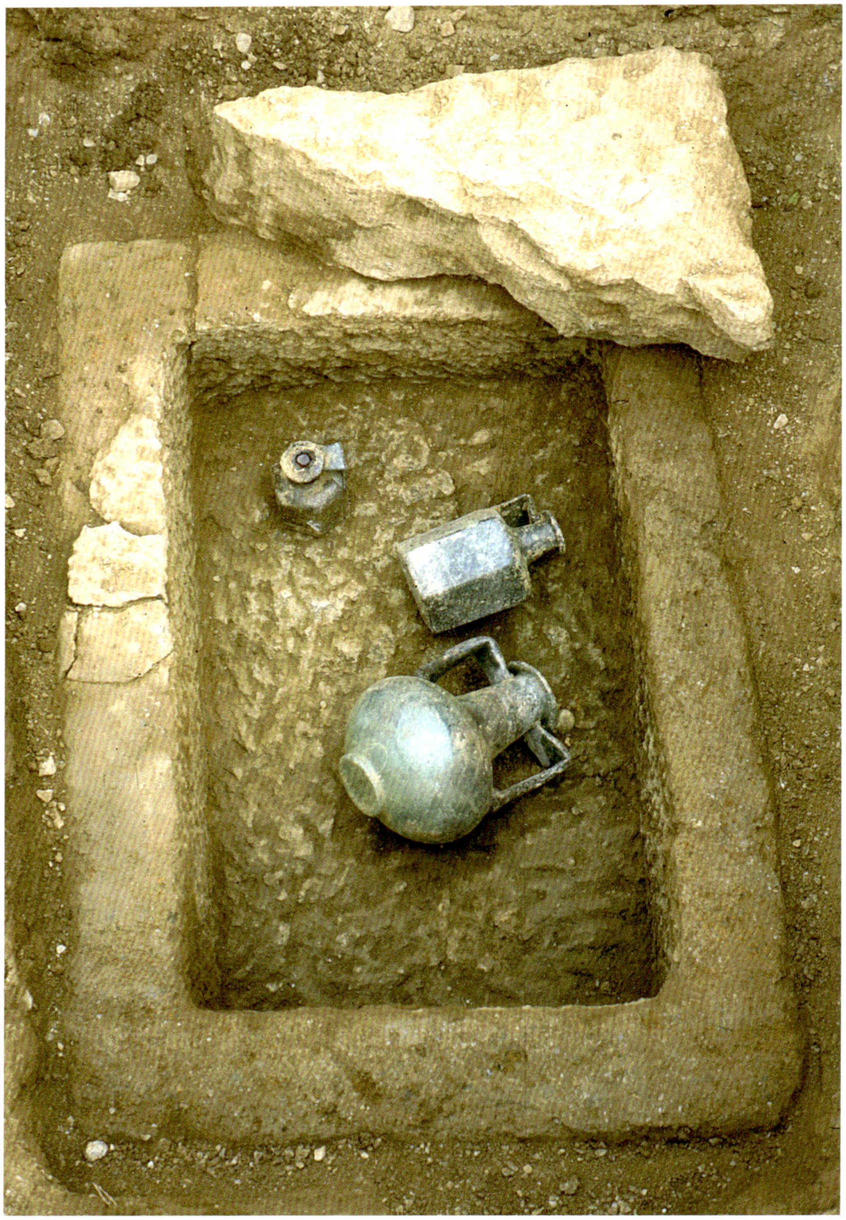

Fig. 11 Leienkaul, Cochem-Zell district. Ash box with three glass vessels of the 2nd century. (GDKE/Landesarchäologie/Koblenz/M. Neumann)

zabern for the manufacture of *terra sigillata* and bricks, Eisenberg for the production of iron, Mayen for the manufacture of mill stones, and Urmitz-Weißenturm and Speicher for rough ceramics. On the other hand, the importance of Andernach and Koblenz can be explained due to their position at the Rhine and thus as a trans-shipment centre for goods of all kinds.

The *vici* underwent a development comparable to that of the villas. After an initial phase in the 1st century, there was a highly positive development during the following two centuries. It was interrupted by the Germanic invasions, and only few settlements managed to once more reach the standard of the preceding couple of centuries.

Graves

Graves and especially the endowment with grave goods and the design above ground provide archaeology with important information about the social structure, but also about the status of the individuals buried there. The analysis of the grave goods also reveals traditional grave rituals as well as new cultural and social influences and trends.

The grave inventories of the upper class in the second half of the 1st century BC differ from the other burials because of the amount and exclusivity of the grave goods (wine amphorae, weapons, chariot burials). While the dead are still being cremated, the marked difference in the quality and quantity of the grave goods disappears with few exceptions during the 1st century AD. Archaeologists are often able to distinguish between graves for women and for men by means of certain grave goods. Specific grave goods provide indications as to special professional knowledge (such as ophthalmologists, dentists or painters). If one considers the grave traditions of the middle imperial time on a supra-regional level, the nearly standardized grave goods were only supplemented by regional, temporarily limited phenomena of the grave cult or by individual and singular grave goods. (Fig. 11)

One also notes that, except for Roman culture, during early imperial times there are archaeologically no or only few foreign influences that are apparent for the rural population in the northern parts of Rhineland-Palatinate. Finds from graves in the Palatinate, however, which are otherwise found mainly in the Elbe area, give an indication of a settlement of Elbe-Germanic groups as early as mid-1st century BC. The considerable standardization of the grave goods contrasts – especially from the 2nd century until the first half of the 3rd century – with the grave structures above ground, which now serve to demonstrate power and prosperity. This is shown impressively by monumental grave structures comparable to the grave tower of Igel (the so-called »Igel Column«) which still stands today. The newly discovered sites of similar grave pillars

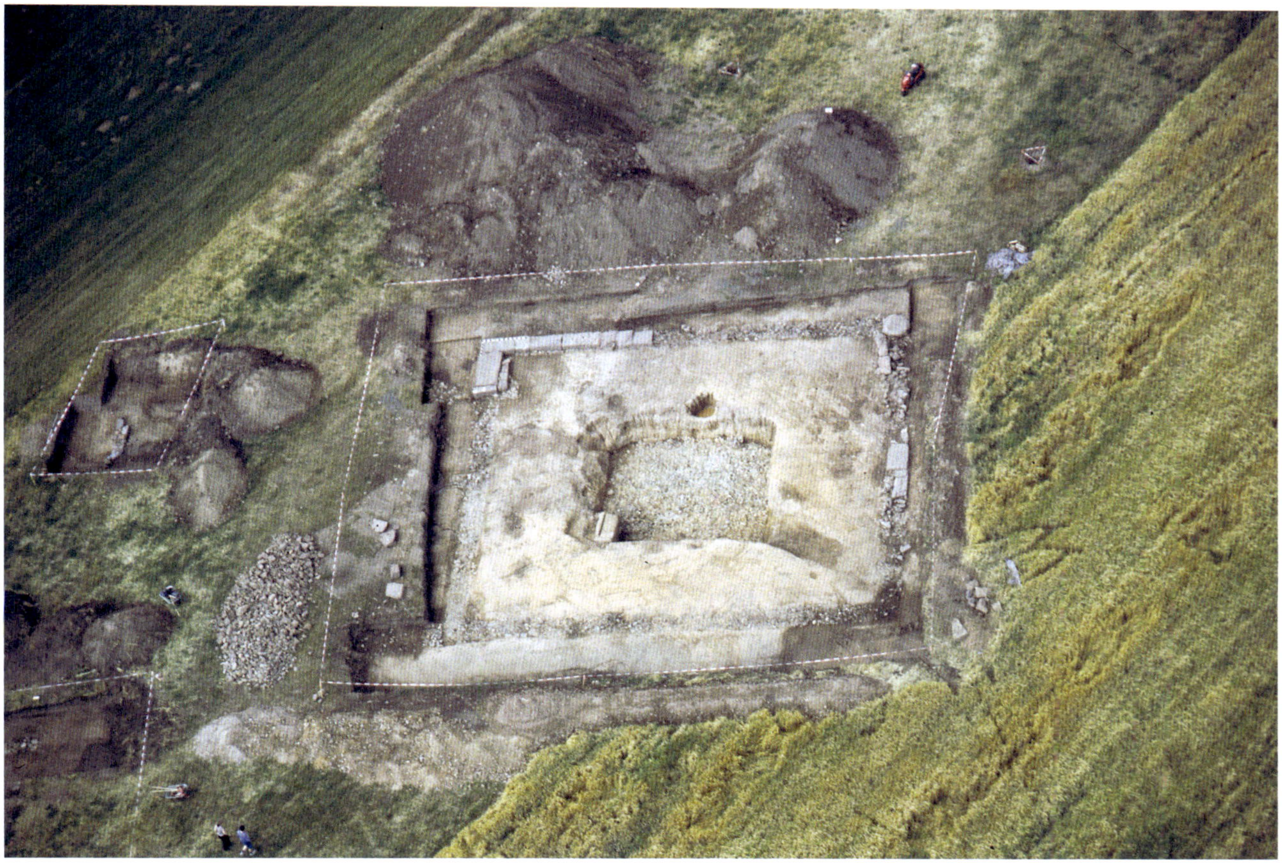

Fig. 12 Duppach-Weiermühle, Vulkaneifel district. Grave memorial A. The broken foundation and the enclosing wall of the memorial are still visible. (P. Henrich)

and the evaluations of sculpture fragments document the wide distribution of this type of monument. The grave monuments from the Vulkaneifel district (Duppach-Weiermühle, Gillenfeld, and Mehren), which all belong to large, well-equipped villas, bear witness to a kind of competition among villa owners trying to outdo one another in building the largest and most exclusive grave monument. (Fig. 12) The solid-stone grave pillars, more than 20 m high and decorated with sculptures painted in colours, usually stood within view of the adjacent road; they were also isolated from the surroundings by a wall.

Monumental grave mounds and grave temples, which continued to be erected, e.g. in Nehren (Fig. 13–14), are further evidence for the display of prosperity and the change from rich grave goods to elaborate grave markings above ground.

The described change in the grave goods custom and the demonstration of a person's high social rank can be recognized in the grave field of the Vicus Belginum. This is the most thoroughly researched grave field in Rhineland-Palatinate and was used continuously from the middle Latène period (3rd century BC) till late antiquity. Rich grave inventories at first and subsequently grave monuments in prominent positions directly facing the road distinguish the graves of the rich and influential people of the vicus. (Fig. 15) A speciality of this grave field are its numerous grave gardens. These are rectangular areas enclosed by a ditch and wall hosting one or several burials. This style of marking graves or grave areas is characteristic of the burials in the Hunsrück and Eifel and has been known since the middle Latène period. Many examples are also found in the Taunus and in the southern Rhineland. We must assume that these grave gardens were the model for rectangular grave areas enclosed by walls from the late 1st to the 3rd century.

During the 3rd century there was a gradual transition towards inhumations rather than cremations. At the same time, rich grave goods and underground monuments again demonstrate the social status of the deceased.

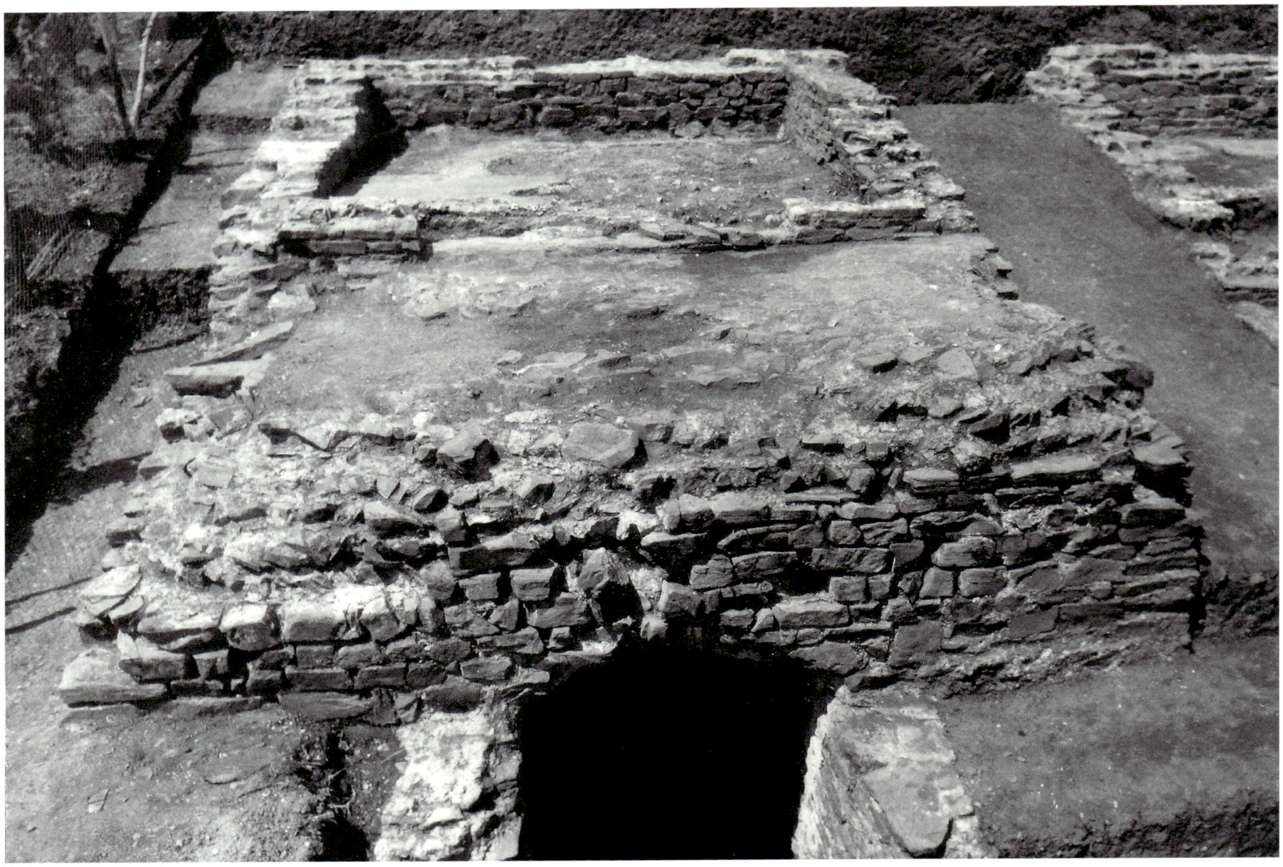

Fig. 13
Nehren, Cochem-Zell district. Western grave building after excavation. (GDKE/Landesarchäologie/Koblenz)

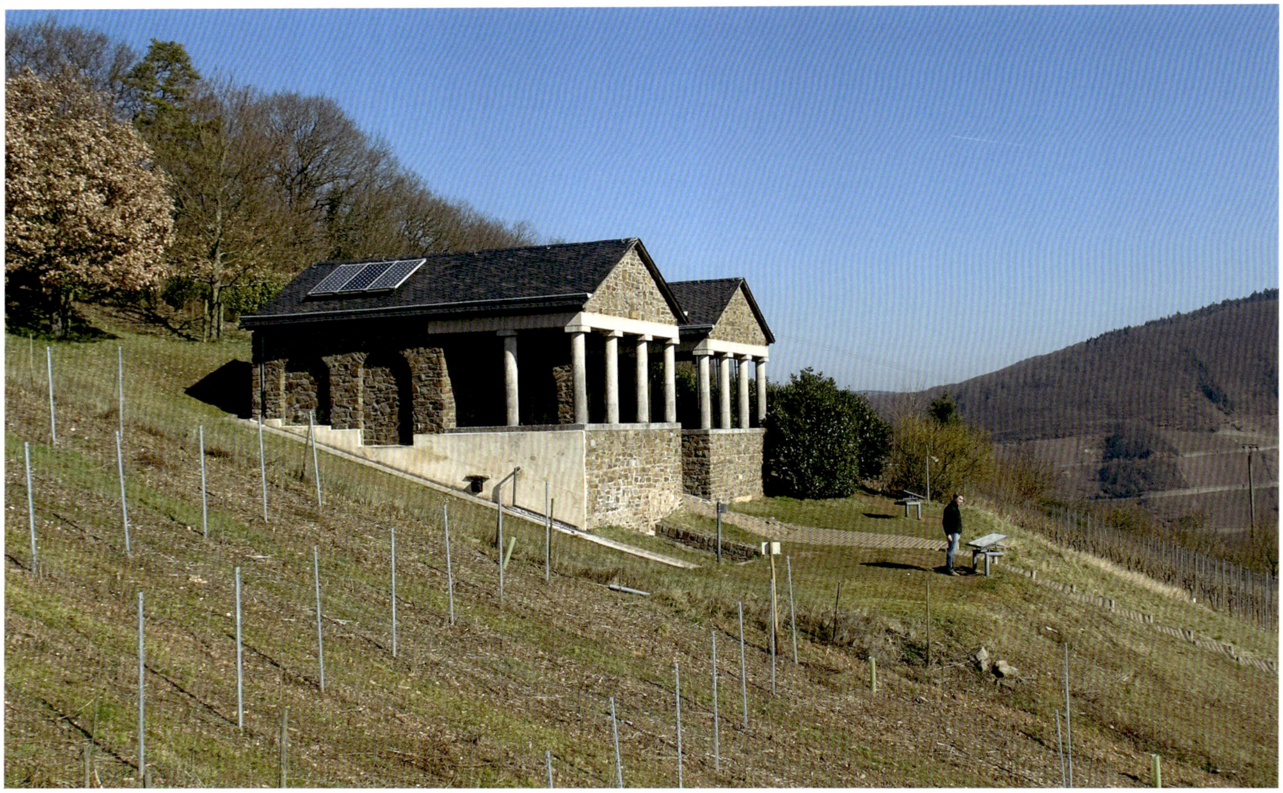

Fig. 14
Nehren, Cochem-Zell district. Reconstruction of the grave complex. (GDKE/Landesarchäologie/Koblenz/C.A. Jost)

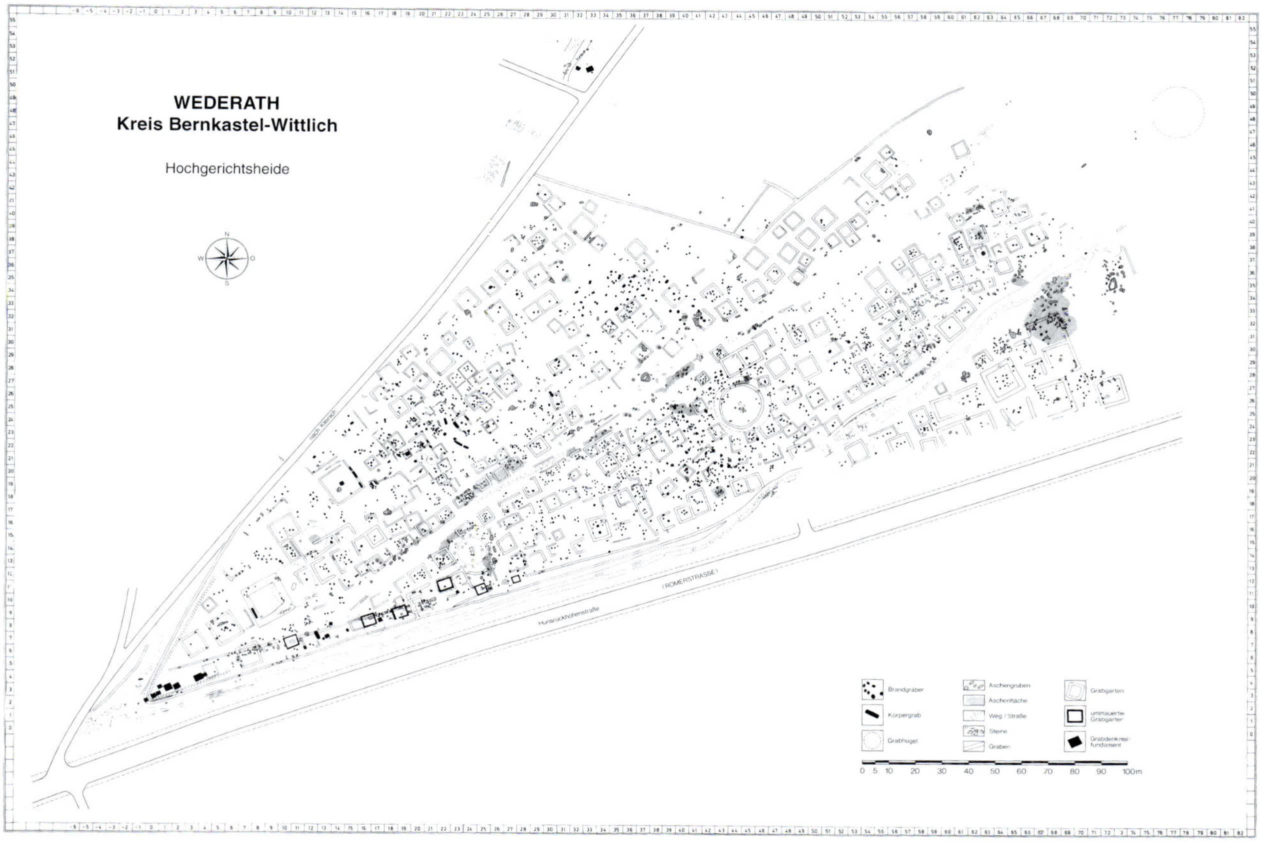

Fig. 15
Wederath, Bernkastel-Wittlich district. Map of the grave field. (GDKE/ Landesmuseum Trier/Dewald)

Bibliography

M. Grünewald, S. Wenzel (Hg.), Römische Landnutzung in der Eifel. Neue Ausgrabungen und Forschungen. RGZM Tagungen 16 (Mainz 2012).

A. Heising (Hg.), Neue Forschungen zu zivilen Kleinsiedlungen (vici) in den römischen Nordwest-Provinzen. Akten der Tagung Lahr 21.–23.10.2010 (Bonn 2013).

P. Henrich (Hg.), Perspektiven der Limesforschung. 5. Kolloquium der Deutschen Limeskommission Köln 2009. Beiträge zum Welterbe Limes 5 (München 2010).

S. Hornung, Das spätrepublikanische Militärlager bei Hermeskeil (Lkr. Trier-Saarburg) – Überlegungen zu den Auswirkungen der römischen Eroberung auf die spätlatenezeitliche Besiedlung im Treverergebiet, in: G. A. Lehmann/R. Wiegels (Hg.), Über die Alpen und über den Rhein – Anfänge und früher Verlauf der römischen Expansion nach Mitteleuropa. Kolloquium Göttingen, 28.–30.11.2012. Abh. Akad. Wiss. Göttingen N.F. 37 (Berlin 2015), 103–132.

M. Scholz, Grabbauten des 1.–3. Jahrhunderts in den nördlichen Grenzprovinzen des Römischen Reiches. Monographien des Römisch-Germanischen Zentralmuseums 103 (Mainz 2012).

The dragon standard from the fort village of Niederbieber

AXEL VON BERG

The fort of Niederbieber is situated in a newly developed area north of the urban district of Niederbieber-Segendorf. It is one of the largest Roman forts on the Upper Germanic Limes. Since the remains were found and documented through archaeological excavations before being built over, the ancient military installation is of central importance in the UNESCO World Heritage Site »Frontiers of the Roman Empire: Upper Germanic-Raetian Limes« in Rhineland-Palatinate.

The fort of Niederbieber existed from about 190 until its destruction in the year 260. It was built during the government of Emperor Commodus (180– 192) and replaced the older fort at Neuwied-Heddesdorf, which was nearer to the Rhine.

The unusual size of the Niederbieber fort indicates that troops of up to 1000 men were housed in barracks there. Stone inscriptions document a *numerus exploratorum Germanicorum Divitiensium* and a *numerus Brittonum*. It seems that during the late period of the fort the *cohors VII Raetorum equitata* had been relocated to Niederbieber. The fort was situated in a strategic position at the northern edge of the Neuwied Basin, about 3.5 km away from the eastern bank of the Rhine. The Limes, which runs from the Rhine over the peripheral ridges of the Westerwald, is about 150 m away northwest of the fort.

First excavations in the Niederbieber fort were already undertaken in the 18th century on instructions by the Wied dynasty. The Imperial Limes Commission subsequently carried out extensive examinations in the years 1897-1912, involving nearly half of the fort area with the well-preserved remains of the main buildings. The State Archaeology undertook further excavations during pumice tuff mining in the years 1963–1968 and 1973–1974. (Fig. 1)

The fort was rectangular with rounded corners and measured 198.50 m × 265.25 m, with an area of 5.2 ha. It was fortified all around by a wall, which went as deep as 2.20 m underground and was up to 2.40 m wide at the bottom. The wall was finished on the outside with a light chalk plaster and red ashlar joints painted on it. In front of the wall there was a 6.0–6.5 m wide ditch around the fort. An earth embankment incorporating the wall walk had been heaped up behind the wall and within the fort. The fort could be accessed on all four sides.

The interior of the fort contained buildings almost wall to wall. Alongside the central headquarters *(principia)* with a square internal courtyard, the commander had his residence *(praetorium)* and there were two additional buildings as storehouses. The long, thin staff barracks were made of wood and arranged parallel to each other both in the southern front part of the fort and on the opposite side. The baths, which would normally be outside the walls of the forts, were within the enclosure in Niederbieber.

A strip of land 100 m wide around the fort remained unbuilt on. Behind it in the south and east lay the large civilian fort village *(vicus)*, where the families of the soldiers had settled together with traders, craftsmen, and innkeepers who made their money from the wealth brought in by the soldiers. The famous equestrian standard was discovered in a pit of the vicus.

The fort and the camp village were destroyed and abandoned in 260. This is indicated by archaeological finds from the fort and in particular by a great number of coins with their final dates. We do not know whether the fort was destroyed in attacks by Germanic tribes; or whether the destruction is to be seen rather as a consequence of clashes between Roman troops in connection with the takeover by the usurper Postumus against

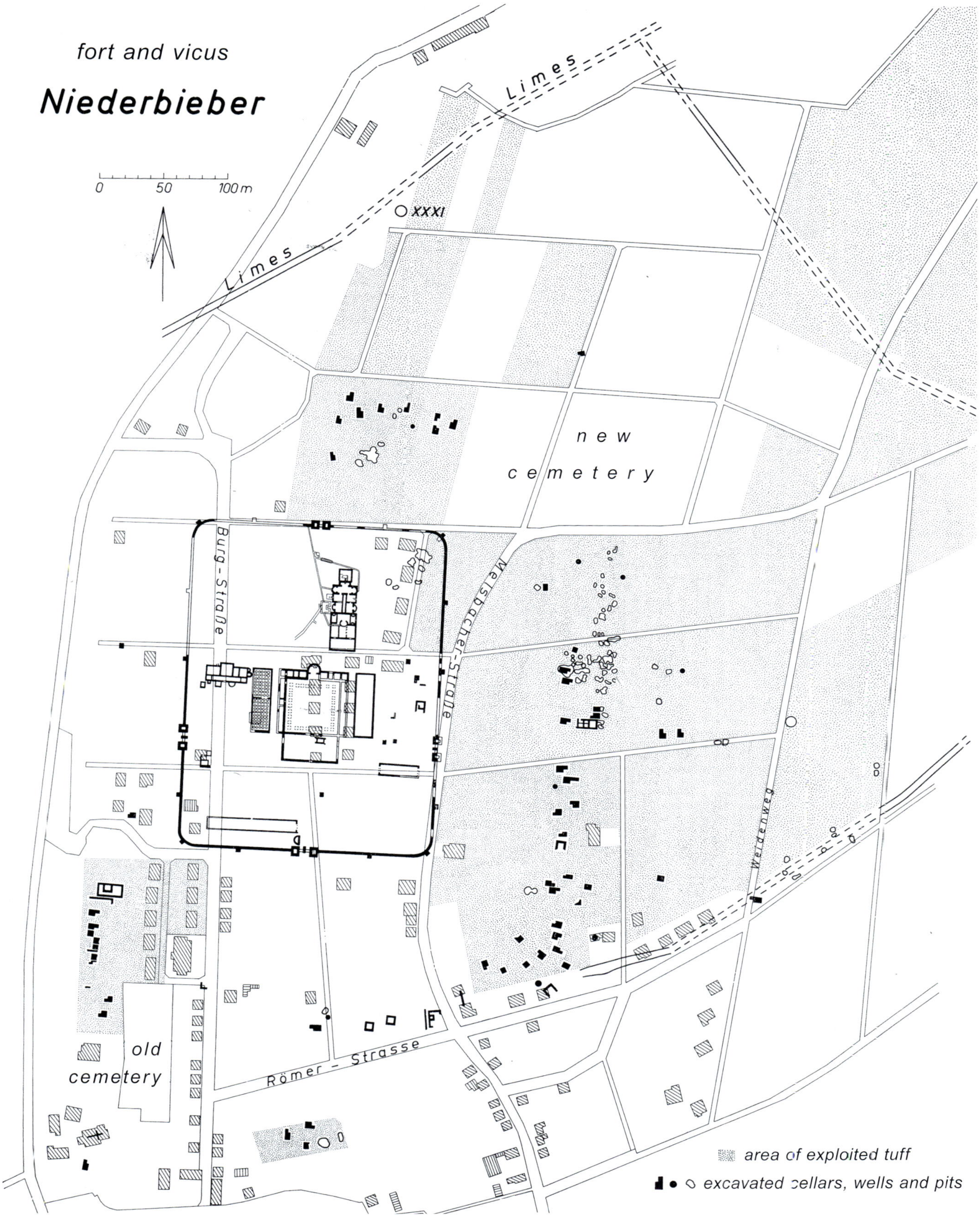

Fig. 1
Niederbieber, city of Neuwied. Overall plan of the fort with the parts of the camp village. (GDKE/Landesarchäologie/Koblenz)

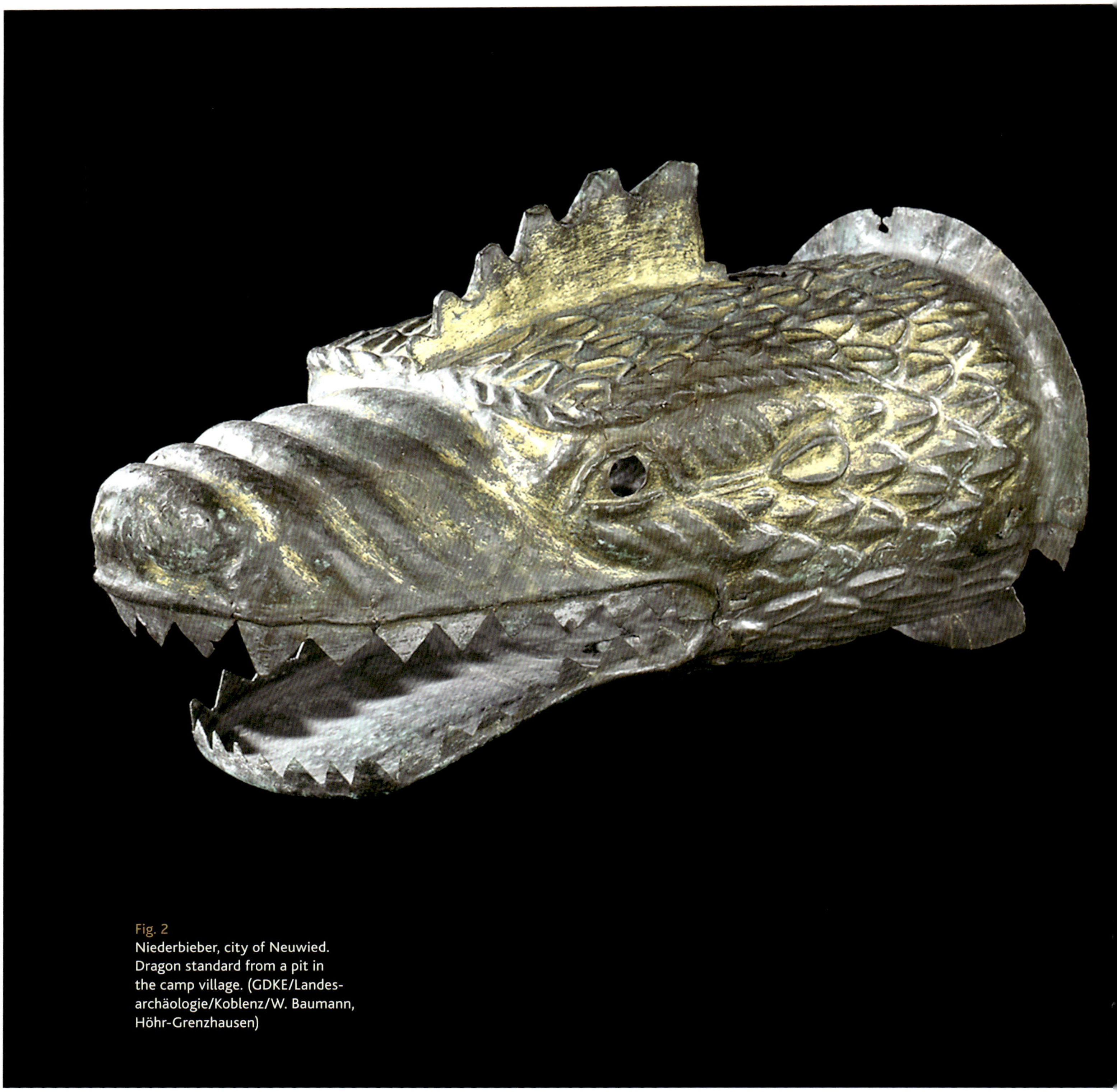

Fig. 2
Niederbieber, city of Neuwied. Dragon standard from a pit in the camp village. (GDKE/Landesarchäologie/Koblenz/W. Baumann, Höhr-Grenzhausen)

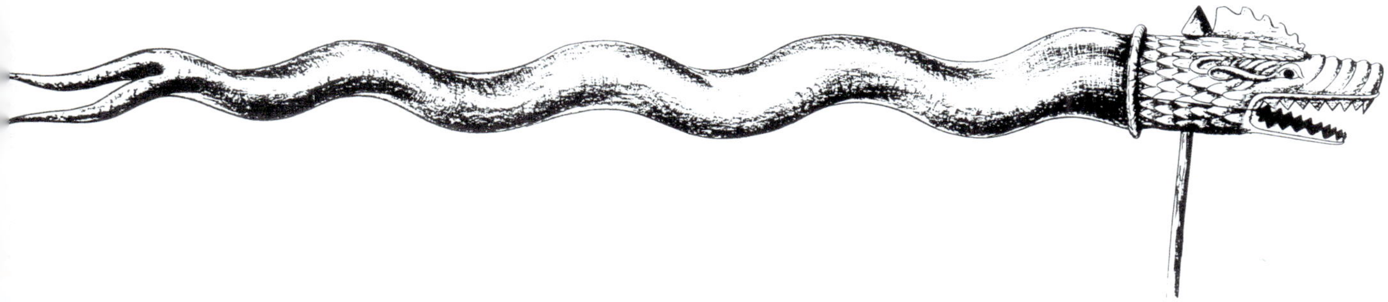

Fig. 3
Reconstruction of the dragon standard. (GDKE/Landesarchäologie/Koblenz/M. Meinen)

the rightful emperor Gallienus and the development of the Imperium Galliarum. The archaeological evidence for the violent destruction of the Niederbieber fort is provided by traces of battles and devastation, such as the burnt layers often observed in the fort and the vicus, the buried coins (hoard finds), and the skeleton remains of dead soldiers.

What caused an immense loss of archaeological findings was, however, the destruction brought about by the intensive building activity since 1945. The Imperial Limes Commission was still able to conduct excavations relatively undisturbed, since at that time the fort was situated in an open agricultural area. After the war, the area of the fort was earmarked as a development area and built on with the exception of a few open spaces. Nobody had any regards for the great cultural and historical importance of the site and the Roman remains which had been known for more than 200 years. With the new state law for the »protection and maintenance of the cultural documents in Rhineland-Palatinate« and the designation of the fort area as a protected excavation site, it was possible to keep the areas of the northern gate and the fort baths largely free of buildings and also to safeguard their foundations in 1986, making them accessible in a park. Since 2005, the fort has been part of the Limes World Heritage Site.

Besides many other finds, a pit filling in the south eastern part of the camp village revealed an equestrian standard made of bronze in the form of a dragon's head *(draco)* with its mouth wide open and a jagged crest. (Fig. 2) The animal's head is 30 cm long and was chased from a copper sheet of thickness 1 mm. There is a circular opening both at the bottom of the neck and on top behind the crest, probably for fixing a holding rod there. The top part of the head is fire gilded, while the lower part is covered with a tin alloy. The copper sheet is bent up at the back; probably, a textile hose was attached there. If the rider held the standard whilst galloping, the air would stream noisily through the open throat and inflate the textile body, which would wriggle in the wind. (Fig. 3) This outstanding piece is a standard of a cavalry unit, which until its discovery was only known from descriptions and pictures. It is the only preserved item of this kind from the Roman Empire to date.

Bibliography

H. Eiden, 10 Jahre Ausgrabungen an Mittelrhein und Mosel, Ausstellungsführer (Koblenz 1976) 36 ff.

H. Eiden, Ausgrabungen an Mittelrhein und Mosel 1963–1976. Tafelband. Trierer Zeitschr. Beiheft 6 (1982) 137 ff.

H.-H. Wegner, Neuwied-Niederbieber. In: H. Cüppers (Hg.), Die Römer in Rheinland-Pfalz (Stuttgart 1990) 501 ff.

The window grille of Niederbieber

AXEL VON BERG

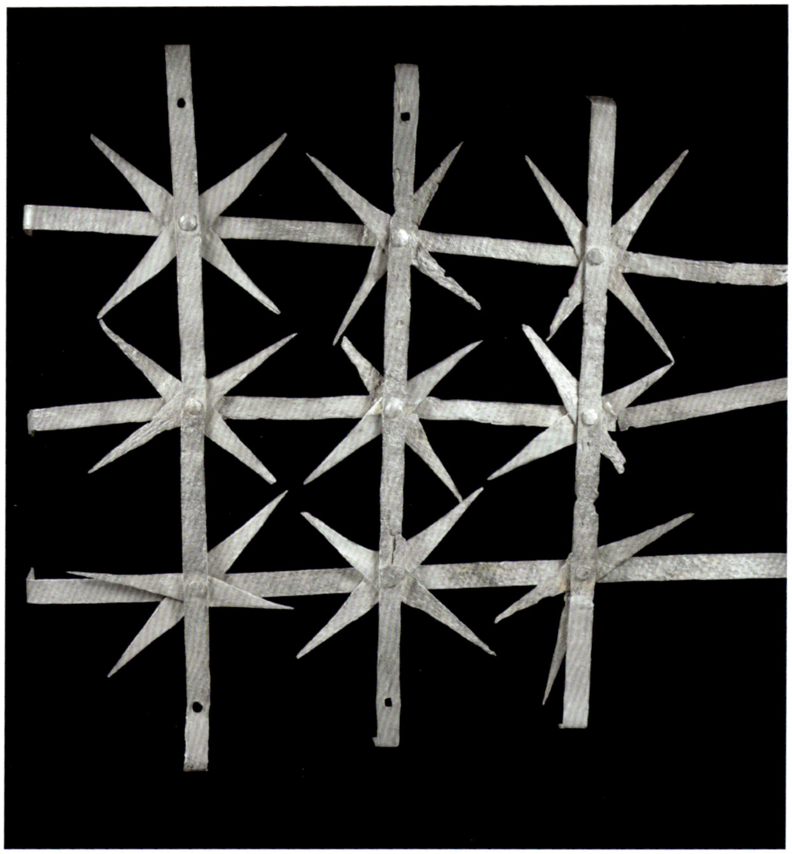

Fig. 1
Niederbieber, city of Neuwied. Iron window grille from an earth cellar in the camp village of the fort. (GDKE/Landesarchäologie/Koblenz/W. Baumann, Höhr-Grenzhausen)

The fort of Neuwied-Niederbieber, erected during the reign of Emperor Commodus (180–192), was surrounded on all sides by a large camp village (*vicus*). Emergency excavations in the years 1963–1968, 1973 and 1974, which were carried out only in partial areas during the large-scale mining of volcanic pumice tuffs, revealed that a 100 m wide line of fire round the wall of the fort had been kept free of civilian houses. The adjoining camp village consisted of buildings generously spaced out without planned roads. There were individual groups of buildings of different size and structure, which were often aligned towards the fort. The houses were simple, mostly long and narrow rectangular buildings, normally built in wattle-and-daub technology with stone foundations, of which often only the cellars have survived.

A nearly intact forged iron window grille was found in an earth cellar in the eastern part of the camp village. (Fig. 1) The grille (measuring 0.59 m × 0.59 m) consists of three horizontal and three vertical flat iron strips. Where the strips cross each other, there are nine four-pointed stars worked in two parts and riveted together with the iron strips arranged at right angles over each other. The flat irons are bent up at the ends and perforated for fixing them into a wooden window frame. The grille elements are movable and were meant to prevent a hand or animal from getting through, thus securing the opening completely, while the four-pointed stars increased the decorative effect of the grille. So far, only a few complete window grilles have been found in the territory of the former Roman Empire. The item from the camp village of Niederbieber dates from the 3rd century and belongs to Type II, which is known via the Gallo-Germanic provinces from northern Italy to as far afield as England.

Bibliography

H. Eiden, Ausgrabungen an Mittelrhein und Mosel 1963–1976. Tafelband. Trierer Zeitschr. Beiheft 6, 1982, 137 f.

P. Kienzle, Geschmiedete römische Fenstergitter aus der Colonia Ulpia Traiana. Xantener Berichte 24 (Xanten 2012) 391 ff.

A. von Berg, C. Jost, W. Baumann, Archäologie. Ausgesuchte Funde vom Mittelrhein (Koblenz 2007) 174 f.

The dagger of Niederbieber

AXEL VON BERG

In 1982, when there were plans for ground excavations in preparation for new buildings, archaeological examinations were conducted within the Roman fort of Neuwied-Niederbieber, and an area in the northern inner part of the fort immediately before the gate was documented. The archaeologists found ten settlement pits, an earth cellar, a drainage pipe, postholes of former timber buildings and a large number of smaller items from the former internal buildings.

Of particular interest is Site 4, a small earth cellar 3.00 m long and 1.90 m wide. The cellar pit was sunk about another 0.80 m into the pumice. The multilayer infill contained mainly burnt-clay remains of a wattle wall construction with daub. Four posts in the corners of the cellar pit once supported a timber superstructure with a simple roof construction. Various items were discovered on the floor of the cellar, mostly remains of different ceramic vessels dating from the middle of the 3rd century, immediately preceding the time when the fort was destroyed. An outstanding find was a completely preserved iron legionary's dagger, a so-called *pugio.* (Fig. 1) The 41.5 cm long weapon is completely made of iron and left undecorated. The wide, double-edged blade has a narrow central ridge. The simple hilt consists of two metal shells worked half-round, ending in a trapezoidal pommel slightly retracted on top. From the 2nd century BC onwards, the dagger formed part of the standard weaponry of the Roman legionaries and was developed from Iberian dagger forms. The *pugio* went out of fashion as a standard weapon at the end of the 3rd century AD. The piece from the cellar pit of Niederbieber belongs to the late forms of this stabbing weapon.

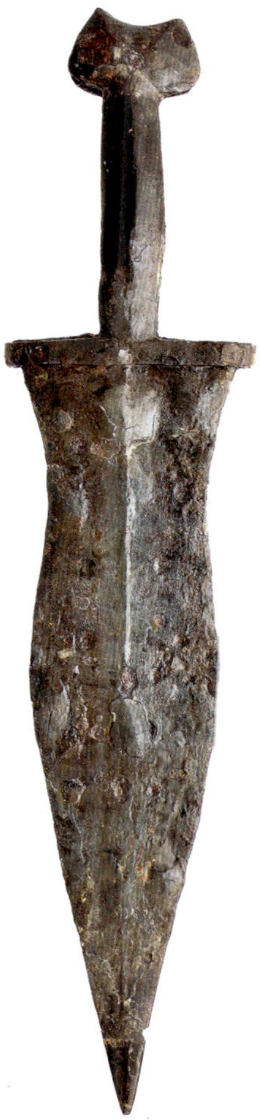

Fig. 1
Niederbieber, city of Neuwied. Iron legionary dagger from a cellar in the fort of Niederbieber. (GDKE/Landesarchäologie/Koblenz/M. Neumann)

Bibliography

A. von Berg, H.-H. Wegner, Niederbieber: in: H.-H. Wegner (Hg.), Ausgrabungen, Funde und Befunde im Bezirk Koblenz. Berichte zur Archäologie an Mittelrhein und Mosel 3. Trierer Zeitschr. Beiheft 14 (Trier 1992) 485 ff.

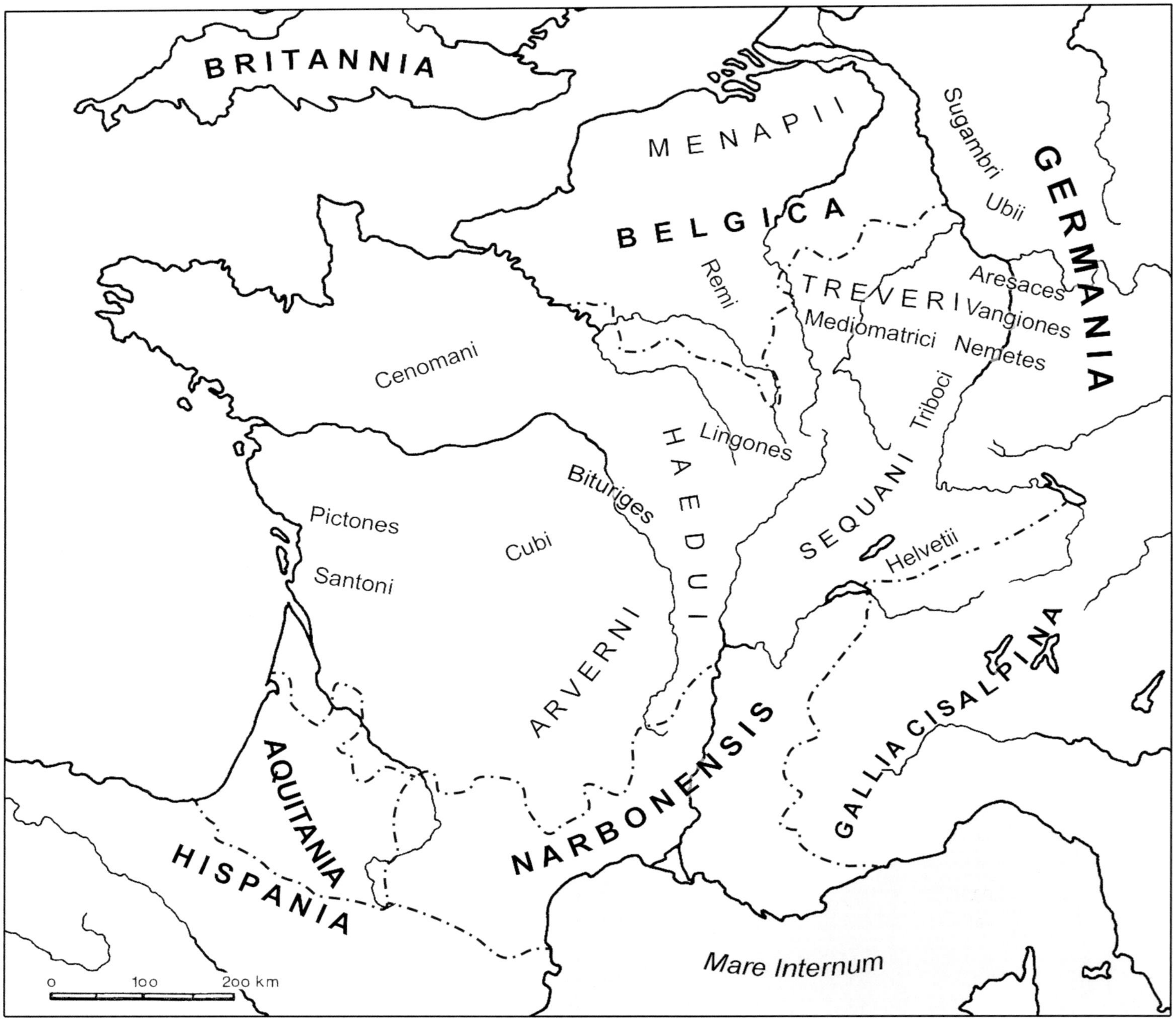
BRITANNIA
MENAPII
BELGICA
GERMANIA
Sugambri
Ubii
TREVERI
Remi
Mediomatrici
Aresaces
Vangiones
Nemetes
Cenomani
Lingones
Triboci
HAEDUI
Bituriges
SEQUANI
Pictones
Cubi
Helvetii
Santoni
ARVERNI
GALLIA CISALPINA
AQUITANIA
NARBONENSIS
HISPANIA
Mare Internum
0
100
200 km

A piece of the Imperium Romanum – The military occupation from the 1st century BC to the 4th century AD

MARION WITTEYER

Conflicts among the tribes of Gaul north of the Roman provinces Gallia Cisalpina (integrated into the Roman Empire around 218 BC) and Gallia Narbonensis (established 125/118 BC), together with the advances of Germanic troops, concentrated the focus of the growing world power of Rome in the 1st century BC to the north. This eventually led to the military intervention by Gaius Julius Caesar, consul in 59 BC and appointed governor for five years over the above-mentioned Gallic provinces. With his campaigns, described by him in detail in his *Commentarii de bello Gallico,* the increasing claim to power stretching as far as the Rhine, which Caesar defined as the border between the Gauls and the Germanic tribes, becomes clear for the first time. After the end of the wars conducted between 58 and 51 BC, Gaul and the regions on the Rhine came under the influence of Rome, but the civil wars after Caesar's return to Italy and the power struggles following his assassination prevented a speedy political and military development and the administrative transformation into a province.

The intrusion of Caesar into Gaul happened at a time of major change with momentous political, social, and economic alterations of the Celtic world, which gained additional impetus through the military actions of Caesar. During the campaigns in Gaul, Roman troops for the first time reached the area of today's Rhineland-Palatinate; the names of the tribes living there and their settlement areas are also mentioned by name for the first time. (Fig. 1) The territory of the large Treverian tribe, who prided themselves in their Germanic origins and who, according to Caesar, had the strongest cavalry amongst all Gallic tribes and considerable fighting forces, is to be localized between the Rhine, Ardennes, Hunsrück, and Eifel. The land of the Mediomatrici, which extended from the southern Palatinate and Upper Alsace to the river Blies area, was immediately south, with an unclear boundary line that may have either been along the river Nahe or south of the mighty oppidum on the Donnersberg. At a later time, the names of other tribes such as the Triboci, Nemetes, and Vangiones are documented for the Palatinate and Rhine-Hesse, and the Aresaces and Caeracates in the Mainz area. Except for the Treveri, who were already living in their settlement areas in pre-Caesarean times, the Germanic Vangiones, Nemetes, and Triboci listed in Ariovist's contingent of tribes are archaeologically documented in the last third of the 1st century BC as being on the left side of the Rhine.

Rome's changing contacts and conflicts with the Treverians and especially with their leaders have left both literary and archaeological traces. The oldest archaeological evidence is a military camp near Hermeskeil (Fig. 2) discovered only a few years ago. The camp of about

Fig. 1
Map with the names of the late Celtic tribes. (GDKE/Landesarchäologie/Mainz/U. Weichhart)

Fig. 2
Hermeskeil, Trier-Saarburg district. Lidar scan with entries of the archaeological findings of the Caesarian military camp. (VFG, Universität Mainz/S. Hornung)

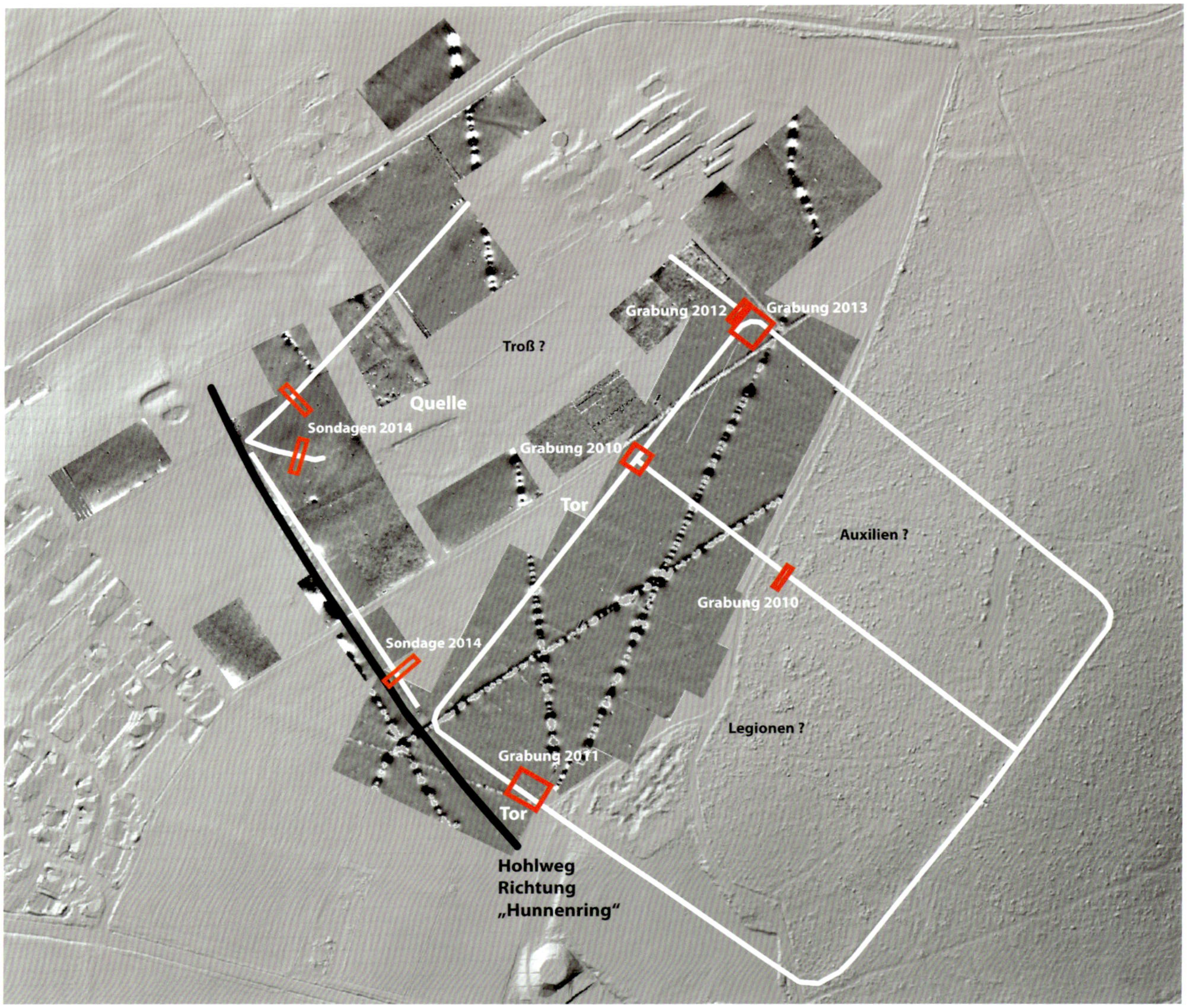

18 ha with its trapezoidal layout was erected on a gradually sloping plateau next to a late Latène-time settlement within view of the so-called Hunnenring of Otzenhausen, an oppidum 5 km away that had already been abandoned. It was secured by a rampart with a V-shaped ditch in front and does not seem to have contained fixed buildings inside, so the soldiers were probably housed in tents. Repairs seem to indicate a longer occupation, at least for several months, perhaps even with a legion and auxiliary troops. The camp, which dates from the middle of the 1st century BC, was probably systematically destroyed by fire by the military before it was abandoned. Besides ceramics, the dating is based on the special iron shoe nails from the soles of Roman *caligae*, the nailed shoes of Roman soldiers since Caesarean times, whose size and appearance show close parallels with the shoe nails from other military bases from the time of the Gallic Wars. (Fig. 3) For the years 53 and 51 BC, battles with the Treverians are documented in connection with their division into a pro-Roman and an anti-Roman group. It is therefore quite plausible to view the erection of the Hermeskeil camp in the context of these events. It would seem that growing economic differences contributed to the development of the opposing groups: in fact, while the western Treverian territory was blooming due to its vicinity to the central Gallic economic area, the development in the eastern parts went in the opposite di-

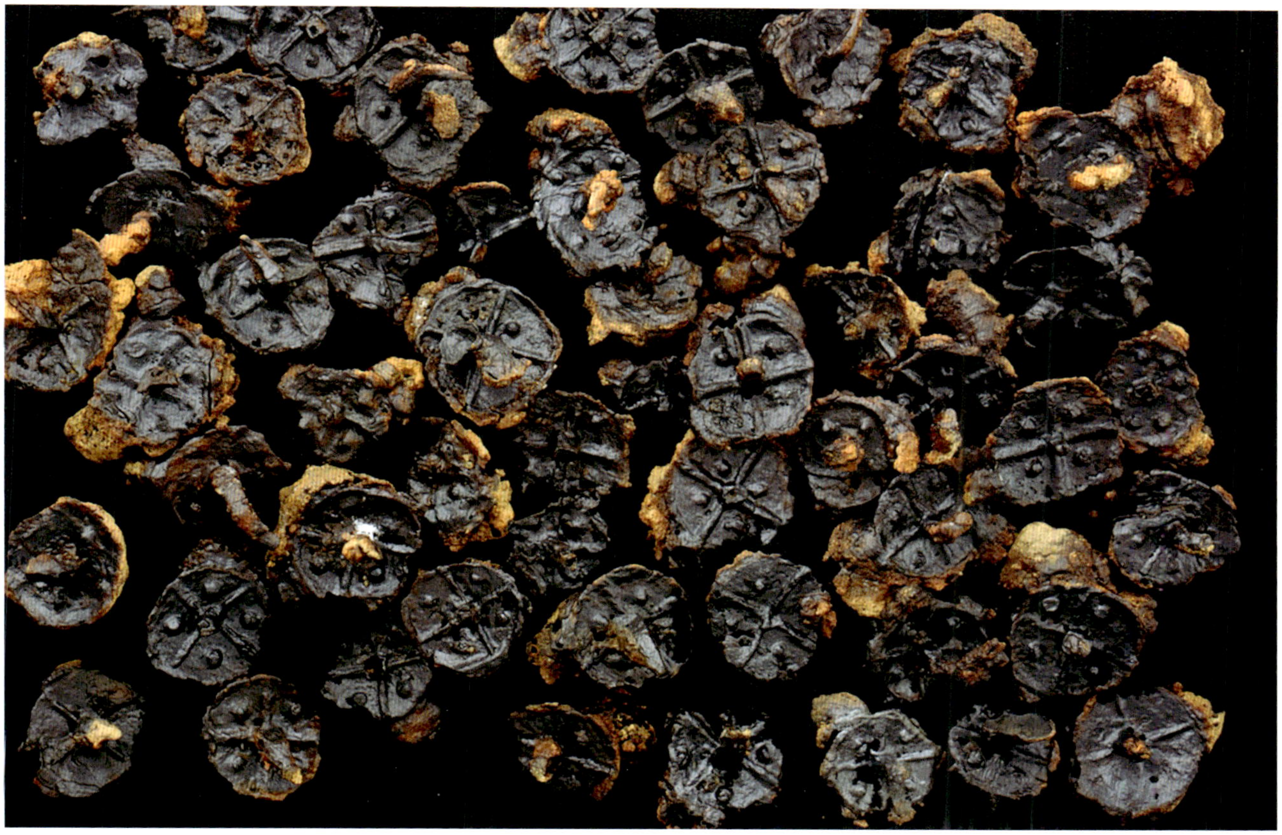

Fig. 3
Hermeskeil, Trier-Saarburg district. Shoe nails from the Caesarian military camp. (GDKE/Landesarchäologie/Trier/D. Bach)

rection, as can be inferred from the decline of formerly important settlements.

The advantages of being situated in a large area are reflected in the economic rise of the tribal centre of the Treverians, the oppidum on the Titelberg. During the 1st half of the 1st century BC, not only had Italic traders settled there, but during the Gallic Wars Roman troops were also barracked in this area. While the quartering of the military was certainly an intrusion into the structure of this centre of territorial dominion, it was obviously also a positive economic factor. Numerous militaria document the presence of legionaries and Germanic auxiliary troops up to Augustan times, just in those decades when the oppidum was in full bloom.

Another event mentioned in Caesar's *commentarii* concerns two legendary bridges which were allegedly constructed in an incredibly short time across the Rhine and which impressively demonstrated the capabilities of Roman military power. In the course of punitive actions against Germanic tribes on the right bank of the Rhine, Roman troops had crossed the river in the years 55 and 53 BC, the second crossing being made explicitly from the territory of the Treverians. At the end of the advances, the bridges were dismantled. There are no archaeological traces, but it appears that the two Rhine crossings took place in the Neuwied Basin; lately, some scholars argued with good reasons that they may have occurred below the mouth of the river Sieg near Bonn.

Even decades after the end of the Gallic Wars, the area of the Treverians continued to be a trouble spot where rebellions repeatedly flared, probably in response to increased pressure from the various measures applied in the course of establishing a province. The administrative survey of Gaul and the infrastructural development of the inner-Gallic road network were beginning to show the ever-growing Roman dominance. A revolt is recorded for the year 30/29 BC, when the Treverians, supported by Germanic tribes, rebelled against Rome, only to be vanquished again after a short time.

An archaeological connection may be established with the long suspected and in the meantime partly

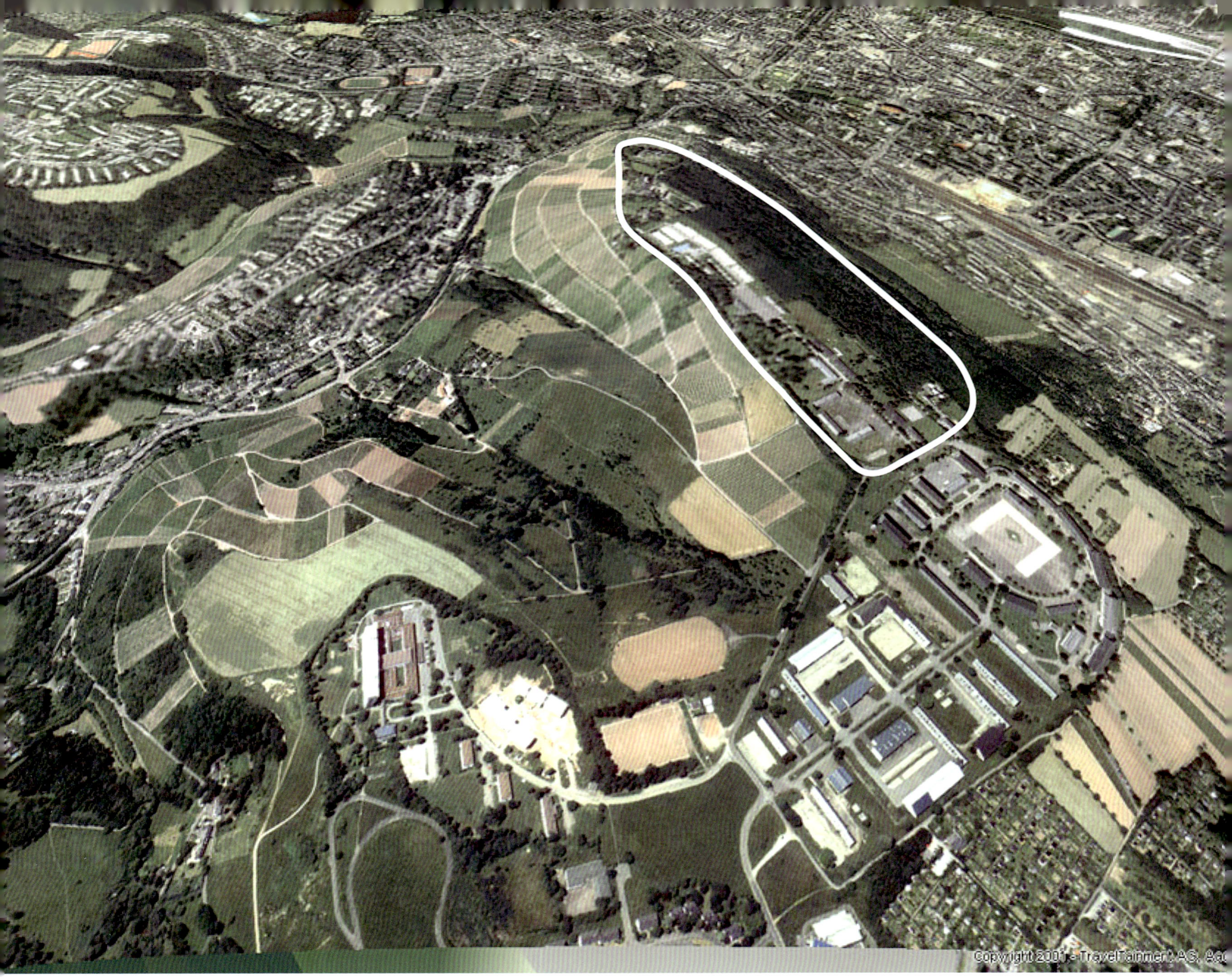

Fig. 4
Trier, Petrisberg, city of Trier. (GDKE/ Landesarchäologie/ Trier/Drawing U. Weichhart)

excavated military base on the Petrisberg near Trier. (Fig. 4) Several pieces of timber and firewood are dated dendrochronologically to have come from the year 30 BC, tallying with the timing of the small find material, which is older than that from the military bases established on the Rhine. The fact that the camp apparently existed only for a short time also fits the historic tradition; it was abandoned, according to plan, around 27 BC. The topographic location high above the town Augusta Treverorum, founded some time later on the banks of the Moselle, marked a strategically important spot from which both the wide Trier valley and the Moselle ford could be controlled. As far as we know, the camp covered an area of approx.50 ha, was secured by ditches on the narrow side across the mountain ridge, contained fixed timber and clay buildings which probably were the *principia,* and the cavalry barracks were constructed lined-up along the main road of the camp.

The camp in Belginum, today's Wederath, which was discovered some 20 years ago on the Hunsrück

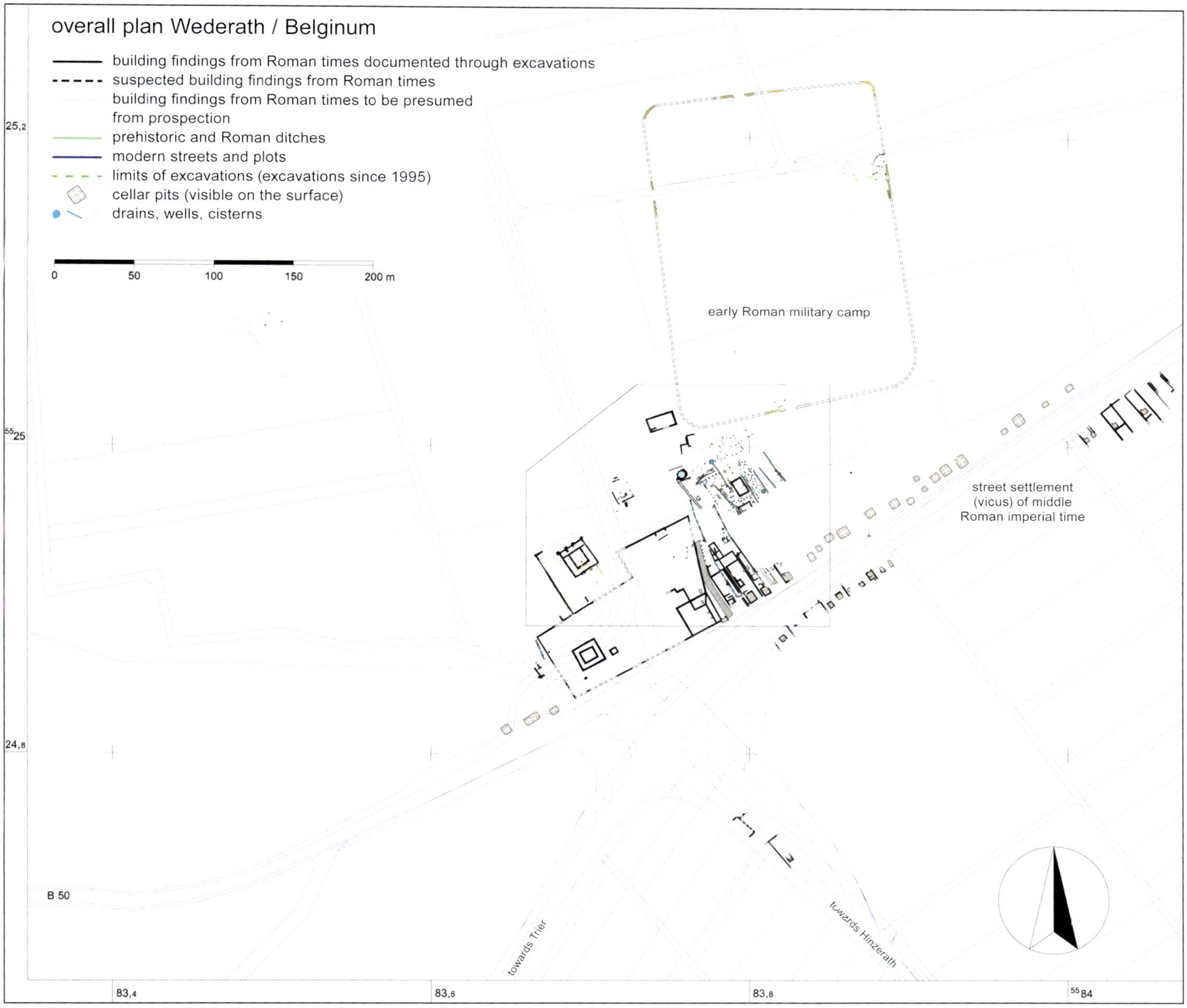

plateau and is situated on the main road from Trier to Mainz (Fig. 5), is difficult to assess for the time being. The military site, apparently established in the vicinity of an existing late Latène building, measured approx. 3 ha, had a rectangular layout and was surround by a timber-and-earth wall with a ditch. The main gate of the camp and the two side entrances were protected by crescent-shaped barriers in the form of *claviculae*. We know nothing about the buildings inside, but it seems that the entire complex was levelled when it was abandoned. So far, we do not know enough about the dating and function of this military installation. The small number of finds allows no closer dating than sometime between 30 BC and 50/70 AD. The proposed interpretations remain just as open. There might have been a connection with the rebellion of 30/29 BC or further unrests in the year 21 AD, or it might have had to do with the extension of the road network in relation to plans for the offensive against the Germanic tribes, or with the safeguarding of a supply route from the in-

Fig. 5
Wederath, Bernkastel-Wittlich district. Plan of the *vicus* of Belginum. (Archäologiepark Belginum/R. Cordie)

Fig. 6
Badenheim, Mainz-Bingen district. Sword grave 67 and 68. (GDKE/Landesarchäologie/Mainz/K.Soukup)

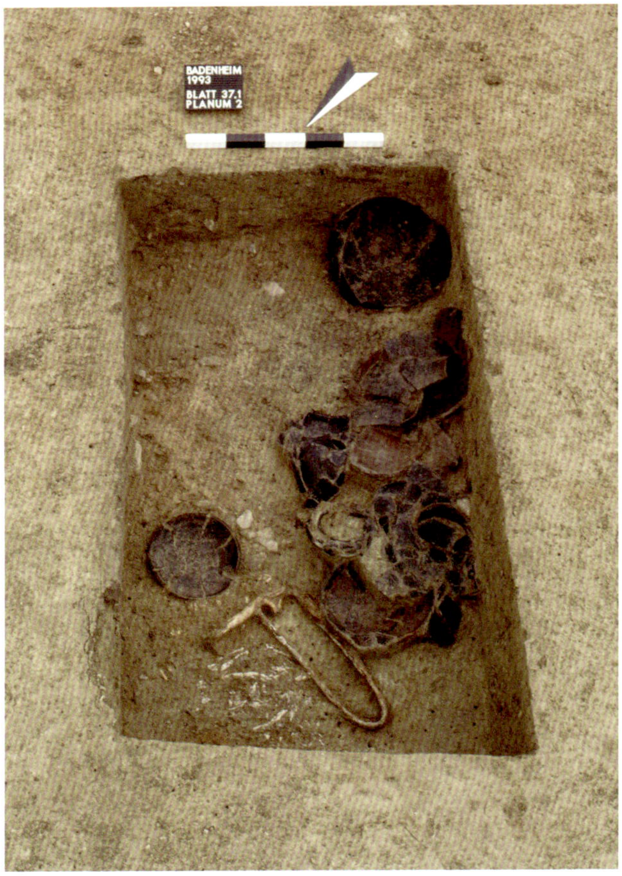

grave 67

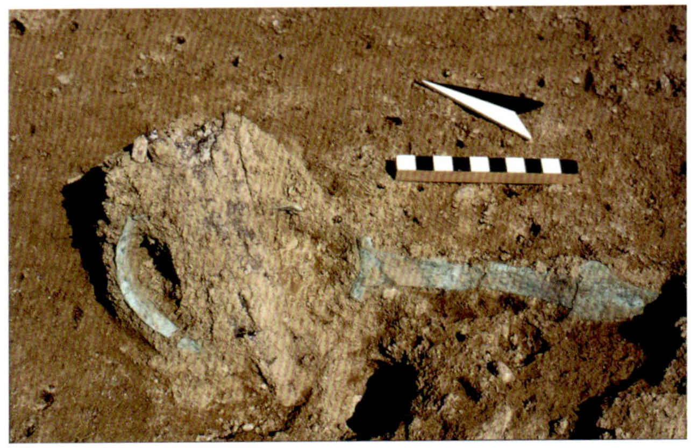

Detail from grave 68

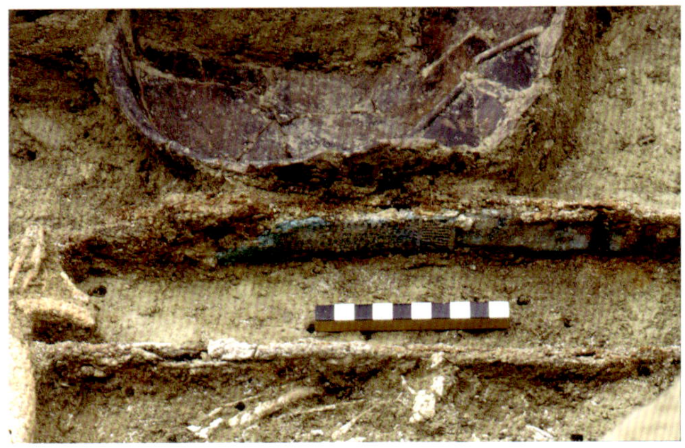

Detail from grave 67

terior of Gaul via further stations for provisioning the troops on the Rhine.

Members of the old local elite, who cooperated with the Romans, were allowed to keep their leading positions and win new social prestige, this time as leaders in the Roman military service. The importance of being a warrior is documented by the continuation of the traditional grave equipment with weapons in tombs at the Moselle, Ahr, and Nahe up to the middle of the 1st century AD. In the Celtic-Roman burial site of Badenheim, Mainz-Bingen district, two weapon graves of Caesarean and Augustan times were excavated in the 1990s, which represent two generations of the leading members of what was probably a family clan. The older grave contained (besides purely late Latène tableware) a ceremonial sword with its scabbard decorated in *opus interrasile*, which had been placed in the grave after having been bent in the traditional manner and thus been made unfit for use. (Fig. 6) The dead of the more recent grave had been provided with a mixed inventory of Celtic and Roman goods. The latter included a bronze sieve for wine consumption, a bronze buckle (potentially military) and, as a sign of the warrior status, a sword *(gladius)*, of which however only the point and the scabbard throat survive. There was also a different group of weapon graves which appeared in the Palatinate since late Augustan-Tiberian times and is to be seen in connection with the groups of Germanic immigrants.

Rome itself had seen a major upheaval during the decades after Caesar's death. The victor in the power struggle for the leadership of the state, Gaius Octavianus, grandnephew and adopted son of Caesar, had practically ended the old order of the republic led by the senate and placed himself as »*primus inter pares*« at the top of the new government system (principate) which he had established. Since 27 BC, Octavian took the name of honour Augustus (the magnificent, the

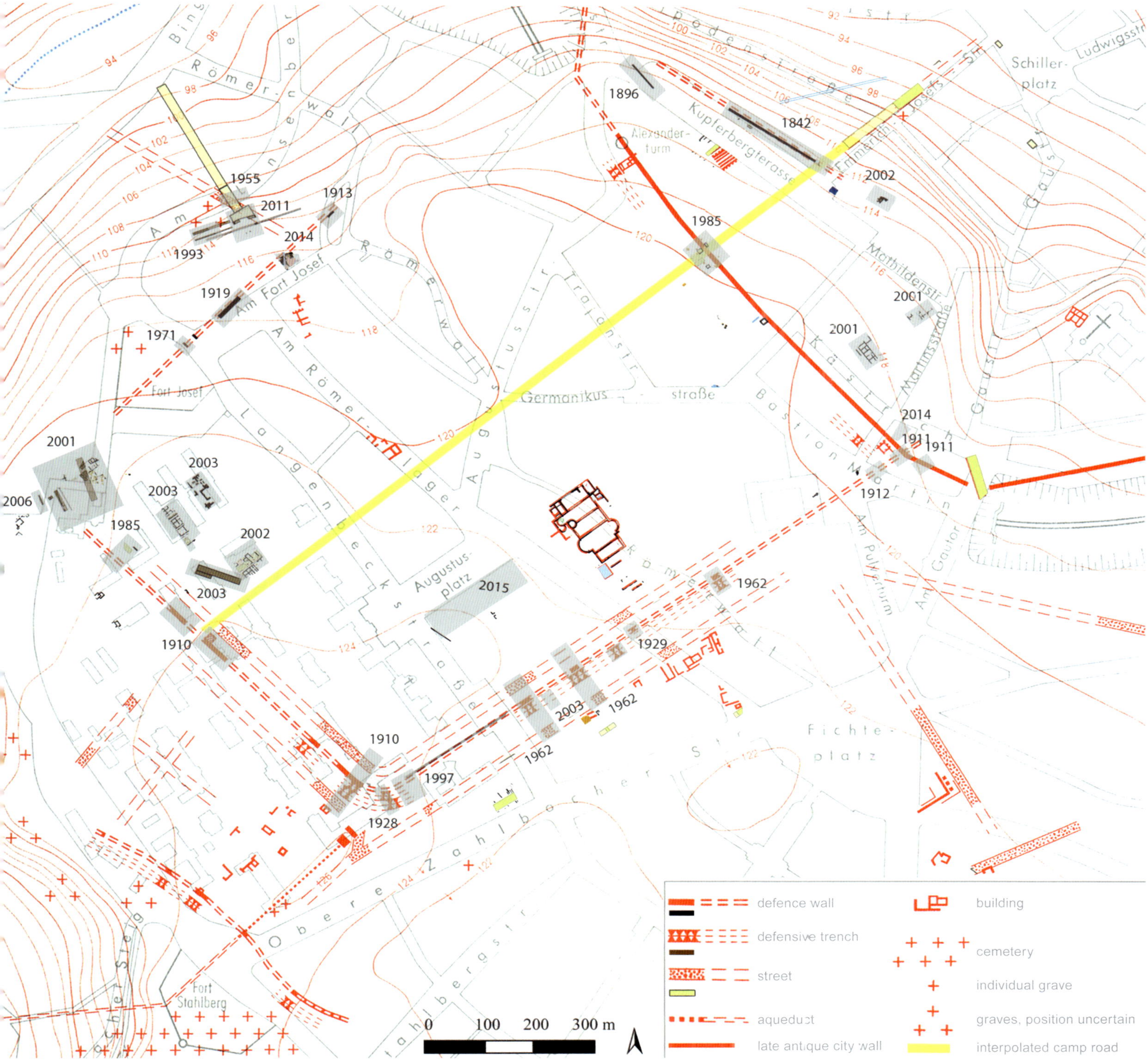

Fig. 7
Mainz, city of Mainz. Plan of the legion camp of Mogontiacum. (RGK/D. Burger)

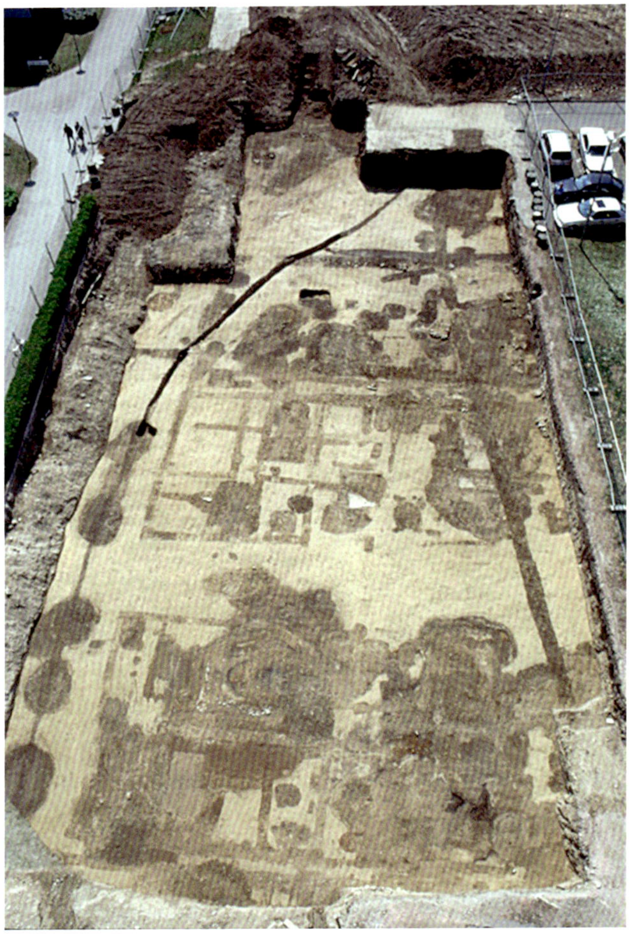

Fig. 8
Mainz, city of Mainz. Barrack buildings of the legion camp. (GDKE/Landes-archäologie/Mainz/K. Soukup)

increaser). The Gallic provinces were established in the same year; from then on, the territory of the Treverians was a part of the province Gallia Belgica. While the conditions here consolidated, and towns and vici developed, the situation at the Rhine border remained dangerous. Conflicts at the Middle and Lower Rhine eventually led to the establishment of military bases in the 2nd decade BC, first in the exposed areas, but then also on the Upper Rhine.

It was the loss of a legionary eagle in the year 16 BC – referred to in Roman sources as a disgraceful defeat of Roman troops *(clades Lolliana)* by the Germanic tribe of the Sicambri, who had advanced to an area left of the Rhine – which triggered a major offensive. The exact target of the campaigns in Germania is controversial: either territorial expansion and establishment of a super-province of Germania, or more or less incident-driven reactions. Strategic locations, from where it was easy to penetrate into Germania (Germania Magna), were selected for the construction of military bases in the framework of the emergent military operations: Vetera/Xanten at the Lower Rhine opposite the mouth of the river Lippe, as the military basis for the planned pincer movement, and Moguntiacum/Mainz opposite the mouth of the river Main at the northern Upper Rhine. To safeguard his own power in the young and as yet politically unstable principate, Augustus also put members of his own family in command of the armies; for instance, he entrusted the Rhine army to his stepson Nero Claudius Drusus. According to literary sources, not later than 11 BC an advance was made from Mainz up the Main to the northeast through the Wetterau district. The construction of the camp (probably intended for two legions right from the beginning) on a prominent area above the river is dated only a little earlier in the years 13/12 BC, but there are some indications of activities there (perhaps by military scouts?) even before the camp was built, such as the dendrodate of timber felled in the winter of 17/16 BC, which was later used in road construction. Little is known of the design of the camp, which existed at the same spot up to late antiquity, or of its construction phases and internal structure. (Fig. 7–8) It seems to have been planned from the outset to be about 36 ha in size with capacity for two legions. There were probably additional camps for additional troop contingents relating to this main base on the Upper Rhine, especially during the offensive phase and because of the high mobility of the army, yet there is no evidence except for Weisenau 3 km away, and even there we cannot be sure of such an early date. The Rhine as an important logistic communication and supply route played a role that is so far barely traceable in archaeological findings. No early port installations have been found until now. It is obvious that they must have existed, since supplies for the troops operating inside Germania could be transported much easier via a combined river and land route. An example is the supply camp of Rödgen approx. 60 km away in the upstream area of Mainz from around 10–7 BC. A military post in Speyer as well as a suspected post in Mutterstadt also belong to that time. In both places, however, finds of Elbe-Germanic origin belong to the oldest find inventory, indicating that Germanic people were living opposite the military base in Mainz, in a strategically and logistically important area. They had probably settled there with Roman support and acted as military settlers with border protection tasks. Further early camps have long been suspected in Worms and Bingen but have not been substantiated so far either through findings or by militaria. Only evidence of early terra sigillata could indicate the existence of a base in Worms during the last decade BC, not later than the 1st decade AD; things are even less clear in Bingen. Further north, Augustan troop bases are documented near Koblenz and Remagen.

An event in the year 9 BC had far-reaching consequences for the development of the military base at Mainz. Although the historical tradition does not actually mention the place name, there are many indications that this was Mainz. Drusus, the supreme commander of the Rhine army, suffered an accident when marching back from the Elbe to his winter camp *(castra hiberna)* in Mainz and died a few days later. His brother and later emperor Tiberius reached Mainz after a spectacular high-speed ride, and from there transported Drusus' body to Rome where it was cremated and buried in the mausoleum of Emperor Augustus. Immediately after Drusus' death, however, the troops had begun to build a grave of honour for their commander at the headquarters in Mainz. Not without political calculation, Augustus himself wrote a funeral poem that was affixed to the cenotaph, a propaganda exercise demonstrating the close connection of the emperor with the army and solidarity in mourning for the stepson. Annual memorial celebrations with a troop parade *(decursio)* and sacrifices *(supplicatio)* were also ordered by a senate resolution, where delegations of all Gallic tribes were required to take part. Mainz had thus been raised as the ritual centre of the Rhine army and a place of political pilgrimage. For these events, which would take place on at least two days of each year, adequate buildings were required. They are identified with the so-called Eichelstein (Fig. 9) in today's citadel in the architectural tradition of the late Republic, and with a previous building of the neighbouring late Roman theatre (Fig. 10); both belonged to a larger memorial district (see below). The connection between the cenotaph and the theatre is also indicated by a cornice with corbels found in the theatre where it had been reused. Its picture zones show weapons, part of a sacrifice scene, and the goddess Victoria with a laurel wreath: a suitable iconographic programme for the ritual zone as symbols of Roman power, victory, and respect for the gods.

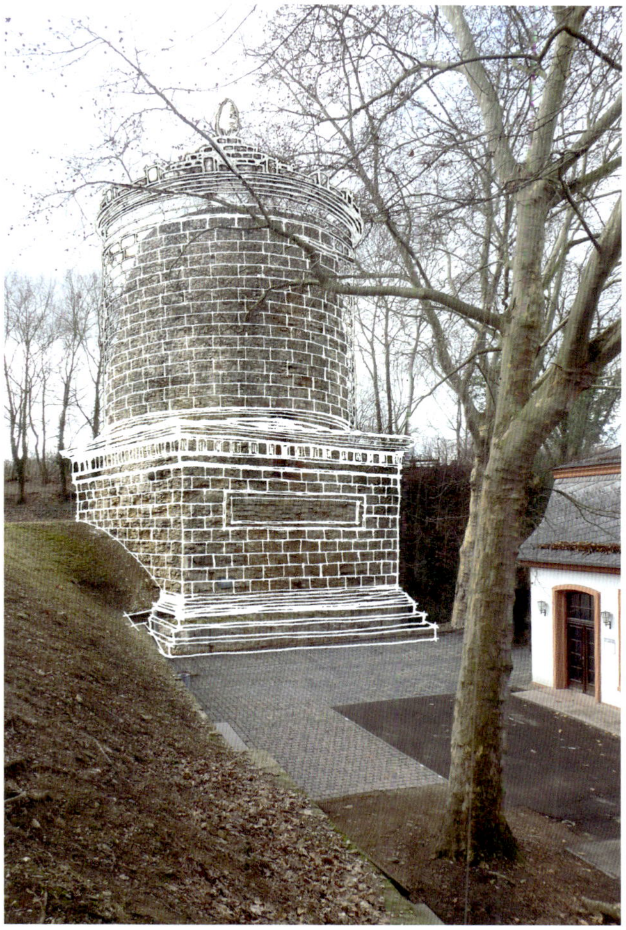

Fig. 9
Mainz, city of Mainz. Drusus cenotaph, reconstruction sketch over original state. (GDKE/Landesarchäologie/Mainz/E. Klingenberg, P. Kneib)

After Drusus' death, Tiberius took over the command of the army in Germania. In 6 AD, Mainz is again the starting point for a pincer attack, this time acting as the northern base together with a yet unidentified military area named Carnuntum in Noricum (Austria) to the south. The objective was the destruction of the Maroboduus realm in Bohemia, but it had to be abandoned due to a major rebellion in Pannonia (Hungary). At that time, the Mainz troops probably set up a base (corresponding to the Mainz camp) at the Main bend near Marktbreit, and it was probably also meant to fulfil administrative tasks as successor camp for Mainz. Germania was in those years considered a provincial territory, and the extension of the territory on the right bank of the Rhine was begun, as can be clearly inferred from the foundation of a town near Waldgirmes in the valley of the river Lahn. This phase came to an abrupt end when in 9 AD the Roman governor, Publius Quinctilius Varus, was decisively defeated with his three le-

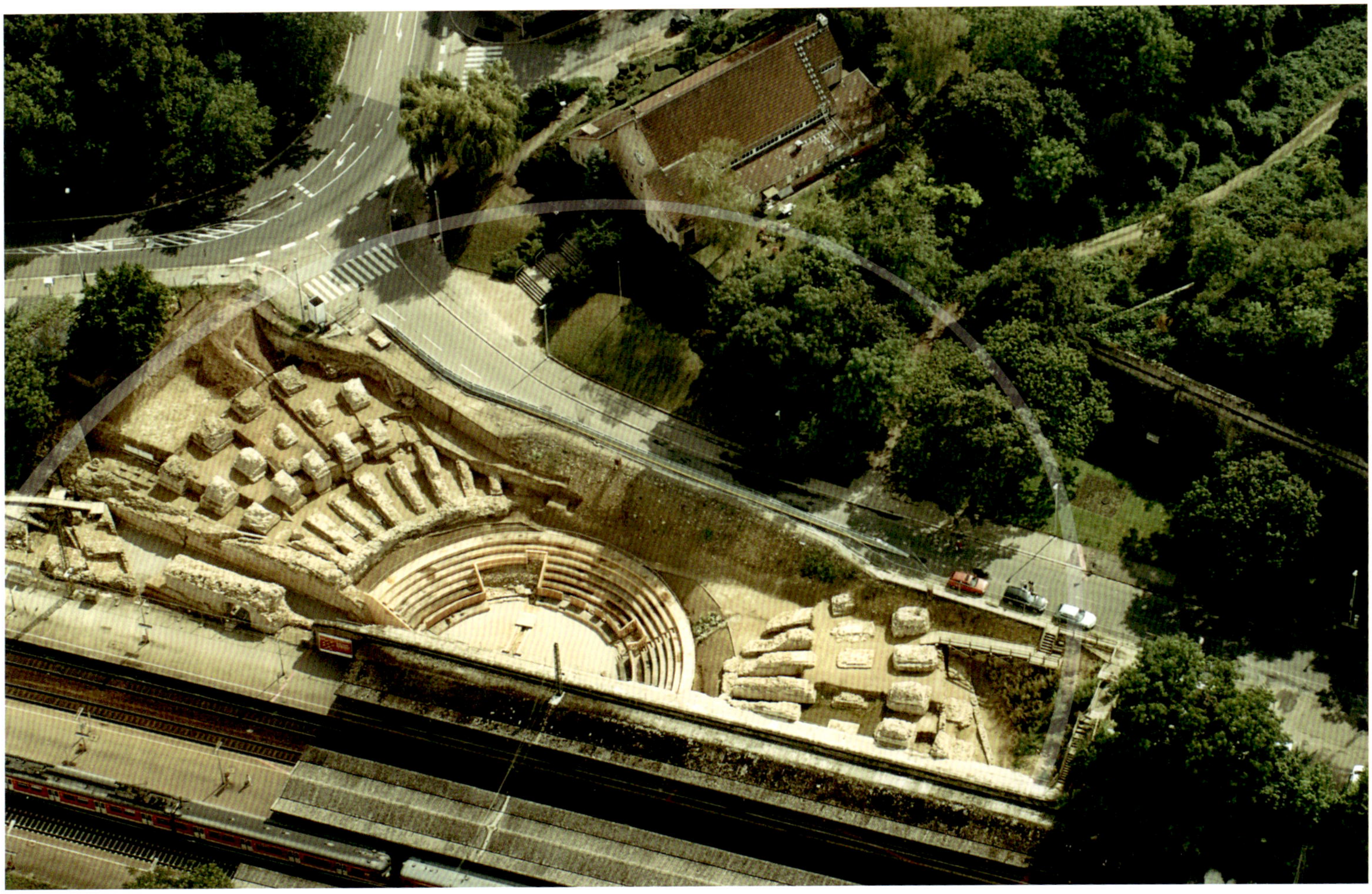

Fig. 10
Mainz, city of Mainz. Late Roman extension of the theatre. (GDKE/Landesarchäologie/Mainz/A. Rath)

gions plus auxiliary troops by Arminius. But the efforts to occupy Germania on the right side of the Rhine were not yet abandoned. When Augustus died in 14 AD and Tiberius succeeded him, there was unrest in the army, which favoured Nero Claudius Drusus Germanicus, the son of Drusus, as the new princeps. Except for a legion in Mainz, the Upper Germanic army was sworn-in without delay, while Germanicus had problems in calming the mutinous troops on the Lower Rhine.

The year 16 AD marked the turning point in the offensive policy concerning Germania: after repeated unsuccessful campaigns, Tiberius recalled his nephew Germanicus to Rome and granted him a triumph as conqueror of Germania. Until then, the Rhine border had belonged to Gaul, but now a strip was separated and divided into two military districts, which formed the basis for the later Germanic provinces. There was also no longer a comprehensive supreme command for the Rhine army. In the new concept of linear border protection, Mainz remained as a military base and as the seat of the Upper Germanic army command *(legatus Augusti exercitus superioris)*. Yet another important event for Mainz is linked to Germanicus. When he died in 19 AD in Syria through poisoning (possibly also with the help of magic practices), the senate passed an edict on how the deceased was to be remembered in the future. They ordered inter alia that commemorative arches were to be erected for the deceased, namely in Rome, Syria, and on the bank of the Rhine near the funerary monument for his father Drusus. The exact location cannot be deduced from this wording, so scholars are still not sure whether the remains of an arch found in 1986 on the right bank of the Rhine near the bridge head of Castellum/Kastel actually belong to the historically documented Germanicus arch, or whether this monument was left of the Rhine and closer to the Eichelstein. Irrespective of this, the important role of Mainz in the personality cult around members of the imperial family is emphasized once more by this second senate resolution marking respect for Germanicus. The synopsis of the architectural remains seen in connection with the Drusus celebrations and of new finds from around the theatre along with the literary sources has recently contributed to the reconstruction of an emperor cult area. According to it, the building ensemble was surrounded by a walled area with its gate oriented towards the Rhine. Within the area was an altar, decorated with a deification scene depicting the focus of the *decursio*, as well as an open area for parades. Besides the Drusus cenotaph and the theatre, the reconstruction also envisages a temple for the emperor cult and the Germanicus arch, where the latter may have been built across the military road leading to Weisenau. Even if much of the above is based on weak indications, this does not diminish the importance of the cults to Mainz. This appears to be reflected in an urban upgrading of the settlement structure, i.e. by the construction of solid roads (dendrodate around 24 AD), a thermal bath (dendrodate around 33 AD), and the bridge across the Rhine (dendrodate 27 AD). The connecting road between the camps, which leads past the Drusus stone, developed at that time into the most important grave road of Mainz and received a Mediterranean aspect with representative grave monuments.

In the years 39 and 50 AD, the Chatti tribe had advanced to some areas on the left bank of the Rhine. The construction of the Rhine bridge at Koblenz (dendrodate 49 AD) was presumably connected with the counter-attack conducted by the Romans from Mainz. The line of forts at the Rhineland-Palatinate section of the Rhine was consolidated by further camps for auxiliary troops. Troops were stationed north of Mainz in Remagen, which still belonged to the command area of the lower army; the forts in Andernach, Urmitz and Koblenz followed the river. After the narrow portion of the Rhine valley, the river border was only secured again in Bingen. Directly opposite Mainz, the Romans manned the bridgehead in Kastel. There was another camp in Wiesbaden, which secured on the one hand the control of the Taunus crossings and on the other the use of the thermal springs for the Mainz military. South of Mainz, the camp of Weisenau was followed by those of Worms, Rheingönheim, and Speyer.

The final years of the government of Emperor Nero (54–68 AD) ended in politically highly unstable conditions, whose effects can be archaeologically traced in many places. This was preceded by the discovery of a conspiracy against Nero. In recognition of the lucky escape of the emperor, the inhabitants of the suburban camp (*canabarii*) at Mainz donated a column to the supreme Roman god Jupiter Optimus Maximus, and this monument (as some sort of sign of loyalty) became a model for numerous later Jupiter columns. The conflicts around Nero eventually led to a year of civil war after his death, with four emperors, from which Vespasian emerged as the winner. From then on, emperorship was no longer tied to family bonds, since it had become clear that the power to bestow the dignity of an emperor lay with the military. The units stationed in Mainz played a significant role in this context. Among the events of the »Year of the Four Emperors« was the so-called Revolt of the Batavi, a rebellion of Germanic and Gallic tribes in 69/70 AD, who at first supported different troops fighting for one or other of the proclaimed emperors, but then came together in a coalition. In the course of events, the troops on the Rhine had even sworn an oath to a Gallic realm, which probably was not meant to detach itself from Rome and rather sought to re-organize the emperorship with the support of the Rhenish troops and of Gaul, but actually made things worse in the process. The relocation of legions and auxiliary troops from the Lower Rhine to Trier now brought the war to the civilian hinterland. According to historical tradition, the decisive battles took place in the area between Trier and Mainz, but the battle sites mentioned by Tacitus have not been localized so far except for Riol. In the end, the rebels were decimated by a superior Roman army and the Imperium Galliarum came to an end. Numerous layers of destruction can be connected to the events of those years; e.g. the impressive hoard from a burnt-down cellar in the fort vicus of Rheingönheim. (Fig. 11)

The foundation of the double sanctuary for the Mater Magna and Isis Panthea in Mainz might also be connected to the conclusion of the crisis-years at the end of Nero's government; at least two construction documents in the form of dedications to both deities for the benefit of the emperor, the senate, the people

Fig. 11
Rheingönheim, city of Ludwigshafen. Burnt-down cellar with hoard. (GDKE/Landesarchäologie/Speyer/B. Fischer)

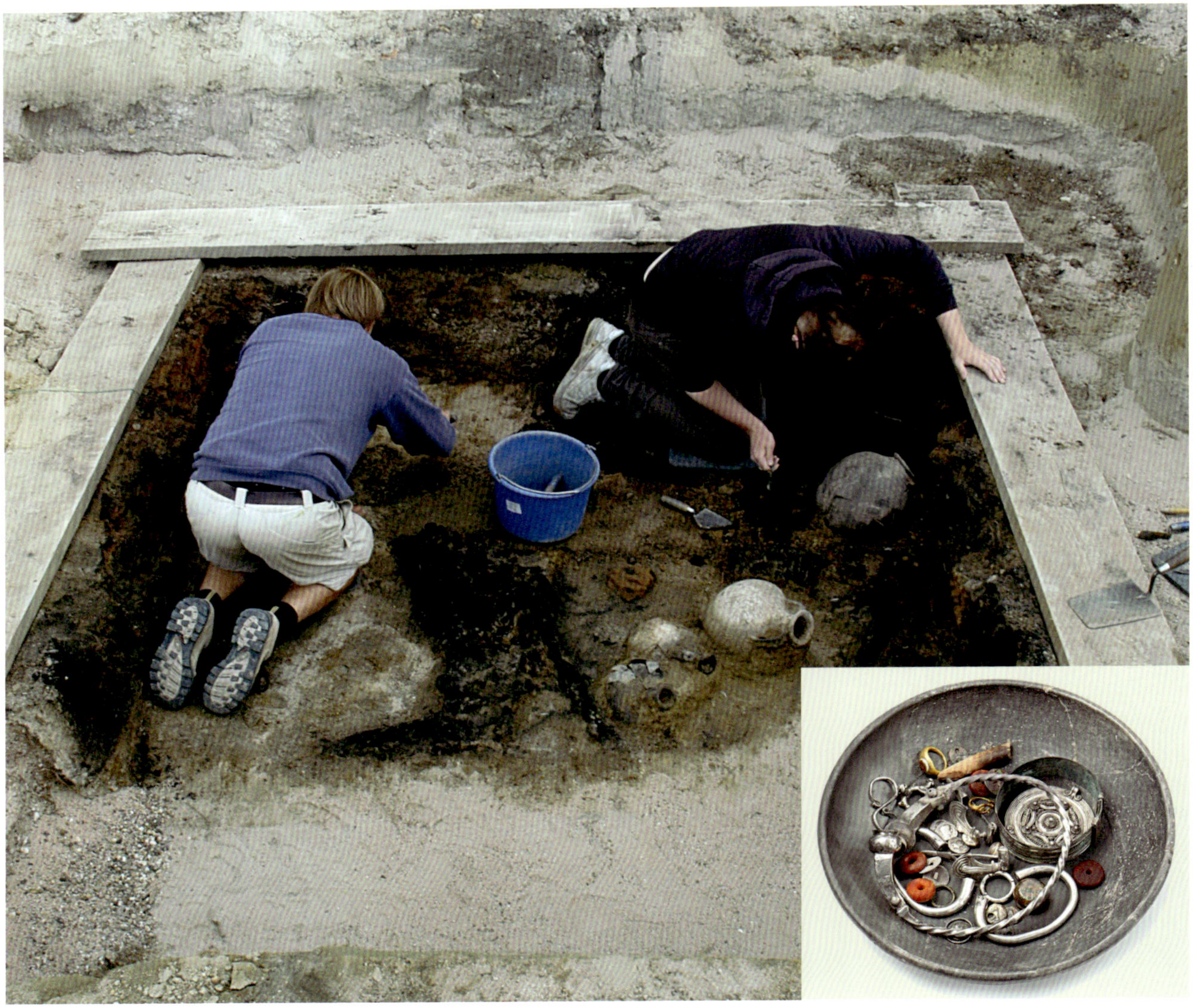

of Rome and the army suggest an important event for the realm as being the reason for the donations by an imperial freed woman and a slave. A third inscription is by a treasurer of a finance procurator under Emperor Vespasian with his office in Trier. The extraordinary feature of the sanctuary excavated around the turn of the millennium is the fact that, besides the official cult followed there, forbidden magic practices were also conducted on a large scale. (Fig. 12)

The reorganisation of border protection by Vespasian led once again to relocations of troops, and some were even disbanded. On the right bank of the Rhine, communication between the Danube and Rhine was shortened through the construction of a road, and the eastern foreland of Mainz was secured by forts; in Bingen, a bridge was built at the outlet of the Nahe into the Rhine. In Mainz itself, the legion camp was rebuilt in stone no later than that time, and the old water supply of the camp, consisting of a wooden water pipe, was replaced by a stone aqueduct. (Fig. 13) Under the subsequent emperor Domitian, new campaigns into the area to the right of the Rhine were started in 83 and 85 AD from Mainz; the target was the territory of the Chatti tribe. To this end, a mighty army was assembled in Mainz, and even the emperor himself came to the Mainz headquarters with his court. Domitian's stay during the first campaign against the Chatti is documented by two epigraphic testimonies, one of which

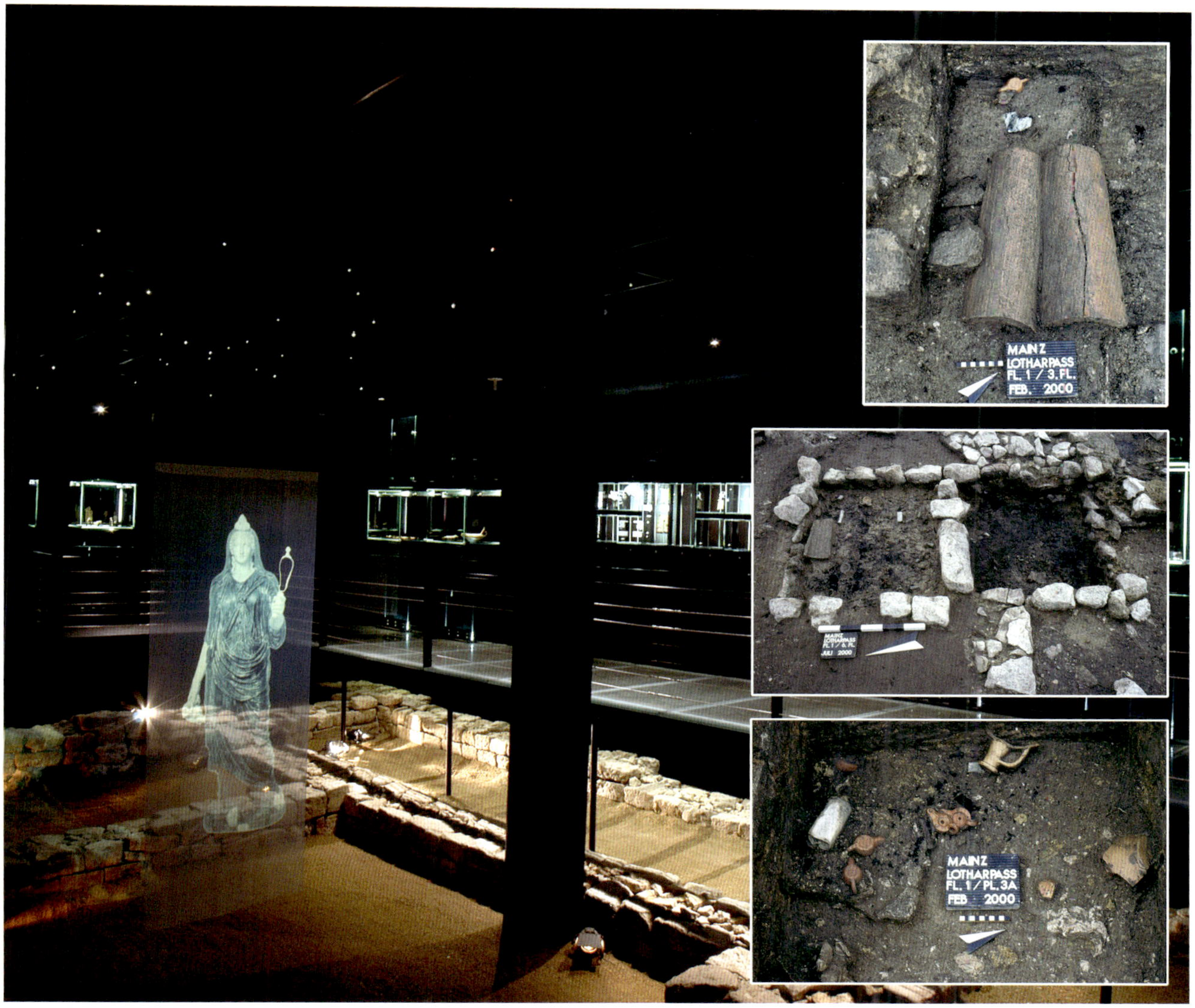

Fig. 12.
Mainz, city of Mainz. View of the display area of the Isis and Mater Magna sanctuary, on the right: findings of a burnt offering place with curse tablets. (GDKE/Landesdenkmalpflege/J. Ernst/E. Klingenberg)

is the tomb inscription for the imperial food taster discovered in 1967. There were territorial gains in the area of the upper Germanic army: in the Neuwied Basin, the Wetterau, and south of the river Main. The result of the war was viewed in different ways in ancient literature. In the end, Domitian was honoured with the epithet »Germanicus« and other compliments while he was still in Mainz, and even in the coin-based propaganda Domitian appeared as the conqueror of Germania. Some scholars suggest there may be a connection to the arch found in Mainz-Kastel due to the emphasis on the Chatti wars.

At present it is still not certain in which historical context a large installation examined in 2013 in

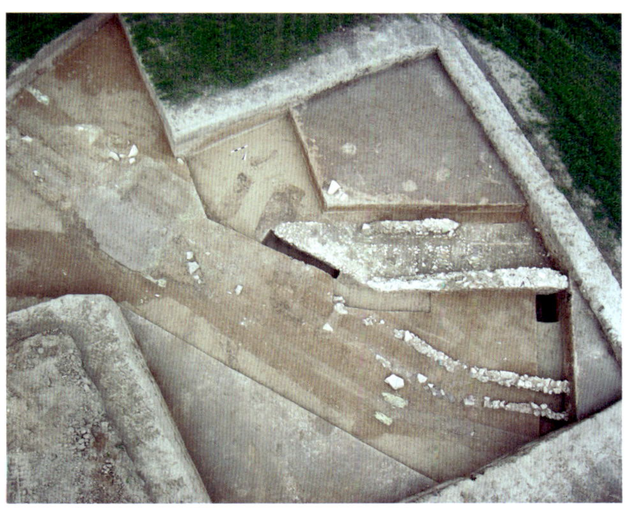

Fig. 13
Mainz, city of Mainz. Wood and stone gutters of the aqueduct. (GDKE/Landesarchäologie/Mainz/K. Soukup)

Fig. 14
Mainz, city of Mainz. Relief block with representation of a German. (GDKE/Landesarchäologie/Mainz/E. Klingenberg)

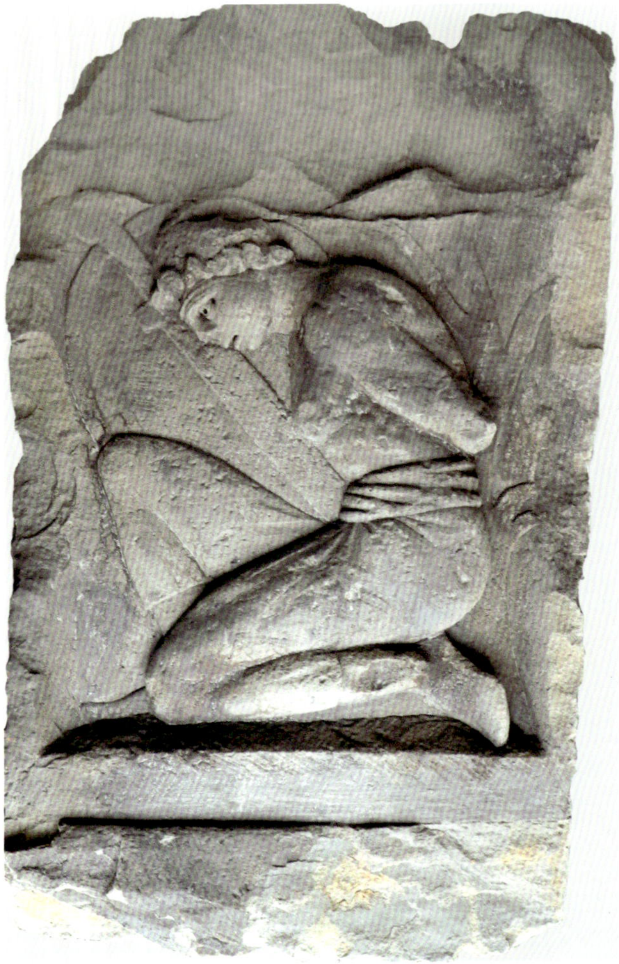

the Gonsbach valley near Mainz is to be placed. In the walls of a late antique architectural complex diverse spolia had been used as building material, among them fragments of tombstones of soldiers' graves and a completely preserved relief block with a good quality representation of a fettered German kneeling before an oval shield and a sword. (Fig. 14) If we are not to assume that the pieces were brought here from nearby Mainz, the original installation would have needed to fulfil a military or public function. This might also be supported by the fact that even the roofs of late antiquity were covered with a large number of militarily stamped tiles. Images like that of the bound German belong to Roman victory symbolism and are a common motif for instance on triumphal arches. The theme of a conquered German also appears on the pedestal reliefs in the Mainz legion camp from the time of Vespasian, displaying the superiority of Rome with over-evident signs. Germans in the pose of prisoners are usually shown in pairs, so one can assume that there was another person on this particular piece as well. The style of the presentation indicates that it belonged to a triumphal monument and not to a tomb, especially since on graves the barbarians are usually shown as vanquished by the victorious Romans on horseback. Only a section of the entire building complex is known so far, but it clearly differs from the usual form by its luxurious finishing elements, such as coloured stone slabs and profiled wall skirting.

Around 85/90 AD, Domitian transformed the areas of the Rhenish army districts under Roman command into the provinces of Upper and Lower Germania (Germania superior/inferior). The attempts to expand into territories on the right side of the Rhine were thus finally concluded. Mainz and Cologne became the seats of the governors *(legatus Augusti pro praetore Germaniae superioris/inferioris)*. The provincial border between the two Germaniae is still reflected today in the Vinxtbach *(ad fines)* north of Koblenz.

Right of the Rhine, the new border was marked from then on by the Limes, originally probably not more than a patrol path with wooden signal towers, which was then gradually developed, first with wooden palisades, later with stone towers and forts as well as ramparts and ditches during the last phase of extension. The small (recently reconstructed) fort of Pohl with a watchtower (Fig. 15) belongs to the group of early installations, perhaps also the fort of Bendorf; the fort of Niederbieber is among the latest. When the Limes was extended, the camps along the Rhine became obsolete and were abandoned one after the other.

In 89 AD, Mainz was once more the scene of a rebellion (known as the Revolt of Saturninus) attempted by the commander of the Upper Germanic troops with the support of the Chatti. The unsuccessful endeavour ended with major changes to the military base at Mainz: reduction of the size of the troops to one legion, which was the *legio XXII Primigenia* from then on until the 4th century.

With the exception of the raids by the Chatti in 162 and 169 AD, conditions in northern Upper Germania remained relatively stable up to the 3rd century AD. Due to conflicts for the throne, which in 193 led to the proclamation of four emperors within one year as had similarly occurred during the 1st century, and the later

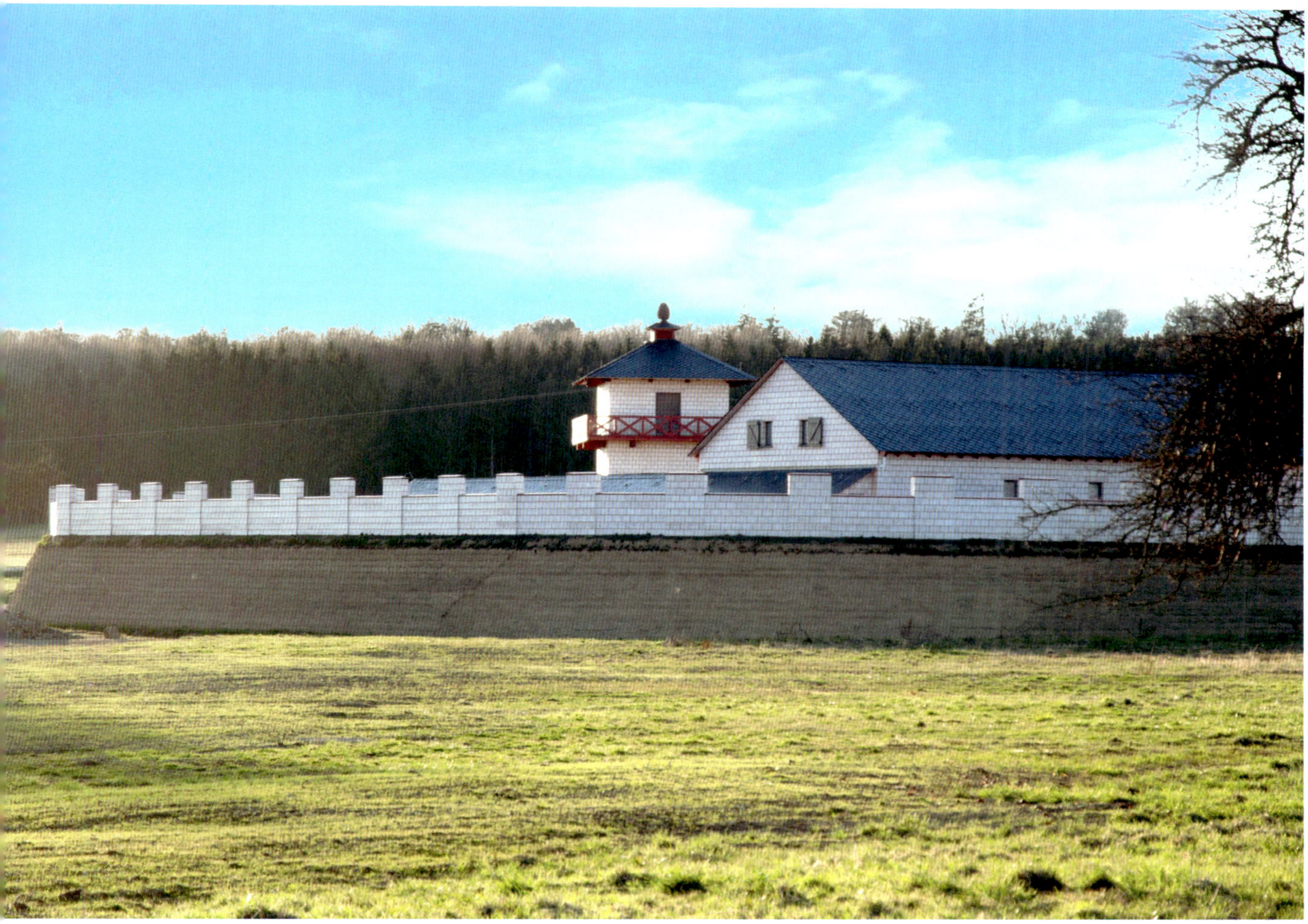

Fig. 15
Pohl, Rhein-Lahn district. Reconstruction of the small fort at the Limes. (Limeskastell Pohl)

revolt of a co-regent against the emperor, the Limes was strengthened by constructing additional forts. It seems that Trier had also been besieged, as witnessed not only by the well-known honorific inscription for the Mainz legion, but also by the Trier hoard of gold coins of more than 2650 pieces.

When troops were relocated for a campaign against the Persians, Chatti and Alamani used the opportunity to invade the Limes area on the right side of the Rhine in 233 AD. The ensuing alternation of unrest, crises, and periods of short-term calm reached a climax in 259/260 AD and during the following years, when the Limes was abandoned. Whilst the Holzhausen fort seems to have been conquered only after a siege, layers of fire debris in the Niederbieber fort indicate a sudden, unexpected end. In the debris, archaeologists found not only the skeleton of a standard bearer, but also a good number of outstanding objects including the dragon head standard. There is a controversial discussion among scholars about the causes of the so-called *Limesfall* (fall of the Limes), but most of them view it as the result of a multi-decade process where the outside threat by Germanic tribes, economic problems, worsening ecological and climatic conditions as well as inner-political conflicts all played a part.

After the first major raid by Germanic tribes in 233 AD, reduction measures can be recognized in many sites, such as the downsizing of baths, which also affected the baths in forts. The forts themselves, perhaps including those of Anhausen and Hillscheid, were also affected by restructuring for smaller contingents. However, the raid of 233 AD was not the only reason for size reduction, but rather yet another event during a continuing phase of decline. Twenty years later, the

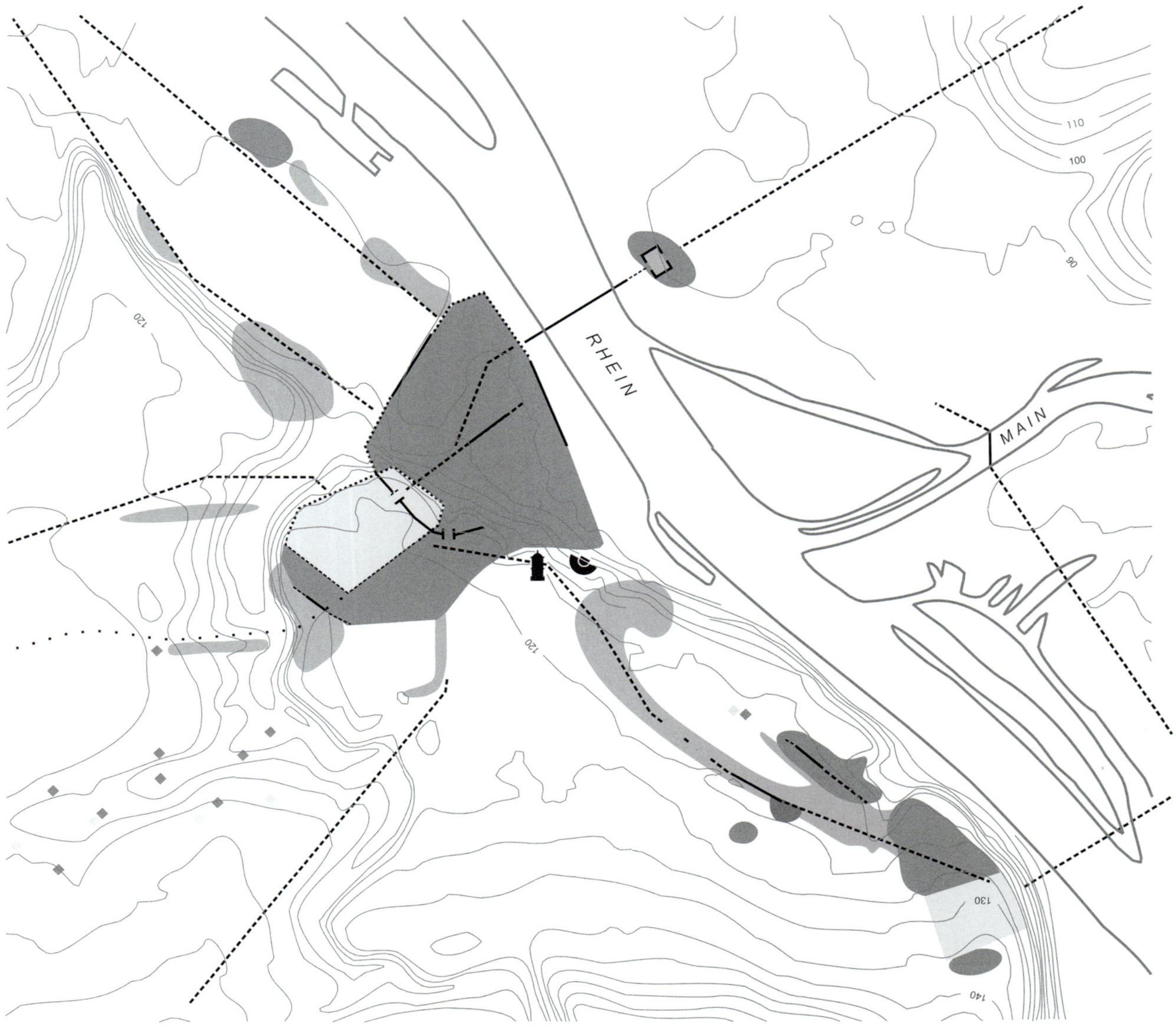

Fig. 16
Mainz, city of Mainz. Schematized city map. (GDKE/Landesarchäologie/Mainz/M. Witteyer, Drawing B. Spannring)

security situation had deteriorated once more, so that it evidently seemed advisable to surround Mainz with a city wall. (Figs. 16–17) Until then, people had clearly felt safe enough under the protection of the legion camp, since Mainz was the only provincial capital in Germania and Gaul that was still unfortified. The repeated withdrawal of troops might have increased the need for more protection, so the construction of the wall may be unequivocally linked to the relocation of troops when Valerian came to power. The wall enclosed the settlement areas on three sides as well as the legion camp and probably also the theatre. Dendrodata of the wall foundations sitting on oak piles in the damp subsoil indicate that the construction works began sometime after the winter of 250/251 AD, and that further works were carried out after the winters of 252/253 and 253/254 AD. The priority given to the stronghold character for the construction of the wall is indicated by the large-scale use of spolia, which were obtained by intentionally pulling down even larger installations, which had been built only a few years earlier.

When the territories on the right side of the Rhine were abandoned, Mainz had become a border town again. The raid by Germanic tribes in 259/260 AD has left only a few traces in the area close to the Rhine, since the attacks were aimed far into Gallic territory.

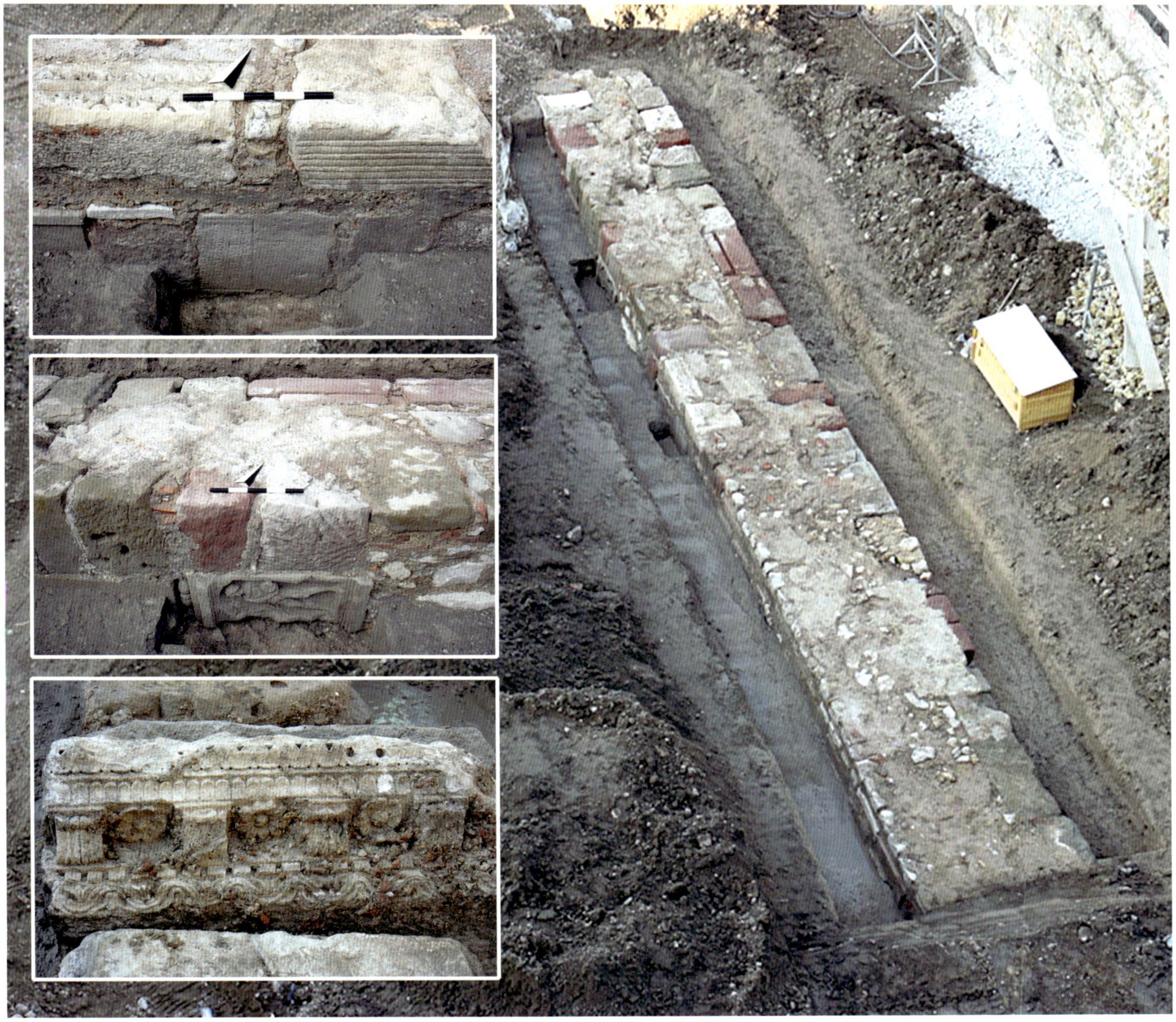

Fig. 17
Mainz, city of Mainz. City wall of the 3rd century with spolia used for building the foundations. (GDKE/Landesarchäologie/Mainz/E. Klingenberg)

The situation is reflected in the hoards of captured spoils of Neupotz and Hagenbach which were dug out in the 1960/80s. Mini-fortifications were erected behind the Rhine line for the protection of the interior; these include the *burgus* of Mittelstrimmig, which can be dated to 23/05/269 AD thanks to an inscription. In Mainz, the building structure of the legion camp seems to have been changed: on the one hand new residential units were created, and on the other many walls were pulled down to their foundations on a large scale. Changes in military tactics also led to changes in military architecture, as can be seen in Remagen, where the old stone wall of the auxiliary camp was enlarged to twice its former width; and in Mainz, both from the wide U-shaped ditch, which now lies far in advance of the camp wall, and the probable double thickness of the wall, presumably implemented during the time of Constantin. The new big buildings included the theatre visible today, which was constructed in the same place as the old theatre from Augustan times, and the building complex in the Gonsbach valley outside the gates, which can perhaps be interpreted as a stud farm with a round training ground. (Fig. 18)

In the course of the 4th century, the former civil settlements of Andernach, Koblenz, Boppard, Bingen, Worms, and Speyer were transformed into walled, for-

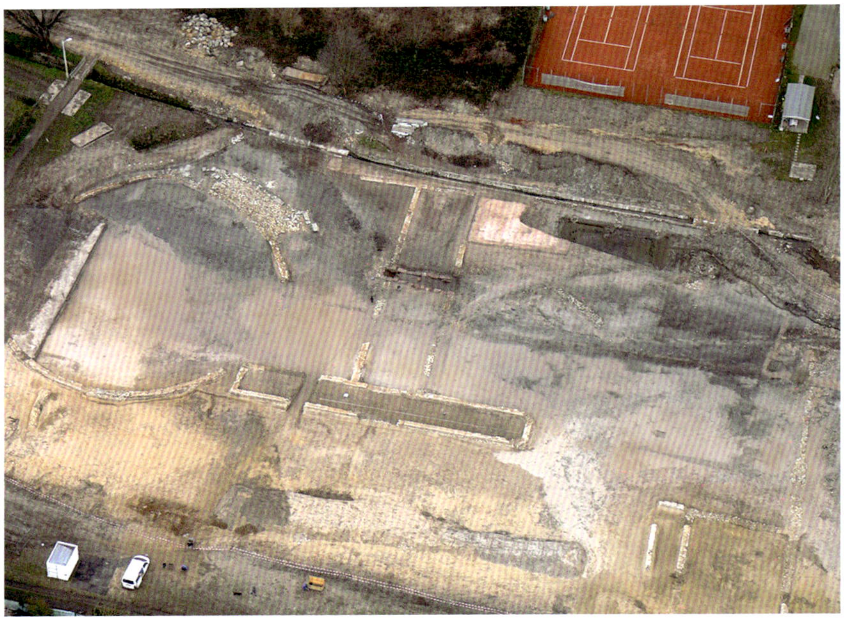

Fig. 18
Mainz, city of Mainz. Architectural complex in the Gonsbach valley. (B. Saile)

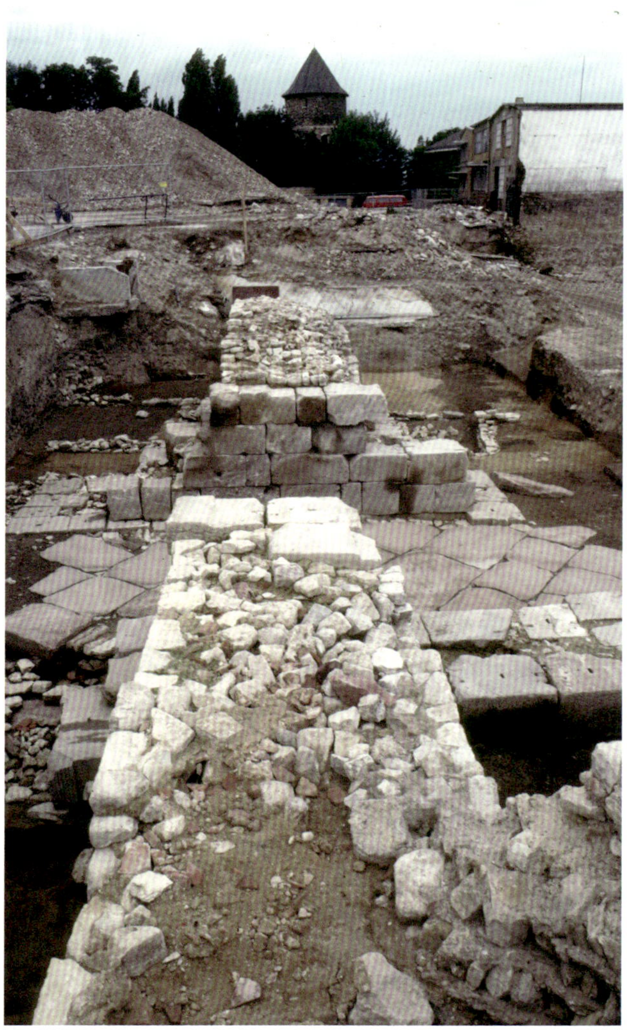

Fig. 19
Mainz, city of Mainz. Late antique city wall with gate and old legion camp road. (GDKE/ Landesarchäologie/ Mainz/G.Rupprecht)

tified cities. After the 22nd Legion had been wiped out in the civil war troubles connected to the usurpation by Magnentius in 350/353 AD, the legion camp in Mainz was abandoned. The gap thus produced in the city wall was filled by a new piece of wall with a city gate (Figs. 19–20) over the old main camp road, and the city wall ring was shortened considerably on the southern side, thus significantly reducing the settlement area as well. Remains of the city gate discovered in 1985 are preserved in situ. The exact course of the wall in this area is not yet completely clear, but we can assume that the theatre remained inside. It appears that it now also served as a fortification. The remaining importance of Mainz as a military base (also in the context of border defence during late antiquity) is documented by several ships, whose wrecks were excavated on the banks of the Rhine in 1981. (Fig. 21) There is dendrochronological evidence of two military boats used in the 4th century; another one may be a bigger row boat from the 2nd quarter of the 5th century.

Bibliography

R. Bockius, Die spätrömischen Schiffswracks aus Mainz. RGZM Monogr. 67 (Mainz 2006).

A. Böhme-Schönberger, Kulturwandel in Badenheim? In: A. Hafner/ S. von Schnurbein (Hg.), Kelten, Germanen, Römer im Mittelgebirgsraum zwischen Luxemburg und Thüringen. Akten Int. Koll. DFG-Schwerpunktprogramm »Romanisierung« 28.–30. September 1998 in Trier (Bonn 2000). W. Boppert, Zur Dekoration der Metopen am Konsolengesims aus dem Theater in Mainz. Mainzer Arch. Zeitschr. 10, 2015, 49–77.

D. Burger, Das Legionslager von Mogontiacum. Nachrichtenbl. Deutsche Limeskommission 10, 2016, 8–11.

H. Cüppers (Hg.), Die Römer in Rheinland-Pfalz (Stuttgart 1990).

Chr. Ertel, Der Kaiserkultbezirk von Mogontiacum (Mainz). Mainzer Arch. Zeitschr. 10, 2015, 1–48.

S. Friedrich, Remagen. Das römische Auxiliarkastell Rigomagus. Ber. Arch. Mittelrhein u. Mosel 16 (Koblenz 2010) 10–439.

C. Gaeng/ J. Metzler/ N. Gaspar/ L. Homan, L'oppidum Gaulois du Titelberg (Luxembourg 2014).

K. J. Gilles, Der römische Goldmünzenschatz aus der Feldstraße in Trier. Trierer Zeitschr. Beih. 34 (Trier 2013).

M. Grünewald, Unter dem Pflaster von Worms. Archäologie in der Stadt (Worms 2012).

J. Haas, Zur Burgusinschrift von Mittelstrimmig, Kreis Cochem-Zell. Ber. Arch. Mittelrhein und Mosel 9. Trierer Zeitschr. Beiheft 28 (Trier 2004) 93–102.

P. Haupt, Ein Nachtrag zu Datierung und Rekonstruktion des augusteisch-tiberischen Militärlagers von Belginum: www.vfg-mz.de/ wp-content/uploads/2012/11/MAOO.pdf.

A. Heising, Die römische Stadtmauer von Mogontiacum-Mainz (Bonn 2008).

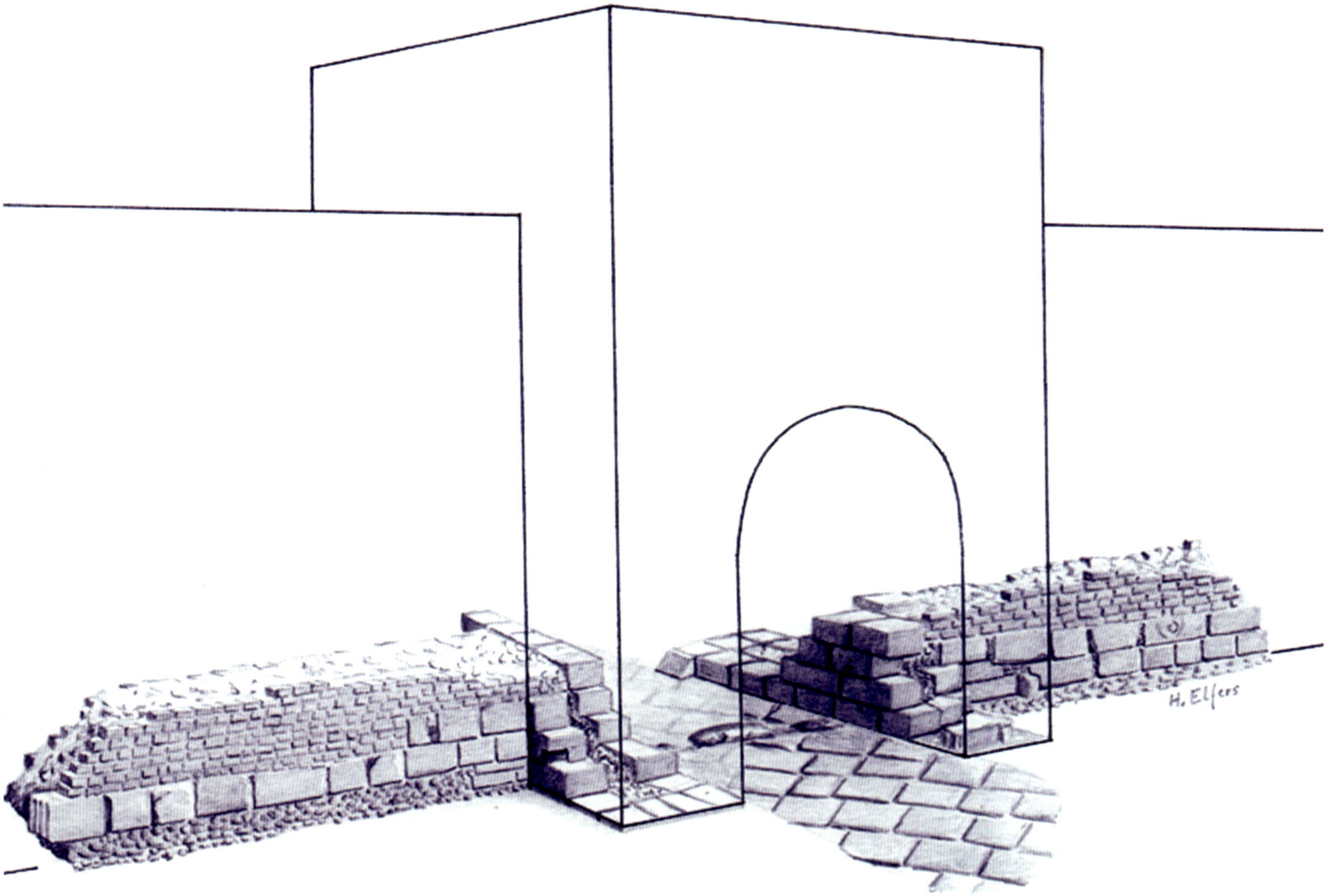

Fig. 20
Mainz, city of Mainz. Block diagram of the late antique city wall with gate and old legion camp road. (GDKE/Landesarchäologie/Mainz/ G. Rupprecht, E. Elfers)

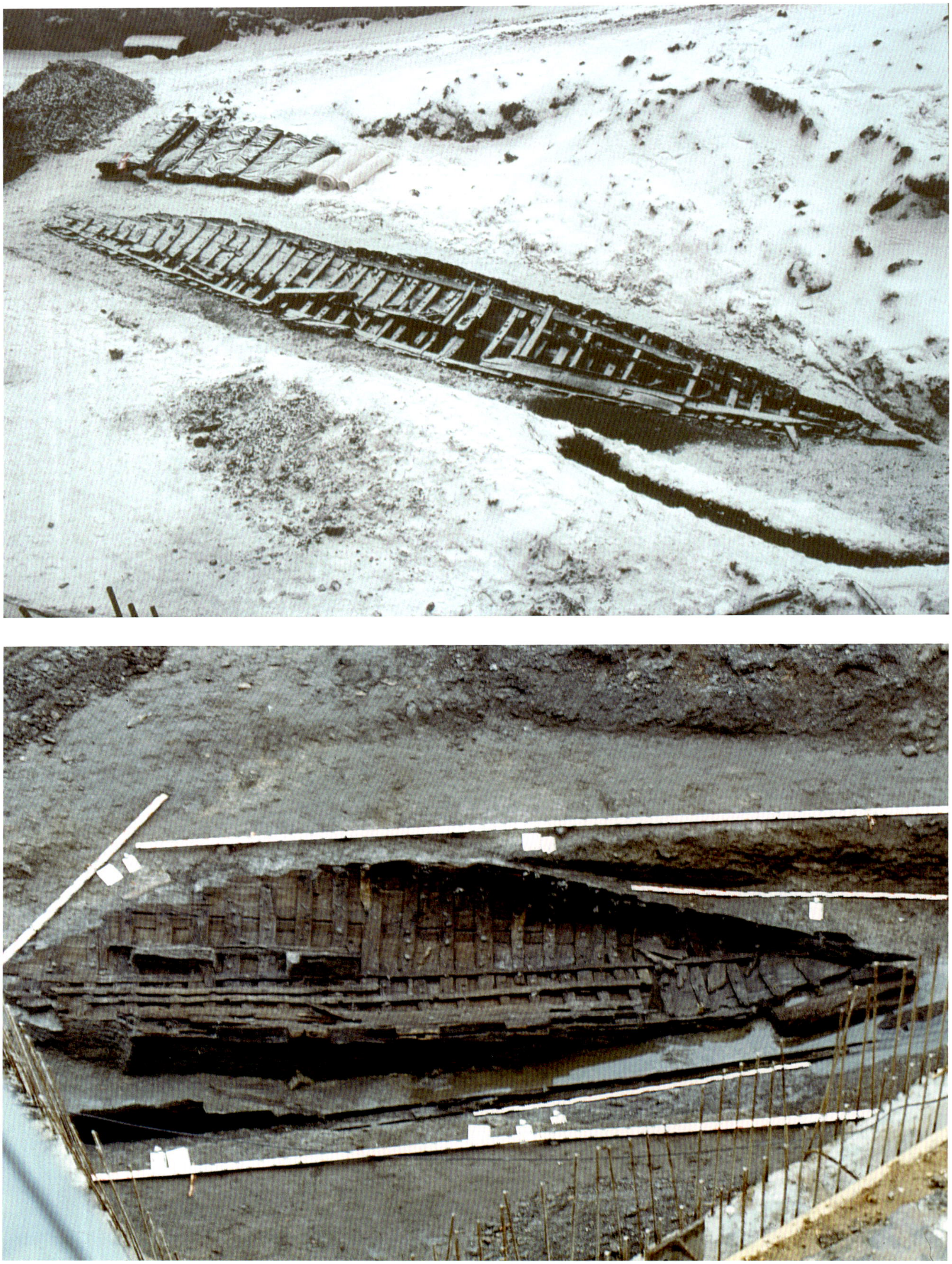

Fig. 21
Mainz, city of Mainz. Late antique ships, top: ship 5, bottom: ship 1. (GDKE/Landesarchäologie/Mainz/G. Rupprecht, M. Witteyer)

S. Hornung, Das spätrepublikanische Militärlager bei Hermeskeil (Lkr. Trier-Saarburg), in: A. Lehmann/ R. Wiegels /Hg.), »Über die Alpen und über den Rhein«. Beiträge zu den Anfängen und zum Verlauf der römischen Expansion nach Mitteleuropa. Abhandl. Akad. Wiss. Göttingen N.F. 37 (Berlin/Boston 2015) 103–132.

B. Hünerfauth, In der Not versteckt. Der Hortfund von Rheingönheim. Arch in der Pfalz 5 (Speyer 2016) 22–25.

C.A. Jost, Der römische Limes in Rheinland-Pfalz. Arch. an Mittelrhein und Mosel 14 (Koblenz 2006).

M. Klein (Hrsg.), Die Römer und ihr Erbe (Mainz 2003).

G. Lenz-Bernhard/ H. Bernhard, Militärische und zivile Strukturen in der Pfalz zur frührömischen Zeit, in: R. Cordie (Hg.), Belginum. 50 Jahre Ausgrabungen und Forschungen (Mainz 2007) 247–295.

H. Löhr, Zum Stand der Untersuchungen im früheströmischen Militärlager auf dem Petrisberg bei Trier. Arch. in Rheinland-Pfalz 2004 (Mainz 2005) 36–39.

E. Schallmayer (Hg.), Limes Imperii Romani. Saalburg-Schr. 6 (Bad Homburg v.d.H. 2004) 135–145.

L. Schwinden, Die Aufstände der Bataver und der Treverer nach Neros Sturz, in: Begleitband zur Ausstellung Nero – Kaiser, Künstler und Tyrann. Schriftenreihe Rhein. Landesmus. Trier 40 (Darmstadt 2016) 309–320.

B. Steidl, Nordbayern zur Zeit Marbods: in: V. Salač/ J. Bemann (Hg.), Mitteleuropa zur Zeit Marbods. 19. Internationales Symposium Grundprobleme der frühgeschichtlichen Entwicklung im mittleren Donauraum (Prag/Bonn 2009) 473–484.

G. Uelsberg (Hg.), Krieg und Frieden. Kelten – Römer – Germanen. Begleitbuch zur Ausstellung im Rheinischen LandesMuseum Bonn (Darmstadt 2007) 200–202.

M. Witteyer, Rituelle Niederlegungen im Heiligtum für Isis und Magna Mater, in: A. Schäfer/ M. Witteyer (Hg.); Rituelle Deponierungen in Heiligtümern der hellenistisch-römischen Welt. Mainzer Arch. Schr. 10 (Mainz 2013) 317–352.

A cornice with corbels from the theatre at Moguntiacum/Mainz

MARION WITTEYER

The Roman history of Moguntiacum/Mainz starts with Nero Claudius Drusus, and with his death (9 BC) and that of his son Nero Claudius Drusus Germanicus (19 AD) the city became a cult centre of the Upper Germanic army.

After the death of these two members of the imperial family, the honours that the Roman senate decreed should be held at their place of activity as commanders made Mainz the scene of annual cultic-political ceremonies where delegations of all Gallic *civitates* had to take part. To perform the celebrations, an adequate place of assembly in the vicinity of the Drusus cenotaph was needed. Because of its size, with capacity for more than 10,000 people, the nearby theatre situated on the slope below was a good choice, although this was not the installation visible today, which dates from late Roman times. Under the later building, remains of the wall under the peripheries of the orchestra area in an older theatre of apparently similar dimensions could nevertheless be documented. There are, however, only few indicators for its dating. The most important is the block of a cornice with corbels, which was probably reused in the crown of the later orchestra as a foundation stone for an altar. (Fig. 1) The projecting parts of the cornice were cut off when it was built in, but were left in situ, so that the decoration could be completed again.

The cornice block is very richly covered with an ornamental decoration. The sima shows a row of acanthus leaves with poppy capsules in between. Below that we see, separated one from the other by smooth mouldings, a bead-and-reel band, a row of egg-and-dart and at the lower end a band of leaf moulding. The main decoration is found on the image fields between the corbels. The latter are decorated alternatively with shells, acanthus leaves, and blossoms. Besides cult implements, the image fields are decorated with weapon motives, partly weapons or defensive arms of the military and partly those of gladiators, as well as scenic representations with shortened depicted sacrifices and the goddess Victoria promising victory.
The site of the cornice as such is no proof that it actually came from the theatre context, but both the Augustan dating and the high quality of the sculpture and the themes of Augustan pictorial propaganda indicate that it belonged to an official state architectural structure, as might be expected in the vicinity of the Drusus cenotaph. For this reason, the integration of the cornice block into the pedestal of the stage *(hyposcaenium/pulpitum)* of the theatre was suggested as the most probable reconstruction. The existence of a theatre is documented for not later than 39 AD; it is mentioned in connection with a *spectaculum* by Sueton (Galba 6.2).

Apart from an assembly place, the community also required further installations to perform the memorial celebrations. Unfortunately, no certain architectural findings could be made so far. Our ideas about the cult ensemble are based mainly on information from written traditions, but now also on remains of sculptures from a lime kiln in the vicinity of the theatre. A large emperor cult area was reconstructed on the basis of the find material discovered in the kiln. It may thus be inferred that the entire complex was surrounded by a wall and had gate openings on the side facing the Rhine. The interior of the area served for the *memoria* of Drusus and Germanicus, and fixed rituals *(decursiones, supplicationes)* were performed here. There most certainly would have been an altar, some architectural remains of which might have been preserved, inter alia the fragment of a representation of an apotheosis. A larger open area, perhaps between the Drusus cenotaph and the altar, was required for parades. The ceremonies

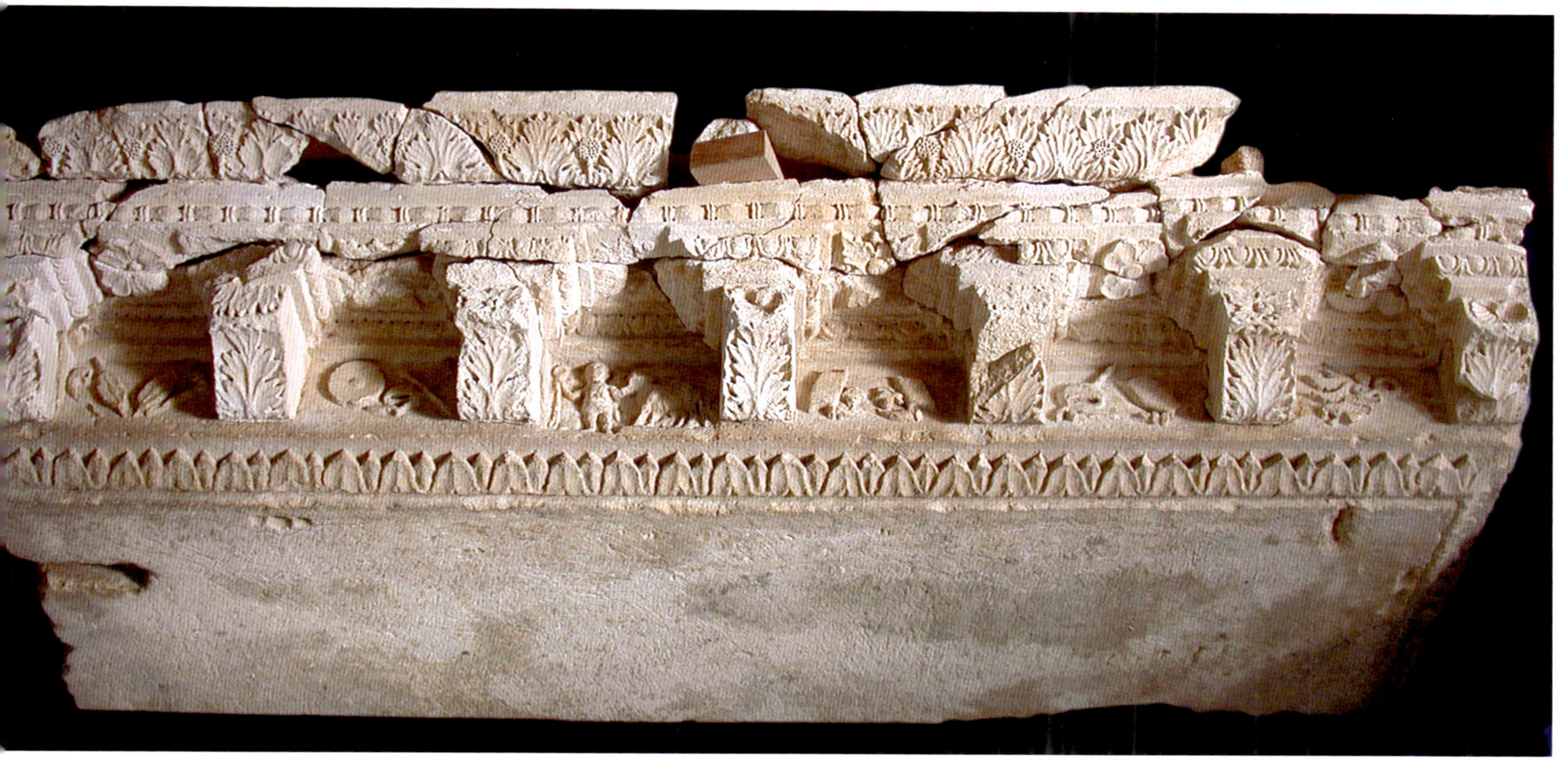

to be performed included animal sacrifices requiring further altars, kitchens and banquet rooms, where food for the participants of the sacrifices was prepared and eaten. Old finds of architectural elements also seem to indicate an impressive temple; the bronze door, which has been known for a long time and is today kept in the museum in Wiesbaden, may have belonged to this construction. The arch erected in honour of Germanicus may also have been located in the vicinity of the buildings mentioned. Even if we cannot be sure about the details, there can be no doubt that a cult was established in Mainz by the army on the occasion of Drusus' death and sponsored by Emperor Augustus. The honours established by then were confirmed once again when honour resolutions were passed after the death of Germanicus, since the relevant celebrations were to take place at the same place as those for his father Drusus.

Fig. 1
Mainz, city of Mainz. Console cornice from the Roman theatre of Mainz. (GDKE/Landesarchäologie/Mainz/E. Klingenberg)

Items of military equipment from Mainz

MARION WITTEYER

It comes as no surprise that an important military base like Moguntiacum/Mainz provides a large number of finds of Roman militaria. A great percentage of the particularly well-preserved weapons does not, however, come from the direct camp area, but from the Rhine or from areas close to the river banks. Most of these objects were found during dredging works in the riverbed for widening its shipping channel. Swords, daggers, and helmets, which nowadays appear very often in illustrations in archaeological publications about the equipment of the Roman army, were thus discovered mainly during gravel dredging works in the 1880s. The quality of the finds made them interesting also for non-Mainz collections, so that some were sold to museums in Germany and abroad, amongst them the so-called sword of Tiberius, kept in the British Museum in London. Part of the finds in the river is certainly due to loss or intentional sinking as a sacrificial offering, while most of the militaria in the legion camp and within the city area had probably been discarded as no longer usable. Various parts of equipment were found embedded in gravel layers, filled together with refuse of all kinds in pits, and in the filling material of the many wet places in the urban area and the river bank zone. Remarkably, some militaria came from the road lined with tombs in Mainz-Weisenau, where they may have been lost in connection with demolition works on the grave monuments.

Before the solid construction of the legion camp in wood and later in stone, tents were used to accommodate the soldiers. Leather remains and iron tent pegs,

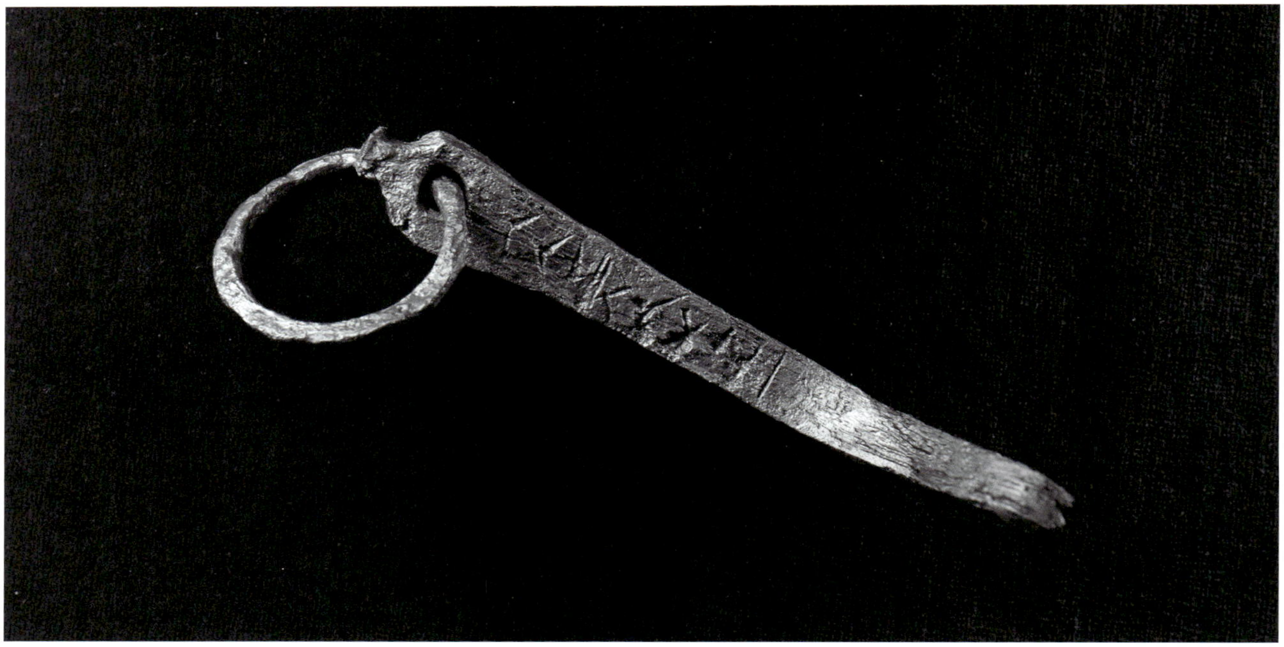

Fig. 1
Mainz, city of Mainz, Universitätsmedizin (Canabae), Tent peg with embossed name »CORONI«; possibly Augustan (GDKE/Landesarchäologie/Mainz/F. Schulz)

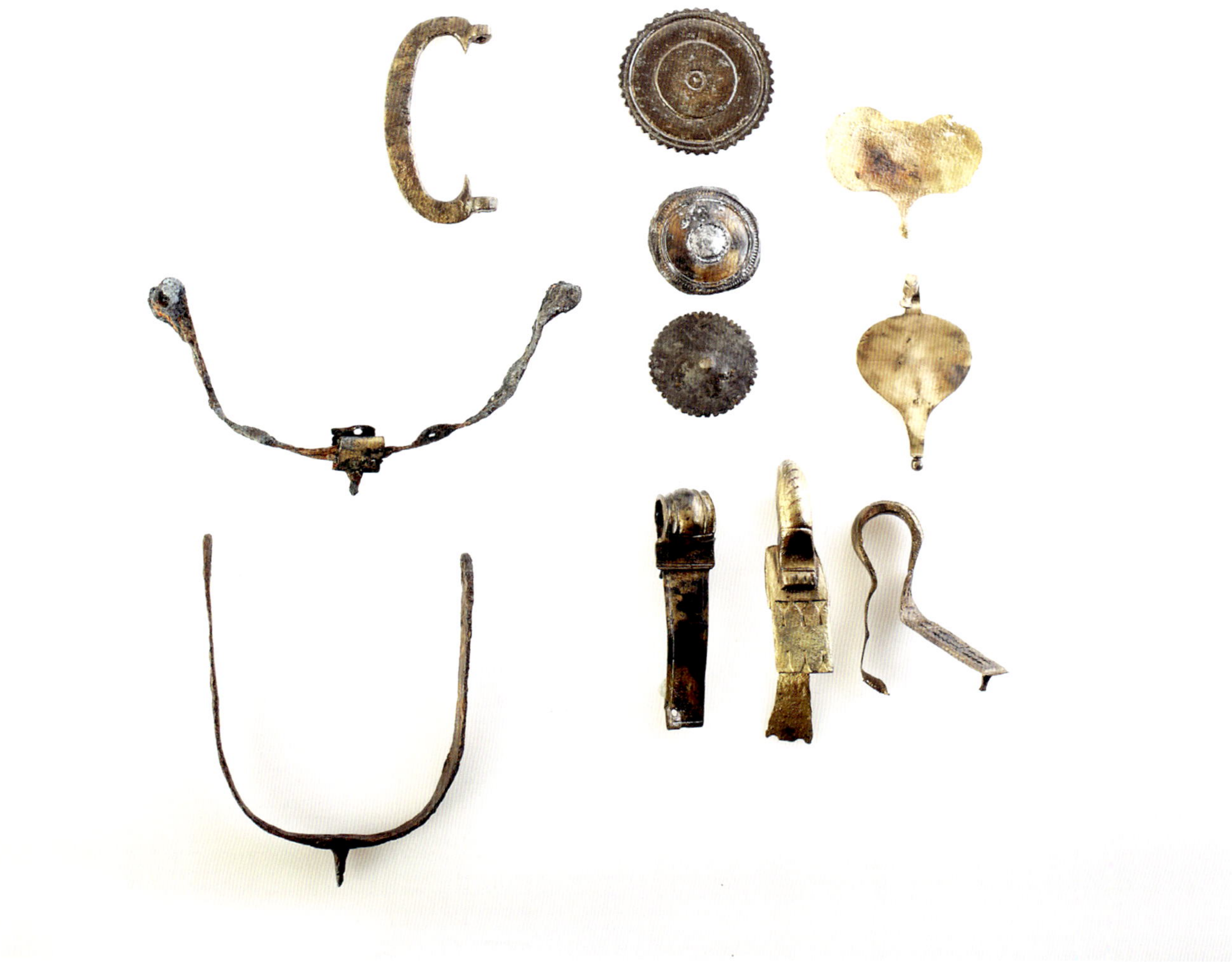

Fig. 2
Mainz, city of Mainz. Holzstraße (Rhine bank area), Various elements of cavalry equipment. 1st century AD. (GDKE/Landesarchäologie/Mainz/E. Klingenberg)

one of them with a name on it (Fig. 1), are witnesses of this. The unusual marking with the name was probably meant to indicate ownership, which might point towards the tent of an officer. So far it is not possible to determine how far the military presence, which continued until late antiquity, is also reflected in the find material, though in the finds of the last decades there seems to be a clear predominance of material from the early imperial period. There also appear to be far more defensive weapons and horse-gear than offensive arms. Finds of horse-gear need not necessarily belong to the militaria, since they do not differ fundamentally from the equipment of horses used by civilians. The major part of the finds consists of pendants fixed to the harnesses. There are far fewer strap holders, strap fittings, and decorative discs, and even fewer snaffles and saddle parts. (Fig. 2) Spurs also belong to the cavalry context, but there are only very few of them. (Fig. 3)

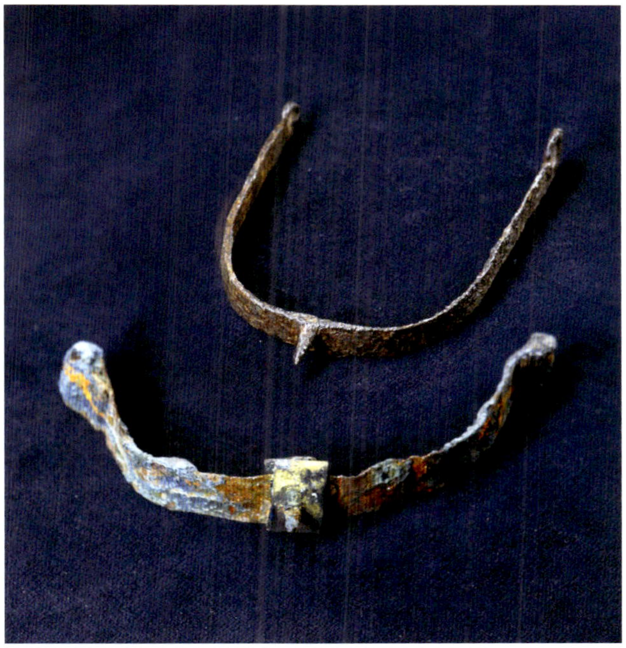

Fig. 3
Mainz, city of Mainz. Holzstraße (Rhine bank area), Detail of Roman spurs. (GDKE/Landesarchäologie/Mainz/F. Schulz)

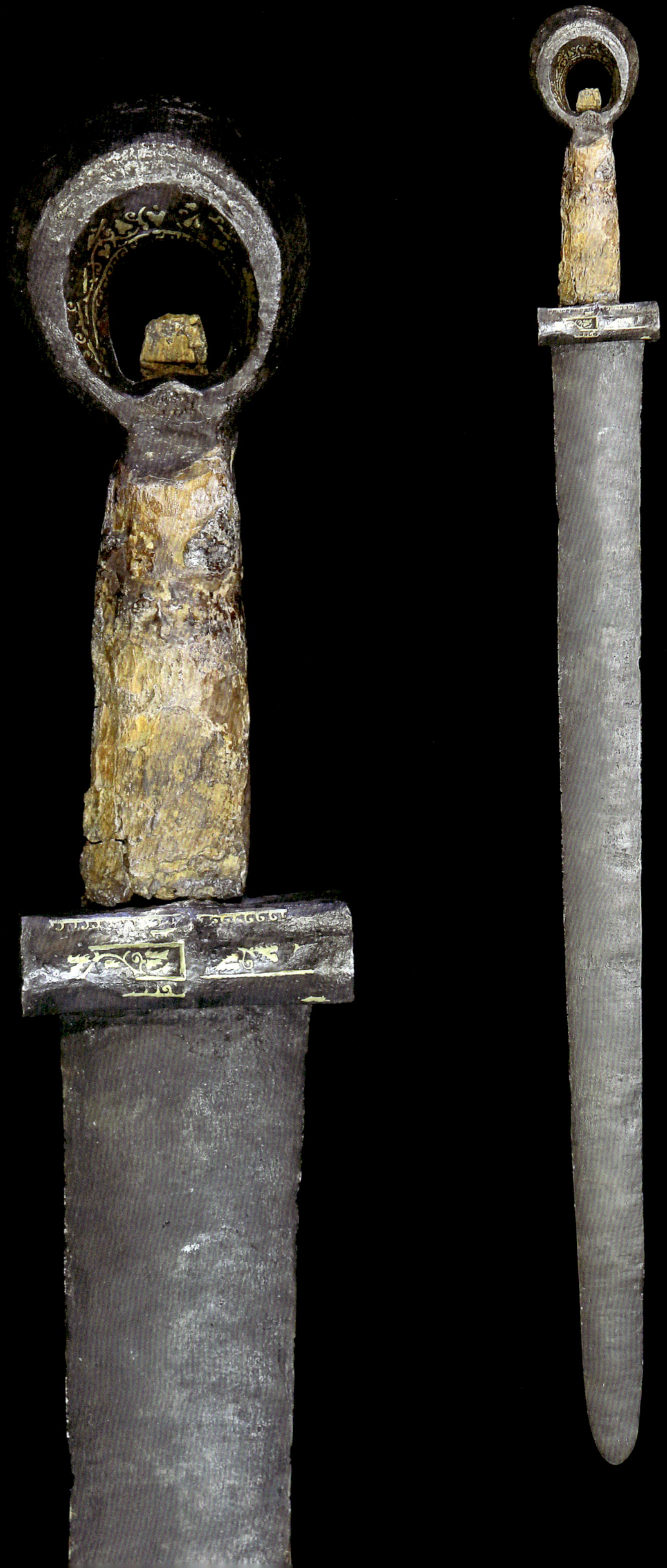

Fig. 4
Mainz, city of Mainz. Löhrstraße (late antique ship cemetery), Ring pommel sword, 2nd half of 2nd century AD. (GDKE/Landesarchäologie/Mainz/F. Schulz)

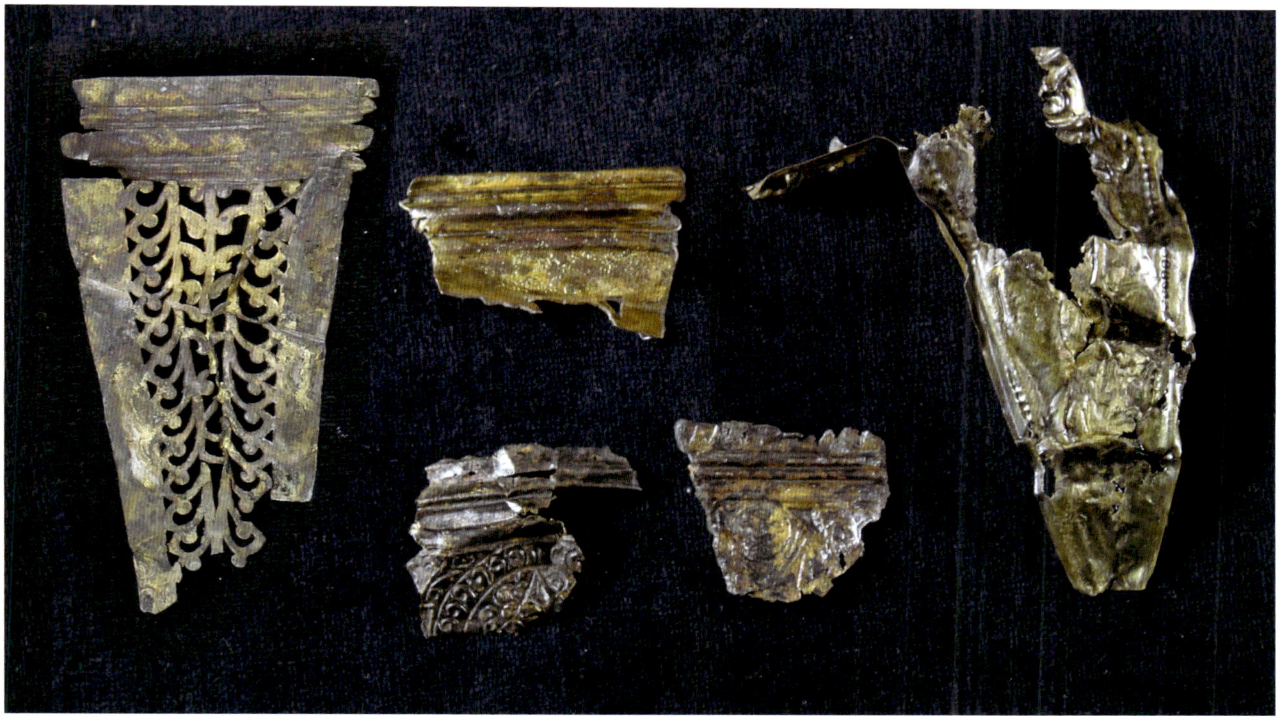

Fig. 5
Mainz, city of Mainz. Holzstraße (Rhine bank area), Fragments of decorated scabbard fittings. 1st century AD. (GDKE/Landesarchäologie/Mainz/F. Schulz)

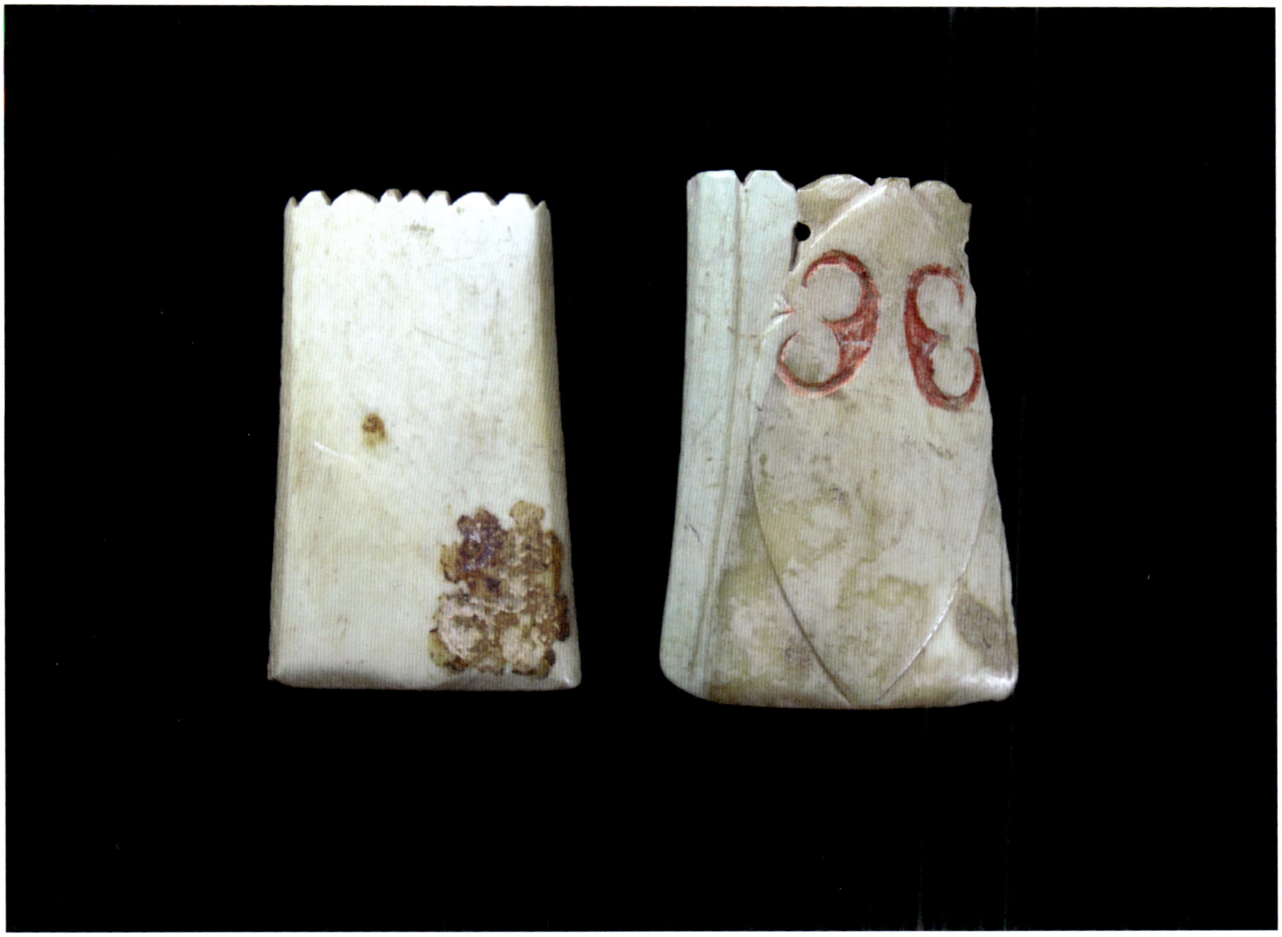

Fig. 6
Mainz, city of Mainz. Kästrich (Legion camp/Canabae), Bone chape with colour remains. 1st half of 3rd century AD. (GDKE/Landesarchäologie/Mainz/F. Schulz)

Except for a completely preserved ring pommel sword (Fig. 4) from the building site of the late antique ships, the remains of offensive weapons are mainly parts of swords, such as guards, scabbard clasps, ornamental scabbard plates (Fig. 5), chapes, and chape buttons. Besides chapes made of non-ferrous metal, some were made of bone and even decorated in colours. (Fig. 6) Organic material, i.e. bone and wood, was also used for making sword hilts. Apart from a sword and a dagger (Fig. 7) for hand-to-hand combat, the *pilum* (Fig. 8) as a special throwing spear for distance combat formed part of the weapon equipment of a legionary.

Lead slingshots (Fig. 8) and bow and arrow were the equipment of special units, which often fought as national formations in the auxiliary troops or were deployed as independent regular troops. Finds of end reinforcements of reflex bows made from bone and three-winged arrow points are clear evidence for archers in Mainz. The relevant units, like the Ituraean units coming from the orient or the *Ala Parthorum et Araborum*, are also documented through tombstones. Shield, helmet, and armour plate were the essential parts of personal protective gear. As a rule, however, only small parts of these were found: from the shield mainly the rim fittings, and from the helmet mostly the cheek pieces, plume holder, and forehead protection. Two recent finds of completely preserved helmets did not come from Mainz, but from an old branch of the Rhine near Eich. (Fig. 9) One helmet went to a private owner, the other is currently in the museum in Worms. Both helmets have been re-worked and thus represent, in a manner of speaking, the latest development of Roman weapons technology.

The various protective armours provide the largest inventory of defensive weapons. Chain mails are documented by S-shaped clasps, while hardly anything survived of the iron chains. Scale armour is also documented though only in small numbers in the form of small metal plates connected by wire. On the other hand, there is a good amount of finds of plate armour

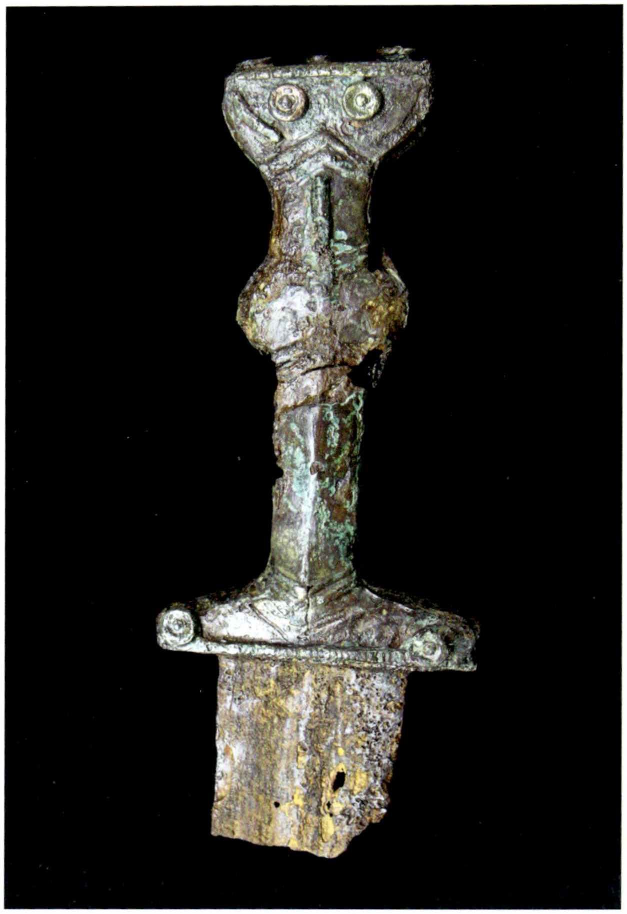

Fig. 7
Mainz, city of Mainz. Helmholtzweg/Pettenkoferweg (Legion camp). Dagger with broken blade. 1st century AD. (GDKE/Landesarchäologie/Mainz/F. Schulz)

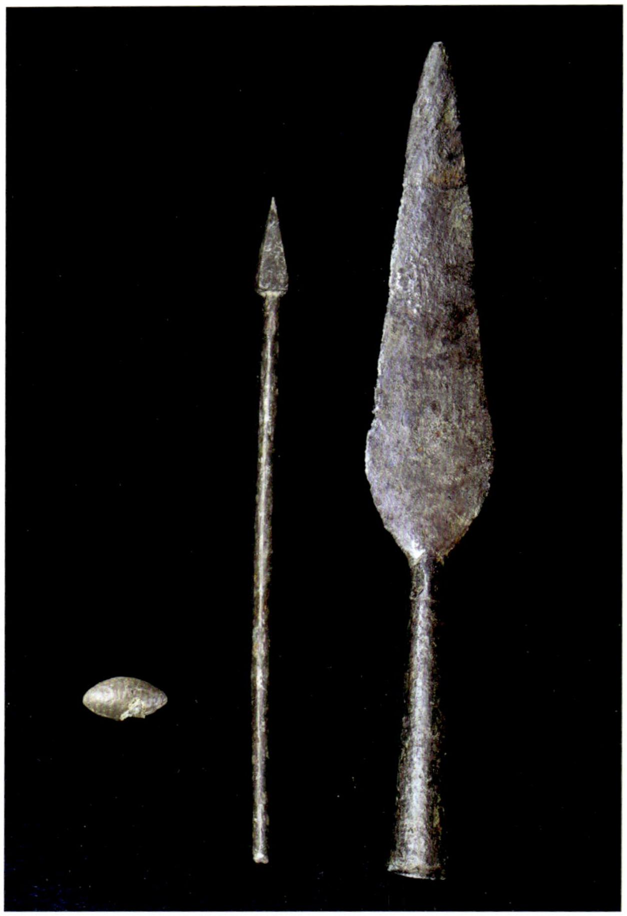

Fig. 8
Mainz, City of Mainz. Holzstraße (Rhine bank zone). Sling lead, pilum and lance point. 1st century AD. (GDKE/Landesarchäologie/Mainz/F. Schulz)

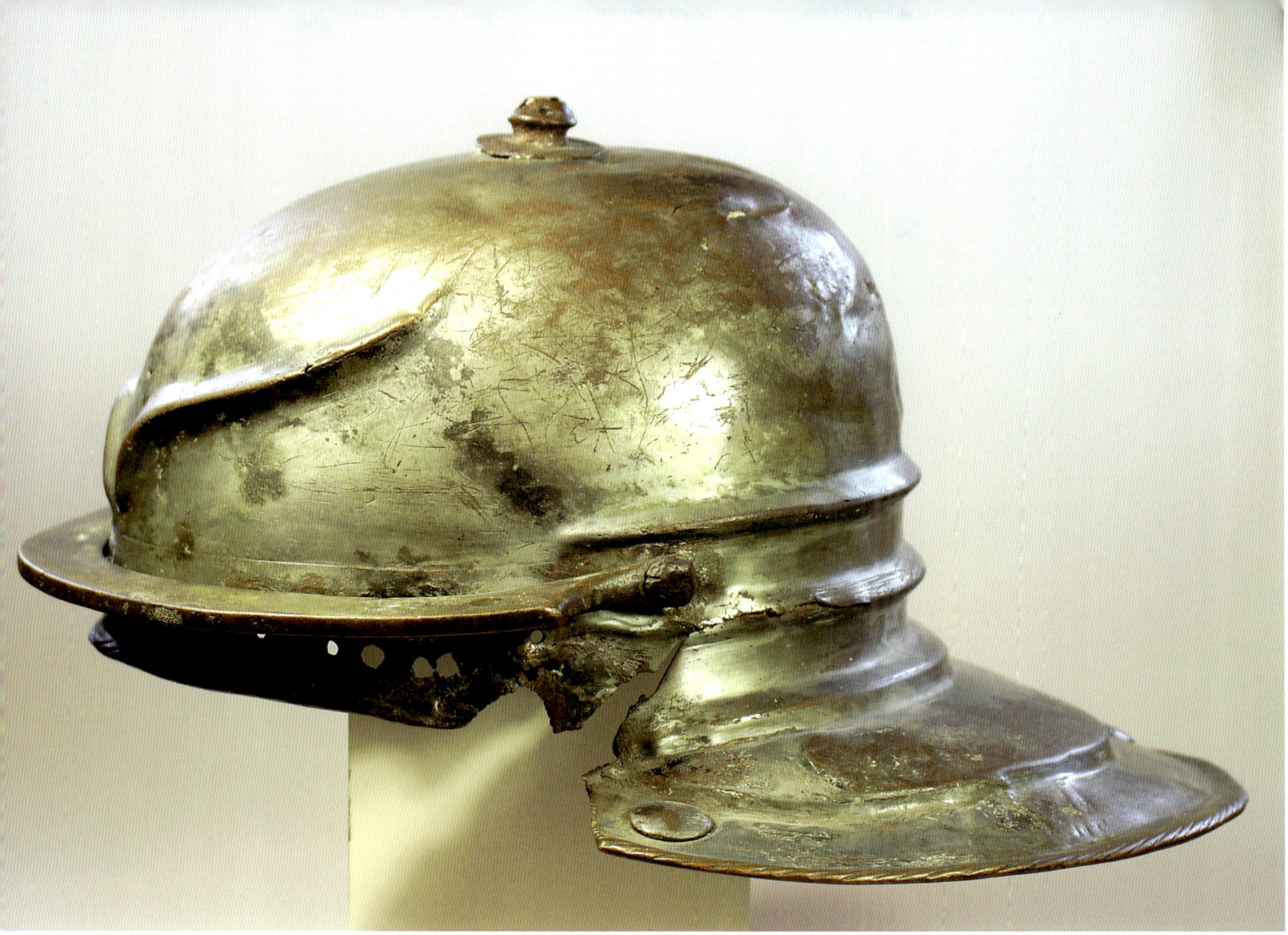

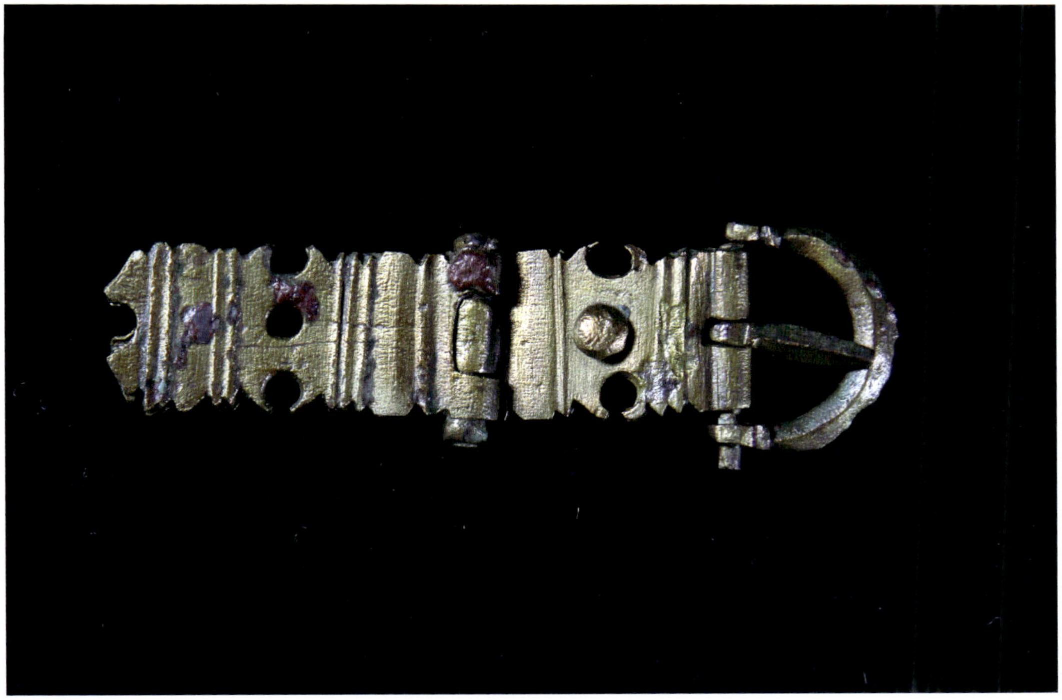

Fig. 9
Eich, Alzey–Worms district. (Gravel pit) Older Augustan helmet type with later changes. (Museum der Stadt Worms/ C. Weißert)

Fig. 10
Mainz, city of Mainz. Augustusplatz (Legion camp). Armour hinge in two parts with buckle. Augustan-Claudian. (GDKE/Landesarchäologie/Mainz/ F. Schulz)

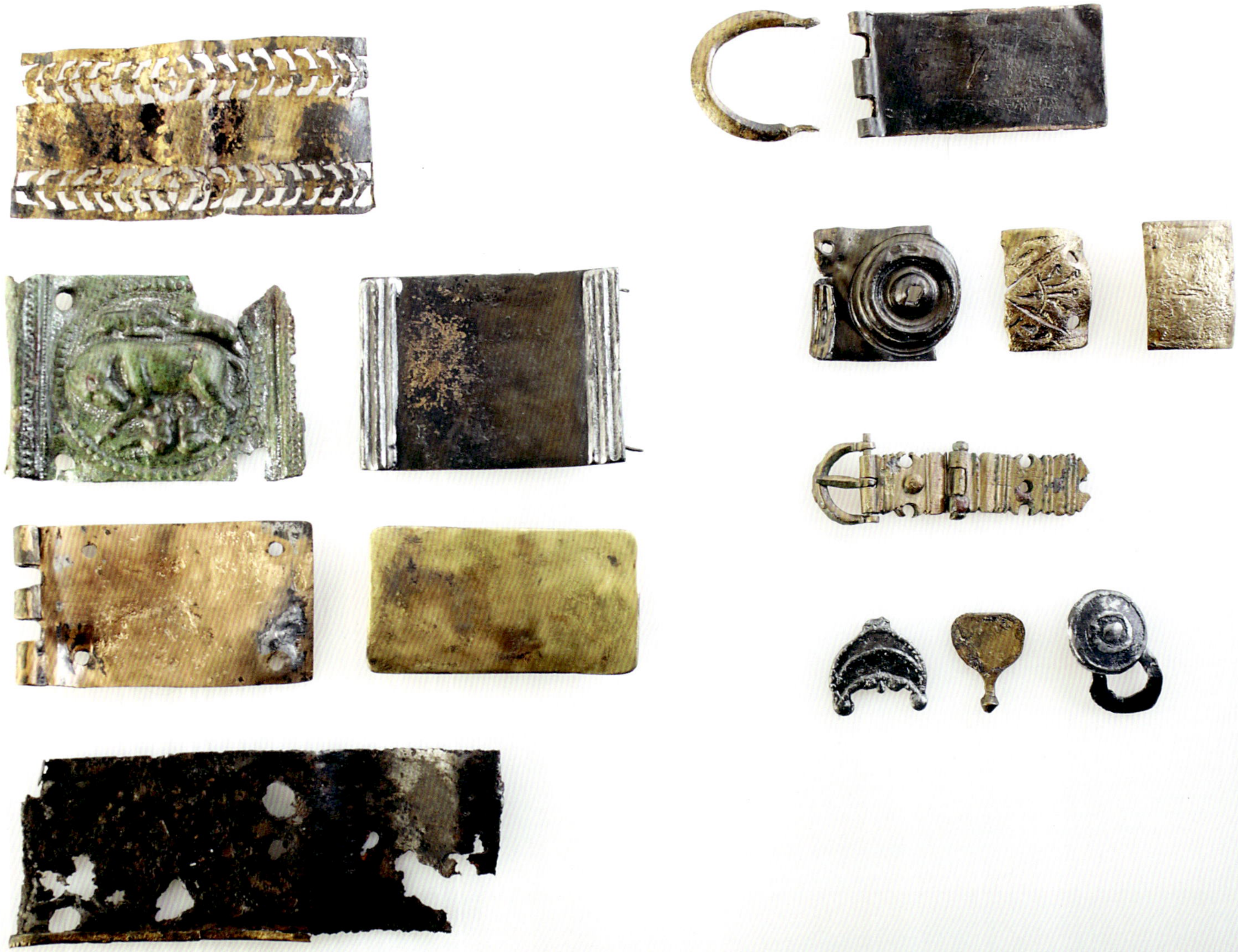

Fig. 11
Mainz, city of Mainz. Holzstraße (Rhine bank area). Fitting foils and other parts of the baldric. (GDKE/ Landesarchäologie/Mainz/ E. Klingenberg)

parts, due to the fact that great numbers of fittings and buckles were needed to fix and lock the individual iron plates. (Fig. 10) Other implements included baldric belts and belt guards. (Fig. 11) Both the belt and the belt guard were made of leather with riveted plate fittings, often lavishly decorated.

One further item of outstanding quality shows the Roman foundation myth of the she-wolf suckling the twins Romulus and Remus. (Fig. 12)

Special decorative elements include round discs with the head of a Julian-Claudian emperor, surrounded by the *lituus* (curved staff of the augurs), a jug or the goddess Victoria. The discs produced as lead casts or in press plate technology are mostly assigned to the fittings of belt guards, while others were used as medallions on scabbards. There was undoubtedly a political-propagandistic statement behind these representations: it is the emperor who is glorified here as the successful commander under the protection of the goddess of victory, and the importance of Rome as the power protecting the world is emphasised. (Fig. 13)

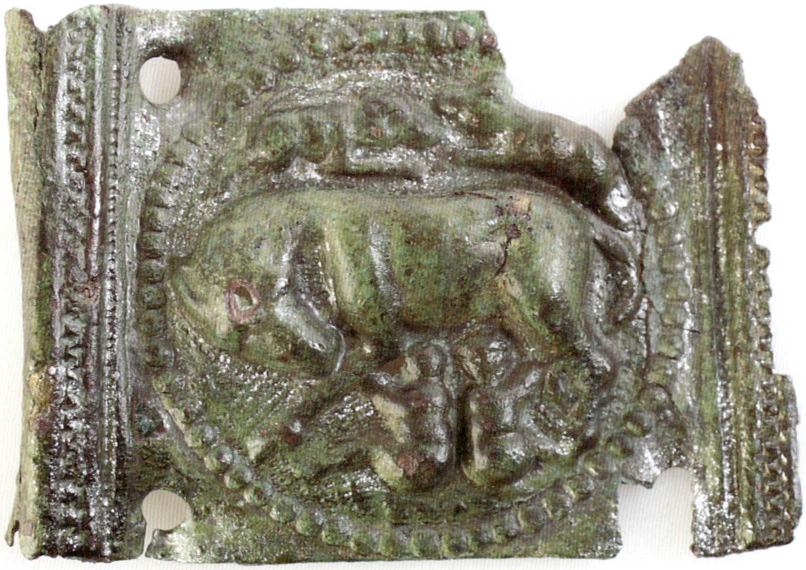

Fig. 12
Mainz, city of Mainz. Kästrich (Legion camp). Belt foil with embossed relief. So-called Lupa foil. Tiberian-Claudian. (GDKE/Landesarchäologie/Mainz/E. Klingenberg)

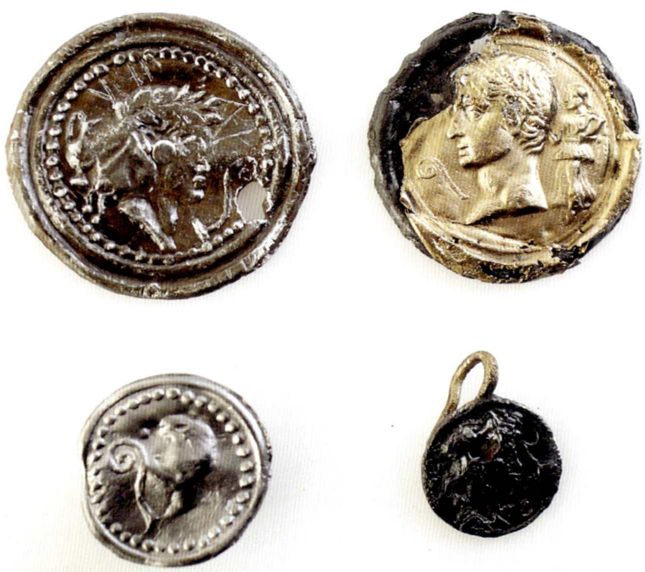

Fig. 13
Mainz, city of Mainz. Holzstraße (Rhine bank area). Sword scabbard medallion and baldric pendant. Julian-Claudian/1st century AD. (GDKE/Landesarchäologie/Mainz/E. Klingenberg)

Bibliography

J. Dolata, Zelthering mit Besitzermarke. In: Imperium – 2000 Jahre Varusschlacht (Darmstadt 2009) 349.

H. Mikler, Ein bichromes römisches Ortband aus Knochen. Mainzer Arch. Zeitschr. 5/6, 1998/99, 163–166.

C. Miks, Ein römisches Schwert mit Ringknauf aus dem Rhein bei Mainz. Mainzer Arch. Zeitschr. 8, 2009, 129–165.

J. Oldenstein, Zwei römische Helme aus Eich, Kreis Alzey-Worms. Mainzer Zeitschr. 83, 1988, 257–270.

G. Rupprecht, Cingulumbeschlag mit Lupadarstellung aus Mainz. Arch. Korrespondenzblatt 17, 1987, 223–225.

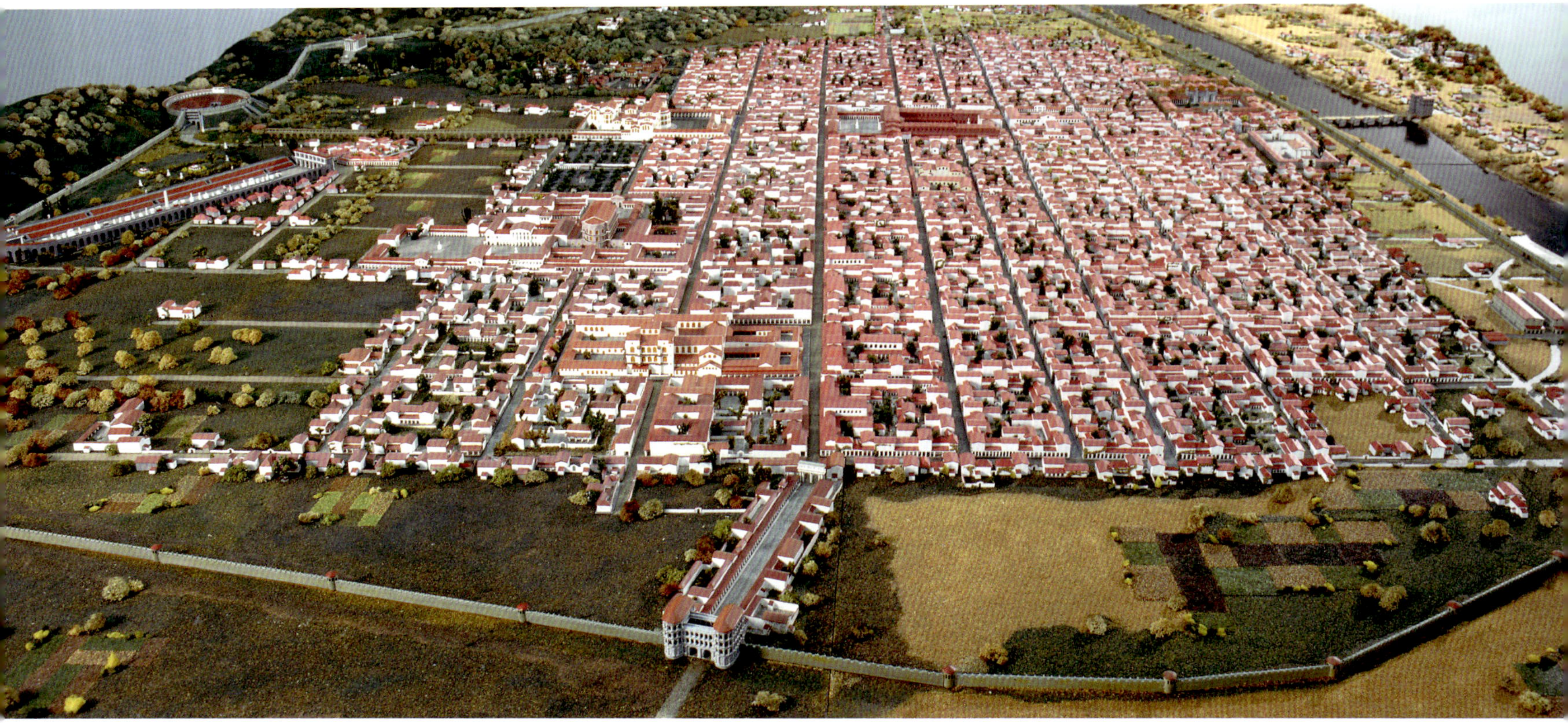

Trier – the Rome of the north

MARCUS REUTER

When the Romans advanced under emperor Augustus across the Alps, many things in Central Europe changed. Whether writing, construction in stone, official coinage, or new gods – a deep cultural change took place at that time in nearly all spheres of life. Cities were undoubtedly among the most important achievements that the Roman conquerors brought with them. There had been major city-like settlements in late Celtic times – the so-called *oppida* –, but these central places did not have public buildings; there are also no indications of urban administrative structures. This was to change completely under Roman rule. New cities were systematically planned by Roman architects and founded throughout the land. With a rectangular street network, public market places, administrative buildings, public baths, temples, and an elaborate water supply and drainage system, these new cities provided surprisingly comfortable living for the time. This was made possible, among other things, by the use of new building materials – namely tiles, stone and mortar – brought to our region for the first time by the newcomers. Together with Roman engineering skills, stone construction opened up new possibilities, especially for monumental buildings, which were considered unfeasible only a few years earlier.

Although many of the newly established settlements had a decidedly urban character, they were not considered to be »cities« in the Roman sense. In fact, the size, number of inhabitants, and architectural appearance were not definitive for the status of a city at that time. The important feature was the formal possession of a city privilege, which was exclusively granted by the Roman emperor. This could sometimes lead to somewhat curious circumstances: in Roman North Africa, for instance, there were small settlements with only a few hundred inhabitants, which nevertheless had a city privilege, while much larger places never got beyond the legal status of village. Even in the area of today's Rhineland-Palatinate there were similar cases, as the example of Moguntiacum, today's Mainz, strikingly shows. This place, with a built-up area of around 90 ha, was not only among the largest Roman settlements in Germany, it was also the seat of the governor of the province of Upper Germania and, as a legion base, also one of the most important administrative and military centres on the Rhine. So it may be somewhat surprising that this place with its thoroughly urban structures – Mainz had an impressive public theatre and also an important city wall from around the mid-3rd century – never gained the legal status of a city. Mainz shared this destiny with many other Roman central locations in Germany that similarly had no formal city privilege, although they

Fig. 1
Trier, city of Trier. Model of the Roman city around 300 AD. (GDKE/Rheinisches Landesmuseum Trier/Th. Zühmer)

resembled cities in appearance. There were thus only very few genuine cities – in the Roman sense – on the Rhine and Moselle and in southern Germany; in the north, these were the *colonia Ulpia Traiana* (Xanten) and the *colonia Claudia Ara Agrippinensium* (Cologne), both of which had the higher-ranking colony privilege. In the south, there were the *municipium Aelium Augustum* (Augsburg) and the *municipium Arae Flaviae* (Rottweil), which as so-called municipal towns possessed only »minor« town privilege. As a fifth city, one must finally mention the *colonia Augusta Treverorum* (Trier), which was by far the largest Roman settlement north of the Alps, with a total of 284 ha of walled city area. Trier, with an estimated population in late antiquity of around 80,000 inhabitants, can be considered as a prime example of a Roman city, since all the characteristics of a large ancient metropolis can be found here. (Fig. 1)

The Moselle bridge, built in the years 17/16 BC, is considered to be the oldest building in the Trier Moselle valley, and its construction must be seen in direct connection with the construction of major long-distance roads from Gaul to the Rhine – especially to Cologne and Mainz. To date, there are only few indications of what the city looked like even under its founder Augustus. It is nevertheless certain that already around the year 4 AD a colossal honorary monument was erected here for Gaius and Lucius, Augustus' grandsons who were adopted by him, both of whom died young. Three preserved limestone blocks bear witness till today of the former 7 m wide inscription. Trier probably had a rectangular street network already at that time, although the city had not reached its later dimensions. The recently discovered larger-than-life head of Livia, the wife of emperor Augustus, shows however that Trier was already an important centre in the Moselle area during its foundational years. Should the portrait have been part of a statue, as one might assume, then this statue of the empress would have been an impressive 4 m high. It is also quite probable that a statue of Augustus of similar size had been erected in Trier. These monumental statues from Trier's early days clearly show that the city had several representative buildings by that time. Unfortunately, little is known of the residential areas during the first decades; the oldest buildings were probably still half-timbered houses (wattle-and-daub technique). The young city must in any case have seen a rapid rise, since in the forties of the 1st century the geographer Pomponius Mela describes Trier as *urbs opulentissima*, i.e. a thriving, affluent city. (Fig. 2) However, Trier appears to have seen a construction boom for large public buildings only after the troubles of the civil war in 69/70, when the monumental forum was built, extending over an area of 140 m × 278 m, for which older private residential dwellings were pulled down. The city thus obtained a representative market place with adjoining hall buildings where trials were also held. In a letter from the city council of Hermopolis in Roman Egypt to a market controller by the name of Demetrius, the Hermopolis forum is characterized as follows: »The urban forum is, on the one hand, a jewel of the city, but on the other it also makes a nice profit, since it generates income from those who lease stands on it«. One may assume that market stalls were also leased to individual traders in Trier. In analogy to other Roman cities, it may further be assumed that there was a fixed weekly market day in the *Colonia Augusta Treverorum*. From a wall graffito in Pompeii we know that the local market of that city always took place on a »dies Saturni«, that is on a Saturday.

On the remains of a small predecessor building at the foot of the Petrisberg, another large building in Trier was erected around the year 100: a large stone and earth amphitheatre, which could accommodate some 18,000 spectators. The oval combat area at its centre, where gladiators fought, animals were baited, and executions took place, had dimensions of ca. 70 m × 49 m. There were also underground rooms from where wild animals as well as gladiators could be conveyed into the arena on lifting platforms. During the 2nd century, the city was enriched by further large buildings, such as a circus, where major chariot races were held for the race-loving people of Trier up until late antiquity. The gigantic Barbara-Thermen, built around the middle of the 2nd century, also served for leisure activities; at the time of its construction, the enormous complex was the second-largest public bath of the whole Roman Empire. The marble sculptures discovered there are evidence of high-quality, if not luxurious internal decorations of the complex. When the population grew and large thermal baths were built, the water supply for the city also had to be reorganized. While the first generations had seen to their water requirements using sim-

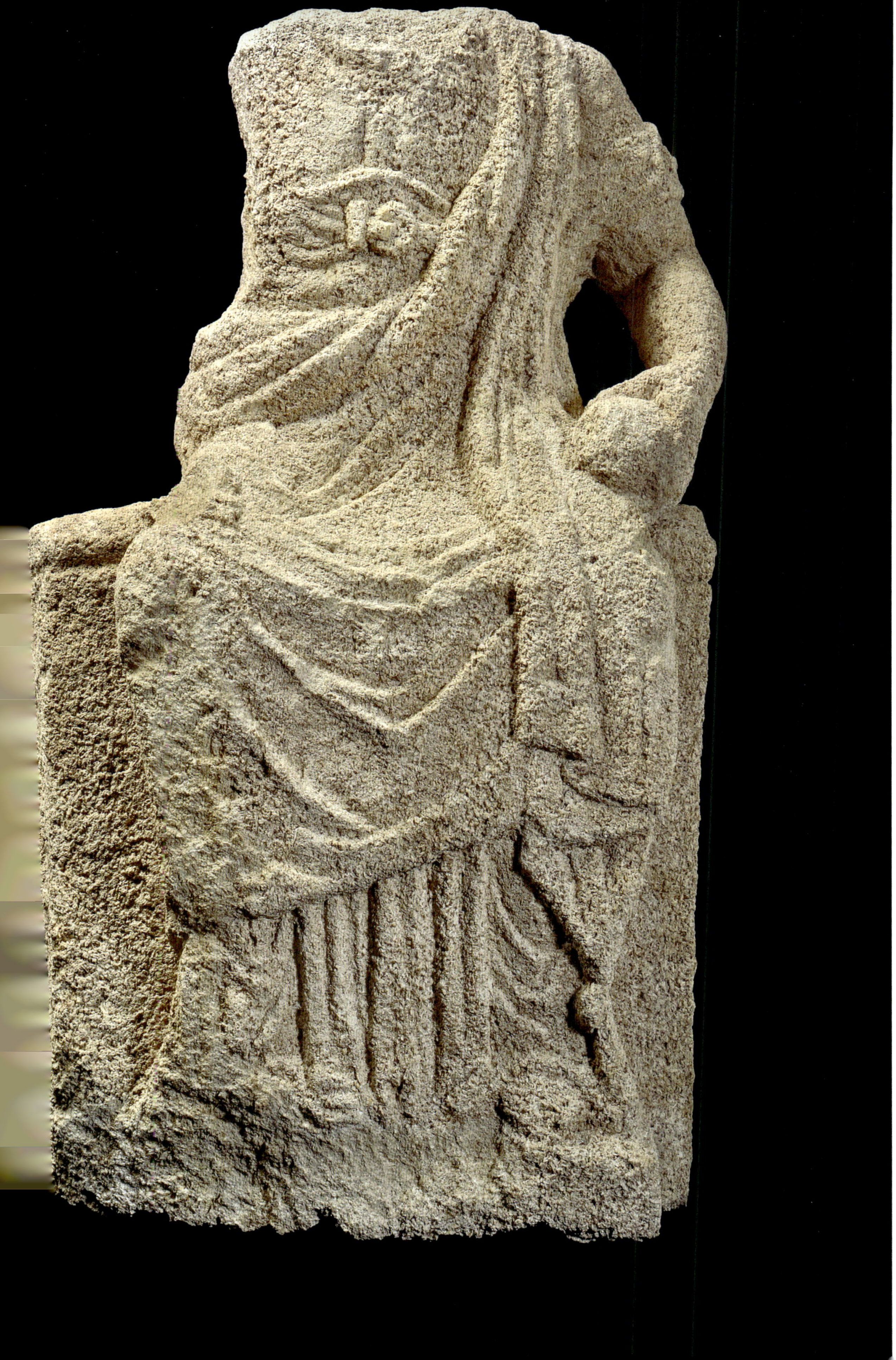

Fig. 2
Trier, city of Trier. Statue of a sitting woman in local costume from the 1st century AD, probably from a grave monument. (GDKE/Rheinisches Landesmuseum Trier/ Th. Zühmer)

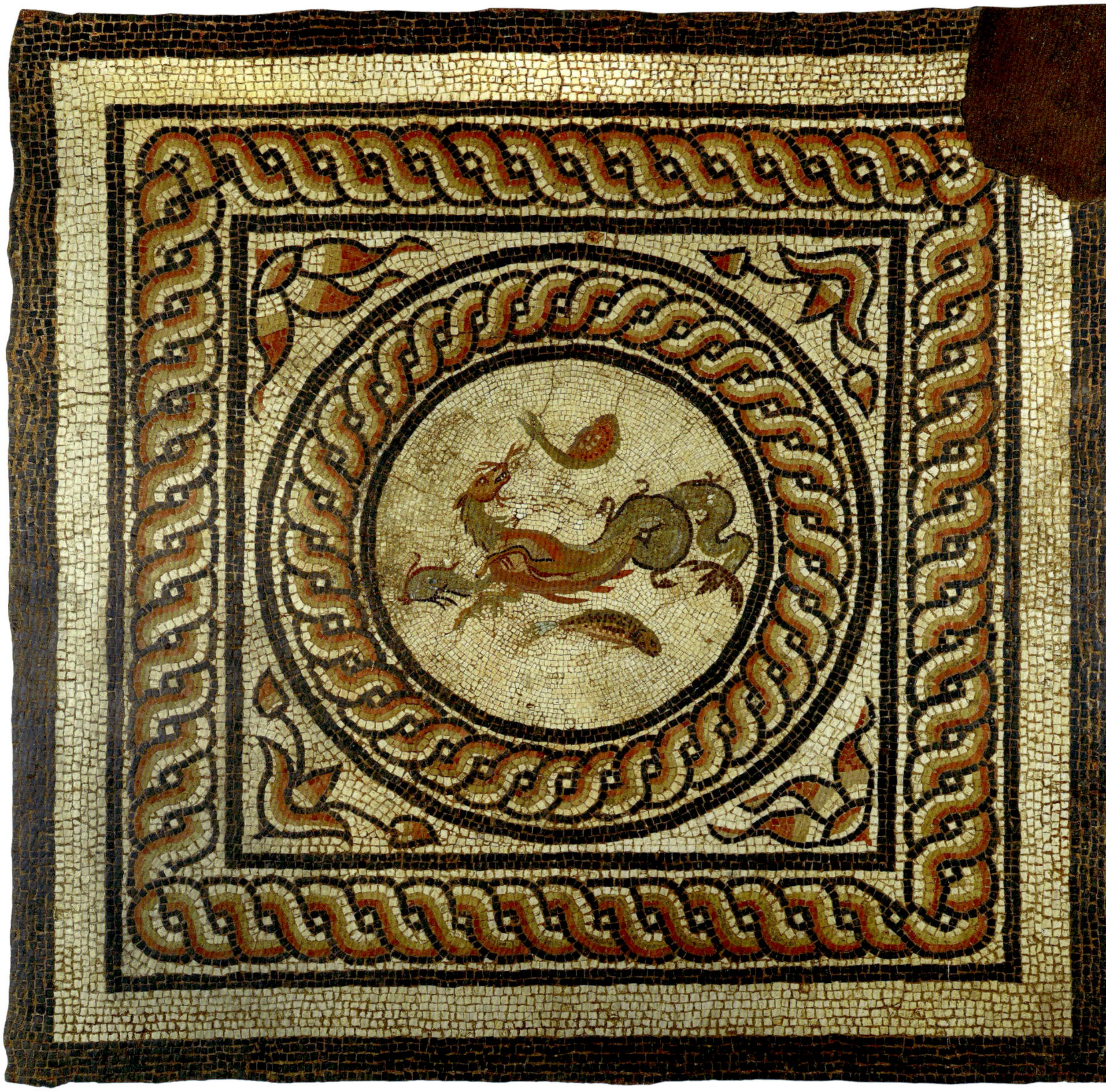

Fig. 3
Trier, city of Trier. Mosaic from the 1st half of the 2nd century with depiction of a sea dragon (Ketos), found in 1998 in Frauenstraße. (GDKE/ Rheinisches Landesmuseum Trier/Th. Zühmer)

ple wells, an elaborate water supply with a stone canal, nearly 13 km long, now brought around 20,000 m³ of water to Trier every day from the nearby Ruwer valley. However, the Ruwer aqueduct was not the only one to supply Trier with water: recent discoveries indicate that there were in total three such long-distance water supply lines into the city, where distribution basins and a large network of smaller lead pipes ensured that water was available over a large area. The drainage system was just as ingenious. Beneath nearly all the streets were stone drains with a slight drop that would carry the waste water to the Moselle. When this highly-developed water supply and disposal system was no longer maintained at the end of late antiquity and the much-diminished population reverted to using simple wells and latrines, it was nearly 1,500 years before Trier once more benefited from a sewerage system in the early 20th century.

The growth of the colonia Augusta Treverorum was accompanied by the construction of numerous monumental temples, of which only the large temple area of the healer god Asclepius shall be mentioned here by way of example. Situated inside the city towards the Moselle, a central podium temple with surrounding courtyards and colonnades was built on an area of 170 m × 88 m towards the end of the 1st century. The numerous remains of the former marble cladding document a highly decorative architectural finishing of the entire complex. Between the years 161 and 169, the financial procurator Titus Iulius Saturninus, who resided in Trier, dedicated a statue to the healer god, which was discovered in 1734 but lost again in the meantime. The personage of the donor leads us to another important role of Trier: cities were not only economic, but also administrative centres. Not only the surrounding areas, the so-called *civitas Treverorum*, were catered for administratively from Trier, but presumably also the entire Roman province of Gallia Belgica. While the official residence of the competent governor has not yet been concretely localized, the present state of research seems to indicate that it might have been Trier. The city certainly housed another administrative authority, namely the financial procurator's office. The taxes from three Roman provinces – from the North Sea to Switzerland – were collected centrally, and at the same time the payment of troops stationed on the Rhine was organized here.

Probably around the end of the 2nd century, another large building project was undertaken in Trier, which changed the appearance of the city considerably: a mighty city wall nearly 6.5 km long and 3 m wide was built, with defensive towers protruding in semicircles. Several imposing city gates, of which the Porta Nigra has survived (it was declared a UNESCO World Heritage in 1986), now allowed control of access to the city. The reasons for the elaborate fortification system are not clear, however, since no warlike intrusions in the Moselle region are documented for the time it was presumably built. Perhaps prestige and public image played a central role for building the city wall of the colonia Augusta Treverorum, as was the case for several other Roman cities.

While we are quite well informed about the appearance of the large public buildings in Roman Trier, this is much less the case when it comes to private living quarters. In most cases, only smaller sections of dwellings were discovered during excavations. In any event, these (unfortunately only selective) insights into private life show an astonishingly high standard of living – for example, a considerable number of high quality mosaics can be found all over the city. (Fig. 3) The quality of many murals originating from Roman dwellings in Trier is just as impressive. Life in the city certainly appears to have borne signs of luxury!

Another important part of the ancient city of Trier, which we know very little of, must have been the port. As one of the most important economic centres in the north-western provinces, the import and export of goods was the basis for Trier's development into a successful metropolis. In particular, it had efficient large potteries, which traded their goods on waterways as far as Britain or Hungary. Wine from the Moselle also reached all northern provinces on ships. In return, many goods from the entire ancient world – and even beyond – came to the colonia Augusta Treverorum on waterways. These included expensive marble from Greece, Italy, Turkey or North Africa. Small labels made of lead, which were inscribed with a pointed object, are particularly intriguing and allow fascinating insights into the world of Roman long-distance trading. One of these labels found in Trier mentions »piper«, i.e. pepper, which in ancient times was imported from India. Another tablet mentions »cinnamon«, which at that time came from Ceylon. All these goods probably reached the Moselle valley on boats, as did thousands of olive oil amphorae from Spain. The lively exchange of goods in Roman Trier is also documented by approx. 3,000 lead seals, once used for sealing goods and letters. They, too, reflect extensive trade connections to the big metropoles of the Roman Empire, for instance to Ephesus or Smyrna in today's Turkey.

During the 3rd century, the political and military situation of the Imperium Romanum slowly began to deteriorate, since inter-Roman civil wars and the first raids by Germanic tribes into the north-western provinces caused increasing uncertainty and a decline of the settlements. An inscription recently discovered in Dalheim in neighbouring Luxembourg tells us that a public bath was destroyed through violent acts by barbarians *(vi barbarorum absumptam),* but then rebuilt under the direction of a Roman centurion of the legio VIII from Strasbourg. There is no archaeological evidence so far that Trier was also affected by warlike intrusions – but there are indications that at least the

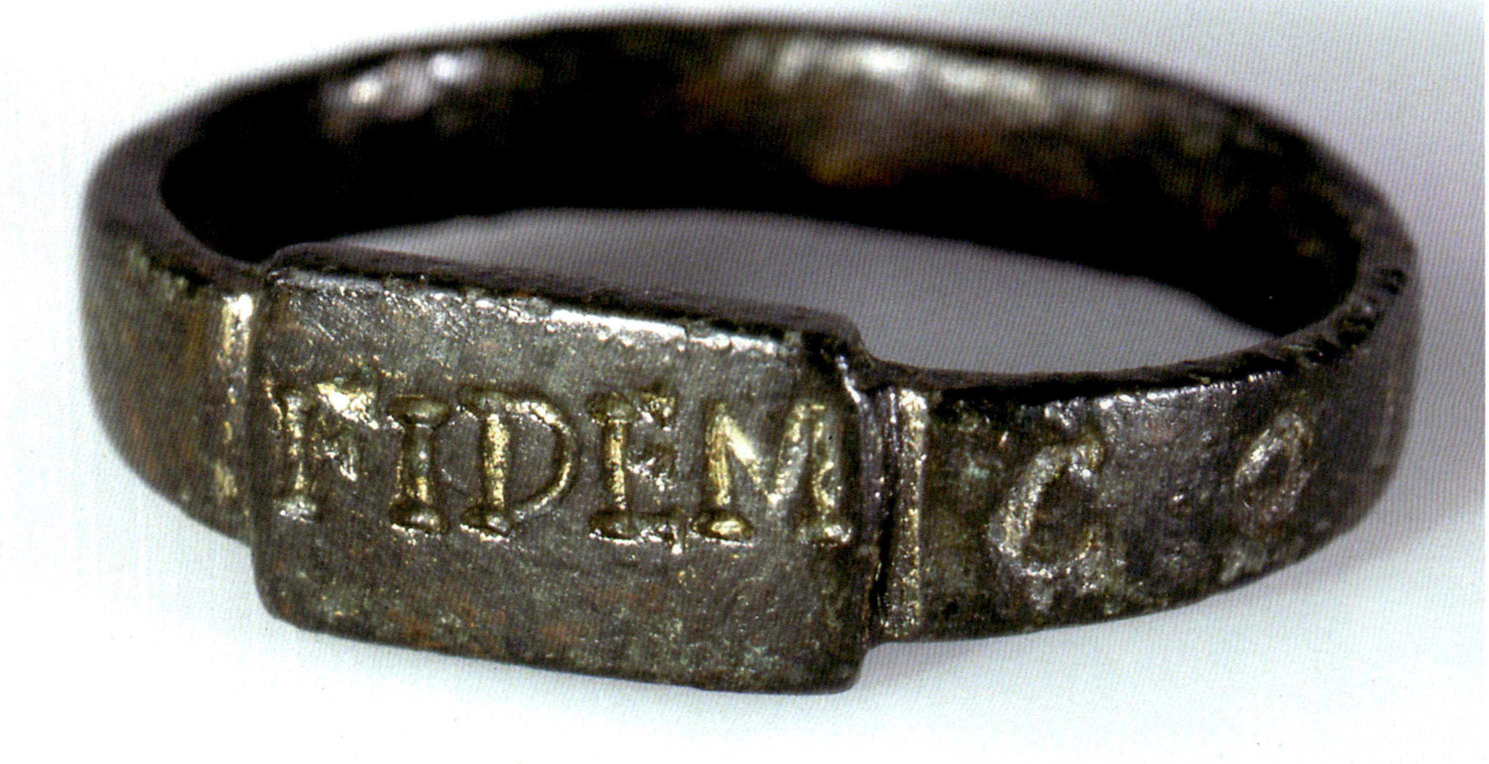

Fig. 4
Trier, city of Trier. Finger ring with inscription »FIDEM CONSTANTINO« – Loyalty to Constantine! (GDKE/Rheinisches Landesmuseum Trier/Th. Zühmer)

environs of the city were subject to plundering and destruction. These troubled times in the Moselle only ended in the late 3rd century, when Trier's finest hour came: the city was raised to the rank of imperial residence, a golden period of nearly 100 years began, and with it a building boom that is unique for the Roman north-western provinces. (Fig. 4) After the residential areas in entire city quarters had been levelled, a palace area about 800 m long with large impressive buildings was created, some of which are visible to this day. These include the imperial thermal baths (250 m × 145 m) and the no less impressive audience hall (the so-called *Konstantinsbasilika*) with a remarkable ceiling height of about 30 metres. An imperial eulogist went into raptures in 310 when describing the monumental buildings of Trier: »I see the gigantic circus, competing with the one at Rome, I think; I am seeing basilicas and the forum, royal buildings and the throne of justice rising to such a height that they are worthy of the stars and the sky, and promise to be their neighbours«.

It thus comes as no surprise that towards the end of the 19th century the famous classical scholar and Nobel Prize winner Theodor Mommsen described ancient Trier as the »Rome of the North«. Nowhere else in central Europe can one experience Roman city life and Roman culture, but also the nascent Christianity (with over 1000 early Christian epitaphs!), as impressively as in Trier. (Fig. 5)

Bibliography

Generaldirektion Kulturelles Erbe Rheinland-Pfalz / Württembergisches Landesmuseum Stuttgart (Hg.), Ein Traum von Rom. Römisches Stadtleben in Südwestdeutschland (Stuttgart 2014).

H. Heinen, Trier und das Trevererland in römischer Zeit (Trier 1985).

M. König (Hg.), PALATIA. Kaiserpaläste in Konstantinopel, Ravenna und Trier (Trier 2003).

J. Krier, Livia Augusta in Trier. Die Wiederentdeckung eines kolossalen Marmorkopfs der Gattin von Kaiser Augustus. Funde und Ausgrabungen im Bezirk Trier 46, 2014, 24–36.

Rheinisches Landesmuseum Trier (Hg.), Trier. Augustusstadt der Treverer (Trier 1984).

Rheinisches Landesmuseum Trier (Hg.), Trier. Kaiserresidenz und Bischofssitz (Trier 1984).

R. Schwinden, 2000 Jahre alt – das Trevererdenkmal für die Söhne des Augustus 4 n. Chr. Funde und Ausgrabungen im Bezirk Trier 36, 2004, 29–40.

U. Wulf-Rheidt, »Den Sternen und dem Himmel würdig«. Kaiserliche Palastbauten in Rom und Trier (Wiesbaden 2014).

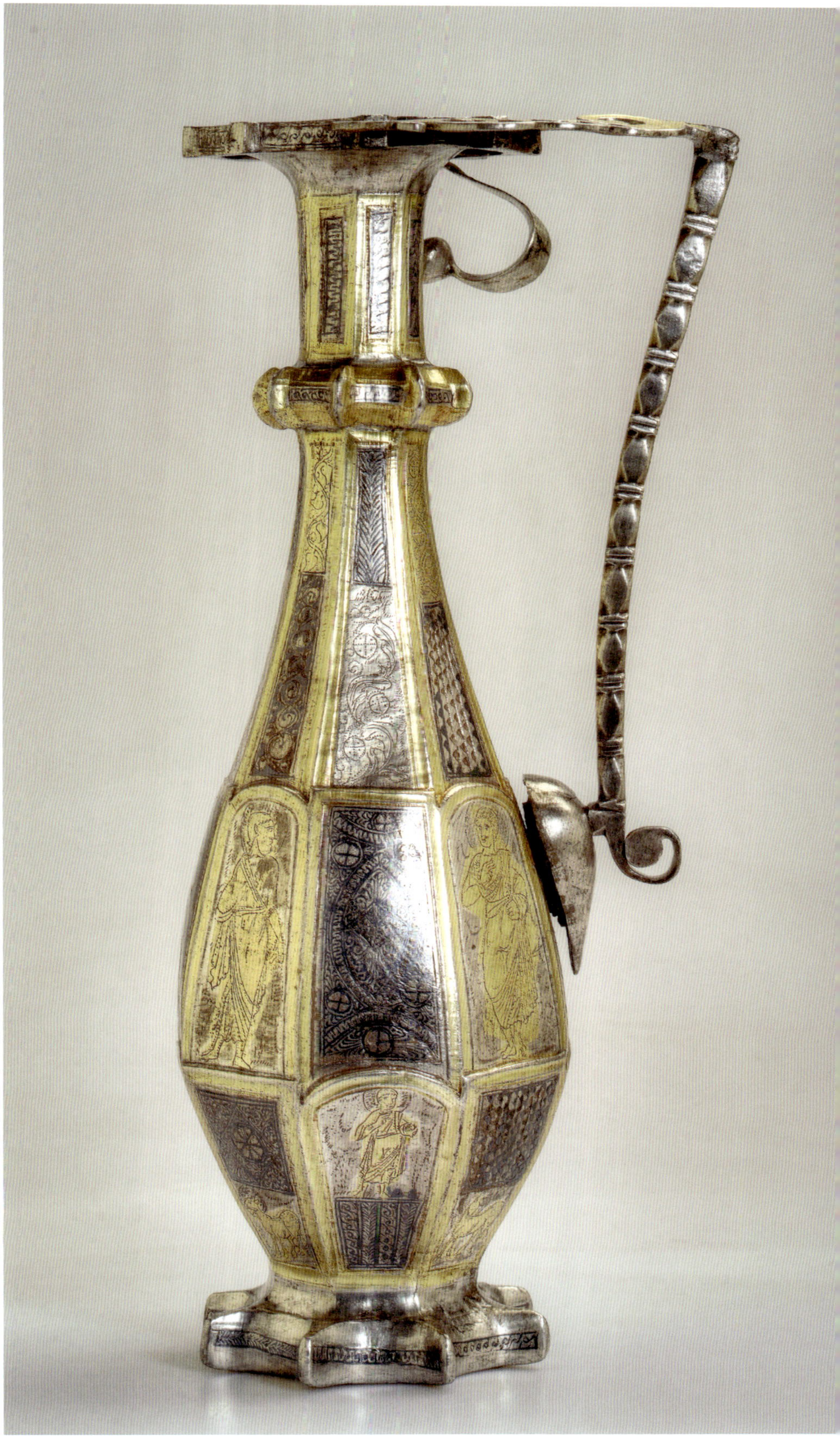

Fig. 5
Trier, city of Trier. A centre of early Christianity. Late antique silver jug with images of saints. (GDKE/Rheinisches Landesmuseum Trier/ Th. Zühmer)

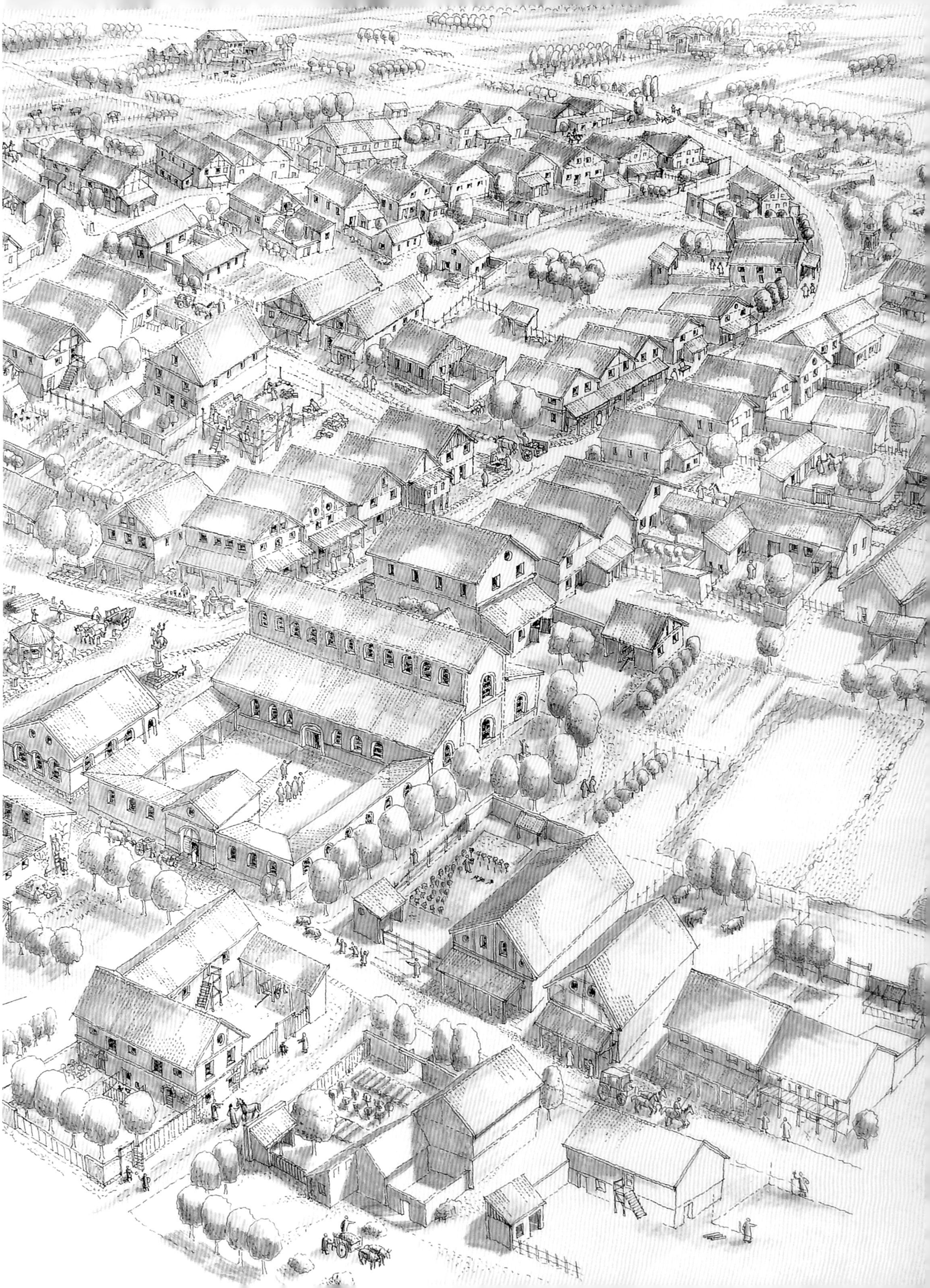

The crisis of the empire – peoples on the move

ULRICH HIMMELMANN

The world of their predecessors would have appeared as a golden era to the people living in the area of today's Rhineland-Palatinate at the end of the 3rd century AD. Just a hundred years earlier, power was wielded by able emperors who regulated their succession through the adoption of suitable successors. All major conflicts had taken place far away to the east, and economic development had been positive over a longer period. The people living east of the Limes in »free Germania«, who carried out a lively trade with the inhabitants of the *Imperium Romanum*, had also profited from this status quo. (Fig. 1)

Yet in the meantime the situation had deteriorated dramatically: quite incredibly, it was the emperor Marcus Aurelius, the wise philosopher-politician, who broke with the tradition of adopted emperors and appointed his son Commodus as successor. This led produced a whole sequence of difficult government changes, which eventually led to one of the most serious crises of the Roman Empire. The era of the »soldier emperors« (235–284) in particular was characterized by a quick succession of military rulers, poor governance, frequent civil wars, and an increasingly dismal economic outlook. Because of the continuing wars in the east, large troop contingents were time and again withdrawn from the western half of the empire, leading to massive invasions by Germanic tribes at the Rhine. Numerous hoard and treasure finds, hidden by their owners during the 3rd century and later abandoned, are associated with these restless times. One example is the hoard of coins of approx. 700 *denarii*, most of them freshly minted, from the reign of Maximinus Thrax, around 235/36, recently excavated in Speyer-Nord. (Fig. 2)

Events reached a dramatic climax in the year 260, when emperor Valerian was taken captive by the Persian king Shapur I – something unimaginable for the Romans until then! While Valerian's son and co-regent Gallienus was tied up militarily in the Balkan, the Roman officer Postumus seized power on the Rhine. The Gallic, Germanic, Britannic, and Spanish provinces were thus practically separated from the Roman Empire and formed the so-called »Gallic Empire« until 274. Postumus, who copied Roman imperial structures with his own senate and consuls, first reigned in Cologne, his successor Tetricus relocating the capital of the *Imperium Galliarum* to Trier.

The loss or abandonment of the areas right of the Rhine falls in this phase. In previous research, the picture of the »Limes Fall« was developed for this development, according to which in the years 259/260 a »tremendous storm of Germanic tribes« had overrun the Limes

Fig. 1
Eisenberg, Donnersberg distr. View of the Roman vicus around mid-3rd century. In the middle of the picture on the left: the centre of the settlement with the forum. (GDKE/Landesarchäologie/Speyer/W. Himmelmann)

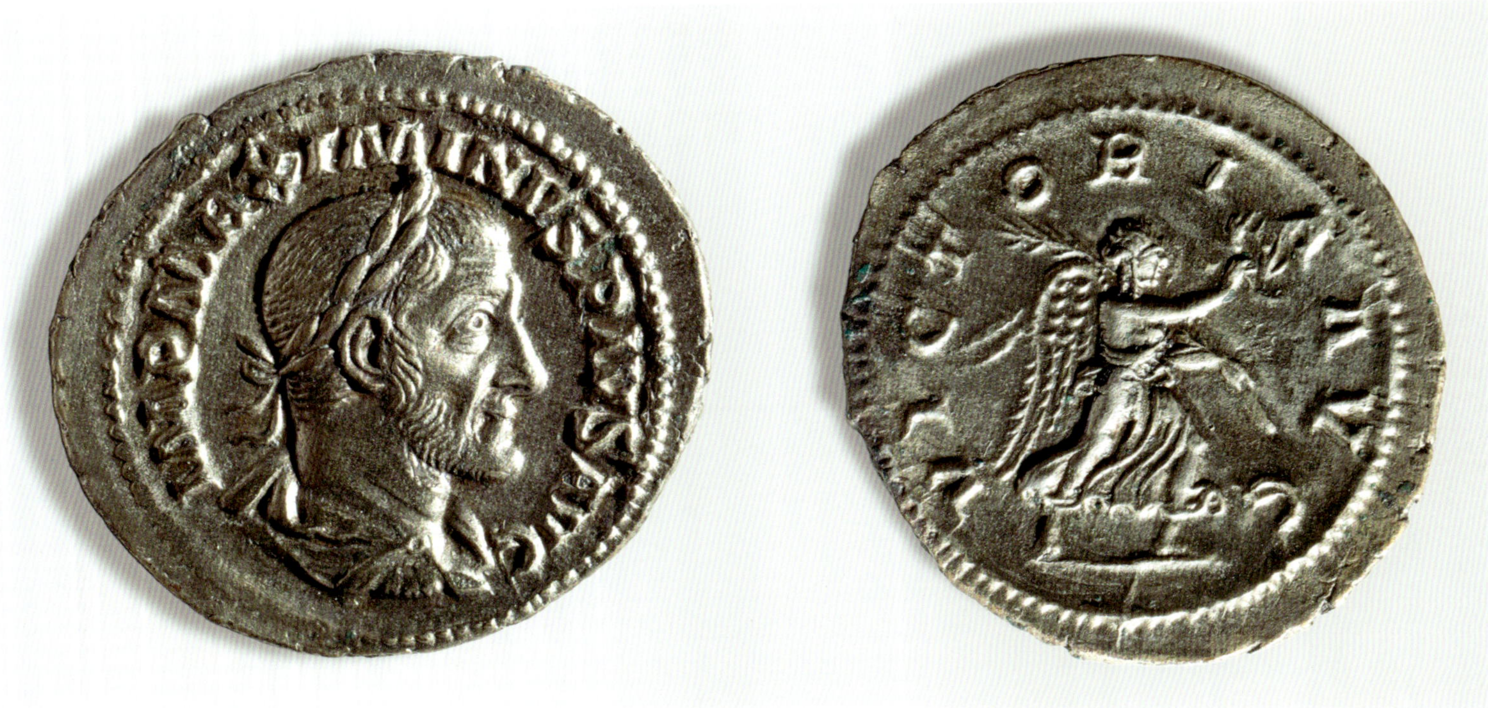

Fig. 2
Speyer, city of Speyer. A denarius of Maximinus Thrax (probably minted in the year 236 AD). (GDKE/Landesarchäologie/Speyer/P. Haag-Kirchner)

»on a broad front« and destroyed the Roman civilisation east of the Rhine. Today, however, we know that this was not one single event, but a process that took decades and was also caused by the inner political weakness of the Roman Empire.

At the same time, extensive Germanic raids to Gaul, Spain, and even Italy occurred: the treasure finds of Hagenbach and Neupotz, which were lost in the Rhine on the way back from plunders, with the finds originating in part from the edge of the Pyrenees, show how deep Germanic units could advance practically unhindered into the Roman Empire at that time. In 268, emperor Claudius II fought against Germanic hordes at Lake Garda, and the energetic emperor Aurelian (270–275) was even compelled to have city walls built in Rome.

The people living in the area of today's Rhineland-Palatinate were obviously negatively affected by these intrusions as well. The archaeological finds, however, show highly diverse developments: in Speyer, the built area of the archaeological city is clearly getting smaller after the middle of the 3rd century, and there are coin-dated fire and destruction layers in many places. A well filled-in during the last third of the 3rd century contained building and fire debris as well as parts of skeletons. The villa rustica of Wachenheim on the other hand, which is only ca. 30 km away, shows a continuous prospering development until mid-4th century, while in the industrial vicus of Rheinzabern, which is also only 30 km away from Speyer, there are clear signs of a decrease in population, although the mass production of terra sigillata continued until the middle of the 4th century. Only the production of classical relief terra sigillata was abandoned after the middle of the 3rd century, which may not, however, necessarily be due only to those restless times, but also to the changed tastes of the clients. The fact that the provincial capital of Moguntiacum/Mainz got city walls for the first time during this phase also shows how threatening the situation had become. At the same time, fortified height settlements developed in formerly unattractive, but easily defendable positions in the Eifel, Hunsrück or the Pfälzer Wald, for instance, and on the »Großer Berg« near Kindsbach.

In 274, the area was once again integrated into the Imperium Romanum, but this did not significantly change the poor security situation. Only Diocletian (284–305) managed to consolidate the situation on a larger scale. This emperor from Dalmatia initiated comprehensive reforms: already during his second

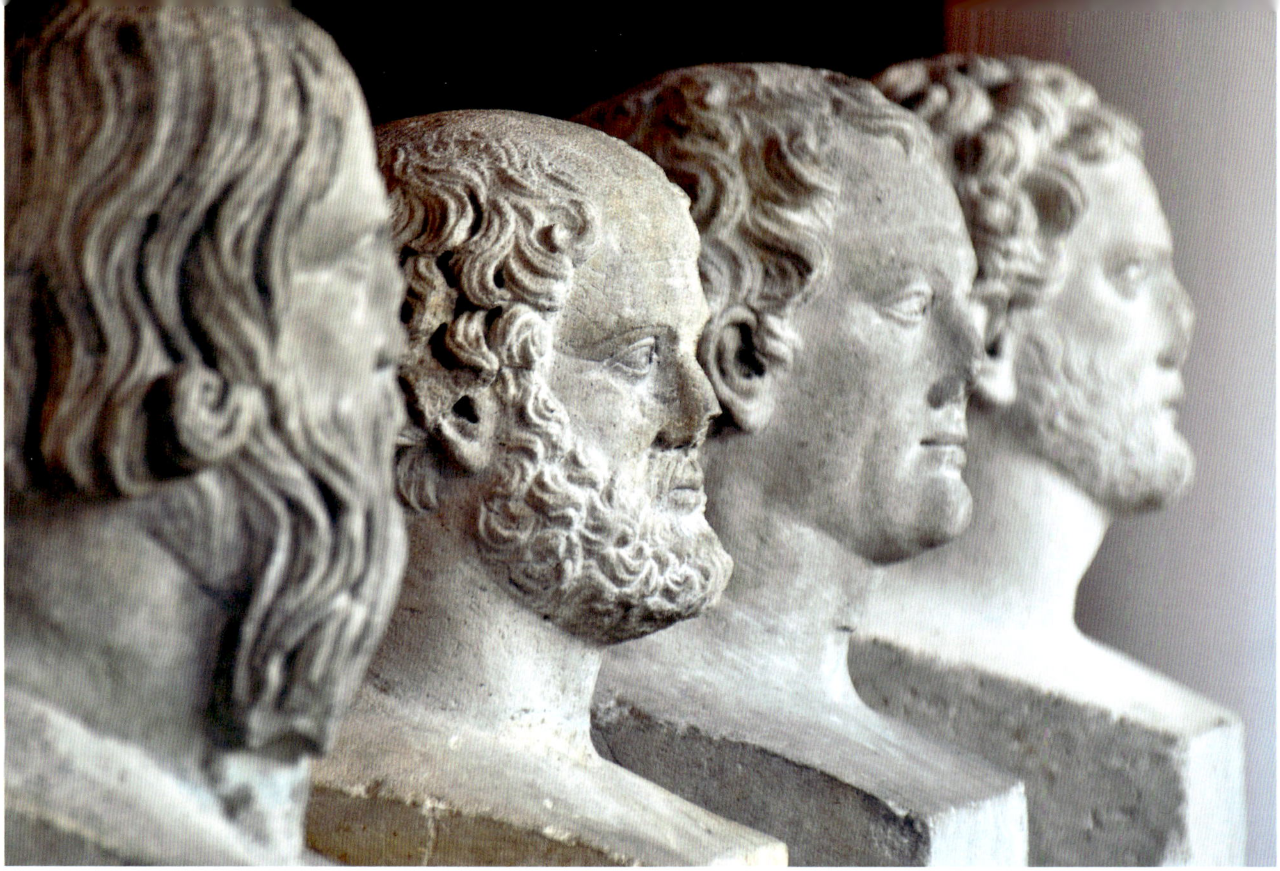

Fig. 3
Welschbillig, Trier-Saarburg distr. Four of the originally 112 herms placed around a large water basin in the centre of the splendid villa complex. (GDKE/ Rheinisches Landesmuseum Trier/Th. Zühmer)

year of government, he introduced the four-emperors rule (tetrarchy), where two senior emperors *(Augusti)* and two junior emperors *(Caesares)* each ruled a manageable part of the Roman Empire. At the same time, a fundamental administrative reform was begun, where the provinces were split up into smaller and more effective units, causing their number to nearly double. The new prefectures established an administrative level above the provinces, and the civil administration was separated off from that of the military. The army was also reorganized: the nominal strength of the legions was drastically reduced, and they were divided into stationary border troops and mobile field units.

Caesar Constantius, who was responsible for Gaul, Germania, and Britain, and his son, who later became emperor Constantine the Great, ruled mostly in Trier. The city on the Moselle, which had already served as the capital for a short time during the last years of the Gallic Empire, was now the official imperial residence. This implied numerous changes not only for the city itself: the imperial construction programme also radiated into the surrounding areas, where many palatial villas and sumptuous country estates were built (e.g. Welschbillig). (Fig. 3)

The highly precarious times are confirmed by the example of the villa at Bodenbach, ca. 80 km north of Trier. It was transformed into a fortress at the end of the 3rd century or the beginning of the 4th century. The main building was surrounded by ditches, and additional defensive walls protected the two sides that were particularly exposed. The safety of the imperial residence of Trier evidently did not reach even as far as the Eifel in those days. For other places in Rhineland-Palatinate, archaeological finds provide an inconsistent picture: while some settlements like Speyer, Worms, Rheinzabern, and Eisenberg remained unfortified, other places like Boppard, Andernach, Bitburg, and Neumagen were equipped with defensive walls. The Remagen fort from the middle imperial time was transformed into a fortification, and the palatial villa in Bad Kreuznach was reworked into a small fortification. While in some country estates (e.g. the villa at the Silberberg in Ahrweiler) only parts of the original building were still used, other villas were in fact enlarged (e.g. Bad Dürkheim-Ungstein). Inhumation tombs with or without grave goods dominate the grave fields of this phase, but cremations can also still be found.

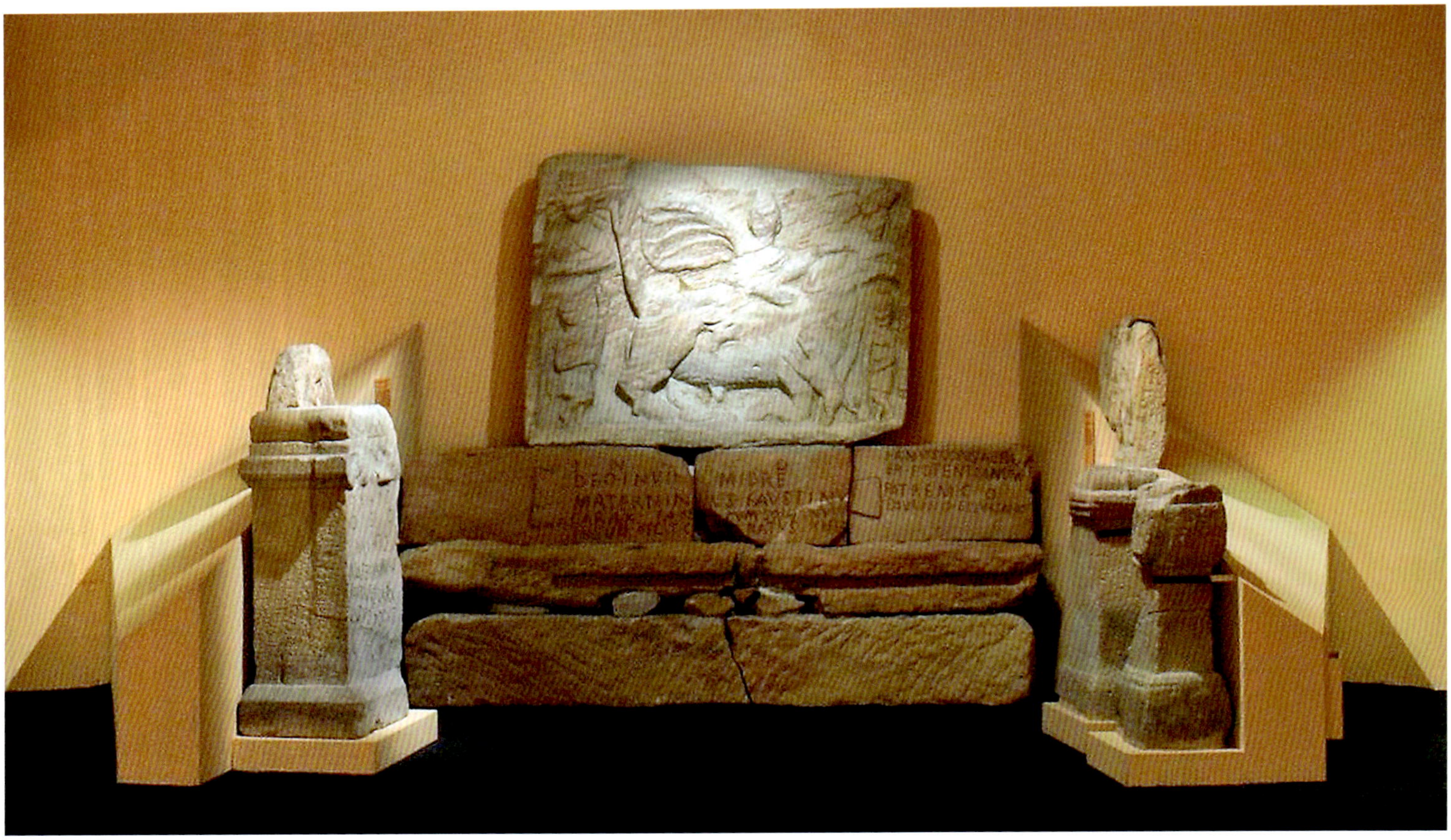

Fig. 4
Gimmeldingen, city of Neustadt. The mithraeum in its present place in the Historisches Museum der Pfalz in Speyer. (Historisches Museum der Pfalz/ P. Haag-Kirchner)

Two Germanic groups, the *Franci* and the *Alamanni*, which would soon gain a major influence on the destiny of our area, appear in Roman documents from this time onwards. While at the end of the 3rd century the Alamanni settled mainly in the area on the right side of the Rhine, which had been abandoned by the Romans, the Franci established themselves at the Lower Rhine during the same period. Members of both groups appeared, on the one hand, as opponents to the Romans, but on the other they are also mentioned as allies *(foederati)* in the direct vicinity of the Rhine border or even as new settlers *(laeti)* in previously depopulated areas within the empire. More and more Franci and Alamanni also served in the Roman army and reached ever higher ranks there.

The tetrarchy system established by Diocletian failed due to the dynastic ambitions of his successors. In 324, Constantine the Great emerged from a civil war as the sole ruler and relocated his residence from Trier to Constantinople. Under his rule, the administrative reforms started by Diocletian were continued. Trier was now the seat of the newly created *prefectura galliarum*, which underlines the importance of the city at that time. Although the fortifications along the Rhine border continued to be strengthened, hoards indicating unrest and warlike events, such as the coin hoard of Mittelstrimmig, were found even in the hinterland.

Although Christianity had been recognized as a religion since 313, practically no traces of any churches from the 4th century have been found so far in Rhineland-Palatinate. This is most likely explained by the fact that these were inconspicuous domestic churches that during excavations can hardly be distinguished from normal dwellings. Only the basilicas in Trier, built under Constantine and his successors, are an exception, and are to be seen as part of the imperial building programme in cities in which the emperor took up residence – comparable to the Constantinian basilicas in Rome and Constantinople. The participation of the Trier bishop Agritius in the Synod of Arles is documented for the year 314. Pagan sanctuaries continued to be erected simultaneously in many areas, including the Mithras sanctuary of Neustadt-Gimmeldingen, consecrated on 25th February 325. (Fig. 4)

After Constantine's death in 337, heavy conflicts broke out over his succession, from which the emperor's sons emerged victorious. The next catastrophe occurred in 350, when the officer Flavius Magnentius rose up against Constans, who ruled in the west. During the subsequent civil war, the entire *legio XXII* from Mainz (see article »A piece of the Imperium Romanum«) and great numbers from the *legio VIII Augusta* from Strasbourg were wiped out. At the same time, various attacks by the Alamanni and Franci led to major destruction along the Rhine, which in many places can be traced archaeologically. In the Palatinate, for instance, many fortified height settlements disappeared. Also in country estates (e.g. Bad Dürkheim-Ungstein) and *vici* (e.g. Eisenberg), destruction can be detected. However, even after the end of the civil war in 353 the situation did not improve much: the border defence on the Rhine collapsed completely over large distances due to the vacuum left by the perished legions.

Things changed only with emperor Valentinian I (364–375), who resided in Trier from 365. He not only sumptuously extended the imperial residence in the city, but also started a major building programme of fortifications along the Rhine. Ancient sources describe dams and fortifications built from the mouth of the river to Lake Constance, with the emperor being personally involved, for example in Altrip, where he not only supervised the building works, but on 19th June 369 also passed several laws. Besides fortifications reminiscent of classic forts (Alzey, Bad Kreuznach), he also had various *burgi* (Eisenberg (Fig. 5), Bad Dürkheim-Ungstein) built in the hinterland to protect civilian settlements and thereby allowing them to recover. In addition, strongly fortified Rhine crossings were set up (e.g. in Altrip) as starting points for advances into enemy territory. On the right-hand (enemy) side of the Rhine, fortified landings for the fast galleys of the Roman Rhine Fleet were situated at regular intervals, such as at the Zullestein, in Mannheim-Neckarau, and in Ladenburg.

Valentinian's fortifications, which are precisely dated through dendrodata or building inscriptions, are of great interest to archaeologists, since they are important fixed points for the chronology of late antiquity. The grave fields of that time hardly show any cremations, and mostly consist of inhumations without grave goods, where the dead were buried in either wooden coffins, stone sarcophagi or stone or tile casings. (Fig. 6) The traditional funerary rites nevertheless persisted in some rural areas, such as Wachenheim and Gönnheim, with rich grave goods and some occasional cremations far into the 5th century.

A few years after the death of Valentinian I (379), his son Gratian relocated the court from Trier to Milan. The catastrophic year 406 – when not only the Goths devastated Italy and Britain suffered a whole series of military uprisings, but also large Germanic units apparently crossed the Rhine border – falls within the rule of Honorius' (395–423). The church father

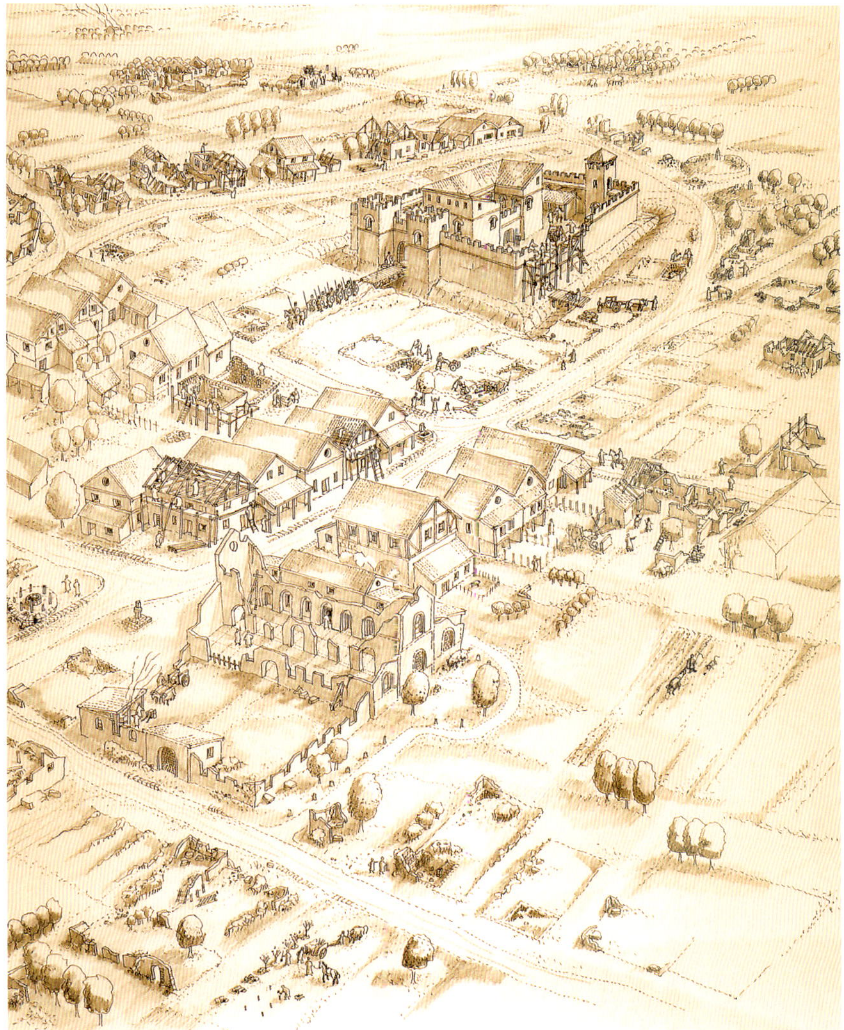

Fig. 5
Eisenberg, Donnersberg distr. The Roman vicus around 370. In the background: the burgus erected at the time of Valentinian I (365–375). It protected the Roman settlement of Eisenberg which remained inhabited until at least the 5th century. (GDKE/Landesarchäologie/Speyer/W. Himmelmann)

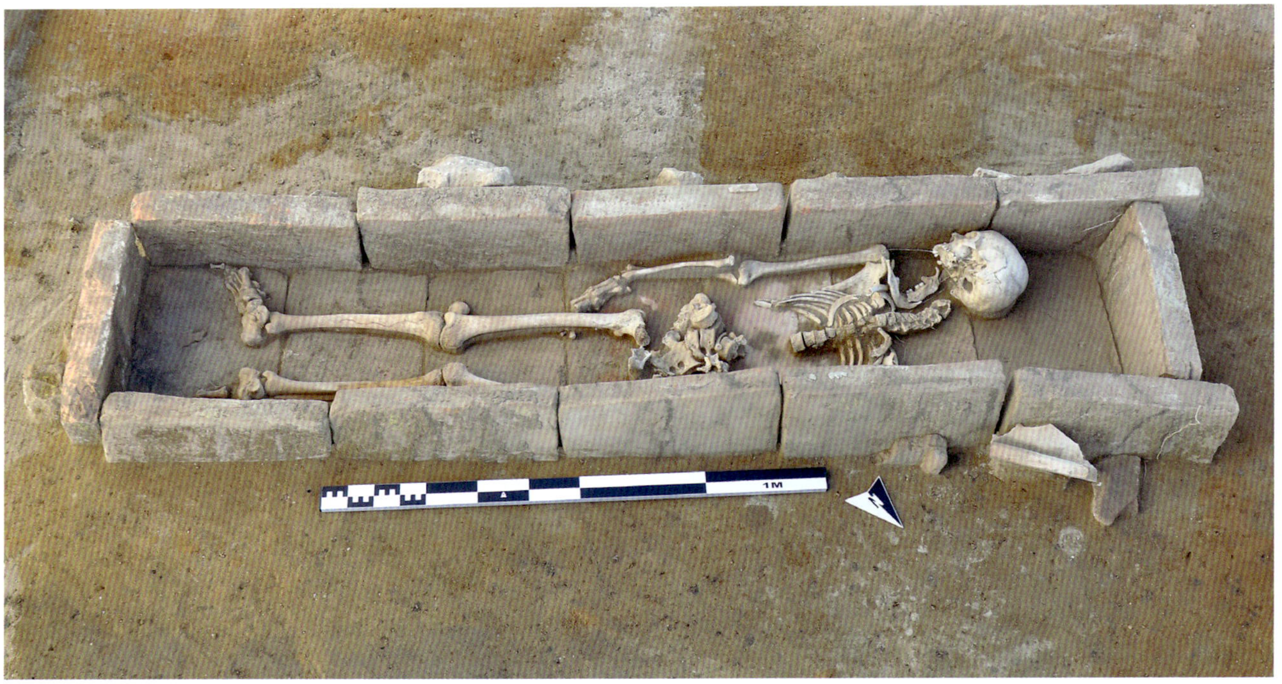

Fig. 6
Speyer-Diakonissenkrankenhaus, city of Speyer. Inhumation burial without grave goods in the grave field of late antiquity. (GDKE/Landesarchäologie/Speyer/A. Zschommler)

Hieronymus described this event – admittedly from the safe haven of Bethlehem – in such drastic terms that historians for a long time considered it to mark the end of Roman civilisation on the Rhine. Thanks to archaeological sources, however, we now have a much more differentiated picture. For the fort of Alzey, for instance, there is proof that it was used for military purposes beyond the middle of the 5th century, and the material remains indicate that »Germanic« troops had taken over the border defence.

As early as the late 4th century, the Romans had reached contractual agreements with barbaric groups, called *foederati*. Under these agreements, which became ever more frequent in the 5th century, the *foederati* committed themselves to fighting for the Romans for money or food, without being formally integrated into the Roman army. The advantages for the Romans were obviously of a financial nature, since these confederates were considerably cheaper than regular soldiers. Ancient sources mention the settlement of Burgundian confederates near Worms, who had to be dislodged again in 436 because of increasing problems with Hun units under the command of the Roman *magister militum* Flavius Aëtius. Barely 15 years later, the same Roman commander fought at the Catalaunian Plains against his former allies, the Huns; he was supported inter alia by Burgundians, Franks, Alans, and Visigoths; Franks and Burgundians also fought on the side of the Huns together with Ostrogoths and Gepids. During these historical events, the treasure of Rülzheim, which shows strong Hunnic-eastern Germanic connections, may have been buried in the ground.

After the death of Aëtius in 454, the influence of the Roman central power in our area visibly diminishes. His successor Aegidius is forced to abandon the cities on the Rhine and retreats to an area in north-western Gaul, which his son Syagrius can still retain as »Roman« *dux* (commander) until 486/87, when he is defeated by the *rex* Clovis I of the Franks. From then on, the western provinces were factually no longer under the rule of the *Imperium Romanum*, but were dominated by former confederates of the Romans who nevertheless relied mainly on established structures, so the transition probably did not mean an interruption of everyday life.

The archaeological finds of that time actually show that there was coexistence: protected by the city walls, »Roman« life continued in many cities in a simplified form. In Speyer, for instance, houses with private baths were still being built well into the 5th century. At the same time, many country settlements were aban-

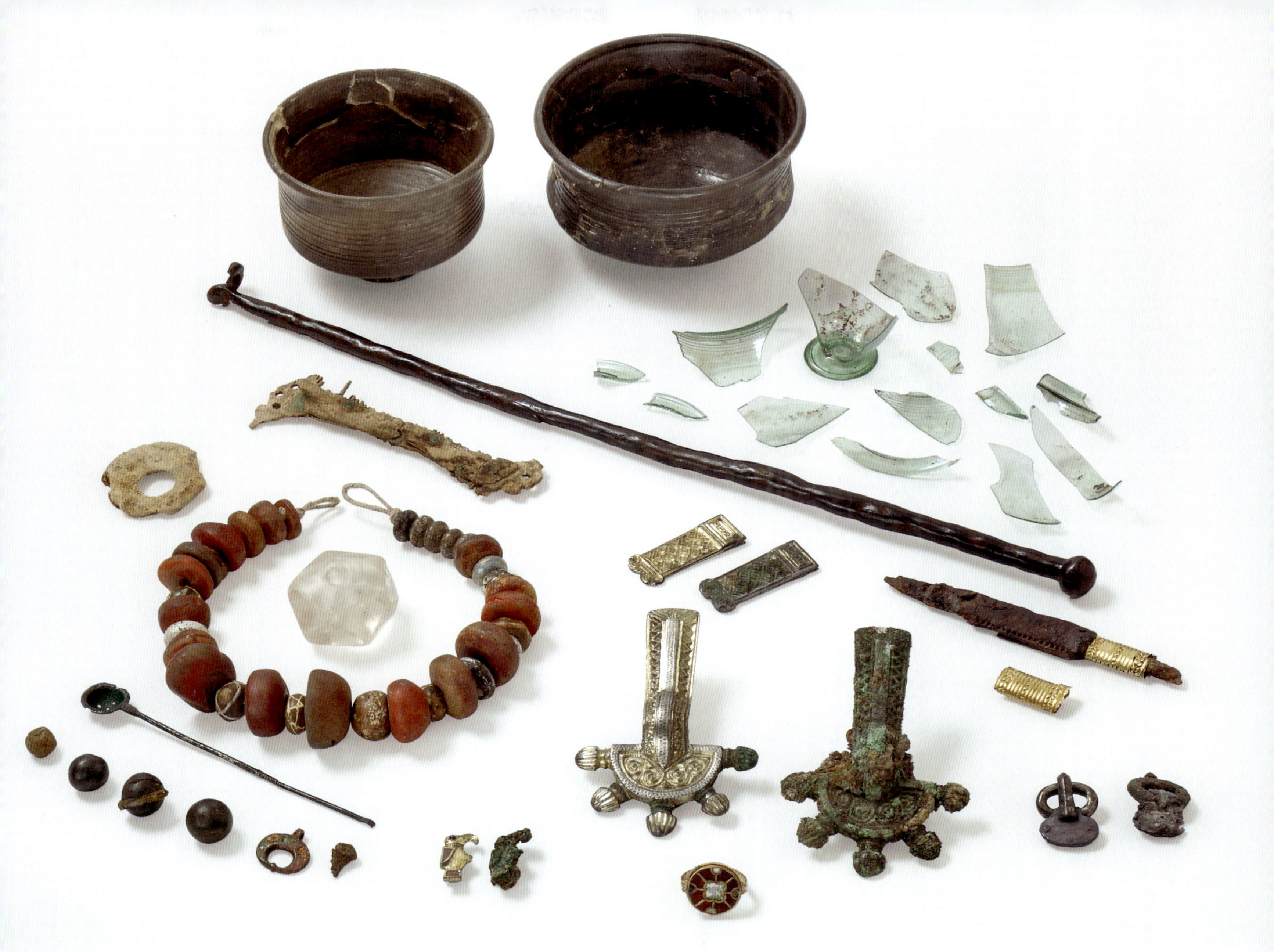

doned or survived only in an extremely reduced form. This was the case for the villa at Wachenheim, where, after several fires, only very few rooms of the formerly representative country estate were repaired, yet the inhabitants nevertheless continued to bury their dead into the late 5th century in the »Roman tradition«. Starting in the last third of the 5th century, new settlements developed, often in the vicinity of those abandoned by the Romans; the new settlers provided their dead with objects of Frankish, Alamannic, North Sea-Germanic, Danube-east Germanic, and eastern Elbe-Germanic imprint. (Fig. 7)

Bibliography

Archäologisches Landesmuseum Baden-Württemberg (Hg.), Die Alamannen. Begleitband zur Ausstellung »Die Alamannen«, Stuttgart/Zürich/Augsburg 1997/98 (Stuttgart 1997).

Badisches Landesmuseum Karlsruhe (Hg.), Römer, Christen, Alamannen – Die Spätantike am Oberrhein. Begleitband zur großen Landesausstellung »IMPERIUM ROMANUM«, Karlsruhe 2005 (Karlsruhe 2005).

H. Bernhard et al., Studien zur Spätantike – Civitas Nemetum. Forschungen zur Pfälzischen Archäologie 7 (Speyer 2017).

H. Cüppers (Hg.), Die Römer in Rheinland-Pfalz (Stuttgart 1990).

Fig. 7
Heßheim, Rhein-Pfalz distr. Grave goods of a young woman buried around the year 500. (GDKE/Landesarchäologie/Speyer/P. Haag-Kirchner)

Late antiquity treasure finds from Mittelstrimmig

AXEL VON BERG

During survey work in 2010, the Koblenz branch of the State Department for Archaeology managed to rescue several treasure finds in the area of the small Roman fort *(burgus)* of Mittelstrimmig in the Cochem-Zell district. The depot includes two late antiquity coin hoards (I–II) with more than 22,000 freshly minted *folles* and a hoard with several bronze vessels (III) from Constantine's time. Its scope and preservation make it one of the significant treasure troves in those regions of the Western Roman Empire that were close both to the border and to the Rhine.

The Roman *burgus* east of the municipality of Mittelstrimmig was conveniently situated at the crossing of two major ancient roads, which since prehistoric times have been among the main routes into the Moselle valley. It was built directly near a Roman settlement area, which had been extended into a larger one-street village *(vicus)* since the 3rd century. Comparable to small towns of today, these Roman road villages served to supply the rural population and were central sites of local economy, trade, and administration outside the big cities.

The economic boom was effected both by the favourable position along the major roads and by the rich ore deposits in the vicinity as well as several temple areas nearby. In the late 3rd century, the *vicus* was fortified with a small military installation, later extended into a heavily fortified *burgus*. A building inscription discovered in 1908 mentions 23rd May 269 as the date when the small fort was completed. An older inscription on the limestone blocks was originally dedicated to a sanctuary at this place. The second, younger text at the back refers to the building of the ancient small fort. During geomagnetic surveys in the area of the *vicus*, the small fortification could be localized and its dimensions recorded. (Fig. 1) A massive rectangular building of 13 m × 18 m was thus detected, consisting of a central internal courtyard with several rooms arranged around it. The fortress is also surrounded by two ditches 50 m long and 5 m wide. The position of the *burgus* is remarkable, since it was not found in the usual place at the top of a hill, but on the slope in the direct vicinity of the civilian settlement. The reason for this was the nearby mining industry, which was to be protected by the small fortress as well as the crossing of the major roads in front of it and the nearby temple areas within range.

Such fortifications in the hinterland region of the Rhine and Moselle were of vital importance for the Western Roman Empire when, starting in the late 3rd century, the military administration tried to effectively counter the attacks occurring time and again in the northern border area. The late antique fortress-building programme, developed to protect the area against invasions and plundering, involved small fortifications which could effectively defend the hinterland with the small military units stationed there. All along the Moselle between Trier and Koblenz, a close series of small hilltop fortifications and heavily guarded *burgi* were built over time; as corn stores and central supply stations, they were also meant to safeguard the supplies of the field army near the border of the empire. The *burgus* of Mittelstrimmig is part of this late Roman building programme of fortresses in the border area of the Rhine and Moselle. During the crisis times of the 3rd and 4th centuries, it served for the protection of the population, their roads and cultic centres and of the economic locations on the heights along the Moselle.

It is known that the ancient settlement area of Mittelstrimmig included several Roman sacred sites. In addition to the Martberg near Pommern on the Moselle, this is one of the biggest ancient cultic centres of the region. The older of the dedicatory inscriptions of the 2nd-3rd century on the limestone blocks discovered in 1908 mentions the deities Mars Smertius, Vindoridius and Boud(a/e/i)na. During the geophysical examinations in the years 2009–2011, four large ancient temple sites were discovered; judging from the find material, they were used until the end of the 4th century.

All three treasure troves (Fig. 2–3) were apparently buried simultaneously and close to each other at the western side of the *burgus* during an acute threat around the year 321. The exclusively freshly minted coins either indicate the deposit of large amounts of money originally meant to be circulated in the region, or they represent the pay of the military unit stationed there.

Coin hoard I was found at about 60 cm below the plough horizon. According to the archaeological findings, a coarse ceramic vessel with a hinged lid from the late antiquity Mayen ceramic works was deposited in a hastily dug pit. The coins were emptied into the vessel and covered with a coarse slate, and then the pit was filled in again.

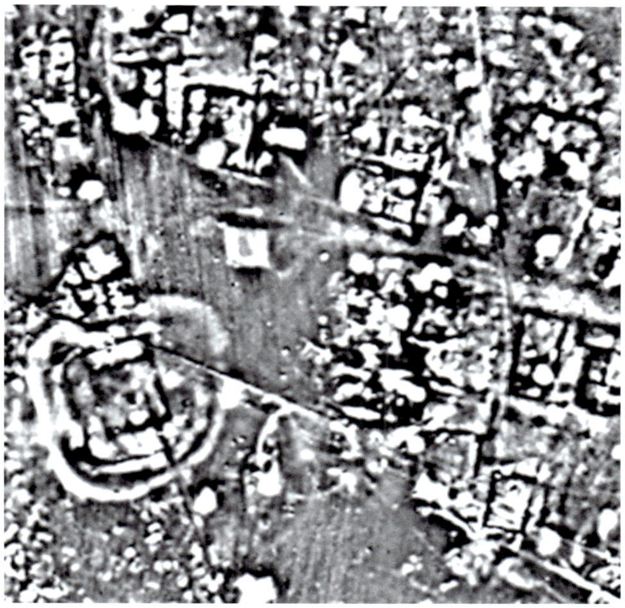

Fig. 1
Mittelstrimmig, Cochem-Zell distr. Geomagnetic image of the burgus with the surrounding ditches of the fortification and further settlement findings. (GDKE/Landesarchäologie/Koblenz/Posselt+Zickgraf)

Coin hoard II was lying at a depth of about 30 cm, and some parts had already been damaged by the passage of ploughs. Here, too, a coarse ceramic vessel of

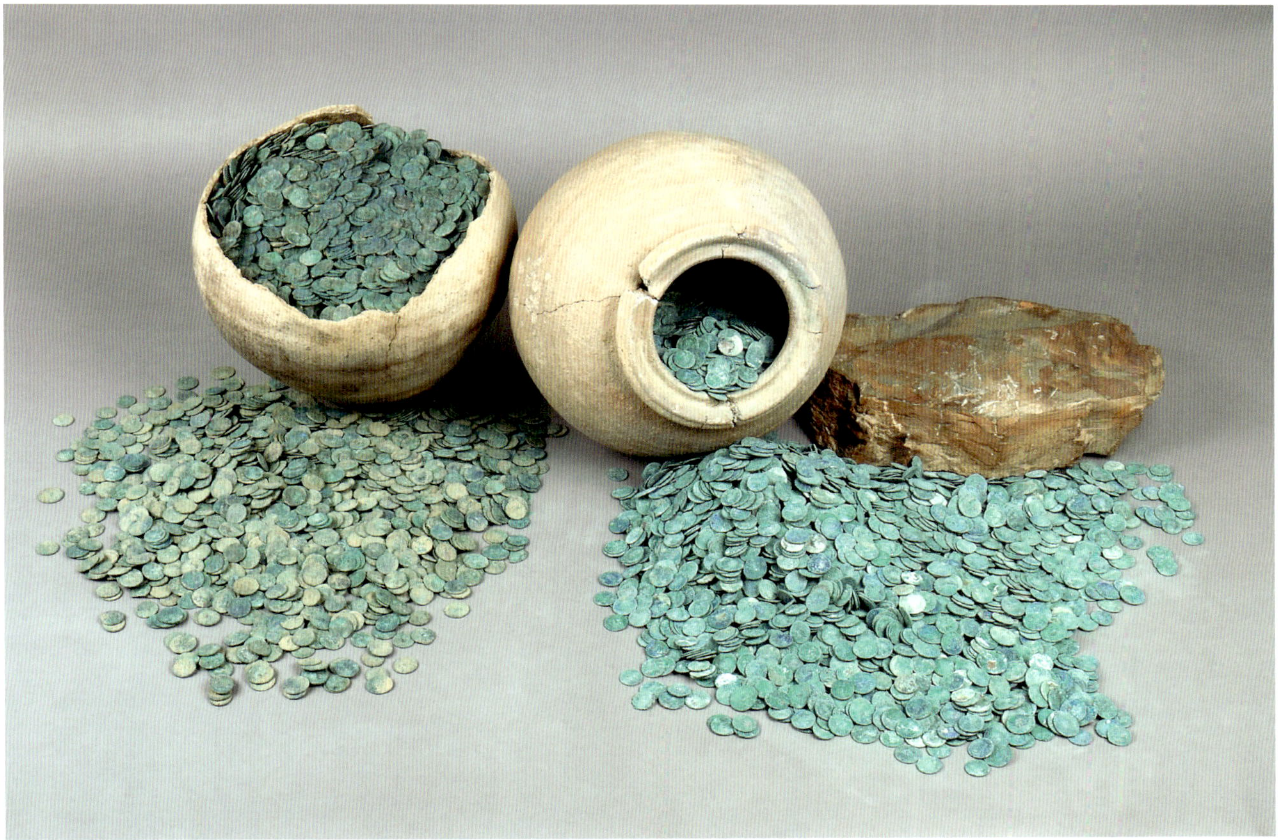

Fig. 2
Mittelstrimmig, Cochem-Zell distr. The coin hoards from the surroundings of the burgus (left: hoard II, right: hoard I). (GDKE/Landesarchäologie/Koblenz/M. Neumann)

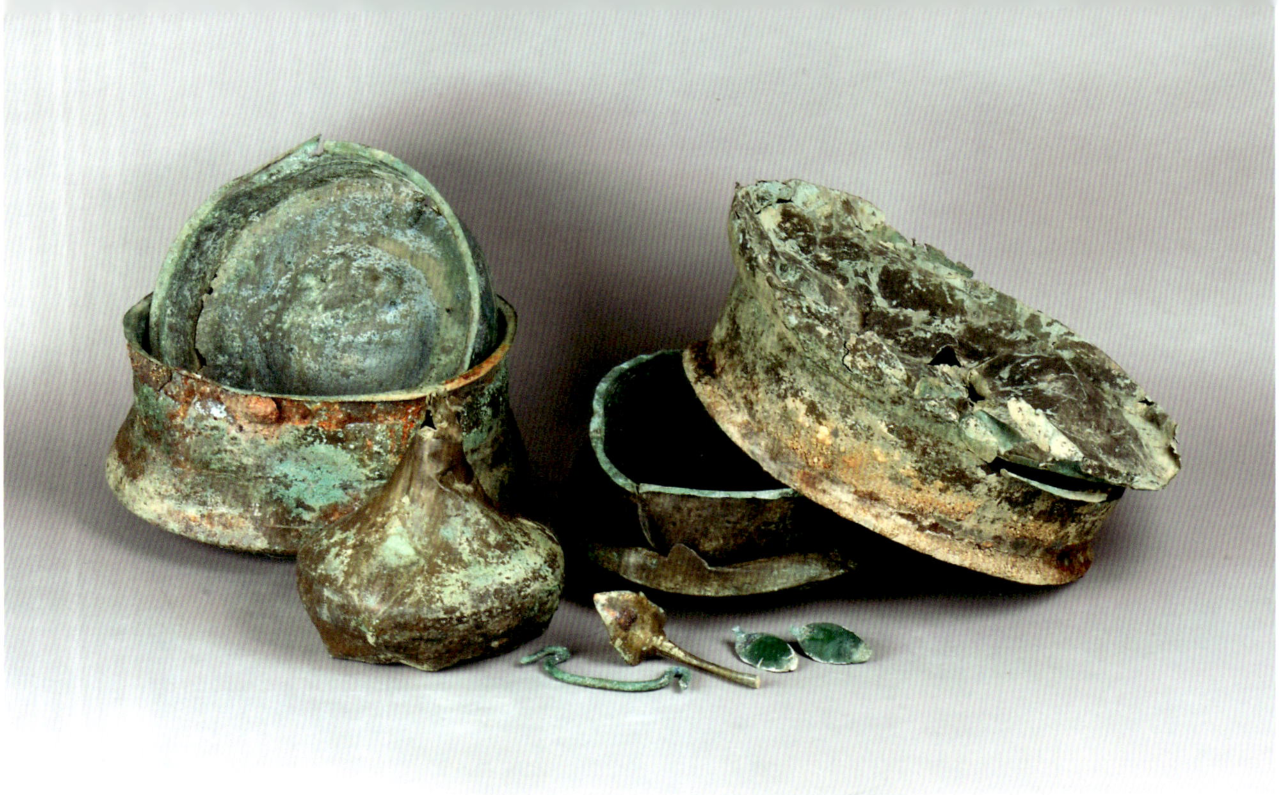

Fig. 3
Mittelstrimmig, Cochem-Zell distr. Hoard with bronze vessels from the surroundings of the burgus. (GDKE/Landesarchäologie/Koblenz/M. Neumann)

Mayen production held the coins that had been poured into it. According to the findings, the vessel also stood in a pit which had been dug quickly and carelessly.

The hoard with the bronze vessels was originally deposited in a square wooden nailed box; charred wooden remains and iron nails in situ allowed its dimensions of about 1 m × 1 m to be reconstructed. The wooden box was also buried in a pit in the soil. It held four big bronze bowls and one bronze pitcher placed one inside the other. (Fig. 3) The fragmented condition of the vessels (some of which had been damaged already during Roman antiquity) indicates that this was just a materials depot.

The coins are nearly all freshly minted late antiquity *folles*, a currency unit typical for that time made from bronze containing copper, which were partly covered with a thin layer of silver. Only imperial issues exist, without the normal barbarized regional mintages. Most of the coins are dated between 310 and 318; the coin series of both deposits ends simultaneously in the year 321. The two coin hoards and certainly the depot with the bronze vessels were buried directly near the small ancient fort at that time. Most of the coins belong to uniform coinages from the time of Emperor Constantine the Great and his son Constantius II. There are also coinages of Licinius I and Licinius II, Crispus, Maximinus Daia, and Allectus. There are only few coinages of the earlier soldier emperors. The coins were minted in Trier, London, Lyon, Arles, Aquileia, and in smaller numbers in Siscia, Tricinium, Rome, Ostia, and Camulodunum (Colchester).

The finds from Mittelstrimmig in the Cochem-Zell district belong to a horizon of comparable hoard finds and depositions that can be found in the Hunsrück, the Eifel as far as Luxembourg, and eastern France. The reason was probably political unrest, but also looting by hordes of Germanic tribes who time and again overran the border fortifications at the Rhine and advanced deep into the Gallic provinces of the Western Roman Empire. The Roman *burgus* of Mittelstrimmig probably disappeared during the constant conflicts and the economic decline of the western empire in the late 4th century. It fell into ruin and was then forgotten for many centuries.

Bibliography

A. von Berg, Schätze im Acker. Archäologie in Deutschland 3, 2011, 56 f.

J. Haas, Zur Burgusinschrift von Mittelstrimmig, Kreis Cochem-Zell, in: H.-H. Wegner (Hg.), Berichte zur Archäologie an Mittelrhein und Mosel 9 (Koblenz 2004) 93 ff.

M. Mohr, Mittelstrimmig: Römischer Vicus. in: H.-H. Wegner (Hg.), Cochem-Zell. Landschaft an der Mosel. Führer zu archäologischen Denkmälern in Deutschland 46 (Stuttgart 2005) 142 ff.

The treasure find of Rülzheim – A Hunnic funerary offering for the dead in the west?

ULRICH HIMMELMANN, RICHARD PETROVSZKY

At the beginning of 2014, the story of the treasure find at Rülzheim attracted extensive press coverage: a year earlier, a young man, who was illegally using a metal detector, had come across an important hoard from late antiquity. Since he did not report the find to experts and with two acquaintances »retrieved the objects from the ground«, all archaeologically relevant traces at the site were irreversibly destroyed. It was only under pressure from police investigations that several months later the looter handed over the known objects to the relevant authorities, yet doubts remain as to whether the entire find was eventually handed in.

Since nearly all information at the site itself was lost due to the illegal and unprofessional excavation, we must rely on studying the Rülzheim finds as they are, as well as on comparisons with other sites for their interpretation and historical classification. The more than one hundred individual pieces still available to us originally belonged to at least eleven objects, nearly all of which show more or less clear traces of destruction in antiquity.

A large number of iron profiled rods covered with sheet silver, some silver chains, and various decorative figures made of sheet silver belong to a folding chair with a back, which is truly unique. Similar chairs with backs were so far only known from pictorial representations in a mosaic (Sidi Ghrib/Tunisia) and on silver objects (the Proiecta Casket from the Esquiline Hill in Rome; a container with lid from the Seuso Treasure). In all the depictions mentioned, female figures are sitting on chairs of this kind.

A large silver plate hacked into three pieces bears at its centre a fire-gilded medallion showing a female head (Fig. 1), which can be interpreted, on the basis of a comparison with a nearly identical representation in the well-known silver treasure from Mildenhall/Great Britain, as Olympias, the mother of Alexander the Great. Comparisons with silver plates and other dishes – for example, from the major silver treasures of Mildenhall, Kaiseraugst, the Esquiline or Carthage – suggest a dating of the Rülzheim plate in the 4th or the beginning of the 5th century. Similar individual pieces, called *missoria*, are often interpreted as diplomatic/imperial gifts *(donativa)* for high-ranking figures.

The second silver vessel is a bowl (Fig. 2) with golden rim fittings of semi-precious stones and a medallion at the centre (Fig. 3) whose filigree design distinguishes it clearly from the bowl itself. There is reason to believe that this is a recycled piece, probably the decorative disc of an imperial or onyx fibula. The bowl also has a suspension ring on the outside which shows clear signs of use. This object seems to be complete, except for some semi-precious stones that are missing. Comparable finds for the vessel, which appears unusual and odd within the Rhineland-Palatinate context, were found in the Pannonian-Transylvanian area: three bowls, in this case made of gold, from the treasure find of Şimleu Silvaniei/Szilágysomlyó II should be mentioned here, because their structure, decoration, and manufacture are nearly identical with the Rülzheim bowl. These bowls are rare even in eastern Europe, and they were only retrieved in find complexes connected with high-ranking figures from among the »barbarian« ruling elite. These vessels are certainly to be seen less as functional and more as prestige objects.

Only the crushed, fully decorated reverse side of a mirror made from sheet silver and bronze has survived. It shows the Three Graces (Fig. 4), a motif found rather frequently on relief mirrors from the second half of the 2nd century and those from the 3rd century.

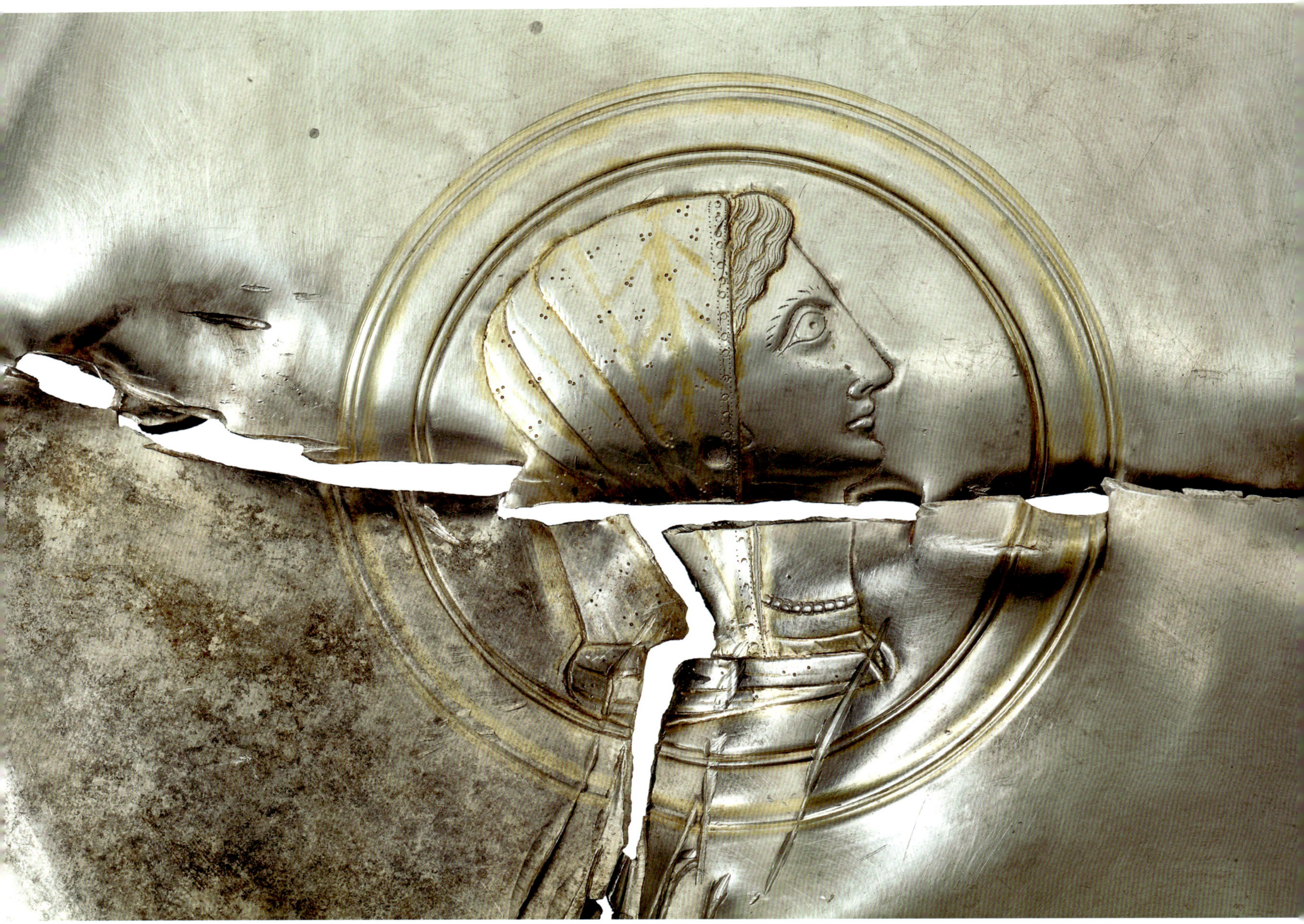

Fig. 1
Rülzheim, Germersheim distr. Depiction of a woman (»Olympias«) in the central medallion of the big silver plate. (GDKE/ Landesarchäologie/Speyer/P. Haag-Kirchner)

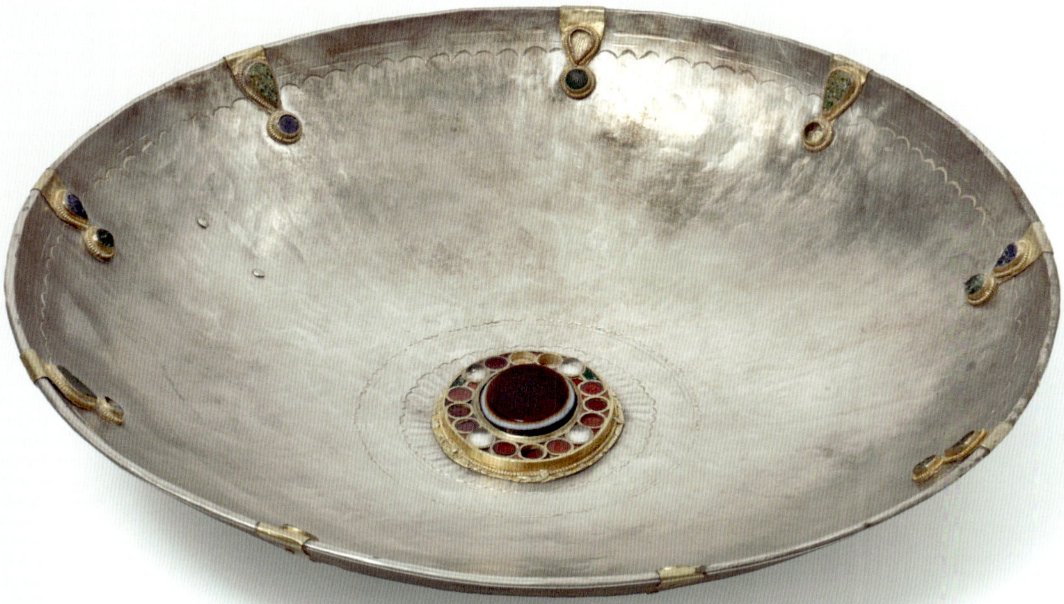

Fig. 2
Rülzheim, Germersheim distr. The silver bowl of the Szilágysomlyó type with an oval gold medallion. (GDKE/Landesarchäologie/Speyer/P. Haag-Kirchner)

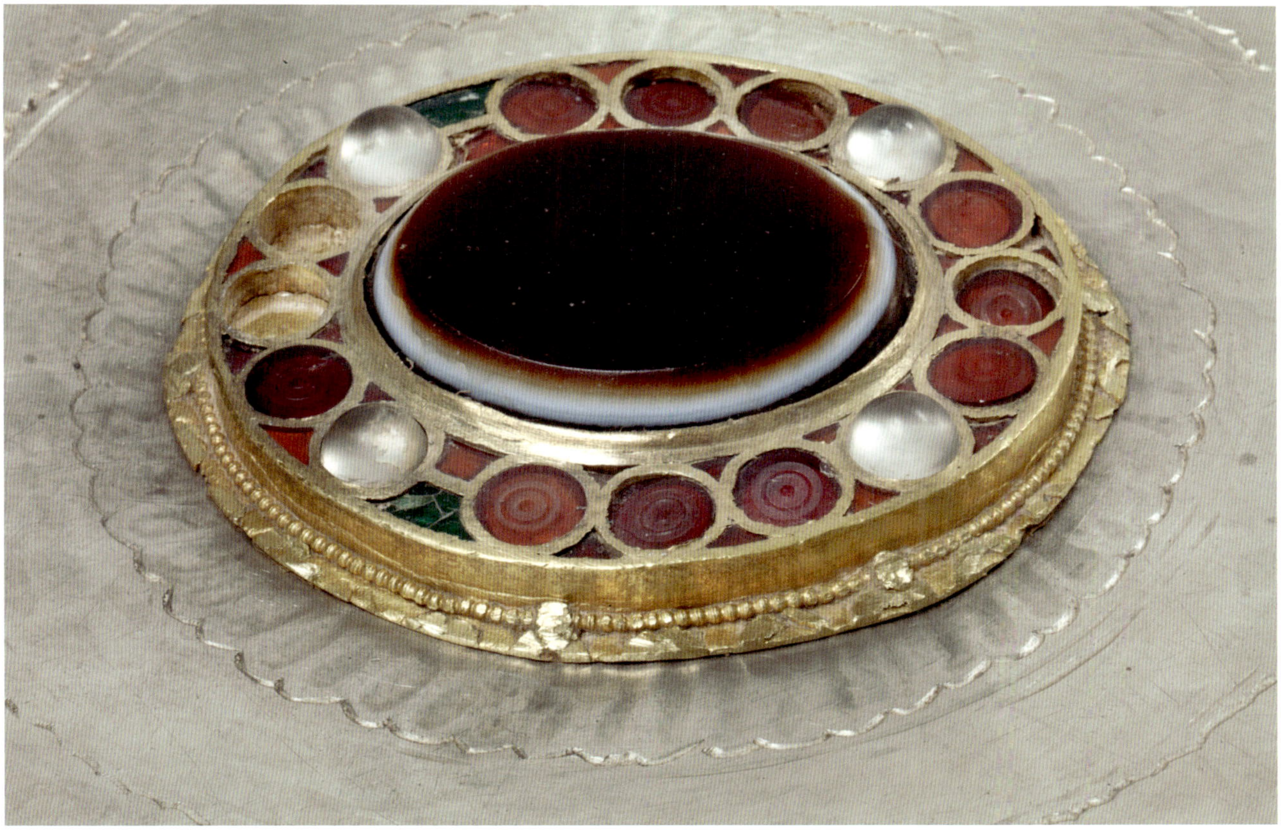

Fig. 3
Rülzheim, Germersheim distr. The medallion of the Rülzheim bowl. (GDKE/Landesarchäologie/Speyer/P. Haag-Kirchner)

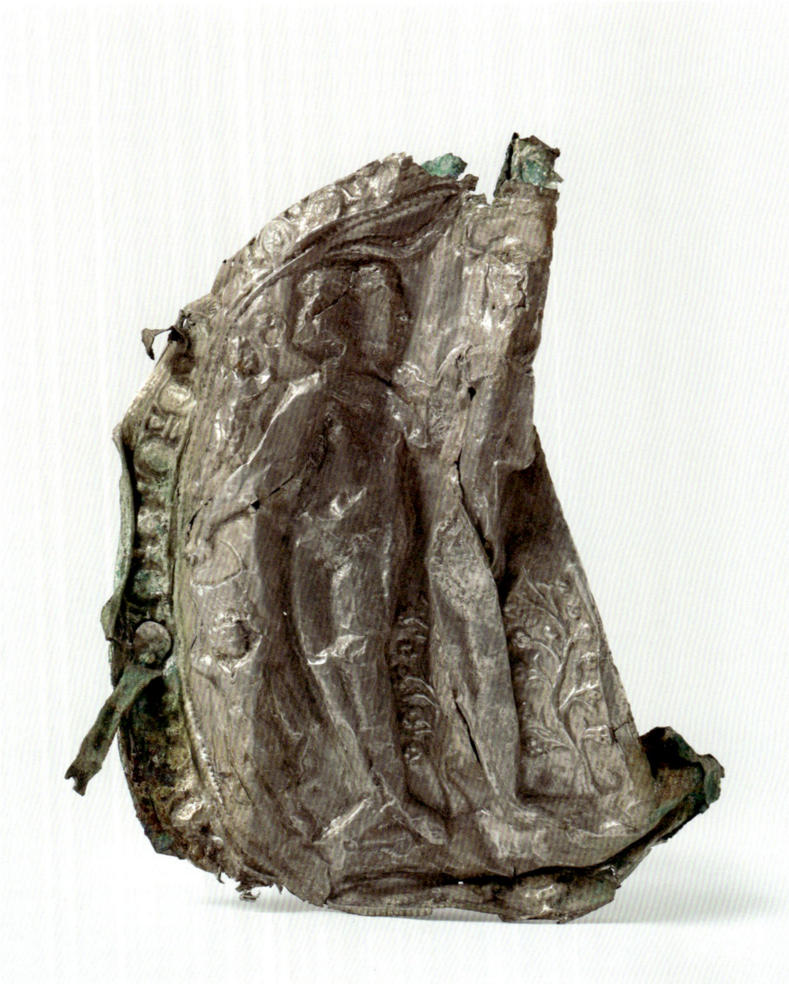

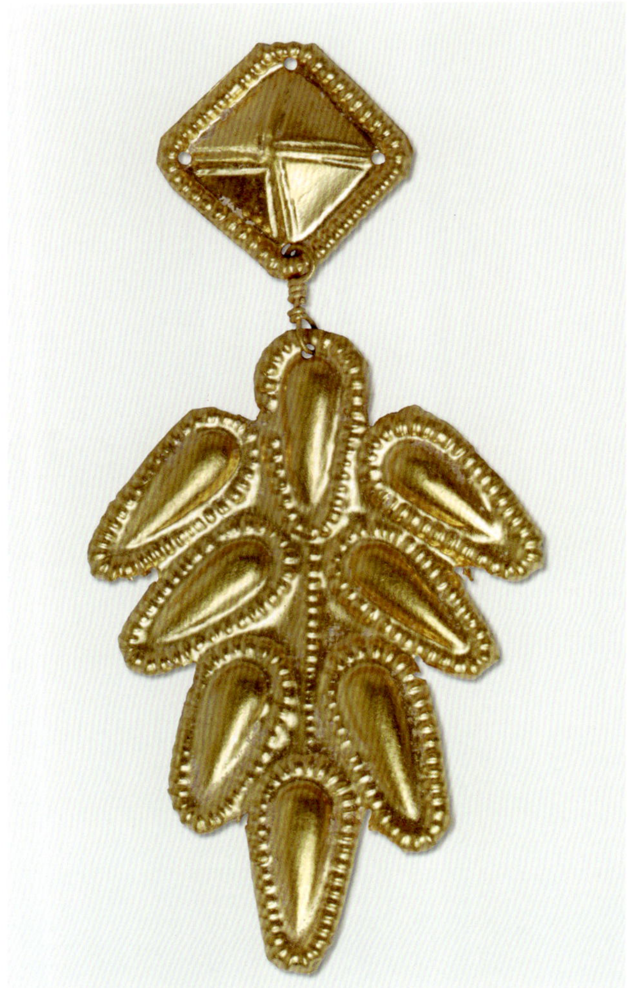

Fig. 4
Rülzheim, Germersheim distr. The back of a mirror with a representation of the Three Graces. (GDKE/Landesarchäologie/ Speyer/P. Haag-Kirchner)

Fig. 5
Rülzheim, Germersheim distr. Detail of a grape-shaped pendant made of gold foil. (GDKE/ Landesarchäologie/Speyer/ P.Haag-Kirchner)

Some fire-gilded silver plate fragments, which are also from a decorated reverse side, indicate that there was a second mirror.

There is a total of 58 well-preserved rhombic appliqués made in identical shapes by press plate procedure from gold foil. There are also another 36 rhombic appliqués of the same style with grape-shaped pendants. (Fig. 5) They were certainly used as garment decoration, for example, on a cloak-like cape in the chest area (Fig. 6), or on the sleeves, but possibly also on some headgear, as documented in a recently recovered female grave near Pförring in Bavaria. Gold tinsel in rhombic or grape form was found mainly in the Pannonian area (Dunapataj-Bödpuszta, formerly Bakodpuszta; Szeged-Nagyszéksós; Rábapordány – grape shaped), but also in Bavaria (Pförring – female grave), and even in a »Vandal« female grave in Carthage (Koudiat Zateur treasure).

A cap-like clasp (Fig. 7) and a kidney-shaped fitting (Fig. 8), both made from gold foil and originally fixed with small golden nails on a soft base, belong to the same as yet unidentified object. The function of the four small peg-like rim fittings made of gold foil (Fig. 9) could not yet be safely determined. A silver sheet cut from a larger object and depicting a hunting lion produced in pressure plate technique also remains enigmatic. (Fig. 10) The strange representation, a leaping male animal with its mouth wide open, its claws extended, and the end of its tail coiled up, shows a stunning similarity to the lions on a pair of gold disc fibula from the treasure find of Şimleu-Silvaniei/Szilágysomlyó II. Another piece of sheet silver

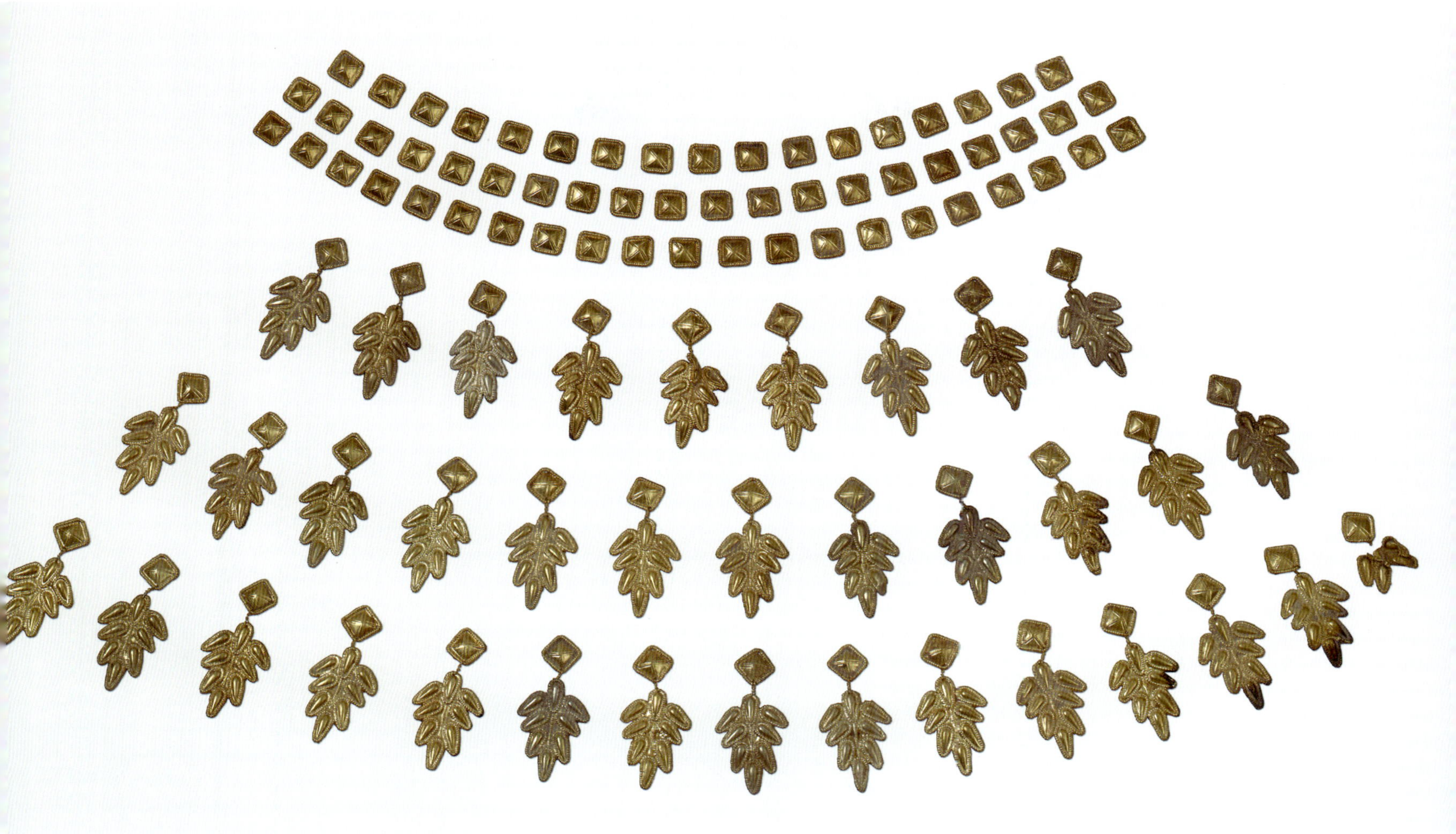

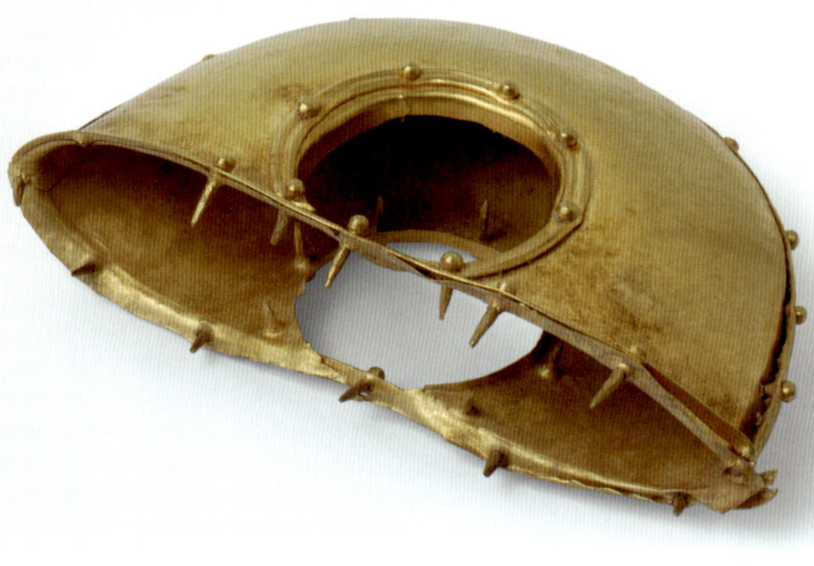

Fig. 6
Rülzheim, Germersheim distr.
All 94 appliques from Rülzheim.
(GDKE/Landesarchäologie/
Speyer/P. Haag-Kirchner)

Fig. 7
Rülzheim, Germersheim distr.
The cap-like clasp. (GDKE/
Landesarchäologie/ Speyer/
P. Haag-Kirchner)

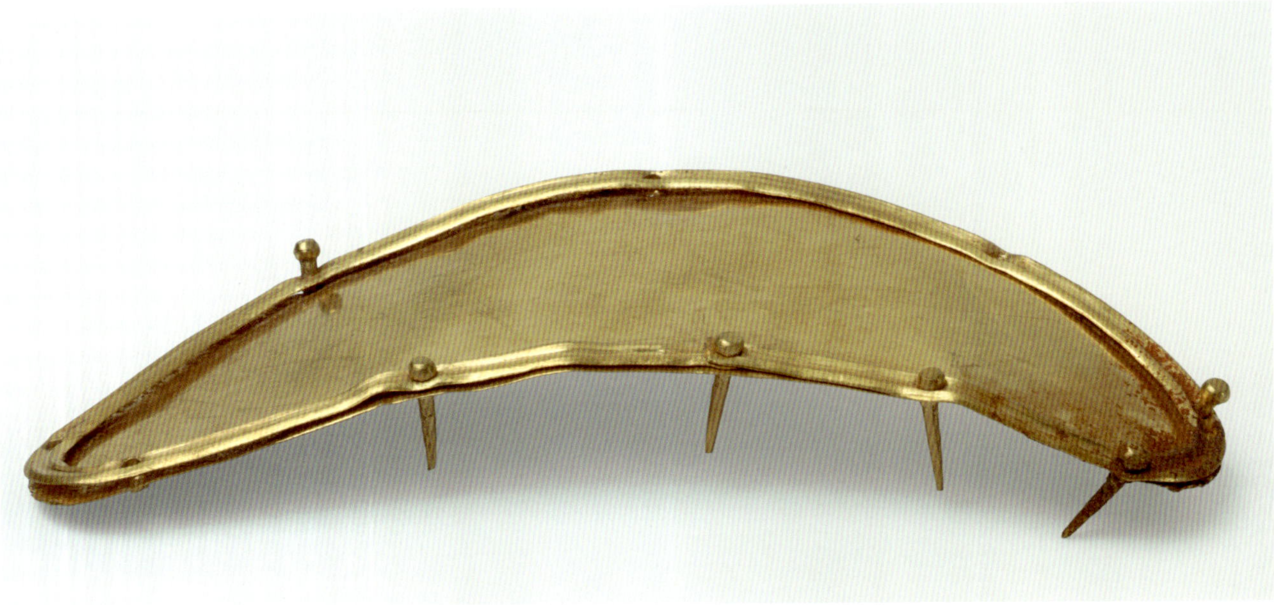

Fig. 8
Rülzheim, Germersheim distr. The kidney-shaped fitting. (GDKE/ Landesarchäologie/Speyer/ P. Haag- Kirchner)

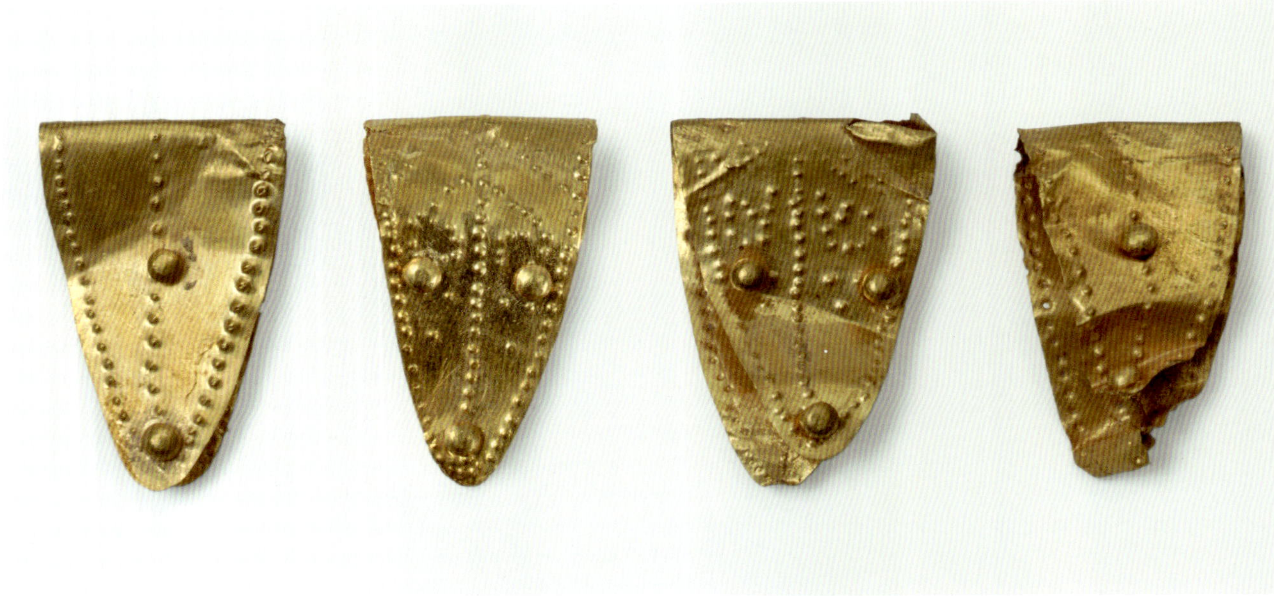

Fig. 9.
Rülzheim, Germersheim distr. The four bracket-like rim fittings made of gold foil. (GDKE/ Landesarchäologie/Speyer/ P. Haag- Kirchner)

cut out from an unknown object does not bear any decorations.

In summary, it can be said that the Rülzheim treasure find represents a unique ensemble for Rhineland-Palatinate. The gender of the objects' owner cannot unequivocally be determined. A large number of the objects show evident signs of having been intentionally destroyed (a folding chair, large silver plate, mirror [?], and a fragment with the image of a lion), with only a few objects showing signs of fire (some appliqués with pendant). At the same time, there are complete, undamaged objects, such as the bowl with the medallion and the two gold and the four rim fittings, whose organic bases, however, did not survive.

When classifying the objects according to their function, one notices that there are ceremonial objects such as silver vessels, furniture (a folding chair) and apparel accessories (gold tinsel, the cap and kid-

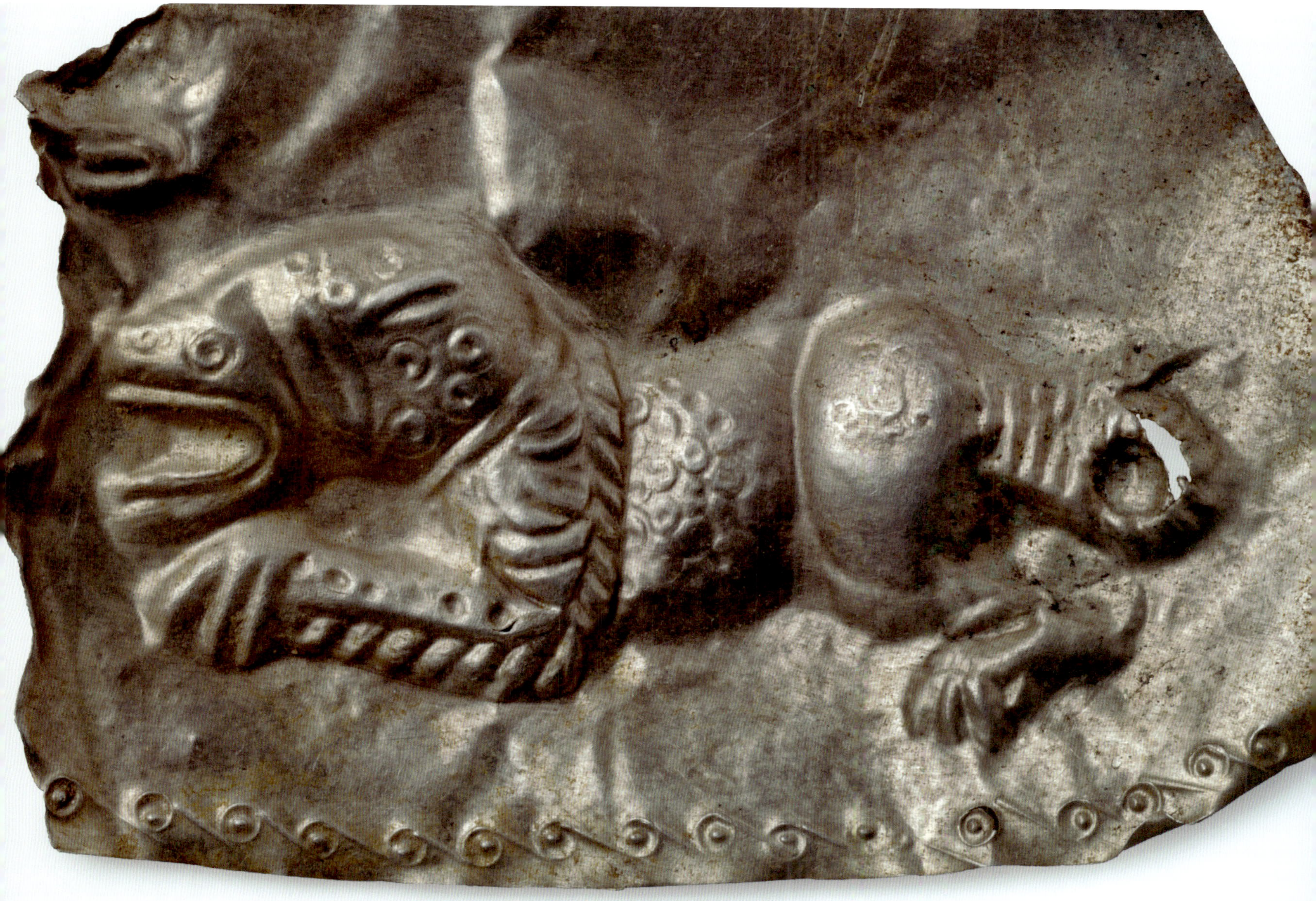

ney shaped fittings, rim fittings), while other decorations (for e.g., arm and finger rings, diadem, necklaces, fibulae, etc.), apparel accessories such as belt and shoe buckles, weapons and harnesses (bridles and saddles) are missing. The origin of the objects also appears heterogeneous: while the folding chair (Fig. 11), the large silver plate, and the mirrors were made in Roman workshops, the silver bowl, the appliqués, the cap and kidney fittings, the rim fittings, and the »lion sheet« very likely were of »barbarian« production.

As far as dating is concerned, comparisons with Pannonian-Transylvanian find complexes suggest that these objects were probably buried in the second quarter of the 5th century, with the Roman objects being somewhat older (mirror, 3rd century; large plate, 4th century; folding chair, 4th century) than those of »barbarian« origin, which all seem to come from the first

Fig. 10
Rülzheim, Germersheim distr. The silver foil with representation of a lion. (GDKE/Landesarchäologie/Speyer/P. Haag-Kirchner)

half of the 5th century. An interpretation as a »standard« grave find appears rather unlikely, since the pit documented during the subsequent excavation was too small, and neither bone nor cremated remains were found in the secondary filling. The composition and condition of the objects also seems to indicate that this is not a scrap metal or treasure find. The comparison with »invocation-offerings« (Pannonhalma, Pecsüszög, Szeged-Nagyszeksos or Bataszek) practised by the Hunnic-Alanic ruling class in south-eastern Europe, which is also dated to the first half of the 5th century, appears to be more convincing. However, the question of how and for what reason the objects or their owner found their way to the area of today's Palatinate remains unanswered.

Bibliography

A. von Berg, U. Himmelmann, Seiner Geschichte beraubt. Der sogenannte Barbarenschatz von Rülzheim. Raubgräberei – Kein Kavaliersdelikt. Begleitheft zur Präsentation (Speyer 2014).

U. Himmelmann, Seiner Geschichte beraubt – der spätantike Schatzfund von Rülzheim. Wissensgesellschaft Pfalz – 90 Jahre Pfälzische Gesellschaft zur Förderung der Wissenschaft, 2015, 165–174.

Fig. 11
Proposed reconstruction of the folding chair of Rülzheim developed by the restorer Holger Becker at LVR-Landes-Museum Bonn (subject to the results of the pending scientific assessment) (Photographic realisation: Jürgen Vogel, LVR-Landes-Museum Bonn)

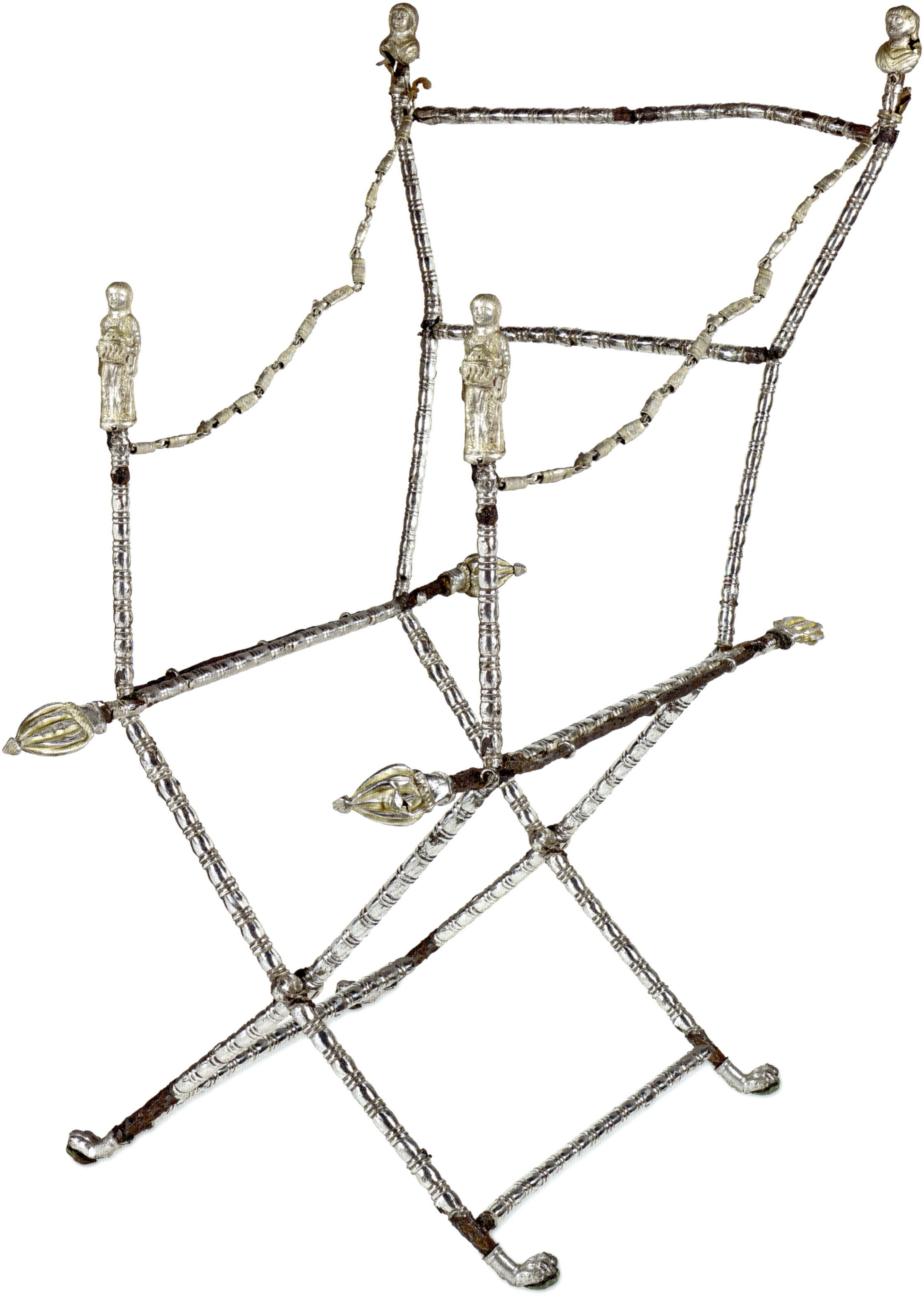

EARLY MIDDLE AGES

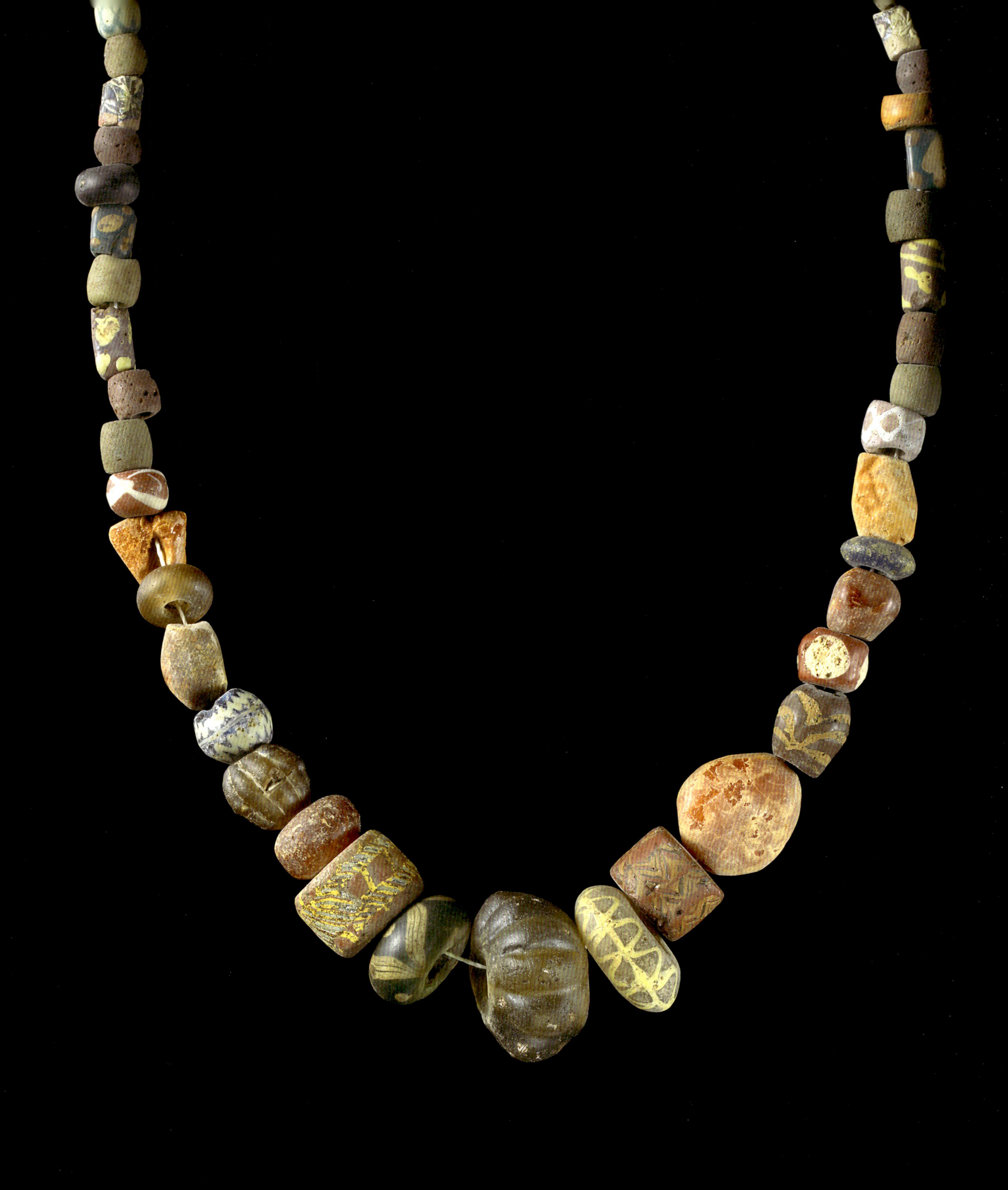

The Merovingian period – The transition from antiquity to the Middle Ages

CLIFF ALEXANDER JOST

After the end of Roman rule and the climax of the so-called Migration period with its major movements of peoples, the early medieval age starts around 480 AD with the Merovingian period. It is named after the Frankish royal dynasty of the Merovingians founded by Clovis (482-511 AD), who ruled the Frankish Empire or its part realms until 751. Clovis and his successors continuously enlarged their sphere of control through expansionist wars, family intrigue, murder, skilful alliances and marriage policies. The territory of today's Rhineland-Palatinate was completely under Frankish rule by the beginning of the 6th century, after Clovis had brought the zones of influence of the Alamanni at the southern Middle Rhine and northern Upper Rhine under his control between 496 and 506. In the end, the Frankish Empire stretched from the Atlantic to the Bavarian Forest and became the central power in early medieval Europe. The Merovingian period comes to an end around 750 AD, when the Carolingian dynasty takes over government in the Frankish Empire.

The Merovingians had founded the Frankish realm in Gaul on the territory of the former Roman Empire. From the beginning, they ruled over an ethnically mixed population. Even after the Franks had come to power, further population groups, in particular Germanic tribes, came to settle there. Whether Huns, Saxons, Anglo-Saxons, Visigoths, Alamanni or Thuringians – they were all considered as belonging to the society of the Franks once they had sworn allegiance to the Frankish king and his officials.

The majority of the population at first consisted of the »Romani«, the successors of the Gallo-Roman provincial population who had remained in the areas of the former Roman western provinces after the Franks had occupied them. Most likely, the Franks could only rise to power there because they were widely accepted by the populous Romani, especially by their elite. By the second half of the 4th century, Franks had taken over key commanding positions in the Roman military. During the 4th and 5th century, they settled, already well adjusted and largely assimilated, amidst the Gallo-Romanic population. They understood and spoke Latin, they knew the Roman world of late antiquity, the organization of the Roman provinces along with their economy and administration and were acquainted with the great cultural achievements of the Romans.

The conversion of Clovis – and with him of the Frankish leadership – to the religion of Rome, i.e. to Catholic Christianity, after the victory over the Alamanni, proved an essential assimilating link, since it brought about the decisive accord with the locals of Romanic origin

Ochtendung, Mayen-Koblenz distr. Neck jewellery made of coloured beads (7th century). Glass beads of different size and colour were used as a rule, but also beads made of other materials such as semi-precious stones and amber. (GDKE/Landesarchäologie/Koblenz/W. Baumann, Höhr-Grenzhausen)

Fig. 1
Rhineland-Palatinate. Selected sites of settlements and grave fields of the Merovingian period. Sites where the State Archaeology conducted major excavations since 1947 are marked in orange-yellow. (GDKE/Landesarchäologie/Koblenz/C. A. Jost, A. Schmidt, based on: SRTM data (NASA) http://ows.terrestris.de/osm/service)

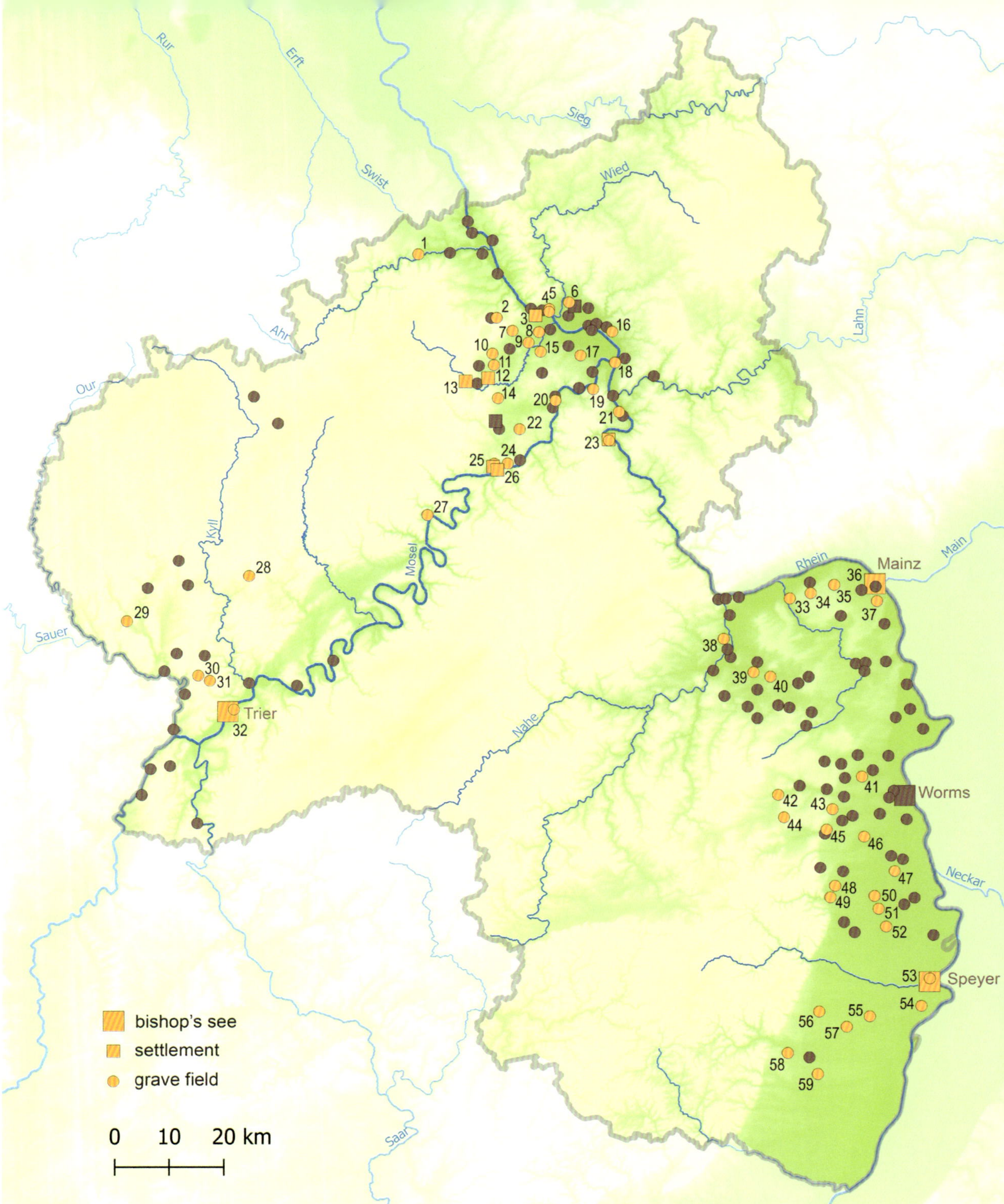

sites:
1 Ahrweiler
2 Kell
3 Andernach
4 Irlich
5 Wollendorf
6 Niederbieber
7 Nickenich
8 Miesenheim
9 Pommerhof
10 Mendig
11 Thür
12 Hausen
13 Mayen
14 Polch
15 Saffig
16 Weitersburg
17 Rübenach
18 Koblenz
19 Lay
20 Gondorf
21 Rhens
22 Münstermaifeld
23 Boppard
24 Müden
25 Karden
26 Treis
27 Eller
28 Spangdahlem
29 Schankweiler
30 Olk
31 Newel
32 Trier
33 Ingelheim
34 Wackernheim
35 Finthen
36 Mainz
37 Hechtsheim
38 Langenlonsheim
39 Badenheim
40 Gau-Bickelheim
41 Mörstadt
42 Marnheim
43 Bockenheim
44 Göllheim
45 Asselheim
46 Dirmstein
47 Eppstein
48 Ungstein
49 Bad Dürkheim
50 Fußgönheim
51 Schauernheim
52 Dannstadt
53 Speyer
54 Heiligenstein
55 Weingarten
56 Edesheim
57 Niederhochstadt
58 Arzheim
59 Insheim

and at the same time assured the new rulers of the support of the mighty Catholic Church.

For the territories of today's Rhineland-Palatinate, the Merovingian period meant major changes in the settlement landscape, but some continuity can also be clearly observed. After a noticeable decrease in the population in the 5th century, as compared to the middle Roman Empire, there is a gradual increase from the early 6th century. In rural areas, numerous small farming settlements develop, which often form the core of medieval villages and eventually the origins of today's towns and cities. Many of these Frankish foundations can still be recognized by their names, which usually end in -heim, -dorf and -ingen. Place names ending in -hofen and -hausen appear from the late Merovingian and the Carolingian periods.

The cities and localities on the Rhine and Moselle, which had continued to exist since Roman times and where the majority of the Romanic population lived, had also regained some of their original importance by the 6th century: first and foremost there was the former imperial residence of Trier, in addition to Mainz, Worms, and Speyer as early episcopal sees. The big cities developed into leading market places, centres of administration, trade, and spiritual and worldly culture, with a wide sphere of influence in the region. In this Christian-dominated environment, the Merovingians succeeded in merging Germanic and Gallo-Roman traditions and thus creating the basis for further development in the Middle Ages.

Archaeology of the Merovingian period

The archaeology of the early Middle Ages is one of graves and a treasure trove of burial finds retrieved from them. The grave fields are normally found at the peripheries of the cities, villages, and farms still in existence today, while the corresponding settlements of the Merovingian period have been studied much less. Their remains are thought to be hidden under our present day localities, but were often removed from there through extensive medieval and modern ground work interventions. The grave fields, however, offer us insights into the settlement pattern of the early Middle Ages, with indications as to the position and size of the dwelling sites, as each settlement usually has its own burial site.

Settlement in the rural area

The distribution of the row grave fields (*Reihengräberfelder*) indicates that the Frankish settlements in the countryside are situated in those settlement areas that are easy to cultivate, that is to say within the fertile and climatically favourable valley and basin landscapes that had earlier been used by the Romans. (Fig. 1) Uplands with poor soils, such as Hunsrück, Eifel, Westerwald, Taunus, and Palatine Uplands, were, however, not settled again until the high Middle Ages. The Franks preferred their traditional timber wood constructions and almost always built their new rural settlements somewhat away from the abandoned stone-built Roman estates *(villae rusticae)*. Sometimes they used the Roman ruins as burial places. While Roman settlements were usually erected on slopes, the Franks preferred locations close to rivers running through valleys.

The largest Merovingian grave field in Rhineland-Palatinate to date with 829 recovered graves – of an estimated number of ca. 1200 original burials – was excavated in 1939–1940 and then in 1966 when a highway was built through a stretch of today's Koblenz-Rübenach. The grave field was used from the second half of the 5th to the middle of the 8th century. Calculations of the number of inhabitants for the settlement associated with the cemetery during the different phases resulted in ca. one hundred at the start with more than double that number by the end. The settlement would therefore have been the size of a village. It was probably situated in the historical town centre of today's Rübenach, 250 m away from the grave field. Most of the early medieval grave fields are indeed much smaller and indicate an open settlement pattern for the rural area, with numerous individual farms and loosely structured small hamlets. Larger village-like settlements were rather the exception.

There is hardly any archaeological evidence as to what the rural settlements of the Franks might have looked like. Only a few early medieval settlements with clear findings from the Merovingian period could be examined on a large scale in Rhineland-Palatinate. The settlement of Neuwied-Gladbach in the Neuwied district (6th-9th century), which had already been discovered in 1937-1938 during pumice mining, was for a long time considered to be the most important site of this kind in Rhineland. Since then, the two settlement sites

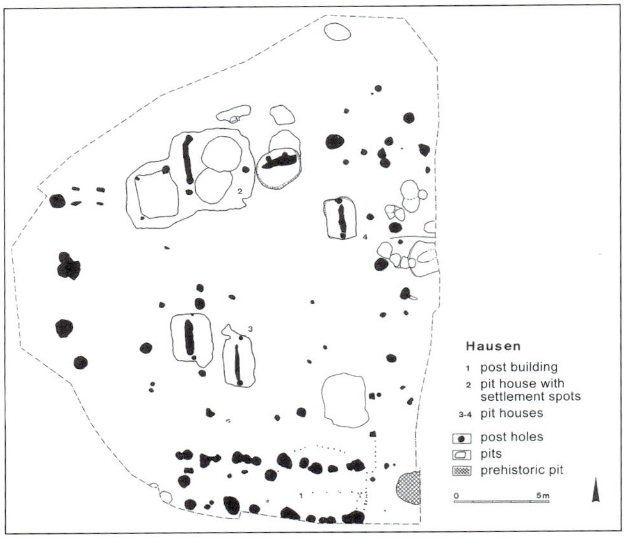

Fig. 2
Mayen-Hausen, Mayen-Koblenz distr. Plan of a portion of the early medieval settlement with post settings, pit houses, and settlement pits. (GDKE/Landesarchäologie/Koblenz/F. Brüninghaus)

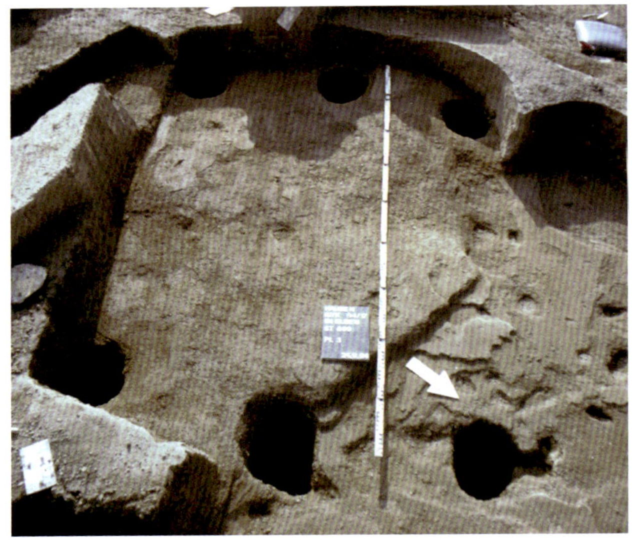

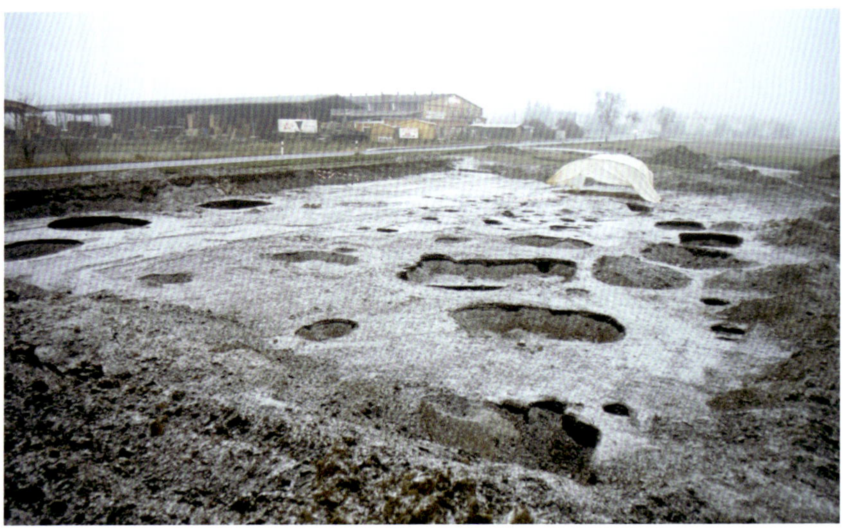

Fig. 3
Mayen-Hausen, Mayen-Koblenz distr. Overview of a part of the excavation area with post settings, pit houses, and settlement pits. (GDKE/Landesarchäologie/Koblenz/F. Brüninghaus)

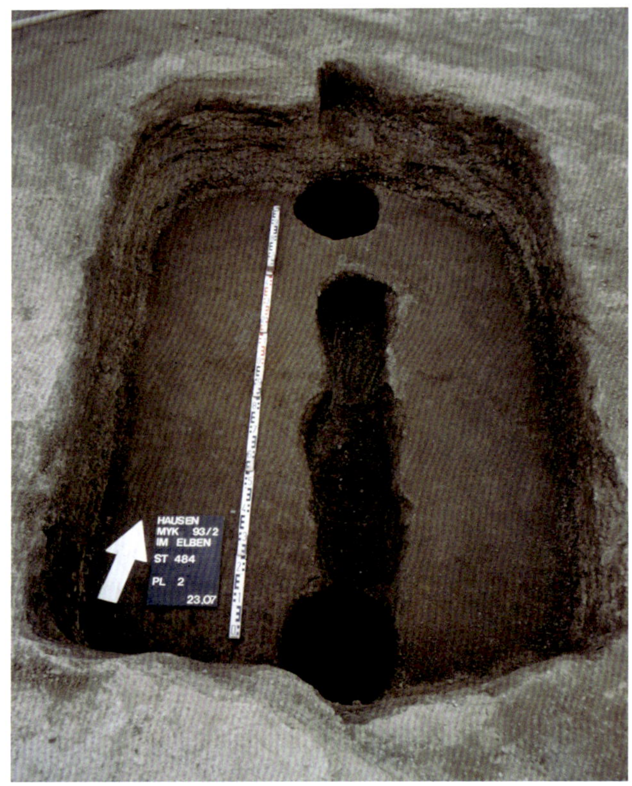

Fig. 4 (top)
Mayen-Hausen, Mayen-Koblenz distr. Excavation find of a Merovingian period pit house with its typical 6-post arrangement. The pit house was covered by later building traces of the settlement. (GDKE/Landesarchäologie/Koblenz/F.Brüninghaus)

Fig. 5 (bottom)
Mayen-Hausen, Mayen-Koblenz distr. Small early-medieval pit house with ridge post settings and traces of a loom stand in the centre. (GDKE/Landesarchäologie Koblenz/F.Brüninghaus)

Speyer-»Im Vogelgesang« (excavation 1978-1982 during building projects) and Mayen-Hausen (Mayen-Koblenz district, excavation 1992-1994 during pumice mining), where a larger section was examined, have significantly widened our knowledge. (Fig. 2–3)

The settlements consisted of several individual buildings with different functions. Most of the houses were of timber-frame construction with a basic structure of wood and clay-clad wattle walls. The roofs were covered with straw, perhaps also with wood shingles. Bigger, one-storey post constructions with a rectangular, mostly one-room layout, at least 4 m in width and 7 m in length, were probably used as dwellings or as barns, sheds or stables. A precise allocation of

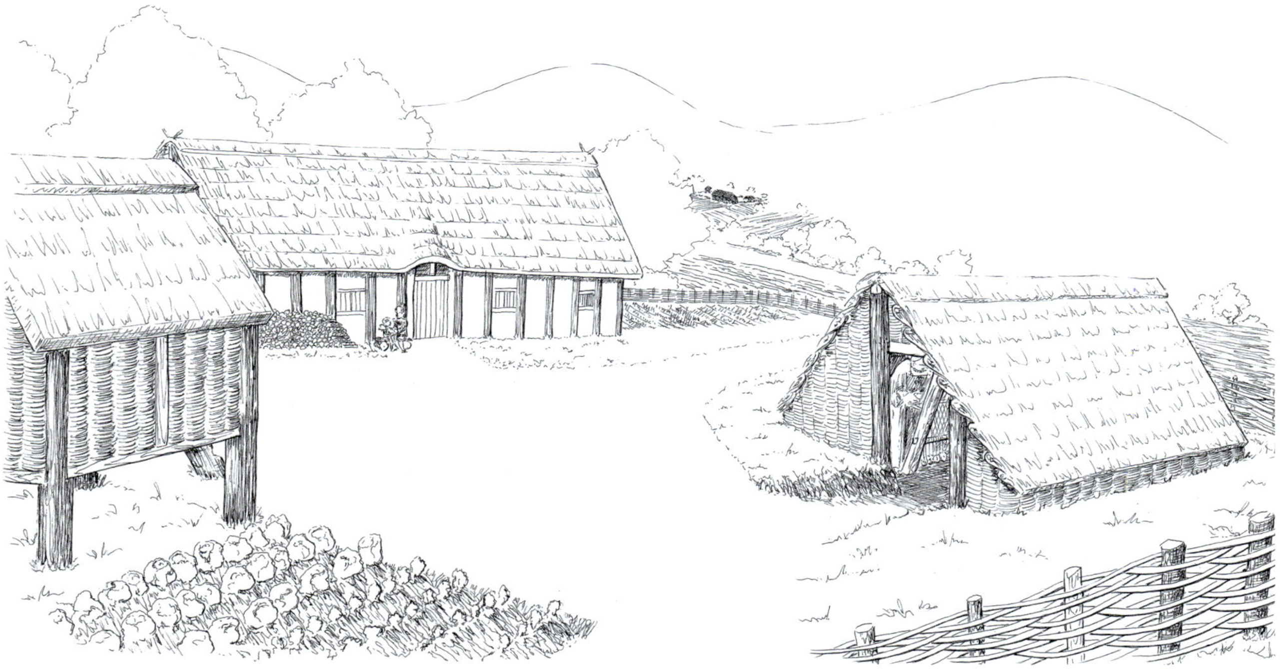

Fig. 6.
Mayen-Hausen, Mayen-Koblenz distr. Reconstruction of a Frankish farm complex according to the archaeological finding. (GDKE/Landesarchäologie/Koblenz/M. Meinen)

functions is rarely possible. Small, square or rectangular wooden buildings with four to six posts were most probably barns for hay and cereals. They probably had an elevated floor to protect the stored goods from damp and pests. One very often comes across so-called pit-houses: small rectangular huts on average just 3 m × 4 m, where the floor was sunk into the ground with postholes in the corners and for the roof ridge. (Fig. 4–5) They sometimes served as cool cellars for storing foodstuffs, but were mainly used as workshops for artisanal activities, especially the production of textiles. This is indicated by the many weaving weights and spindle whorls found in them, but also by traces of looms on the floor. Drinking water came from wells with wooden or drywall-stone casings. Pits of various shapes and depths had formed during clay removal and were used as supply and waste pits. Rows of small postholes and traces of small flat ditches indicate fences and enclosures within the settlement site.

The distribution of the various building traces in the settlement Speyer-»Vogelgesang«, situated at the southern border of modern-day Speyer, also allows differentiated statements about the spatio-temporal development of the settlement site. It extended along a terrace edge on the northern bank of an ancient waterbody of the Rhine and was founded at the beginning of the Merovingian period at the end of the 5th century. Until it was abandoned in the 13th century, the form of the settlement changed from one or two farmsteads in a small group of farms to a slightly bigger village, and also relocated from the southeast to the northwest over a wide area. During the Merovingian utilization phase, three farming units existed in the south-eastern settlement area; they had one post structure each, with a layout of up to 6 m × 10 m and the corresponding four-post barns on stilts and pit-houses. (Fig. 6)

The early medieval settlement of Mayen-Hausen also shows a shift of the settlement centre. At first, the settlement was ca. 700 m outside and to the east of today's Mayen district of Hausen. According to the finds, it existed from the late 5th century to the 12th century. Thereafter, it was deserted, and the settlement was moved into the area of today's village centre, where the durable construction method of using stone and placing the church in the centre, which became the norm again around 1200, contributed to making it permanent.

Urban settlements: towns (*civitates*), former fort locations (*castra*) and small-town-village settlements (*vici*)

The situation in the urban area differed from that in rural zones. Most of the towns and fort locations, which had been fortified since late Roman times by solid walls, as well as small-town village settlements with vicus character in economically favourable locations with good transport facilities for trade, continued to exist in the early Middle Ages and as a rule have survived until today. It seems that a large share of the Romani, who had remained in the former Roman province, lived there side by side with the Franks, who had moved to the region earlier.

For the former imperial residence and early episcopal see of Trier, the settlement finds from the Merovingian period, which have been unearthed time and again during excavations in the city since the middle of the 1990s – combined with the results from old excavations – indicate an at least loosely continued settlement protected by the formidable old Roman city wall. The late antique street grid and the bridge across the Moselle also continued to exist in the early days. Settlement concentrations within the city area have to date been detected around St. Irminen, the Constantinian double church (i.e. cathedral and Church of Our Lady), the palace hall (so-called basilica), the imperial thermal baths, and the Altbach valley. (Fig. 7) The double church of the cathedral and the Church of Our Lady were rebuilt under bishop Nicetius (who died after 561) and liturgical elements were added (ambo and solea). The remains of other large antique buildings were often reused for differing purposes. Other areas of the former city territory were abandoned and used for agriculture.

Several house outlines of a hamlet-like settlement of the 7th–9th centuries were documented during the old excavations between 1926 and 1934 in the Gallo-Roman temple area of the Altbach valley. Most of the houses followed the wall contours of Roman temples. Two completely new buildings had dry wall foundations for a half-timbered wall.

Near the Moselle, in the northwest of the former city area, a convent for members of the Frankish nobility was founded in the 7th century over the ruins of the monumental late Roman warehouses (horrea). The name St. Maria in horreo (later St. Irminen-Oeren) shows that the original function of the antique building complex was still known in medieval times. During archaeological examinations in 1926 and 1996, parts of the early medieval convent with building remains and waste chutes were unearthed. A large quantity of excavated items, indicating metal, glass, and textile manufacturing close by, or the Merovingian potter's kiln in the Altbach valley, which shows that pottery was produced there, are evidence of industrial production in the urban area. Wine continued to be grown in Trier and along the Moselle and the Rhine, while coins were minted in Trier from the second half of the 6th century.

The fact that Trier was continuously inhabited during the 6th and 7th centuries can be shown archaeologically above all through the large grave fields and Christian cult sites north and south of the city walls established in late Roman times along the arterial roads. This is shown most impressively by the long-term excavations in St. Maximin, with a proven uninterrupted sequence from a late antique cemeterial building to an early medieval church.

The Romanic urban population pursued the antique tradition of marking graves with a tombstone. The more than 1100 late antique and early medieval tombstones with signs, decorations, and Christian inscriptions in Latin underline the importance of Trier as a centre of early Christendom with a wide sphere of influence in the region. In addition, in many other cities, former fort locations, and vicus-like settlements along the Rhine and Moselle – such as Mainz, Andernach, Boppard, Bingen,Worms or Karden and Kobern-Gondorf – the tombstones with early Christian inscriptions from the 4th to the 7th century bear witness to the continuity of the Romanic population and language, as well as to the uninterrupted presence of Christian communities between late antiquity and the early Middle Ages. (Fig. 8)

The Christian community in the fort location of Boppard had established itself during the 5th century. Excavations from 1963 to 1966 beneath today's St. Severus church uncovered quite completely the layout of the first ascertained community church and baptistery. The design and size of the building are typi-

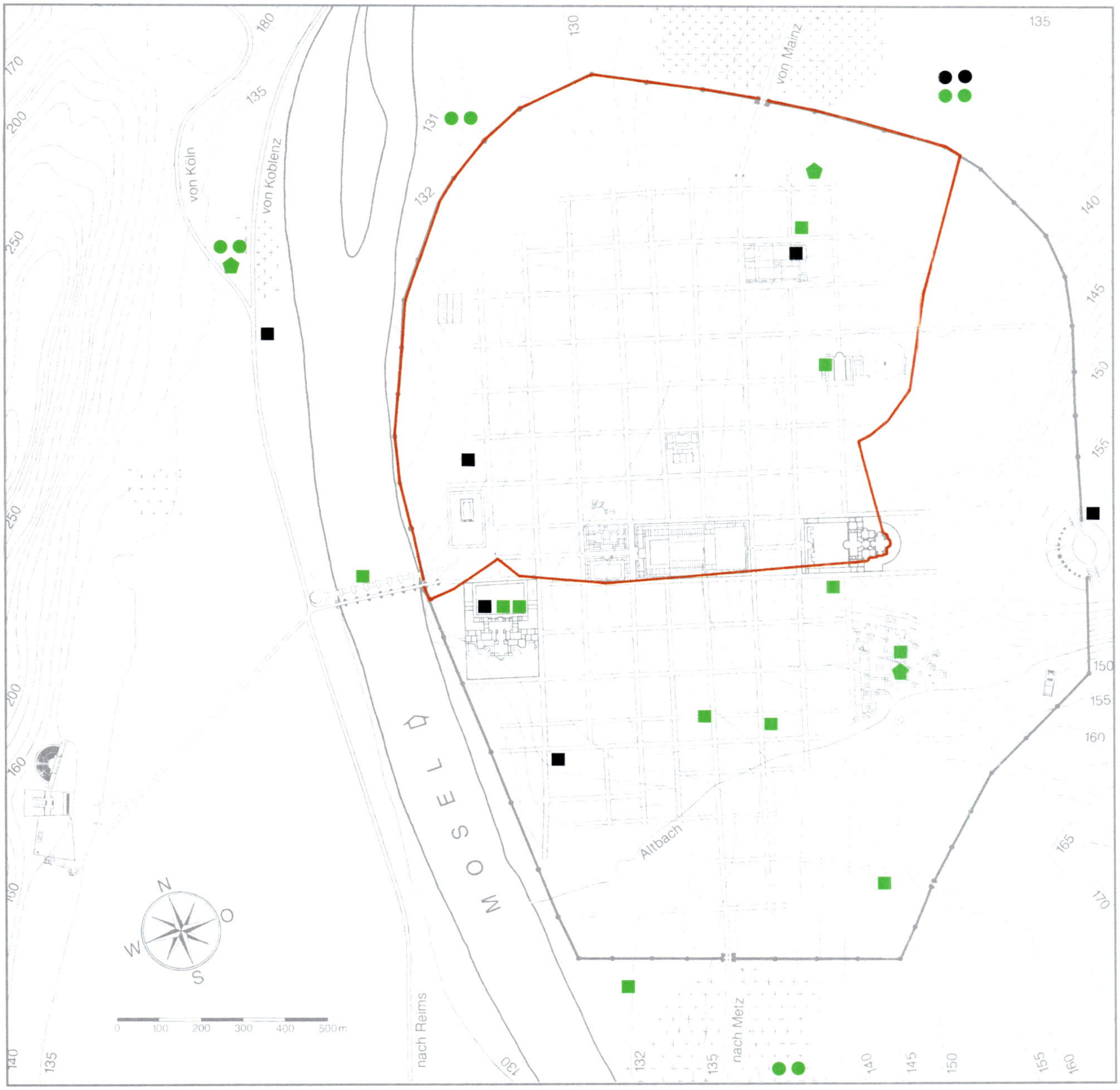

Find and find distribution of the 6th/7th century in Trier

	6th century	7th century
Individual find	■	■ (green)
Settlement find		⬟ (green)
grave/graves	●●	●● (green)

— Course of the high medieval city wall

Fig. 7
Trier, city of Trier. Distribution of Merovingian period finds of the 6th to the 7th century (after L. Clemens). (GDKE/Rheinisches Landesmuseum Trier/Scientific basis: L. Clemens, Graphic design: F. Dewald)

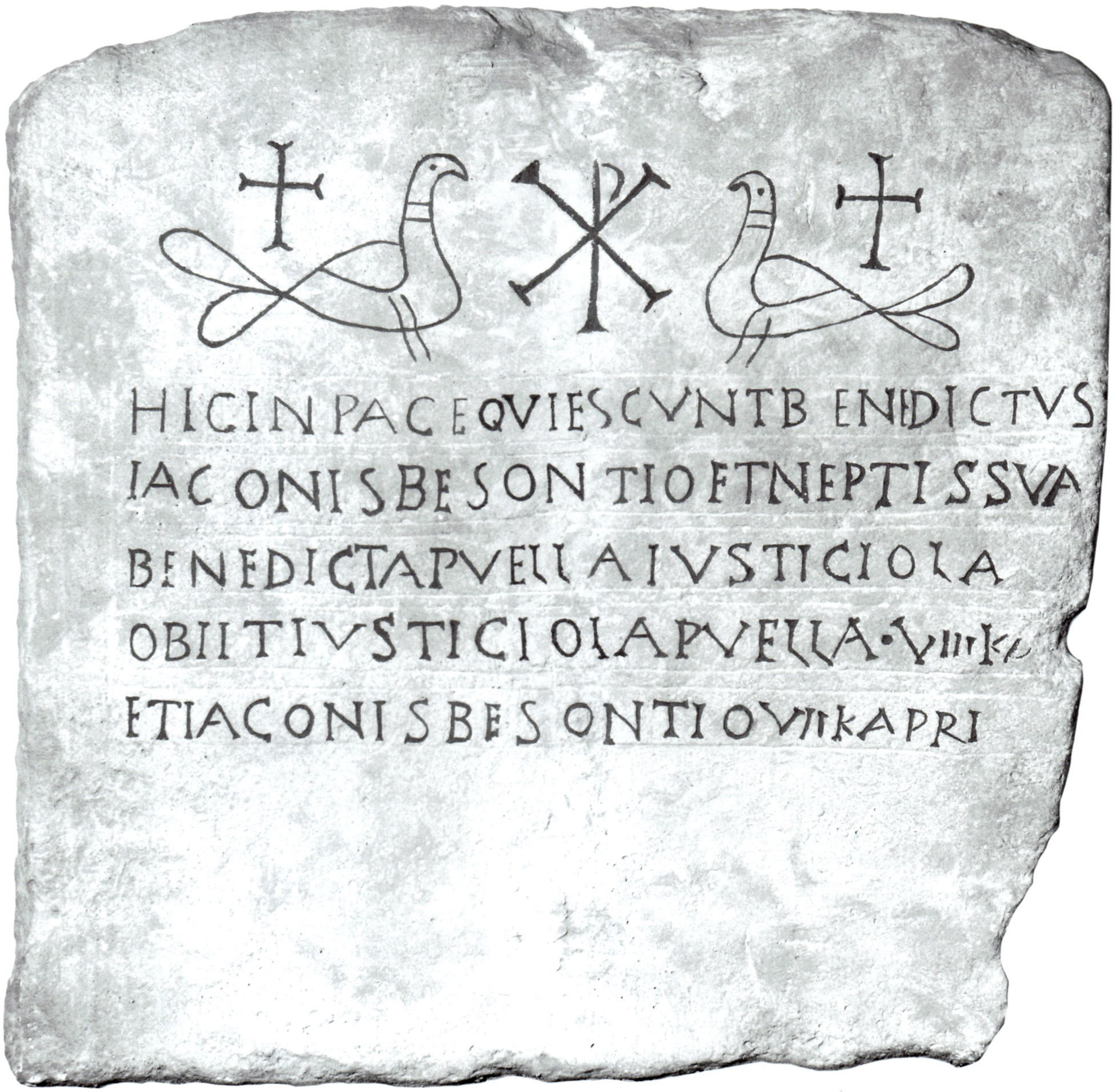

Fig. 8
Boppard, Rhein-Hunsrück distr. Tombstone of Besontio and Justiciola from the 5th or the first half of the 6th century. »Here rest in peace the highly praised deacon Besontio and his niece, the highly praised girl Justiciola. The girl Justiciola died on March 25th, the deacon Besontio on March 26th« (GDKE/Landesarchäologie/Koblenz/M. Neumann)

cal for church architecture in the second half of the 6th century. (Fig. 9) Parts of the city wall and walls of the bath at the Roman fort had been used for a hall building of 32 m in length and 9 m in width, with a semi-circular apse in the east and a lateral addition with four rooms in the south. Its characteristic elements are the keyhole-shaped elevated pulpit structure (ambo), leading from the altar room to the central nave via a 5 m long passage (solea); and the seven-sided baptismal font (piscina) with a round interior, located in a separate baptistery in the west of the nave. (Fig. 10–11) The font has an internal diameter of 1.30 m and is sunk into the ground; it was provided with a circumferential lower step and a water drain. The square indentations in the pedestal frame of the font once held the seven wooden supports of a canopy (ciborium).

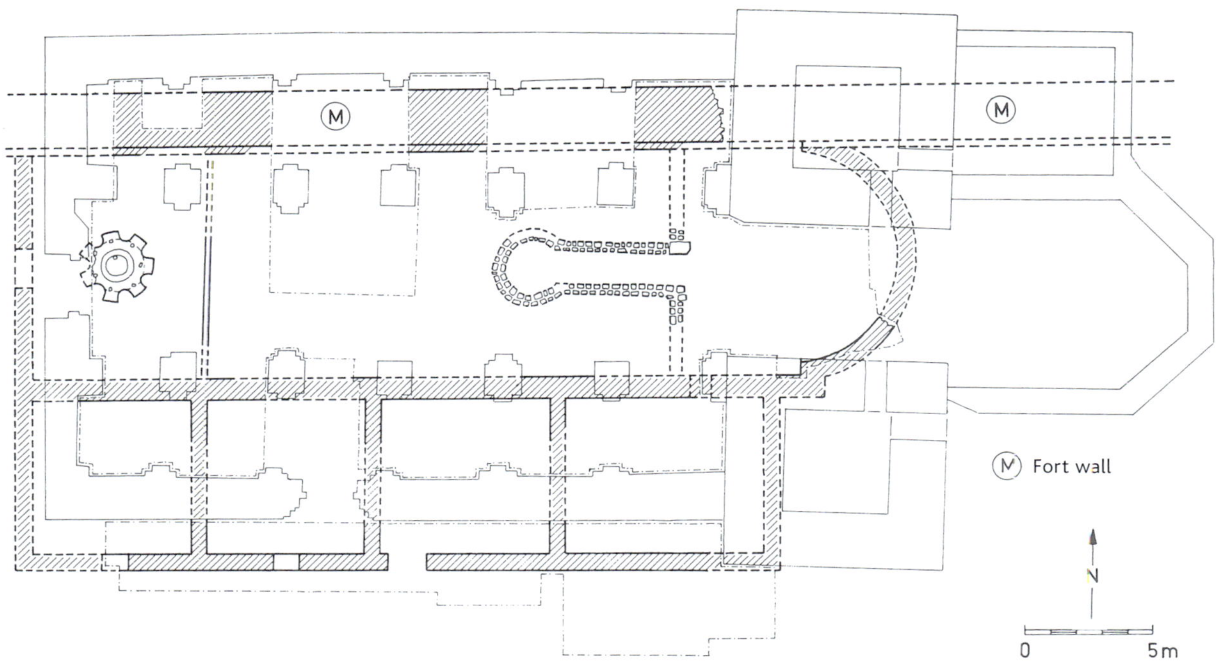

Fig. 9
Boppard, Rhein-Hunsrück distr. Layout of the early Christian church from the second half of the 6th century under today's St. Severus church. In the north the church building included the city wall, in the east the semi-circular apse of the Roman fort bath. (GDKE/Landesarchäologie/Koblenz/F. Dewald)

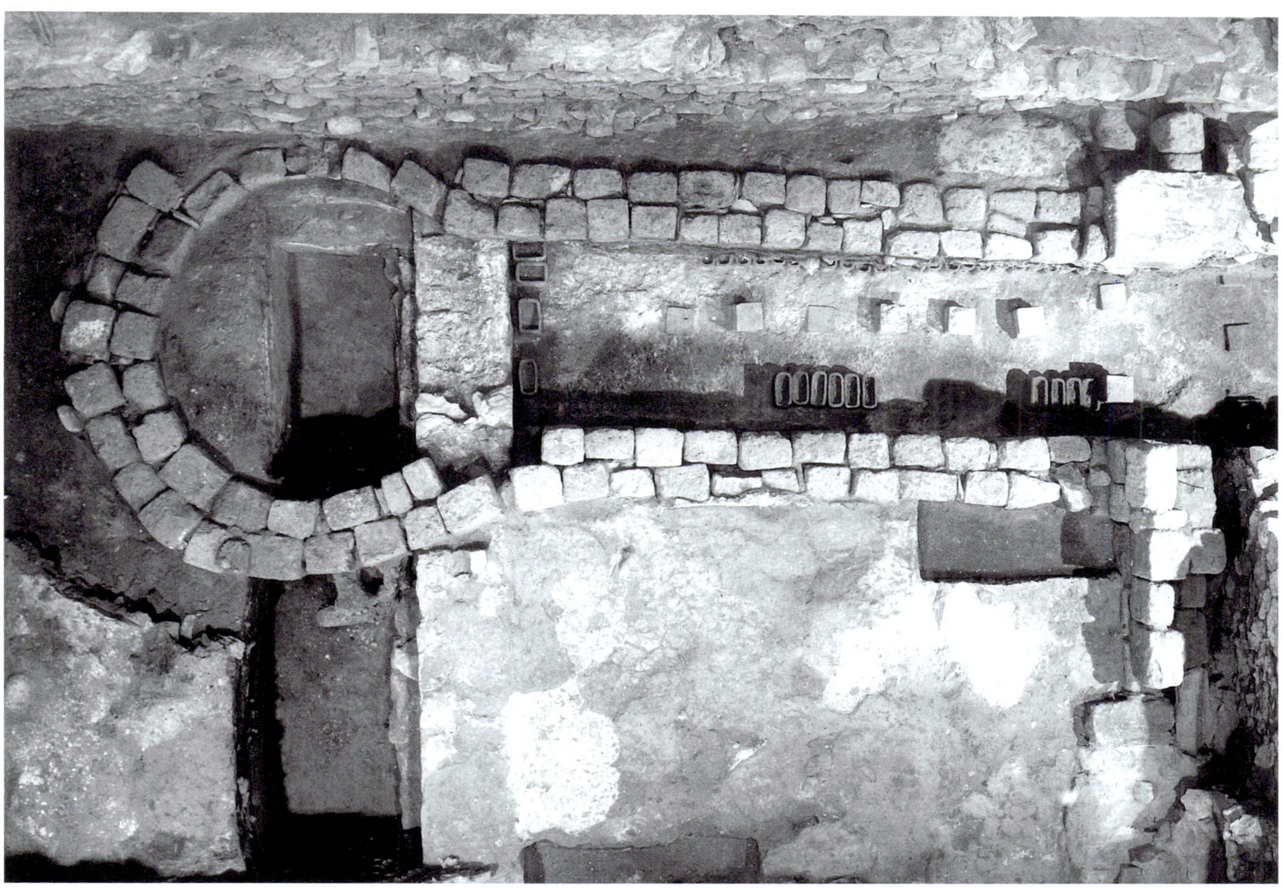

Fig. 10
Boppard, Rhein-Hunsrück distr. Keyhole-shaped base for a chancel complex with ambo and solea in the early Christian church; beneath: pillars as support for the heating system of the Roman fort bath. (GDKE/Landesarchäologie/Koblenz/Foto Klein, Boppard)

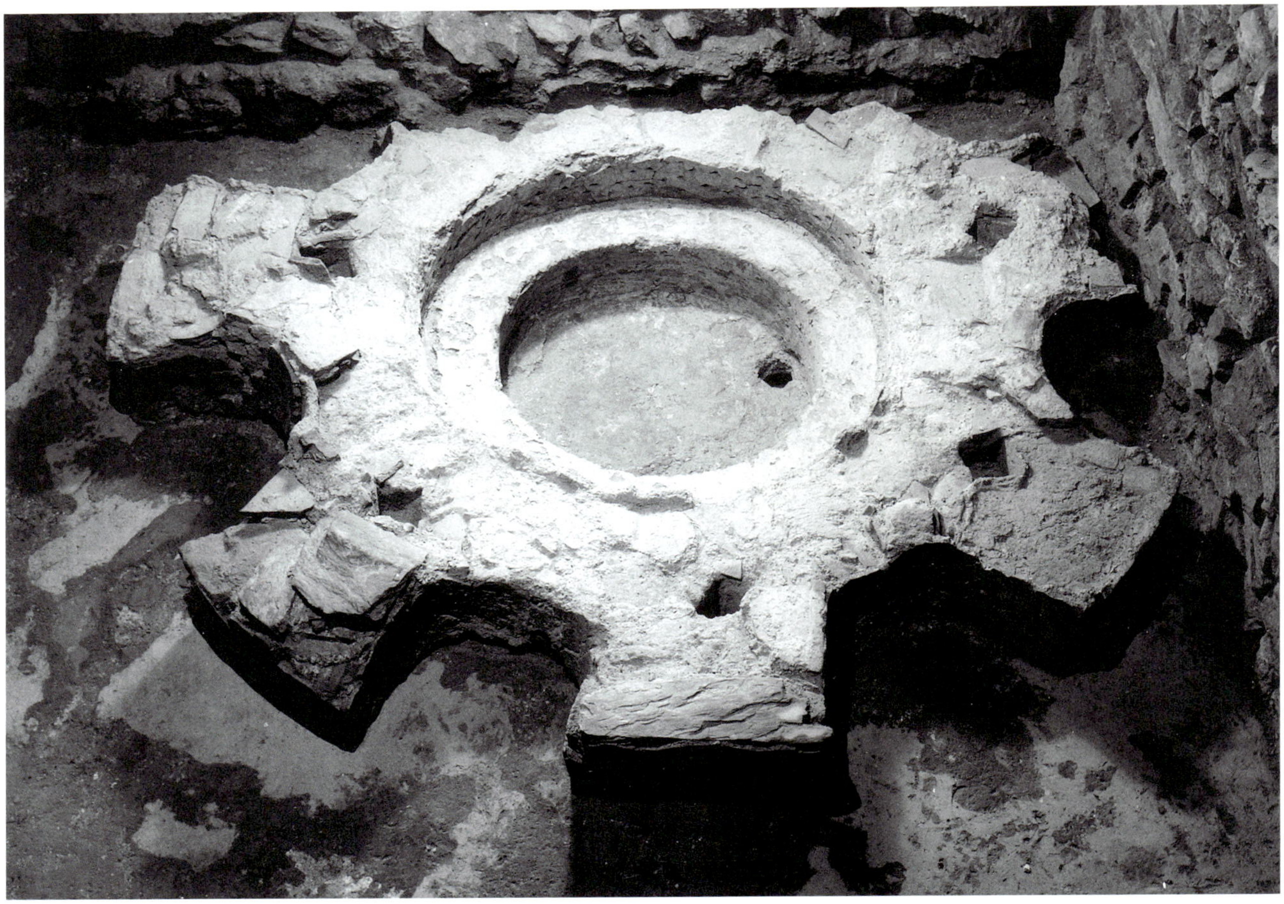

Fig. 11
Boppard, Rhein-Hunsrück distr. Baptismal font in a separate room in the west of the early Christian church. The border of the base with seven semi-circular indentations has square holes in which seven wooden support posts once stood supporting a baldachin-like superstructure of the basin. (GDKE/Landesarchäologie/Koblenz/Foto Klein, Boppard)

As a previously important centre for the production of pottery, the vicus Mayen, located at the eastern edge of the Eifel, is a good example of specialist handicrafts and commerce largely continuing far beyond the 5th century. The economic location profited from the continued existence of the important long-distance Roman road leading from the two cities of Metz and Trier on the Moselle via the Eifel to Andernach on the Rhine, which was important for the exchange of goods.

In late antiquity and in the early Middle Ages, Mayen was a leading place of pottery production. (Fig. 12) From the end of the 5th century onwards, the potteries were only operating on the right bank of the river Nette near today's castle of Genovevaburg – the cleared pottery area in the late antique vicus on the left bank of the Nette now being used as a burial place (»Eich« grave field) – but the production of the so-called »Mayen ware« continued without interruption. Construction excavations especially between 1974 and 1981 during building works on both sides of today's Siegfriedstraße provided important information about the medieval pottery area of Mayen. Several pottery kilns and clay pits filled with pottery waste as well as heaps of misfired pottery were found. (Fig. 13) Further examinations from 1986 to 1987, when an underground garage was built, uncovered parts of the pottery settlement with 51 pit-houses from the 5th to 9th century, overbuilt by kilns of the 9th to 14th century. (Fig. 14)

There is continuity also in the production of millstones, which was another important industry of Mayen. Basalt lava was still mined in the basalt quarries nearby and processed into millstones, although on a smaller scale. The existing infrastructures were used for trade. The products were transported on the still intact Roman road to Andernach, where the Rhine port remained the most important hub for the onward transport of the products aboard ships.

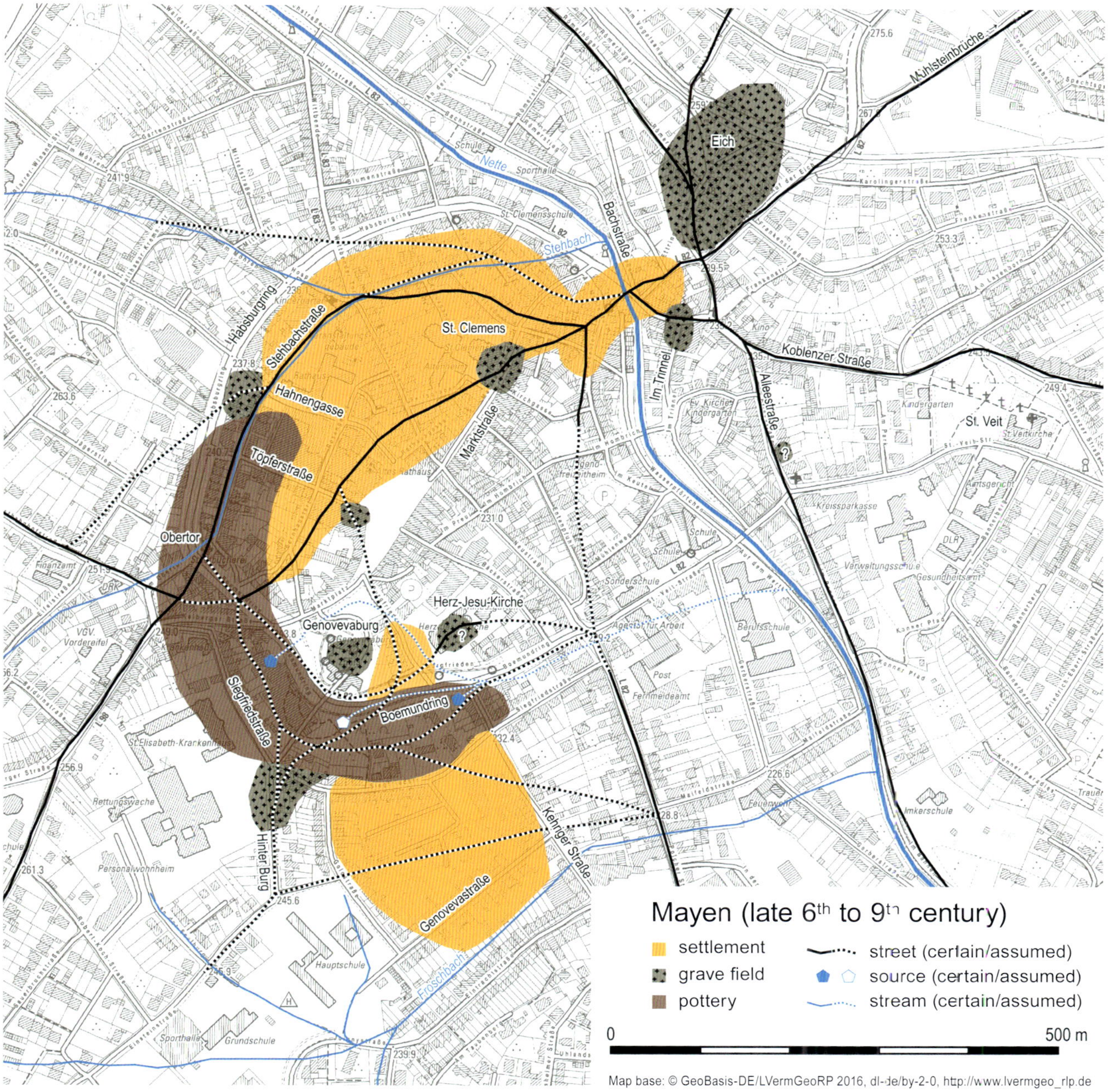

Fig. 12
Mayen, Mayen-Koblenz distr. Mapping of the sites from the early Middle Ages with settlement, grave field, and pottery areas. (after L. Grunwald). (RGZM/Scientific basis: L. Grunwald, Graphic design: B. Streubel)

Row grave fields (Reihengräberfelder)

The grave fields used over several generations from the 5th to the first half of the 8th century are still the most important archaeological source for studying the early Middle Ages. Because of the more or less regular arrangement of the graves in rows – even if not always in strict chronological order – they are commonly referred to as row grave fields. (Fig. 15–16)

Many of the grave fields have been known since the 19th century, when they were searched mainly by treasure hunters and antiquarians, though not in a scientific manner. Therefore, exact details about the context of the finds are often missing, and the grave inventories are not always completely documented either. Thus, the row grave fields examined systematically and using modern methods of assessment during the last 70 years by branches of the Department for Archaeology in

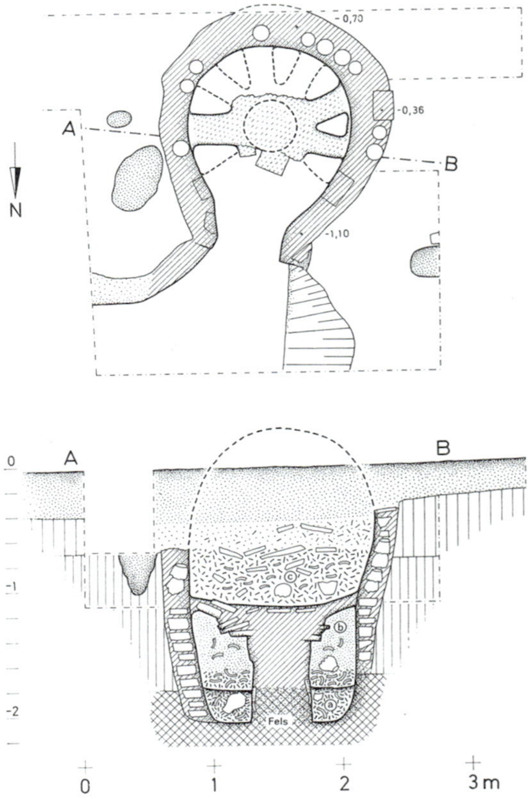

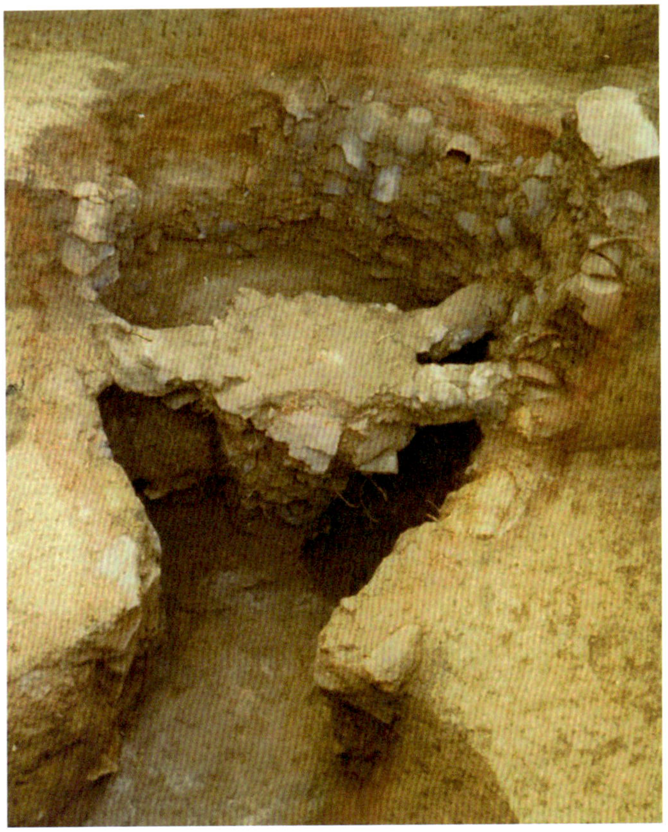

Fig. 13
Mayen, Mayen-Koblenz distr. Pottery kiln (kiln 2) in Siegfriedstraße in the archaeological excavation finding. Late 5th to early 6th century. View of the fire box and firing chamber. Layout and profile drawing. (GDKE/Landesarchäologie/Koblenz/Photo: H. Gadenz, Graphic design: F. Dewald)

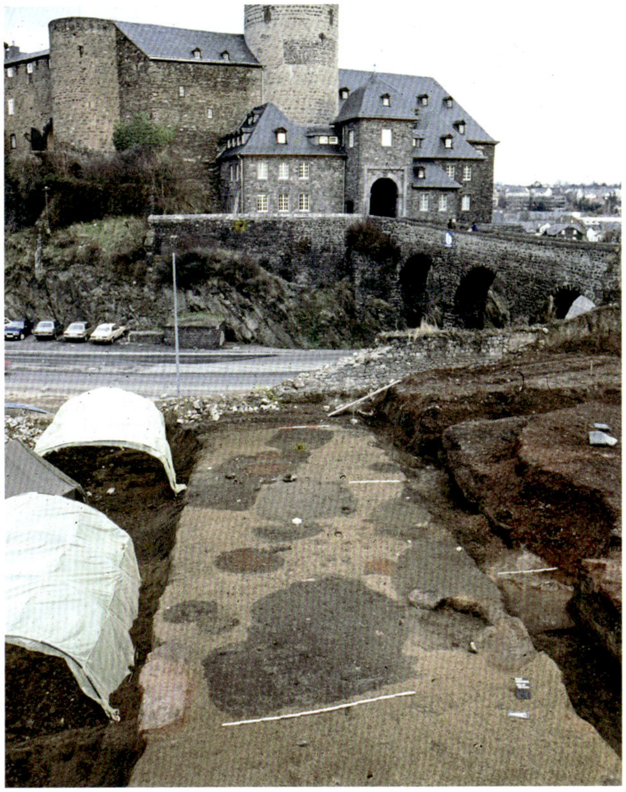

Fig. 14
Mayen, Mayen-Koblenz distr. Overview of a part of the excavation area near Genovevaburg with pit houses, clay extraction pits, and kilns of the 5th to the 14th century. (GDKE/Landesarchäologie/Koblenz/M. Neumann)

Rhineland-Palatinate are of particular importance (cf. Fig. 11). Most of them were unearthed since the 1970s during the development of new building areas, and in the Middle Rhine Basin often also through the exploitation of pumice sand. The capacity of the Frankish row grave fields depends on the size of the corresponding settlement and the period these cemeteries were used, ranging from a few dozen to several hundreds of burials. The dead were buried uncremated in stretched back position with the head in the west looking to the east. (Fig. 17–18) Deviations from the east-west orientation are often due to the terrain. Besides burials in simple earth graves, usually in wooden coffins or on biers (Totenbretter), there are graves built with stone slabs or dry walls. A few graves are marked by particularly lavish tombs, for instance by large, wood-clad grave chambers, wooden buildings erected over the graves, and grave mounds or circular pits. The use of sarcophagi and tombstones followed the burial traditions of the Gallo-Roman provincial population. Groups of graves within a row grave field sometimes indicate spatially separated burial areas of family or farm communities.

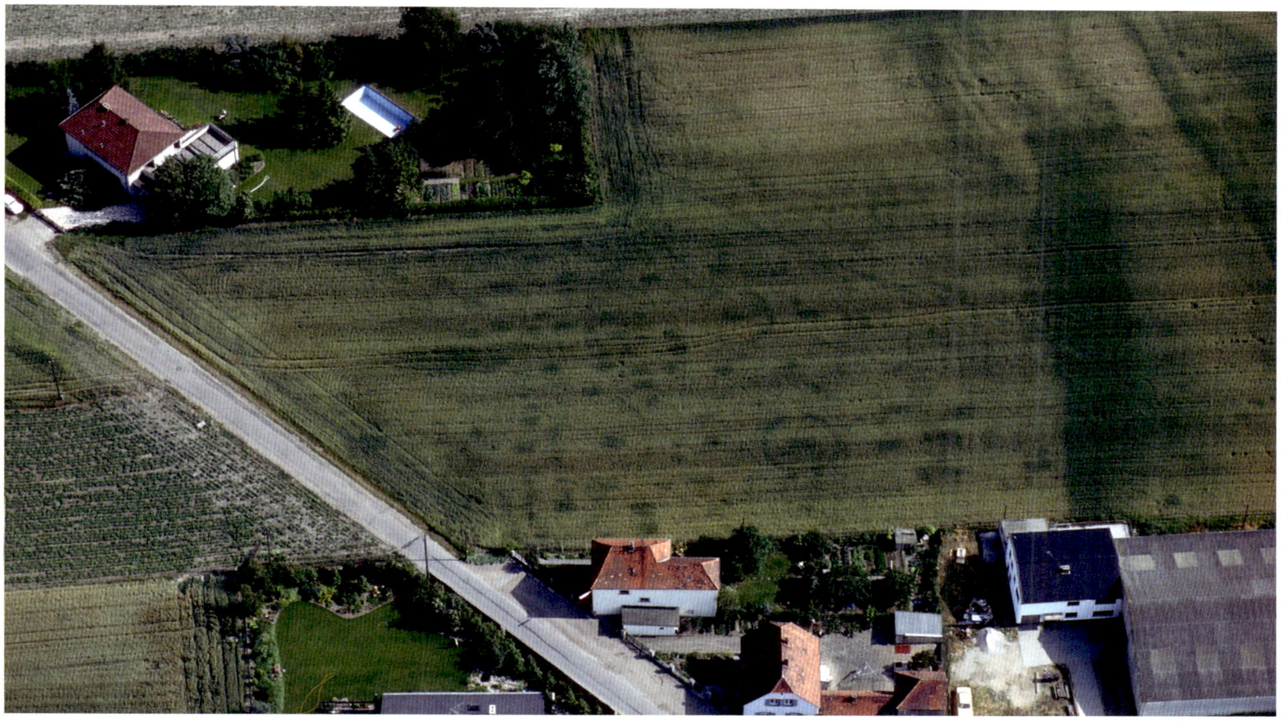

Fig. 15
Ormsheimer Hof, city of Frankenthal. Aerial photo of the early-medieval row grave field with simple graves and chamber graves in circular ditches recognizable in the natural cover. (GDKE/Landes-archäologie/Speyer/O. Braasch)

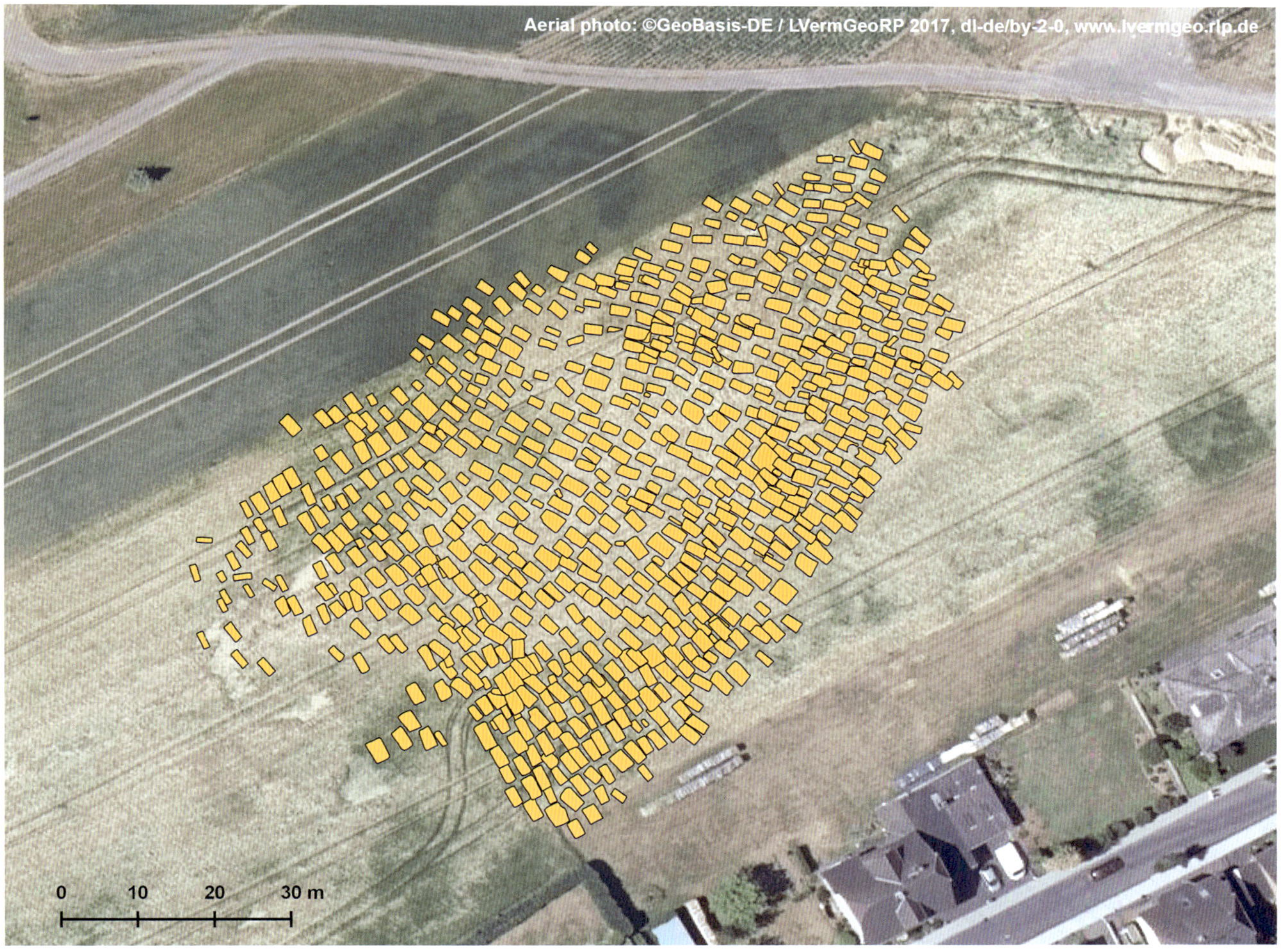

Fig. 16
Thür, Mayen-Koblenz distr. Aerial photo with inserted map of the big early-medieval row grave field with approx. 750 burials of the Merovingian and Carolingian period. (GDKE/Landesarchäologie/Koblenz/F. Gebert, Y. Schäfer, E. Schneider)

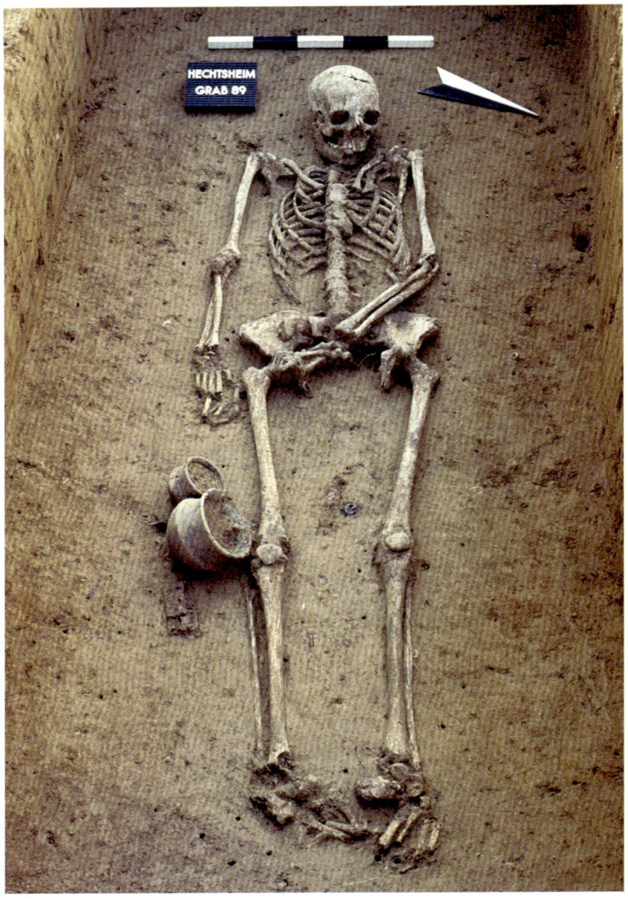

Fig. 17
Hechtsheim, city of Mainz. Grave of an adult woman (25-39 years) from the first half of the 6th century. (GDKE/Landesarchäologie/Mainz)

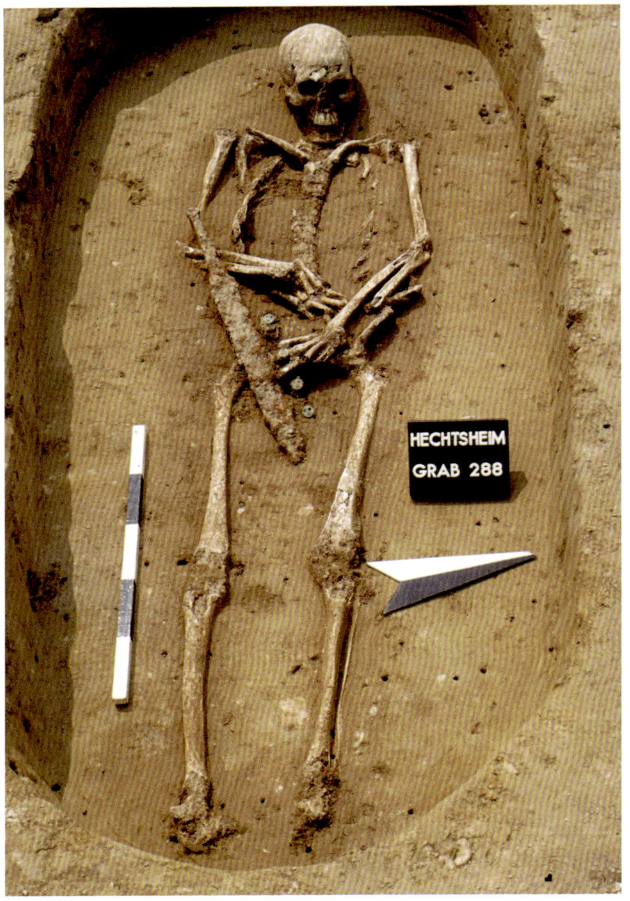

Fig. 18
Hechtsheim, city of Mainz. Grave of an adult man (25-35 years) from the second half of the 7th century, i.a. with a broad seax with bronze scabbard rivets. (GDKE/Landesarchäologie/Mainz)

The relatives equipped the dressed dead with rich goods for the afterlife: men were buried with weapons, belts, and personal belongings; women in their customary dress with jewellery, amulets, and other personal implements, including tools for textile processing. Keys among grave goods symbolized the leading position of the woman in the household. Moreover, vessels with drink and victuals for the deceased were placed in the graves. The grave goods were meant to help the dead maintain the rank due to them also in the afterlife. They also offered relatives a good opportunity to clearly display the social status and prosperity of the family during the public funeral rites.

Detailed analyses, such as those conducted in the completely excavated and anthropologically examined row grave field of Mainz-Hechtsheim, allow many insights into the social ranking of the local society, with a division into upper, middle, and lower classes. (Fig. 19) Considering the time of burial within the overall use of the row grave fields (often over many generations), the different expenditure for the grave structures as well as the type, size, and quality of the grave goods provide indications about the economic circumstances and the social rank of the deceased men and women. Aspects such as age – small children and the elderly usually only received modest grave goods – ethnicity, and the religious background of the dead also played a role in equipping the graves with goods.

Graves of above-average wealthy individuals

In nearly every examined row grave field there are graves of men, women, and children that stand out from most of the other burials through particularly precious and prestigious grave goods. The men at the top of the social hierarchy were entitled, according to their status, to a rich supply of weapons, exclusive rid-

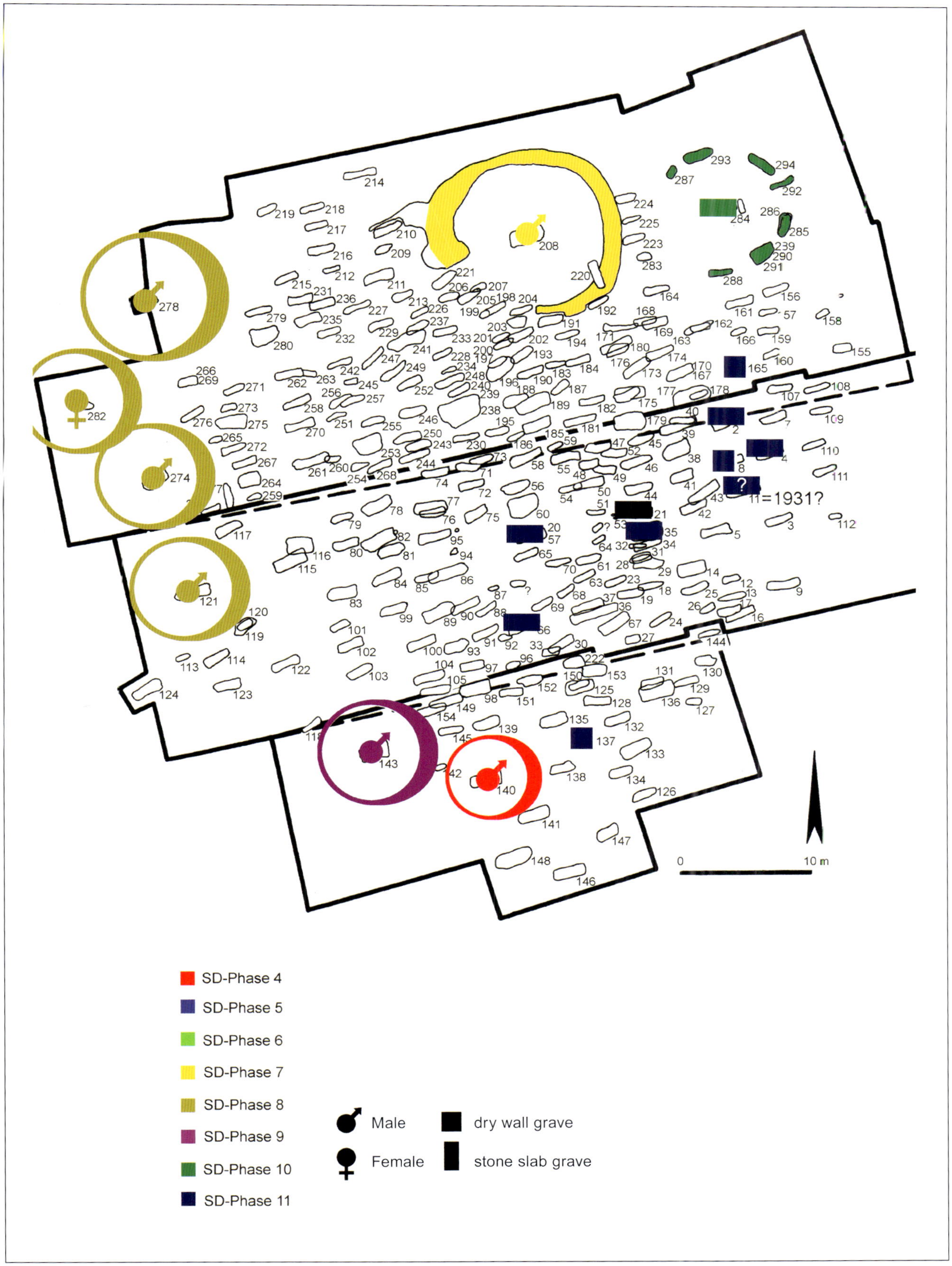

Fig. 19
Hechtsheim, city of Mainz. Plan of the grave field with prominent grave complexes of different times (SD phases 4-11, approx. 510-700) and genders marked in colours (after: U. Koch). Graves surrounded by a circular ditch or by a circular space not occupied by other burials could indicate former grave mounds or other grave structures. (GDKE/Landesarchäologie/Mainz/U. Koch, REM Mannheim)

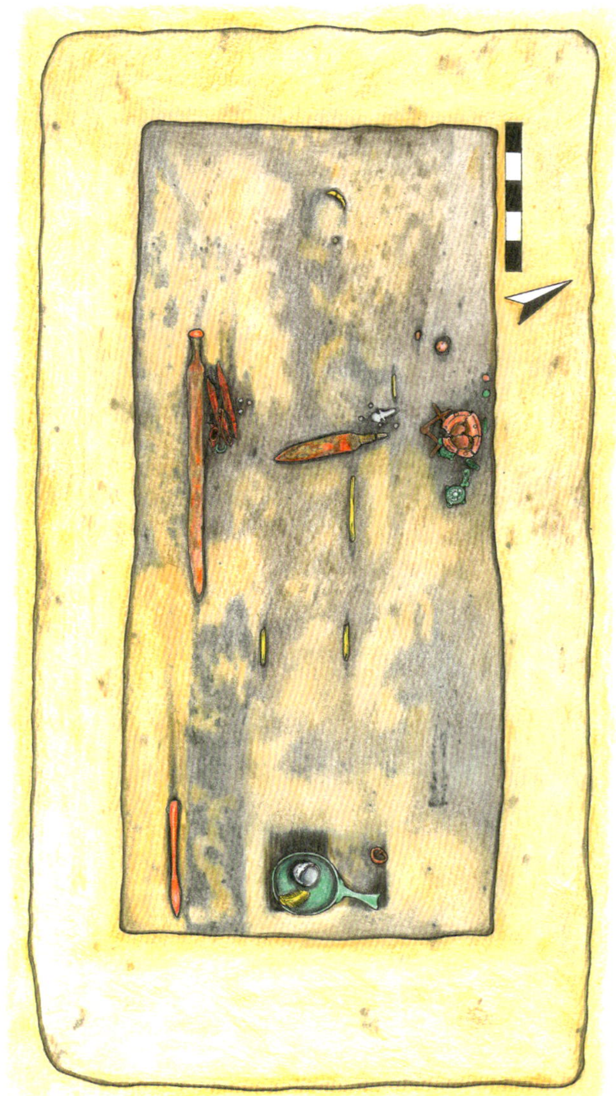

Fig. 20
Münstermaifeld, Mayen-Koblenz distr. Drawing of the excavation finding of male grave 164 with skeleton remains and grave goods. (GDKE/Landesarchäologie/Koblenz/F. Houben)

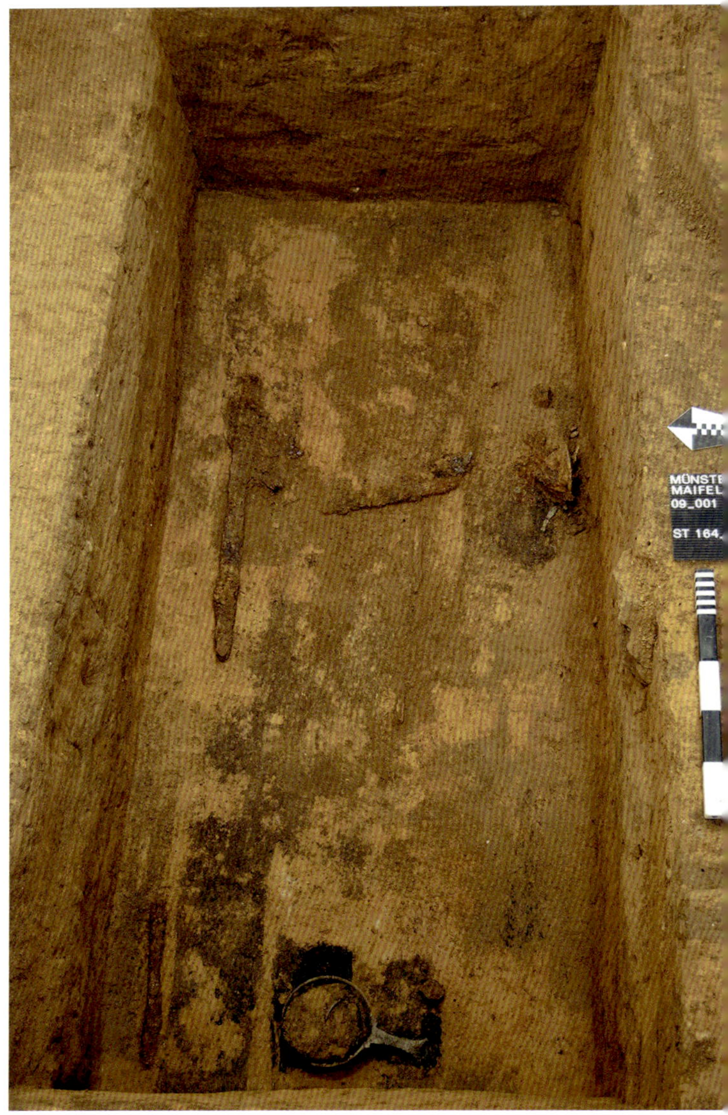

Fig. 21
Münstermaifeld, Mayen-Koblenz distr. Excavated grave chamber of male grave 164. (GDKE/Landesarchäologie/Koblenz/M. Gensty)

ing equipment, and bronze tableware. Sometimes riding horses were killed and buried in a separate grave pit near their master. Women were given gold jewellery and bronze tableware.

Grave goods of a horseman and noble landlord: Münstermaifeld, grave 164

The male grave 164 stands out among the early medieval graves of Münstermaifeld, Mayen-Koblenz district, through its elaborate tomb with a wooden chamber and its rich grave goods. It can be dated to the first decades of the 7th century. (Fig. 20–21) Discolouration of the soil and charred wood remains suggest that a wooden grave chamber had been built inside the grave pit.

According to the prevailing custom of the time, the man was buried with weapons considered a sign of his rank. Parts of grave goods made of organic materials were only preserved in the form of a few mineralized traces together with metals. They can nevertheless be deduced from the metallic components of the finds. On a wooden shield to the left of the dead person, an iron shield boss with a coniform cover and a mushroom-shaped pointed button had once been riveted. It protected the hand holding the iron shield grip on the inside. The lance was found in the southwest corner of the grave chamber. It consisted originally of a

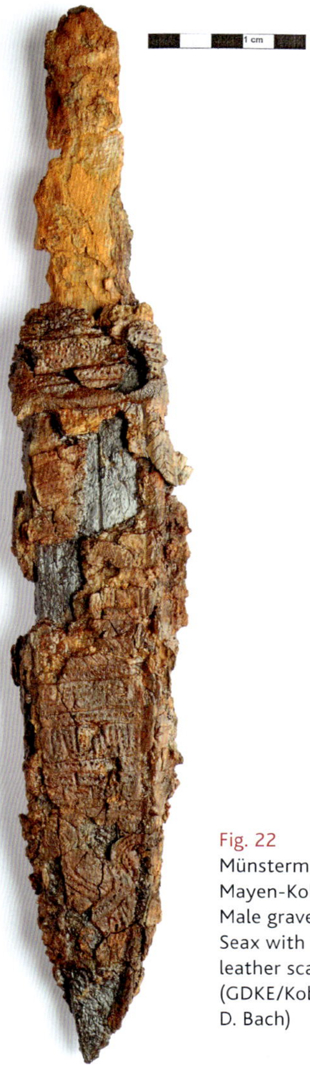

Fig. 22
Münstermaifeld, Mayen-Koblenz distr. Male grave 164. Seax with decorated leather scabbard. (GDKE/Koblenz/ D. Bach)

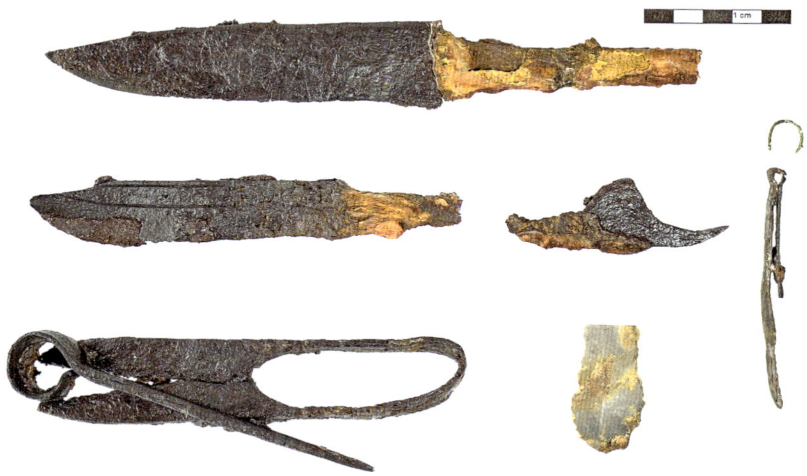

Fig. 23
Münstermaifeld, Mayen-Koblenz distr. Male grave 164. Contents of a pouch with knife, small razor blade, scissors, awl, fire steel with flint, and pincers. (GDKE/ Landesarchäologie/ Koblenz/D. Bach)

long wooden shaft, on which the surviving iron point was fixed with two big decorated bronze rivets. The double-edged long sword, the so-called spatha with an iron pommel hilt, was on the right side of the dead person. The remains of organic material adhering to the iron blade seem to suggest that the sword was originally kept in a wooden scabbard, covered on the outside with leather and lined on the inside with animal skin. The single-edged short sword, the so-called seax, had been placed in the pelvic area of the body. (Fig. 22) Major remains of the leather scabbard are preserved, and one can still make out the peculiar impressed decoration, which was probably coloured, consisting of geometrical patterns, rows of dots, and interlacing ornamentation towards the point. Only the silver thorn of a buckle with a shield-like base and three silver rivets remain of the dead man's belt. The corresponding buckle with fittings consisted of organic material and did not survive. Three more small silver rivets probably belonged to the belt pocket. It contained a man's typical personal effects: a knife, a shaving blade, an awl for working leather, scissors, a punch (fire steel) with flint stone, and pincers. (Fig. 23)

The riding equipment was on the left side of the body next to the shield. It consists of an iron snaffle and several decorative fittings and strap holders of bronze that were fixed to the leather straps of the bridle. (Fig. 24) They are decorated with Germanic animal-style ornaments.

In the mouth of the dead individual was a small gold coin (triens) known as »Charon's penny«. (Fig. 25) According to antique tradition, it was meant to guarantee the crossing into the realm of the dead. It is a so-called Merovingian *Monetärmünze* (monetary coin), which displays verso the master responsible for minting Medulfus (MEDULFO MO), and recto Campo Trecio (CAM*POTRE) as the place where the coin was minted. Today this would correspond to the old town of Trois-champs in the northern French department Haute-Marne.

A heavy bronze-cast drinking bowl with handle was found at the feet. (Fig. 26) The handled bowl, which reached Münstermaifeld as an imported item,

Fig. 24
Münstermaifeld, Mayen-Koblenz distr. Male grave 164. Snaffle with strap holder and decorative fittings of the bridle. (GDKE/Landes-archäologie/ Koblenz/D. Bach)

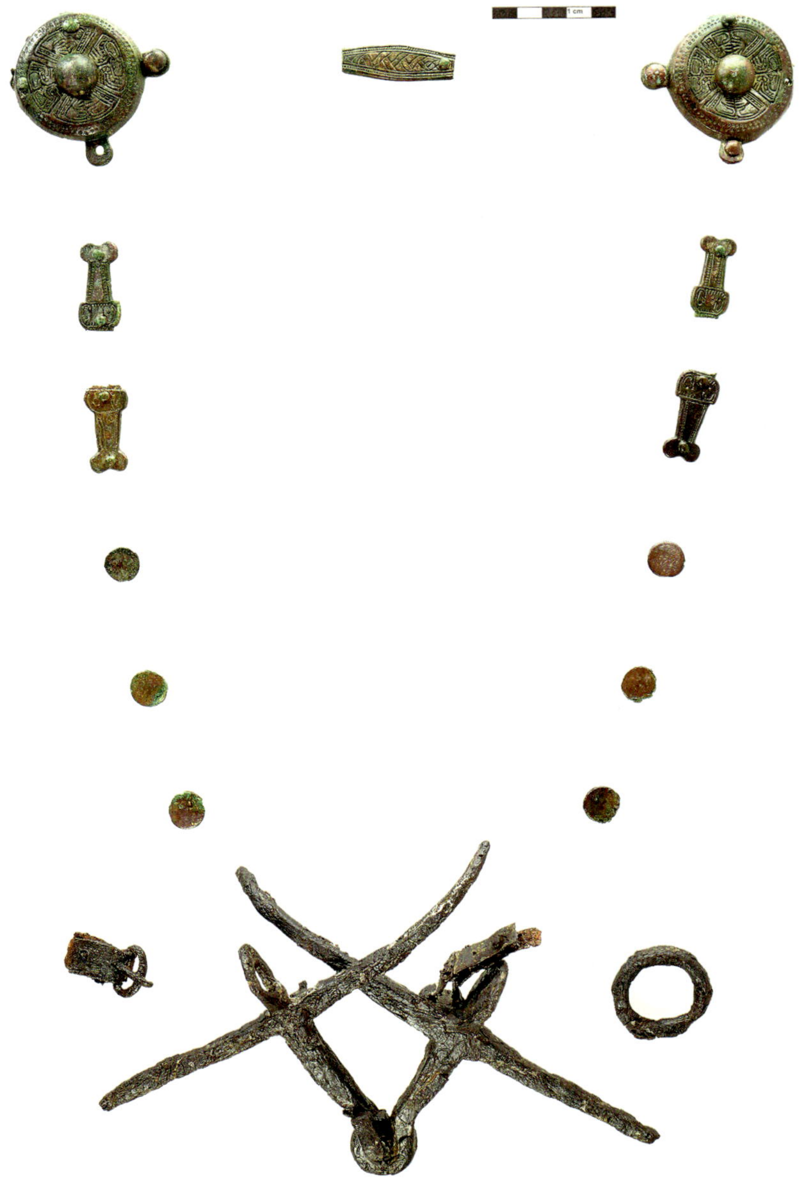

Fig. 25
Münstermaifeld, Mayen-Koblenz distr. Male grave 164. Merovingian monetary coin. Gold. (GDKE/ Landesarchäologie/ Koblenz/G. Forneck)

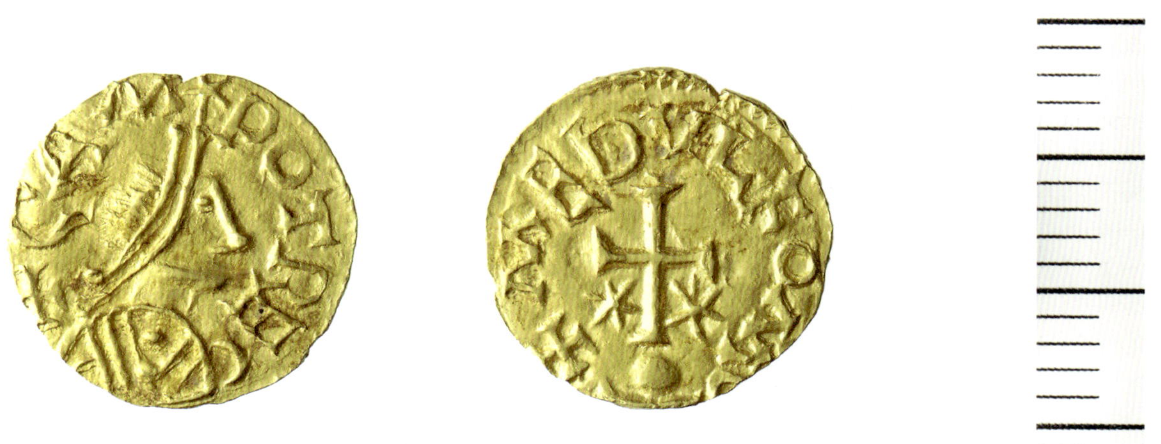

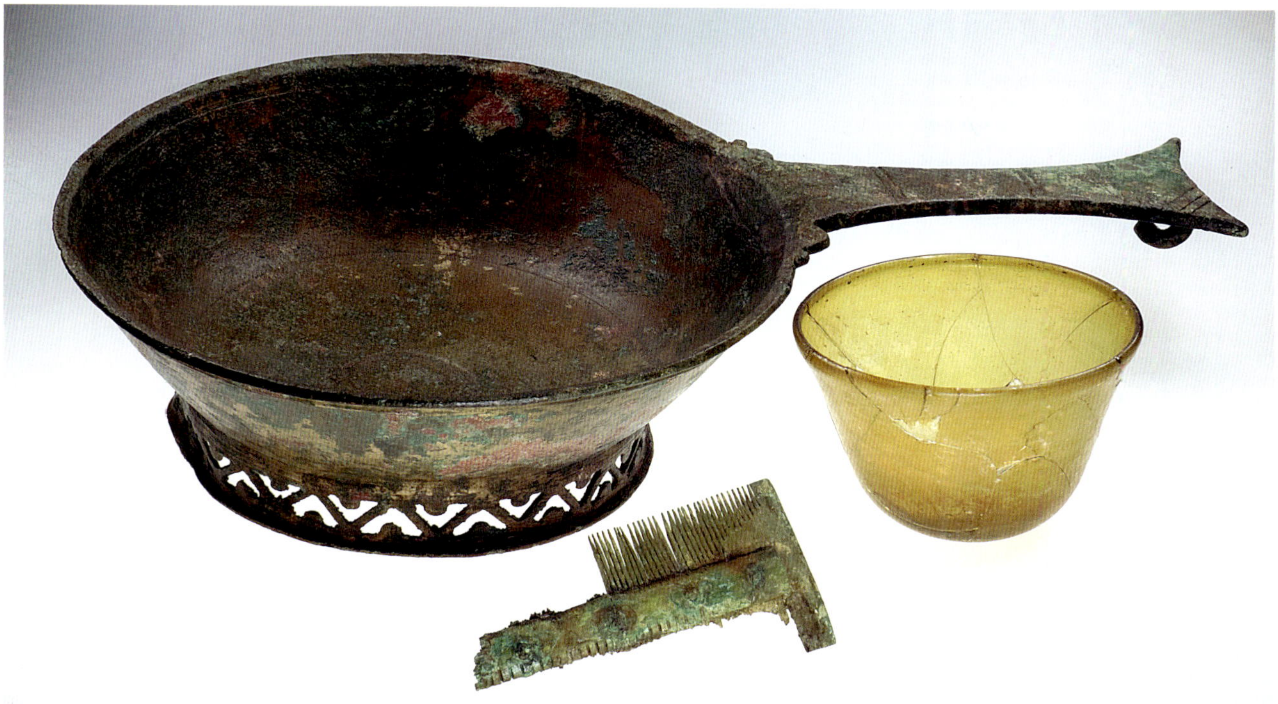

Fig. 26
Münstermaifeld, Mayen-Koblenz distr. Male grave 164. Bronze bowl with handle from a Byzantine workshop of the Mediterranean area, tumbler made of yellowish glass, and comb made from antler. (GDKE/Landesarchäologie/Koblenz/M. Neumann)

belongs to the so-called Coptic bronze tableware. The exact origin of the vessels is still a subject of debate. Egypt, Italy, and the eastern Mediterranean area have been suggested as regions where the bowl may have been manufactured. The bronze vessel certainly served various purposes, inter alia for washing one's hands before and after a meal. It therefore shows not only the far-reaching trade connections, but also the adoption of Mediterranean table manners within the Frankish leading class. Another drinking vessel of yellowish glass (so-called tumbler) and a double-toothed comb made from antlers were found in the bowl. Long, well-groomed hair was considered as a sign of strength and display of higher social status, especially among men.

The precious grave goods with a considerable number of weapons in grave 164 thus evidently single out the deceased as a member of the privileged local upper class. The addition of the horse bridle makes it clear that he was a horseman. The bronze tableware represents him as a host and thus as a noble landlord.

Grave goods of a woman from the wealthy upper class: Münstermaifeld, grave 108

Women were buried during Frankish times in their festive clothes with the corresponding jewellery for both clothing and body. The female grave 108 from the grave field of Münstermaifeld, Mayen-Koblenz district, which can be dated by the grave goods as being from the second half of the 7th century, is a good example. (Fig. 27) The position of the finds in grave 108 provides information about clothes and the way to wear them, and the quality of the finds indicates the social standing of the deceased. The woman could have been a noble landlady in her lifetime. This is suggested by the golden filigree disc fibula and the splendid silvery belt set. According to the anthropological examination of the skeleton remains, this was an adult woman who died when she was between 20 and 30 years old.

The woman was decorated with a pair of silver earrings. Only the left earring has survived intact, with just a few fragments of the right one. The earrings consisted of a wire-shaped loop with hook and eye clasp and a decorative double-leafed capsule on it. The deceased wore a silver finger ring on her left hand. The

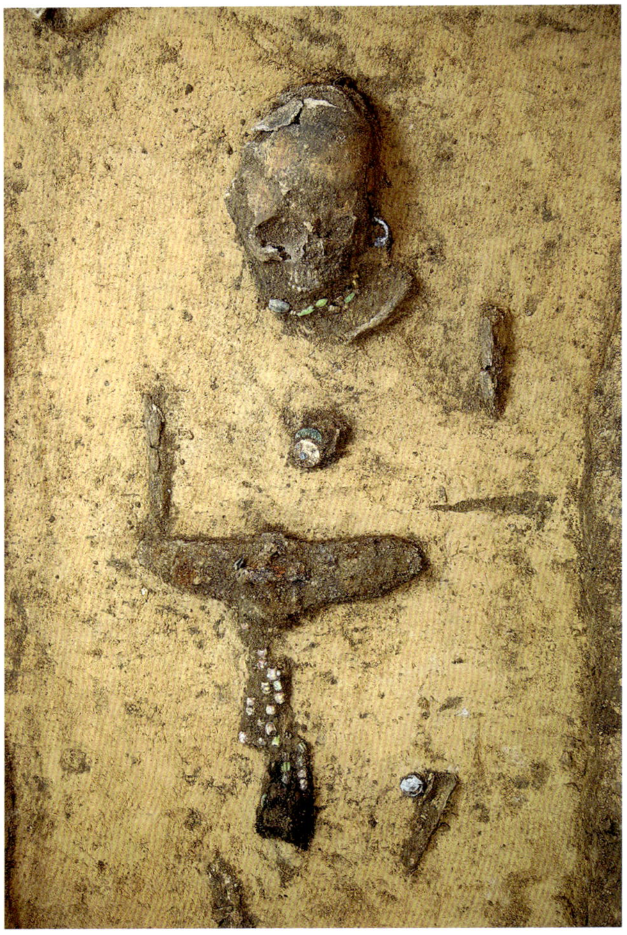

Fig. 27
Münstermaifeld, Mayen-Koblenz distr. Female grave 108 with customary dress and jewellery goods in the excavation finding. (GDKE/Landesarchäologie/Koblenz/M. Gensty)

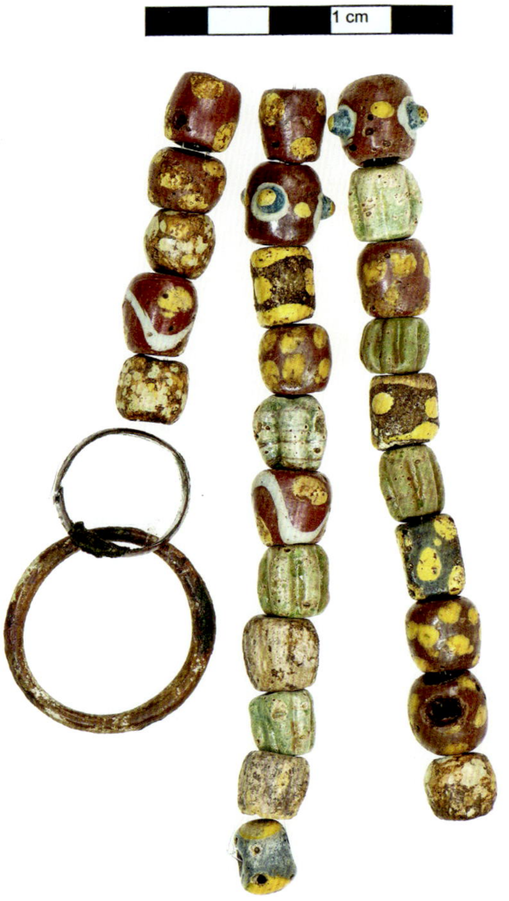

Fig. 28
Münstermaifeld, Mayen-Koblenz distr. Female grave 108. Pendant with three strands of glass beads and two bronze rings. (GDKE/Landesarchäologie/Koblenz/M. Neumann)

soldered round ornamental plate is decorated with rows of small punches at the rim. The necklace, whose beads did not go all round but reached perhaps up to the shoulder, was mostly strung with small yellow beads and green almond-shaped beads of opaque glass, together with a double-conical amber bead. A decorative pendant affixed to the centre of the belt consisted of three individual strands with glass beads of different sizes, many of them decorated in colour, plus two bronze rings. (Fig. 28)

At the height of the woman's chest was a filigree disc fibula. (Fig. 29) A twirled gold thread was applied round the edge and at the base of the bent sides of the golden cover sheet of the fibula. In the centre there is a dark blue glass pearl in a round setting. It is surrounded crosswise by four triangular settings with transparent light green glass inserts. The areas in between are filled with filigree ornaments consisting of U-shaped slings with rolled-up ends and small rings of twirled or smooth gold thread. The golden disc fibula originally held together a cape-like cloak belonging to the woman made of high-quality fabric. This is indicated by fragments of a delicate tissue in twill or satin weave still adhering to the iron needle at the back of the fibula.

The solid iron belt fitting with silver and brass damascening is the most striking find in the grave. (Fig. 30) It was attached to a leather belt by which the woman gathered her dress at waist level. The two-part fitting consists of a buckle with a triangular fitting profiled at the sides and a corresponding counter fitting of the same shape and size. The face sides of the set are extensively damascened with individual silver threads. Individual reticle groups and the thread-shaped symmetrical network in the silver-plated bases are made of brass and served decorative purposes. The fittings

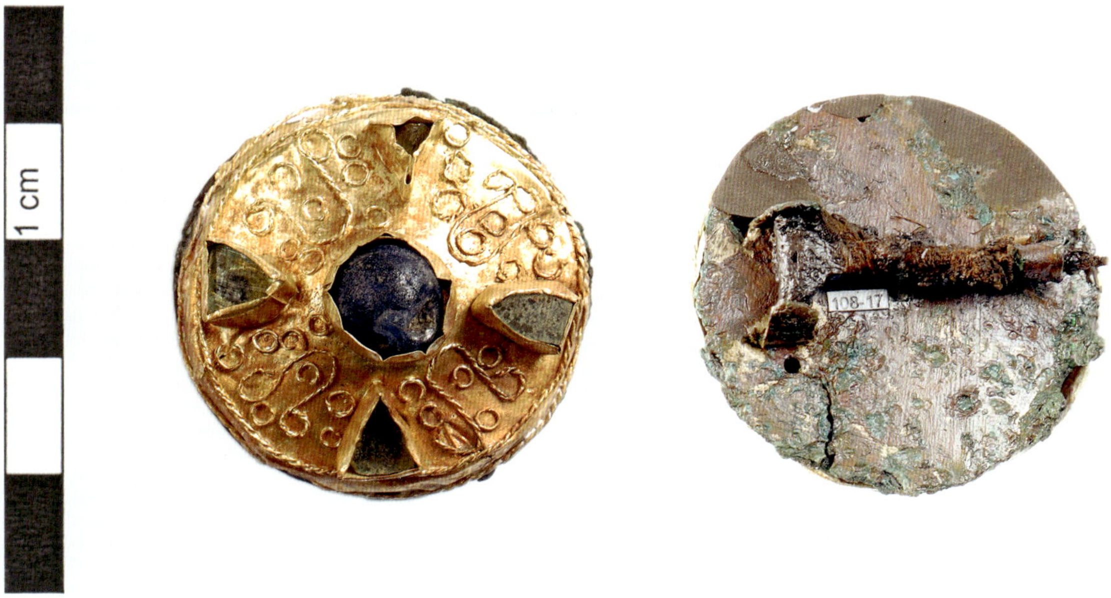

Fig. 29
Münstermaifeld, Mayen-Koblenz distr. Female grave 108. Filigree disc fibula. (GDKE/ Landesarchäologie/ Koblenz/D. Bach)

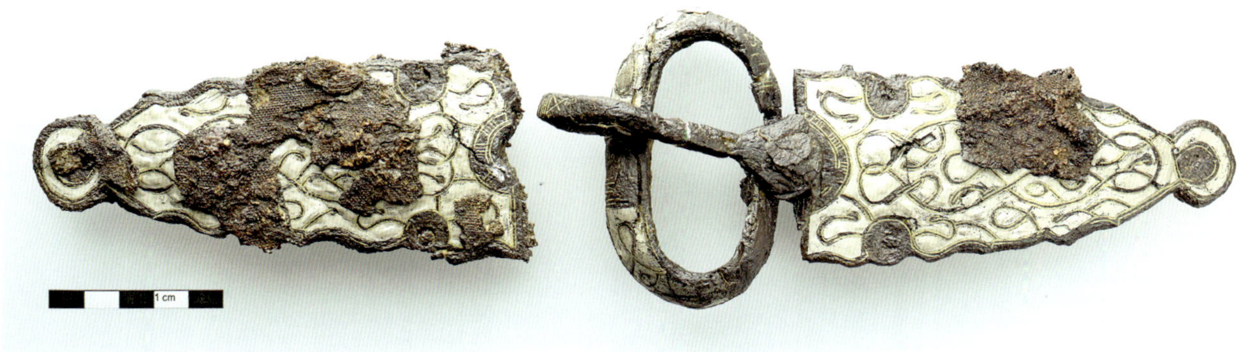

Fig. 30
Münstermaifeld, Mayen-Koblenz distr. Female grave 108. Two-part belt set made of iron with silver and brass damascene inlaying and textile remains. (GDKE/ Landesarchäologie/ Koblenz/D. Bach)

were fixed on the belt with three eyes cast on the backs. Only a few examples of belt fittings of this size from female graves are known from Frankish grave fields in Rhineland. They rather belonged to women's attire in the western Frankish area. This could indicate that the fitting or its owner came from today's northern France.

Male and female graves in the countryside with particularly rich grave goods probably belonged to the owners of larger farms. Sometimes, the leading family of a place can be traced over several generations. They sometimes established their own separate burial places at the edge of large grave fields, where memorials or first small churches were later built. Well-known examples are the richly endowed graves of Flonheim, Alzey-Worms district, which were discovered already in 1883 when a new church was built; the oldest grave from the time around 500 contained a sword with a gold-coated hilt (so-called gold hilt spatha) as a ceremonial weapon.

Grave goods and funeral rites originating in foreign lands

Grave goods of foreign origin, especially coins, cast (so-called Coptic) bronze vessels, and other luxury goods as well as accessories and decorations of women's apparel show the far-reaching trade connections or personal relations of the Frankish upper class. Specific forms among the grave goods and distinctive features of funeral customs could also give indications of the ethnic origins of the deceased. Especially in the row grave fields of Rhine-Hesse and the Anterior Palatinate, forms of fibulae and ceramics from the Elbe-Germanic cultural sphere appear repeatedly during the first half of the 6th century; as with the burial of horses and dogs, this circumstance led scholars to assume the presence of demographic groups from today's central Germany, i.e. probably mostly from Thuringia. Ceramic vessels of North Sea Germanic forms and the south-north orientation of graves are indications of either recently migrated or settled inhabitants nonetheless originating from Saxon or Anglo-Saxon areas in today's North Sea coastal area. These people were almost always quickly acculturated, so that the newly arrived Germanic groups of people can no longer be documented archaeologically after the second generation.

Since the late 4th century, the Romani usually buried their dead without grave goods. In towns and places with a remaining Romanic population, the Romani and Franks as well as newcomers of other Germanic origin mostly used common cemeteries or those which were close to each other, such that the Germanic people became accustomed to Christian burial traditions. With the growing influence of Christianity, the goods in the graves decreased from the middle of the 7th century onwards, since according to Christian ideas of the afterlife they were of no benefit for one's salvation. Consequently, people would thoroughly plunder any such graves, even those of their ancestors, looking for valuables and recyclable materials. The tradition of grave goods was only rarely continued far into the 8th century. At that time, most of the row grave fields were abandoned and the cemeteries were relocated next to the new churches erected in the settlements, unless these had been built on an already existing burial place, as in Münstermaifeld.

Bibliography

H. Ament, Die Franken im Rheinland. In: Merowingerzeit – Europa ohne Grenzen. Archäologie und Geschichte des 5. bis 8. Jahrhunderts. Ausstellungskatalog Berlin (Berlin 2007) 212–226.

B. Bienert, Merowingerzeitliche Besiedlung. Archäologische Befunde in den südlichen Rheinlanden. Geschichtlicher Atlas der Rheinlande IV/13 (Bonn 2008).

B. Bienert, Zur frühmittelalterlichen Besiedlung Triers und des Trierer Landes. In: H. H. Anton, A. Haverkamp (Hrsg.), 2000 Jahre Trier. Bd. 2. Trier im Mittelalter (Trier 1996) 119–159.

Ch. Engels, Das merowingische Gräberfeld Eppstein, Stadt Frankenthal (Pfalz). Internationale Archäologie 121 (Rahden/Westfalen 2012).

F.J. Felten, Antikes Erbe und germanische Eigenart. Archäologische Beiträge zur Geschichte des frühen Mittelalters. In: L. Clemens, F. J. Felten, M. Schnettger (Hrsg.), Kreuz – Rad – Löwe. Rheinland-Pfalz. Ein Land und seine Geschichte. Bd. 1. Von den Anfängen der Erdgeschichte bis zum Ende des Alten Reiches (Mainz 2012) 213–234.

M. Grünewald, U. Koch, A. Wieczorek, Zwischen Römerzeit und Karl dem Großen. Die frühmittelalterlichen Grabfunde aus Worms und Rheinhessen im Museum der Stadt Worms im Andreasstift. 3 Bde. (Lindenberg im Allgäu 2009).

L. Grunwald, Produktion und Warendistribution der Mayener Ware in spätrömischer und frühmittelalterlicher Zeit. In: Ch. Later, M. Helmbrecht, U. Jecklin-Tischhauser (Hrsg.), Infrastruktur und Distribution zwischen Antike und Mittelalter. Studien zu Spätantike und Frühmittelalter 8 (Hamburg 2015) 191–207.

U. Koch, Das frühmittelalterliche Gräberfeld von Mainz-Hechtsheim. Mainzer Archäologische Schriften 11 (Mainz 2011).

U. Leithäuser, Das merowingerzeitliche Gräberfeld Dirmstein, Kreis Bad Dürkheim. Universitätsforschungen zur Prähistorischen Archäologie 204 (Bonn 2011).

S. Ristow, Frühes Christentum im Rheinland. Die Zeugnisse der archäologischen und historischen Quellen an Rhein, Maas und Mosel. Jahrbuch 2006 des Rheinischen Vereins für Denkmalpflege und Landschaftsschutz (Köln, Münster 2007).

E. Saal, Das merowingerzeitliche Gräberfeld von Rhens, Kreis Mayen-Koblenz. Beiträge zur frühmittelalterlichen Chronologie an Mittelrhein und unterer Mosel. In: H.-H. Wegner (Hrsg.), Berichte zur Archäologie an Mittelrhein und Mosel 20 (Koblenz 2014) 157–485, Taf. 1–64.

A. Wieczorek, P. Perin, K. v. Welck, W. Menghin (Hrsg.), Die Franken – Wegbereiter Europas. Vor 1500 Jahren: König Chlodwig und seine Erben (Mainz 1996).

Wealth, power and salvation – The medieval grave field below Münsterplatz in Münstermaifeld

CLIFF ALEXANDER JOST

The imposing collegiate church and today's Catholic parish church of St. Martin and St. Severus rises in the centre of the city of Münstermaifeld in the Mayen-Koblenz district, visible from afar from the highest point of the Maifeld, an extremely fertile high plain of the Middle Rhine Basin. (Fig. 1) Today's church dates from the 12th to the 14th century, but its origins probably go back to the Merovingian period. According to a later tradition, the archbishop of Trier, Modoald, is said to have founded the church in the first half of the 7th century in honour of Saint Martin. To the south of the collegiate church there was a large medieval cemetery. An unknown number of graves had already been uncovered and cut into between 1840 and 1899 at the southern side of Münsterplatz square adjacent to the church (during house and sewer building works), and in 1962 north of the square within the transept of the church during central heating building works. In the process, individual early medieval grave goods were unearthed, mainly from the second half of the 6th century.

From 2008 to 2010, the Koblenz branch of the Department of Archaeology Rhineland-Palatinate examined a large section of the grave field in the course of the extension of Münsterplatz. Over an area of ca. 1500 m², ca. 530 graves could be documented, which were not only situated very close to each other, but in part also up to ten layers on top of each other. (Fig. 2) A boundary for the grave field was only found towards the east by the excavations, hence a considerably higher number of burials may be assumed. Most of the graves without grave goods date from the 9th to the 14th century. In 45 graves, however, Frankish grave goods from the time between the later 6th century and the first half of the 8th century were recovered. After that time, the tradition of grave goods was discontinued, just as in other places, because of the ever-growing influence of the Church. Garment components in the form of disc fibulae with representations of saints, crosses, and animals were found only in ten graves datable to the period from the 9th to the 11th century.

It was surprising that the Frankish burials of Münstermaifeld – except for some disturbances by earlier building measures at Münsterplatz and at the collegiate church – were mostly untouched. They hardly showed any traces of the planned opening and robbing of graves which was otherwise already so widespread in Rhineland in antiquity. Perhaps the sacrosanct position near the church protected the graves. It appears that the grave field was also spared plundering by professional treasure hunters and antiquarians, who were very active especially in the area of the Middle Rhine and Moselle during the second half of the 19th century.

Some of the Frankish graves were endowed with particularly precious grave goods. These not only show the high social rank of the deceased, but also the contacts and far-reaching trade connections of the local Merovingian upper class, which point mainly to the west of the Frankish Empire, but also to the south in the dominion of the Longobards in today's northern Italy, and also as far as the eastern Mediterranean area. The male members of the local leading family were buried in wooden chamber graves with a set of weapons and riding gear as status symbols distinguishing them as warriors and horsemen. Bronze tableware in the grave identified them as hosts and thus as noble landlords or heads of a farming community. The noble lady would stress the wealth of the family through her dress and jewellery, which is documented in these graves especially through golden filigree disc fibulae.

The position of the early medieval farm settlement associated with the grave field is unknown. It was probably in the direct vicinity of today's Münstermaifeld.

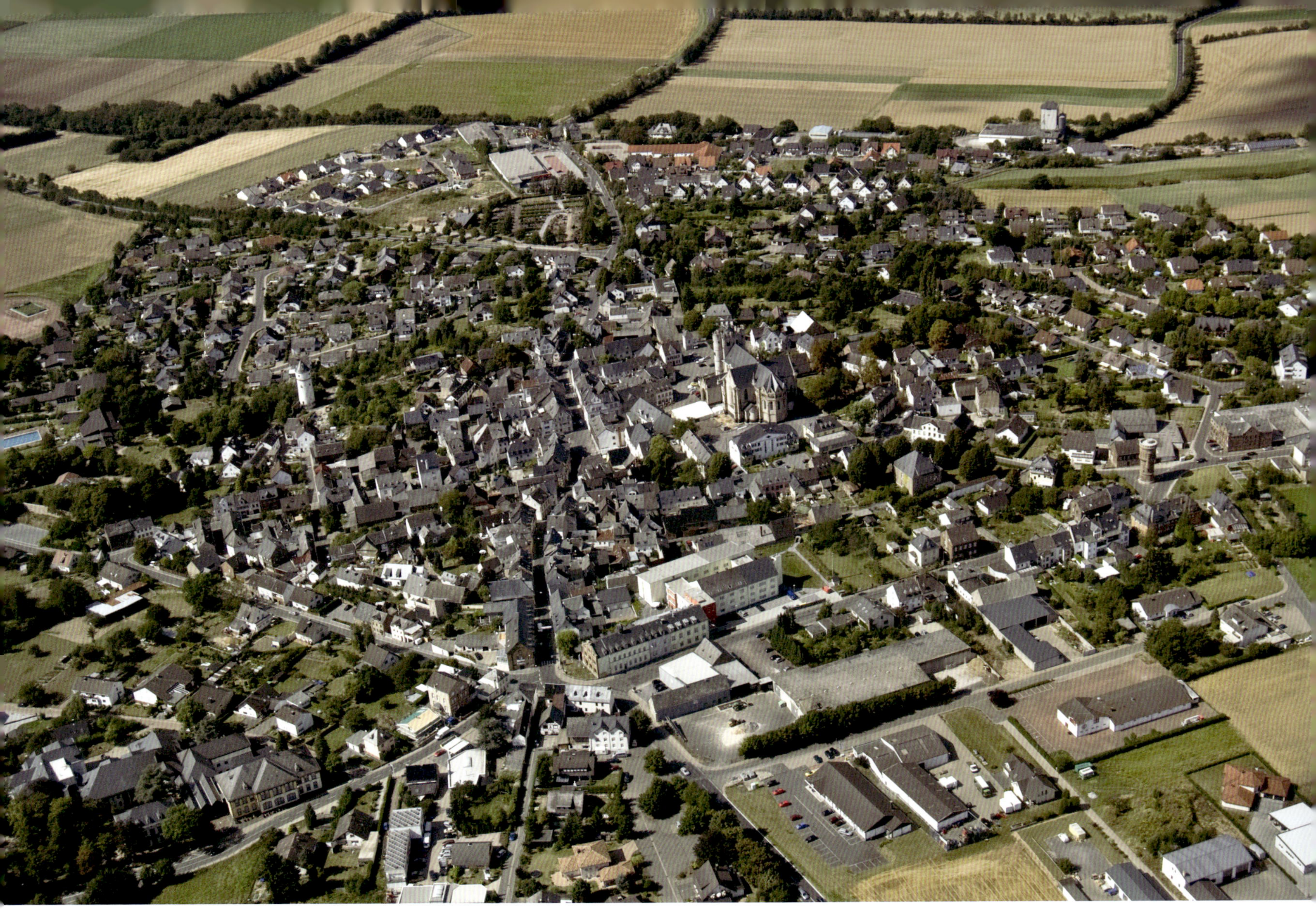

Fig. 1 Münstermaifeld, Mayen-Koblenz distr. Aerial photo of 2009. In the centre, the former collegiate church St. Martin and St. Severus' church with the excavation tent on the Münsterplatz located in the south. (C.A. Jost)

But it was most likely a member of the Merovingian leading class and early Christian, who erected a small grave chapel on the pre-existing cemetery, i.e. the original building beneath today's St. Martinskirche.

Snaffle and bridle from male grave 142

The male grave 142 was disturbed over its entire length by modern drains and sewer works. For this reason, the skeleton and the grave goods, which had once been placed on or next to the deceased, were lost. There can, however, be no doubt, judging from the grave structure of a large wooden chamber and the grave goods that were placed inside it – including a shield, a spearhead, a big bronze bowl, and an elaborate bridle (Fig. 3) – that this was the grave of an individual from the leading social class, probably a noble landlord. The grave can be dated to the decades around the year 600.

The iron snaffle bit and the metal fittings from the bridle were found in the grave chamber on the assumed right side of the body. The leather straps from the bridle have not survived. The structure of the bridle can nevertheless be reconstructed quite reliably on the basis of the find situation of the iron snaffle, strap holders, small buckles, and metallic decorations. (Fig. 4) The iron snaffle is a full cheek snaffle with a two-part (i.e. single-jointed) mouthpiece. The mouthpiece and snaffle still show remains of a decoration of circumferential grooves. The snaffle bit of the mouth-

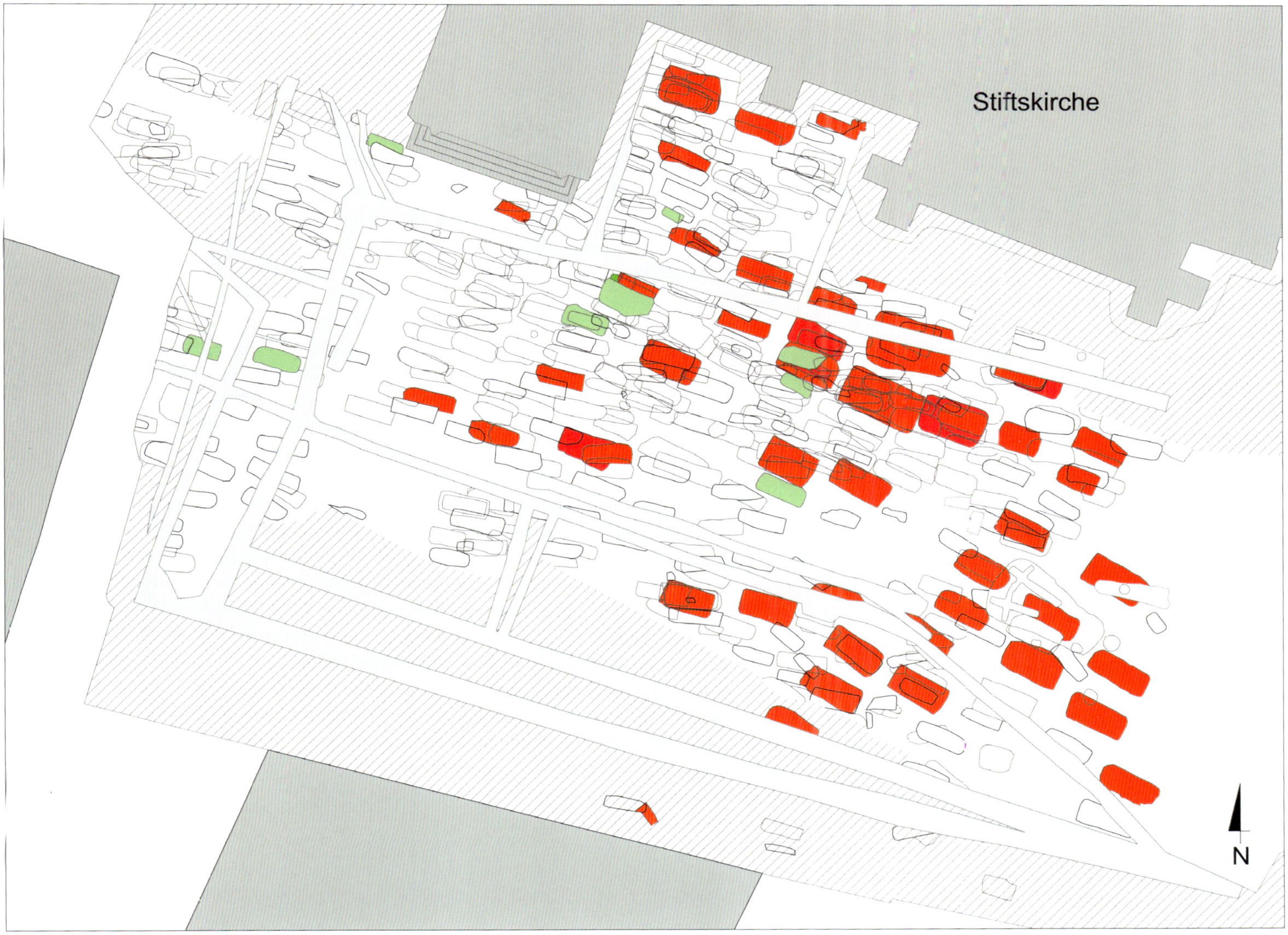

piece is 13 cm long and corresponds to that of a large horse. The long shanks on the side were meant to prevent the mouthpiece from shifting in the mouth. The upper halves of the shanks are bent slightly backwards and end in small coniform pointed buttons. The strap holders for the reins were fixed to the snaffle in the outer horizontal eyes of the extended mouthpiece. The strap holders for the cheek strap of the driving bridle were hung in these eyes at right angles to the mouthpiece at the back of the shanks.

The fittings of the bridle are cast from bronze and partly tin or silver-plated. The decoration was done in chip-carving and punching technique. (Fig. 5) The two strap-cross fittings with a round base plate and four rivet holders placed eccentrically were placed left and right of the horse's head at the crossing of the cheek and neck strap and the brow and throat strap. A large decorative rivet with a grooved edge is mounted in the centre of the base plate. Around it, there is a chip-carved four-field ornament bordered by crosspieces with step, interlacing and animal claw patterns, and at the edge of the outside we find a ribbon filled with a step pattern. The three oblong, symmetrically-shaped decorative fittings with fish-tail ends were fixed in the middle on the brow strap running at right angle across the forehead, and at the sides of the left and right cheek strap. They are silver-plated and decorated with small circular and triangular punches. The decorations of the head bridle also include 17 bronze rivets with a flat disc hat, which were affixed in groups of two and three on

Fig. 2
Münstermaifeld, Mayen-Koblenz distr. The map of the 2008 –2010 excavations shows a dense occupancy of the graveyard used for a long time, with graves close to and on top of each other. The graves with Frankish grave goods of the late 6th to the first half of the 8th century are marked red, the graves with disc fibulae from the 9th to the first half of the 11th century are marked green. (GDKE/Landes-archäologie/Koblenz/ C. A. Jost, M. Gensty)

Fig. 3
Münstermaifeld, Mayen-Koblenz distr. Snaffle and harness from male grave 142. (GDKE/Landesarchäologie/Koblenz/D. Bach)

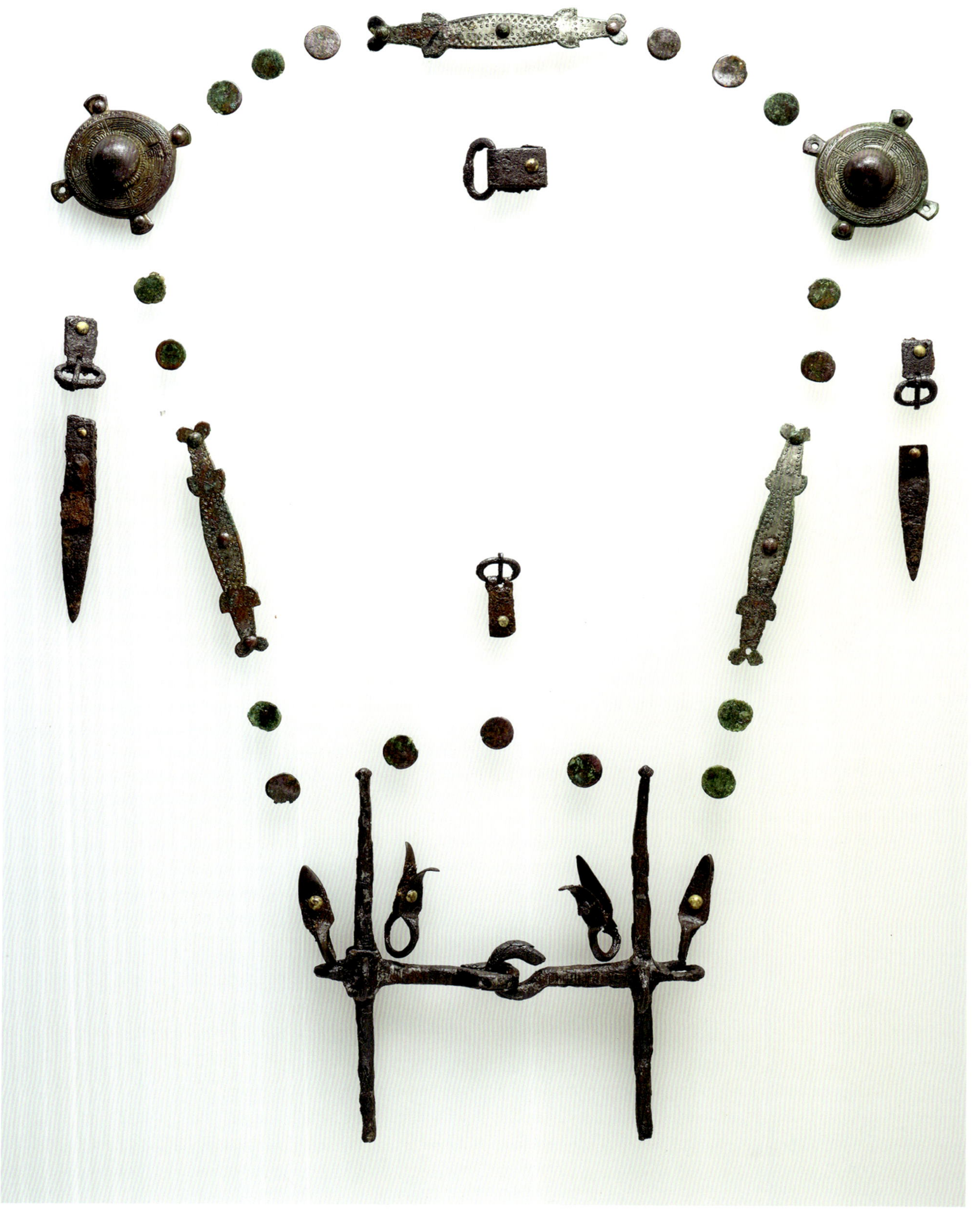

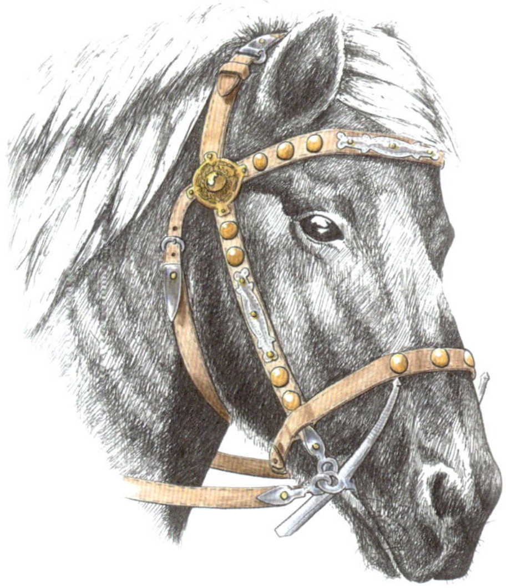

Fig. 4
Münstermaifeld, Mayen-Koblenz distr. Reconstruction of the harness from grave 142. (GDKE/Landesarchäologie/Koblenz/M. Meinen)

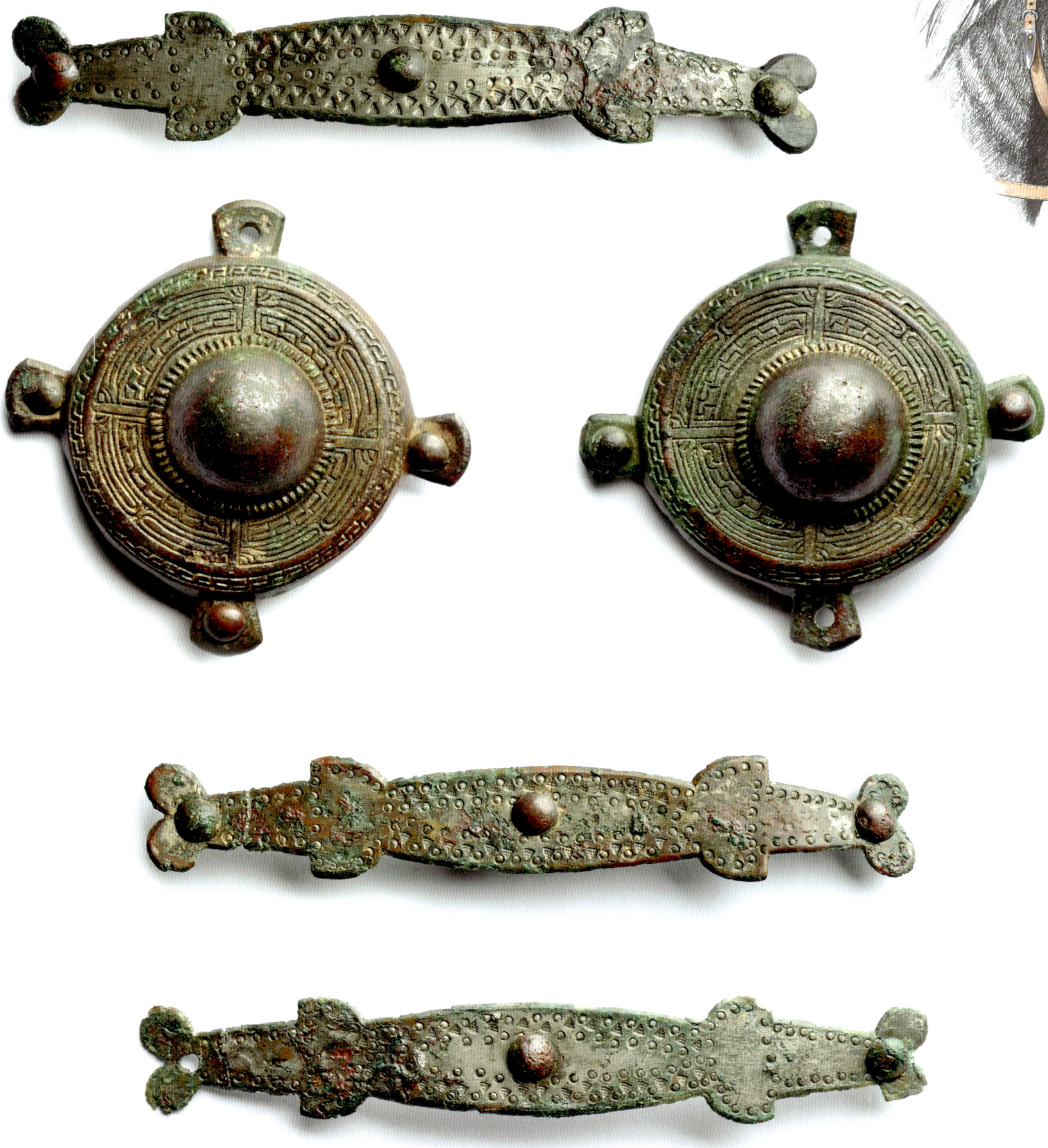

Fig. 5
Münstermaifeld, Mayen-Koblenz distr. Strap cross fittings and decorative fittings of the harness from grave 142. Length of the decorative fittings approx. 13 cm. (GDKE/Landesarchäologie/Koblenz/D. Bach)

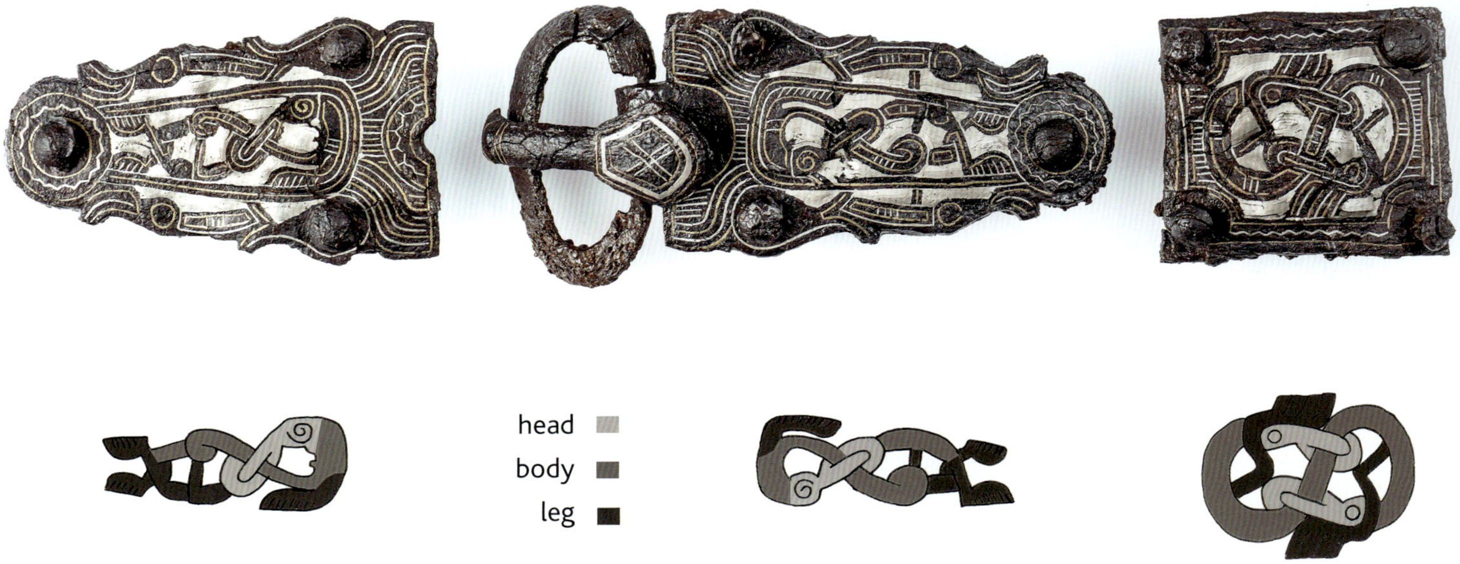

Fig. 6 Münstermaifeld, Mayen-Koblenz distr. Three-part belt set made of iron with silver and brass damascening from male grave 198. Beneath: schematic drawing of the animal pictures. Length of the triangular counter-fitting (left) 7.8 cm. (GDKE/Landesarchäologie/Koblenz/Photo: D. Bach, Graphic design: M. Meinen)

the left and right cheek strap, on the brow strap, and possibly on the nose strap. An iron strap eyelet with a rectangular fitting was probably riveted to the neck strap, while three small iron buckles with a single-rivet rectangular fitting were apparently used for buckling the chin strap below the chin of the horse, and the throat strap on both sides of the horse's head. The latter are combined with two iron strap-end fittings.

The horse's harness from grave 142 is particularly important because it is complete and the find position of the objects was exactly documented. During the excavation, the snaffle bit and the bridle decoration were plastered and retrieved en bloc and prepared solely in the restoration workshop under laboratory conditions.

Belt set in three parts with animal ornaments from male grave 198

The only dress elements preserved in the graves of males are the metal buckles and belt fittings. These were subject to fast-changing fashion trends and are therefore also an important find group for dating purposes. In the 7th century, wide waist belts with three-piece sets of fittings were very popular.

The set from the waist belt of the man of grave 198 (Fig. 6), decorated in the so-called Germanic animal style (Animal Style II), is to be dated to the time around or shortly after the middle of the 7th century. The three-piece belt set consists of a buckle with fitting, counter fitting, and back fitting. The buckle and counter fitting are triangular with profiled sides, whereas the back fitting is square. The belt fittings are forged from iron and the front sides damascened in two colours with inserts of silver and brass. The shining decorations made a particularly effective contrast with the iron base.

The central motif of the damascene inlaying is an animal style decoration. The ornamental animal depictions stand out from the damascened silver background: the internal designs were done with fine silver and brass wires. A backward-looking animal, biting its own body, fills the central zone of the buckle and counter buckle fitting, which is surrounded by a U-shaped frame. The animal head is marked by the eye in the form of a spiral and the two long-stretched jaws, clamping the body. The upper jaw bites over the lower jaw, which is turned back towards the top. The neck and body of the animal are shown as a wide band with individual horizontal lines, twisted around itself as if it were plaited. The animal legs consist of four thighs ending in three feet with claws. The two outer areas of the fittings are each filled with two animal heads, the contours of which follow the edge of the profiling of the fitting. The animal heads can be recognized mainly by the big round eyes – they are marked by rivet caps on the heads in front – and by the wide-open mouths with the jaws turned upwards and downwards. The animal ornaments of the square back fitting show two animals entwined in the form of a figure of eight. The picture zone is framed on the long sides by a wave band, and on the narrow sides by striped damascening. The four rivets on the back fitting only served as a decoration, just like the rivets on the buckle and the counter buckle. The fittings were attached to the belt on the undersides with flange eyes. The width of the belt strap (3.5 – 4.5 cm) can be inferred from the inside dimension of the buckle and the width of the fittings. Attached to the belt was a pocket for everyday objects as well as the scabbard of a single-edged long sword (so-called broad seax).

Broad seax with fittings of the scabbard and by-knife from male grave 287

During the 7th century, the seax became the prevailing weapon of the Frankish man. One can ascertain that it was highly esteemed due to the scabbards, which were now often richly decorated with ornamental and edge rivets. One sample of remarkable quality is the broad seax from male grave 287. (Fig. 7) It can be dated to the time around or shortly after the middle of the 7th century.

On both sides of the blade, the seax is decorated with an interlacing ornament, which is extremely rare in Rhineland. The interlacing decorations are triple on the front side and double on the back; they run near the back edge of the sword and are set between two decorative grooves which underline the form of the seax blade. The blade of the broad seax is 41.5 cm long and 5.0 cm wide. The hilt is quite short (12.5 cm) and meant for wielding the weapon single-handedly. What has survived are major organic remains of both the hilt

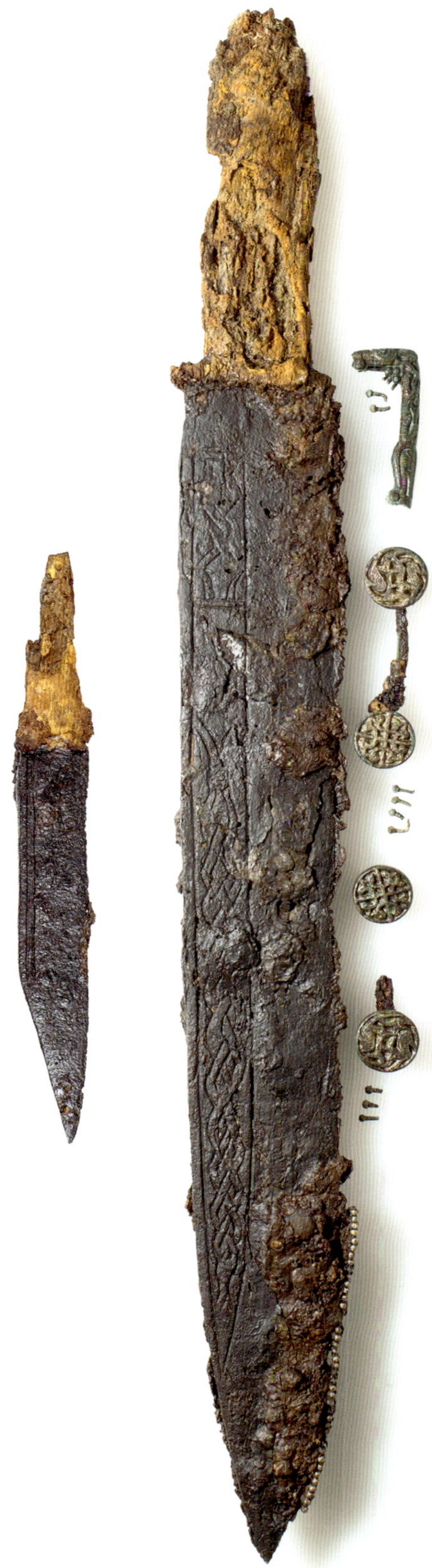

Fig. 7
Münstermaifeld, Mayen-Koblenz distr. Broad seax with decorated blade, fittings of the sword scabbard, and the so-called by-knife from male grave 87. Total length of seax: 54 cm, total length of knife: 21 cm. (GDKE/Landesarchäologie/Koblenz/D. Bach)

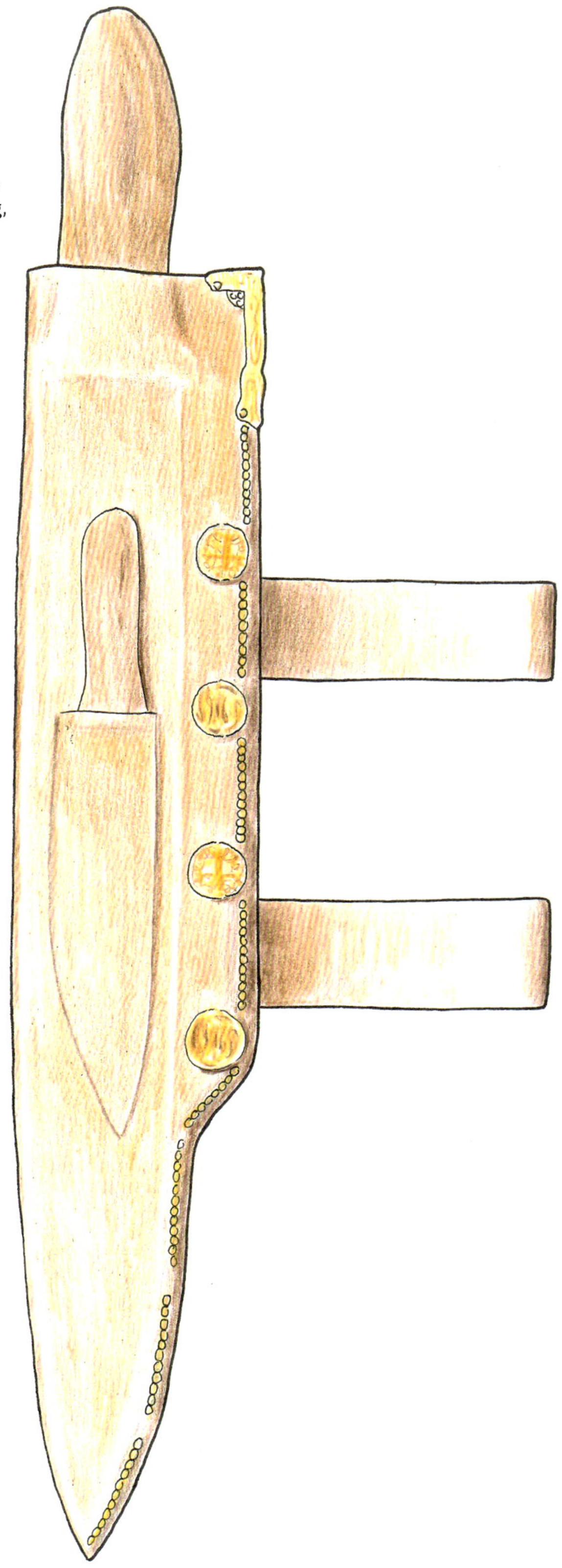

Fig. 8
Münstermaifeld, Mayen-Koblenz distr. Reconstruction of the seax scabbard from grave 287 with bronze decorative rivets, edge fitting, and so-called by-knife. (GDKE/ Landesarchäologie/Koblenz/ M. Meinen)

wood at the hilt tang and the leather of the scabbard, which during restorations were preserved mainly on the back of the blade.

The richly decorated scabbard consisted of a broad leather strip folded round the back of the blade and held together with a seam of variable width by many small bronze rivets on the side of the cutting edge. The upper end of the widened scabbard seam was protected by a rectangular bronze edge-fitting. On the front side, it has a decoration with interlacing ornament, which was cast together with it and ends in a long-stretched animal head on the longer side of the angle fitting. Four big bronze rivets, decorated alternatively with a cross and an animal ornament, served for fixing two iron carrier handles on the scabbard. They held the two carrier straps needed for attaching the scabbard to the belt. (Fig. 8)

In the grave, the seax was placed on the right side of the deceased near his feet, together with the belt and a belt pocket. A 21 cm long knife, found directly on the seax blade, is to be regarded as a so-called by-knife. In the 7th century, the knife was no longer worn in the belt pocket as before, but in a knife sheath fixed on the seax scabbard, where it was always ready for use.

Filigree disc fibulae from female graves 313, 181, and 256

In the 7th century, women would close their cape-like cloak with a single large disc fibula, as in the Mediterranean area. The fibulae were not only fashionable items of jewellery, but also status symbols. Ladies of the wealthy upper class adorned themselves with golden disc or quatrefoil fibulae.

The structure of the gold disc fibulae is always in two parts: a thin golden cover foil was fixed on a bronze base plate with the needle required for pinning it to the cloak. This foil was decorated on the front side with golden filigree wire – hence the name filigree disc fibulae – and coloured stone and glass inserts in soldered box settings.

The filigree disc fibulae from the graves of Münstermaifeld were found in dress position in the centre of the chest. Only the quatrefoil fibula from female grave 313 had been displaced and damaged by a bell casting pit of the 16th-17th century that had been built over the

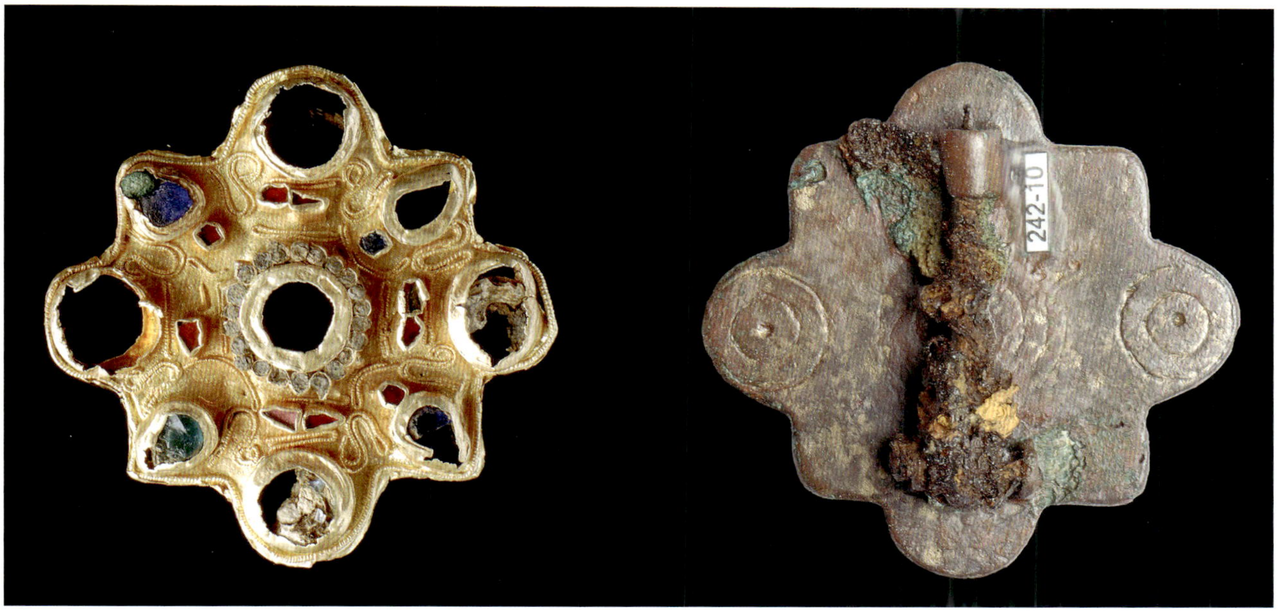

Fig. 9
Münstermaifeld, Mayen-Koblenz distr. Quatrefoil filigree fibula from female grave 313. Golden cover foil, length 4.4 cm. Bronze base plate, length 4.5 cm. (GDKE/ Landesarchäologie/Koblenz/ D. Bach)

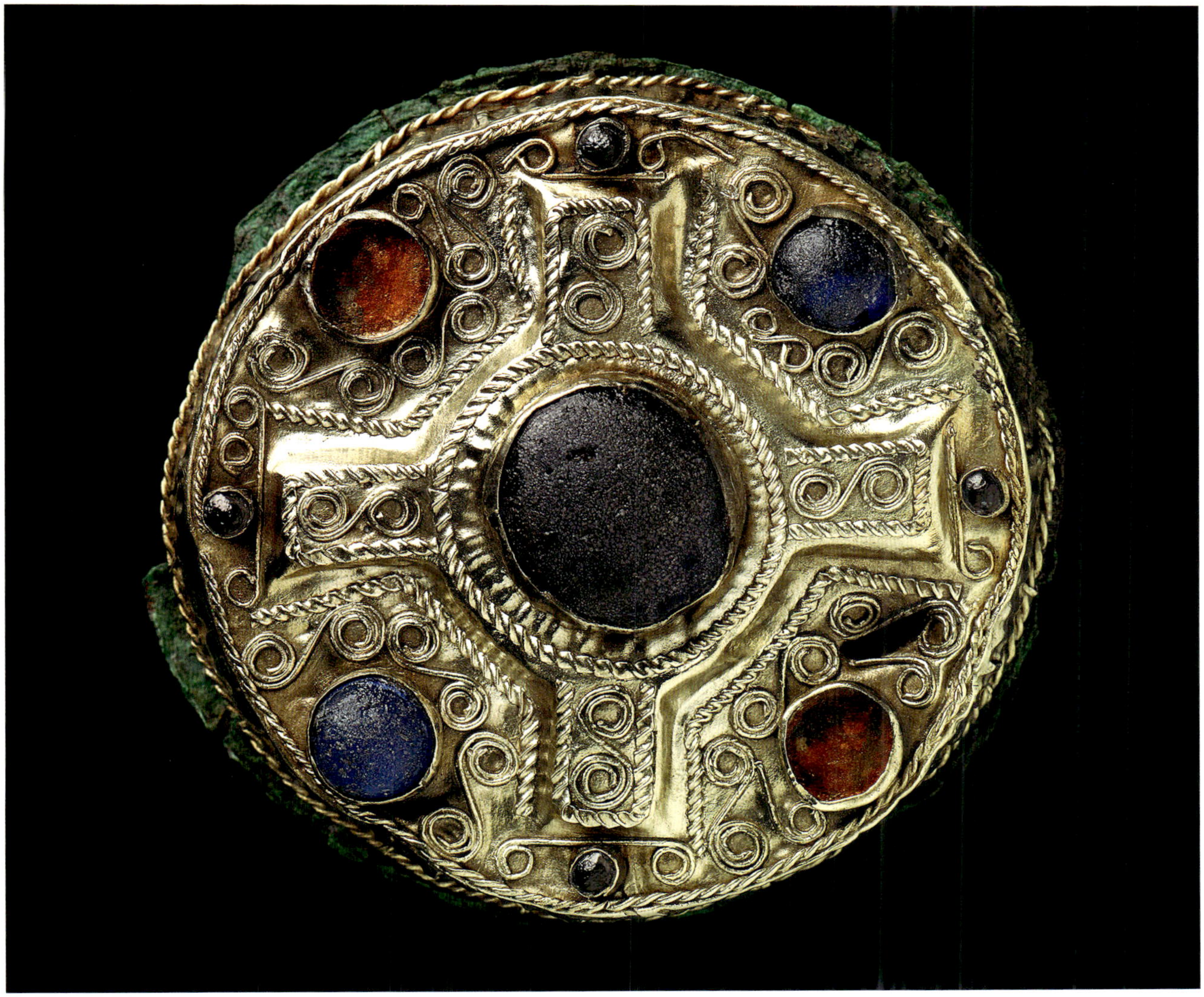

Fig. 10
Münstermaifeld, Mayen-Koblenz distr. Filigree disc fibula with cross motif from female grave 181. Diameter 4.2 cm. (GDKE/ Landesarchäologie/Koblenz/ W. Baumann)

Fig. 11
Münstermaifeld, Mayen-Koblenz distr. Small filigree disc fibulae worn as a pair from female grave 256. Diameter 1.9 cm and 2.4 cm. (GDKE/Landesarchäologie/Koblenz/D. Bach)

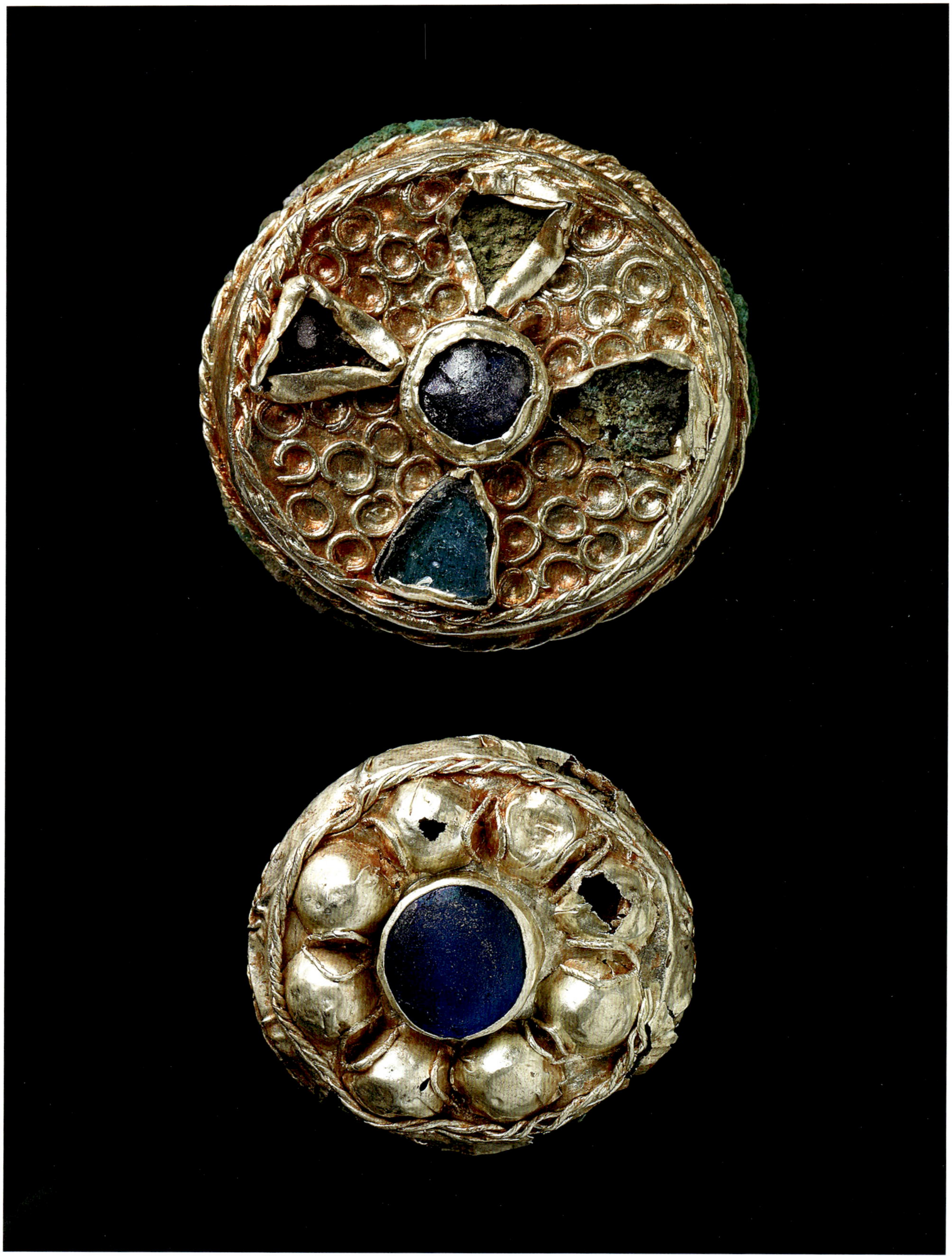

grave. The base plate of the fibula and the cover foil decorated with golden notched filigree wire were found in the grave separated from each other. (Fig. 9) Most of the coloured glass and stone inserts have fallen out. The round setting in the centre is surrounded by a ring of 22 small pipe settings. All the inserts are missing. Round and drop-shaped settings are fixed in the semi-circular bulges and corners of the quatrefoil. Three of them hold remains of inserts, one of turquoise glass and two of blue glass. Only ten of the former twelve symmetrically arranged small triangular and square settings in the central section of the fibula have survived. They are filled with inserts of red garnet, one of them with blue glass.

The circular disc fibula from grave 181 (Fig. 10) displays reduced colours. The round inserts all consist of dark blue glass. The front side of the fibula shows as its main motif a plastically formed symmetrical cross, which is probably to be regarded as a Christian symbol of salvation. The gold ground is covered with spiral loops of smooth gold wire. A twirled gold wire is arranged around the circular glass insert in the middle, around the cross and also around the edge of the fibula at the cover foil, as well as at the base of the wavy side foil.

The two small filigree disc fibulae from grave 256 (Fig. 11) can be dated to the early 8th century. The edge and the side foil at the base are decorated with a twirled gold wire. The front side of one of the fibulae shows a cruciform decoration, consisting of a central round setting with a dark blue glass insert and of four triangular settings with two inserts of dark green and red-brown glass that are still intact. The areas in between are densely covered with small rings of smooth gold wire. The second fibula has a blue glass insert in the middle, which is surrounded by eight hemispheric hollow studs made of gold foil. The two small fibulae were originally joined by a fine chain made of silver wire. Worn as a pair, this would correspond to the fashion trend of the late Merovingian period in the Rhineland area.

Disc fibula with picture of a falconer from female grave 147

This extraordinary disc fibula with figurative decoration on the silver cover foil from female grave 147 was also used as a cloak clasp. (Fig. 12) The remains of the skeleton and the precious grave goods retrieved are indicative of the grave of an elderly lady who died around the middle or in the third quarter of the 7th century. Her dress with one single fibula corresponded to the fashion of the time.

The disc-shaped pressed-foil fibula has a diameter of 4.8 cm. The round base plate and the 1.0 cm wide foil strip at the edge setting are made of bronze, while the needle with the spiral spring at the back is made of iron. The front side of the fibula is a silver foil in which the picture of a horseman with his falcon was impressed convexly with a pressing mould. This is perhaps the earliest figural depiction of a falconer in Central Europe. The picture is relatively naturalistic and detailed. Elements of the so-called Germanic animal style are missing. Whilst the casing of the Münstermaifeld fibula was most probably manufactured by a local craftsman, the decorated pressed foil possibly reached the region as an import. There can be no doubt, however, that the artist had access to a model for his picture, presumably from the late antique and early Byzantine cultural circle of the Mediterranean area.

The medallion-like ornamental foil shows (in profile to the left) an unarmed horseman on his galloping stallion with a raptor on his hand. The picture is framed by an imprinted beaded border. At the lower edge of the picture, a horizontal bar resting on two short vertical supports forms the base for the group of figures. The rider appears in an upright position with a somewhat larger than life head. His angular chin has no beard and his wavy hear reaches down his neck. The trunk of the rider is shown in a simplified manner, with the arms looking somewhat awkward. The strongly angled arm in front holds the bridle, the one at the back, more extended, holds the bird on his hand. The left leg is covered with closely fitting trousers, the foot is in a half-high bucket top boot.

The horse is shown in a galloping jump. The ears are erect, the eye and the mouth are wide open. The mane is carefully and strikingly groomed. One can recognize the chest strap of the harness with a round decorative plaque (phalera) on the side and a waist belt going around the rear of the horse. On the side of the horse, below the rider, a ring-shaped object is hanging down, possibly a stirrup.

The bird sitting on the arm of the rider behind his back is characterized as a raptor by its hooked beak.

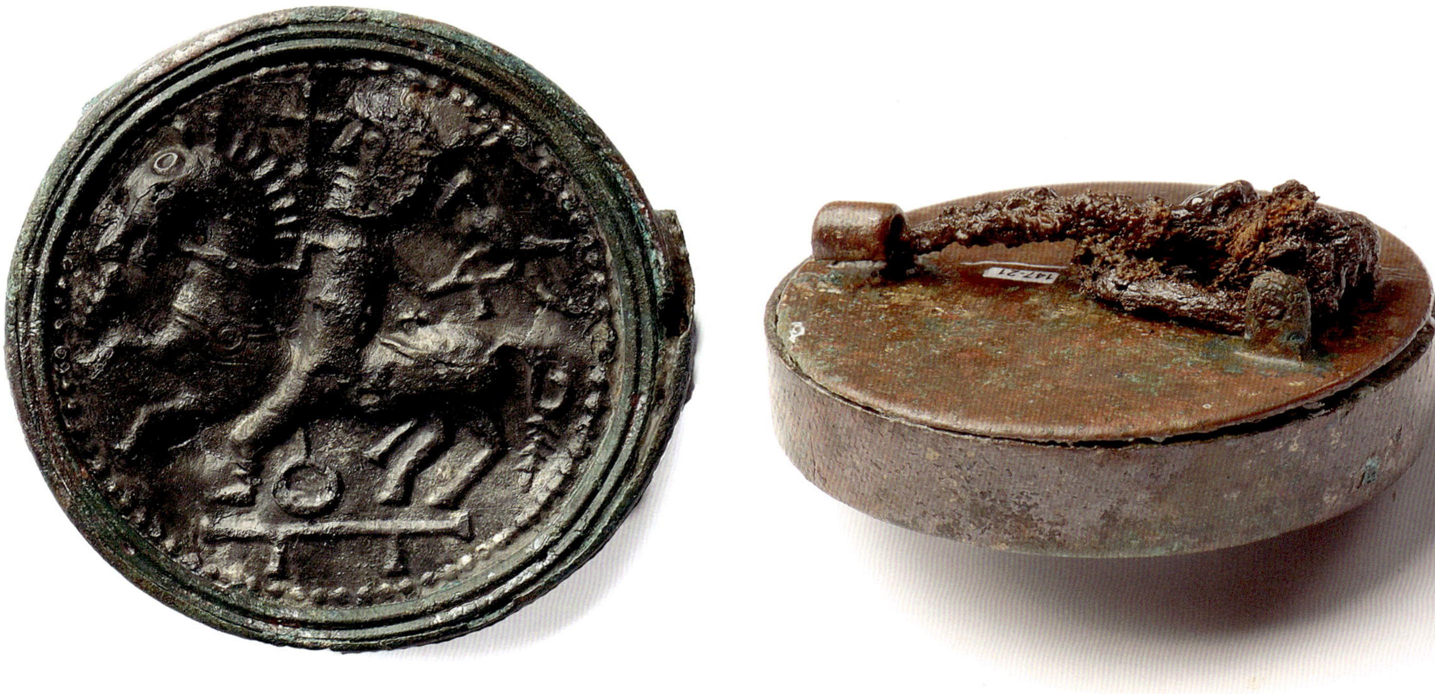

Fig. 12
Münstermaifeld, Mayen-Koblenz distr. Disc-shaped pressed-foil fibula with representation of a falconer from female grave 147. Diameter 4.8 cm. Front and back. (GDKE/Landesarchäologie/Koblenz/D. Bach)

Its upright position, the long retrices and the pointed flight feathers could indicate a falcon, a raptor particularly suitable for hawking on horseback. The leather straps of the jess by which the rider holds the hunting bird also seem to be depicted.

The Münstermaifeld fibula evidently shows a detail from a hunting scene. The hunt, the horse, and the falcon reflect the status of the horseman. The motif of the noble hunter on horseback, who ostentatiously carries the hunting falcon on his extended arm, is linked to similar figural depictions known from late antique mosaics of the western Mediterranean coast of North Africa from Carthage and Hergla (second half of the 5th to the early 6th century), or from the high and late Middle Ages, for instance on the Bayeux Tapestry (second half of the 11th century) or in the Falcon Book of emperor Frederic II (1194–1250) and in the Codex Manesse (first half of the 14th century). The motif of the picture is so far unique for the Merovingian period. The frequent mention of falconry and hawking birds in the Germanic collections of laws from the 6th – 8th century, as well as bones of raptors among grave goods in some opulently endowed male and female graves of that time, are an indication that hunting with hawking birds was very popular during the Merovingian period, especially among the distinguished leading class.

On the basis of other early medieval representations of horsemen, we can be quite certain that the image also had a religious meaning. For the Münstermaifeld fibula, the symbols added to the figure of the rider, i.e. the cross as a sign of salvation in front of the rider and the two palm twigs before and behind the horse, certainly imply a religious reference. Here, a Christian ruler or even Christ himself is visibly depicted as a heroic hunter. The former owner was certainly aware of the Christian meaning of the precious fibula and used it on purpose as her jewellery, thus not only demonstrating her high social rank but also her religious belief.

Bibliography

H. Ament, Die archäologischen Funde des frühen Mittelalters aus dem westlichen Deutschland im Museum für Vor- und Frühgeschichte Berlin. Staatliche Museen zu Berlin – Preußischer Kulturbesitz. Museum für Vor- und Frühgeschichte. Bestandskatalog 10 (Berlin 2006) 154–157, Taf. 56, 1–13.

U. Back, Frühmittelalterliche Grabfunde beiderseits der unteren Mosel. BAR International Series 532 (Oxford 1989), 166–169, Taf. 28–29, 1–3.

C. A. Jost, Mittelalterliche Bauhütte und Friedhof in Münstermaifeld. Archäologie in Deutschland 3, 2009, 54–55.

C. A. Jost, Vor Grabraub bewahrt: kostbare Funde im Schutz der Kirche. Archäologie in Deutschland 1, 2010, 52.

C. A. Jost, A depiction of a falconer on a disc brooch of the 7th century from the cemetery of Münstermaifeld, District of Mayen-Koblenz, south-western Germany. In: K.-H. Gersmann, O. Grimm (eds.), Premodern Falconry and Bird Symbolism – Interdisciplinary and Practical Considerations: The Global Perspective in Relation to Northern Europe (Schleswig 2017, im Druck).

THE MIDDLE AGES

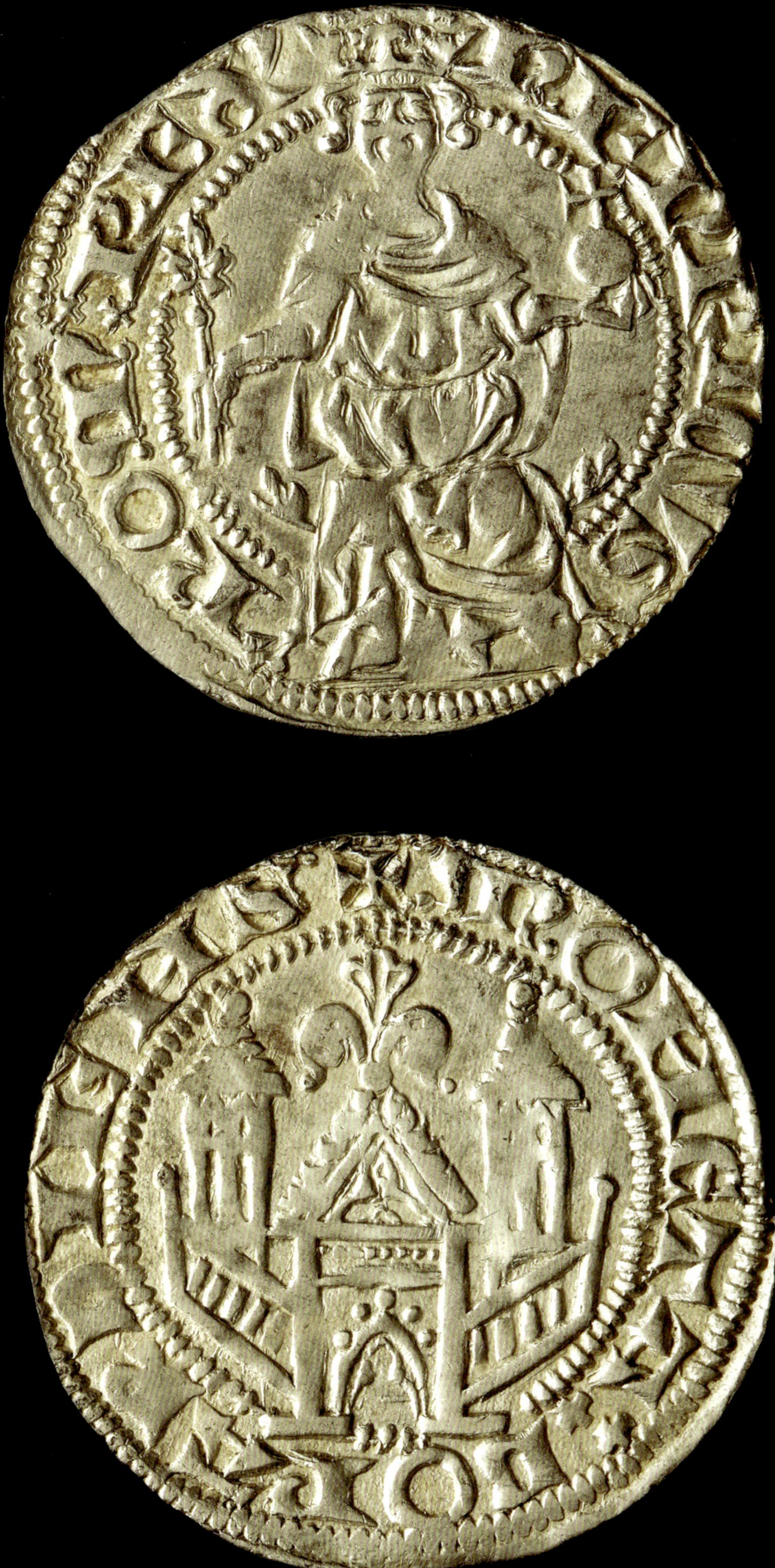

The Middle Ages

LUKAS CLEMENS

During the Middle Ages, the area of today's Rhineland-Palatinate, like many others, was characterized by the manorial estates of royalty, nobility, and the church. (Fig. 1) The self-reliant demesnes of the land owners with the accompanying terra salica had dependent small farms attached to them, the tenants of which had to perform services and pay taxes. During the high Middle Ages, this bipartite system was dissolved at staggered intervals associated with a clear reduction in the self-reliant manorial system, as well as a widespread grant of manorial land, formerly cultivated by the landlords themselves, to farmers and vintners.

Ecclesiastical organisational structures in the area under examination included some territories of the archdiocese of Mainz and of the associated suffragan dioceses of Worms and Speyer. In the west, the archdiocese of Trier bordered on the diocese of Mainz. Among the relevant territories, the archbishoprics of Mainz and Trier should be mentioned as well as the archbishopric of Cologne and the County Palatinate of the Rhine, along with smaller estates and legal titles along the Rhine, and thus four of the seven electorates whose owners had elected the king of the Holy Roman Empire since the 13th century. The region of the middle/northern Upper Rhine had developed into a central royal territory since Carolingian times. Numerous court meetings and synods under the chairmanship of a king or emperor were held at the royal residences of Worms, Frankfurt, Mainz, and Ingelheim. When the Salians rose to become the ruling dynasty in the realm (1024–1125), the imperial estates in that area and in the neighbouring Palatinate to the west grew even more through territories and privileges later transferred to the Hohenstaufen dynasty.

The high and late Middle Ages differ in their general climatic conditions, with long-term effects on the development of the cultural landscape and settlement conditions. A warm phase lasting until the late 13th century favoured a general population increase, leading to the concentration and new development of localities and forest clearings with the subsequent development of areas for agriculture. Major clearing measures are documented by pollen graphs of the Eifel maars, which for the 12th and 13th centuries show a drastic decrease of forest indicators and high figures for cereals and grasses, but also an increased presence of broom and juniper. Besides the trends towards cereal farming, which have been highlighted by agriculture historians for some time already, an equally striking increase of heather also shows the spread of heathland. Pollen analyses from the Palatinate Forest also confirms a progressive thinning of the forests characterized by inventories of oak with a few beech trees. The turn to the 14th

Bell, Mayen-Koblenz district. Denarius of Heinrich VII. of Luxembourg as German king (1308-1313). The obverse shows the king on the throne with sceptre and orb, the reverse a building with two towers and a gate and a lily on the gable of the gate. The name of the imperial mint MONETA BOPARDIENS(is) (Boppard) is also recognizable. (GDKE/Landesarchäologie/Koblenz/W. Baumann, Höhr-Grenzhausen)

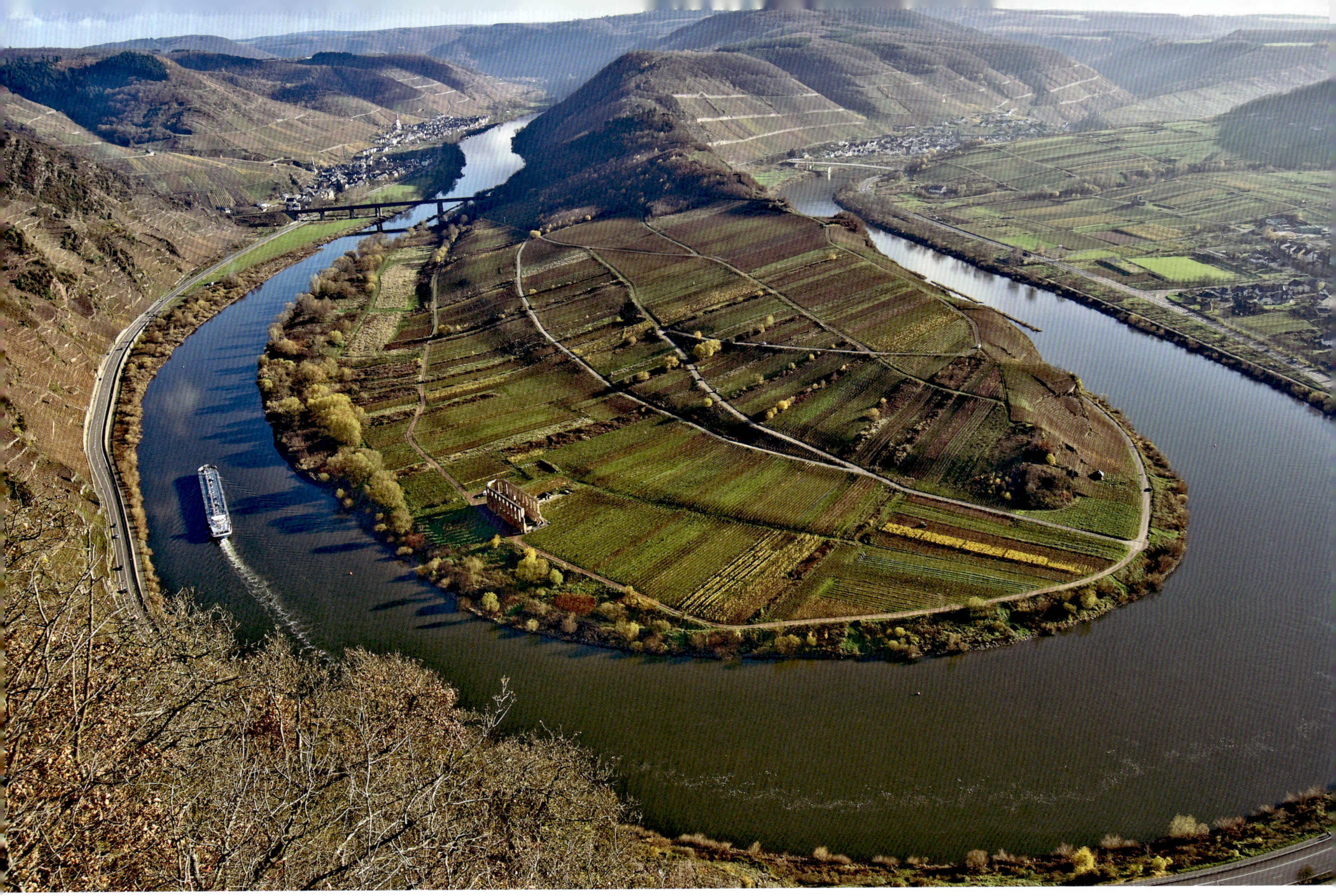

Fig. 1
Bremm, Cochem-Zell district. Ruins of the Stuben monastery with surrounding agricultural areas. (GDKE/Landesarchäologie/Koblenz/C. A. Jost)

century marks the beginning of long-term climatic changes, which are characterized as a »small ice age«. Cold and wet years dominated the subsequent period, despite moderate weather periods and even extremely hot years time and again. Frequent crop failures and profit cuts, supply crises and the famine it caused, as well as the outbreak of the plague in the middle of the 14th century (Fig. 2) along with subsequent epidemics led to drastic demographic losses, which were reflected in the upper Nahe, Westerwald, western Palatinate, and Palatinate Forest in dramatic abandonment processes. Pollen counts indicate a parallel recovery of the forests.

In the following, we shall be looking at some fields of medieval research to which the Department of Archaeology of Rhineland-Palatinate contributed new data over the last few decades.

Palaces (Pfalzen): Centres of power of travelling kings and emperors

The palaces, with their architectural triad of aula regia (hall), church, and royal residence were centres of royal power. Major archaeological investigations and architectural studies of the palace at Ingelheim, built under Charlemagne, identified some essential components of the Carolingian centre of power and reconstructed the further development of the ensemble, which is documented in the rulers' itineraries until mid-14th century and still recognizable in today's urban landscape. The original plan shows numerous references to antiquity, including a monumental semi-circular porticoed building, which recalls the architecture of Roman fora and was fitted with numerous spolia. According to the

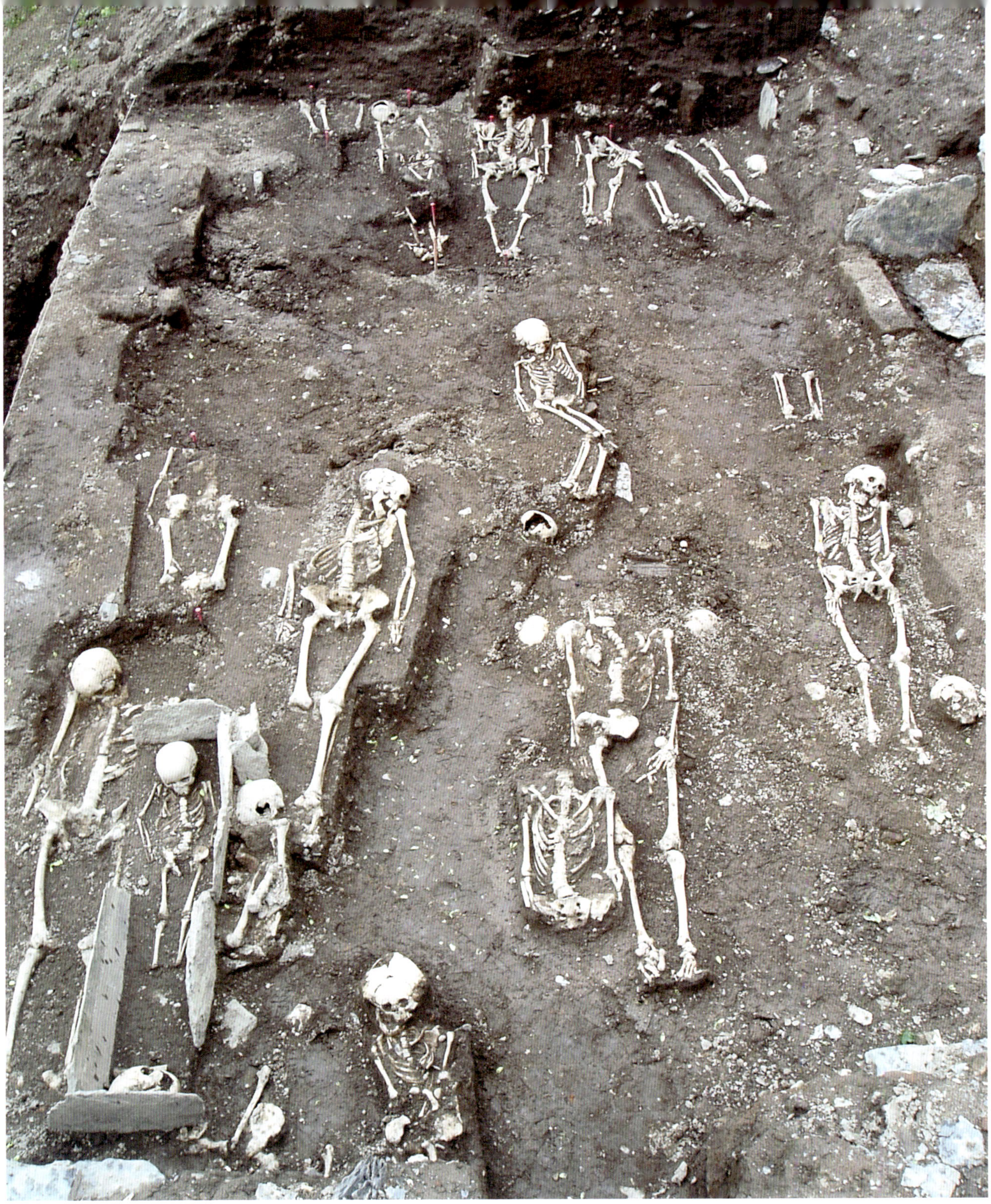

Fig. 2
Andernach, Mayen-Koblenz district. Medieval cemetery near the Marienkirche with possible epidemic victims from the 14th century. (GDKE/Landesarchäologie/Koblenz/F. Brüninghaus)

Poeta Saxo, marble columns from Rome and Ravenna were also used for building the palace of Charlemagne in Ingelheim. Together with still surviving capitals of Mediterranean origin, this information would suggest that here – as in Aachen – people tried to express the concept of a transfer of Rome [to the north] and the imperial idea connected with the caput mundi. The archaeological proof that the aqueduct (seven kilometres in length) providing the palace with water was not – as suggested by its architecture – of antique origin, but

Fig. 3
Pilligerheck, Cochem-Zell district. A witness of inner-Carolingian tensions. Obverse of a Carolingian coin (denarius) from a hoard find hidden after 855. (Liebenstein-Gesellschaft)

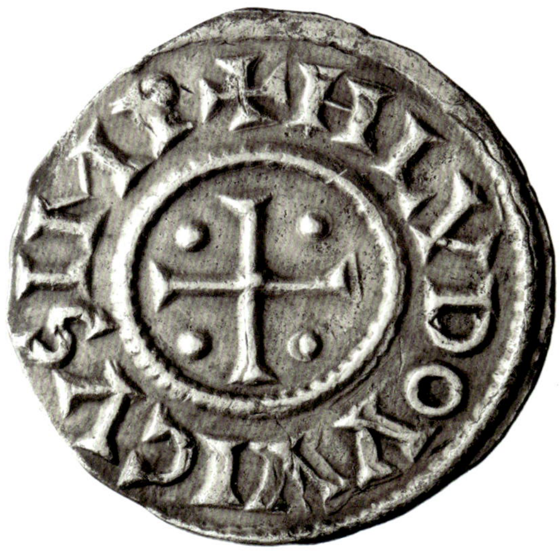

Fig. 4
Pilligerheck, Cochem-Zell distr. A witness of inner-Carolingian tensions. Reverse of a Carolingian coin (denarius) from a hoard find hidden after 855. (Liebenstein-Gesellschaft)

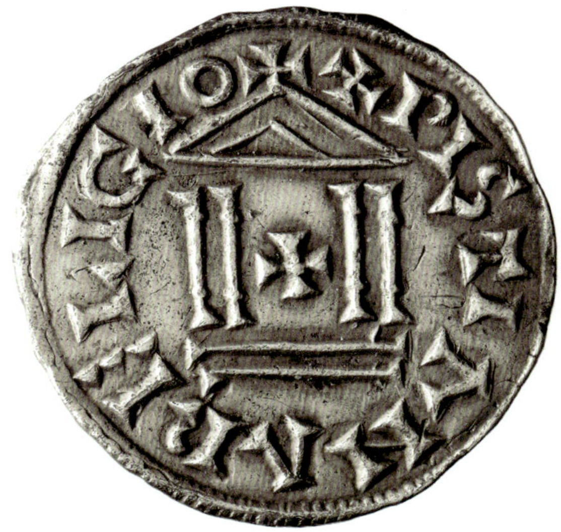

dates from Carolingian times, is unique to this day, standing as an impressive testimony to the adaptation of antique technology and architecture.

The Frisian trade

The regions of today's Rhineland-Palatinate were connected with the major long-distance northern trade routes to England and Scandinavia mainly via the river systems of the Rhine and Moselle, and via the Rhône and Saône to the Mediterranean in the south.

Trade with the countries bordering the North Sea and the Baltic Sea was dominated by the Frisians. The appearance in the Middle Rhine and in Trier of silver coins (sceattas) dating from the late 7th and 8th centuries, which were circulating in England, Frisia, and Jutland, documents early contacts with this currency area. In the 9th century, Frisian long-distance traders maintained a network of permanent establishments along the Rhine; those of Duisburg, Cologne, Mainz, and Worms were documented in the literary tradition. For Trier, a hagiographic source witnesses the presence of fresones, who undertook trade journeys overseas in the service of the abbey of St. Maximin. The existence of coin fibulae, which can be found as far as the Baltic Sea region and appear in significant numbers in Frisia and also in places along the Middle Rhine (Andernach, Koblenz, Mainz) and in Trier, is a striking element: the people carrying them probably were long-distance traders, and the fibulae referred to their activity and were thus symbolic. The appearance of sceattas and coin fibulae in Andernach is an indication that the place was included in Frisian long-distance trade, since millstones and semi-finished products made of Mayen and Niedermendig basalt were shipped from here. Corresponding pieces can be found in Jutland, England, and Frisia. Other products exported from the Frankish realm included swords (documented in great numbers in the Baltic Sea area in the form of blades bearing Ulfberht inscriptions even though they were time and again prohibited from being exported), wine, cereals, jewellery, Rhenish ceramic products, glasses and textiles, but also used materials from antiquity, such as mosaic tesserae and bronze coins as well as fragments of statues such as raw material for glass beads and non-ferrous metal products. Frisians introduced among other things furs, walrus tusks, and amber as imports to the region. We cannot be sure whether a comb with a bronze grip, which was unquestionably made in Haithabu and found in the area of the Trier convent settlement of St. Irminen, can be considered as a trade item or rather as a personal effect, either of a

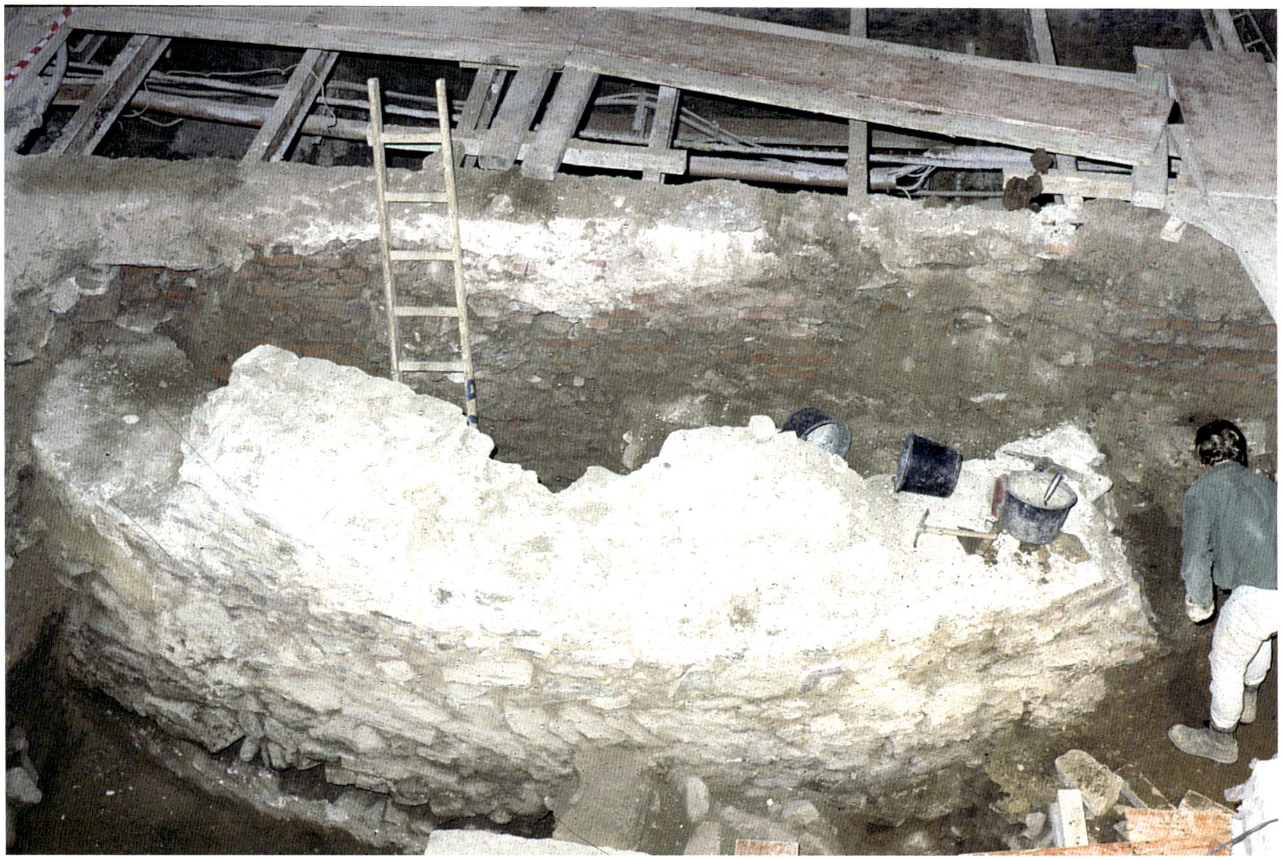

Fig. 5
Koblenz, city of Koblenz. Carolingian apse in the church St. Castor. (GDKE/Landesarchäologie/Koblenz/F. Gebert)

Frisian trader or a foreign visitor. The finds of numerous sceattas and coin fibulae on the bank of the Rhine in Mainz from the area of the building site Hilton II in Löhrstrasse, where the famous Roman ships were also discovered, suggest that the Frisian settlement, mentioned in the Annales Fuldenses as situated in the optima pars of the city when it was destroyed by fire in 886, was here or in the vicinity. We can be quite certain that it was located in the port area, which – as we know from archaeological examinations »Auf dem Brand« – was a riverside strip situated outside the Roman city wall that had been fortified from the mid-7th century by a palisade and rampart-and-ditch system.

The Viking incursions

Incursions by Normans seriously affected the trade connections even beyond the estuaries of the Meuse and the Rhine.

Since the 30s of the 9th century, Viking forces threatened the northern and north-western coasts of Francia at first, but soon also regions situated upstream. Viking armies spent the winter in the lower Rhine-Meuse area from around the 840s. At the beginning of the 880s, the (arch)bishops of Mainz and Worms had the old Roman city fortifications strengthened in view of imminent Scandinavian attacks. In 882, Norman units sailed up the Rhine, and also from Koblenz along the Moselle to eventually plunder Trier for four days from Maundy Thursday. At the upper Moselle, they were confronted by troops led by the bishop of Metz, who died during the ensuing combat together with his colleague from Trier and the count of Metz. Probably because of increasing resistance, the Normans withdrew from the region. But in that very year and again in 893, they destroyed the Eifel monastery of Prüm.

Archaeological studies in the collegiate church of St. Castor outside Koblenz (Fig. 5), both at Trier cathedral and in the area of the abbey church of St. Maximin

Fig. 6
Jewish settlements in the middle Rhine area, approx. 1000-1400. (Arye-Maimon-Institut, Trier University)

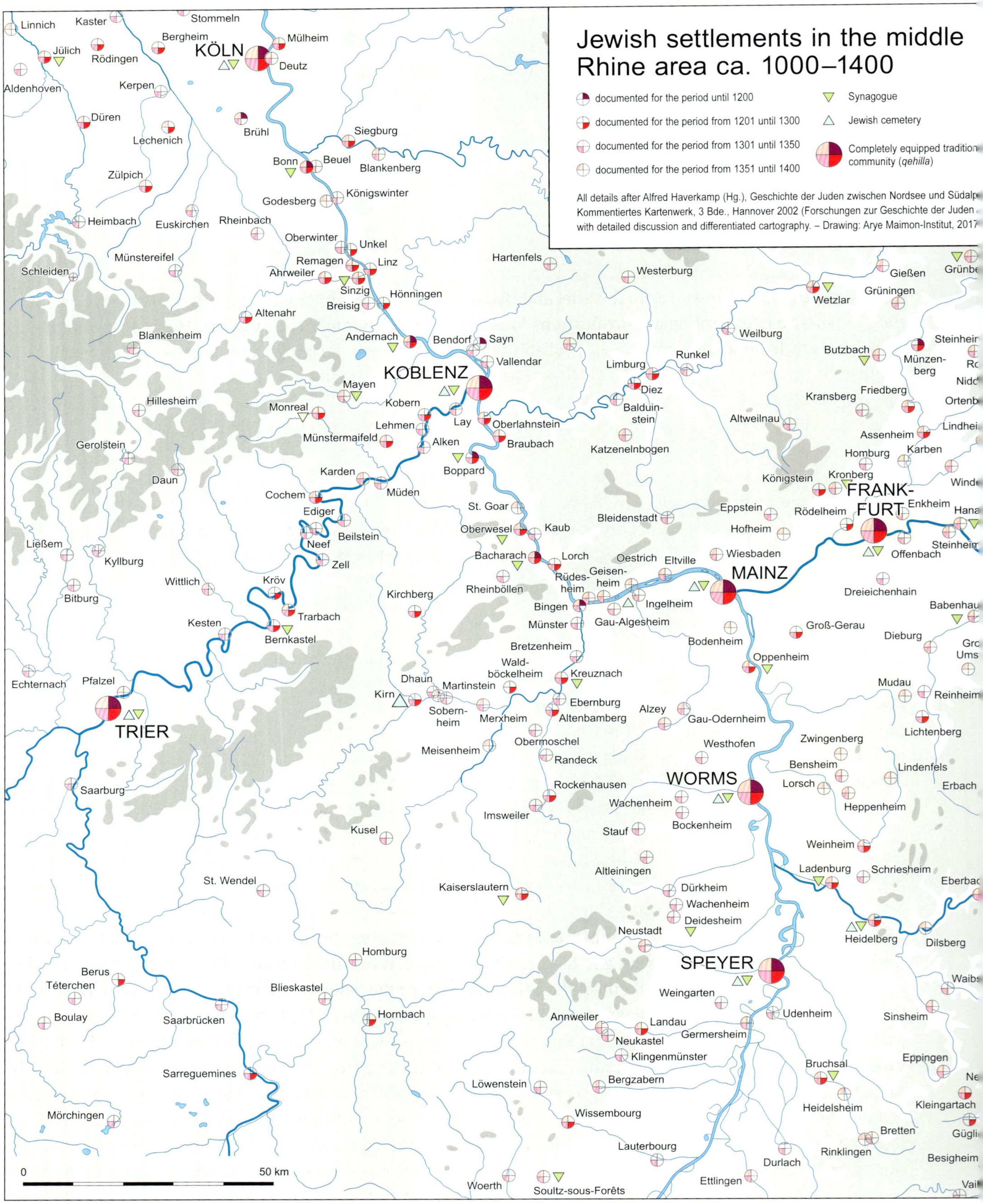

outside the city, uncovered traces of fires and building structures, which were interpreted as a reflection of the Norman destruction. A clear (although short-term) reduction of cereal pollens in the sediment profiles of the Eifel maars during the last third of the 9th century and a subsequent clear increase in the cereals curve may also be connected with the Norman raids. The drastic decrease in these settlement indicators supports the assumption that not only urban centres and important spiritual institutions, but also rural areas suffered destruction by the Scandinavians. For many places in the Middle Rhine area as well as in the Eifel and Hunsrück, small-size late Carolingian fortifications located on heights are documented, which were probably built because of the uncertain times (conflicts among the Carolingians themselves, Norman incursions, etc.) by both the archbishops or bishops and the local nobility. (Fig. 3-4) The nobility succeeded in developing larger domains on the basis of their own holdings and rights, but also via the institution of the bailiwick (*Vogtei*) as representative of ecclesiastical institutions in worldly matters.

Jewish life in a Christian environment

Jewish long-distance traders from the Mediterranean area travelled through the Frankish Empire already in the early Middle Ages, but permanent Jewish settlements and the ensuing development of community structures did not occur till the 10th and 11th centuries, first in the cathedral cities of Mainz, Trier, Worms, and since 1084, also in Speyer. (Fig. 6) Until the persecution of the Jews prior to the First Crusade, the Jewish population represented between 10 and 15 % of the local urban population. An outstanding role in the spiritual life of the Jews in the Holy Roman Empire was played by the communities of Speyer, Worms, and Mainz, which gave themselves common legal statutes (the Takkanot Kehillot SchUM); they were put down in writing in the 13th century and served as a template for other communities. Some of them are still applicable in Ashkenazi Judaism. While the partly preserved synagogues and mikvaot in Speyer and Worms as well as individual Jewish tombstones from Mainz, Speyer, Trier, and the highly important Jewish cemetery of Worms – with its more than 2,500 tombstones – were already examined well and sometimes even in an exemplary manner in archaeological, architectural, epigraphic, and Judaic studies, this applies so far only selectively to the archaeology and topography of the urban »Jewish quarters«, where Christians and Jews lived side by side. Individual smaller excavations in the Jewish quarter of Worms have repeatedly documented imported pottery of the high and late Middle Ages. Floor tiles with reliefs also indicate a higher social milieu. A prick spur from the high Middle Ages indicates the presence of mounted warriors; imported types of spices and fruit seem to show long-distance commercial relations of the inhabitants. The Trier Jew Muskinus, who died in 1336 after managing the financial affairs of the Trier archbishop Baldwin of Luxembourg for some time, is an example of the close relationships between Jews and Christians. His seal with a circumscription in Hebrew and Latin was found during excavations on the Trier cattle market, where the Jewish cemetery of the city on the Moselle had been before. Major treasure finds refer time and again to the greatest catastrophe of the Jews before the Shoah, i.e. the Black Death pogroms of 1349. The silver hoard discovered near Lingenfeld on the road from Speyer to Germersheim can be dated to that time by means of its mintage. It presumably belonged to some inhabitants of Speyer, who had tried to escape the persecutions.

Investigation of town centres

There have been many archaeological insights into medieval urbanism of today's Rhineland-Palatinate, especially in the cathedral cities, but also for instance in Andernach (Fig. 7), Koblenz, and Treis-Karden. (Fig. 8) During the city centre excavations that began in some places after the destruction of World War II and which have intensified (especially in the cathedral cities) since the 1980s, scholars focused at first on the continued existence of urban centres from older roots or on their first beginnings. After the demographic decline resulting from the collapse of Roman rule and the Migration period, a resettlement of ancient city areas occurred from the 7th century onwards, with buildings now mainly made of wood. (Fig. 9) In Trier, city archaeology has shown that the ancient street pattern was kept up and maintained until the turn to the 10th cen-

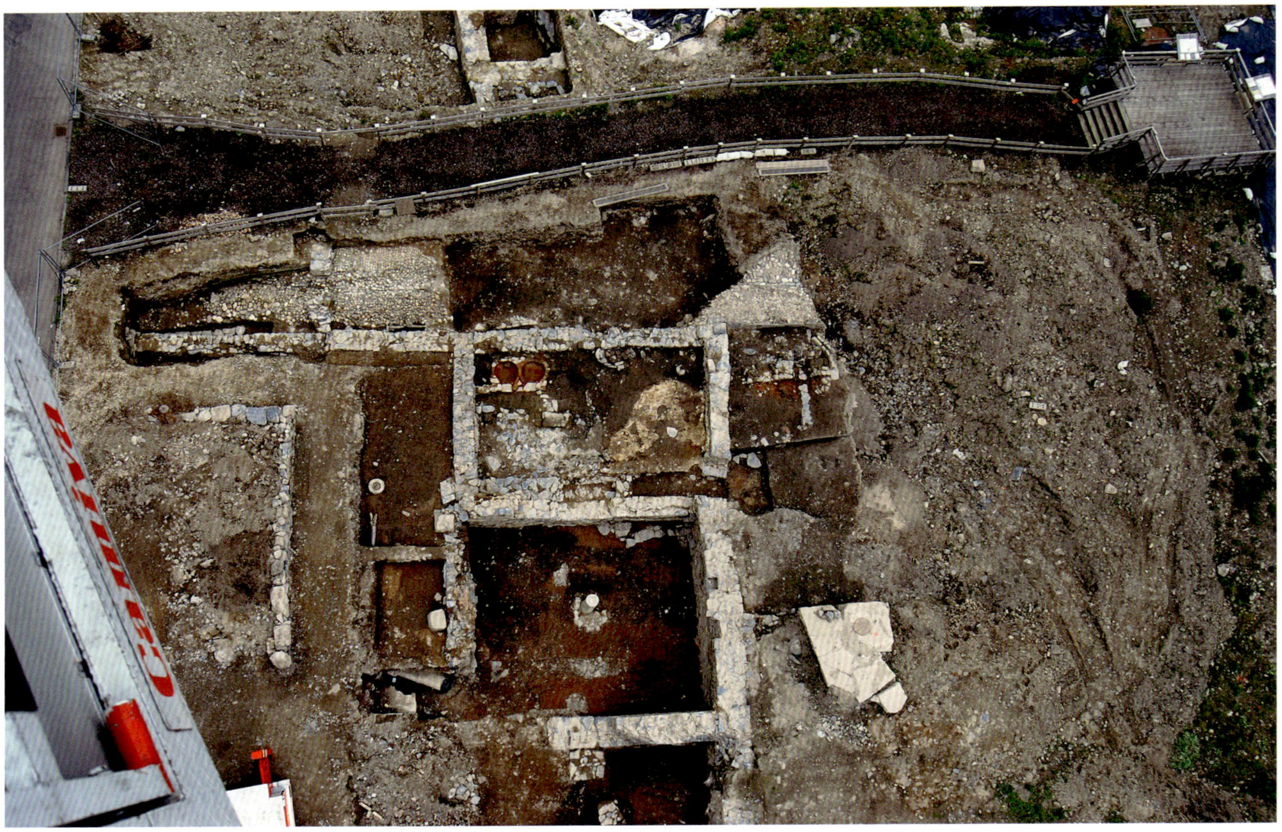

Fig. 7
Andernach, Mayen-Koblenz district. Medieval cellar below a former factory. (GDKE/Landesarchäologie/Koblenz/F. Brüninghaus)

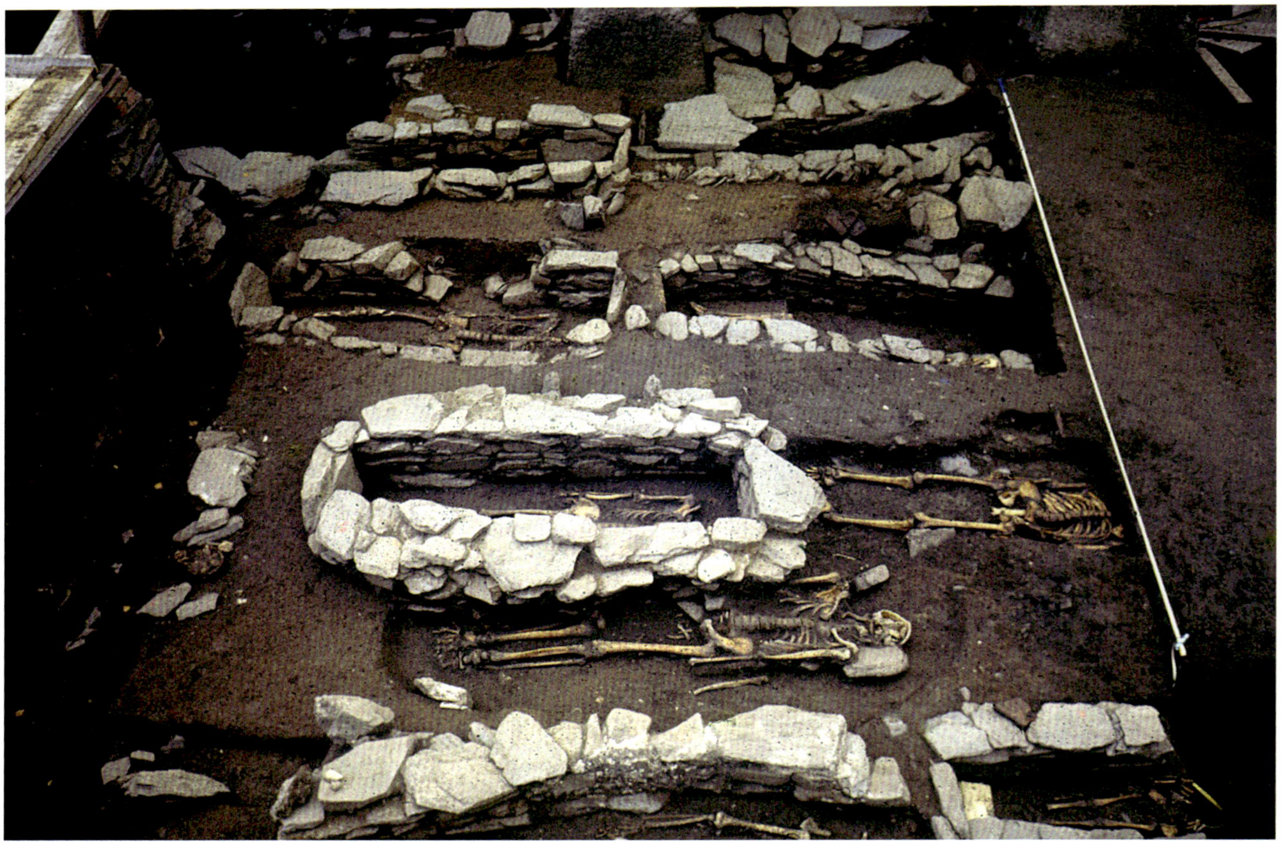

Fig. 8
Treis-Karden, Cochem-Zell district. Grave field around St. Castor's church in Karden. (GDKE/Landesarchäologie/Koblenz/H. Gadenz)

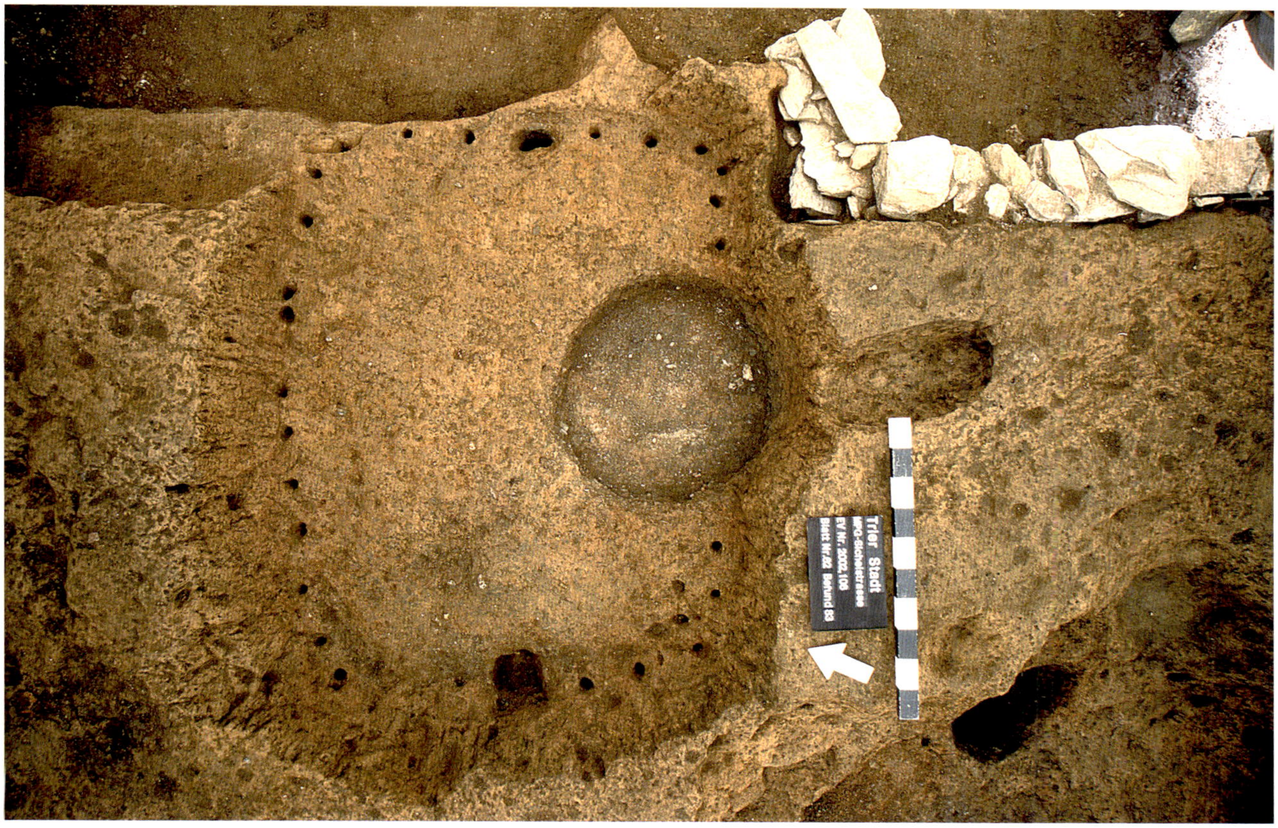

Fig. 9
Trier, city of Trier. Pit hut from the Middle Ages in the area of the antique city. (GDKE/Landesarchäologie/Trier/B. Kremer)

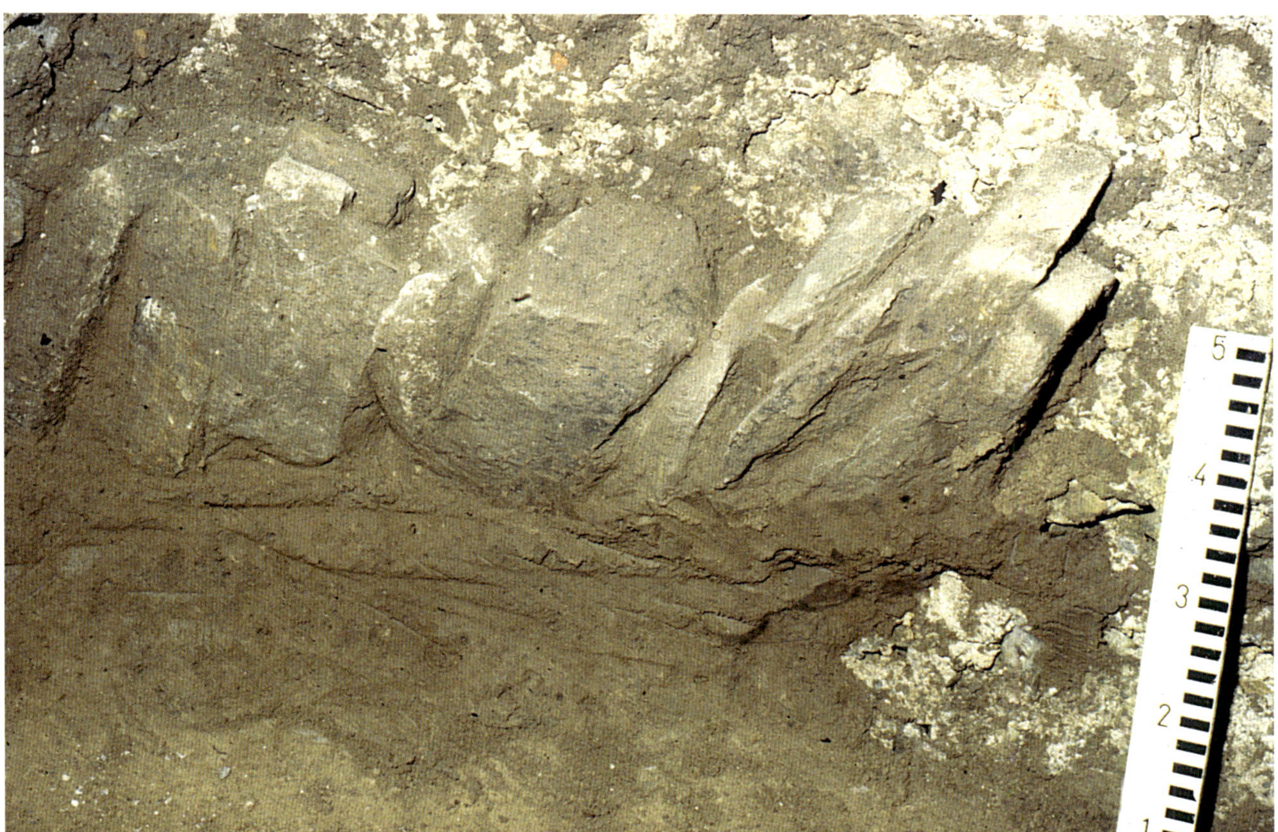

Fig. 10
Koblenz, city of Koblenz. Remains of Roman foundations in St. Castor's church. (GDKE/Landesarchäologie/Koblenz/F. Gebert)

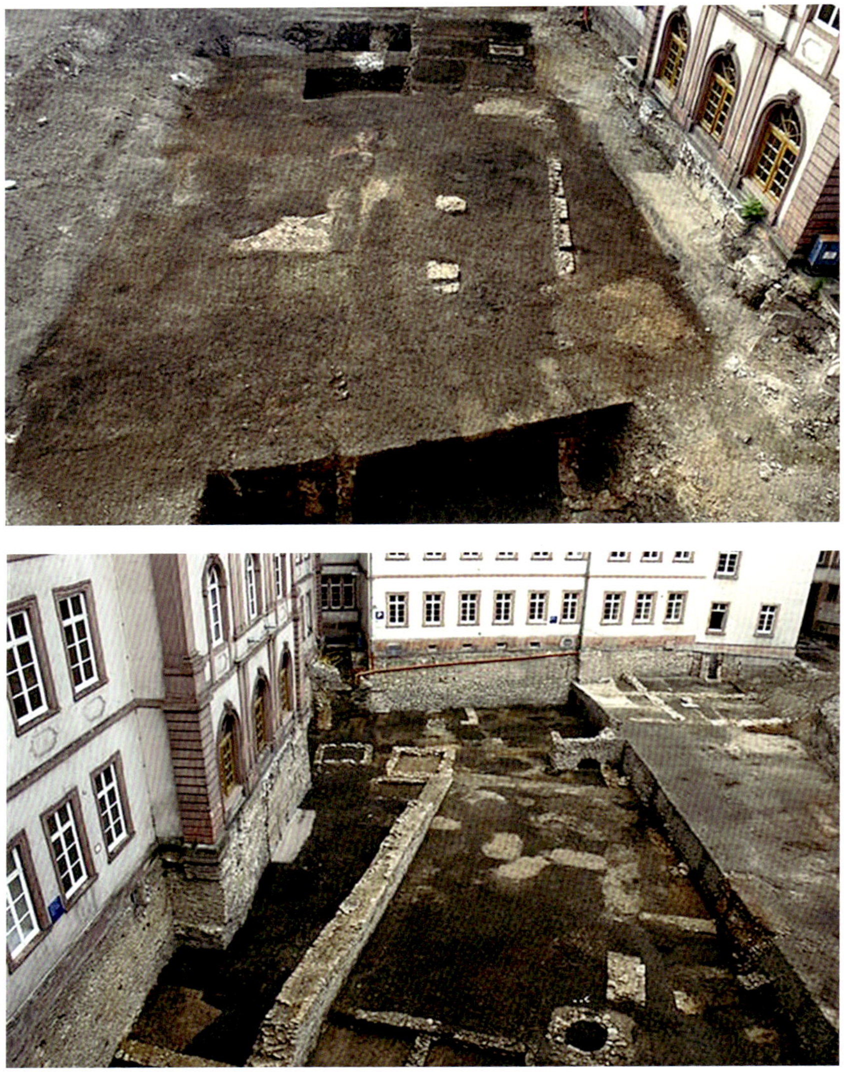

Fig. 11
Mainz, city of Mainz. Excavation area at Dalberger Hof with remains of late medieval buildings. (GDKE/Landesarchäologie/Mainz/R. Knöchlein)

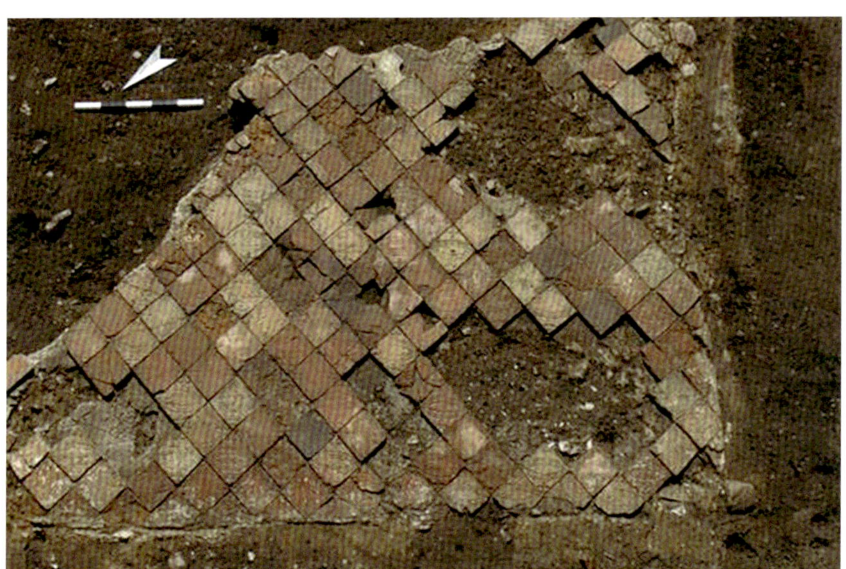

Fig. 12
Mainz, City of Mainz. Floor in Dalberger Hof with decorated floor tiles. (GDKE/Landesarchäologie/Mainz/R. Knöchlein)

tury. New roads gradually developed from beaten paths between the ruins, and the new main axis connected the Roman bridge across the Moselle with the market in front of the cathedral. Nevertheless, the ancient remains still characterized the settlements far into the high Middle Ages. As architectural trends changed from wooden buildings into an increasing amount of stone structures, the ancient buildings generally degenerated into quarries and fell into oblivion. (Fig. 10)

Another subject of city archaeology is further urban development through the extension and increasing density of buildings within settlements, including the development of plot structures. An example of this is the area of the Younger Dalberger Hof in Mainz, where, in the immediate vicinity of the Jewish quarters inferable from written tradition, an area of approx. 1,200 m² was excavated. Its history has been documented since antiquity, with the area being resettled during the high Middle Ages. More recent destruction by a late medieval fire over the entire area can also be traced. (Fig. 11–12)

Other studies deal with the origins and course of development of city fortifications. Regarding constructions, studies regarding the tower houses of urban elites and the churches and residential complexes of spiritual institutions are to be mentioned here. Small finds time and again testify to the high mobility of urban dwellers. For instance, the weight of a throwing weapon used by horse people for catching animals, which was found in Löhrstraße in Mainz, proves contact with Asiatic steppe nomads during the high Middle Ages. The evidence of leaden pilgrim's insignia on the hat or robe permits assertions on the attractiveness of pilgrimage sites. (Fig. 13) Cloth seals made of lead and attached to rolls of fabric as signs of quality reflect the standing of centres of textile production in the late Middle Ages and early Modern Age: over 500 pieces have been found so far during city excavations in Trier alone. Besides local textile lead seals, they also include seals from England, the Netherlands, neighbouring Lorraine, and the Rhenish cloth production area as well as from the southern German linen and fustian production centres. (Fig. 14)

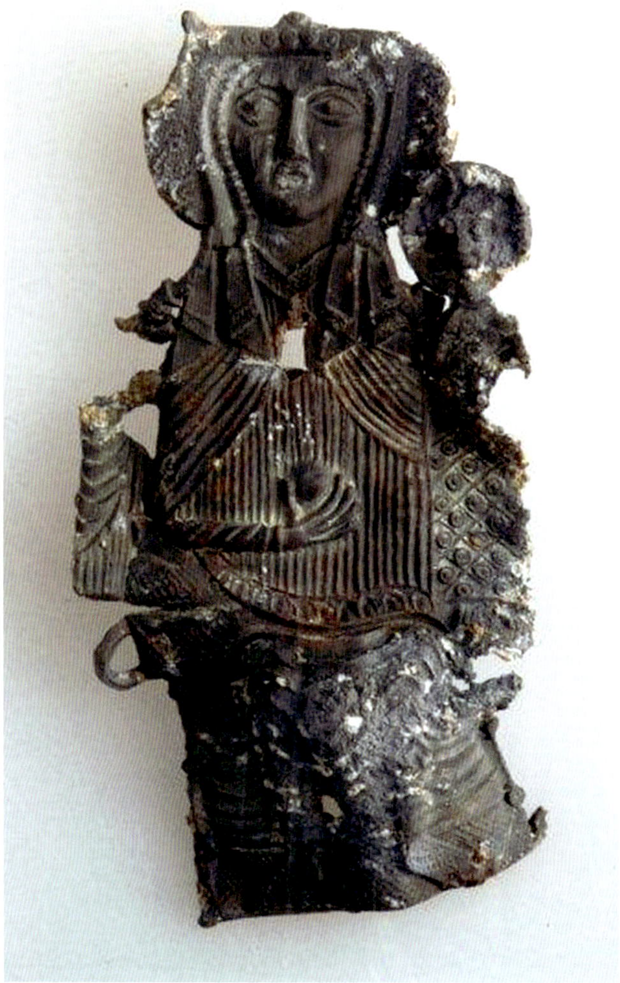

Fig. 13
Andernach, Mayen-Koblenz district. Tin pilgrim badge. (GDKE/Landesarchäologie/Koblenz/M. Neumann)

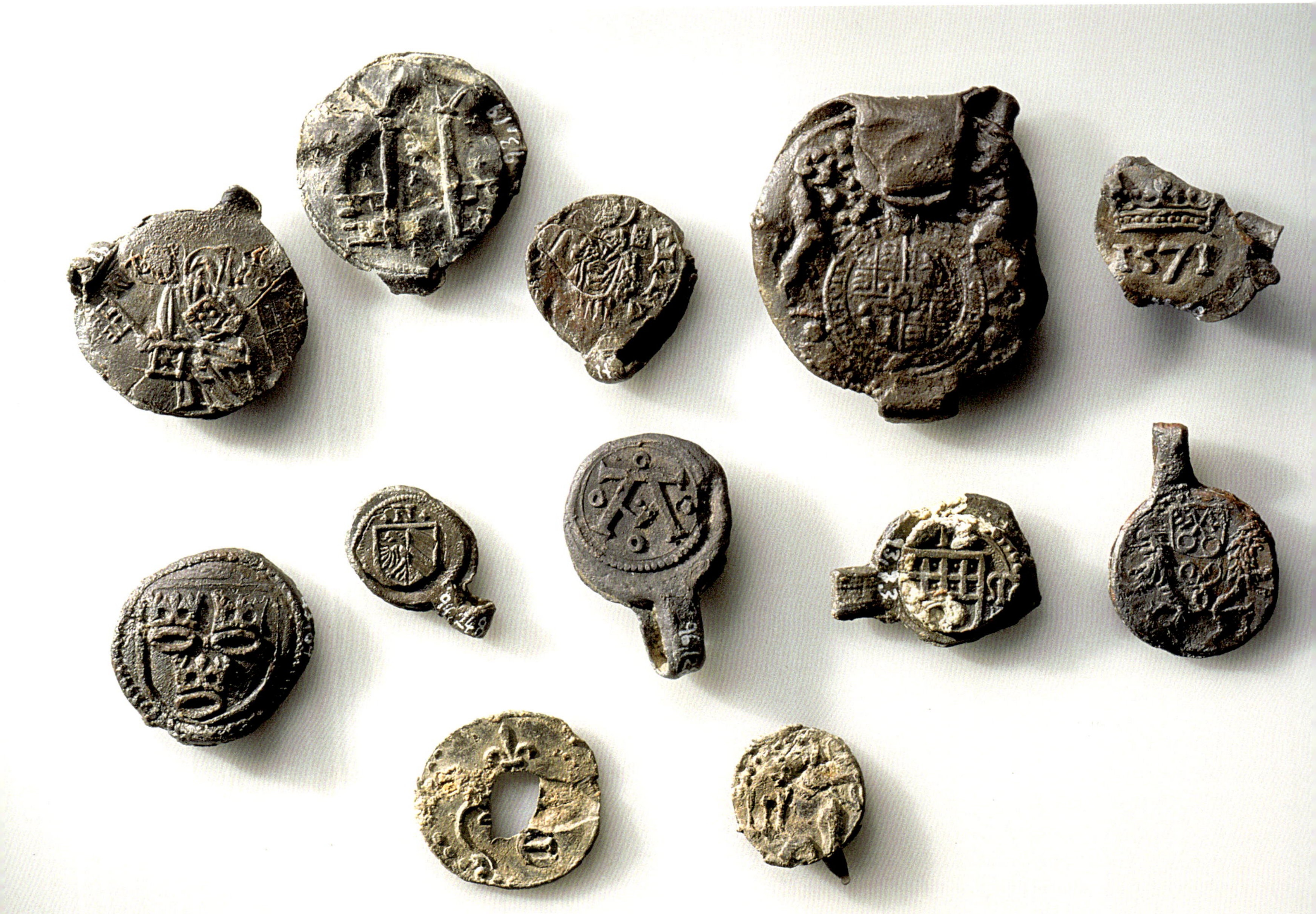

Fig. 14
Trier, city of Trier. Lead seals for fabrics from excavations in the inner city. (GDKE/Rheinisches Landesmuseum Trier/D. Zühmer)

Bibliography

L. Clemens, Die Archäologie des Mittelalters und der Frühen Neuzeit in Trier, In: Rettet das archäologische Erbe in Trier. Zweite Denkschrift der Archäologischen Trier-Kommission. Schriftenreihe des Rheinischen Landesmuseums Trier 31 (Trier 2005) 41–47.

M. Grünewald, Unter dem Pflaster von Worms. Archäologie in der Stadt (Lindenberg/Allgäu 2012).

E. Wamers, Die frühmittelalterlichen Lesefunde aus der Löhrstraße (Baustelle Hilton II) in Mainz mit Beiträgen von Peter Berghaus und Christian Stoess. Mainzer Archäologische Schriften 1. (Mainz 1994).

A medieval weapons hoard near Andernach

AXEL VON BERG

In 1954, pumice tuff was quarried south of Andernach on the low terrace directly in front of the flat valley of the river Nette, near its estuary into the Rhine on a plot used for agriculture. After the approx. 40 cm thick topsoil had been removed, an irregularly rectangular pit filling, approx. 1 m long and 0.50 m wide, was discovered in the pumice layers. Carbonized wood remains near the edges of the pit indicate a former wooden pit lining or box that was sunk into the hastily dug pit. Inside, there were 15 iron weapons lying on top of each other: six seax blades, five axes, three lance or spear heads and an angon. (Fig. 1) The seax blades were those of a short seax from the 6th century, three broad seaxes from the 7th century, and a long seax from the 8th century. The hilts had plainly been altered at some later time. The preserved pommels were made from lead and bronze and consist of recycled (mostly Roman) pieces. The ring pommel of the long seax has clear parallels to Roman rein-guides in the context of ancient chariots. The bronze grommet of the broad seax belongs to the bronze pommel ends of Roman pieces of furniture. Even the lead pommel of another broad seax seems to have been recycled.

The five axes in the find belong to different Merovingian and Carolingian types and are also to be dated differently. The angon in combination with later winged spear heads is also unusual. The overall impression is that of a collection of Merovingian weapons adapted to new requirements by using older pieces. This find is unique for the Middle Rhine area. The dating of the individual weapons extends from end-6th century to late 8th century, and they were subsequently reworked. There are many indications that the Andernach find is to be seen as a weapons hoard in the context of activities in Viking times. Merovingian-Frankish weapons in particular were very popular with North Germanic tribes towards the end of the early Middle Ages because of their quality and were thus often adapted to their requirements. The fact that the weapons were hidden near the Rhine at Andernach could be seen in the context of the Viking raids during the last decades of the 9th century.

Bibliography

A. Willemsen, Wikinger am Rhein (Utrecht 2004) 119 ff.

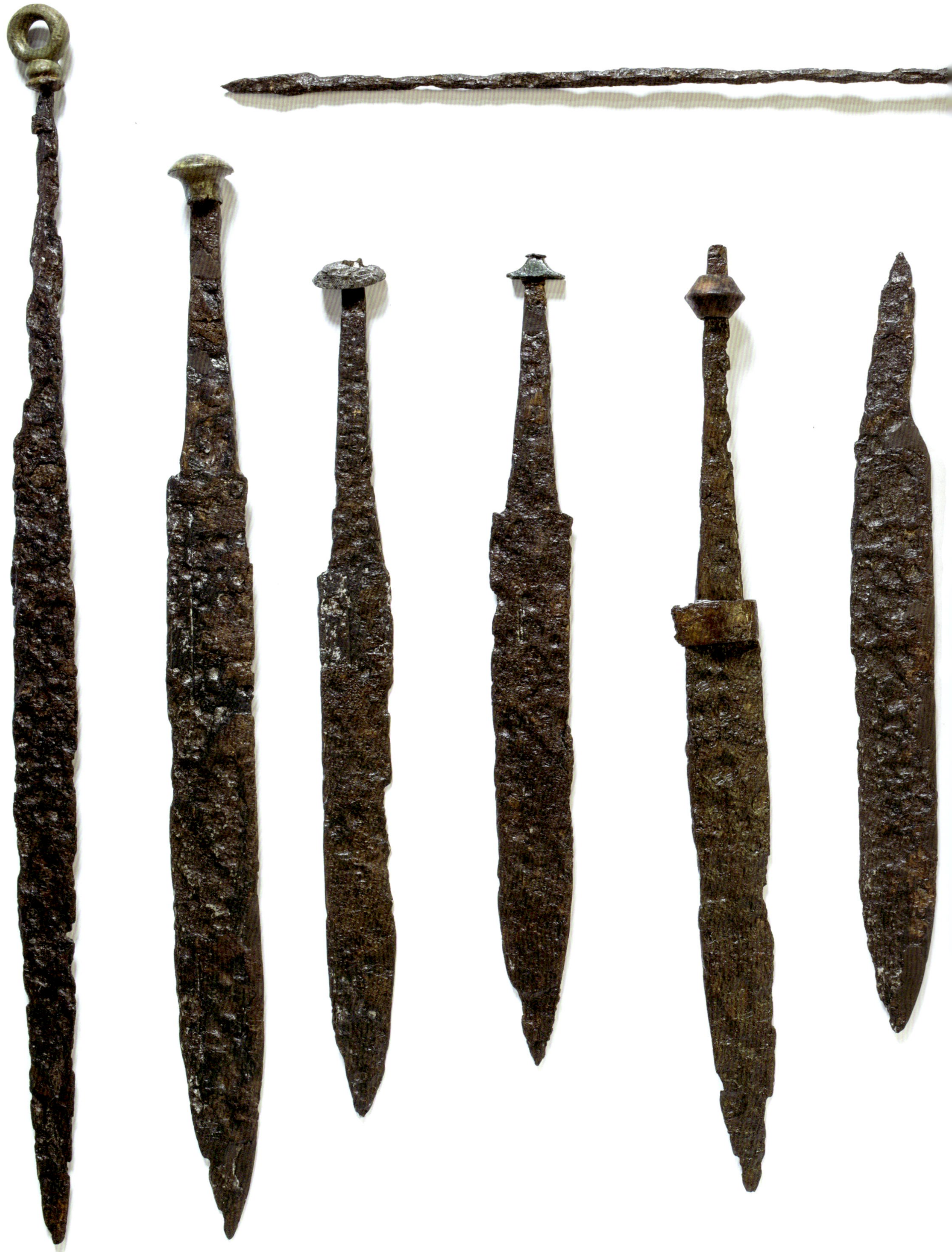

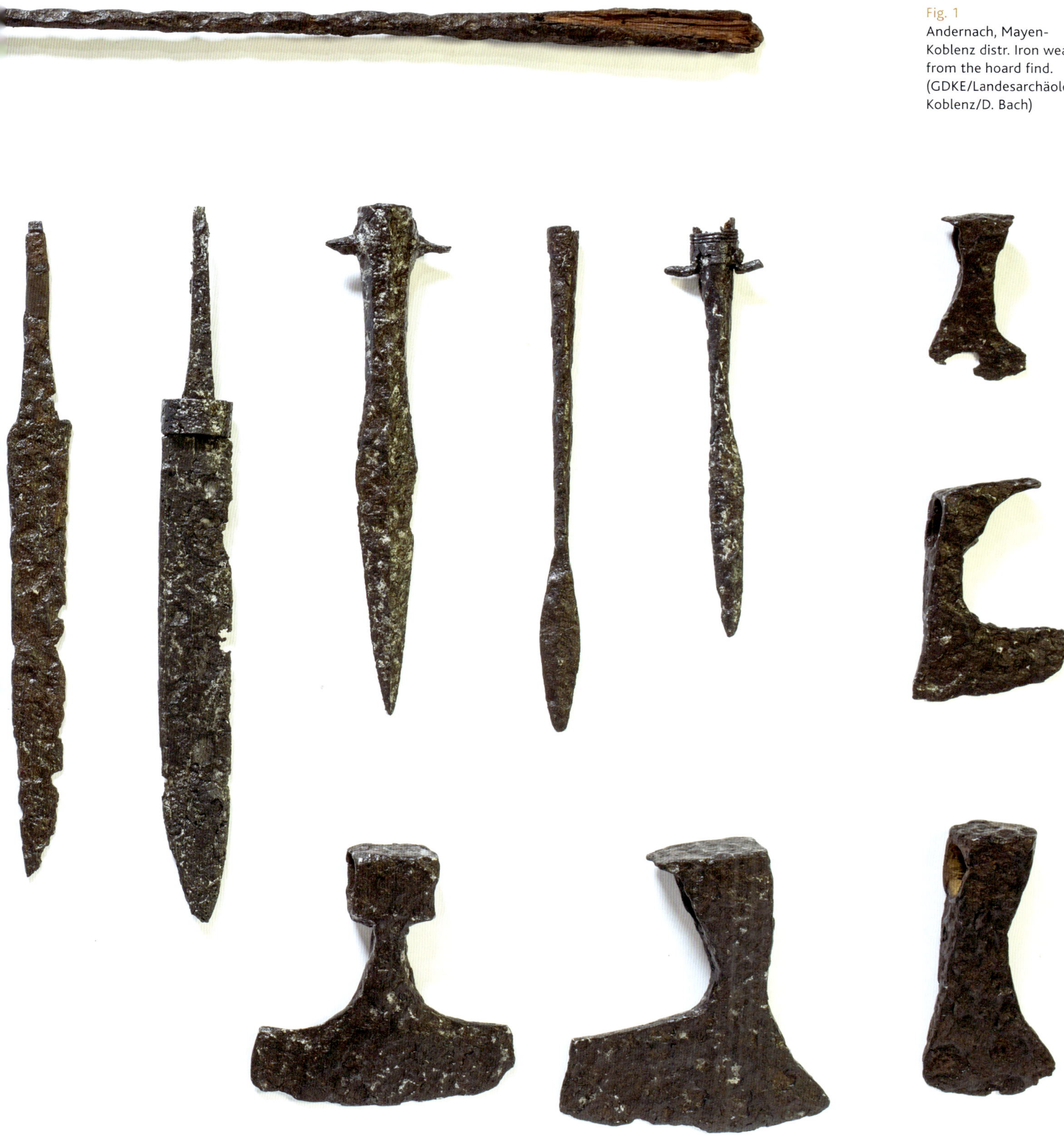

Fig. 1
Andernach, Mayen-Koblenz distr. Iron weapons from the hoard find. (GDKE/Landesarchäologie/Koblenz/D. Bach)

The man with the helmet from Andernach

AXEL VON BERG

Fig. 1 Andernach, Mayen-Koblenz distr. Radial eye-decorated shoulder blade with scratched representation of a warrior with medieval conical helmet. (GDKE/ Landesarchäologie/Koblenz/ M. Neumann)

From 2008 to 2014, extensive excavations were undertaken in Andernach in the Mayen-Koblenz district near the Rhine in the ancient port area. Settlement remains from late Celtic times up to the Modern Age were examined. The surveys were necessary since the malt factory, which had been built there at the end of the 1950s, was demolished and there were plans to redevelop the entire area. Various archaeological findings, such as building layouts, thermal baths, roads of the ancient cadastre, and numerous workshops were uncovered over an area of 6,000 m^2. In addition, the massive walls of the Roman city fortifications run all along the side facing the Rhine. In front of the ancient walls, a Roman harbour basin could be localized: today it is dry and filled-in, but it was once situated in a protected bay along the old course of the Rhine. The port of Andernach was very important up to medieval times as a loading point for millstone products and volcanic ashlars from the eastern Eifel.

Since the ancient port area was to be built over, several sondages were performed in the former basin during the excavations to establish the depth and dimensions of the harbour basin. At a depth of approx. 8 m below the level of today's fill, the older layers of ancient and medieval use of the basin could be recorded. The finds from the layers date from early Roman times to the 15th century. Much organic material, such as wood, leather, and bone remains could be recovered besides pottery and coins and many items of everyday use from the peaty layers of the harbour bottom.

A very special piece was found among the well-preserved bones, remains of production, workpieces, and offal: a fragmentary shoulder blade of a young cow covered with small circle ornaments. On the surface of the bone, the engraving of a human face is recognizable in the middle of one of the linear alignments of the ornamental sequences. (Fig. 1) The image shows a warrior with a pointed conical helmet and a clearly recognizable nasal armour piece. The helmet also shows vertical and horizontal decoration with small circles. Because of its characteristic form, the high pointed cone helmet with nasal armour can be related to helmet types of the 10th/11th centuries, which are often documented in northern European/Viking Period find contexts. A direct parallel to the piece at Andernach is the antler carving of a warrior wearing a nasal helmet with small circle decorations from Sigtuna in Sweden. The piece from the Andernach harbour basin is so far the only depiction of an early medieval warrior with a nasal helmet in Rhineland-Palatinate.

Bibliography

A. von Berg, Mann mit Helm. Archäologie in Deutschland 6, 2009, 54–55.

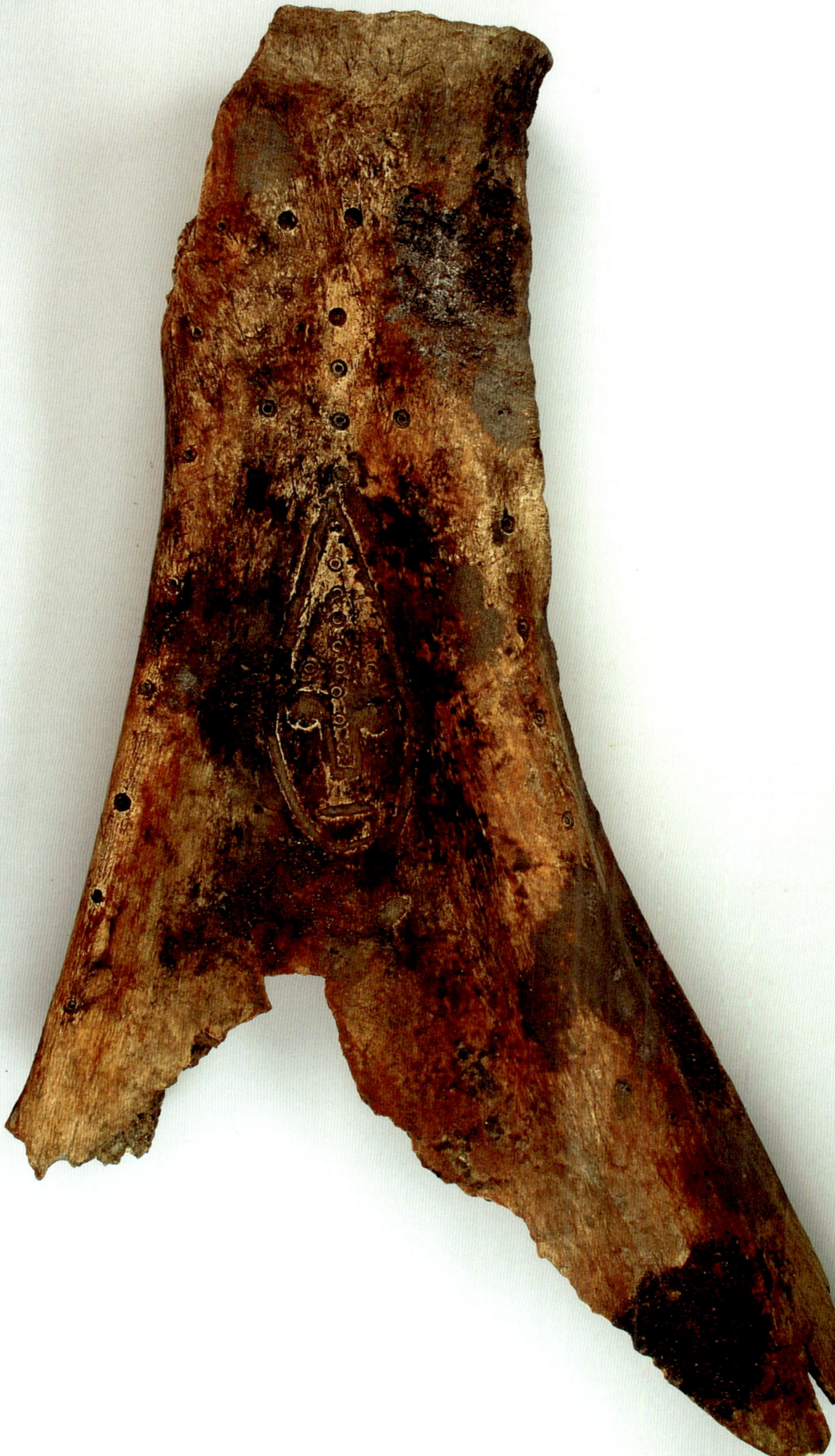

Frisian »twins« on the Middle Rhine – Two sceattas from Rhens

RALF FISCHER ZU CRAMBURG

In the grave field of Rhens, dating back to the Merovingian Period and discovered in 1990, the burial of a mounted warrior going back to the period around 760 was among those unearthed. Besides everyday tools, the pouch lying in the grave contained two small silver coins, which had clearly been minted from the same die. The obverse carries a highly abstract head in lateral view, from which the gently curving hair stands out. (Fig. 1) The reverse side seems to show the two-line (pseudo) inscription »ToT« and »/.\« in a dotted square. (Fig. 2) In numismatic studies, these coins are referred to as »sceattas«. Because of the recognisable hairstyle, our special variety is defined as the »porcupine« type. Under the term »sceattas«, small, compact silver coins are understood, which were first minted in England, later also in Frisia and perhaps even in Denmark. It is related to the German term »Schatz« (treasure) and derives from the old English *sceatt*, which was originally used for a gold weight. Only from the 17th century onwards was it used for early silver coinages, which were known to the contemporaries as *peningas*. The term has nevertheless prevailed in numismatics to distinguish the early Anglo-Saxon and Frisian silver coins from the broader Frankish *denarii*.

Sceattas appear in numerous variations. The abstract representations comprise human figures, birds and other animals, in addition to crosses, plants and creatures, which have been classified into various categories. These include other types besides our »porcupine«, such as »dragon«, »wolf«, and »Wodan monster«. The terminology is dominated by British research, and it distinguishes four phases of sceatta production, namely: 1st »Preliminary« (approx. 675–680), 2nd »Primary« (approx. 680–710), 3rd »Intermediate continental« (approx. 695–740), and finally »Secondary« (approx. 710–760). The total number of coins minted was likely very high; for the porcupine type alone, it is estimated that some 5 million coins were issued during the third and fourth phases (approx. 720 to 760).

The assignment of the types of coins to particular authorities remains a challenge. The minting of the continental sceattas was probably ordered by private individuals, who needed them for trading and traffic and would hire (if necessary even itinerant) coiners, and they were probably produced in the big Frisian trading centres such as Dorestadt and Domburg. The rich variety of the coins and their restrikes might also indicate other issuing places of regional importance. The inferior and copper (re)strikes in particular may have been minted in the periphery of the currency area. In particular, the possibility cannot be excluded that some of the low grade sceattas from the last (»secondary«) phase were even minted in the Middle Rhine.

The import of sceattas also had a long-term effect on the continental currency system. After the collapse of the Western Roman Empire and its monetary economy, the first coin to dominate was the *tremissis* of the Byzantine golden *solidus* and its restrikes. The introduction of the silver denarius was a consequence of the continuing depreciation of these gold coins. They disappeared practically completely from monetary transactions, so that the solidus only survived as a unit of accounting valued at 40 denarii. In the late 7th century, the solidus calculation at 12 denarii, which had been imported from England together with the sceattas, was introduced as well. In England, the gold (*thrymsa*/shilling) and silver penny (Lat. *denarius*), weighing 1.3 g each, had about the same weight as the continental tremisses or denarii. Unlike England, where the shilling really was a gold coin, on the continent the solidus at 12 pennies remained a mere unit of accounting without an actual coin. In Great Britain,

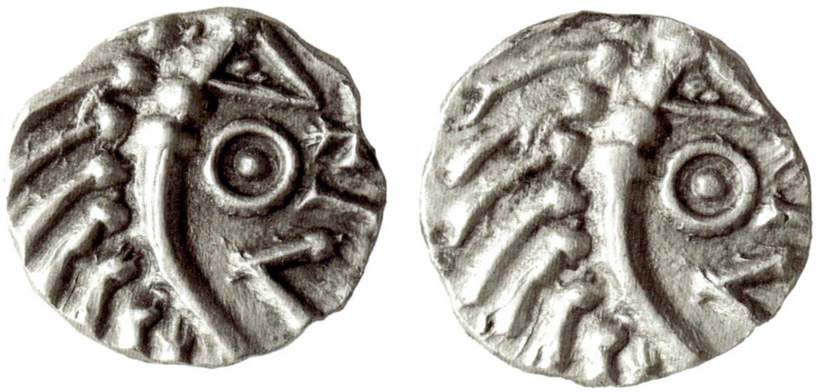

Fig. 1
Rhens, Mayen-Koblenz distr. Sceattas from the burial of a Merovingian warrior (obverse). (Liebenstein-Gesellschaft)

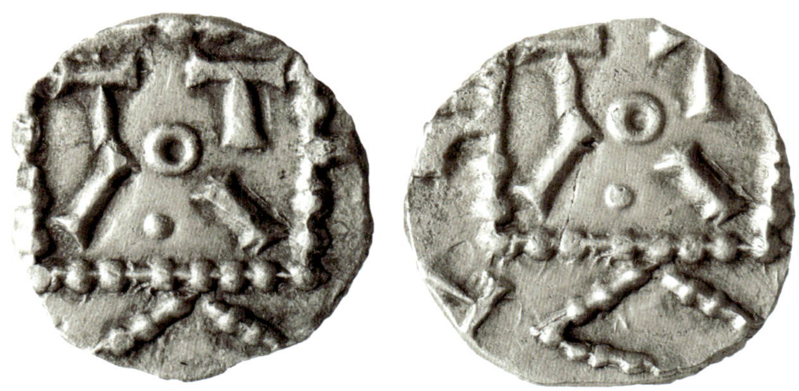

Fig. 2
Rhens, Mayen-Koblenz distr. Sceattas from the burial of a Merovingian warrior (reverse). (Liebenstein-Gesellschaft)

however, the shilling at 12 pence was not abolished until 1971, when the British pound was converted to the decimal system.

In Germany, sceattas are discovered regularly as individual finds. The Anglo-Frisian coins probably reached as far as the Upper Rhine area mainly through Frisian traders, whose establishments along the Rhine in Carolingian times are documented as far as Mainz and Worms. The large number of finds from Mainz from the first half of the 8th century seems to indicate that they were a well-established currency there and that the monetary economy was comparatively advanced. Besides the two Rhens pieces, coins have been found (in the Middle Rhine region) at Andernach, Boppard, Kaltenengers, Koblenz-Lay, Remagen and near Nassau (Fig. 3); not all of them have yet been published. Here, too, the sceattas are a manifestation of trade activities which extended from the Frankish Empire on the left bank of the Rhine via England in the west, and from the Frisian North Sea coastal area as far as Scandinavia and the southern Baltic Sea coasts. One cannot underestimate the importance of the Rhine as a major transportation route and at the same time as the eastern border of the diffusion of trade and currency. Sceattas remained the popular currency here until the beginning of the Carolingian period.

Fig. 3
Sites of sceattas in Rhineland-Palatinate (Liebenstein-Gesellschaft, Graphic: GDKE/Landesarchäologie/M. Schwab, Map base: SRTM data [NASA]/ows.terrestis.de/osm/service)

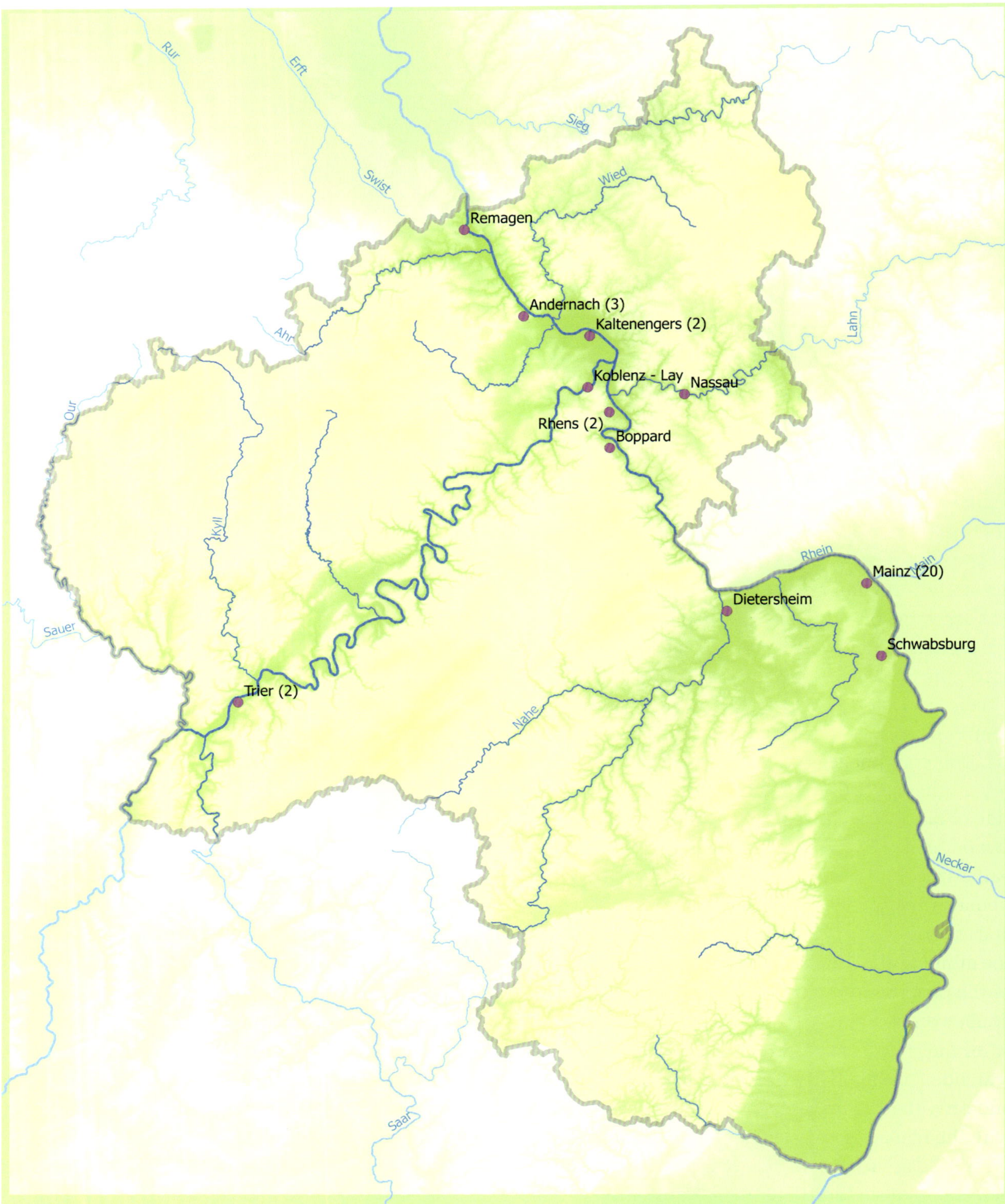

Bibliography

E. **Saal**, Das merowingerzeitliche Gräberfeld in Rhens, Landkreis Mayen-Koblenz. Beiträge zur frühmittelalterlichen Chronologie und Siedlungsgeschichte an Mittelrhein und unterer Mosel. Berichte zur Archäologie an Mittelrhein und Mosel 20 (Koblenz 2014) 157–551.

R. **Wiechmann**, Sceatta. In: Reallexikon der Germanischen Altertumskunde 26 (Berlin/New York 2004) 558–564.

Carolingian coin fibulae from Andernach

AXEL VON BERG

Two early medieval coin fibulae were discovered in 1970 during excavation works in the city of Andernach; more precisely in the area of the early medieval grave field at St. Peter's church. The fibulae pair was discovered in a grave surrounded by stones.

These cast coin fibulae are so-called »pseudo-coin fibulae« in the style of genuine fibulae with original gold or silver coins worked into them. (Fig. 1) Cast, pseudo-coin fibulae with coin imitations had a purely decorative function and were worn as a typical women's accessory on the dress. This pair shows as its central element the obverse and reverse side of a *triens* according to the wide-spread Dorestad coin type of the 7th century. Dorestad was one of the best-known trade centres of the 7th–9th centuries on the North Sea in Frisia. The coin images are shown mirror-inverted and the motifs are sunken into the surface. On the front side of one of the fibulae, the obverse side of the coin can be seen with the stylized image of a ruler and the barbarized circumscription *DORESTATFIT*. The other fibula shows the reverse side of the coin with a cross and the circumscription *MADALINUSM (monetarius)* of the mint master. These objects with the cast imitations of the obverse and reverse side of the triens were no doubt worn as a pair. A three-line pearl-rim decoration surrounds the central image of the coin imitation. The rear sides of the fibulae are smooth and undecorated and carry the needle holders which were cast together with the fibulae. The diameter of both decorative fibulae is 3.0 cm; the material is bronze, containing a high percentage of tin to imitate silver. Signs of wear on the edges and of the needle holders indicate that they were worn for a long time.

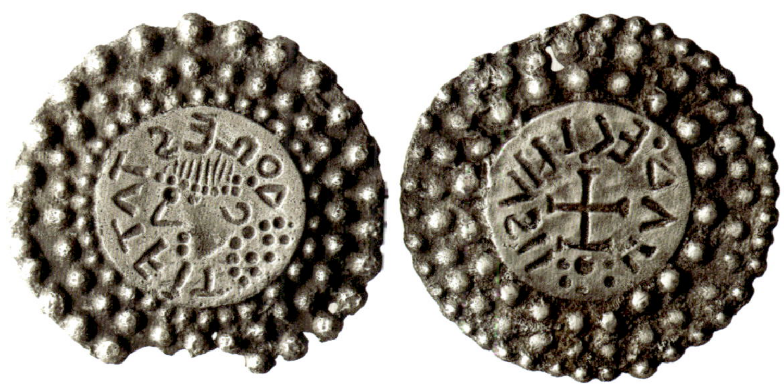

Fig. 1
Andernach, Mayen-Koblenz distr. Cast coin fibulae with imitation of obverse and reverse of a Dorestad coin from a burial near St. Peter. (GDKE/Landesarchäologie/Koblenz/Liebenstein-Gesellschaft)

These pseudo-coin fibulae were used in the northern core regions of the Carolingian Empire, with find centres on the Middle Rhine and the Frisian North Sea coast. On the basis of these Frisian coins and the coin fibulae, it is possible to trace trade relations to the north, which serviced the entire North and Baltic Sea area. The two pseudo-coin fibulae from Andernach were probably manufactured in the North Sea coastal region and reached Andernach through trading with the Frisians or as personal belongings. Jewellery of this type with a wide pearl-rim appears to have been produced since the middle of the 9th century.

Bibliography

L. **Grunwald**, Bestattungsritus und Sachgut der Karolingerzeit im Moselmündungsgebiet. Berichte zur Archäologie an Mittelrhein und Mosel 17 (Koblenz 2011) 381 f.

The palace *(Pfalz)* of Ingelheim on the Rhine

HOLGER GREWE

The Frankish Empire, and until the 14th century also the (Holy) Roman Empire, were not ruled from a capital city but from a number of different residences. The king practiced a travelling rule, which is also referred to as »itinerant kingship«. The residences usually had a palace *(Pfalz)*, whose representative building was used for government business, such as court days and imperial assemblies, and served at the same time as a temporary residence for the king and his courtiers.

Only a few representatives of this group of monuments have survived. Many of the palace sites mentioned in the annals and documents cannot be localized, and where this is possible, all too often the soil archive was destroyed. Quite unexpectedly, several of Charlemagne's palaces have survived in unusually good condition. However, this is no coincidence, since 9th-century historians had already noted that Charles had a wonderful Church of Our Lady built in Aachen and *palatia operis egregii*, magnificent palaces, in Nijmegen and Ingelheim. Once they had this imperial charisma, posterity obviously considered it worthwhile to continue using and maintaining these structures.

The fact that the complexes at Aachen and Ingelheim can be reconstructed more or less reliably (on the basis of scientifically documented findings) did in fact involve major efforts in archaeology. In the area named »Im Saal« near Ingelheim on the Rhine, where excavations started in 1889, the studies had already reached a high intensity in the years from1960–1970. Since 1993, further excavations and sondages could be performed with the assistance of the Department of Archaeology.

The excavations and their finds revealed something quite astonishing, namely a monumental architecture with a unique design from the time around 800, decorated with a large number of recycled antique Roman building elements. (Fig. 1) These include marble capitals and columns, and precious wall and floor slabs made of porphyry. They were once components of representative architecture, which could be found in many areas of the Imperium Romanum. Identical materials and stylistic elements can be seen in the late antique remains of the imperial city of Trier. We assume today that precious architectural sculpture, such as a Corinthian capital only rediscovered in 2010 (Fig. 2), had reached Trier during the time of Constantine from stores and production sites in central Italy and was then transported via the Moselle and Rhine to the building site of Charlemagne's at Ingelheim around 800. This building site was distinguished from others not only by recycling the precious architectural sculpture, but also by its size and the extraordinary building plan establishing a symmetrical arrangement of the building components. According to the archaeological evidence provided by the remains of walls, most of which are only preserved in the soil, it was divided into three groups of buildings: firstly, a semi-circular building with a centrally located gate; secondly, a transverse building attached to it, which was connected at the side to a long rectangular construction (these two groups of buildings were accessed from the court side via porticos in antique style); and thirdly, a wing with the palace hall and narthex.

The peripheral buildings surrounding one quadratic and one half-moon shaped court are unique among the palaces of Carolingian time. Archaeologists explain the fact that there are gaps between these peripheral buildings by the state of research: no excavations could be performed there so far, or, if there have been excavations, they did not provide clear results, since the soil documents were already destroyed.

It is wholly evident that Carolingian builders were inspired by antique architecture, not only regarding

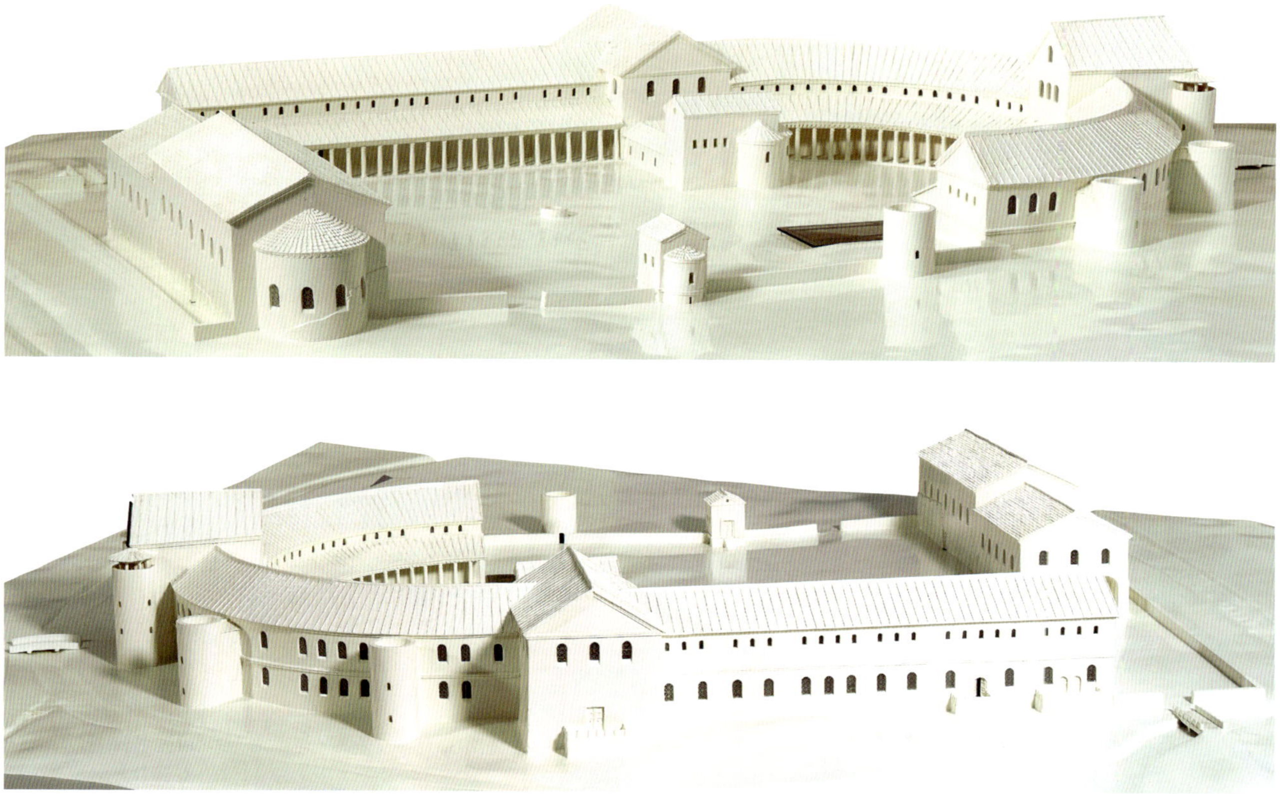

Fig. 1
Ingelheim, Mainz-Bingen distr. The imperial palace at Ingelheim around 800, volume modell, scale 1:100 (after H. Grewe 2006/ Stadt Ingelheim am Rhein. Photo: V. Iserhardt)

features, but also regarding the large dimensions of the buildings up to the arrangement of the entire complex. This interpretation is strongly supported by the observation that even technical structures, such as the big aqueducts and long-distance water pipes of Roman cities, were echoed in Ingelheim. A 6.8 km long subterranean canal, which used to be referred to as a »Roman-Carolingian long-distance aqueduct«, can today be safely dated to the end of the 8th century thanks to radiocarbon data and stratified find material.

Medievalists by now agree that these phenomena are to be interpreted neither as an imitation nor as a programme unilaterally inspired by the Roman heritage (»Carolingian Renaissance«). The palace of Ingelheim is an example of how traditional building elements were adopted, but also that these elements found their way into new spatial concepts. Let us look once more at architectural sculpture: besides the antique marble capitals, there are also numerous pieces with original Carolingian-period design, such as the truncated pyramid transoms or a remarkable figural-

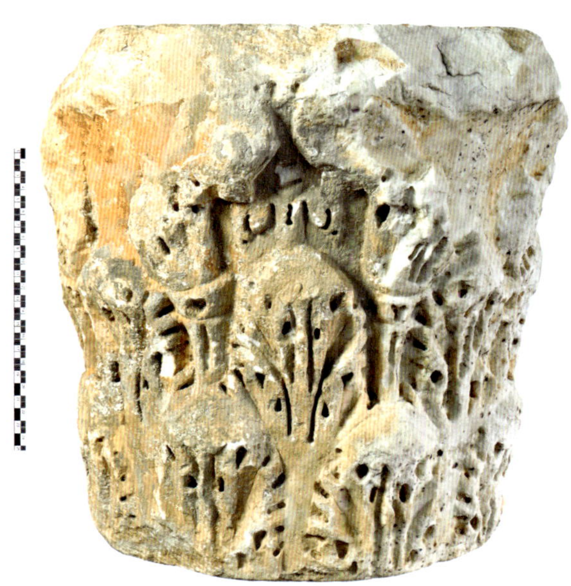

Fig. 2
Ingelheim, Mainz-Bingen distr. Marble Corinthian capital, rediscovered 2010 (private collection). 2nd-3rd century AD. Originally most probably from Italy/Rome (Stadt Ingelheim am Rhein. Photo: D. Wolf)

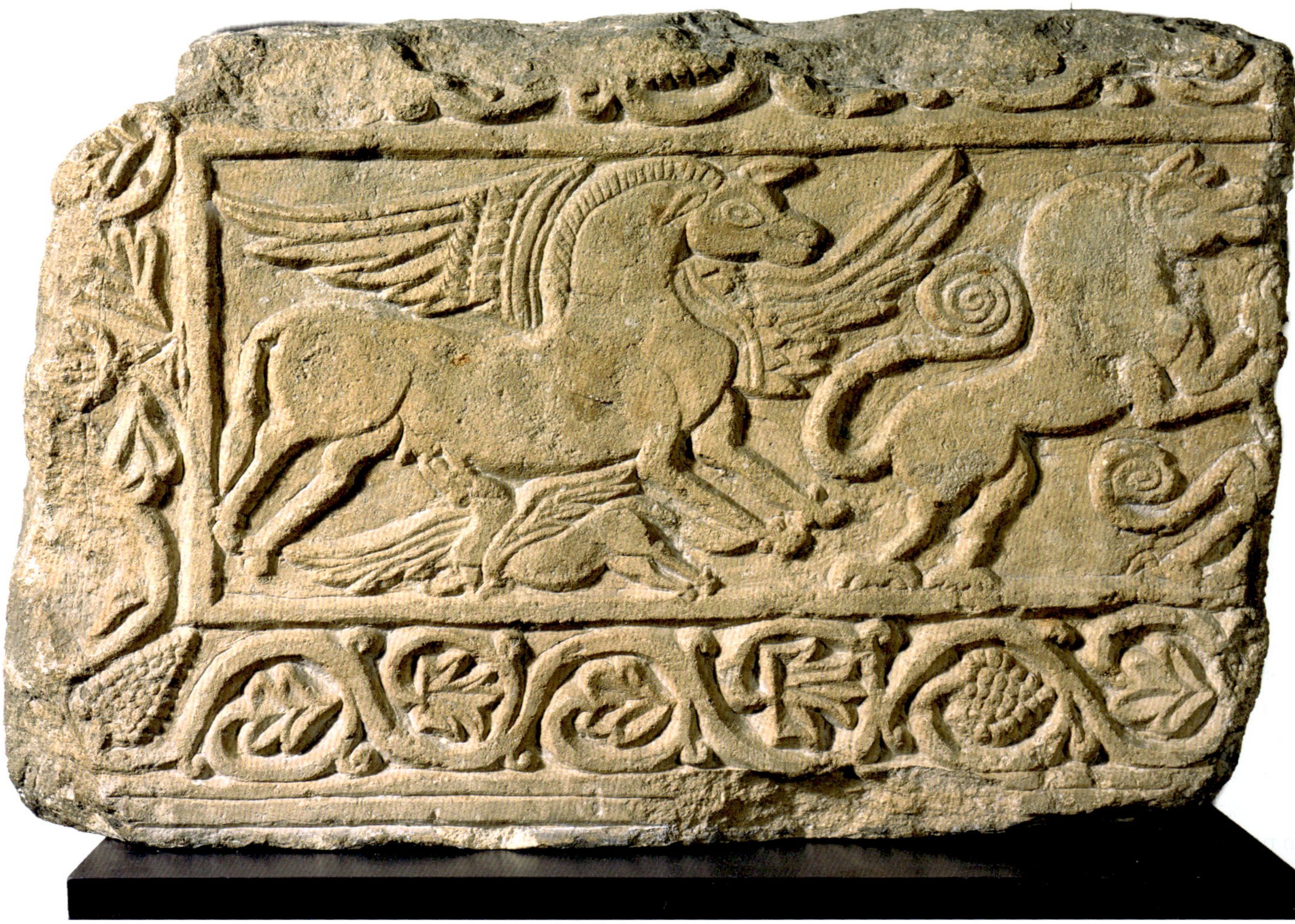

Fig. 3
Ingelheim, Mainz-Bingen distr. Fragmented limestone plate with mythical creatures and pampres. 1st half of the 8th century or around 800 (GDKE/Landesmuseum Trier)

ly-decorated relief plate of Langobardic origin or inspired by Langobardic models. (Fig. 3) This »winged horse relief« clearly points out that many different technical and stylistic influences impacted art and architecture around 800.

For the time being, it is not possible to decipher these phenomena, let alone the programme behind them. One can however state that where material, form, complexity or skill had produced objects of exceptional quality, these *realia* of (late) Roman antiquity had a latent influence on the production of the Carolingian period.

Under the hands of the archaeologists, the soil of Ingelheim revealed yet another precious and unique find: during excavations in the palace settlement, a gold coin with the image of Charlemagne was discovered in 1996. It shows a bust of Charlemagne with laurel wreath and emperor's cloak. Also imprinted on the obverse side is an abbreviated form of the imperial title: *D(ominus) N(oster) KARLUS IMP(erator) AUG(ustus) REX F(rancorum) ET L(angobardorum)*. The coin measuring 19.5 mm and weighing 4.18 g follows the form and weight of the Roman solidus. This piece, which was minted after 800 in Arles, presents a yet unsolvable conflict with the coin reform of 794, which was meant to introduce a monometallic silver coinage into the entire Frankish Empire. (Fig. 4)

The palace of Ingelheim is a relic of Charlemagne's *renovatio imperii*. The great importance given to it by the Carolingians and subsequent dynasties as a seat of government was maintained until the middle of the 11th century. From then on, the king resided there

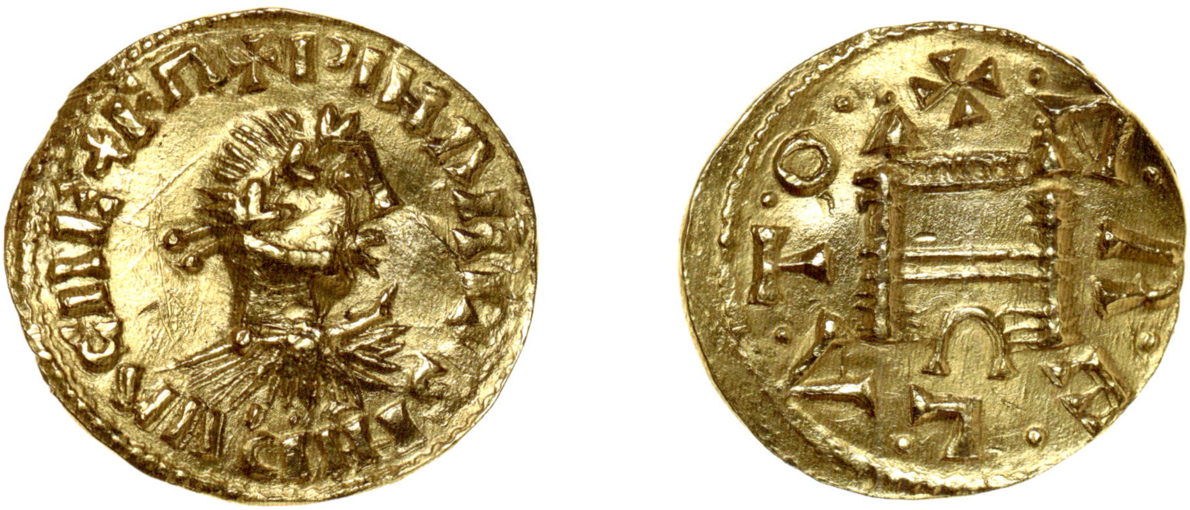

Fig. 4
Ingelheim, Mainz-Bingen distr. Gold coin with the head of Charlemagne. Front and rear. Probably around 800-814. From Arles (Stadt Ingelheim am Rhein. Photo: V. Iserhardt)

less frequently, until the palace and the entire ground at Ingelheim were pledged to County Palatine of the Rhine. Today, the monument is included among the »Archaeological treasures of the Rhine and Moselle«, after excavations brought it to light once again, at least in parts.

Bibliography

C. Ehlers, »Auch herrliche Paläste baute er...« – Karl der Große in Ingelheim nach den Schriftquellen. In: H. Grewe (Hg.), Auf den Spuren Karls des Großen in Ingelheim. Entdeckungen – Deutungen – Wandlungen (Petersberg 2014).

H. Grewe, Pfalzen Karls des Großen. In: Deutsches Historisches Museum (Hg.), Kaiser und Kalifen. Karl der Große und die Mächte am Mittelmeer um 800 (Mainz 2014) 158–181.

H. Grewe, Das Nachwirken römischer Stadtarchitektur – ausgewählte Aspekte am Beispiel der Pfalz Karls des Großen in Ingelheim. In: Ein Traum von Rom. Römisches Stadtleben in Südwestdeutschland. Ausstellungskatalog Stuttgart und Trier 2014 (Stuttgart 2014) 346–357.

P. Haupt, Die karolingische Wasserleitung bei Ingelheim, Kr. Mainz-Bingen. In: Frontinus-Gesellschaft (Hg.), Wasser auf Burgen im Mittelalter. Geschichte der Wasserversorgung 7 (Mainz 2007) 183–189.

P.-H. Martin, Eine Goldmünze Karls des Großen. In: Numismatisches Nachrichtenblatt 46, 1997, 351–55.

B. Schulze-Böhm, Die Bauskulptur der karolingischen Pfalz Ingelheim. Zur Ausstattung frühmittelalterlicher Herrschaftsarchitektur. In: H. Grewe (Hg.), Archäologie und Bauforschung in der Pfalz Ingelheim am Rhein, im Druck.

A prick spur from Schlüsselgasse in Worms

LUKAS CLEMENS

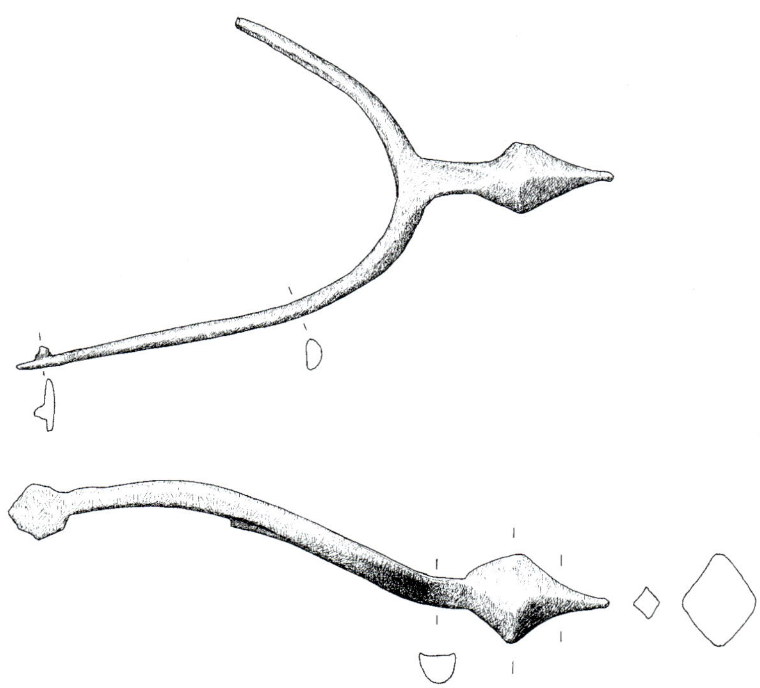

Fig. 1
Worms, city of Worms. Prick spur from Schlüsselgasse. (after M. Diederich)

During an archaeological exploration undertaken in 1980 in the Jewish quarter of Worms, in Schlüsselgasse to be precise, which branches off as a cul-de-sac to the southwest between the houses Judengasse 50 and 52, a fire debris horizon was discovered containing find material from the high Middle Ages, including relief tiles and imported Pingsdorf pottery. The most interesting among the metal finds is an 11 cm long iron prick spur with a double pyramid spike, a slightly-bent neck, and diamond-shaped ends, one of which is still preserved. (Fig. 1) Riding equipment of this kind is often found on castle sites from the high Middle Ages. They all date from the 12th century. The find from Worms is indicative of the presence of armed riders. We cannot say whether the owner was a Jew or a Christian, since the two communities often lived in close vicinity to one another. Armed or knight-like Jews are in fact documented especially in connection with Rhineland in the high Middle Ages. For instance: members of the Jewish community of Mainz, who in 1096 had fled from the crusaders under count Emicho von Flonheim into the archiepiscopal castle, defended themselves unsuccessfully with arms against the mob. The continuation of the *Gesta Treverorum* informs us about the personal physician of the Trier archbishop Bruno (1102-1124), a Jew by the name of Josua, who stood out by his knightly way of life *(quem circumdabat militaris habitus)*. In the context of armed Jews, there is an interesting Hebrew source which recalls a siege of the city of Worms in 1201 with the participation of Jews in combat. Furthermore, in the 60s and 70s of the 13th century, a Jew by the name of Michael is mentioned, who had first participated in the service of the nobleman Frederick of Eberstein in a feud against the Mainz archbishopric and later fought together with count Henry of Leiningen against the city of Worms.

Bibliography

N. Goßler, Untersuchungen zur Formenkunde und Chronologie mittelalterlicher Stachelsporen in Deutschland (10.–14. Jahrhundert), In: Bericht der Römisch-Germanischen Kommission 79, 1998, 479–664.

M. Grünewald, Unter dem Plaster von Worms. Archäologie in der Stadt (Lindenberg/Allgäu 2012) bes. 176–187.

C. Magin, »Waffenrecht« und »Waffenverbot« für Juden im Mittelalter – zu einem Mythos der Forschungsgeschichte, In: Aschkenas 13, 2003, 17–33.

M. J. Wenninger, Von jüdischen Rittern und anderen waffentragenden Juden im mittelalterlichen Deutschland, In: Aschkenas 13, 2003, 35–82.

A bone comb with bronze shaft fittings from Trier

LUKAS CLEMENS

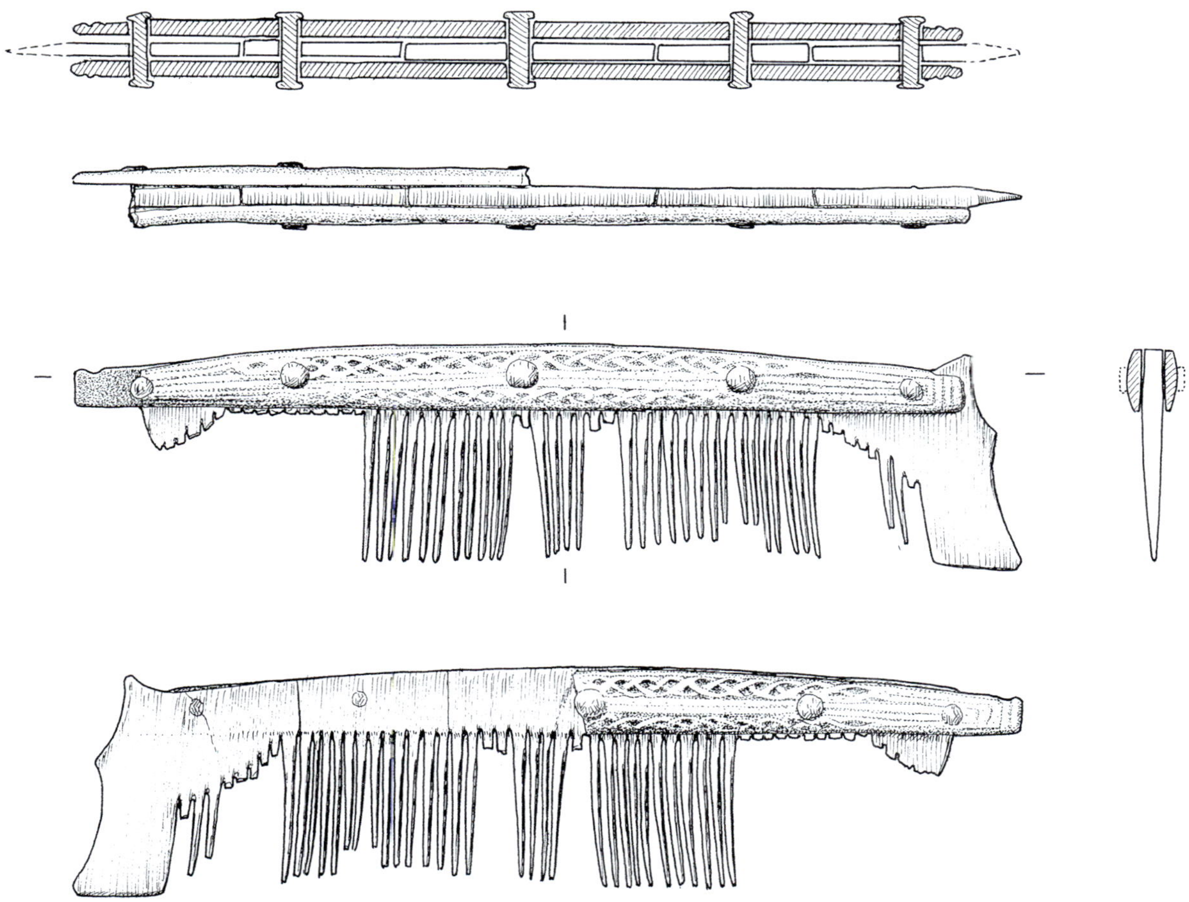

Fig. 1
Trier, city of Trier. Drawing and reconstruction of a bone comb with bronze shaft fittings. (after M. Diederich)

During preparations for the construction of a new kitchen tract within the area of the Vereinigte Hospizien in Trier in 1996, a section of the early medieval settlement of the noble nuns' convent of St. Maria *ad horrea* or *in horreo* (later St. Irminen-Oeren) was examined; it had been established around the middle of the 7th century in the late antique warehouses (*horrea*) near the Moselle. The documented finds include a partly excavated pit-hut: its surviving northern side with three post settings, one of which had visibly been renewed

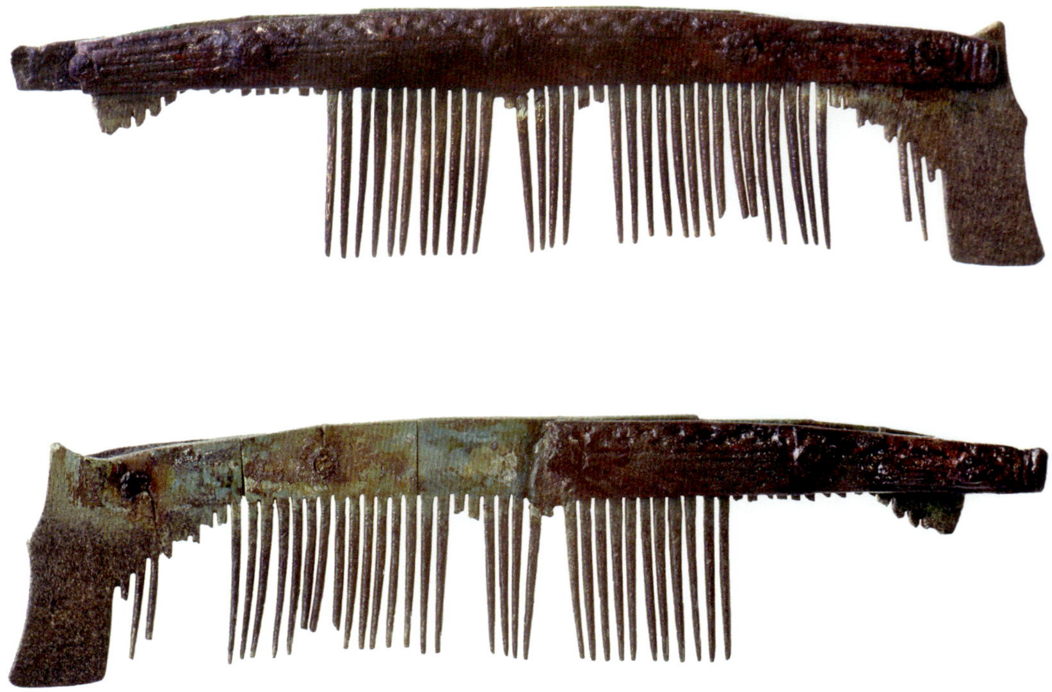

Fig. 2
Trier, city of Trier: Bone comb with bronze shaft fittings, front and back. (GDKE/Landesmuseum-Trier/T. Zühmer)

once, was 3.80 m long. The much stronger middle post (with a diameter of 40 cm, while the outer posts were 18 cm and 24 cm) implies a central function within the building structure. The western and eastern sides could still be examined over a length of about 3.10 m. On all three preserved sides of the building were small ditches, approx. 10 cm wide and 10 cm deep, which probably served to hold boards or planks. The rich find material of the infill contained among other things a pressed foil fibula and a denarius of Charles III, minted in Trier between 911 and 923. In the outer area, a coin fibula was also recovered. The unusual find is a bone comb, whose relatively intact recovery still has a length of 12 cm and whose side grip and teeth are up to 3 cm, with bronze shaft fittings and braid decoration. (Fig. 1) The comb is joined to the shaft fittings by five bronze rivets. (Fig. 2) There are parallels from the Baltic Sea area, especially from Kosel in Schleswig-Holstein, Birka, Gotland, Staraja Ladoga or Kaup in East Prussia (as well as from Frisia – Almenum near Harlingen, Aalsum, Groningen province). The easternmost site detected so far is Bolšoe Timerevo near Jaroslavl in Russia. (Fig. 3) The piece may have been manufactured in the commercial centre of Haithabu on the river Schlei, where numerous fragmented moulds for making bronze shaft fittings but also the finished pieces themselves were found. The site where they were discovered together with other finds is safely datable to the 10th century. The piece from Trier is evidence of the inclusion of the Moselle region in the Frisian trade with the North and Baltic Sea area; this is supported by finds of coins (sceattas) and dress components, but also by reports of miracles. The biography of Saint Maximin, written around mid-8th century, tells us of miraculous healing attributed to him after his death. He is reported to have healed 13 people within one year, including three Frisians. The version of the *Vita sancti Maximini* revised in 839 mentions a Frisian by the name of Ibbo, who in the service of the abbey named after Saint Maximin undertook trips overseas, i.e. to England and

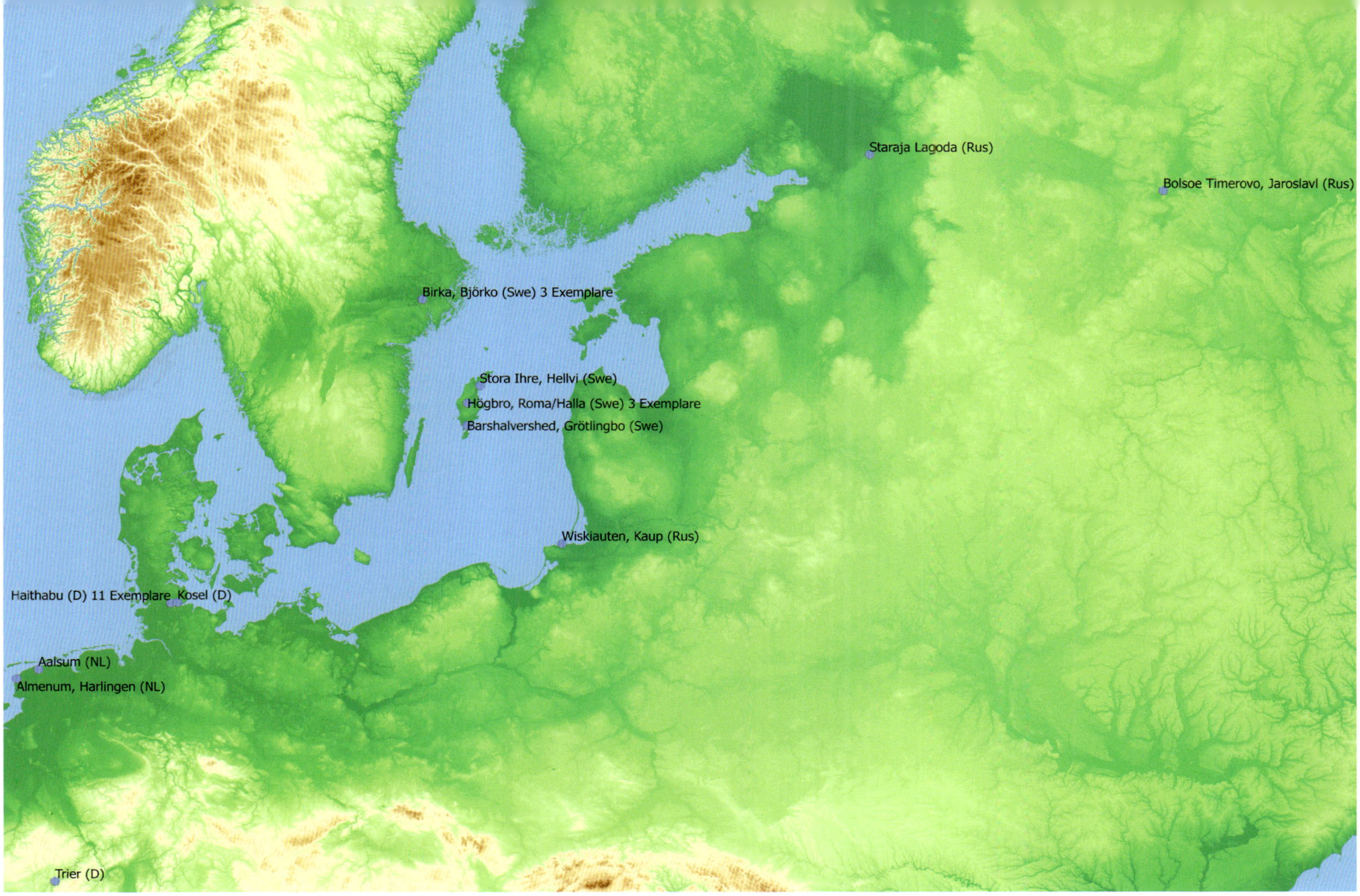

Scandinavia. According to the miracle report, when he and his ships were caught in a storm, he prayed to the monastery's patron saint and was saved.

Bibliography

L. Clemens, Archäologische Beobachtungen zu frühmittelalterlichen Siedlungsstrukturen in Trier. In: S. Felgenhauer-Schmiedt, A. Eibner, H. Knittler (Hg.), Zwischen Römersiedlung und mittelalterlicher Stadt. Archäologische Aspekte zur Kontinuitätsfrage (Beiträge zur Mittelalterarchäologie in Österreich 17 (Wien 2001) 43–66.

M. Müller-Wille, Hedeby und sein Umland. Archäologische Zeugnisse des Handels, In: B. Hardh, L. Larsson, D. Olausson, R. Petré (Hg.), Trade and Exchange in Prehistory. Studies in Honour of Berta Stjernquist (Lund 1988) 271–278.

D. Meier, Die wikingerzeitliche Siedlung von Kosel (Kosel-West), Kreis Rendsburg-Eckernförde. Offa-Bücher 76 (Neumünster 1994) bes. 154–156.

K. Petry, Monetäre Entwicklung, Handelsintensität und wirtschaftliche Beziehungen des oberlothringischen Raumes vom Anfang des 6. bis zur Mitte des 12. Jahrhunderts. Trierer Petermännchen. Wissenschaftliche Reihe 2 (Trier 1992) bes. 332–333.

Vita S. Maximini antiqua (I), In: Acta Sanctorum, Mai VII (Antwerpen 1688) 21–25, hier 24

Bruno Krusch (Hg.), Lupus von Ferrieres, Vita Maximini (II), In: Monumenta Germaniae Historica, Scriptores rerum Merovingicarum I,2 (Hannover 1896) 74–82, hier 80–81.

Fig. 3
Map showing the distribution of bone combs with bronze shaft fittings after Müller-Wille 1988 and Meier 1994 with the new find from Trier. (GDKE/Landesarchäologie/Schwab, Map base: SRTM data NASA/ows.terrestris.de/osm/service)

The Treasure of Lingenfeld

WERNER TRANSIER

The Treasure of Lingenfeld was found on 24 November 1969 in an agricultural estate during excavation works for the enlargement of a barn. Six silver vessels (Fig. 1), golden jewellery, and at least 2,369 coins were contained in a broken pot. The find was not reported to the agency in charge of archaeological monuments and was distributed among the finders at the find spot. Except for the jewellery and some coins, 95 % of the treasure could be reconstructed. Only three of the silver vessels and a few hundred coins are kept in the Historical Museum of the Palatinate in Speyer and thus publicly owned.

The dating of the find results from the youngest coins in the find: 1,514 hellers from the years 1346-1349 minted by the imperial city of Speyer. (Fig. 2) Nearly 80 % of all the coins were minted in Speyer. Hellers from Schwaebisch Hall and Frankfurt, and pfennige from Strasbourg, Basel, Offenburg, Laufenburg, and Solothurn are also represented in considerable numbers.

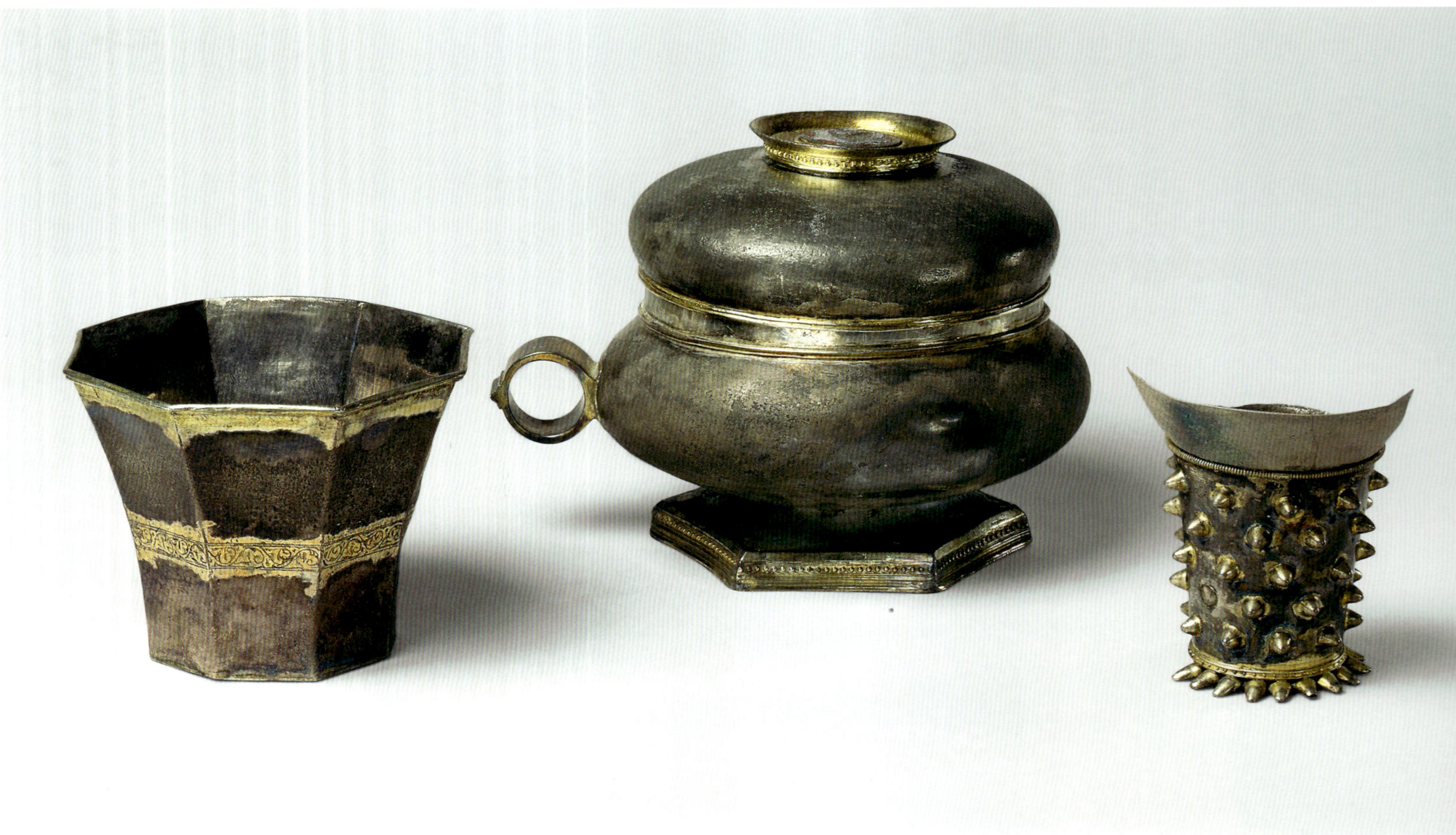

Fig. 1 Lingenfeld, Germersheim distr. Silver vessel from the treasure of Lingenfeld. (Historisches Museum Speyer)

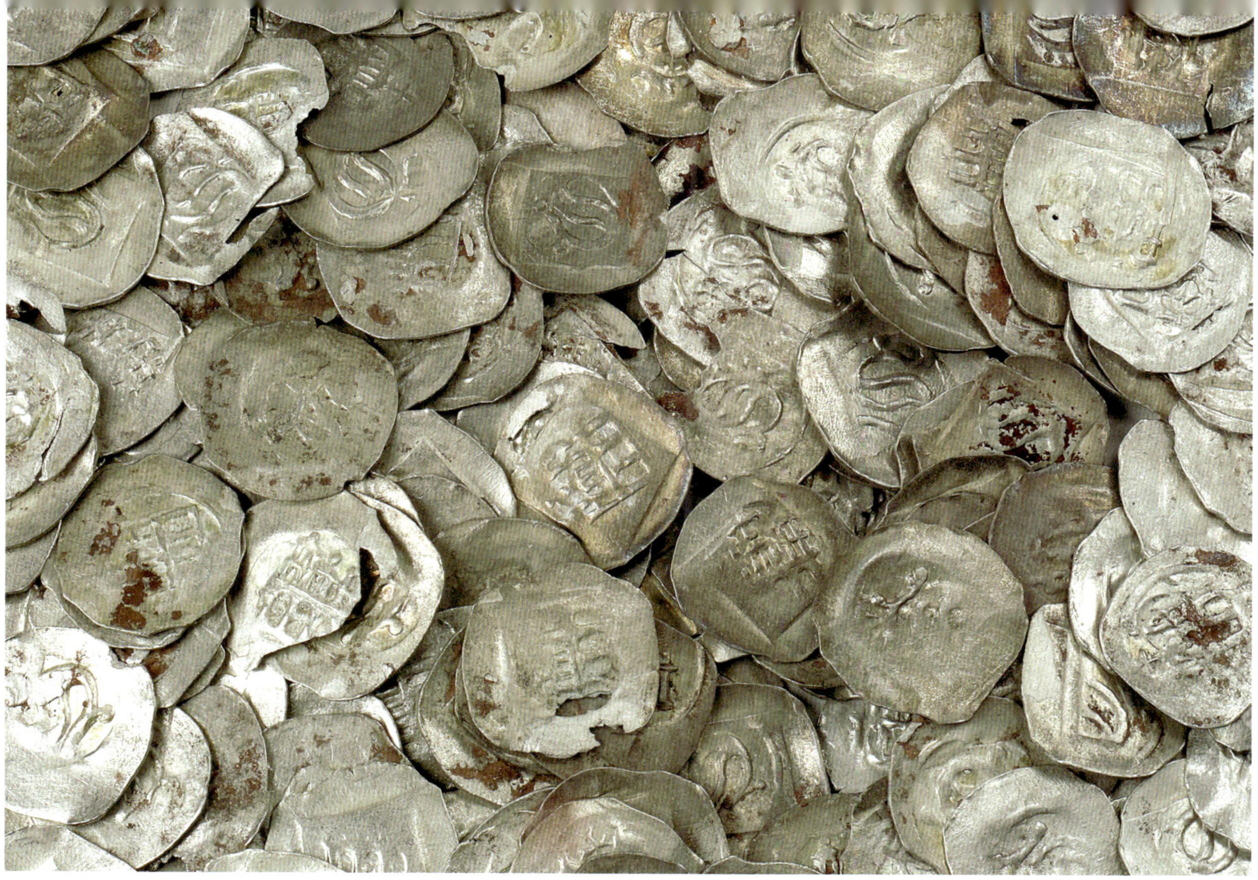

Fig. 2.
Lingenfeld, Germersheim distr. Heller of the city of Speyer (1347–1349) from the treasure of Lingenfeld. (Historisches Museum Speyer)

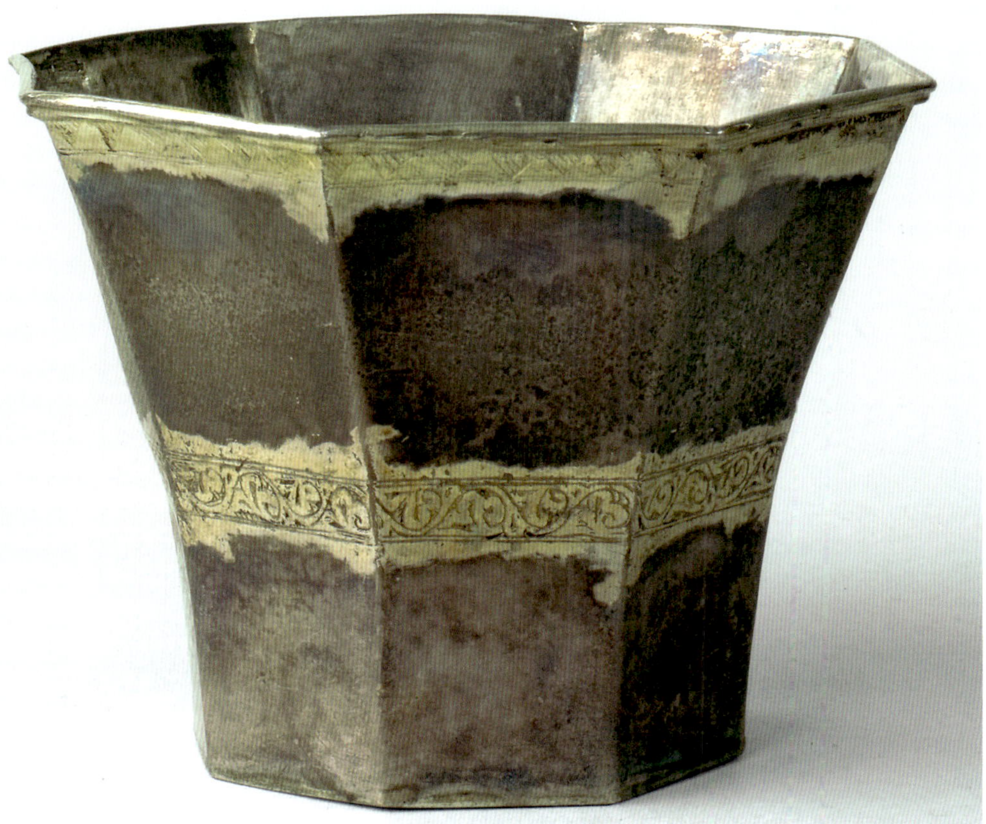

Fig. 3
Lingenfeld, Germersheim distr. Octagonal beaker, silver, partly gilded. (Historisches Museum Speyer)

Fig. 4
Lingenfeld, Germersheim distr. Double beaker with coat of arms, silver, partly gilded. (Historisches Museum Speyer)

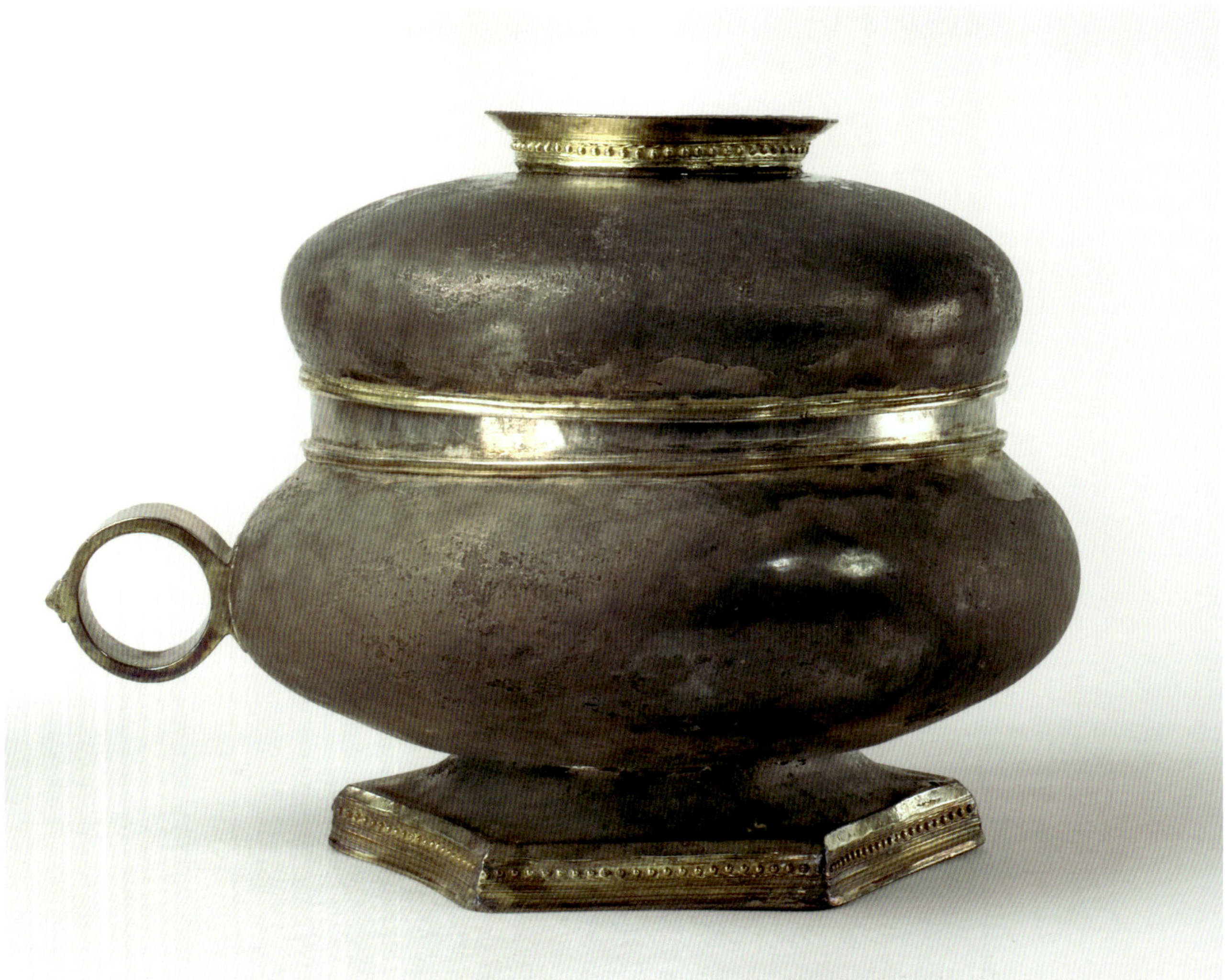

Except for the large number of coins from Speyer, the composition of the find is not unusual for the Upper Rhine area. The high percentage of Speyer coins is an indication that the treasure was put together in that city or its immediate surroundings. The partly gilded silver vessels of high quality are the only pieces from the Palatinate area which have been preserved from this epoch. They are drinking vessels of different types: an octagonal, partly gilded beaker (Fig. 3), a round double beaker with an enamelled coat of arms inserted in the top part (Fig. 4), and a partly gilded shaft (with foot) of a goblet. Vessels like that could only be afforded by well-off households.

There are a number of treasure finds of similar composition from this epoch in the area of the Holy Roman Empire, of which the find at Erfurt is larger than all the other finds taken together. The finds of Colmar, Erfurt, and Weissenfels contained Jewish wedding rings. This links them to the anti-Jewish pogroms of 1348/1349 before the outbreak of the plague, when Jews were wrongly blamed with causing the epidemic by poisoning the wells and subsequently killed in many cities as a »precaution«. A comparison of the sequence of pogroms in various cities suggests that these excesses occurred with the approval of the authorities in charge of protecting Jews, since they directly benefited from the killing of Jews who were mainly active in money lending. The fear of the plague and death was used for a bloody debt redemption at the expense of the Jewish creditors. (Fig. 5)

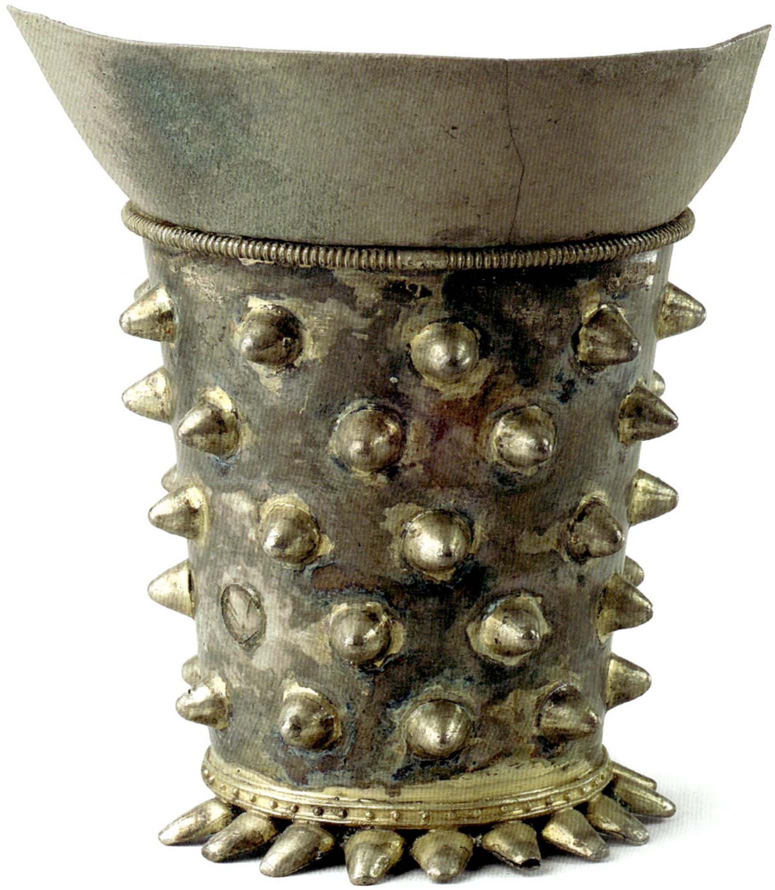

Fig. 5
Lingenfeld, Germersheim distr. Fragment of a beaker with nubs, silver, partly gilded. (Historisches Museum Speyer)

On the basis of their composition, which is identical except for the Jewish wedding ring (silver vessels, jewellery, coins), it is likely that the other finds are to be linked to the Black Death pogroms as well. The owner of the Lingenfeld treasure was obviously one of the Jewish money lenders from Speyer. The wave of pogroms did not hit the Jews unexpectedly. Before the killings in Speyer, which started on 25 January 1349, the owner (and the treasure) must have been on his way to the territory of the Electoral Palatinate near Germersheim, where the Jews had already been driven away or murdered at the end of 1348. He certainly sustained material losses. We do not know whether he survived.

Bibliography

H. Ehrend, G. Stein, F. Wielandt, Der Münzschatz von Lingenfeld (Speyer 1975).

G. Stein, Der Schatzfund von Lingenfeld, In: Die Juden von Speyer. Hg. von der Bezirksgruppe Speyer, Historischer Verein der Pfalz (Speyer 2004) 125–131.

M. Stürzebecher, Der Schatzfund aus der Michaelisstraße in Erfurt, In: Die mittelalterliche jüdische Kultur in Erfurt, Bd. 1 Der Schatzfund, Archäologie – Kunstgeschichte – Siedlungsgeschichte. Thüringisches Landesamt für Denkmalpflege und Archäologie (Weimar 2010) 60–304, bes. 158–185.

The seal matrix of the Trier Jew Muskinus

ANDREAS LEHNERTZ

The only surviving private seal matrix of a Jew of the medieval realm was found in 1988 during archaeological excavations at the Trier cattle market (Viehmarkt) and had probably been placed in the grave of one of the seven individuals buried there. (Fig. 1) The medieval Jewish cemetery must have been located here, as suggested by the name *Jüdemerstraße* (»Jewish wall road«) situated to the west at today's St. Antonius church. There are many indications that this church was built on part of the Jewish cemetery, which was desecrated in 1349 during the Black Death pogroms. The former building of St. Antonius church is documented for the first time in 1406 as *nuwe capelle in Judemer gaßen*.

Muskinus was one of the most influential Jews of the Trier prince-archbishopric and worked from not later than 1323 until his death in September 1336 in the financial administration of archbishop Balduin of Luxembourg (1307–1354), who called him his *negociator*. The brilliant Jewish financier was in charge of the archiepiscopal central payments office; it appears that entries were recorded in Hebrew and translated into Latin at the end of the financial year. In community matters, he also appeared often as *parnas* (community leader) of the Jews of Trier.

The seal matrix was very likely smashed after Muskinus died in September 1336 and put in his grave with him. Breaking the seal was the normal procedure when a seal keeper died, but his wife or children could sometimes continue using it. Putting a broken seal in the grave of the deceased is already known from Christian graves. Most of the Jewish graves from the Middle Ages however no longer exist today, since the cemeteries were destroyed. For those few still intact, the peace of the dead is being respected, which makes them inaccessible for research. For this reason, finds like Muskinus' seal matrix remain rare fortuities.

The bronze seal has an eye in the form of a trefoil at the upper end of its shaft; it allowed the seal keeper to fix it with a string or chain for displaying it round his neck or on his belt. The circumscription and the image are in Gothic style and still show numerous details, which could only be seen on very few Jewish seals of the medieval realm in such high quality and concentration. (Fig. 2) The size of the seal face is typical for the private seals of Jews of approx. 20–40 mm, but also for the seals of citizens who were legally associated with Jews.

The seal of Muskinus is no doubt a highly representative legal object, which is linked to the position of the seal keeper working as a financial administrator of Balduin and as parnas of the Jewish community. Muskinus had previously used another seal, the impression of which is documented on a deed of 1330. Ownership of more than one seal has been documented only in exceptional cases even for Christian citizens. This item is thus an expression of an increased self-confidence and need for a display in status of the Jewish elite.

The image of the seal shows a stylized tree of life feeding two birds of paradise in the circular foil. The remarkable aspect of the image is that these are not motifs that one could call specifically Jewish. They are rather an expression of a Christian-Jewish canon of seal images, since both depictions are also well-known from Christian seal keepers. Nonetheless, the motifs were undoubtedly interpreted differently by Christians and Jews. The tree of life refers to the Torah, depicted as the source of life, as indicated until today by the name of the two poles on which the Torah is rolled and unrolled: tree of life (*etz chaim*). However, the image of the seal refers in particular to messianic symbols, since the tree and the birds both relate to paradise.

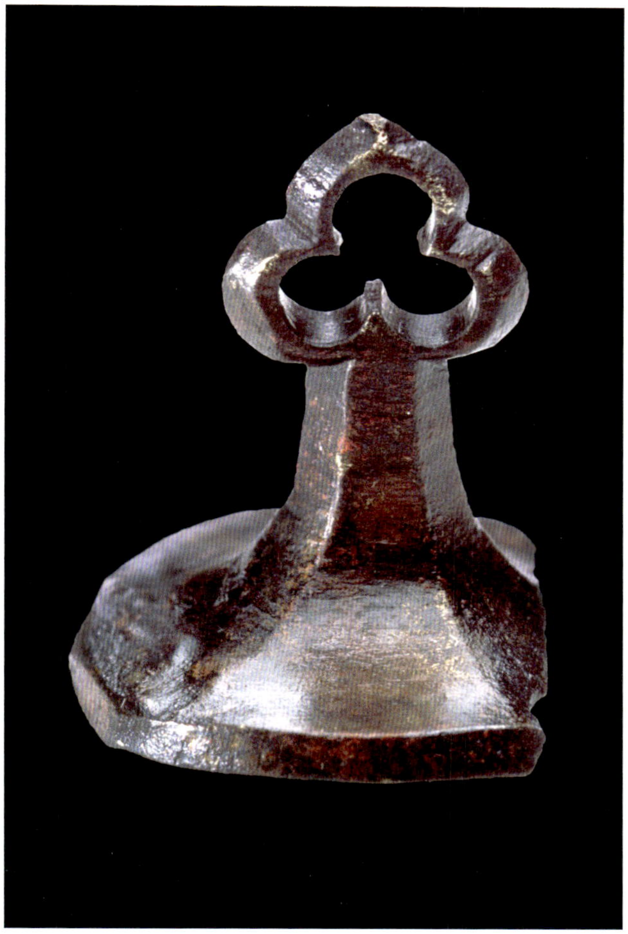

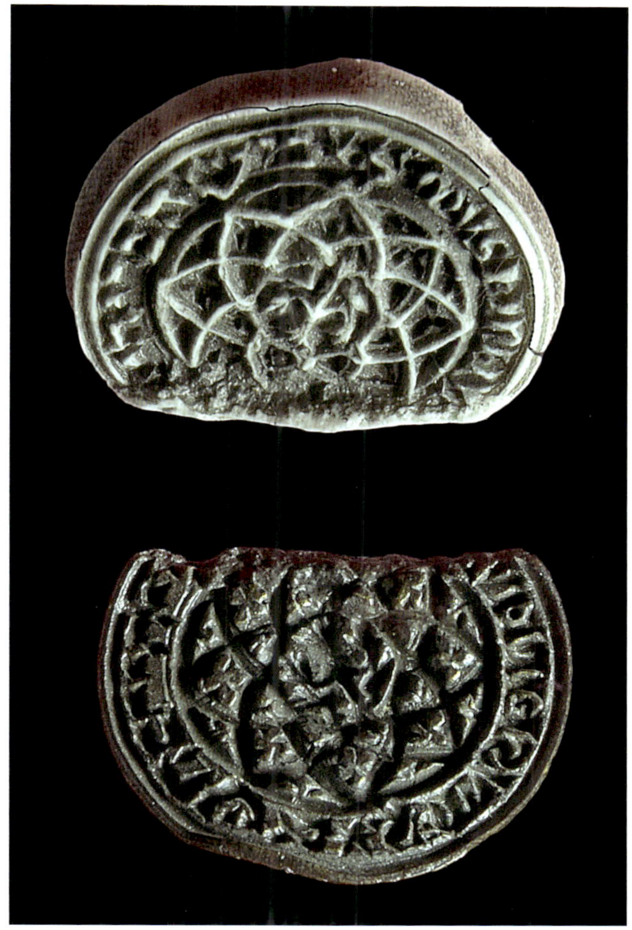

Fig. 1
Trier, Landesmuseum Trier. Smashed seal of Muskinus. (GDKE/Landesmuseum Trier/Th. Zühmer)

Fig. 2
Trier, Landesmuseum Trier. Sealing matrix (top) and impression (bottom) of the seal. Circumscription left: * s(igillvm) mvskini . ivd[ei] […]; right: […] [אל] משה ב״ר יחי* (Engl.: Moses, son of master Jechi[el] […]). (GDKE/Landesmuseum Trier/ Th. Zühmer)

Bibliography

L. **Clemens**, Archäologische Beobachtungen zur Trierer Judengemeinde im Mittelalter, In: Synagogen, Mikwen, Siedlungen. Jüdisches Alltagsleben im Lichte neuer archäologischer Funde, hg. v. Fritz Backhaus und Egon Wamers. Schriften des Archäologischen Museums Frankfurt 19 (Frankfurt a. M. 2004) 165–177.

A. **Haverkamp**, Die Juden im mittelalterlichen Trier, In: Trierisches Jahrbuch 19, 1979, 5–57.

In English:

A. **Lehnertz**, Two Seals of Muskinus the Jew (Moshe b. Yehiel, d. 1336), the Archbishop of Trier's Negociator, In: A Companion to Seals in the Middle Ages, ed. Laura Whatley (Leiden, 2019), 243–263.

The Dalberger Hof in Mainz

RONALD KNÖCHLEIN

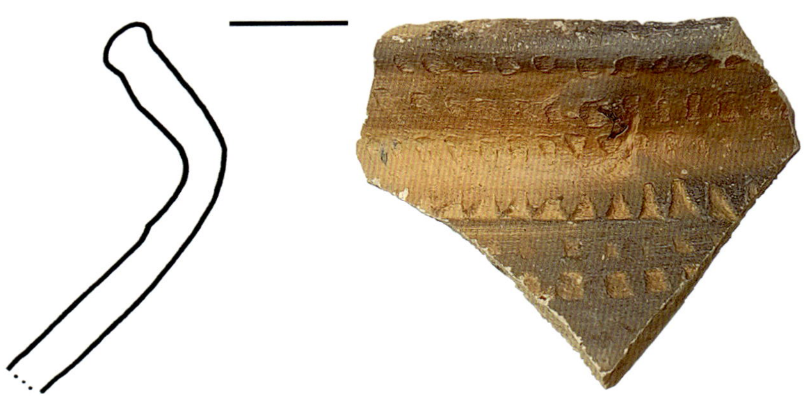

Fig. 1
Mainz, city of Mainz. Early Middle Ages. Badorf pottery of the 8th–9th century with roller stamp decoration. (GDKE/Landesarchäologie/Mainz/R. Knöchlein))

After the examination of the Roman cult area at Römerpassage, the excavations by the Mainz branch in the inner area of the Dalberger Hof in the block made up of Emmeransstraße, Klarastraße, and Ottiliengasse is the most outstanding undertaking of the past 20 years in the city centre of Mainz. More than two thirds of the ca. 1800 m² of the internal courtyard could be studied, mostly in closely associated partial areas, from spring 2008 to spring 2009. The quality and variety of the findings and finds make this excavation a particularly valuable source for the settlement history of the old city of Mainz from the time around the birth of Christ until today.

The entire stretch of some 450 years of Roman times can be documented with impressive building findings, supported by rich find material. In antiquity, these were residential quarters for the local average population: without elements of luxury, but very solid in the usual Roman architectural quality. In this context, several well-preserved hearths plus walking levels are remarkable. A solid pile foundation was essential for erecting buildings on ground that was at all times (and still is) more or less soaked because of the high groundwater level. This building practice was repeatedly documented at this site as well. Because of the good preservation conditions for wood, some wooden piles provided dendrodata of the 1st and 2nd century AD. Other wooden building findings from Roman times were also studied: e.g. a latrine (around 154) and a well-shaft very carefully clad with wood and built around the year 250.

The present state of the excavations already allows us to determine that the settlement was used throughout the late 4th, 5th and 6th centuries and during the younger Frankish period (7th–9th century). (Fig. 1) This is remarkable insofar as no complete abandonment to the west occurred in post-Roman times' i.e. outside the core of the post-antique residual settlement along the city wall on the side of the Rhine in a strip from St. Quintin in the north through the Brand to the area of the cathedral in the south (St. Martin, St. Marien, St. Johannis). Apparently, the above-mentioned residual settlement strip in the east, which was dominated by the bishop, was joined in Merovingian times (and especially since the 7th century) by farm settlements of the regional Frankish upper class. The bishops of that time typically came from this group. For instance, the name of the nearby Betzelsgasse still reminds us of the estate of bishop Petilin. We do not know which particular group settled in the area of the later Dalberger Hof. The foundation of estates outside the continuously inhabited core, but still within the former antique city area, is a phenomenon that can also be noted elsewhere (e.g. the former settlements Böheim, Musil, Castel, and Bergentheim in Trier).

The local settlement tradition established in Frankish times appears to have continued into the high Middle Ages (historically 911/913–1250). The find quantity

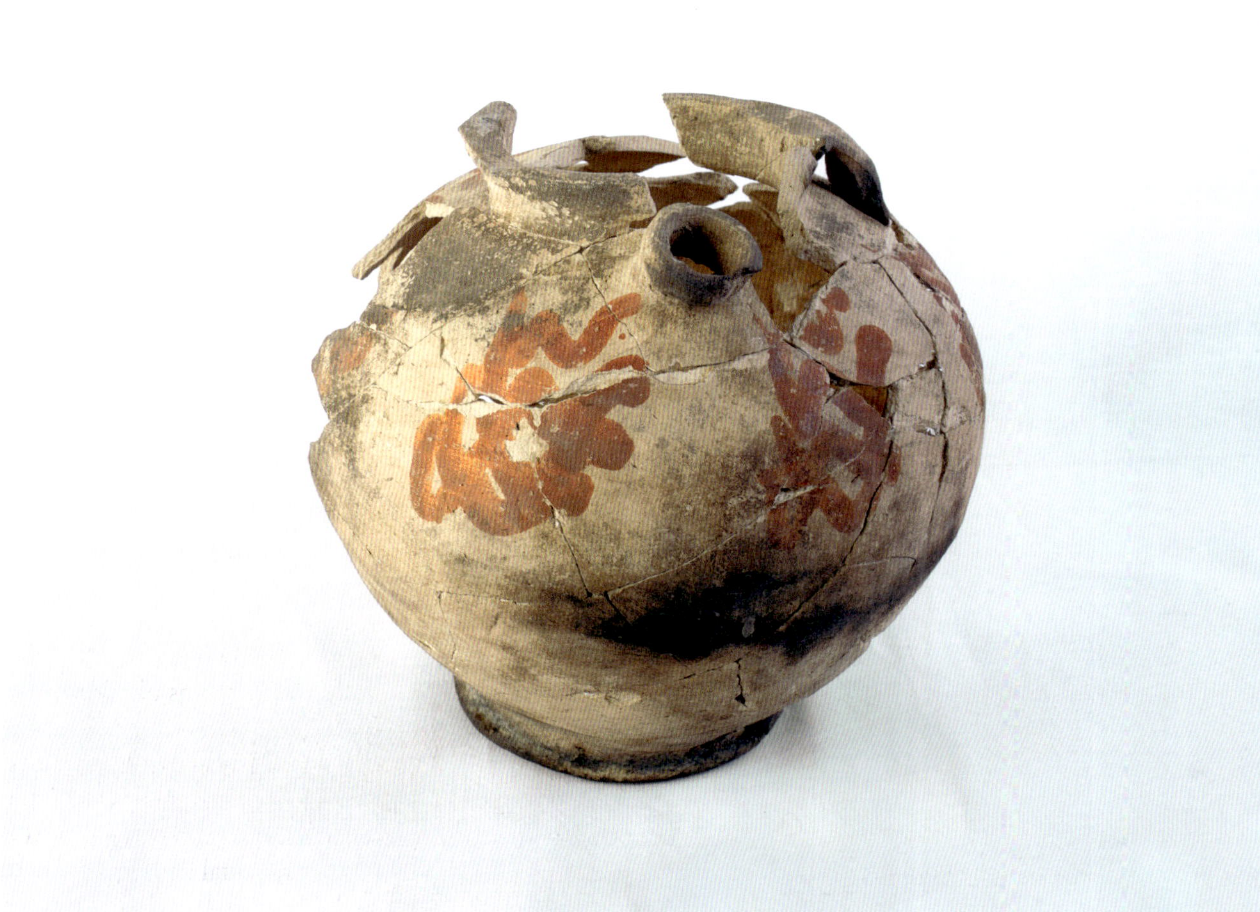

Fig. 2
Mainz, city of Mainz. High Middle Ages. Pingsdorf-type pottery with red paint. (GDKE/Landesarchäologie/Mainz/R. Knöchlein)

varies at the same rhythm as in other parts of the old city area: finds for the Frankish time and the early high Middle Ages until about 1100 (Fig. 2) are comparatively rare, while there is plenty of material for the following periods. (Fig. 3)

Especially during the early high Middle Ages (10th–11th century), the area around the Dalberger Hof is connected to the presence of Jews, who represented a good portion of the Mainz residents. (Fig. 4) This presence can be divided into the following main stages: 10th century – (23 August)1349; 1355–1438; 1445–1471; from 1583 onwards. The oldest and by far the longest period (10th century – 1349) with some 400 years is the one to which the notion »SchUM« and the chain of associations connected with it can be attached concretely. The contemporary use of the abbreviation SchUM is documented for the first time in 1220 in Mainz (Takkanot Schum) on the occasion of a meeting of rabbis, when the close cooperation of the Jewish communities of Speyer, Worms, and Mainz became evident; for example, in establishing common codes of conduct in religious-ethical, social, and economic matters as templates for the entire western Jewry. The Dalberger Hof is situated in the centre of the widely dispersed settlement area of Jewish people, which can be inferred from sources of late medieval/early modern times. (Fig. 5) It should, however, be noted that there was no closed Jewish residential area in the sense of a ghetto in medieval Mainz and that Christians and Jews lived closely together. Moreover, the sources do not tell us clearly whether the real estate formerly owned by Jews were only cultivated plots or actually the residences of Jew-

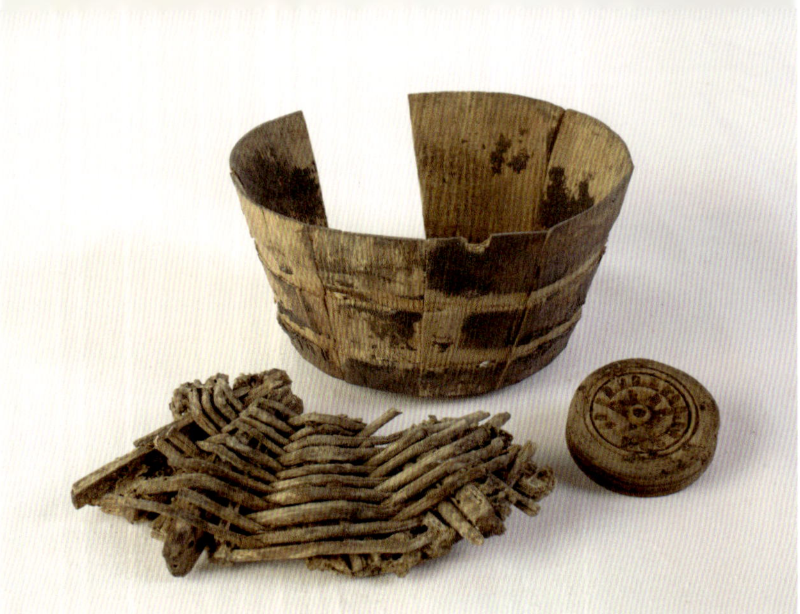

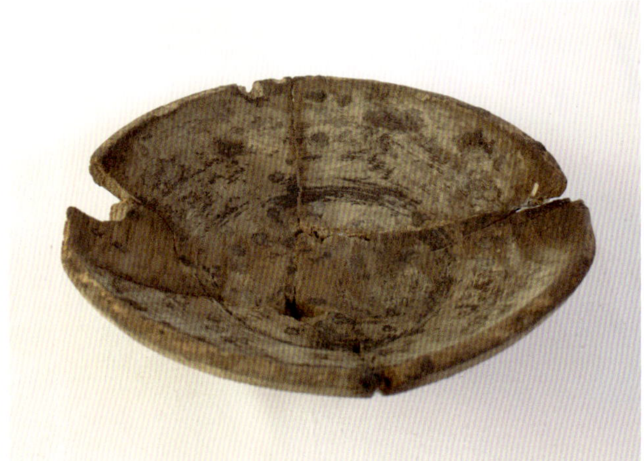

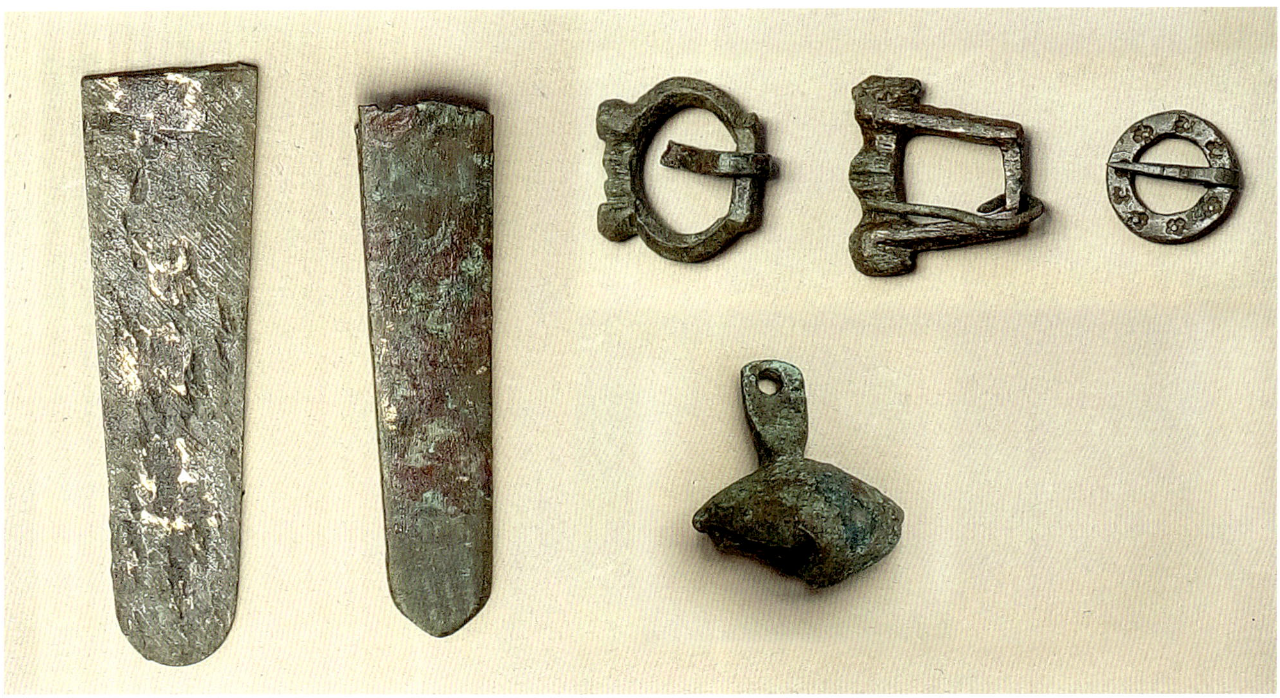

Fig. 3
Mainz, city of Mainz. Late Middle Ages. Metal and wood finds. (GDKE/Landesarchäologie/Mainz/R. Knöchlein)

ish families. In any case, no previous Jewish ownership is mentioned for the area of the later Dalberger Hof in the topographic sources of the 15th and 16th centuries. The buildings »Zum bunten Mantel«, »Zum Frohen«, »Zum Schlegel«, »Zur Setzrebe«, and »Zum Juckel«, which stood here in the 15th century, were owned by citizens, patricians, nobility, and the church. Various excavation findings (walls, wells, and latrine shafts) can be assigned to them. In later times (16th –17th century), this complex situation was replaced by nearly exclusive occupancy by the houses of the aristocracy, a reflection of the new political situation brought about by the Mainz Diocesan Feud of 1461/1462. Inter alia, direct evidence of the family behind the Brendelscher Hof was found during excavations. To date, the Jewish neighbours have not become noticeable in the area of the Dalberger Hof through relevant finds (objects with Jewish symbols, Hebrew graffiti etc.). Nevertheless, it is expected that the archaeological sources will provide further information about the common everyday life of the two groups (Christians and Jews), in spite of their seemingly dissimilar social and cultural traditions.

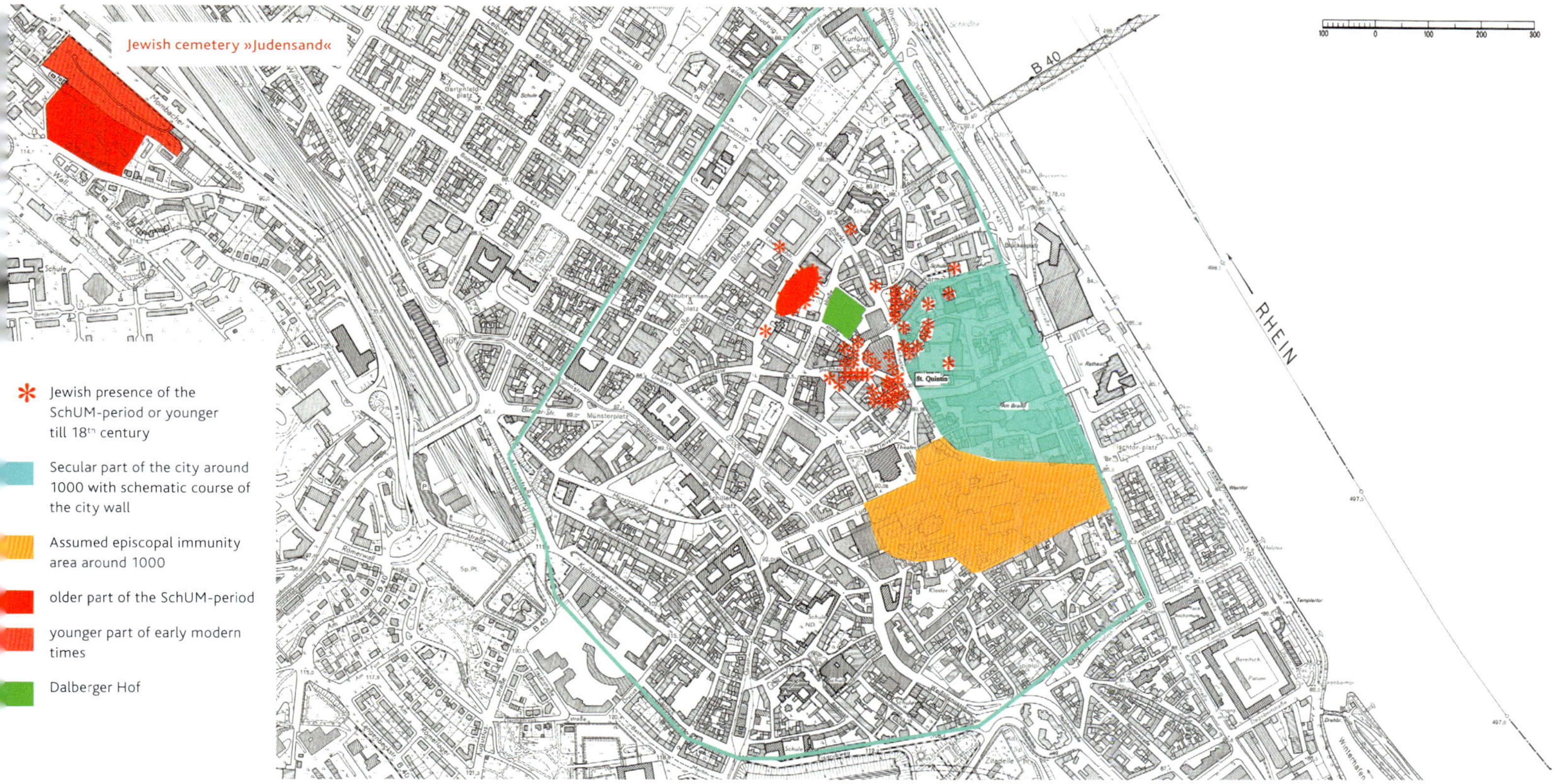

dence: G. Rupprecht, in: GDKE (Hrsg.), Die SchUM-Gemeinden Speyer Worms Mainz. Auf dem Weg zum Welterbe (2013) 189–196. – P. Heberer, in: ibid. 432–441. – L. Falck, in: Kulturdenkmäler in Rheinland-Pfalz 2.2 (1988) 14–37; vor allem Plan 24f.

Fig. 4
Jewish presence in Mainz. (GDKE/Landesarchäologie/Mainz/G. Rupprecht)

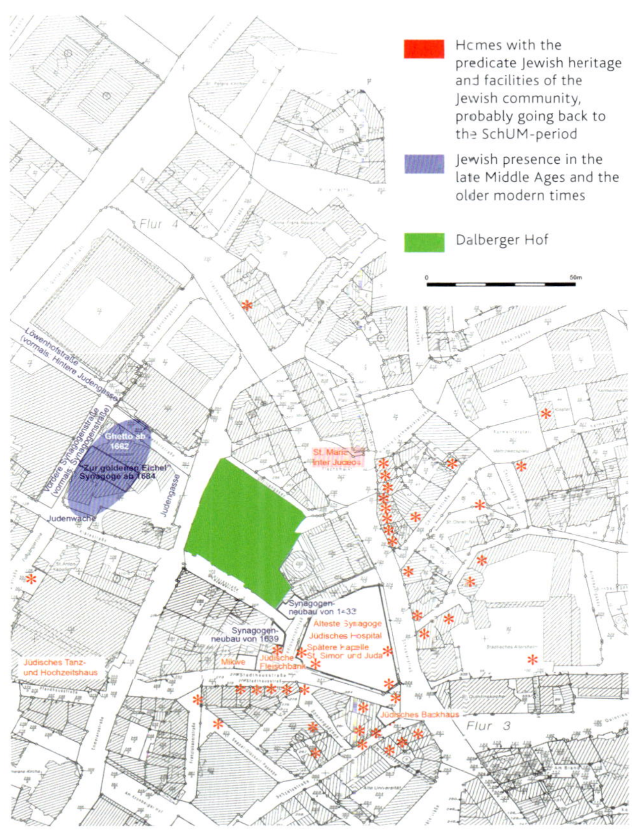

Fig. 5
Jewish presence in the inner city of Mainz. (GDKE/Landesarchäologie/Mainz/R. Knöchlein)

Bibliography

L. **Clemens**, Jüdisch-christliche Nachbarschaften im Profil – Die jüdischen Siedlungsareale in Speyer, Worms und Mainz während des Mittelalters, In: Blickpunkt Archäologie 2016, H. 1, 10–16, bes. 14–15.

L. **Falck**, Mainz im frühen und hohen Mittelalter (Mitte 5. Jahrhundert bis 1244). Geschichte der Stadt Mainz 2 (Düsseldorf 1972) 118.

L. **Falck**, Mainz in seiner Blütezeit als freie Stadt (1244 bis 1328). Geschichte der Stadt Mainz 3 (Düsseldorf 1973) 75–76; 141.

L. **Falck**, Von der fränkischen Zeit bis zum Ende des 18. Jahrhunderts, In: Denkmaltopographie Bundesrepublik Deutschland. Kulturdenkmäler in Rheinland-Pfalz. Stadt Mainz 2.2. Altstadt (Düsseldorf 1988) 18; 26.

THE MODERN ERA

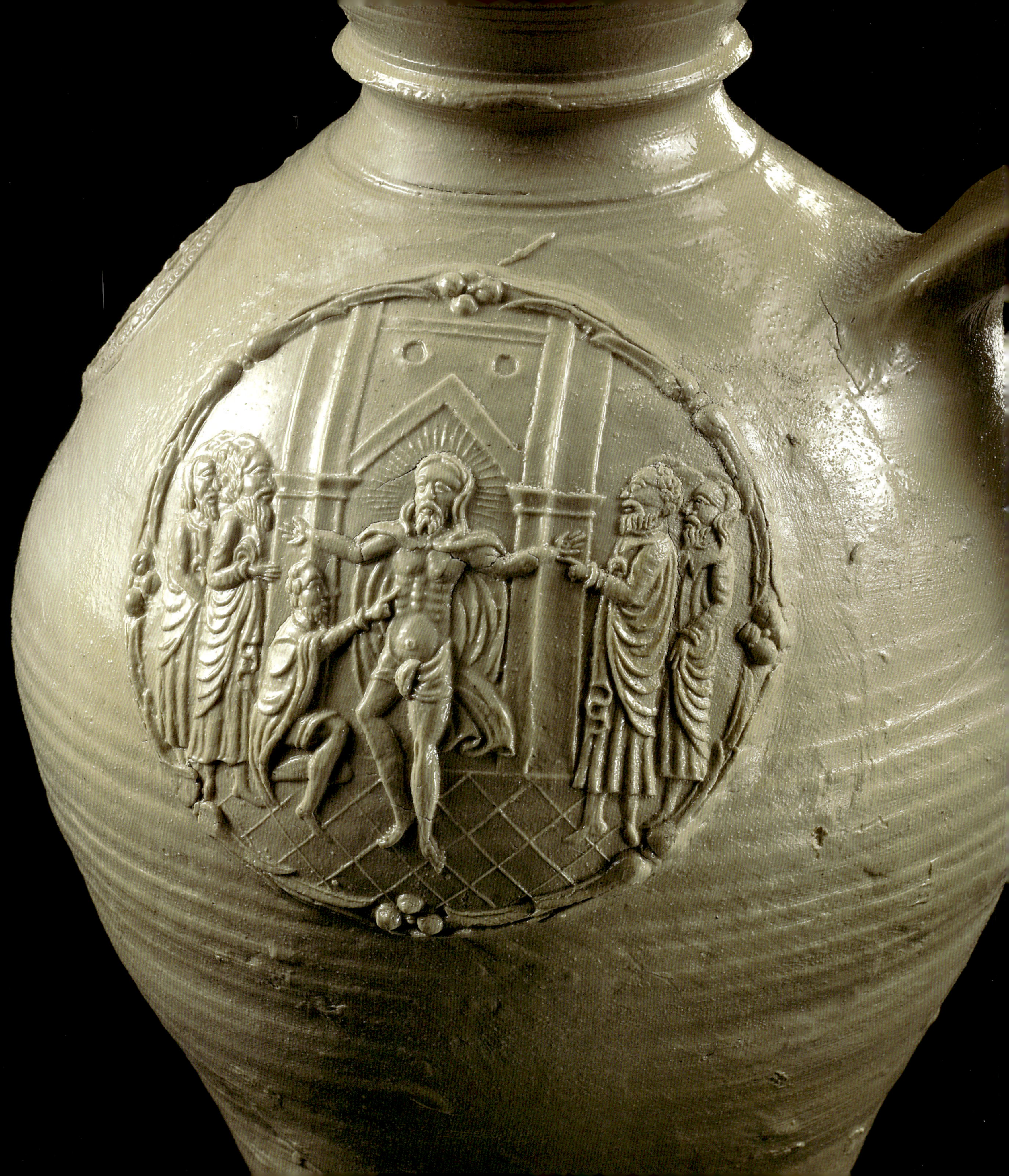

The Modern Era

MICHAEL SCHWAB

In archaeology, the periodization of history until the Middle Ages is based upon significant changes in the find material. While palaeontology deals with the evolution of our planet and life before the dawn of modern man, archaeology – with its tripartition into Stone, Bronze, and Iron Ages – is guided by the prevailing material available to man during each respective period. Iron, however, continued to be the prevailing material for centuries. The subsequent Roman Age and the Migration Period, as well as the (early) Middle Ages, contrast with the preceding epochs by way of new cultural influences, which are also reflected in the archaeological finds. From the Middle Ages on, however, archaeology often follows the periodization determined by historians. This periodization is made in retrospect from the insight that historical events have led to a radical change in human society. There are several, sometimes interwoven events and developments that cannot always be dated exactly. The beginning of the Modern Era is thus often established at the turn from the 15th to the 16th century, with historians arguing as to which major historical event marks the start of the Modern Era. Events often quoted as possible markers for the start of modern history are the Christian »recapture of Spain«, the so-called Reconquista; the discovery of America in 1492; and also the start of the Reformation.

One invention from this early Modern Era is to a certain extent both a blessing and a curse for the branch of archaeology dealing with the remains of this age (»Neuzeitarchäologie« in German): the invention of movable type by Johannes Gutenberg from Mainz. With the aid of this printing technology, the volume of available publications and literary sources multiplies within a very short time. In addition, administration becomes more professional and the decisions taken are fixed in writing and collected in archives. Neuzeitarchäologie therefore has access to a very large collection of written sources. On the other hand, this increasing availability of written sources also gives the impression that a sufficient number of historical sources are extant. Neuzeitarchäologie has hardly made an appearance in Germany until now. Only the results of industrial archaeology are attracting attention to a wide extent, but its roots are rather to be found in the history of technology.

Koblenz, city of Koblenz. Representation of a scene from the bible on a funnel neck pitcher made from greyish Siegburg stoneware. Similar medallion applications, but also house brands or coats of arms, can often be found on the typical Renaissance drinking pottery from the Rhine area (16th century). (GDKE/Landesarchäologie/Koblenz/W. Baumann, Höhr-Grenzhausen)

It is precisely this juxtaposition of archaeological finds and written sources that Neuzeitarchäologie, just like historical archaeology or post-medieval archaeology, has to face. Besides the usual archaeological working method, scholars also deal with historical sources (written and oral tradition, images, etc.) to draw their conclusions. Archaeologists dealing with the

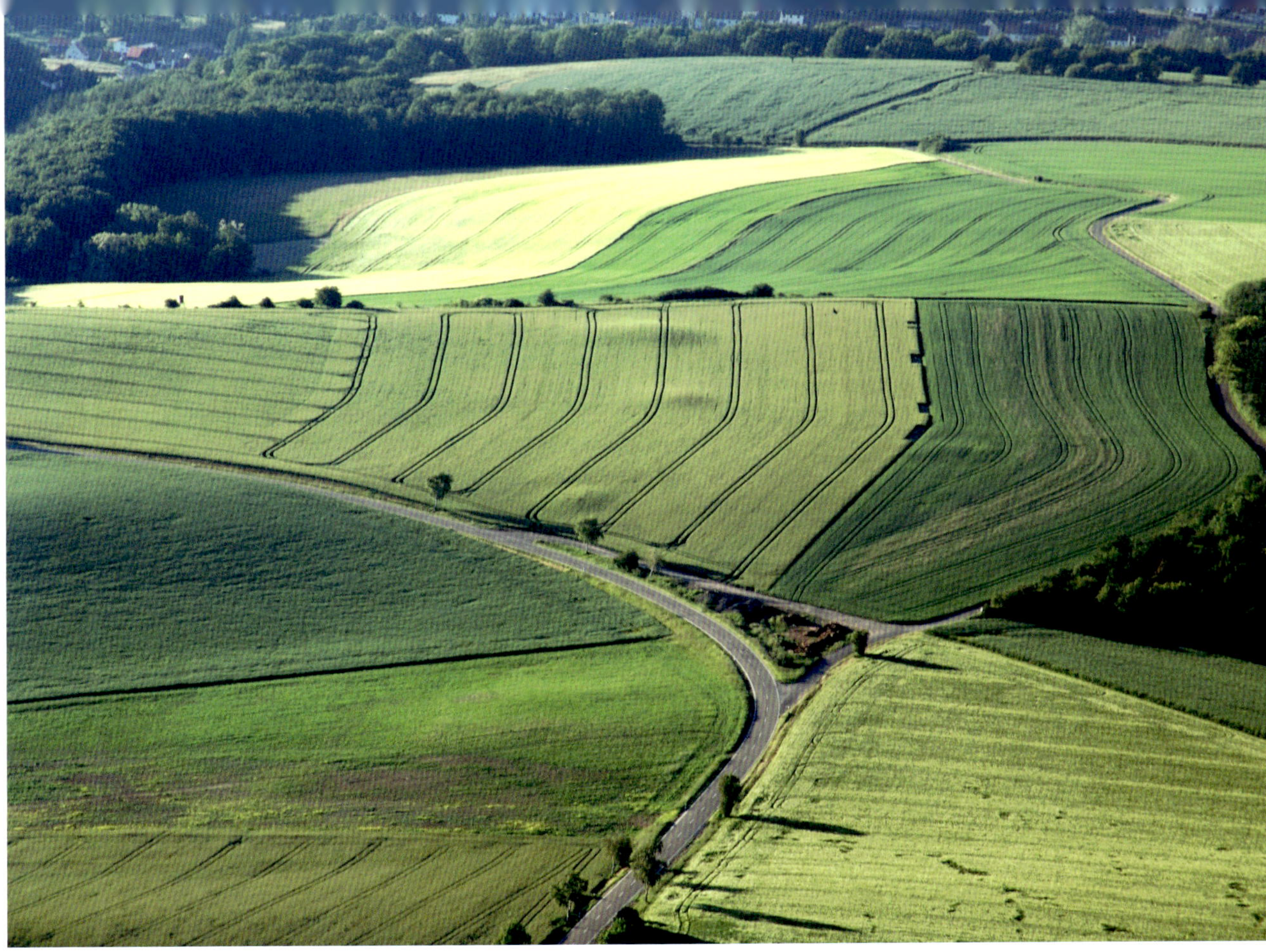

Fig. 1
Contwig, Südwestpfalz distr. Aerial photo of a field with clearly recognizable circular humps. (GDKE/Landesarchäologie/Speyer)

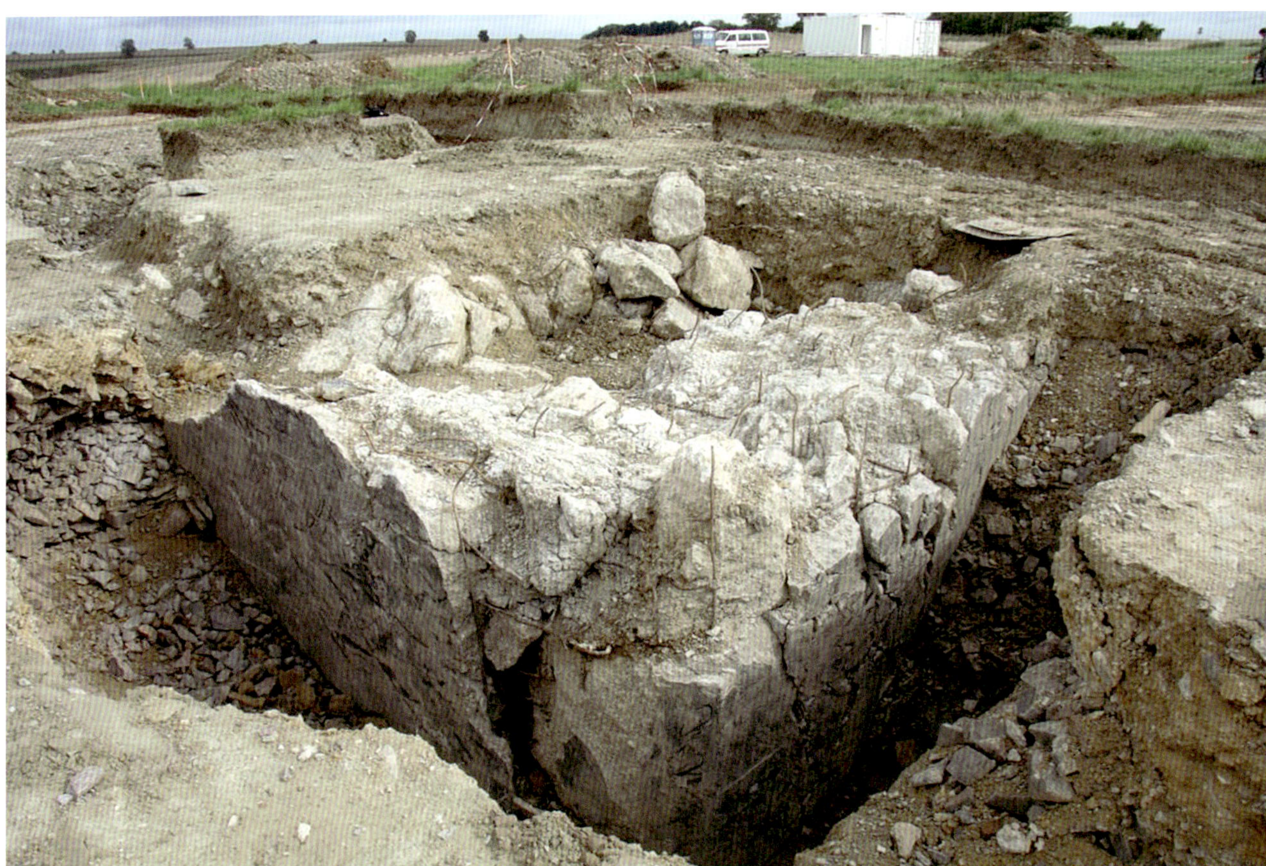

Fig. 2
Contwig, Südwestpfalz distr. Excavation of remains of bunkers. (GDKE/Landesarchäologie/Speyer)

remains of the Modern Era archaeologists hence also need to know and be able to apply the methods of historians. After studying archive materials on the construction of the Westwall (*Siegfried Line*), for instance, scholars found out that circular elevations in a field near Contwig (Fig. 1), which had been considered to be burial mounds, were in fact remains of bunkers. (Fig. 2)

But even the impression of an increasing availability of written sources has to come to terms with reality soon: in most cases, the early writing of history was done on the order or from the viewpoint of the rulers. So it is only their story that is told. Only few written sources of the early Modern Era dealt with the way of life of the greater part of the population. Moreover, enormous quantities of written sources were lost in modern times: natural disasters, fires, and inadequate storage have during all ages irretrievably destroyed archives. During the last few centuries, the ever more brutal forms of warfare, which can be seen, for example, in the large-scale destruction of residential areas, have time and again ruined archives and libraries where written sources were being kept. Huge amounts of documents were destroyed at the end of World War II so that they would not fall into enemy hands. For this time in particular, there is thus only a rather limited amount of processed literary sources available, and the results of archaeological studies have in the meantime occupied an indispensable place in the study of the relevant events.

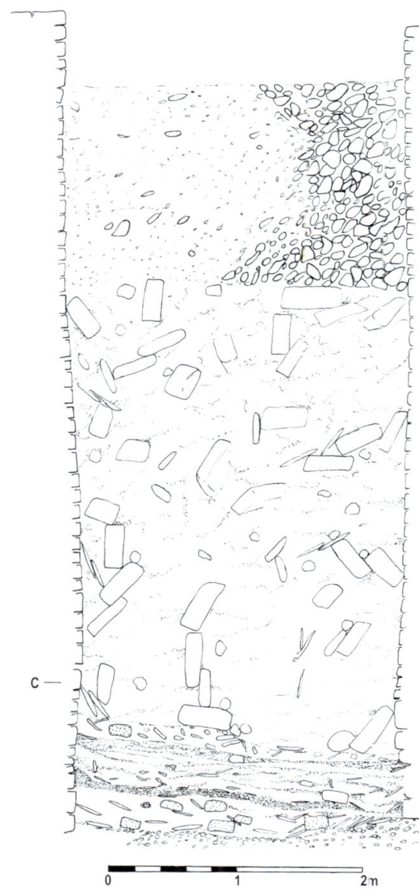

Fig. 3
Koblenz, city of Koblenz. Drawing of a sewer shaft filled with refuse, with dating. (GDKE/ Landesarchäologie/ Koblenz)

Rhineland-Palatinate has been characterized by high settlement continuity since the Middle Ages. Once established, settlements are no longer abandoned. Even areas devastated by diseases and war are repopulated in most cases after some time. The centre of worldly and religious power has been concentrated since the Middle Ages in big cities and settlements. The redevelopments of historic districts and town centres are therefore welcome opportunities for the Department of Archaeology to look at the past of these places. Rich finds are made time and again, proving that a certain settlement was used for several centuries, and thereby providing important information about the way people used to dwell, work, and live until well into the Modern Era. The established findings provide astonishing results and supplement the historical tradition on the development of the respective places and cities. The find material, especially from sewers and cesspools, allows (with the help of the most diverse scientific methods) conclusions to be made regarding food, health, social rank, and commercial and economic relationships, and also regarding the agricultural situation in the settlements and their surroundings. (Fig. 3) The items found mirror poverty and wealth in the population, which receive only scant mention in the surviving written sources. The large redevelopment areas in cities, the construction of underground garages in inner-city areas, the individual renovation of poor building material carried out plot-by-plot, as well as the development of infrastructures in towns and the establishment of commercial and industrial facilities near settlements offer unique insights into the settlement and living conditions of the Modern Era due to the sometimes substantial intrusions into settlement areas that had previously grown undisturbed.

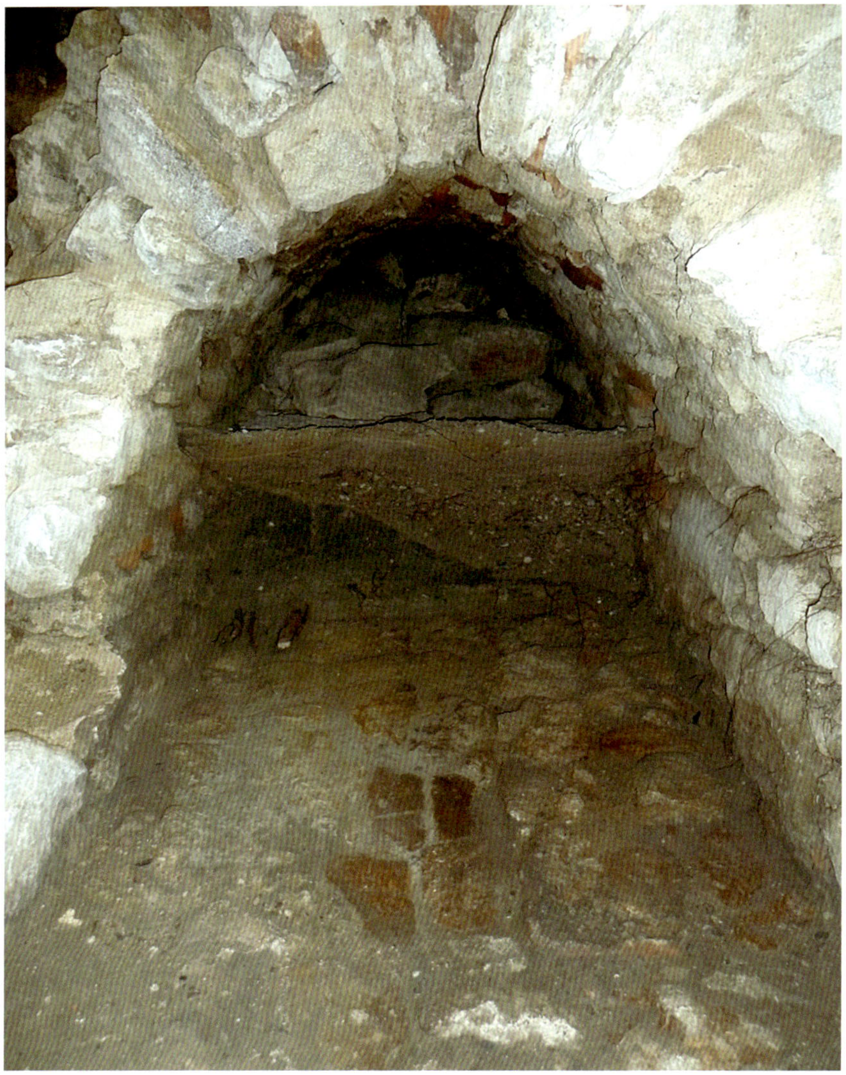

Fig. 4
Mainz, city of Mainz. Sewer from the year 1658, discovered during building works in the Landesmuseum Mainz. (GDKE/Landesarchäologie/Mainz/J. Dolata)

(Fig. 4) The results of these excavations are therefore indispensable as a source of historical knowledge.

The Rhine as a waterway has always been a lifeline for the exchange of goods and ideas. People live and travel on the river. The Rhine waters the fields, allows fishing, and supplies drinking water. But it was also the border between different areas of power. Especially during the last few centuries, with the revival of national states, the Rhine time and again became a strategic target of political and military plans. When those plans were implemented, the areas to the west of the river, especially the Palatinate, became the scene of acts of war. France and the German Empire had been fighting for the regions west of the Rhine since the middle of the 16th century. Ownership and government changed time after time on the basis of peace treaties, but none lasted long. Neuzeitarchäologie must therefore also frequently deal with the war legacies on the European continent. The city of Landau, in particular, which had been under French control since 1648, shows these changes on a very small scale. Louis XIV had the city transformed into a modern fortification by his military architect Vauban, and it changed its occupier four times during the War of the Spanish Succession alone (1702-1714). The finds around the lunette 38 provide a snapshot of the storming of the fortress on 12 July 1713 by French troops. The French and their kings, especially Napoleon I, were able to extend their sphere of influence into the areas far east of the borders of today's Rhineland-Palatinate. After the collapse of the Napoleonic empire and the Congress of Vienna of 1815, today's Rhineland-Palatinate came under the rule of the Prussians, Hessians, and Bavarians. Except for a few changes within the territories in favour of Prussia, the external borders remained stable. (Fig. 5)

After World War I, these borders are almost literally cast in concrete. With the construction of the so-called »Maginot line« (a combination of fortresses, bunkers, and barriers for protecting its borders against attacks by neighbouring states including Italy and Belgium), France in 1930 starts to secure its eastern border. From 1936 onwards, a line of fortifications of 630 kilometres in length is built on the western border of the then German Reich. Some 264 km of this line, known today as the »Westwall« (»Siegfried Line«), extend over the area of Rhineland-Palatinate. Since 2015, the state has participated in the activities of the foundation »Grüner Wall im Westen – Mahnmal ehemaliger Westwall« and is thus committed to safeguarding the largest surface monument in the state. The foundation also safeguards the relics in the »Western Air Defence Zone« which was directly connected with the fortifications of the »Siegfried Line«. The foundation is the vehicle to organise measures of nature and heritage conservation and of political education. Archaeological findings around these installations complete the picture when written sources are missing. During construction works in the former barracks of the French army in Landau, for example, a British sea mine was discovered in a filled-in bomb crater. The mine had been stored in the »Siegfried Line« as »war booty«, since parts of the fortress

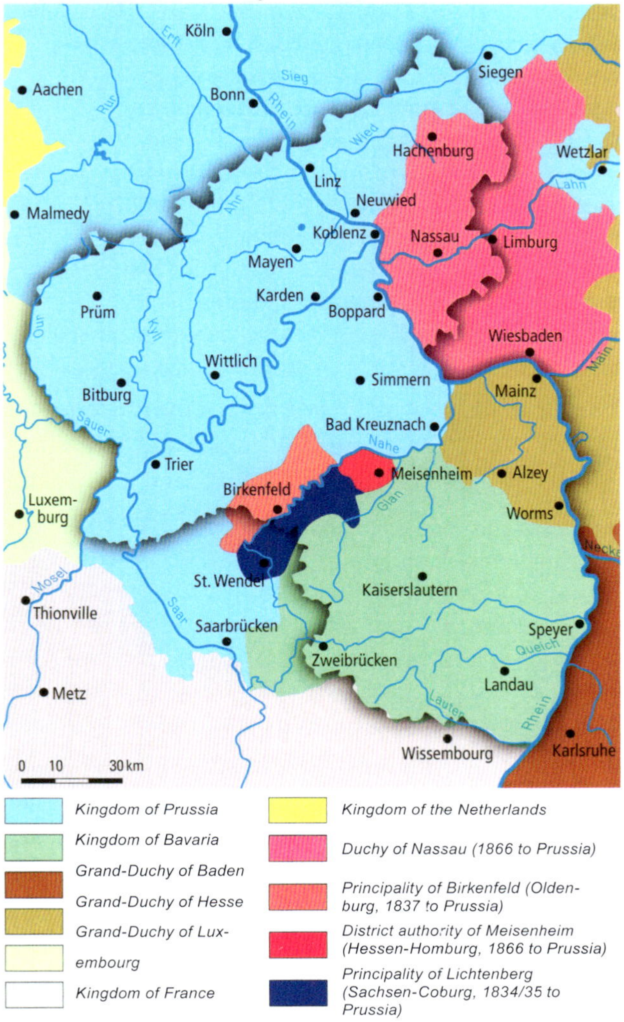

Fig. 5
The political order in the areas of today's Rhineland-Palatinate around 1815. (LvermGeo RLP)

had been used as a depot between 1940 and 1944, including use by the German navy. (Fig. 6) In 1944, the outlook of World War II changes: after the Allied landing in Normandy, the combat operations return to German territory. The »Siegfried Line« is overrun in just a short time and once again the Rhine becomes the target of Allied operations. While attempts are being made from the east to establish the Rhine once more as a border, the Allied aim is to cross the river coming from the west. Within a few weeks, the armies of the USA, Great Britain, and France reach the Rhine and cross it. For this reason, military equipment from the time of the World Wars can also be found inside the state. (Fig. 7) Unexploded bombs repeatedly cause interruptions in building works but also in archaeological excavations. During the war, bomb craters were filled with material which was to be disposed of; for instance, with the weapons that the German troops handed over to the Allies when they were disarmed. The events before and during World War II mark a deep break in history. Relics of World War II are witnesses of historical events. They have recently come more and more under the scrutiny of research and gained considerable importance for the study of this period.

Besides archaeological and historical studies, there is also the »human« aspect to be considered, especially with regard to finds from the World Wars. Not everyone killed by war can be found and identified. It is often only the personal belongings (jewellery, papers, insignia, etc.) or military equipment (weapons, troop insignia, etc.) of these victims that allow the competent authorities to identify them. Unfortunately, frequently one finds the mortal remains of victims only to discover they were robbed of such belongings long after the end of the war. From a legal point of view, all military goods – i.e. airplanes, vehicles, and weapons,

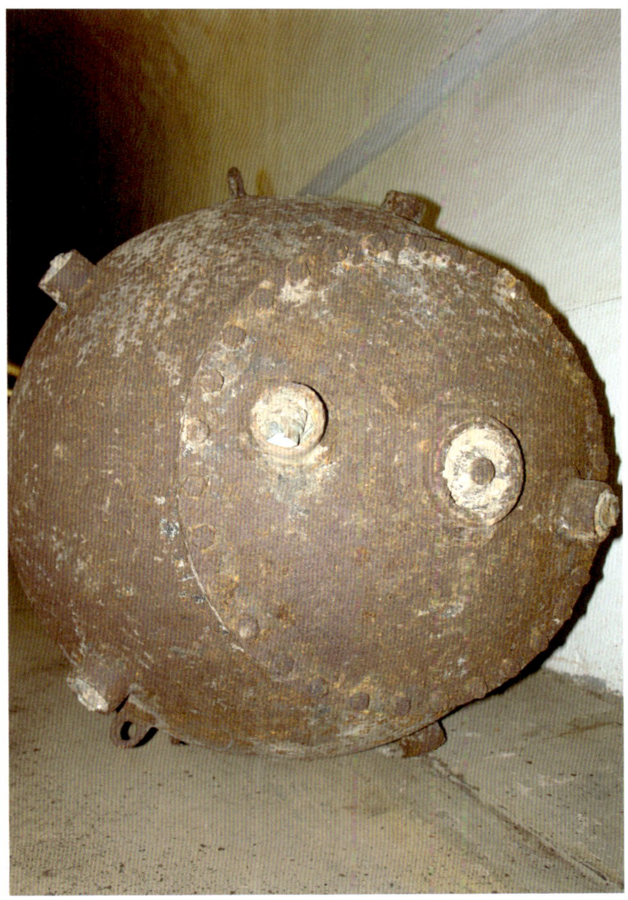

Fig. 6
British water mine found during clearing works around today's Westwallmuseum in Pirmasens. (Westwallmuseum Pirmasens)

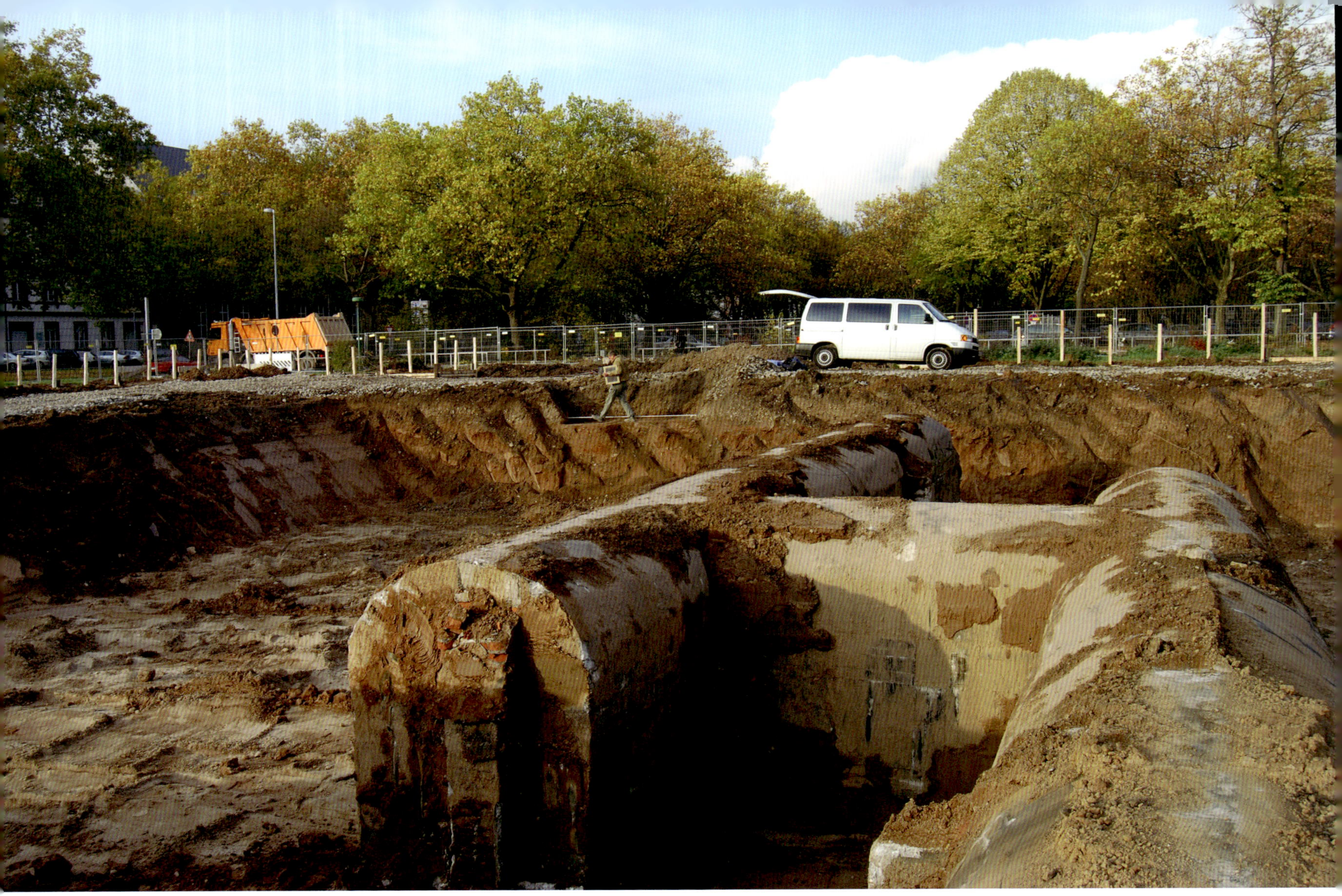

Fig. 7
Koblenz, city of Koblenz. Air raid shelters of World War II excavated during building works in the square in front of the Electoral Palace. (GDKE/ Landesarchäologie/ Koblenz/ M. Neumann)

but also the equipment of fallen soldiers – are still the property of the warring nations or their successors. The personal belongings have become the property of the heirs of the deceased. People taking possession of any such item are appropriating material that is considered to be »without custodian« but not »ownerless«; in addition, this prevents clarifying the destiny of a person killed in the war and sometimes even prevents families from coming to terms with their loss. However, even people killed in the war whose origin cannot be determined through their personal belongings can regain their identity under certain circumstances through medical examinations. Clearly defined scientific standards for the recovery of the mortal remains must be observed for this, but only few institutions can guarantee such standards. These include, besides the Department of Archaeology, the police, and the department of public prosecution.

A find from the Weberbach valley in Trier shows which objects have now come into the focus of our work through Neuzeitarchäologie. Not only that, the find also highlights how supplementary studies in other fields of research can help establish in what way a certain find ended up »in the ground« and even whether owners of the find can still be established.

Whilst during the reconstruction of the Federal Republic of Germany after World War II archaeological studies were hardly possible, because of the high demand for living and working space, the finds from the Modern Era were simply ignored even during the following decades: the idea was that this material would not

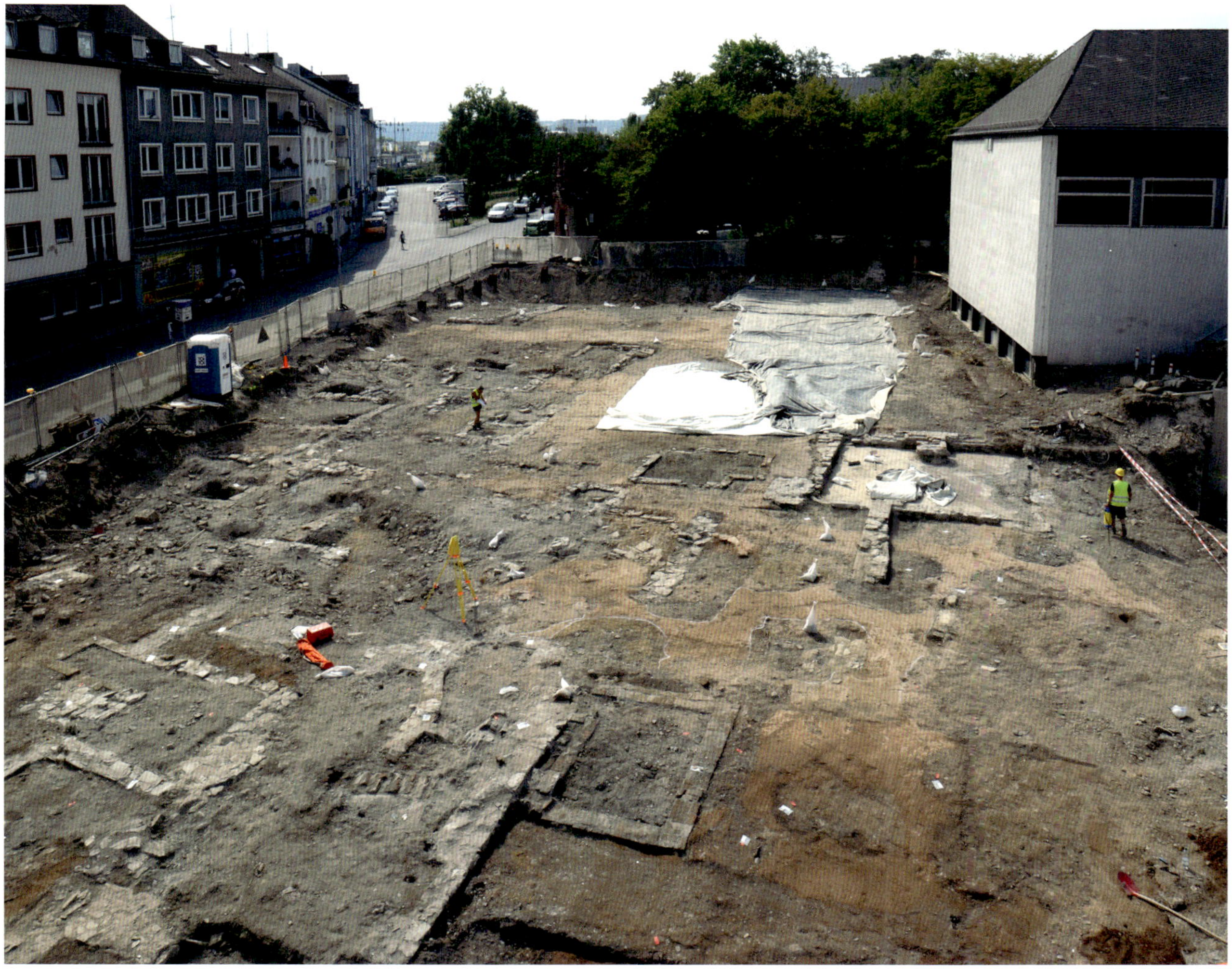

Fig. 8
Koblenz, city of Koblenz. Excavation in Weißergasse. (GDKE/Landesarchäologie/Koblenz/J. Schamper)

be required because of the allegedly widely available written sources. During those years, only particularly elaborate objects, precious metal, and coins were studied scientifically. During the reconstruction of historic districts of various municipalities in the last few years, it was possible to collect a wealth of information about the development of the respective locality. In the unearthed ruins of a former convent in the city centre of Koblenz, for instance, remains from the Palaeolithic right up to traces of World War II operations were found. (Fig. 8)

In the meantime, many cities and villages have recognized the importance of the existing historic building stock for (culture) tourism purposes. Their restoration, renovation, and development are therefore pushed forward, and in this context the Department of Archaeology has an opportunity to look at the past of the relevant site. During excavations in the inner city of Koblenz, waste pits were found from time to time. A well filled to the top with china, glass bottles, and bits of metal was examined by the participants of the Voluntary Social Year, the Voluntary Ecological Year and of a German-French exchange programme at the Koblenz branch of the Department of Archaeology. Archive documents confirmed that the individual objects were filled in before 1910/14. A comparison with old Koblenz address books showed that there had been a china shop, a delicatessen, and a beer seller in this area. The composition of the find material revealed a striking correspondence with the goods sold in these shops. The results of this work and the finds were then made accessible to the public in 2015 within the frame-

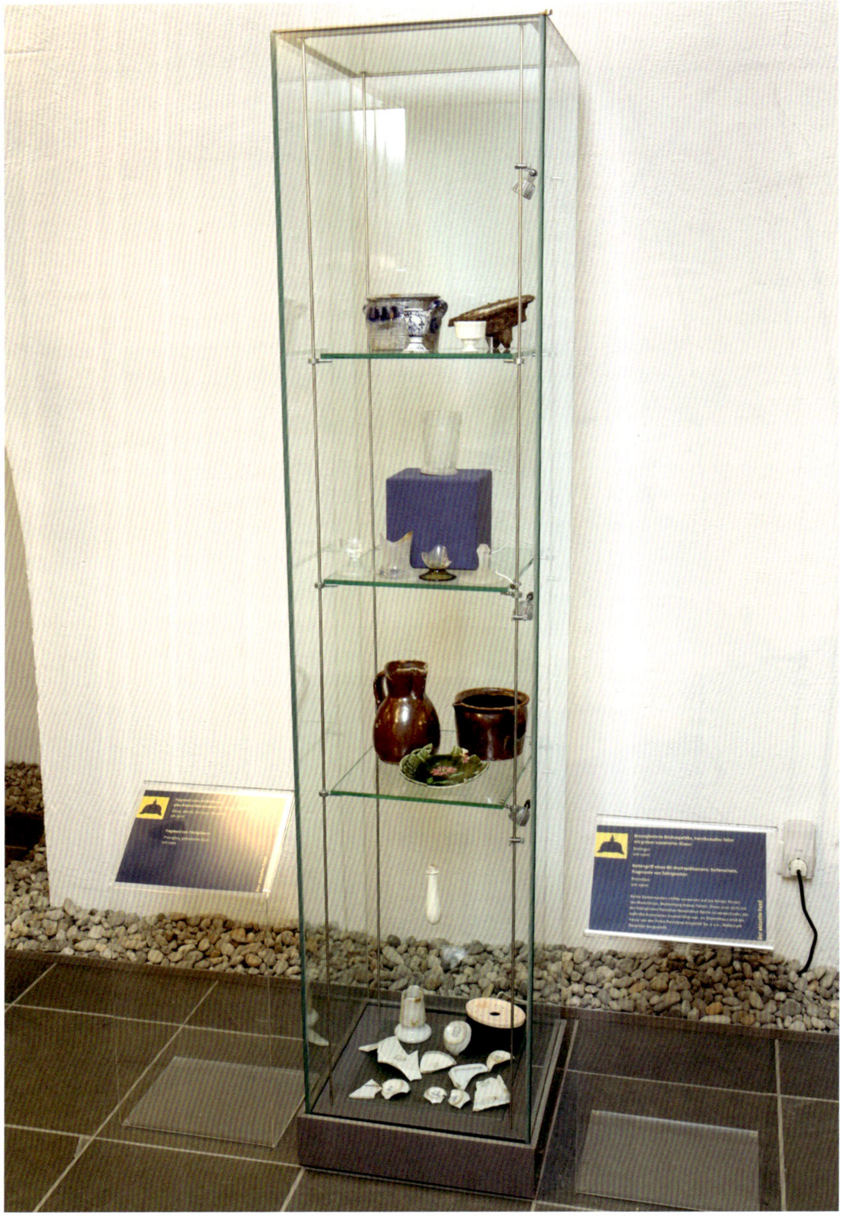

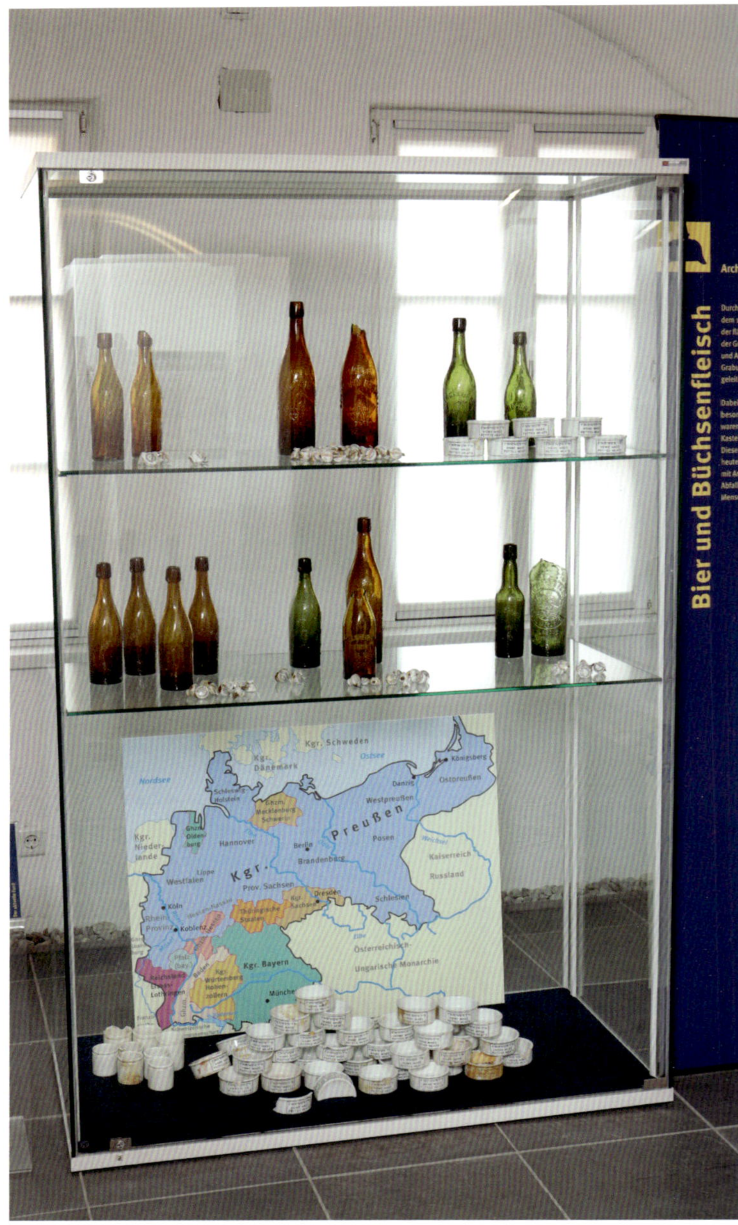

Fig. 9
Showcase of the exhibition »Beer and Canned Meat«, Haus der Archäologie, Landesmuseum Koblenz. (GDKE/Landesmuseum Koblenz/U. Pfeuffer)

work of the special exhibition »Recent finds«, under the title »Beer and Canned Meat«, held in the House of Archaeology of the Landesmuseum Koblenz in Ehrenbreitstein fortress. As often happens, the find was mostly composed of waste and provided interesting insights into the everyday life of people of the 19th and early 20th centuries. (Fig. 9-10)

The churches located in larger municipalities also offer opportunities for historical-archaeological studies and provide important information. In Rhineland-Palatinate, special legal provisions apply to churches and religious communities, provided that they have their own, state-recognized organisation in charge of heritage protection and maintenance. Although the dioceses do have offices of this kind, the Department of Archaeology can also time and again examine the findings in important sacred buildings in connection with construction and renovation works. Major excavations were undertaken in the churches St. Kastor and Liebfrauenkirche in Koblenz, in St. Kastor church in Karden, in St. Clemens near Mayen, in the parish church of Dausenau, in the Jacobus-Kapelle of Lahnstein, and in the chapel on Burg Sayn.

Neuzeitarchäologie thus deals with a section of the history of mankind that has only lasted for a few centuries. It is, nevertheless, a critical factor for the study of this period due to the many cultural and political upheavals and the accompanying loss of written sources during this short time. Right from the beginning, its work has been organized in an interdisciplinary manner, and it often provides the material bases for other – including scientific – branches of research. Within the framework of the work of the Department of Archaeology in the General Department of Cultural Heritage Rhineland-Palatinate, Neuzeitarchäologie will supplement the picture we have of our past and will certainly revise information from time to time.

Fig. 10
Showcase of the exhibition »Beer and Canned Meat«, Haus der Archäologie, Landesmuseum Koblenz. (GDKE/Landesmuseum Koblenz/U. Pfeuffer)

Bibliography

B. Scholkmann/H. Kenzler/R. Schreg, Archäologie des Mittelalters und der Neuzeit (Darmstadt 2016).

Mittel- und Ostdeutscher Verband für Altertumsforschung e.V. (Hg.), Bodendenkmäler der Neuzeit. Nachrichtenblatt der Landesarchäologie. Ausgrabungen und Funde 40, 1/1995 (Berlin 1995).

H.-H. Wegner/A. von Berg, Jäger – Bauern – Keltenfürsten. 50 Jahre Archäologie an Mittelrhein und Mosel. Archäologie an Mittelrhein und Mosel 13 (Koblenz 2001).

C. Theune, Grundlagen und Perspektiven einer Archäologie des 20. Jahrhunderts, In: Deutscher Verband für Archäologie (Hg.), Blickpunkt Archäologie 3/2015 (München 2015) 164–176.

B. Arndt/U. Müller, Klasse trotz Masse? Zu einer Archäologie des 19. bis 21. Jahrhunderts, In: Deutscher Verband für Archäologie (Hg.), Blickpunkt Archäologie 3/2015 (München 2015) 177–183.

The lunette 38 in Landau/Palatinate – The last battle

BETTINA HÜNERFAUTH

Between 1688 and 1692, French troops developed the town of Landau into a fortification on the orders of king Louis XIV according to a plan by the military architect Sébastien le Prestre de Vauban. (Fig. 1) The fortress had already withstood various sieges during the War of the Palatine Succession between 1688 and 1697. After 1697, France had to give back the entire occupied Electoral Palatinate to the right of the Rhine, but Alsace and Landau as a garrison town remained French. During the imperial rule between 1704 and 1713, the southern front of the fortress, which until then had been a weak point in the defence belt, was massively extended. The fortress belt received six new fortifications, the so-called lunettes. A lunette (»little moon« in French) is an independent fortification outside the actual fortress and is connected to the main building by underground galleries and covered passages. During the War of the Spanish Succession 1701–1714, lunette 38 in particular played an important role during the sieges. After 1871, when the fortress was completely outdated from a military viewpoint, it was razed, and barracks were built on the area. In connection with the Bundesgartenschau (horticultural and landscaping show) of 2015, this area was included in the plans for modern residential units. Because of the well-known razing of the fortress, the developers expected to find only few traces of the walls. Instead, the subsequent archaeological finding of lunette 38 showed that the stone fortification was still excellently preserved. (Fig. 2)

During the excavation in the summer of 2014 conducted by the Department of Archaeology Speyer, a central area of the lunette, the so-called »Eugenschanze«, was documented in detail. The two fortification works on the offensive side, built of granite quarry stone, were excavated over a length of 35 m each and up to a height of 1.80 m. The upper part was made of carefully dressed sandstone blocks. This meant that only the part visible above ground had actually been demolished. In front of this fortification was a ca. 15 m wide ditch, and behind its supporting wall there was a vaulted chemin de ronde built with regularly hewn sandstone ashlar. The extremely carefully built underground corridor, which could still be used during the excavations over a length of ca. 65 m, had eleven loopholes and a sally port with a groined vault behind it leading into the ditch. Due to the construction rights already established, the impressive fortress remains unfortunately could not be preserved.

In the north-eastern excavation area, a mass grave of nine individuals was uncovered. (Fig. 3) It is most probably connected with the siege of 1713, as is evidenced mainly by the numerous musket bullets and flint stones found. The youngest of the buried individuals was just 15 years old, whilst the oldest was over 60. The skulls showed effects of blunt force, and the extremities revealed several fractures. The impressions on the bones were probably caused by musket bullets; bite marks from dogs or other animals, which would indicate that the corpses lay above ground for a long time, could not be detected on the bones, for which reason it appears that the fallen soldiers were buried soon after their death. Another interesting and typical finding on soldiers' skeletons are the so-called »pipe holes«, almost half-round, worn-down spots in the front teeth of the upper and lower jaw, which appear circular when the teeth are closed and are the result of the exaggerated smoking of tobacco in clay pipes. It was not possible to establish on which side the men had fought, since the few metallic objects found were not significant in this respect.

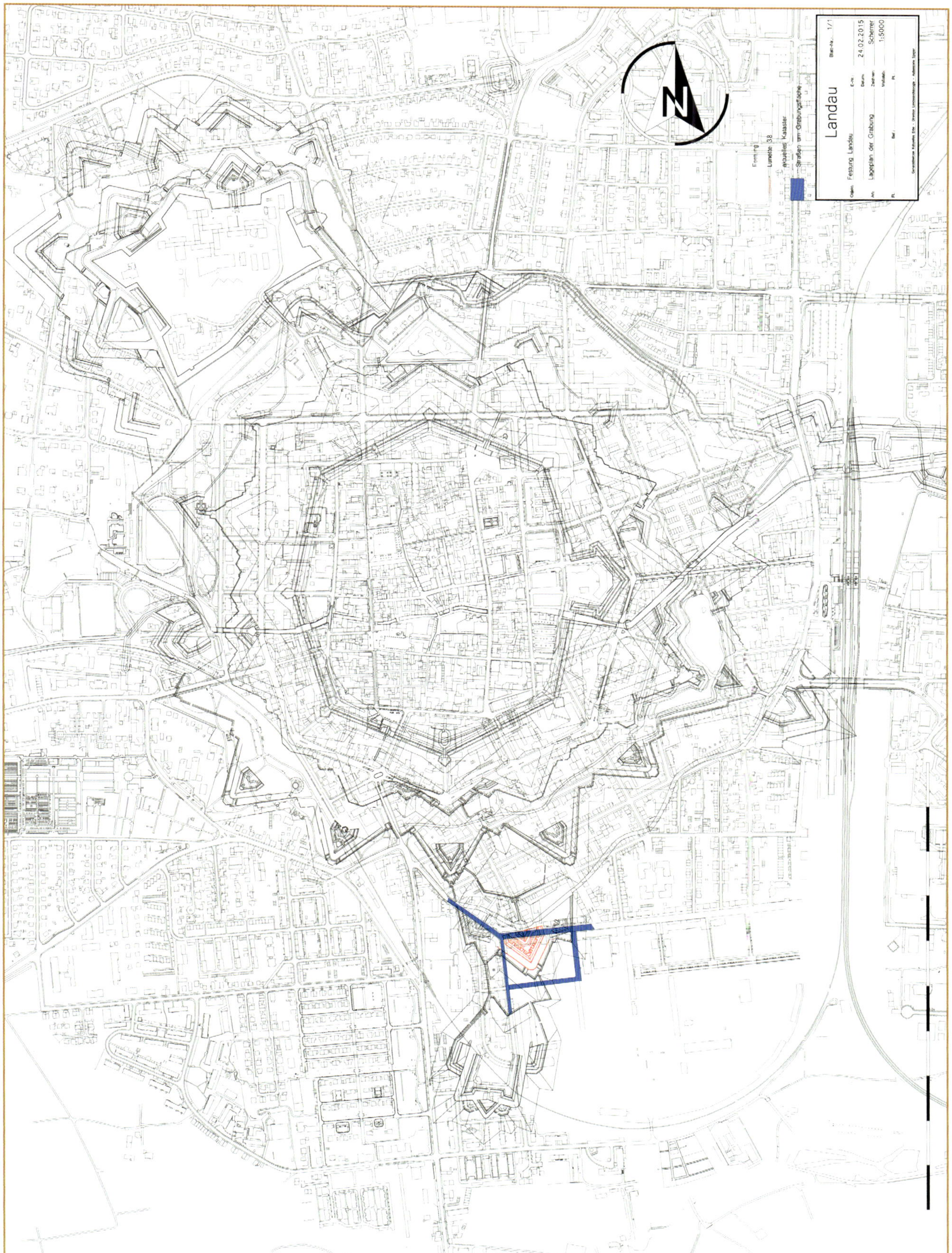

Fig. 1
Landau, city of Landau. Overall plan of the Landau fortress with the excavation area of Lunette 38 marked in blue. (GDKE/Landesarchäologie/Speyer/Map: Stadtarchiv Landau)

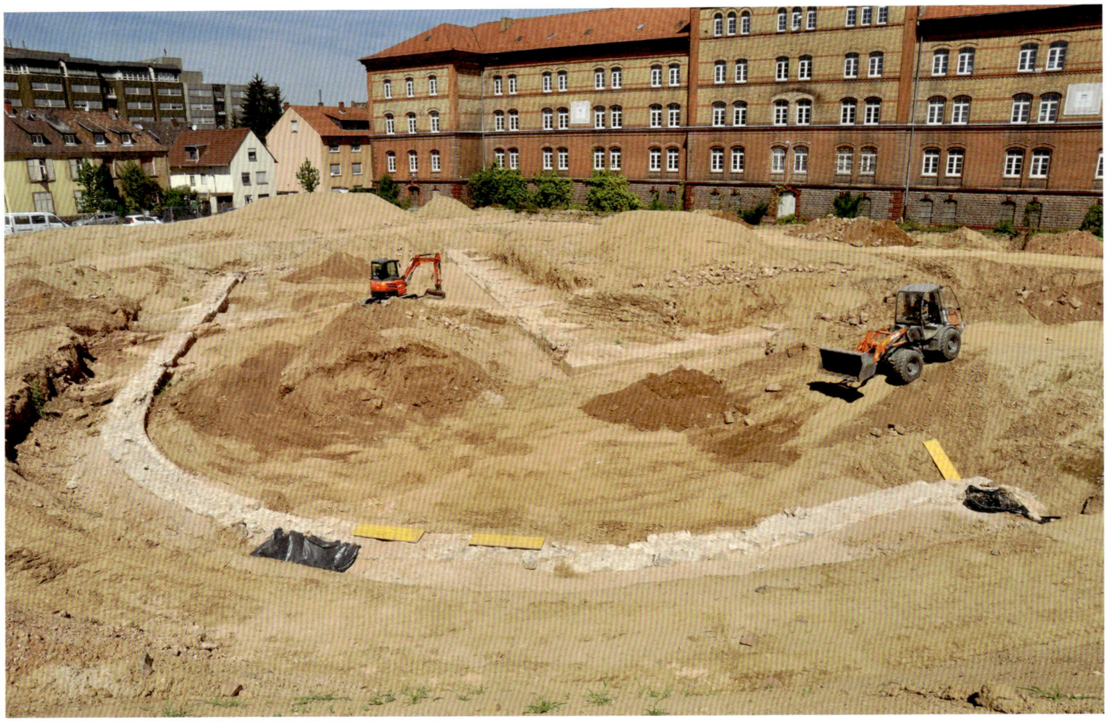

Fig. 2
Landau, city of Landau. Lunette 33 during excavations in summer 2014. (GDKE/ Landesarchäologie/Speyer/ F. Krämer & P. Scherrer)

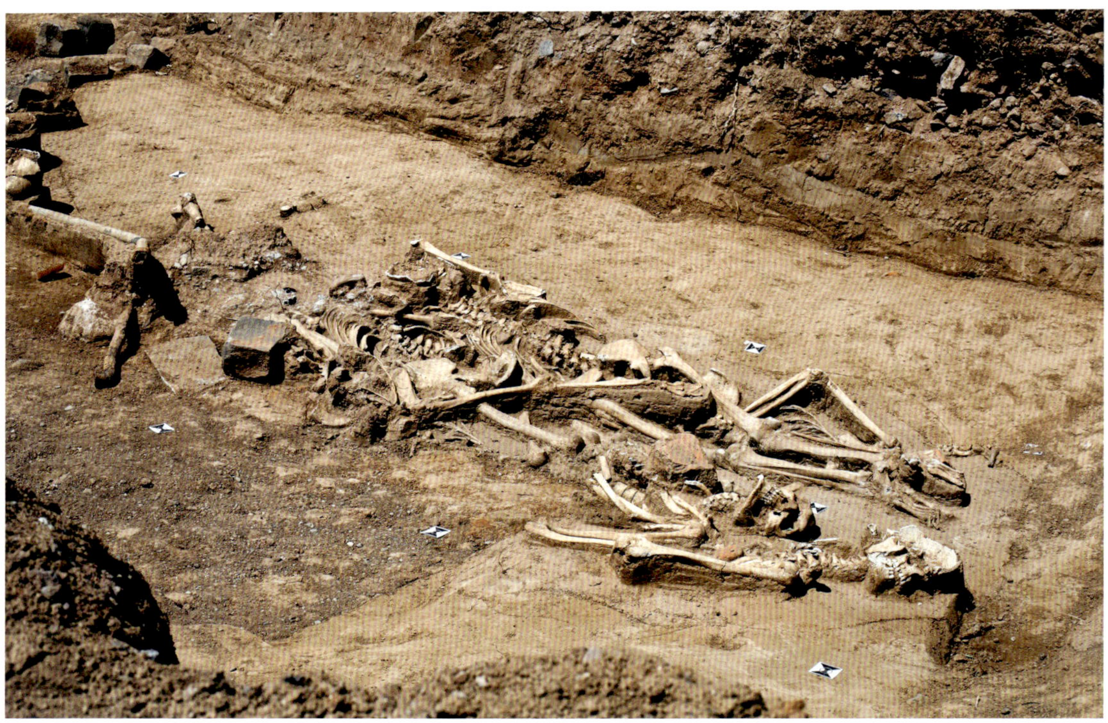

Fig. 3
Landau, city of Landau. View of the mass grave of nine individuals. (S. Kiem)

Bibliography

E. **Heuser**, Die dritte und vierte Belagerung Landaus im Spanischen Erbfolgekrieg 1704 und 1713 (Landau 1896).

J. **Finkbeiner**, Garnisonsbauten in Landau: 1680–1816 (Neustadt/ Wstr. 2007).

F. **Krämer**/P. **Scherrer**, Landau-Lunette 38, ADP 4, Speyer (in Vorbereitung).

M. **Martin**, Kleine Geschichte der Stadt Landau (Karlsruhe 2006).

A return to family ownership after more than 70 years

JOACHIM HUPE

It is probably rather an exception when archaeologists, following excavations, are able to return finds to the legal owners, but this is precisely what happened in 2015 in Trier. The Trier branch of the Department of Archaeology conducted investigations during the years 2014-2015 on a derelict inner-city area allocated to a new building project. The excavation area along the street »Weberbach« had been built up with Gothic city houses up until World War II, (Fig. 1) which were then severely damaged during air raids on Trier in December 1944 and not rebuilt after the war. When the former owners sold one of the plots of ruins to the city of Trier in the 1960s, they included a clause in the sales contract stating that any valuables hidden in the ground were to be returned to the family.

To their great surprise, at the beginning of 2015, the staff of the Department of Archaeology came across the remains of a stone-walled cabinet (Fig. 2) within the

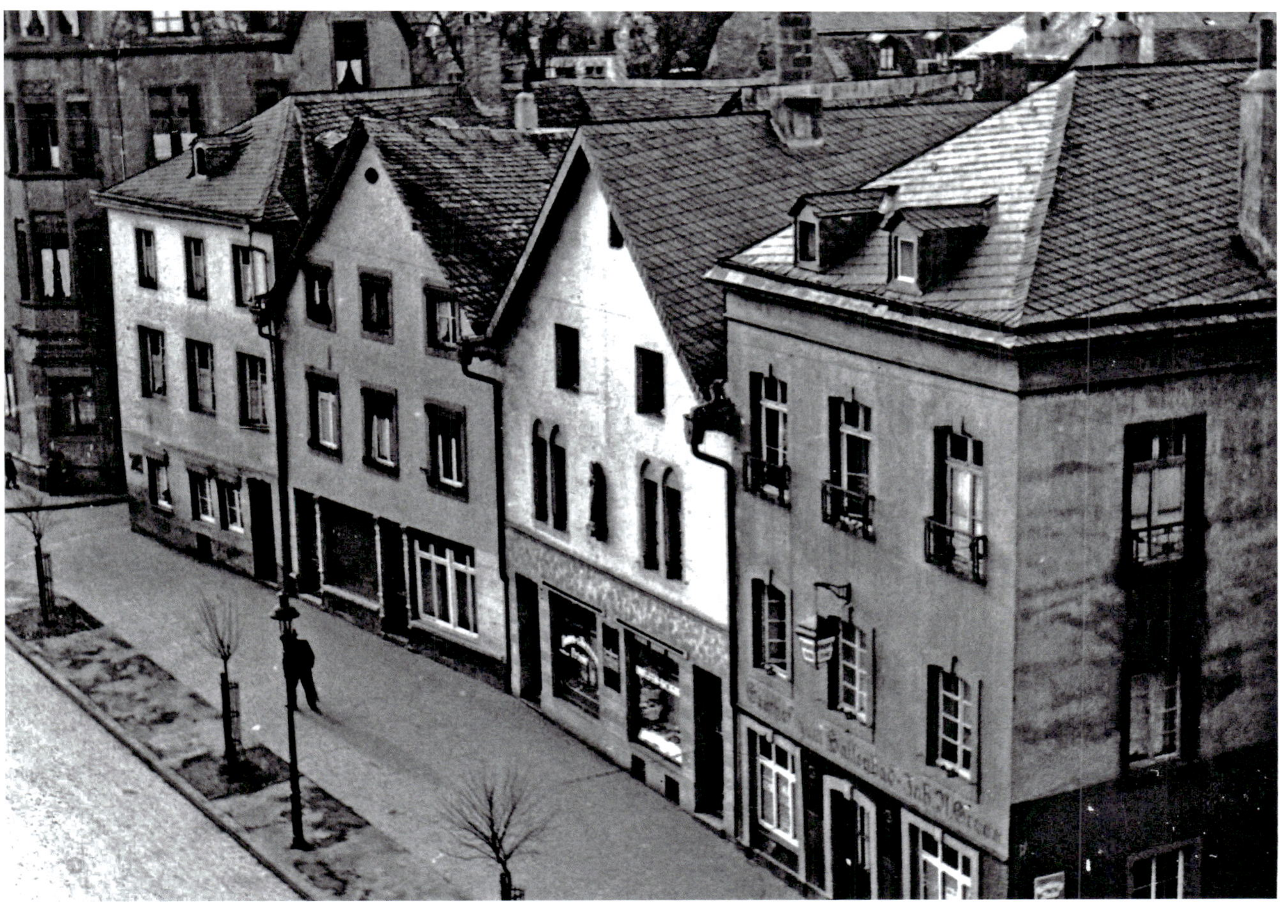

Fig. 1
Trier, city of Trier. Weberbach street (1930s). Historical view of the buildings destroyed during the war. The ruins of the house on the right contained the family property. (Stadtarchiv Trier)

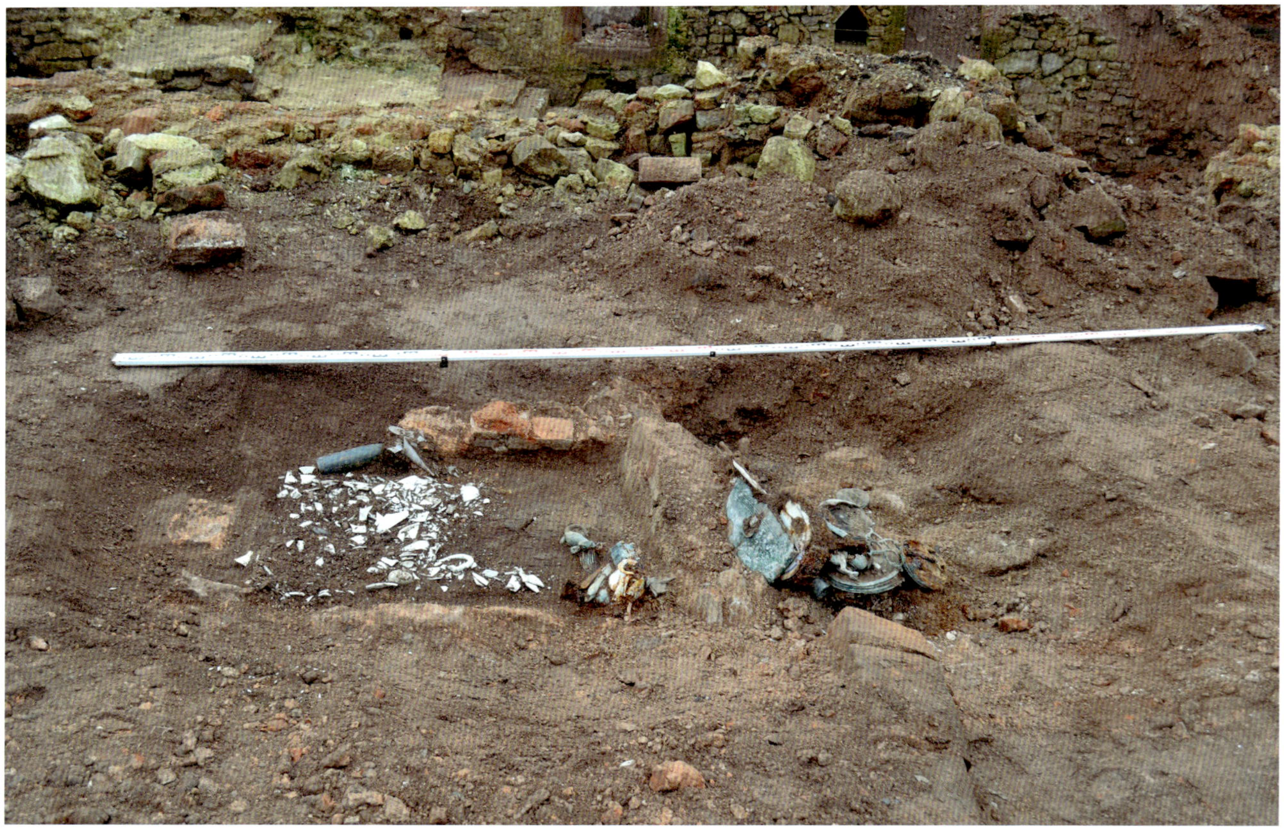

Fig. 2
Trier, city of Trier. Weberbach street. Destroyed wall cabinet with content on the ground floor of the former house. (GDKE/Landesarchäologie/Trier/B. Kremer)

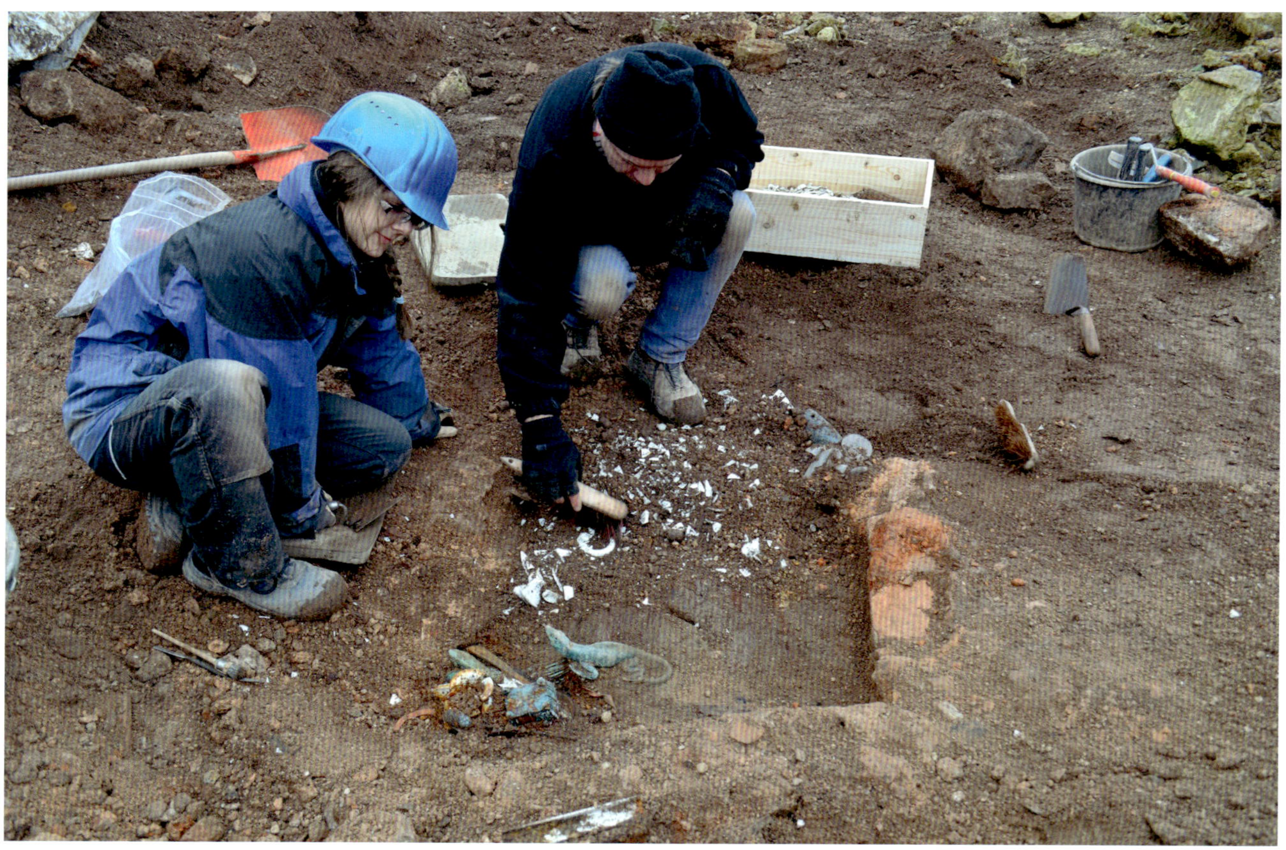

Fig. 3
Trier, city of Trier. Weberbach street. Unexpected encounter during the excavation in January 2015. (GDKE/Landesarchäologie/Trier/B. Kremer)

ruins of the house destroyed during the war. It contained many everyday objects and collector's items belonging to the family: china, metal tableware, cutlery, and other household goods, decorations and pocket watches, a large collection of coins and other items. The find complex comprised over three hundred objects, including some odd things such as a solid bronze lizard. (Fig. 3)

There was no difficulty in identifying the rightful owner, who was still residing in Trier. Her parents had run a hotel in the house on Weberbach (street) until the war; she herself had spent her early childhood there. The objects salvaged were collector's items and souvenirs from the personal belongings of her father (Fig. 4), who had been seriously wounded in World War I and fell in the eastern theatre of war in 1944. Her elder brother also fell in World War II. The mother was forced to leave the items behind during air raids, and after the war they could no longer be salvaged. »There are memories connected with each item – the finds will now keep us busy for some time«, the daughter stated, visibly moved when the find was handed over to her by the Department of Archaeology in Trier in March 2015. A total of 12 find boxes, filled to the top with house inventory, were thus returned to the family.

Probably nobody would have thought that the far-sighted clause in the sales contract of 1967 would one day come into effect.

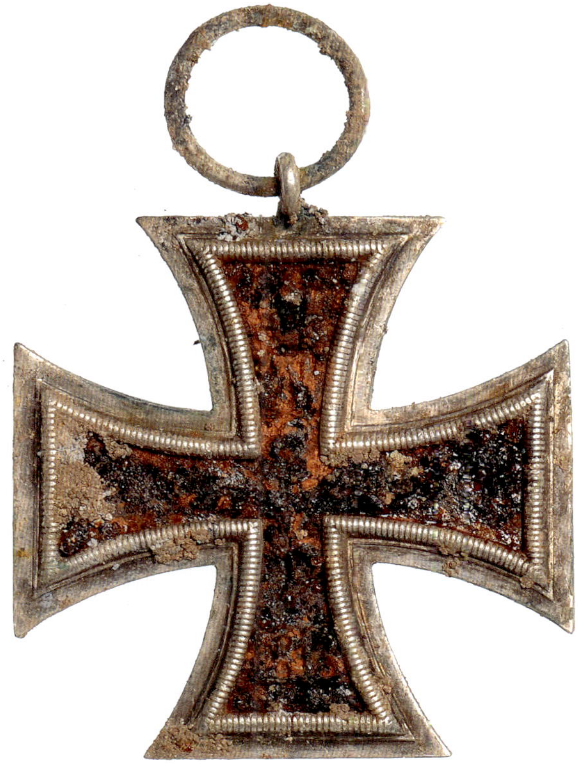

Fig. 4
Trier, city of Trier. Weberbach street. Iron cross (2nd class) 1914/18, blackened cast iron with silver alloy. (GDKE/Landesarchäologie/Trier/B. Kremer)

List of Authors

Marc Bentz, M.A., Generaldirektion Kulturelles Erbe Rheinland-Pfalz, Direktion Landesarchäologie, Außenstelle Speyer.

Dr. Dr. Axel von Berg, Generaldirektion Kulturelles Erbe Rheinland-Pfalz, Direktion Landesarchäologie.

Prof. Dr. Lukas Clemens, Universität Trier, Fachbereich III – Mittelalterliche Geschichte.

Dr. Ralf Fischer zu Cramburg, Liebenstein-Gesellschaft, Koblenz.

Holger Greve, M.A., Forschungsstelle Kaiserpfalz Ingelheim.

Dr. Peter Henrich, Generaldirektion Kulturelles Erbe Rheinland-Pfalz, Direktion Landesarchäologie, Außenstelle Koblenz.

Dr. Ulrich Himmelmann, Generaldirektion Kulturelles Erbe Rheinland-Pfalz, Direktion Landesarchäologie, Außenstelle Speyer.

Bettina Hünerfauth, M.A., Generaldirektion Kulturelles Erbe Rheinland-Pfalz, Direktion Landesarchäologie, Außenstelle Speyer

Dr. Joachim Hupe, Generaldirektion Kulturelles Erbe Rheinland-Pfalz, Direktion Landesarchäologie, Außenstelle Trier.

Dr. Cliff Alexander Jost, Generaldirektion Kulturelles Erbe Rheinland-Pfalz, Direktion Landesarchäologie, Außenstelle Koblenz.

Dr. Ronald Knöchlein, Generaldirektion Kulturelles Erbe Rheinland-Pfalz, Direktion Landesarchäologie, Außenstelle Mainz.

Andreas Lehnertz, M.A., Universität Trier, Fachbereich III – Arye Maimon-Institut für Geschichte der Juden.

Dr. Herbert Lutz, Naturhistorisches Museum der Stadt Mainz/Landessammlung für Naturkunde.

Dr. Hans Nortmann, Generaldirektion Kulturelles Erbe Rheinland-Pfalz, Direktion Landesarchäologie, Außenstelle Trier.

Dr. Richard Petrovszky, Historisches Museum der Pfalz, Speyer.

Markus Poschmann, Generaldirektion Kulturelles Erbe Rheinland-Pfalz, Direktion Landesarchäologie, Erdgeschichte/Koblenz

Dr. Marcus Reuter, Generaldirektion Kulturelles Erbe Rheinland-Pfalz, Direktion Landesmuseum Trier.

Petra Schäfers, Generaldirektion Kulturelles Erbe Rheinland-Pfalz, Direktion Landesarchäologie, Erdgeschichte/Mainz.

Dr. Rüdiger Schulz, Generaldirektion Kulturelles Erbe Rheinland-Pfalz, Direktion Landesarchäologie, Außenstelle Speyer.

Michael Schwab, M.A., Generaldirektion Kulturelles Erbe Rheinland-Pfalz, Direktion Landesarchäologie.

Dr. Werner Transier, Historisches Museum der Pfalz, Speyer.

Dr. Marion Witteyer, Generaldirektion Kulturelles Erbe Rheinland-Pfalz, Direktion Landesarchäologie, Außenstelle Mainz.

Dr. Andrea Zeeb-Lanz, Generaldirektion Kulturelles Erbe Rheinland-Pfalz, Direktion Landesarchäologie, Außenstelle Speyer.